1,001 DELICIOUS RECIPES for People with Diabetes

EDITED BY
**Sue Spitler and
Linda Eugene, R.D., C.D.E.**
with Linda R. Yoakam, R.D., M.S.

Surrey Books
Chicago

1,001 DELICIOUS RECIPES FOR PEOPLE WITH DIABETES
is published by Surrey Books, Inc.,
230 E. Ohio St., Suite 120, Chicago, IL 60611.

This book is manufactured in the United States of America.

Library of Congress Cataloging-in-Publication data:

1,001 delicious recipes for people with diabetes / edited by Sue Spitler
and Linda Eugene, with Linda R. Yoakam.
    p. cm.
  Includes index.
  ISBN 1-57284-041-2 (pbk.)
    1. Diabetes—Diet therapy—Recipes. I. Title: One thousand and
one delicious recipes for people with diabetes. II. Spitler, Sue.
III. Eugene, Linda. IV. Yoakam, Linda R.

RC662. A16 2001
641.5'6314—dc21   2001049376

Editorial and production: *Bookcrafters, Inc., Chicago*
Art direction and book design: *Joan Sommers Design, Chicago*
Nutritional analyses: *Linda R. Yoakam, R.D., M.S.*
Cover illustrations: *Vicki Rabinowitz*

For prices on quantity purchases or for free book catalog,
contact Surrey Books at the above address.

This title is distributed to the trade by Publishers Group West.

Other Surrey Books titles for people with diabetes, include:
  The Free and Equal® Cookbook
  The Free and Equal® Dessert Cookbook
  Light and Easy Diabetes Cuisine
  The Microwave Diabetes Cookbook
  The Restaurant Companion

CONTENTS

ACKNOWLEDGMENTS

The publisher, editors, and staff of Surrey Books wish to thank the seven innovative authors who contributed to this cookbook:

Linda Eugene
Ruth Glick
Carole Kruppa
Kim Lila
Carol Munson
Sue Spitler
Desirée Witkowski

Thanks and appreciation also to co-Editor Sue Spitler and her associate Pat Molden, co-Editor Linda Eugene, R.D., C.D.E., Editorial Assistant Leona Pitej, Art Director Joan Sommers, Managing Editor Gene DeRoin, and Nutritionist Linda R. Yoakam, R.D., M.S.

FOREWORD

At the University of Chicago we are doing extensive research on diabetes mellitus, with the goal of finding a cure for a disease that affects about 16 million people in the U.S. That is nearly a 40 percent increase in the past decade. Almost all of these patients (90 percent) have a form of the disease called Type 2 that is often tied to obesity and resistance to insulin (whereas in Type 1 the cause is absence of insulin).

Until we find a cure for Type 2 diabetes, we will continue to counsel our patients that they can reduce symptoms dramatically by losing weight, which they can do by adopting an easy-to-follow meal plan that is low in saturated fats and simple carbohydrates, * and by becoming moderately active. That's it: diet and exercise.

And now we have proof. As I write this Foreword, the Diabetes Prevention Program results have been announced. This multi-center National Institutes of Health-sponsored trial was ended a year early because the result showed beyond a doubt that lifestyle modification—moderate weight loss and exercise—can actually prevent the onset of diabetes mellitus in at-risk adults, young and old, from a wide variety of ethnic groups.

Diabetes is a complex disease involving insulin production and blood sugar levels, but to the person who has it, it has a great deal to do with food—what is all right to eat and what is not. Working with your doctor or diabetes educator, you will learn how your body processes food, and the two of you will work as a team to develop a diet and exercise program suited to your needs so that you can stay in control.

Here is where *1,001 Delicious Recipes for People with Diabetes* can be very helpful. The editors—culinary expert Sue Spitler, registered dietitian Linda Yoakam, and certified diabetes educator Linda Eugene, with whom I work at the University of Chicago—have chosen recipes that are easy to make, good to eat, and fit easily into a diabetic meal plan. They have tested and selected hundreds and hundreds of good tasting, healthy recipes, including desserts, that will meet your needs as well as those of a non-diabetic spouse and active children.

Until we find a cure for diabetes, there is hope, and plenty of good eating.

—Louis H. Philipson, M.D., Ph.D.
Section of Endocrinology, Department of Medicine
University of Chicago, Chicago, Illinois

*See *Report of the Dietary Guidelines Committee on the Dietary Guidelines for Americans, 2000* (U. S. Dept. of Agriculture, Agricultural Research Service, Washington, D.C., 2000).

INTRODUCTION

"Contrary to popular myth, there is no 'diabetes diet.'" So states the Mayo Clinic newsletter. In fact, medical and nutritional professionals have transformed the diabetes diets of yesteryear into contemporary meal planning that includes just about any foods you like as long as nutrition, balance, and moderation are given careful attention. No longer are foods labeled as "good," "bad," or "forbidden." No longer does a diagnosis of diabetes mean a life-sentence of bland, boring, and unappetizing meals.

That's why we are able to put together this collection of *1,001 Delicious Recipes for People with Diabetes*. It offers a practically endless range of recipes from appetizers to desserts and accompanies each with the nutritional data you need to stay within your meal-planning goals.

Even though people with diabetes do not have to give up favorite dishes and the treats they like, including sweets and snacks, it is important to plan meals carefully, both for nutritional quality and quantity. It is even more important for those with diabetes than for the general population to choose foods that are low fat, limited carbohydrate, low salt, high fiber, and rich in vitamins and minerals. Limiting calorie intake, of course, is essential, and even though you can eat moderate portions of just about anything, weight gain can be a serious threat to controlling diabetes.

BALANCING YOUR DIET

For people with diabetes, controlling carbohydrate intake can be of major importance since carbohydrates spike glucose levels most dramatically. Carbohydrates are found in foods with natural or added sugar such as breads, crackers, cereals, potatoes, fresh fruits and juices, milk, table sugar, jams, and jellies. Other foods contain carbohydrates in combination with proteins and fats; some examples are cakes, ice cream, doughnuts, pizza, potato chips, and soups.

A healthy and nutritious meal plan will include a variety of foods from all six food groups: bread (or starch), fruit, milk, vegetable, meat, and fat. Despite their glucose-raising effect, carbohydrates (which are found in all of the food groups except meat and fat) are not discouraged in the diets of people with diabetes. Although specific nutrition goals that reflect blood glucose targets and other medical aims should be discussed with your doctor or registered dietitian, the following guidelines for daily allowances of carbohydrate, protein, and fat can form the basis of a balanced meal plan.

Calories per day	50% Carbohydrates	20% Protein	30% Fat
1500	188 gm	75 gm	50 gm
1800	225 gm	90 gm	60 gm
2000	250 gm	100 gm	66 gm
2200	275 gm	110 gm	73 gm

Knowing your carbohydrate, protein, and fat limits will help you choose recipes that meet these goals, and you can continue to eat most of your favorite foods. If you look at the nutrition data we have supplied with every recipe in *1,001 Delicious Recipes for People with Diabetes*, you will be surprised at what a wide variety of recipes you can enjoy while staying within your target nutrient range. Note, too, that meal-plan consistency is very important. To keep blood sugar at a consistent level, try to eat the same quantity of food and the same proportions of carbohydrate, protein, and fat each day.

THE "EXCHANGE" SYSTEM VS. COUNTING CARBOS

A variety of meal-planning strategies can be used to control your diabetes. Keep in mind that there is no single meal plan that is appropriate for everyone. Individualizing your meal plan is the key to successful control of blood glucose levels. Also remember that, as discussed by the American Diabetes Association and the American Dietetic Association, meal planning for diabetes is really little more than establishing a healthy way of eating. People with diabetes today eat the same foods as people without diabetes.

Two popular meal-planning strategies are in wide use among people with diabetes. One is the "exchange" system, wherein foods are divided into six basic food groups according to the nutrients they contain. Foods in the same group with similar nutrients can be exchanged, or substituted for one another, to meet the daily-allowed quantity of that particular food group. A registered dietitian can best assist people in deciding how many exchanges, or servings, of which foods should be allowed at each meal. However, until meeting with a registered dietitian, the following meal plan can serve as a guide. To use the exchange list method, simply compare the number of exchanges recommended in the chart below with the number contained in each recipe.

Breakfast	A.M. Snack	Lunch	P.M. Snack	Dinner	Bedtime
2 bread	1 bread	3 meat	1 fruit	3 bread	2 bread
1 fruit		2 bread		3 meat	1 meat
1 milk		1 fruit		2 vegetable	
1 meat		1 vegetable		1 fat	
1 fat		1 milk			
		1 fat			

Another method of meal planning for people with diabetes is to count the number of carbohydrate grams eaten. This number is given for each recipe in the book to help a person using this method stay within daily prescribed limits and yet enjoy a wide variety of foods. Of course, for a balanced diet one needs more than just carbohydrates, so we have included suggested quantities of other nutrients in this hypothetical meal plan.

Breakfast	A.M. Snack	Lunch	P.M. Snack	Dinner	Bedtime
60 gm carbo.	15 gm carbo.	45 gm carbo.	15 gm carbo.	55 gm carbo.	15 gm carbo.
1 oz. meat		2 oz. meat		3 oz. meat	
1 tsp. fat		1/2 cup veg.		1 cup veg.	
		1 tsp. fat		1 tsp. fat	

NUTRITIONAL INFORMATION

These delicious and nutritious recipes for people with diabetes were created using the highest quality low-fat ingredients available. Low-fat meats such as skinless chicken breasts, beef eye of round, and pork tenderloin were selected instead of higher-fat cuts. Many nutritious fat-free and reduced-fat dairy products are called for such as fat-free milk, fat-free half-and-half, low-fat cheeses, and low-fat sour cream. Egg whites and liquid egg substitute were chosen in place of their higher-cholesterol equivalents. Fat-free, reduced-sodium broths were used. Vegetable cooking spray usually replaces higher-fat liquid oils for sauteing foods. A variety of herbs, spices, and seasonings enhance flavors while keeping sodium content down.

Recipes throughout the 16 chapters reflect the highest nutritional standards and follow the guidelines recommended by the United States Department of Agriculture for the general population as well as for people with diabetes:

- Eat a variety of foods
- Choose a diet with plenty of grain products, vegetables, and fruit
- Choose a diet low in fat, saturated fat, and cholesterol
- Choose a diet moderate in sugars
- Choose a diet moderate in salt and sodium
- If you drink alcoholic beverages, do so in moderation

The specific nutritional data and diabetic exchanges provided for recipes are not infallible. Nutritional analyses are derived using prestigious nutritional software programs, but they are meant to be used as guidelines only. Figures are based on laboratory values of ingredients, so results may vary slightly depending on the brand of ingredient used and the method of preparation. Other factors that can affect the accuracy of nutritional data include variability in sizes, weights, and measures of fruits, vegetables, and other foods. There is also a possible 20 percent error factor in the nutritional labeling of prepared foods.

Exchange values are averages. If the carbohydrate content of a day's intake is estimated using the exchanges shown, there may be a significant difference between the estimate and the actual values consumed.

Ingredients noted as "optional," "to taste," or "as garnish" are not included in the nutritional data. When alternate choices or amounts of ingredients are given, the ingredient or amount listed first has been used for analysis. Similarly, data is based on the first, or fewer, number of servings where a range is shown.

ENJOY YOURSELF

Even though you have diabetes, you can see how, with a little knowledge and effort, you can eat delicious food, enjoy meals with friends, and take steps to keep glucose controlled. Now you have our "1,001" best wishes for happy and healthy dining, to which we say, *bon appétit!*

— Sue Spitler, Linda Eugene, R.D., C.D.E., and
Linda R. Yoakam, R.D., M.S.

ONE

Appetizers

CURRY DIP

Sweet potatoes and broccoli are particularly good with this dip.

12 servings (2 generous tablespoons each)

1¹/₂	cups fat-free mayonnaise
¹/₂	cup fat-free sour cream
¹/₄	cup thinly sliced green onions and tops
1¹/₂-2	teaspoons prepared horseradish
1¹/₂-2	teaspoons curry powder
2-3	teaspoons sugar
2-4	teaspoons lemon juice
	Salt and white pepper, to taste
	Assorted vegetable relishes, as dippers
	Pita Chips (see p. 652)

Per Serving
Calories: 34
% Calories from fat: 1
Fat (gm): 0
Saturated fat (gm): 0
Cholesterol (mg): 0
Sodium (mg): 393
Protein (gm): 0.7
Carbohydrate (gm): 8
Exchanges
Milk: 0.0
Vegetable: 0.0
Fruit: 0.0
Bread: 0.5
Meat: 0.0
Fat: 0.0

1. Mix mayonnaise, sour cream, green onions, horseradish, curry powder, and sugar. Season to taste with lemon juice, salt, and white pepper. Refrigerate several hours for flavors to blend.

2. Spoon dip into bowl; serve with vegetable relishes and Pita Chips for dipping (not included in nutritional data).

PINE NUT SPINACH PÂTÉ

Toasted pine nuts provide the flavor accent in this unique dip.

12 servings (about 2 tablespoons each)

1	package (10 ounces) frozen, thawed, chopped spinach
¹/₄	cup coarsely chopped onion
¹/₄	cup coarsely chopped celery
1	clove garlic
2-3	teaspoons lemon juice
¹/₂	teaspoon dried dill weed
1-2	tablespoons toasted pine nuts *or* slivered almonds
¹/₂	package (8-ounce size) fat-free cream cheese, softened
	Salt and pepper, to taste
	Bruschetta (see p. 653)

Per Serving
Calories: 19
% Calories from fat: 21
Fat (gm): 0.5
Saturated fat (gm): 0.1
Cholesterol (mg): 0
Sodium (mg): 73
Protein (gm): 2.1
Carbohydrate (gm): 1.9
Exchanges
Milk: 0.0
Vegetable: 0.5
Fruit: 0.0
Bread: 0.0
Meat: 0.0
Fat: 0.0

1. Drain spinach well between layers of paper toweling. Process spinach, onion, celery, garlic, lemon juice, and dill weed in food processor until almost smooth; add pine nuts and process until coarsely chopped, using pulse technique. Stir mixture into cream cheese; season to taste with salt and pepper. Refrigerate several hours for flavors to blend.

2. Spoon pâté into crock or bowl; serve with Bruschetta (not included in nutritional data).

WILD MUSHROOM PÂTÉ

This pâté is most flavorful when made with wild mushrooms, although brown or white mushrooms can be used.

8 servings (about 2 tablespoons each)

Olive oil cooking spray

12 ounces coarsely chopped shiitake, *or* portobello, mushrooms

1/2 cup chopped onion

2-4 cloves garlic, minced

1/4 cup dry sherry *or* vegetable broth

2 tablespoons grated fat-free Parmesan cheese

2-3 teaspoons lemon juice

Salt and pepper, to taste

Bruschetta *or* Whole Wheat Lavosh (see pp. 653, 659)

Per Serving
Calories: 42
% Calories from fat: 2
Fat (gm): 0.1
Saturated fat (gm): 0
Cholesterol (mg): 0
Sodium (mg): 14
Protein (gm): 1.4
Carbohydrate (gm): 8.4
Exchanges
Milk: 0.0
Vegetable: 1.5
Fruit: 0.0
Bread: 0.0
Meat: 0.0
Fat: 0.0

1. Spray skillet with cooking spray; heat over medium heat until hot. Add mushrooms, onion, garlic, and sherry; cook, covered, over medium heat until mushrooms are wilted, about 5 minutes. Cook, uncovered, over medium to medium-low heat until vegetables are very tender and all liquid absorbed, 8 to 10 minutes. Cool.

2. Process mushroom mixture and Parmesan cheese in food processor until smooth. Season to taste with lemon juice, salt, and pepper. Refrigerate 2 to 3 hours for flavors to blend.

3. Spoon pâté into a crock or mound on a serving plate. Serve with Bruschetta or Whole Wheat Lavosh (not included in nutritional data).

BEAN AND VEGETABLE SPREAD

A delicious and nutritious spread for snacking, or to serve as party fare.

12 servings (about 3 tablespoons each)

Vegetable cooking spray
3/4 cup chopped carrot
1/2 cup chopped onion
2 cloves garlic, minced
2 tablespoons vegetable broth *or* water
1 1/2 cups cooked dried, *or* canned, rinsed, drained soybeans *or* garbanzo beans
1 cup reduced-fat, *or* fat-free, sour cream
2 tablespoons minced parsley
1-2 teaspoons lemon juice
Salt and pepper, to taste
Assorted vegetables, Easy Herb Lavosh (see p. 652), or melba toast, as dippers

Per Serving
Calories: 56
% Calories from fat: 29
Fat (gm): 2
Saturated fat (gm): 0.3
Cholesterol (mg): 0
Sodium (mg): 17
Protein (gm): 5
Carbohydrate (gm): 5.6
Exchanges
Milk: 0.0
Vegetable: 1.0
Fruit: 0.0
Bread: 0.0
Meat: 0.5
Fat: 0.0

1. Spray small skillet with cooking spray; heat over medium heat until hot. Add carrot, onion, garlic, and broth; cook, covered, over medium heat until vegetables are tender and dry, 5 to 8 minutes. Cool.

2. Process soybeans and sour cream, using pulse technique, until smooth. Stir in vegetable mixture and parsley; season to taste with lemon juice, salt, and pepper. Refrigerate several hours for flavors to blend.

3. Spoon spread into bowl; serve with vegetables, Easy Herb Lavosh, or melba toast (not included in nutritional data).

ROASTED GARLIC AND HERB CANNELLINI DIP

Another good-for-you dip that tastes terrific! Italian cannellini beans are white kidney beans that are similar in flavor and appearance to navy or Great Northern beans.

6 servings (about ¼ cup each)

1 can (15 ounces) cannellini, *or* Great Northern, beans, rinsed, drained
1 teaspoon minced roasted garlic
1 tablespoon olive oil
1 tablespoon prepared horseradish
2 tablespoons minced chives
½ teaspoon dried oregano leaves
½ teaspoon dried basil leaves
2-3 drops hot pepper sauce
2-3 teaspoons lemon juice
Salt and white pepper, to taste
Pita Chips (see p. 652)
Assorted vegetables, as dippers

Per Serving
Calories: 75
% Calories from fat: 25
Fat (gm): 2.8
Saturated fat (gm): 0.3
Cholesterol (mg): 0
Sodium (mg): 167
Protein (gm): 5.3
Carbohydrate (gm): 13.1
Exchanges
Milk: 0.0
Vegetable: 0.0
Fruit: 0.0
Bread: 1.0
Meat: 0.0
Fat: 0.5

1. Process beans, garlic, olive oil, and horseradish in food processor until smooth. Mix in chives, herbs, and hot pepper sauce. Season to taste with lemon juice, salt, and white pepper. Refrigerate 1 to 2 hours for flavors to blend.

2. Spoon dip into bowl; serve with Pita Chips and vegetables (not included in nutritional data).

SUN-DRIED TOMATO HUMMUS

Sun-dried tomatoes and herbs embellish this Mediterranean favorite.

8 servings (about 1/4 cup each)

1 can (15 ounces) garbanzo beans, rinsed, drained
1/3 cup fat-free plain yogurt
2-3 tablespoons tahini (sesame seed paste)
3 cloves garlic
3 tablespoons sun-dried tomato bits *or* 4 sun-dried tomato halves (not in oil), finely chopped
1 teaspoon dried oregano leaves
1 teaspoon dried mint leaves
2-3 teaspoons lemon juice
Salt and white pepper, to taste
Pita Chips (see p. 652) *or* pita breads, cut into wedges, as dippers

Per Serving
Calories: 73
% Calories from fat: 21
Fat (gm): 1.7
Saturated fat (gm): 0.2
Cholesterol (mg): 0.2
Sodium (mg): 256
Protein (gm): 3.6
Carbohydrate (gm): 11.4
Exchanges
Milk: 0.0
Vegetable: 0.0
Fruit: 0.0
Bread: 1.0
Meat: 0.0
Fat: 0.0

1. Process garbanzo beans, yogurt, tahini, and garlic in food processor until smooth. Stir in sun-dried tomato bits and herbs; season to taste with lemon juice, salt, and white pepper. Refrigerate 1 to 2 hours for flavors to blend.

2. Spoon hummus into serving bowl; serve with Pita Chips (not included in nutritional data).

EGGPLANT CAVIAR

Middle Eastern flavors will tempt you to second helpings!

6 servings (generous 2 tablespoons each)

1 large eggplant (1 1/2 pounds)
1/2 cup chopped tomato
1/4 cup finely chopped onion
3 cloves garlic, minced
1/4 cup fat-free plain yogurt
2 teaspoons extra-virgin olive oil
1/2 teaspoon dried oregano leaves
1-2 tablespoons lemon juice

Per Serving
Calories: 59
% Calories from fat: 28
Fat (gm): 2.1
Saturated fat (gm): 0.3
Cholesterol (mg): 0.2
Sodium (mg): 19
Protein (gm): 1.8
Carbohydrate (gm): 10.1
Exchanges
Milk: 0.0
Vegetable: 1.5
Fruit: 0.0
Bread: 0.0
Meat: 0.0
Fat: 0.5

Salt and pepper, to taste
2 ripe pitted olives, sliced
Lavosh or pita bread wedges, as dippers

1. Pierce eggplant in several places with fork; place in baking pan. Bake at 350 degrees until eggplant is soft, 45 to 50 minutes. Cool.

2. Cut eggplant in half; scoop out pulp with spoon. Mix eggplant, tomato, onion, garlic, yogurt, olive oil, and oregano in bowl; season to taste with lemon juice, salt, and pepper. Refrigerate 3 to 4 hours for flavors to blend.

3. Spoon eggplant mixture into bowl; garnish with olives. Serve with lavosh (not included in nutritional data).

ROASTED ZUCCHINI AND GARLIC SPREAD

A great recipe for summer when garden zucchini are abundant.

12 servings (about 2 tablespoons each)

Olive oil cooking spray
1¼ pounds zucchini, cut into 1-inch pieces
1 small onion, cut into wedges
2 garlic cloves, peeled
⅓ cup fat-free plain yogurt
2 tablespoons finely chopped parsley
Lemon juice, to taste
Salt and cayenne pepper, to taste
Sliced vegetables, as dippers
Baked tortilla chips *or* Pita
Chips (see p. 652), as dippers

Per Serving
Calories: 14
% Calories from fat: 6
Fat (gm): 0.1
Saturated fat (gm): 0
Cholesterol (mg): 0.1
Sodium (mg): 7
Protein (gm): 1
Carbohydrate (gm): 2.6
Exchanges
Milk: 0.0
Vegetable: 0.5
Fruit: 0.0
Bread: 0.0
Meat: 0.0
Fat: 0.0

1. Line jelly roll pan with aluminum foil and spray with cooking spray. Arrange zucchini, onion, and garlic in single layer on pan. Bake at 425 degrees until vegetables are very tender, about 15 to 20 minutes for garlic, 25 to 30 minutes for zucchini and onion. Cool.

2. Process vegetables in food processor, using pulse technique, until coarsely chopped. Stir in yogurt and parsley; season to taste with lemon juice, salt, and cayenne pepper. Serve with sliced vegetables and baked tortilla chips (not included in nutritional data).

EGGPLANT MARMALADE

Minced roasted garlic is very robust in flavor. It can be purchased in jars, or regular minced garlic can be substituted. A quick kitchen tip—ginger-root does not have to be peeled before using! The eggplant mixture can be refrigerated up to 2 weeks.

12 servings (about 3 tablespoons each)

2	medium eggplant (1¼ pounds each), unpeeled
⅓	cup coarsely chopped onion
2	tablespoons minced roasted garlic
2-3	tablespoons minced gingerroot
3	tablespoons light brown sugar
1½	teaspoons fennel seeds, crushed
2	tablespoons red wine vinegar
2	teaspoons dark sesame oil
⅓	cup golden raisins
⅓	cup vegetable broth
2-3	tablespoons toasted pine nuts or slivered almonds
	Whole wheat lavosh, broken into pieces, as dippers

Per Serving
Calories: 75
% Calories from fat: 21
Fat (gm): 1.9
Saturated fat (gm): 0.3
Cholesterol (mg): 0
Sodium (mg): 6
Protein (gm): 1.6
Carbohydrate (gm): 14.9
Exchanges
Milk: 0.0
Vegetable: 2.0
Fruit: 0.5
Bread: 0.0
Meat: 0.0
Fat: 0.0

1. Cut eggplant into ½-inch slices; cut slices into scant ½-inch cubes. Combine eggplant, onion, garlic, gingerroot, brown sugar, and fennel seeds; arrange in single layer on aluminum foil-lined and greased large jelly roll pan. Drizzle with combined vinegar and oil.

2. Bake at 425 degrees until eggplant is browned and wrinkled, about 1½ hours, stirring every 30 minutes. Stir raisins into mixture; drizzle with broth and toss. Bake until broth is absorbed, 10 to 15 minutes longer. Stir in pine nuts and cool. Refrigerate overnight for flavors to blend.

3. Spoon eggplant marmalade into serving bowl; serve with lavosh (not included in nutritional data).

CHUTNEY CHEESE SPREAD

Enjoy these flavors inspired by India. Ginger contributes "heat" as well as flavor to the spread, so adjust according to your taste. Make Pita Chips with curry powder or ground cumin.

8 servings (2 generous tablespoons each)

1	package (8 ounces) fat-free cream cheese, softened
1	cup (4 ounces) shredded reduced-fat Cheddar cheese
$1/2$	cup chopped mango chutney, divided
$1/4$	cup finely chopped onion
2	tablespoons chopped raisins
1-2	teaspoons finely chopped gingerroot
1	clove garlic, minced
$1/2$-1	teaspoon curry powder
1-2	tablespoons chopped cashews
	Thinly sliced green onion tops, as garnish
	Pita Chips (see p. 652) *or* Whole Wheat Lavosh (see p. 659), as dippers

Per Serving
Calories: 116
% Calories from fat: 21
Fat (gm): 2.6
Saturated fat (gm): 1.1
Cholesterol (mg): 7.6
Sodium (mg): 367
Protein (gm): 7.4
Carbohydrate (gm): 14.6
Exchanges
Milk: 0.0
Vegetable: 0.0
Fruit: 1.0
Bread: 0.0
Meat: 0.5
Fat: 0.5

1. Mix cheeses, 2 tablespoons chutney, onion, raisins, gingerroot, garlic, and curry powder until blended (do not beat or fat-free cream cheese will become thin in texture). Refrigerate 1 to 2 hours for flavors to blend.

2. Mound spread on plate; spoon remaining 6 tablespoons chutney over or around spread. Sprinkle with cashews and green onion tops; serve with Pita Chips (not included in nutritional data).

ROASTED GARLIC AND THREE-CHEESE SPREAD

For best flavor, make this dip a day in advance.

12 servings (2 generous tablespoons each)

1 small head garlic
Olive oil cooking spray
1 package (8 ounces) fat-free cream cheese, softened
1¹/₂-2 ounces goat cheese
¹/₄ cup grated fat-free Parmesan cheese
¹/₈ teaspoon white pepper
2-4 tablespoons fat-free milk
Minced parsley *or* dried tomato bits, as garnish
Vegetable relishes and assorted crackers, as dippers

Per Serving
Calories: 43
% Calories from fat: 28
Fat (gm): 1.3
Saturated fat (gm): 0.9
Cholesterol (mg): 3.8
Sodium (mg): 142
Protein (gm): 4.7
Carbohydrate (gm): 2.5
Exchanges
Milk: 0.0
Vegetable: 0.0
Fruit: 0.0
Bread: 0.0
Meat: 0.5
Fat: 0.5

1. Cut off top of garlic head to expose cloves. Spray garlic lightly with cooking spray and wrap in aluminum foil; bake at 400 degrees until very tender, 35 to 40 minutes. Cool; gently press cloves to remove. Mash cloves with fork.

2. Mix cheeses, garlic, and white pepper in medium bowl, adding enough milk to make desired spreading consistency. Refrigerate 2 to 3 hours for flavors to blend.

3. Spoon mixture into serving bowl; sprinkle with parsley or dried tomato bits. Serve with vegetable relishes and crackers (not included in nutritional data).

STUFFED VEGETABLES

Vegetables can also be stuffed with any of the spread recipes in this chapter.

12 servings (4 pieces each)

Per Serving
Calories: 55
% Calories from fat: 24
Fat (gm): 1.5
Saturated fat (gm): 0.9
Cholesterol (mg): 3.8
Sodium (mg): 145
Protein (gm): 5.4
Carbohydrate (gm): 5.2
Exchanges
Milk: 0.0
Vegetable: 0.5
Fruit: 0.0
Bread: 0.0
Meat: 0.5
Fat: 0.5

12 cherry tomatoes
12 cucumber slices, 3/4 inch thick
12 yellow summer squash slices (3/4 inch thick)
12 medium mushrooms
1 cup Roasted Garlic and Three-Cheese Spread (1/2 recipe) (see p. 10)
   Parsley sprigs, ripe olive slices, chopped sun-dried tomato, as garnish

1. Cut tops off tomatoes; cut thin slices off bottoms, if necessary for tomatoes to stand up securely. Remove seeds from tomatoes using tip of vegetable peeler or melon baller. Scoop out centers of cucumber and squash slices with melon baller. Remove stems from mushrooms.

2. Using pastry bag or small spoon, fill vegetables with spread. Garnish with parsley, olives, and sun-dried tomato.

MUSHROOMS STUFFED WITH ORZO

Enjoy flavor accents of tangy goat cheese and a trio of fresh herbs. Serve with Cilantro Pesto or Spinach Pesto (see pp. 287, 419).

4 servings (3 mushrooms each)

Per Serving
Calories: 86
% Calories from fat: 24
Fat (gm): 2.6
Saturated fat (gm): 0.6
Cholesterol (mg): 3.4
Sodium (mg): 18
Protein (gm): 5.3
Carbohydrate (gm): 13
Exchanges
Milk: 0.0
Vegetable: 1.0
Fruit: 0.0
Bread: 0.5
Meat: 0.0
Fat: 0.5

12 large mushrooms
   Vegetable cooking spray
1 tablespoon finely chopped shallot
2 cloves garlic, minced
1 tablespoon finely chopped fresh, *or* 1 teaspoon dried, basil leaves
2 teaspoons finely chopped fresh, *or* 1/2 teaspoon dried, oregano leaves
1/2 teaspoon finely chopped fresh, *or* 1/8 teaspoon dried, thyme leaves

¹/₄ cup (2 ounces) orzo, cooked
1 tablespoon goat cheese *or* reduced-fat cream cheese
Basil *or* oregano sprigs, as garnish

1. Remove stems from mushrooms and chop coarsely. Reserve caps. Spray medium skillet with cooking spray; heat over medium heat until hot. Saute mushroom stems 2 to 3 minutes. Add shallot, garlic, and chopped herbs; saute until shallot is almost tender, about 3 minutes. Stir in orzo and goat cheese; cook until orzo is warm, 1 to 2 minutes.

2. Spoon orzo filling into reserved mushroom caps and place in 13 x 9-inch baking pan. Bake at 350 degrees, covered with aluminum foil, until mushroom caps are tender, about 15 minutes. Remove foil and bake 5 minutes longer.

3. Arrange mushrooms on serving plates; garnish with herb sprigs. Serve warm.

CURRIED ONION CROUSTADES

The Croustades can be filled with onion mixture and refrigerated several hours before baking.

8 servings (2 each)

Vegetable cooking spray
2 cups chopped onions
2 cloves garlic, minced
1 teaspoon curry powder
¹/₂ teaspoon ground cumin
2 tablespoons flour
1 cup fat-free half-and-half *or* fat-free milk
2 tablespoons dried fruit bits
1 tablespoon minced cilantro
Salt, cayenne, and black pepper, to taste
Croustades (see p. 654)
4 teaspoons chopped almonds

Per Serving
Calories: 151
% Calories from fat: 29
Fat (gm): 5.1
Saturated fat (gm): 0.3
Cholesterol (mg): 0
Sodium (mg): 600
Protein (gm): 6.9
Carbohydrate (gm): 20.9
Exchanges
Milk: 0.0
Vegetable: 1.0
Fruit: 0.0
Bread: 1.0
Meat: 0.0
Fat: 1.0

1. Spray large skillet with cooking spray; heat over medium heat until hot. Add onions, garlic, curry powder, and cumin; cook, covered, over low heat until onions are very soft, about 20 minutes. Stir in flour; cook 2 minutes longer, stirring frequently.

2. Stir half-and-half and fruit bits into onion mixture; heat to boiling. Reduce heat and simmer until thickened, stirring constantly. Stir in cilantro; season to taste with salt, cayenne, and black pepper.

3. Spoon slightly rounded tablespoon onion mixture into each Croustade; sprinkle each with 1/4 teaspoon almonds. Bake at 425 degrees, 10 minutes.

ARTICHOKE-STUFFED APPETIZER BREAD

For easy entertaining, assemble this appetizer a day or two in advance. Bread pieces removed from the loaf can be used to make fresh bread crumbs or croutons.

8 servings (2 pieces each)

1 package (8 ounces) fat-free cream cheese, softened

1 can (14 ounces) artichoke hearts, drained, chopped

1/2 cup chopped red bell pepper

1/2 cup chopped celery

1/4 cup chopped pitted green, *or* black, olives

2 teaspoons drained capers, optional

1 clove garlic, minced

1/4 teaspoon dried basil leaves

1/4 teaspoon dried oregano leaves

1-2 teaspoons white wine vinegar *or* lemon juice

Salt and white pepper, to taste

1 loaf French bread (8 ounces; about 15 inches long)

Per Serving
Calories: 151
% Calories from fat: 29
Fat (gm): 5.1
Saturated fat (gm): 0.3
Cholesterol (mg): 0
Sodium (mg): 600
Protein (gm): 6.9
Carbohydrate (gm): 20.9
Exchanges
Milk: 0.0
Vegetable: 1.0
Fruit: 0.0
Bread: 1.0
Meat: 0.0
Fat: 1.0

1. Mix softened cream cheese with artichoke hearts, bell pepper, celery, olives, capers, garlic, and herbs; season to taste with vinegar, salt, and white pepper.

2. Slice bread lengthwise in half. Remove bread from centers of bread halves, using paring knife or serrated grapefruit spoon, leaving 3/4-inch shell of bread.

3. Spoon filling into each bread half; press halves together firmly and wrap in plastic wrap. Refrigerate 2 hours or until serving time. Cut into 16 pieces.

CURRIED PINWHEELS

Make these easy appetizers up to 2 days in advance and refrigerate until ready to serve.

12 servings (3 each)

6 pieces luncheon-size lavosh (5-inch)

1¹/₂ packages (8-ounce size) fat-free cream cheese, softened

2 tablespoons fat-free mayonnaise

1-2 teaspoons spicy brown mustard

1 clove garlic, minced

1-1¹/₂ teaspoons curry powder

¹/₂ teaspoon ground cumin

¹/₄ teaspoon cayenne pepper

¹/₂ cup finely chopped apple

¹/₄ cup chopped celery

¹/₄ cup finely chopped green onions and tops

¹/₄ cup chopped dry-roasted peanuts

³/₄ cup chopped mango chutney

Per Serving
Calories: 114
% Calories from fat: 14
Fat (gm): 1.8
Saturated fat (gm): 0.3
Cholesterol (mg): 0
Sodium (mg): 237
Protein (gm): 5.7
Carbohydrate (gm): 18.6
Exchanges
Milk: 0.0
Vegetable: 0.0
Fruit: 1.5
Bread: 0.0
Meat: 0.0
Fat: 0.0

1. Brush lavosh lightly with water and place between damp kitchen towels until softened enough to roll, 10 to 15 minutes.

2. Mix cream cheese, mayonnaise, mustard, garlic, curry, cumin, and cayenne pepper in small bowl; spread about 3 tablespoons mixture on each lavosh. Combine remaining ingredients, except chutney, and sprinkle over cream cheese. Roll lavosh tightly; wrap each roll in plastic wrap and refrigerate at least 4 hours.

3. Cut each roll into 6 pieces and arrange on plate. Serve with chutney.

MUSHROOM BRUSCHETTA

Use any desired wild mushrooms for richest flavor, and make this filling up to 2 days in advance. Heat briefly before assembling and broiling the bruschetta.

12 servings (1 each)

Vegetable cooking spray
1/4 cup chopped red bell pepper
1/4 cup chopped yellow bell pepper
2 green onions and tops, thinly sliced
2 cloves garlic, minced
2 cups chopped portobello, shiitake, *or* white mushrooms
1 teaspoon dried basil leaves
1/4 teaspoon dried thyme leaves
2-3 tablespoons fat-free grated Parmesan cheese
Few drops balsamic vinegar
Salt and pepper, to taste
Bruschetta (see p. 653)
1/4 cup (2 ounces) shredded reduced-fat mozzarella cheese

Per Serving
Calories: 92
% Calories from fat: 17
Fat (gm): 1.7
Saturated fat (gm): 0.7
Cholesterol (mg): 2.5
Sodium (mg): 194
Protein (gm): 4.4
Carbohydrate (gm): 14.6
Exchanges
Milk: 0.0
Vegetable: 0.5
Fruit: 0.0
Bread: 1.0
Meat: 0.5
Fat: 0.0

1. Spray medium skillet with cooking spray; heat over medium heat until hot. Saute bell peppers, onions, and garlic 2 to 3 minutes. Add mushrooms; cook, covered, over medium heat until wilted, about 5 minutes. Stir in herbs and cook until mushrooms are tender and all liquid is gone, 8 to 10 minutes. Stir in Parmesan cheese; season to taste with balsamic vinegar, salt and pepper.

2. Spoon mushroom mixture on Bruschetta and sprinkle with mozzarella cheese; broil until cheese is melted, 1 to 2 minutes. Serve warm.

SPINACH-CHEESE MINI-QUICHES

The tiny fillo shells, delicious and wonderfully crisp, are available in the frozen food section of supermarkets. Pie pastry for a double-crust pie (see p. 764) can be substituted; roll pastry to scant 1/4 inch thickness and cut into 2 1/2-inch rounds. Fit pastries into muffin cups and crimp top edges with tines of fork.

1 1/2 dozen (1 per serving)

1 1/4	cups fat-free cottage cheese
1/4	cup grated fat-free Parmesan cheese
2	tablespoons fat-free milk
2	tablespoons flour
1/2	cup finely chopped fresh spinach
1/2	teaspoon dried oregano leaves
1/2	teaspoon dried thyme leaves
	Salt and white pepper, to taste
2	eggs
1 1/2	dozen frozen, thawed mini-fillo shells

Per Serving
Calories: 48
% Calories from fat: 30
Fat (gm): 1.6
Saturated fat (gm): 0.2
Cholesterol (mg): 23.7
Sodium (mg): 61
Protein (gm): 3.9
Carbohydrate (gm): 4.3
Exchanges
Milk: 0.0
Vegetable: 0.0
Fruit: 0.0
Bread: 0.5
Meat: 0.0
Fat: 0.5

1. Mix cottage cheese, Parmesan cheese, milk, flour, spinach, oregano, and thyme; season to taste with salt and white pepper. Stir in eggs.

2. Arrange fillo shells on cookie sheet; fill with cheese mixture. Bake at 325 degrees until puffed and beginning to brown on the tops, about 20 minutes.

CHEESE AND SPINACH SQUARES

Lots of cheese and spinach are a team in these terrific appetizer squares. Substitute fat-free Swiss or mozzarella cheese for the Cheddar, if you prefer.

12 servings (2 each)

Vegetable cooking spray
1-2 tablespoons unseasoned dry bread crumbs
2 cups fat-free cottage cheese
1¹/₂ cups (6 ounces) shredded fat-free Cheddar cheese
2 eggs
6 tablespoons all-purpose flour
1 package (10 ounces) frozen, thawed chopped spinach, well drained
¹/₄ cup thinly sliced green onions and tops
¹/₄ cup chopped roasted red pepper *or* pimiento
¹/₄ cup finely chopped parsley
¹/₈ teaspoon ground nutmeg
¹/₄ teaspoon cayenne pepper
¹/₂ teaspoon black pepper

Per Serving
Calories: 81
% Calories from fat: 11
Fat (gm): 1
Saturated fat (gm): 0.3
Cholesterol (mg): 35.5
Sodium (mg): 231
Protein (gm): 11.8
Carbohydrate (gm): 6.7
Exchanges
Milk: 0.0
Vegetable: 1.0
Fruit: 0.0
Bread: 0.0
Meat: 1.0
Fat: 0.0

1. Spray 13 x 9-inch pan with cooking spray; coat bottom and sides of pan with bread crumbs.

2. Combine cheeses and eggs in bowl; stir in remaining ingredients until blended. Pour into prepared pan and bake at 350 degrees until set and lightly browned, 35 to 40 minutes. Cool 10 minutes before cutting into squares.

BAKED SPINACH BALLS

Often laden with butter, these savory treats have been made skinny with no loss in flavor.

12 servings (2 each)

2 cups herb-seasoned bread stuffing cubes

1/4 cup grated fat-free Parmesan cheese

1/4 cup chopped green onions and tops

2 cloves garlic, minced

1/8 teaspoon ground nutmeg

1 package (10 ounces) frozen, thawed chopped spinach, well drained

1/4-1/3 cup vegetable broth

2 tablespoons margarine, melted

Salt and pepper, to taste

2 egg whites, beaten

Per Serving
Calories: 66
% Calories from fat: 31
Fat (gm): 2.3
Saturated fat (gm): 0.4
Cholesterol (mg): 0
Sodium (mg): 211
Protein (gm): 3
Carbohydrate (gm): 8.5
Exchanges
Milk: 0.0
Vegetable: 0.0
Fruit: 0.0
Bread: 0.5
Meat: 0.0
Fat: 0.5

1. Combine stuffing cubes, Parmesan cheese, onions, garlic, and nutmeg in medium bowl. Mix in spinach, broth, and margarine; season to taste with salt and pepper. Mix in egg whites.

2. Shape mixture into 24 balls. Bake at 350 degrees until spinach balls are browned, about 15 minutes.

FIVE-SPICE POTSTICKERS

Purchased wonton wrappers make this recipe simple to prepare. Wonton wrappers can be cut into circles with a 2¹/₂-inch cutter, if you like. Wontons can be assembled up to 1 day in advance; dust lightly with flour and refrigerate in single layer on plate, covered tightly with plastic wrap.

12 servings (4 each)

Vegetable cooking spray
2 cups sliced Chinese cabbage
¹/₂ cup shredded carrot
¹/₄ cup thinly sliced green onions and tops
¹/₄ cup thinly sliced celery
1-2 teaspoons minced gingerroot
1 clove garlic, minced
1 tablespoon wheat germ
1 tablespoon reduced-sodium tamari soy sauce
¹/₄-¹/₂ teaspoon hot chili paste
¹/₄-¹/₂ teaspoon five-spice powder
2 ounces light tofu, cut into small cubes *or* coarsely crumbled
48 wonton, *or* gyoza, wrappers
1 egg white, beaten
Tamari Dipping Sauce (recipe follows)

Per Serving
Calories: 119
% Calories from fat: 6
Fat (gm): 0.8
Saturated fat (gm): 0.1
Cholesterol (mg): 2.9
Sodium (mg): 653
Protein (gm): 5.8
Carbohydrate (gm): 21
Exchanges
Milk: 0.0
Vegetable: 2.0
Fruit: 0.0
Bread: 1.0
Meat: 0.0
Fat: 0.0

1. Spray wok or large skillet with cooking spray; heat over medium heat until hot. Stir-fry cabbage, carrot, green onions, celery, gingerroot, and garlic over medium to medium-high heat until cabbage is wilted, 2 to 3 minutes. Remove from heat; stir in wheat germ, tamari soy sauce, chili paste, and five-spice powder. Add tofu, toss lightly, and cool.

2. Spoon ¹/₂ tablespoon filling on wonton wrapper; brush edges of wrapper with egg white. Fold wrapper in half and press edges to seal. Repeat with remaining filling, wrappers, and egg white.

3. Heat large saucepan of water to boiling. Add wontons, 6 to 8 at a time, and simmer, uncovered, until wontons rise to the surface, 2 to 3 minutes. Remove from water with slotted spoon and drain. Repeat with remaining wontons.

4. Spray wok or large skillet with cooking spray; heat over medium heat until hot. Add single layer of wontons and cook until browned on the bottom, 2 to 3 minutes. Spray tops of wontons lightly with cooking spray; turn and cook until browned. Repeat with remaining wontons. Serve hot with Tamari Dipping Sauce.

Tamari Dipping Sauce

makes about 3/4 cup

> 1/2 cup reduced-sodium tamari soy sauce
> 2 tablespoons rice wine vinegar
> 4 teaspoons lemon juice

1. Mix all ingredients; refrigerate until ready to use.

CRANBERRY-CHEESE WONTONS

Dried cranberries and gingerroot add a lively accent to these unusual cheese wontons. When fried at the correct temperature, deep-fried foods absorb almost no fat.

12 servings (2 each)

> 3/4 package (8-ounce size) fat-free cream cheese
> 3 tablespoons chopped dried cranberries
> 2 tablespoons finely chopped chives
> 1/2-3/4 teaspoon minced gingerroot
> 1 tablespoon minced parsley
> Salt and white pepper, to taste
> 24 wonton wrappers
> 1 egg white, beaten
> Vegetable oil, for frying
> 1/3 cup jalapeño jelly, heated, *or* Tamari Dipping Sauce (see recipe above)

Per Serving
Calories: 91
% Calories from fat: 10
Fat (gm): 1
Saturated fat (gm): 0.1
Cholesterol (mg): 2
Sodium (mg): 184
Protein (gm): 3.9
Carbohydrate (gm): 15.8
Exchanges
Milk: 0.0
Vegetable: 0.0
Fruit: 0.5
Bread: 0.5
Meat: 0.5
Fat: 0.0

1. Mix cream cheese, cranberries, chives, gingerroot, and parsley in small bowl; season to taste with salt and white pepper.

2. Spoon 1/2 tablespoon filling on wonton wrapper; brush edges of wrapper with egg white. Fold wrapper in half and press edges to seal. Repeat with remaining filling, wrappers, and egg white.

3. Heat 2 inches oil in large saucepan to 375 degrees. Fry wontons, 6 to 8 at a time, until golden, 1 to 2 minutes. Drain very well on paper toweling. Serve hot with jalapeño jelly or Tamari Dipping Sauce.

MIXED VEGETABLE EGG ROLLS

The dark oriental sesame oil in this recipe has a more distinctive sesame flavor than the light domestic brands. Spinach, alfalfa sprouts, and black beans add a new dimension to these egg rolls.

12 servings

1 tablespoon sesame seeds
2-3 teaspoons dark sesame oil
2 green onions and tops, sliced
1 tablespoon minced gingerroot
2 cloves garlic, minced
2 cups shredded spinach
1/2 cup chopped water chestnuts
1/2 cup shredded carrot
1/2 cup sliced small mushrooms
1 can (15 1/2 ounces) black beans, rinsed, drained
1-1 1/2 teaspoons tamari soy sauce
  Salt and pepper, to taste
2 egg whites
1 cup alfalfa sprouts
12 egg roll wrappers
  Peanut, *or* vegetable, oil, for frying
  Plum Sauce (recipe follows)

Per Serving
Calories: 101
% Calories from fat: 12
Fat (gm): 1.6
Saturated fat (gm): 0.2
Cholesterol (mg): 0
Sodium (mg): 342
Protein (gm): 5.8
Carbohydrate (gm): 19
Exchanges
Milk: 0.0
Vegetable: 1.5
Fruit: 0.0
Bread: 1.0
Meat: 0.0
Fat: 0.0

1. Saute sesame seeds in sesame oil in large skillet until beginning to brown, 1 to 2 minutes. Add green onions, gingerroot, and garlic; saute until onions are tender, 1 to 2 minutes. Add spinach, water chestnuts, carrot, and mushrooms; cook, covered, over medium heat until spinach and mushrooms are wilted. Stir in beans and soy sauce; season to taste with salt and pepper. Cool 5 to 10 minutes; stir in egg whites and alfalfa sprouts.

2. Spoon about ¹/₃ cup vegetable mixture near corner of 1 egg roll wrapper. Brush edges of wrapper with water. Fold bottom corner of egg roll wrapper up over filling; fold sides in and roll up. Repeat with remaining filling and wrappers.

3. Heat about 2 inches oil in deep skillet or large saucepan to 375 degrees. Fry egg rolls until golden, 4 to 5 minutes. Drain on paper toweling; serve hot with Plum Sauce.

Plum Sauce

makes about 1 cup

> ³/₄ cup oriental plum sauce
> 2-3 tablespoons reduced-sodium tamari soy sauce
> 2 tablespoons rice wine vinegar *or* cider vinegar
> 1 tablespoon grated gingerroot
> 1-2 teaspoons light brown sugar
> 1 green onion and top, thinly sliced
> 2 cloves garlic, minced

1. Mix all ingredients; refrigerate until ready to serve.

TORTELLINI KEBABS WITH MANY-CLOVES GARLIC SAUCE

A fun party food, but also a great idea for a casual meal. Serve 3 to 4 skewers each for an entrée, and accompany with broiled tomato halves, a crisp green salad, and Garlic Bread (see p. 657).

8 servings (2 each)

> 1¹/₂ packages (9-ounce size) mushroom tortellini, cooked
> 5 cups assorted whole, cubed, and sliced vegetables (mushroom caps, cherry tomatoes, bell peppers, zucchini, broccoli florets, artichoke hearts, etc.)
> Olive oil cooking spray
> Many-Cloves Garlic Sauce (recipe follows)

Per Serving
Calories: 146
% Calories from fat: 26
Fat (gm): 5
Saturated fat (gm): 1.8
Cholesterol (mg): 25.3
Sodium (mg): 171
Protein (gm): 7.4
Carbohydrate (gm): 23.3
Exchanges
Milk: 0.0
Vegetable: 2.0
Fruit: 0.0
Bread: 1.0
Meat: 0.0
Fat: 0.5

1. Alternate tortellini and vegetables on 16 long skewers and arrange on broiler pan. Spray generously with cooking spray and broil 6 inches from heat source 4 minutes; turn kebabs, spray with cooking spray, and broil 3 to 4 minutes longer.

2. Arrange tortellini kebabs on serving platter; serve with Many-Cloves Garlic Sauce.

Note: Cook firm vegetables such as broccoli and carrots until crisp-tender before using.

Many-Cloves Garlic Sauce

makes about 2 cups

          25 cloves garlic, peeled
           1 tablespoon olive oil
        1³/4 cups fat-free reduced-sodium chicken
              broth, divided
         1/4 cup dry white wine, *or* chicken broth
           2 tablespoons flour
           2 tablespoons finely chopped parsley
              Salt and white pepper, to taste

1. Cook garlic in oil in medium skillet, covered, over medium to medium-low heat until tender, about 10 minutes. Cook, uncovered, over medium-low to low heat until garlic cloves are golden brown, about 10 minutes. Mash cloves slightly with a fork.

2. Add 1¹/2 cups broth and wine to skillet and heat to boiling. Mix flour and remaining 1/4 cup broth and stir into boiling mixture. Boil, stirring constantly, until thickened, about 1 minute. Stir in parsley, salt, and pepper.

APPLE-CABBAGE STRUDELS

Serve hot or at room temperature. The strudels can be assembled several hours in advance; refrigerate, tightly covered. Spray tops of strudels generously with cooking spray before baking.

12 servings (2 pieces each)

Butter-flavored vegetable cooking spray
1/2 cup thinly sliced onion
2 cloves garlic, minced
3 cups thinly sliced cabbage
1/3 cup apple cider *or* apple juice
1 1/2 cups chopped, peeled apples
1/4 cup dark raisins
1-1 1/2 teaspoons curry powder
Salt and pepper, to taste
8 sheets frozen, thawed fillo pastry

Per Serving
Calories: 146
% Calories from fat: 21
Fat (gm): 3.5
Saturated fat (gm): 1.6
Cholesterol (mg): 5.2
Sodium (mg): 354
Protein (gm): 5.9
Carbohydrate (gm): 23.3
Exchanges
Milk: 0.0
Vegetable: 2.0
Fruit: 0.0
Bread: 1.0
Meat: 0.0
Fat: 0.5

1. Spray large skillet with cooking spray; heat over medium heat until hot. Saute onion and garlic until tender, about 5 minutes. Add cabbage and apple cider; cook, covered, over medium heat until cabbage is wilted, about 5 minutes. Stir in apples, raisins, and curry powder; cook, uncovered, until apples are crisp-tender and mixture is almost dry, 5 to 8 minutes. Season to taste with salt and pepper. Cool.

2. Place 1 sheet fillo on clean kitchen towel; spray with cooking spray. Top with second sheet of fillo and spray. Repeat with 2 more sheets of fillo. Spoon half the cabbage mixture evenly along short edge of fillo, leaving a 1-inch space from the edges. Roll up from short edge, tucking ends under; place seam side down on greased cookie sheet. Repeat with remaining fillo, cooking spray, and cabbage mixture. Spray tops of strudels generously with cooking spray.

3. Bake strudels at 400 degrees until golden, about 15 minutes. Cool slightly; cut diagonally into 1-inch pieces with serrated knife.

ONION AND BLUE CHEESE FOCACCIA

Expect rave reviews when serving this delicious appetizer. Serve larger portions as a bread with entrée salads too.

8 servings

Olive oil cooking spray
2 cups thinly sliced onions
4 cloves garlic, minced
1/2 teaspoon dried rosemary leaves
Salt and pepper, to taste
1 focaccia (Italian flat bread, 10 ounces)
1/4 cup chopped sun-dried tomatoes (not in oil)
2-3 ounces crumbled blue cheese
2 tablespoons grated fat-free Parmesan cheese

Per Serving
Calories: 146
% Calories from fat: 21
Fat (gm): 3.5
Saturated fat (gm): 1.6
Cholesterol (mg): 5.2
Sodium (mg): 354
Protein (gm): 5.9
Carbohydrate (gm): 23.3
Exchanges
Milk: 0.0
Vegetable: 2.0
Fruit: 0.0
Bread: 1.0
Meat: 0.0
Fat: 0.5

1. Spray large skillet with cooking spray; heat over medium heat until hot. Cook onions and garlic, covered, over medium heat until wilted, about 5 minutes. Cook, uncovered, over low heat until tender and lightly browned, about 15 minutes. Stir in rosemary and season with salt and pepper.

2. Arrange onions on focaccia; sprinkle with sun-dried tomatoes and cheeses. Bake at 350 degrees until focaccia is hot and cheese melted, about 15 minutes. Cut into wedges.

SWISS CHEESE AND SPINACH PINWHEELS

Wonderful sandwiches, because they can be made in advance and refrigerated up to 2 days! Always ready for hungry appetites!

8 servings (2 slices each)

1 large whole wheat lavosh (16-inch size)
1 package (8 ounces) fat-free cream cheese, softened
1 tablespoon fat-free sour cream
2 tablespoons minced onion
1 teaspoon crushed fennel seeds
10 slices (7½ ounces) fat-free Swiss cheese
4 cups loosely packed spinach leaves
2 medium tomatoes, thinly sliced
⅓ cup sliced pitted black olives

Per Serving
Calories: 177
% Calories from fat: 29
Fat (gm): 5.8
Saturated fat (gm): 0.9
Cholesterol (mg): 0
Sodium (mg): 782
Protein (gm): 13.4
Carbohydrate (gm): 18.4
Exchanges
Milk: 0.0
Vegetable: 1.0
Fruit: 0.0
Bread: 1.0
Meat: 1.0
Fat: 0.5

1. Place lavosh between 2 damp clean kitchen towels; let stand until lavosh is softened enough to roll, 10 to 15 minutes.

2. Mix cream cheese, sour cream, onion, and fennel seeds in small bowl; spread mixture on lavosh. Arrange Swiss cheese, spinach, tomatoes, and olives on cheese. Roll up lavosh tightly; wrap in plastic wrap and refrigerate at least 4 hours, no longer than 2 days.

3. Trim ends; cut into scant 1-inch slices to serve.

SLICED MUSHROOM PINWHEELS

Easy to make and carry, lavosh sandwiches are great for picnics, as well as home dining.

8 servings

1 large whole wheat lavosh (16-inch size)

4 ounces mushrooms

1 package (8 ounces) fat-free cream cheese, softened

1 tablespoon fat-free sour cream

1 teaspoon minced garlic

1-2 teaspoons Parisian, *or* Dijon-style, mustard

1 medium onion, thinly sliced

1/3 cup thinly sliced red bell pepper

3 tablespoons fat-free Italian salad dressing

Per Serving
Calories: 122
% Calories from fat: **27**
Fat (gm): 3.7
Saturated fat (gm): 0.7
Cholesterol (mg): 0
Sodium (mg): 309
Protein (gm): 6.5
Carbohydrate (gm): 16
Exchanges
Milk: 0.0
Vegetable: 1.0
Fruit: 0.0
Bread: 1.0
Meat: 0.0
Fat: 0.5

1. Place lavosh between 2 damp clean kitchen towels; let stand until lavosh is softened enough to roll, 10 to 15 minutes.

2. Remove mushroom stems and chop; slice mushroom caps. Mix cream cheese, chopped mushroom stems, sour cream, garlic, and mustard in small bowl; spread mixture on lavosh. Toss sliced mushrooms, onion, and bell pepper with salad dressing; arrange on cheese. Roll up lavosh tightly; wrap in plastic wrap and refrigerate at least 4 hours, no longer than 2 days.

3. Trim ends; cut into scant 1-inch slices to serve.

SWEET ONION TARTE TATIN

You'll hear raves when you serve this beautiful upside-down tart! For best flavor, use one of the sweet onions, such as Vidalia.

6 to 8 servings

Butter-flavored vegetable cooking spray
1 tablespoon granulated, *or* light brown, sugar
2½ pounds small, sweet onions, peeled, cut crosswise into halves
Salt and pepper, to taste
⅓ cup raisins
1 teaspoon dried thyme leaves
¼ teaspoon ground allspice
1½ cups vegetable broth
2 teaspoons balsamic vinegar
Onion Tarte Crust (recipe follows)

Per Serving
Calories: 291
% Calories from fat: 25
Fat (gm): 8.3
Saturated fat (gm): 1.6
Cholesterol (mg): 0
Sodium (mg): 126
Protein (gm): 5.9
Carbohydrate (gm): 49.8
Exchanges
Milk: 0.0
Vegetable: 3.0
Fruit: 0.5
Bread: 1.5
Meat: 0.0
Fat: 1.5

1. Spray 12-inch skillet with ovenproof handle with cooking spray; heat over medium heat until hot. Sprinkle bottom of skillet with sugar. Place onion halves, cut sides down, in skillet, fitting as many as possible in skillet. Cut remaining onion halves into pieces, or chop coarsely, and fill in any spaces between onion halves. Sprinkle onions lightly with salt and pepper.

2. Sprinkle raisins, thyme, and allspice over onions. Cook, uncovered, over medium heat until onions begin to brown, 8 to 10 minutes. Add broth and vinegar and heat to boiling. Reduce heat and simmer, covered, until onions are tender, 20 to 25 minutes. Heat to boiling; reduce heat and simmer rapidly, uncovered, until liquid is almost gone.

3. Make Onion Tarte Crust. Roll pastry on floured surface into 13-inch circle. Ease pastry into skillet, covering onions; tuck in edges to fit. Bake at 375 degrees until pastry is lightly browned and juices are bubbly, 30 to 35 minutes. Cool in pan on wire rack, 10 minutes; place large serving plate over skillet and invert tart onto plate. Serve warm or room temperature.

Onion Tarte Crust

makes 1 crust

$1^1/2$ cups all-purpose flour
$1/2$ teaspoon baking powder
$1/2$ teaspoon ground thyme leaves
Pinch salt
4 tablespoons cold margarine, cut into pieces
5-6 tablespoons ice water

1. Combine flour, baking powder, thyme, and salt in medium bowl; cut in margarine until mixture resembles coarse crumbs. Add water a tablespoon at a time, mixing lightly with a fork after each addition until dough just holds together. Refrigerate, covered, at least 30 minutes before rolling.

CRAB PIE

32 servings

2 teaspoons all-purpose flour
$1/8$ teaspoon dried thyme, crushed
$1/8$ teaspoon pepper
1 cup no-cholesterol real egg product
$1/4$ cup chopped red bell pepper
1 can ($13^1/2$ ounces) artichoke hearts, drained and chopped
6 ounces imitation crab, diced
Vegetable cooking spray
32 fillo pastry sheets, cut into squares
3 tablespoons low-fat grated Parmesan cheese
2 tablespoons chives
1 tablespoon low-fat margarine

Per Serving
Calories: 75
% Calories from fat: 18
Fat (gm): 1.5
Saturated fat (gm): 0.3
Cholesterol (mg): 1.2
Sodium (mg): 192
Protein (gm): 3.3
Carbohydrate (gm): 11.7
Exchanges
Milk: 0.25
Vegetable: 0.0
Fruit: 0.0
Bread: 0.75
Meat: 0.25
Fat: 0.25

1. Combine flour, thyme, pepper, and egg product in a bowl. Add peppers, artichokes, and crabmeat. Stir well.

2. Preheat oven to 350 degrees. Coat muffin tins with cooking spray. Gently press fillo squares into each muffin cup allowing the ends to overlap the top. Spoon the crabmeat mixture evenly into the fillo cups. Sprinkle with cheese and chives. Brush the edges of the fillo with margarine.

3. Bake for 20 minutes or until filling is set and edges of the phyllo are golden brown.

SQUASH AND MUSHROOM GALETTE

Any flavorful wild mushroom, such as shiitake, oyster, or cremini, can be substituted for the portobello mushrooms. This elegant entrée tart can also be cut into smaller wedges and served as a first course.

4 to 6 servings

1	pound acorn, *or* butternut, squash, cut into halves, seeds discarded
1/2	cup thinly sliced leek (white parts only)
1	small onion, chopped
1	medium red bell pepper, chopped
2	portobello mushrooms, sliced
8	cloves garlic, minced
1 1/2	teaspoons dried sage leaves
1	tablespoon olive oil
	Salt and pepper, to taste
	Galette Pastry Dough (recipe follows)
1/2	cup shredded fat-free Cheddar cheese
2	tablespoons grated Parmesan cheese
1	egg white, beaten

Per Serving
Calories: 339
% Calories from fat: 18
Fat (gm): 7.1
Saturated fat (gm): 1.7
Cholesterol (mg): 58.3
Sodium (mg): 338
Protein (gm): 16.5
Carbohydrate (gm): 54
Exchanges
Milk: 0.0
Vegetable: 1.0
Fruit: 0.0
Bread: 3.0
Meat: 1.0
Fat: 1.0

1. Place squash, cut sides down, in baking pan. Bake at 375 degrees until very tender, about 1 hour. Scoop squash from shells into large bowl and mash with fork.

2. Saute leek, onion, bell pepper, mushrooms, garlic, and sage in oil in large skillet until tender, about 5 minutes. Mix into squash; season to taste with salt and pepper.

3. Roll Galette Pastry Dough on lightly floured surface to 14-inch circle; transfer to cookie sheet or large pizza pan. Spoon vegetable mixture evenly on dough, leaving 2-inch border around edge; sprinkle with cheeses. Fold edge of dough over edge of vegetable mixture, pleating to fit.

4. Brush edge of dough with beaten egg white. Bake at 400 degrees until dough is golden, about 25 minutes. Cut into wedges; serve warm.

Galette Pastry Dough

makes 1 crust

- 1 teaspoon active dry yeast
- 1/3 cup warm water (115 degrees)
- 1 egg, beaten
- 3 tablespoons fat-free sour cream
- 1 1/2 cups all-purpose flour
- 1/4 teaspoon salt

1. Stir yeast into warm water in medium bowl; let stand 5 minutes. Add egg and sour cream to yeast mixture, mixing until smooth. Stir in flour and salt, making a soft dough. Knead dough on lightly floured surface until smooth, 1 to 2 minutes.

SPRING VEGETABLE TERRINE

Spring asparagus and peas are baked in a delicate herb-seasoned egg custard, which is easily unmolded and sliced to serve.

4 servings

- Vegetable cooking spray
- 1/3 cup thinly sliced green onions and tops
- 1 medium red bell pepper, finely chopped
- 2 cloves garlic, minced
- 1 1/2 pounds fresh asparagus, cut into 1-inch pieces
- 1 package (10 ounces) frozen peas, thawed
- 1 cup fat-free half-and-half
- 2 tablespoons flour
- 1 tablespoon margarine
- 3/4 teaspoon dried tarragon leaves
- 1/4 teaspoon ground allspice
- 1/2 teaspoon pepper
- 1 cup no-cholesterol real egg product

Per Serving
Calories: 224
% Calories from fat: 15
Fat (gm): 3.8
Saturated fat (gm): 0.7
Cholesterol (mg): 0
Sodium (mg): 277
Protein (gm): 16.5
Carbohydrate (gm): 32.4
Exchanges
Milk: 0.5
Vegetable: 3.0
Fruit: 0.0
Bread: 1.0
Meat: 0.5
Fat: 0.0

1. Spray medium skillet with cooking spray; heat over medium heat until hot. Saute green onions, bell pepper, and garlic until tender, about 5 minutes. Stir in asparagus and peas; set aside.

2. Whisk half-and-half and flour until smooth in small saucepan. Heat to boiling; boil, whisking constantly, until thickened, about 1 minute. Remove from heat and stir in margarine, tarragon, allspice, and pepper. Whisk about half the mixture into egg product; whisk egg product back into saucepan.

3. Line the bottom of $8^1/2$ x $4^1/2$-inch loaf pan with parchment paper; spray lightly with cooking spray. Combine vegetable and half-and-half mixtures and pour into pan.

4. Bake, uncovered, at 350 degrees 40 minutes or until sharp knife inserted near center comes out clean. Let stand 10 minutes on wire rack before removing from pan. Invert onto serving plate; carefully remove parchment paper and cut into thick slices.

BLACK BEAN DIP WITH BAKED TORTILLA CHIPS

If a chunkier dip is desired, coarsely mash $^1/2$ cup of the beans and reserve. Make dip as directed, then stir the mashed beans into the dip.

12 servings (about 2 tablespoons each)

Vegetable cooking spray
$^1/2$ cup thinly sliced green onions and tops
1-2 cloves garlic, minced
1 can (15 ounces) black beans, rinsed, drained
$^3/4$ cup (3 ounces) shredded reduced-fat Cheddar cheese
$^1/4$ teaspoon salt
$^1/3$ cup vegetable broth *or* water
1-2 tablespoons finely chopped cilantro
Baked tortilla chips

Per Serving
Calories: 48
% Calories from fat: 21
Fat (gm): 3.8
Saturated fat (gm): 0.5
Cholesterol (mg): 3.8
Sodium (mg): 254
Protein (gm): 4.5
Carbohydrate (gm): 7
Exchanges
Milk: 0.0
Vegetable: 0.0
Fruit: 0.0
Bread: 0.5
Meat: 0.0
Fat: 0.0

1. Spray small skillet with cooking spray; heat over medium heat until hot. Saute onions and garlic until tender, about 3 minutes.

2. Process black beans, cheese, and salt in food processor or blender until almost smooth, adding enough broth to make desired dipping consistency. Mix in onion mixture and cilantro. Spoon dip into bowl; serve with tortilla chips (not included in nutritional data).

PINTO BEAN AND AVOCADO DIP

Avocado and tomato brighten this well-flavored bean dip. Increase the amount of jalapeño chili if you dare—or use the seeds and veins for maximum hotness.

12 servings (about 2 tablespoons each)

1 can (15 ounces) pinto beans, rinsed, drained
3/4 cup finely chopped onion
2 cloves garlic
1/2 jalapeño chili, seeds and veins discarded, minced
3 tablespoons finely chopped cilantro
1 large tomato, chopped
1/2 medium avocado, chopped
2- 3 tablespoons medium or hot salsa
Salt and pepper, to taste
Baked tortilla chips

Per Serving
Calories: 54
% Calories from fat: 25
Fat (gm): 3.8
Saturated fat (gm): 0
Cholesterol (mg): 0
Sodium (mg): 153
Protein (gm): 3
Carbohydrate (gm): 8.3
Exchanges
Milk: 0.0
Vegetable: 0.5
Fruit: 0.0
Bread: 0.5
Meat: 0.0
Fat: 0.0

1. Process beans in food processor or blender until smooth; add onion, garlic, jalapeño chili, and cilantro. Process, using pulse technique, until blended. Mix in tomato, avocado, and salsa; season to taste with salt and pepper. Refrigerate 1 to 2 hours for flavors to blend.

2. Spoon dip into serving bowl; serve with tortilla chips (not included in nutritional data).

CHILI CON QUESO

This popular dip is generally made with full-fat Mexican Chihuahua, Monterey Jack, Muenster, or Cheddar cheese. Our "skinny" version is made with reduced-fat pasteurized processed cheese product for creamy texture and fat-free Cheddar cheese for added flavor.

12 servings (about 2 tablespoons each)

Vegetable cooking spray

5 medium anaheim, *or* 2 medium poblano, chilies, seeds and veins discarded, cut into halves

1 small onion, chopped

1 small tomato, chopped

1/2 teaspoon dried oregano leaves

2 cups (8 ounces) shredded reduced-fat pasteurized processed cheese product

1 cup (4 ounces) shredded fat-free Cheddar cheese

2-4 tablespoons fat-free milk

Baked tortilla chips

Per Serving
Calories: 70
% Calories from fat: 26
Fat (gm): 1.9
Saturated fat (gm): 0.7
Cholesterol (mg): 12.8
Sodium (mg): 274
Protein (gm): 8.7
Carbohydrate (gm): 15.2
Exchanges
Milk: 0.0
Vegetable: 0.0
Fruit: 0.0
Bread: 1.0
Meat: 1.0
Fat: 0.0

1. Line jelly roll pan with aluminum foil; spray with cooking spray. Place chilies, skin sides up, on pan. Bake at 425 degrees until peppers are browned and soft, 20 to 25 minutes. Cool slightly; cut into strips.

2. Spray small saucepan with cooking spray; heat over medium heat until hot. Saute onion, tomato, and oregano until onion is tender, about 5 minutes. Add cheeses and chilies; cook over low heat until melted, stirring in milk for desired consistency. Serve warm in serving bowl with tortilla chips for dipping (not included in nutritional data).

SOMBRERO DIP

The ingredients in this appetizer dip are layered in smaller and smaller circles, resembling the top of a sombrero when finished! Use Florida avocados for making the Guacamole, as they are lower in fat than California avocados!

6 servings

Vegetable cooking spray

1/4 cup chopped poblano chili *or* green bell pepper

1/4 cup chopped onion

4-5 leaves romaine lettuce

1 1/2 cups Refried Beans (see p. 447) *or* 1 can (15 ounces) refried beans

1/2 cup Red Tomato Salsa (see p. 724) *or* prepared salsa

1/2 cup cooked crumbled Chorizo (1/4 recipe) (see p. 166)

1/2 cup chopped romaine lettuce

1/2 cup chopped tomato
Guacamole (recipe follows)

1/4 cup (1 ounce) shredded fat-free Cheddar cheese

1/2 cup fat-free sour cream

1 green onion and top, thinly sliced
Baked tortilla chips

Per Serving
Calories: 175
% Calories from fat: 16
Fat (gm): 3.2
Saturated fat (gm): 0.7
Cholesterol (mg): 23.7
Sodium (mg): 214
Protein (gm): 13.3
Carbohydrate (gm): 25
Exchanges
Milk: 0.0
Vegetable: 2.0
Fruit: 0.0
Bread: 1.0
Meat: 1.0
Fat: 0.0

1. Spray small skillet with cooking spray; heat over medium heat until hot. Saute poblano chili and onion until tender, 3 to 5 minutes; reserve.

2. Line a dinner-size serving plate with lettuce leaves; spoon Refried Beans in a circle on lettuce, 2 inches from edge of lettuce. Spoon Red Tomato Salsa over beans, leaving edge of beans showing.

3. Combine Chorizo and reserved sauteed vegetables; sprinkle over salsa. Sprinkle chopped lettuce and tomato over Chorizo mixture, leaving edge of Chorizo showing. Spoon Guacamole over chopped lettuce, leaving edge of lettuce showing; sprinkle with Cheddar cheese. Spoon sour cream in large dollop on top; sprinkle with green onion. Serve with tortilla chips for dipping (not included in nutritional data).

Guacamole

makes about ²/₃ cup

- 1 medium avocado, peeled, pitted
- ¹/₂ small onion, finely chopped
- ¹/₂ small jalapeño chili, seeds and veins discarded, minced
- 1-2 teaspoons finely chopped cilantro
  Salt and white pepper, to taste

1. Coarsely mash avocado in small bowl (mixture should be chunky, rather than smooth). Mix in onion, jalapeño chili, and cilantro. Season to taste with salt and pepper.

QUESO FUNDIDO

This melted cheese mixture is spooned onto warm tortillas, topped with a sprinkling of Chorizo, onion, and cilantro, and rolled—tuck up the end for easy eating! The Chorizo used is about ¹/₄ of the recipe; freeze the remaining Chorizo mixture, or cook for another meal.

8 servings

Vegetable cooking spray
- ¹/₄ cup chopped red bell pepper
- ³/₄ cup (3 ounces) shredded fat-free Cheddar cheese
- ¹/₂ cup (2 ounces) cubed reduced-fat pasteurized processed cheese product
- ¹/₄-¹/₃ cup fat-free milk
- 8 corn, *or* flour, tortillas, warm
- ¹/₂ cup cooked crumbled Chorizo (¹/₄ recipe) (see p. 166)
- 2 tablespoons finely chopped green onions and tops
- 2 tablespoons finely chopped cilantro

Per Serving
Calories: 112
% Calories from fat: 15
Fat (gm): 1.9
Saturated fat (gm): 0.7
Cholesterol (mg): 12.8
Sodium (mg): 274
Protein (gm): 8.7
Carbohydrate (gm): 15.2
Exchanges
Milk: 0.0
Vegetable: 0.0
Fruit: 0.0
Bread: 1.0
Meat: 1.0
Fat: 0.0

1. Spray small saucepan with cooking spray; heat over medium heat until hot. Saute bell pepper until tender, 2 to 3 minutes. Add cheeses; cook over low heat until melted, stirring in milk for desired consistency.

2. Spoon about 2 tablespoons cheese mixture in center of each tortilla; sprinkle with Chorizo, green onions, and cilantro and roll up.

BEEF EMPANADAS

Pork tenderloin or chicken breast can be substituted for the beef in this recipe. The raisins and spices lend a sweet flavor to the traditional meat filling.

10 servings (3 each)

12 ounces boneless beef eye of round steak, fat trimmed
Vegetable cooking spray
1/4 cup finely chopped onion
3 cloves garlic, minced
2 small tomatoes, finely chopped
1/3 cup raisins
2 tablespoons slivered almonds, optional
1 tablespoon cider vinegar
1/2 teaspoon ground cinnamon
1/8 teaspoon ground cloves
3 tablespoons finely chopped cilantro
Salt and pepper, to taste
Empanada Pastry (recipe follows)
2 tablespoons fat-free milk

Per Serving
Calories: 159
% Calories from fat: 29
Fat (gm): 5.1
Saturated fat (gm): 1.5
Cholesterol (mg): 16.5
Sodium (mg): 57
Protein (gm): 8.7
Carbohydrate (gm): 19.5
Exchanges
Milk: 0.0
Vegetable: 0.0
Fruit: 0.0
Bread: 0.5
Meat: 0.5
Fat: 0.0

1. Cut beef into 2-inch cubes and place in saucepan with 2 inches water; heat to boiling. Reduce heat and simmer, covered, until beef is tender, about 15 minutes. Drain, reserving meat and 1/2 cup broth. Shred beef finely.

2. Spray large skillet with cooking spray; heat over medium heat until hot. Saute onion and garlic until tender, about 5 minutes. Add reserved beef and 1/2 cup broth, tomatoes, raisins, almonds, vinegar, cinnamon, and cloves; cook over medium heat until broth has evaporated but mixture is still moist, about 10 minutes. Stir in cilantro; season to taste with salt and pepper.

3. Roll 1/2 of the Empanada Pastry on floured surface to 1/8 inch thickness; cut into 3-inch rounds with cookie cutter. Place scant tablespoon meat mixture on each piece pastry. Brush edges of pastry with water; fold in half and crimp edges firmly by hand or with tines of fork. Make cut in top of each pastry with sharp knife. Repeat with remaining pastry and meat mixture. Brush tops of pastries lightly with milk.

4. Bake empanadas on greased cookie sheets at 400 degrees until golden, 15 to 20 minutes. Serve warm.

Empanada Pastry

  1¹/₄ cups all-purpose flour
    1 tablespoon sugar
  ¹/₄ teaspoon baking powder
  ¹/₈ teaspoon salt
    3 tablespoons vegetable shortening
    1 teaspoon lemon juice *or* distilled white vinegar
  3-4 tablespoons fat-free milk *or* water

1. Combine flour, sugar, baking powder, and salt in small bowl; cut in shortening until mixture resembles coarse crumbs. Mix in lemon juice and milk, a tablespoon at a time, to form soft dough. Refrigerate until ready to use.

JICAMA WITH LIME AND CILANTRO

Very simple, and incredibly tasty!

4 servings

    1 medium jicama, peeled, thinly sliced
      Salt, to taste
      Lime juice, to taste
  1-2 tablespoons finely chopped cilantro

Per Serving
Calories: 17
% Calories from fat: 2
Fat (gm): 0
Saturated fat (gm): 0
Cholesterol (mg): 0
Sodium (mg): 0
Protein (gm): 0.5
Carbohydrate (gm): 3.8
Exchanges
Milk: 0.0
Vegetable: 1.0
Fruit: 0.0
Bread: 0.0
Meat: 0.0
Fat: 0.0

1. Arrange jicama slices on large serving plate; sprinkle very lightly with salt. Sprinkle with lime juice and cilantro.

PASTA PIZZA

Pizza flavors on a pasta crust!

6 servings

4	sun-dried tomatoes (not in oil)
4	ounces reduced-fat turkey Italian sausage, casing removed
1	cup sliced mushrooms
1/2	cup chopped onion
1	tablespoon finely chopped fresh, *or* 1 teaspoon dried, oregano leaves
1	tablespoon finely chopped fresh, *or* 1 teaspoon dried, basil leaves
1/4	teaspoon salt, optional
1/4	teaspoon pepper
	Vegetable cooking spray
6	ounces fettuccine, cooked
1	egg white, beaten
1	tablespoon finely chopped parsley
1 1/2	ounces goat cheese *or* reduced-fat cream cheese

Per Serving
Calories: 168
% Calories from fat: 29
Fat (gm): 5.7
Saturated fat (gm): 1.6
Cholesterol (mg): 21.6
Sodium (mg): 281
Protein (gm): 9.1
Carbohydrate (gm): 21.6
Exchanges
Milk: 0.0
Vegetable: 2.0
Fruit: 0.0
Bread: 1.0
Meat: 0.5
Fat: 0.5

1. Place tomatoes in small bowl; pour hot water over to cover. Let stand until tomatoes are softened, about 15 minutes; drain. Chop tomatoes.

2. Cook sausage in medium skillet over medium heat until browned; drain and crumble. Drain any excess fat from skillet. Add mushrooms, onion, and tomatoes and saute until tender, about 5 minutes. Stir in oregano, basil, salt, and pepper.

3. Spray 10-inch skillet with cooking spray; heat over medium heat until hot. Combine fettuccine, egg white, and parsley; place in skillet and pat into an even layer with pancake turner.

4. Spoon sausage-vegetable mixture in even layer over pasta; dot with cheese. Cook over medium to medium-high heat, covered, 5 minutes. Uncover and cook 5 minutes more or until pasta is lightly browned on bottom. Cut into wedges to serve.

TWO

Soups: First Course
AND
Entrée

DILLED BEET SOUP

Scrub beets well, as the cooking liquid is reserved for use in the soup. It's not necessary to peel beets before cooking, as the skins slip off easily after cooking.

8 servings (about 1¼ cups each)

12	medium beets, tops trimmed, scrubbed (about 3 pounds)
3	cups water
2-3	chicken bouillon cubes
³/₄-1	cup dry red wine *or* chicken broth
1¹/₂-2	teaspoons dried dill weed
2-3	tablespoons red wine vinegar
	Salt and pepper, to taste
8	thin lemon slices
	Finely chopped chives, as garnish

Per Serving
Calories: 53
% Calories from fat: 2
Fat (gm): 0.2
Saturated fat (gm): 0
Cholesterol (mg): 0
Sodium (mg): 319
Protein (gm): 1.4
Carbohydrate (gm): 8.8
Exchanges
Milk: 0.0
Vegetable: 2.0
Fruit: 0.0
Bread: 0.0
Meat: 0.0
Fat: 0.0

1. Heat beets, 3 cups water, and bouillon cubes to boiling in large saucepan; reduce heat and simmer, covered, until beets are tender, 30 to 40 minutes. Let stand until cool; drain, reserving cooking liquid. Slip skins off beets and cut into scant 1-inch pieces.

2. Add enough water to reserved cooking liquid to make 6 cups. Process beets, wine, reserved cooking liquid, and dill weed in food processor or blender container until smooth. Season to taste with vinegar, salt, and pepper.

3. Heat soup and serve warm, or refrigerate until chilled and serve cold. Pour soup into bowls; garnish each with a lemon slice and sprinkle with chives.

HERBED CUCUMBER SOUP

This soup is very delicate in flavor. Use a serrated grapefruit spoon to seed cucumbers quickly and easily.

6 servings (about 1 1/3 cups each)

Vegetable cooking spray
1/2 cup chopped onion
6 medium cucumbers, peeled, seeded, chopped (about 3 pounds)
3 tablespoons flour
4 cups reduced-sodium fat-free chicken broth
1 teaspoon dried mint *or* dill weed
1/2 cup fat-free half-and-half
Salt and white pepper, to taste
Paprika, as garnish
6 thin slices cucumber

Per Serving
Calories: 83
% Calories from fat: 4
Fat (gm): 0.4
Saturated fat (gm): 0.1
Cholesterol (mg): 0
Sodium (mg): 139
Protein (gm): 6.8
Carbohydrate (gm): 12.5
Exchanges
Milk: 0.0
Vegetable: 2.0
Fruit: 0.0
Bread: 0.0
Meat: 0.5
Fat: 0.0

1. Spray large saucepan with cooking spray; heat over medium heat until hot. Saute onion until tender, 3 to 5 minutes. Add cucumbers and cook over medium heat 5 minutes; stir in flour and cook 1 to 2 minutes longer.

2. Add broth to saucepan; heat to boiling. Reduce heat and simmer, covered, 10 minutes. Process soup in food processor or blender until smooth; stir in mint and half-and-half; season to taste with salt and pepper. Cool; refrigerate until chilled, 3 to 4 hours.

3. Pour soup into bowls; sprinkle lightly with paprika and top each with a cucumber slice.

CUCUMBER AND SORREL SOUP

If cucumbers are mild in flavor, they do not need to be peeled. Fresh sorrel, available in the spring, gives a lemony flavor to this soup.

6 servings (about 1¼ cups each)

Vegetable cooking spray
¼ cup plus 2 tablespoons sliced green onions and tops, divided
1 clove garlic, minced
3 cups chopped seeded, peeled cucumbers (about 1½ pounds)
1 cup coarsely chopped sorrel *or* spinach
2 cups fat-free milk
2 cups reduced-sodium fat-free chicken broth
1 tablespoon cornstarch
2 tablespoons water
Salt and white pepper, to taste
1½ cups Herb Croutons (½ recipe) (see p. 655)

Per Serving
Calories: 77
% Calories from fat: 8
Fat (gm): 0.6
Saturated fat (gm): 0.2
Cholesterol (mg): 1.5
Sodium (mg): 247
Protein (gm): 6.2
Carbohydrate (gm): 11.5
Exchanges
Milk: 0.0
Vegetable: 3.0
Fruit: 0.0
Bread: 0.0
Meat: 0.0
Fat: 0.0

1. Spray large saucepan with cooking spray; heat over medium heat until hot. Saute ¼ cup green onions and garlic until tender, 3 to 4 minutes. Add cucumbers and sorrel and cook over medium heat 5 minutes.

2. Add milk and broth to saucepan; heat to boiling. Reduce heat and simmer, covered, until cucumbers are tender, 5 to 10 minutes. Process soup in food processor or blender until smooth; return to saucepan.

3. Heat soup to boiling. Mix cornstarch and water; whisk into boiling soup. Boil, whisking constantly, until thickened, about 1 minute. Season to taste with salt and white pepper. Cool; refrigerate until chilled, 3 to 4 hours.

4. Pour soup into bowls; top with Herb Croutons and remaining 2 tablespoons green onions.

EGGPLANT SOUP WITH ROASTED RED PEPPER SAUCE

Grilling gives the eggplant a distinctive smoky flavor. For indoor cooking, eggplant can be oven roasted. Pierce eggplant in several places with fork; place in baking pan. Bake at 350 degrees until eggplant is soft, 45 to 50 minutes.

4 servings (about 1 1/2 cups each)

2 medium eggplant (about 2 1/2 pounds)
3/4 cup chopped onion
1/4 cup chopped green bell pepper
2 cloves garlic, minced
1 tablespoon extra virgin olive oil
4-5 cups reduced-sodium fat-free chicken broth
   Salt and white pepper, to taste
   Roasted Red Pepper Sauce
   (recipe follows)

Per Serving
Calories: 164
% Calories from fat: **22**
Fat (gm): 4.1
Saturated fat (gm): 0.6
Cholesterol (mg): 0
Sodium (mg): 180
Protein (gm): 9.1
Carbohydrate (gm): 24.6
Exchanges
Milk: 0.0
Vegetable: 5.0
Fruit: 0.0
Bread: 0.0
Meat: 0.0
Fat: 1.0

1. Pierce eggplant in several places with fork. Grill over medium hot coals, turning frequently, until eggplant is very soft, about 30 minutes. Cool until warm enough to handle; cut eggplant in half, scoop out pulp, and chop coarsely.

2. Saute onion, bell pepper, and garlic in oil in large saucepan until tender, 5 to 8 minutes. Add broth and eggplant to saucepan; heat to boiling. Reduce heat and simmer, covered, 10 minutes.

3. Process soup in food processor or blender until smooth. Season to taste with salt and white pepper. Refrigerate until chilled, 4 to 6 hours.

4. Pour soup into bowls; swirl about 3 tablespoons Roasted Red Pepper Sauce into each.

Roasted Red Pepper Sauce

makes about 3/4 cup

2 large red bell peppers, cut into halves
1 teaspoon sugar

1. Place peppers, skin sides up, on broiler pan. Broil 4 to 6 inches from heat source until skins are blistered and blackened. Place peppers in plastic bag for 5 minutes; remove and peel off skins.

2. Process peppers and sugar in food processor or blender until smooth. Refrigerate until ready to use.

Note: 1 jar (12 ounces) roasted red peppers, drained, can be substituted for the peppers in the recipe.

GAZPACHO

Gazpacho is Spanish in origin, but popularly served throughout Mexico and South America. Easy to make, this is a wonderful soup to keep on hand in summer months.

6 servings (about 1½ cups each)

5 large tomatoes
2 cups reduced-sodium tomato juice
2 cloves garlic
2 tablespoons lime juice
1 teaspoon dried oregano leaves
1 small seedless cucumber, coarsely chopped
1 cup chopped yellow bell pepper
1 cup chopped celery
6 green onions and tops, thinly sliced, divided
2 tablespoons finely chopped cilantro
Salt and pepper, to taste
Avocado Sour Cream (recipe follows)
Hot pepper sauce, optional

Per Serving
Calories: 76
% Calories from fat: 17
Fat (gm): 1.6
Saturated fat (gm): 0.3
Cholesterol (mg): 0.1
Sodium (mg): 46
Protein (gm): 3.3
Carbohydrate (gm): 15.1
Exchanges
Milk: 0.0
Vegetable: 2.0
Fruit: 0.0
Bread: 0.0
Meat: 0.0
Fat: 0.5

1. Cut tomatoes into halves; remove and discard seeds. Chop tomatoes; reserve 1 cup. Process remaining tomatoes, tomato juice, garlic, lime juice, and oregano in food processor or blender until smooth.

2. Mix tomato mixture, reserved tomatoes, cucumber, bell pepper, celery, 5 green onions, and cilantro in large bowl; season to taste with salt and pepper. Refrigerate until chilled, 3 to 4 hours.

3. Serve soup in chilled bowls; top each with a dollop of Avocado Sour Cream and sprinkle with remaining green onion. Serve with hot pepper sauce.

Avocado Sour Cream

makes about 2/3 cup

> 1/2 medium avocado, peeled, chopped
> 1/4 cup fat-free sour cream
> 2 tablespoons fat-free milk
> Salt and white pepper, to taste

1. Process all ingredients in food processor until smooth; season to taste with salt and white pepper.

WHITE GAZPACHO

Something different that is sure to please!

4 servings (about 1 cup each)

> Vegetable cooking spray
> 1 large onion, sliced
> 4 cloves garlic, minced
> 1-2 cups fat-free milk
> 1/2-1 vegetable bouillon cube
> 1 cup plain fat-free yogurt
> 2 teaspoons lemon juice
> 2 dashes hot pepper sauce
> Salt and white pepper, to taste
> 1/3 cup chopped, seeded cucumber
> 1/3 cup chopped, seeded yellow tomato
> 1/3 cup cubed avocado
> Finely chopped cilantro *or* parsley, as garnish

Per Serving
Calories: 109
% Calories from fat: 27
Fat (gm): 3.4
Saturated fat (gm): 0.6
Cholesterol (mg): 2
Sodium (mg): 196
Protein (gm): 6.7
Carbohydrate (gm): 14.3
Exchanges
Milk: 0.5
Vegetable: 2.0
Fruit: 0.0
Bread: 0.0
Meat: 0.0
Fat: 0.5

1. Spray large saucepan with cooking spray; heat over medium heat until hot. Cook onion and garlic over medium-low heat until very tender, about 15 minutes. Add milk and bouillon cube; cook over medium-high heat, stirring frequently, until mixture is hot and bouillon cube is dissolved.

2. Process soup, yogurt, lemon juice, and hot pepper sauce in food processor or blender until smooth. Season to taste with salt and white pepper. Cool; refrigerate until chilled, 3 to 4 hours.

3. Stir cucumber, tomato, and avocado into soup; pour into bowls and sprinkle with cilantro.

BEAN GAZPACHO

Pureed beans contribute a creamy texture and subtle flavor to this unusual gazpacho. Canned pinto beans, rinsed and drained, can be substituted for the dried.

8 servings (about 1¹/₃ cups each)

Per Serving
Calories: 260
% Calories from fat: 13
Fat (gm): 3.8
Saturated fat (gm): 0.2
Cholesterol (mg): 0
Sodium (mg): 642
Protein (gm): 12.9
Carbohydrate (gm): 47.1
Exchanges
Milk: 0.5
Vegetable: 2.0
Fruit: 0.0
Bread: 2.5
Meat: 0.5
Fat: 0.0

4 cups cooked dried pinto beans, divided
1 quart reduced-sodium tomato juice
3-4 tablespoons lime juice
2 teaspoons reduced-sodium Worcestershire sauce
1 jar (16 ounces) thick and chunky mild, *or* medium, salsa
1 cup chopped, seeded, peeled cucumber
1 cup thinly sliced celery
¹/₂ cup chopped onion
¹/₂ cup chopped green bell pepper
2 teaspoons minced roasted garlic
¹/₂ small avocado, peeled, chopped
1¹/₂ cups Herb Croutons (¹/₂ recipe) (see p. 655)

1. Process 2 cups beans, tomato juice, lime juice, and Worcestershire sauce in food processor or blender until smooth; pour into large bowl. Mix in remaining 2 cups beans and remaining ingredients, except avocado and Herb Croutons. Refrigerate until chilled, 3 to 4 hours.

2. Mix avocado into soup and pour into bowls; sprinkle with Herb Croutons.

CHILLED PEA SOUP

A refreshing soup for hot sultry days; serve with a ripe tomato salad and crusty bread or rolls.

6 servings (about 1 cup each)

Per Serving
Calories: 257
% Calories from fat: 4
Fat (gm): 1.1
Saturated fat (gm): 0.2
Cholesterol (mg): 0
Sodium (mg): 274
Protein (gm): 17.4
Carbohydrate (gm): 46.6
Exchanges
Milk: 0.5
Vegetable: 0.0
Fruit: 0.0
Bread: 3.0
Meat: 0.5
Fat: 0.0

- 1/2 cup chopped onion
- 1/2 teaspoon dried marjoram leaves
- 1/4 teaspoon dried thyme leaves
- 2 cups reduced-sodium fat-free chicken broth
- 2 packages (20 ounces each) frozen peas
- 2 cups sliced romaine lettuce
- Salt and white pepper, to taste
- 1/2 cup fat-free sour cream *or* fat-free half-and-half
- Paprika, as garnish

1. Saute onion, marjoram, and thyme in large saucepan until onion is tender, about 5 minutes. Stir in broth, peas, and lettuce; heat to boiling. Reduce heat and simmer, covered, until peas are tender, 5 to 8 minutes.

2. Process soup in food processor or blender until smooth; season to taste with salt and pepper. Cool; refrigerate until chilled, 3 to 4 hours.

3. Stir sour cream or half-and-half into soup; pour into bowls and sprinkle with paprika.

SNOW PEA SOUP

Make this soup a day in advance so that flavors can blend.

6 servings (about 1¹/₄ cups each)

¹/₂ cup sliced green onions and tops
¹/₂ cup chopped onion
1 tablespoon margarine
1 pound snow peas, trimmed
4 cups coarsely chopped romaine lettuce
4 cups reduced-sodium fat-free chicken broth
¹/₂ teaspoon dried tarragon leaves
¹/₂ teaspoon dried mint leaves
Salt and white pepper, to taste
6 tablespoons plain fat-free yogurt
Fresh mint *or* tarragon sprigs, as garnish

Per Serving
Calories: 87
% Calories from fat: 23
Fat (gm): 2.2
Saturated fat (gm): 0.4
Cholesterol (mg): 0.3
Sodium (mg): 153
Protein (gm): 7.7
Carbohydrate (gm): 8.7
Exchanges
Milk: 0.0
Vegetable: 2.0
Fruit: 0.0
Bread: 0.0
Meat: 0.0
Fat: 0.5

1. Saute onions in margarine in large saucepan until tender, about 5 minutes. Add snow peas and lettuce; saute 3 to 4 minutes longer. Add broth, tarragon, and mint; heat to boiling. Reduce heat and simmer, covered, 15 minutes or until snow peas are very tender.

2. Process soup in food processor or blender until smooth; strain. Season to taste with salt and white pepper. Serve warm, or refrigerate and serve cold.

3. Pour soup into bowls; garnish each with a tablespoon of yogurt and fresh herb sprigs.

SUMMER SQUASH SOUP

Use zucchini or yellow summer squash in the soup.

6 servings (about 1¼ cups each)

Vegetable cooking spray
½ cup chopped shallots
¼ cup sliced green onions and tops
2 cloves garlic, minced
4 medium zucchini, chopped
1 cup cubed, peeled Idaho potato
4 cups reduced-sodium fat-free chicken broth
1 cup chopped kale *or* spinach leaves
1-1½ teaspoons dried tarragon leaves
¼-½ cup fat-free half-and-half
Salt and white pepper, to taste
6 thin slices zucchini
6 thin slices yellow summer squash
Cayenne pepper, as garnish
1½ cups Sourdough Croutons
(½ recipe) (see p. 655)

Per Serving
Calories: 106
% Calories from fat: 4
Fat (gm): 0.5
Saturated fat (gm): 0.1
Cholesterol (mg): 0
Sodium (mg): 175
Protein (gm): 7.4
Carbohydrate (gm): 17.9
Exchanges
Milk: 0.0
Vegetable: 2.0
Fruit: 0.0
Bread: 0.5
Meat: 0.5
Fat: 0.0

1. Spray large saucepan with cooking spray; heat over medium heat until hot. Saute shallots, green onions, and garlic until tender, about 5 minutes. Add chopped zucchini and potato; saute 5 to 8 minutes longer.

2. Add broth, kale, and tarragon to saucepan; heat to boiling. Reduce heat and simmer, covered, until vegetables are tender, 10 to 15 minutes.

3. Process soup in food processor or blender until smooth; return to saucepan. Stir in half-and-half; season to taste with salt and white pepper. Heat and serve warm, or refrigerate and serve chilled.

4. Pour soup into bowls. Garnish each with a slice of zucchini and summer squash; sprinkle lightly with cayenne pepper and Sourdough Croutons.

CHAYOTE SQUASH SOUP WITH CILANTRO CREAM

Chayote squash, often called a "vegetable pear," is native to Mexico. Readily available in supermarkets, the squash is light green in color and delicate in flavor.

6 servings (about 1 cup each)

Vegetable cooking spray
1 large onion, chopped
2 cloves garlic, minced
3 tablespoons flour
3 large chayote squash, peeled, pitted, sliced
3 cans (14½ ounces each) reduced-sodium fat-free chicken broth, divided
½ cup water
Salt and white pepper, to taste
Cilantro Cream (recipe follows)
Finely chopped cilantro, as garnish

Per Serving
Calories: 68
% Calories from fat: 4
Fat (gm): 0.3
Saturated fat (gm): 0.1
Cholesterol (mg): 0.2
Sodium (mg): 79
Protein (gm): 6.8
Carbohydrate (gm): 10.5
Exchanges
Milk: 0.0
Vegetable: 2.0
Fruit: 0.0
Bread: 0.0
Meat: 0.5
Fat: 0.0

1. Spray large saucepan with cooking spray; heat over medium heat until hot. Saute onion and garlic until tender, about 5 minutes. Stir in flour; cook over medium heat 2 minutes, stirring constantly.

2. Add squash and 1 can broth to saucepan; heat to boiling; reduce heat and simmer, covered, until squash is tender, 15 to 20 minutes. Process mixture in food processor or blender until smooth; return to saucepan. Add remaining broth and water; season to taste with salt and white pepper. Heat over medium heat and serve warm, or refrigerate and serve chilled.

3. Serve soup in bowls; drizzle with Cilantro Cream and sprinkle with cilantro.

Cilantro Cream

makes about ½ cup

⅓ cup fat-free sour cream
1 tablespoon finely chopped cilantro
¼-⅓ cup fat-free milk

1. Mix sour cream and cilantro in small bowl, adding enough milk for desired consistency.

SWEET RED PEPPER SOUP

Use jarred roasted peppers for this soup, or roast 2 medium red bell peppers yourself. To roast peppers, cut in half and discard seeds. Place peppers, skin sides up, on aluminum foil-lined jelly roll pan; broil 4 inches from heat source until skin is blackened. Place peppers in plastic bag 5 minutes to loosen skins; peel and discard skins.

4 servings (about 1 cup each)

Vegetable cooking spray
1 medium onion, chopped
1/2 small jalapeño chili, seeds and veins discarded, minced
1 clove garlic, minced
1 jar (5 ounces) roasted red peppers, drained
1 cup reduced-sodium tomato juice
1 can (14 1/2 ounces) vegetable, *or* chicken, broth
1/4 teaspoon dried marjoram leaves
Salt and pepper, to taste
1/4 cup fat-free sour cream
1 small green onion and top, thinly sliced

Per Serving
Calories: 60
% Calories from fat: **3**
Fat (gm): 0.2
Saturated fat (gm): 0
Cholesterol (mg): 0
Sodium (mg): 62
Protein (gm): 2.8
Carbohydrate (gm): 13.3
Exchanges
Milk: 0.0
Vegetable: 2.0
Fruit: 0.0
Bread: 0.0
Meat: 0.0
Fat: 0.0

1. Spray medium saucepan with cooking spray; heat over medium heat until hot. Saute onion, jalapeño chili, and garlic until tender.

2. Process onion mixture, red peppers, and tomato juice in food processor or blender until smooth. Return mixture to saucepan and add vegetable broth and marjoram; heat to boiling. Reduce heat and simmer, covered, 15 minutes; season to taste with salt and pepper.

3. Serve soup warm, or refrigerate and serve cold. Serve soup in bowls; top each with dollop of sour cream and sprinkle with green onion.

POBLANO CHILI SOUP

Poblano chilies give this soup its extraordinary flavor. Readily available in most large supermarkets, they can vary in flavor from mild to very picante. Taste the peppers before making this soup; if they are too picante for your taste, substitute some green bell peppers and decrease the amount of jalapeño chili.

8 servings (about 1 cup each)

Vegetable cooking spray

2 medium onions, chopped

4 medium poblano chilies, seeds and veins discarded, chopped

1/2-1 small jalapeño chili, seeds and veins discarded, finely chopped

2 cans (14½ ounces each) reduced-sodium fat-free chicken broth

3 cups tomato juice

1/2 teaspoon ground cumin

1/2-1 cup water, divided

Salt and pepper, to taste

Minced cilantro, as garnish

Per Serving
Calories: 88
% Calories from fat: 3
Fat (gm): 0.4
Saturated fat (gm): 0
Cholesterol (mg): 0
Sodium (mg): 498
Protein (gm): 6.4
Carbohydrate (gm): 18.2
Exchanges
Milk: 0.0
Vegetable: 3.5
Fruit: 0.0
Bread: 0.0
Meat: 0.0
Fat: 0.0

1. Spray large saucepan with cooking spray; heat over medium heat until hot. Saute onions and chilies until onions are tender, about 5 minutes. Add broth; heat to boiling. Reduce heat and simmer, covered, until chilies are very tender, about 5 minutes.

2. Process broth mixture in food processor or blender until smooth; return to saucepan. Add tomato juice, cumin, and enough water for desired consistency; heat to boiling. Reduce heat and simmer, uncovered, 10 minutes. Season to taste with salt and pepper. Serve soup in bowls; sprinkle with cilantro.

CREAMED CORN SOUP

Garnish this colorful soup with a sprinkling of finely chopped cilantro or parsley.

6 servings (about 1 cup each)

Vegetable cooking spray
1/2 cup chopped onion
1 medium Idaho potato, peeled, cubed
2 cloves garlic, minced
1 can (15 1/2 ounces) whole-kernel corn, drained
3 tablespoons all-purpose flour
1/2 teaspoon ground coriander
1/8 teaspoon cayenne pepper
2 cans (14 1/2 ounces each) vegetable, *or* chicken, broth
1 cup fat-free milk
2 medium tomatoes, chopped
Salt and pepper, to taste
Paprika, as garnish

Per Serving
Calories: 144
% Calories from fat: 6
Fat (gm): 1
Saturated fat (gm): 0.2
Cholesterol (mg): 0.7
Sodium (mg): 313
Protein (gm): 5.2
Carbohydrate (gm): 31.2
Exchanges
Milk: 0.0
Vegetable: 0.0
Fruit: 0.0
Bread: 2.0
Meat: 0.0
Fat: 0.0

1. Spray large saucepan with cooking spray; heat over medium heat until hot. Saute onion, potato, and garlic until onion is tender, about 5 minutes. Stir in corn, flour, coriander, and cayenne pepper; cook 1 to 2 minutes, stirring frequently. Stir in broth and heat to boiling; reduce heat and simmer, covered, until potato is tender, about 10 minutes.

2. Process mixture in food processor or blender until almost smooth; return to saucepan. Stir in milk and tomatoes; heat just to boiling. Reduce heat and simmer, uncovered, 5 minutes. Season to taste with salt and pepper. Serve soup in bowls; sprinkle with paprika.

GARLIC SOUP WITH TOASTED BREAD

Traditionally a whole beaten egg is slowly stirred into the simmering soup before serving, similar to Chinese egg drop soup—try this for a change of pace!

4 servings (about 1 cup each)

1 tablespoon vegetable oil
6-8 cloves garlic, finely chopped
$^1/_2$ teaspoon ground cumin
$^1/_4$ teaspoon ground oregano leaves
$^1/_4$ teaspoon cayenne pepper
2 cans (14$^1/_2$ ounces each) reduced-sodium fat-free chicken broth
Salt, to taste
4 slices firm bread (French *or* sourdough)
Vegetable cooking spray
Finely chopped cilantro, as garnish

Per Serving
Calories: 124
% Calories from fat: 30
Fat (gm): 4.3
Saturated fat (gm): 0.6
Cholesterol (mg): 0
Sodium (mg): 216
Protein (gm): 6.8
Carbohydrate (gm): 14.7
Exchanges
Milk: 0.0
Vegetable: 0.0
Fruit: 0.0
Bread: 1.0
Meat: 0.0
Fat: 1.0

1. Heat oil in medium saucepan until hot; add garlic and cook over low heat until garlic is very soft and very lightly browned, 5 to 8 minutes. Stir in cumin, oregano, and cayenne pepper; cook 1 to 2 minutes. Add broth to saucepan; heat to boiling. Reduce heat and simmer, covered, 5 minutes. Season to taste with salt.

2. Spray both sides of bread slices generously with cooking spray; cook in large skillet, over medium heat, until golden on both sides. Place slices of bread in bottoms of 4 shallow bowls; ladle soup over. Sprinkle with cilantro.

CREAM OF TOMATO SOUP

This tastes just like the favorite-brand canned tomato soup we all remember! Canned tomatoes are necessary for the flavor, so don't substitute fresh.

4 servings (about 1¹/₄ cups each)

2 cans (14¹/₂ ounces each) no-salt whole tomatoes, undrained

2-3 teaspoons beef bouillon crystals

2 cups fat-free milk

3 tablespoons cornstarch

¹/₈ teaspoon baking soda

2 teaspoons sugar

1-2 tablespoons margarine

Salt and pepper, to taste

Per Serving
Calories: 143
% Calories from fat: 23
Fat (gm): 3.9
Saturated fat (gm): 0.8
Cholesterol (mg): 2
Sodium (mg): 628
Protein (gm): 6.5
Carbohydrate (gm): 22.9
Exchanges
Milk: 0.5
Vegetable: 2.0
Fruit: 0.0
Bread: 0.5
Meat: 0.0
Fat: 0.5

1. Process tomatoes and liquid in food processor or blender until smooth; heat tomatoes and bouillon crystals in large saucepan to boiling. Mix milk and cornstarch; whisk into boiling mixture. Boil, whisking constantly, until thickened, about 1 minute.

2. Add baking soda, sugar, and margarine to soup, stirring until margarine is melted. Season to taste with salt and pepper. Ladle into bowls.

TWO-TOMATO SOUP

The concentrated flavor of sun-dried tomatoes enhances the flavor of garden-ripe tomato soup.

6 servings (about 1¹/₄ cups each)

Olive oil cooking spray

1 cup chopped onion

¹/₂ cup sliced celery

¹/₂ cup chopped carrot

2 teaspoons minced roasted garlic

4 cups reduced-sodium fat-free chicken broth

4 cups chopped ripe tomatoes *or* 2 cans (16 ounces each) reduced-sodium whole tomatoes, undrained, coarsely chopped

Per Serving
Calories: 118
% Calories from fat: 5
Fat (gm): 0.7
Saturated fat (gm): 0.1
Cholesterol (mg): 0
Sodium (mg): 255
Protein (gm): 7.5
Carbohydrate (gm): 21.3
Exchanges
Milk: 0.0
Vegetable: 3.0
Fruit: 0.0
Bread: 0.5
Meat: 0.0
Fat: 0.0

1 large Idaho potato, peeled, cubed

1/2 cup sun-dried tomatoes (not in oil)

1-2 teaspoons dried basil leaves

1/2 cup fat-free half-and-half *or* fat-free milk

2-3 teaspoons sugar

Salt and pepper, to taste

Finely chopped basil *or* parsley, as garnish

1. Spray large saucepan with cooking spray; heat over medium heat until hot. Saute onion, celery, carrot, and garlic until tender; 5 to 8 minutes. Add broth, tomatoes, potato, sun-dried tomatoes, and basil; heat to boiling. Reduce heat and simmer, covered, until vegetables are tender, 10 to 15 minutes.

2. Process soup in food processor or blender until smooth; return to saucepan. Stir in half-and-half and cook over medium heat until hot through, 3 to 5 minutes. Season to taste with sugar, salt, and pepper.

3. Pour soup into bowls; sprinkle with basil or parsley.

SUN-DRIED TOMATO AND LINGUINE SOUP

For this skinny pasta soup, be sure to use plain sun-dried tomatoes rather than the ones packed in oil. One-half cup of uncooked orzo can be substituted for the linguine, if preferred.

4 servings (about 1 cup each)

2 sun-dried tomatoes (not in oil)

Vegetable cooking spray

1/2 cup thinly sliced celery

2 tablespoons thinly sliced green onions and tops

2 cloves garlic, minced

2 cans (15 ounces each) reduced-sodium chicken broth

2 ounces linguine, uncooked, broken into 2- to 3-inch pieces

1-2 teaspoons lemon juice

Salt and pepper, to taste

Per Serving
Calories: 68
% Calories from fat: 11
Fat (gm): 0.9
Saturated fat (gm): 0
Cholesterol (mg): 0
Sodium (mg): 71
Protein (gm): 3.6
Carbohydrate (gm): 12.1
Exchanges
Milk: 0.0
Vegetable: 1.0
Fruit: 0.0
Bread: 0.5
Meat: 0.0
Fat: 0.0

1. Place tomatoes in small bowl; pour hot water over to cover. Let tomatoes stand until softened, about 15 minutes; drain. Coarsely chop tomatoes.

2. Spray medium saucepan with cooking spray; heat over medium heat until hot. Saute celery, green onions, and garlic until tender, 5 to 7 minutes. Stir in chicken broth; heat to boiling.

3. Add linguine and tomatoes to boiling broth. Reduce heat and simmer, uncovered, until pasta is al dente, about 10 minutes. Season with lemon juice, salt, and pepper.

RIPE TOMATO AND LEEK SOUP

Use the summer's ripest tomatoes for this soup, cooking only briefly to maintain their sweetness. Peel the tomatoes, or not, as you prefer.

6 servings (about 1¹/₄ cups each)

2	cups sliced leeks (white parts only) (about 8 ounces)
3	cloves garlic, minced
1	tablespoon margarine *or* olive oil
6	large tomatoes (about 2¹/₂ pounds)
4	cups reduced-sodium fat-free chicken broth
¹/₂-1	teaspoon dried basil leaves
	Salt and white pepper, to taste
6	tablespoons fat-free sour cream *or* plain fat-free yogurt
	Basil sprigs, as garnish

Per Serving
Calories: 120
% Calories from fat: 19
Fat (gm): 2.6
Saturated fat (gm): 0.5
Cholesterol (mg): 0
Sodium (mg): 173
Protein (gm): 7.3
Carbohydrate (gm): 17.7
Exchanges
Milk: 0.0
Vegetable: 3.0
Fruit: 0.0
Bread: 0.0
Meat: 0.5
Fat: 0.5

1. Saute leeks and garlic in margarine in large saucepan until tender, about 8 minutes. Add tomatoes, broth, and basil to saucepan; heat to boiling. Reduce heat and simmer, covered, 10 minutes.

2. Process soup in food processor or blender until smooth; season to taste with salt and white pepper. Heat and serve soup warm, or refrigerate and serve chilled.

3. Pour soup into bowls; garnish each with a tablespoon of sour cream and a basil sprig.

CREAM OF ARTICHOKE AND MUSHROOM SOUP

Shiitake or cremini mushrooms can be substituted for the portobello mushrooms. Serve with Sourdough Croutons (see p. 655), if desired.

4 servings (about 1 cup each)

3/4 cup chopped portobello mushrooms
2 tablespoons finely chopped onion
1 tablespoon margarine
1 tablespoon flour
3 cups fat-free milk
1 vegetable bouillon cube
1 package (9 ounces) frozen artichoke hearts, cooked, finely chopped
Salt and white pepper, to taste
Paprika, as garnish

Per Serving
Calories: 135
% Calories from fat: 22
Fat (gm): 3.6
Saturated fat (gm): 0.8
Cholesterol (mg): 3
Sodium (mg): 422
Protein (gm): 9.2
Carbohydrate (gm): 18.9
Exchanges
Milk: 1.0
Vegetable: 1.0
Fruit: 0.0
Bread: 0.0
Meat: 0.0
Fat: 0.5

1. Saute mushrooms and onion in medium saucepan in margarine until tender, about 5 minutes. Stir in flour; cook 1 minute longer. Stir in milk and bouillon cube; heat to boiling. Boil, stirring constantly, until thickened, about 1 minute.

2. Stir artichoke hearts into soup; simmer, uncovered, 5 minutes. Season to taste with salt and white pepper. Pour soup into bowls; sprinkle with paprika.

FRESH BASIL SOUP

For flavor variation, try another favorite garden herb, such as rosemary, oregano, lemon thyme, or marjoram.

6 servings (about 1 cup each)

4 cups reduced-sodium fat-free chicken broth
1 cup firmly packed basil leaves
1 cup firmly packed parsley sprigs
1/2 cup chopped onion
1 teaspoon sugar
2 cups cubed, peeled potatoes
1 cup fat-free milk

Per Serving
Calories: 157
% Calories from fat: 13
Fat (gm): 2.2
Saturated fat (gm): 0.5
Cholesterol (mg): 0.7
Sodium (mg): 166
Protein (gm): 8.2
Carbohydrate (gm): 25.8
Exchanges
Milk: 0.0
Vegetable: 2.0
Fruit: 0.0
Bread: 1.0
Meat: 0.5
Fat: 0.5

1/4 cup all-purpose flour
1 tablespoon margarine
Salt and white pepper, to taste
Finely chopped parsley, as garnish

1. Heat broth, basil, parsley, onion, and sugar to boiling in medium saucepan. Simmer, covered, 30 minutes. Strain, discarding herbs and onion; return broth to saucepan.

2. Add potatoes to saucepan; heat to boiling. Reduce heat and simmer, covered, until potatoes are tender, about 15 minutes. Mix milk and flour; stir into saucepan and heat to boiling. Boil until thickened, 1 to 2 minutes, stirring constantly. Stir in margarine; season to taste with salt and white pepper.

3. Pour soup into bowls; sprinkle with parsley.

CREAM OF BROCCOLI SOUP

Fat-free half-and-half lends a wonderful richness to this soup.

6 servings (about 1 cup each)

2 pounds broccoli
Vegetable cooking spray
1 cup chopped onion
3 cloves garlic, minced
1/2 teaspoon dried thyme leaves
1/8 teaspoon ground nutmeg
3 1/2 cups reduced-sodium fat-free chicken broth
1/2 cup fat-free half-and-half *or* fat-free milk
Salt and white pepper, to taste
6 tablespoons fat-free sour cream
2-3 teaspoons fat-free milk
1 1/2 cups Croutons (1/2 recipe) (see p. 655)

Per Serving
Calories: 117
% Calories from fat: 5
Fat (gm): 0.7
Saturated fat (gm): 0.1
Cholesterol (mg): 0
Sodium (mg): 210
Protein (gm): 10.1
Carbohydrate (gm): 18.2
Exchanges
Milk: 0.0
Vegetable: 2.0
Fruit: 0.0
Bread: 0.5
Meat: 0.5
Fat: 0.0

1. Peel broccoli stalks; cut broccoli into 1-inch pieces. Spray large saucepan with cooking spray; heat over medium heat until hot. Saute onion and garlic until tender, 3 to 5 minutes. Stir in broccoli, thyme, and nutmeg; cook 2 minutes longer.

2. Add broth to saucepan; heat to boiling. Reduce heat and simmer, covered, until broccoli is very tender, about 10 minutes.

3. Process soup in food processor or blender until smooth. Return soup to saucepan; add half-and-half and heat over medium heat until hot. Season to taste with salt and white pepper. Pour soup into bowls. Mix sour cream and milk; swirl about 1 tablespoon mixture into soup in each bowl. Sprinkle with Croutons.

HERBED BROCCOLI AND PASTA SOUP

A wonderfully versatile soup, as any vegetable in season and any choice of herb can be substituted for the broccoli and thyme. For an entrée soup, 12 ounces of cubed cooked chicken breast can be added during the last 10 minutes of cooking time.

6 servings (about 1 cup each)

3 cans (15 ounces each) reduced-sodium chicken broth

4 cloves garlic, minced

2-3 teaspoons dried thyme leaves

3 cups small broccoli florets

2¹/₄ cups (6 ounces) fusilli (spirals), uncooked

2-3 tablespoons lemon juice

¹/₄ teaspoon salt

¹/₈ teaspoon pepper

Per Serving
Calories: 125
% Calories from fat: 8
Fat (gm): 1.1
Saturated fat (gm): 0.2
Cholesterol (mg): 0
Sodium (mg): 134
Protein (gm): 6.4
Carbohydrate (gm): 23
Exchanges
Milk: 0.0
Vegetable: 0.5
Fruit: 0.0
Bread: 1.5
Meat: 0.0
Fat: 0.0

1. Heat chicken broth, garlic, and thyme to boiling in medium saucepan. Stir in broccoli and fusilli. Reduce heat and simmer, uncovered, until broccoli is tender and pasta is al dente, about 10 minutes.

2. Stir in lemon juice, salt, and pepper.

DILLED CARROT SOUP

Carrots team with dill for a fresh, clean flavor.

6 to 8 servings (about 1½ cups each)

Vegetable cooking spray
1½ cups chopped onions
2 cloves garlic, minced
6 cups reduced-sodium fat-free chicken broth
1 can (16 ounces) reduced-sodium diced tomatoes, undrained
2 pounds carrots, cut into ½-inch slices
1 medium Idaho potato, peeled, cubed
2-3 tablespoons lemon juice
1-1½ teaspoons dried dill weed
Salt and white pepper, to taste

6 tablespoons plain fat-free yogurt
2 tablespoons shredded carrot
Dill, *or* parsley, sprigs, as garnish

Per Serving
Calories: 156
% Calories from fat: 3
Fat (gm): 0.5
Saturated fat (gm): 0.1
Cholesterol (mg): 0.3
Sodium (mg): 245
Protein (gm): 10
Carbohydrate (gm): 28.7
Exchanges
Milk: 0.0
Vegetable: 4.0
Fruit: 0.0
Bread: 0.5
Meat: 0.0
Fat: 0.0

1. Spray large saucepan with cooking spray; heat over medium heat until hot. Saute onions and garlic until tender, about 5 minutes. Add broth, tomatoes and liquid, sliced carrots, and potato; heat to boiling. Reduce heat and simmer, covered, until vegetables are tender, about 15 minutes.

2. Process soup in food processor or blender until smooth. Stir in lemon juice and dill weed; season to taste with salt and white pepper.

3. Serve soup warm, or refrigerate and serve chilled. Pour soup into bowls; garnish each with a tablespoon of yogurt, a teaspoon of shredded carrot, and dill sprigs.

CREAM OF CAULIFLOWER SOUP WITH CHEESE

Fat-free half-and-half adds a wonderful rich creaminess to the soup. Substitute broccoli for the cauliflower another time.

6 servings (about 1 cup each)

Vegetable cooking spray

1/2 cup chopped onion

2 cloves garlic, minced

2 tablespoons flour

3¹/2 cups reduced-sodium fat-free chicken broth

12 ounces cauliflower, cut into florets

1 large Idaho potato, peeled, cubed

1/4-1/2 cup fat-free half-and-half *or* fat-free milk

3/4 cup (3 ounces) shredded reduced-fat Cheddar cheese

Salt and white pepper, to taste

Ground mace *or* nutmeg, as garnish

Per Serving
Calories: 108
% Calories from fat: 20
Fat (gm): 2.3
Saturated fat (gm): 1.1
Cholesterol (mg): 7.6
Sodium (mg): 312
Protein (gm): 8.8
Carbohydrate (gm): 12.2
Exchanges
Milk: 0.0
Vegetable: 2.0
Fruit: 0.0
Bread: 0.0
Meat: 0.5
Fat: 0.5

1. Spray large saucepan with cooking spray; heat over medium heat until hot. Saute onion and garlic until tender, about 10 minutes. Stir in flour; cook 1 to 2 minutes longer. Add broth, cauliflower, and potato; heat to boiling. Reduce heat and simmer, covered, until vegetables are tender, 10 to 15 minutes.

2. Remove about half the vegetables from the soup with a slotted spoon and reserve. Puree remaining soup in food processor or blender until smooth. Return soup to saucepan; stir in reserved vegetables, half-and-half, and cheese; cook over low heat until cheese is melted, 3 to 4 minutes, stirring frequently. Season to taste with salt and white pepper.

3. Pour soup into bowls; sprinkle lightly with mace or nutmeg.

POTATO CHOWDER

A basic soup that is versatile—substitute any desired vegetables, such as carrots, zucchini, green beans, or corn, for part of the potatoes for a delectable vegetable chowder.

6 servings (about 1 cup each)

1 cup chopped onion
$^1/_4$ cup thinly sliced celery
2 tablespoons margarine
3 tablespoons flour
2 cups reduced-sodium chicken broth
$3^1/_2$ cups peeled, cubed Idaho potatoes
$^1/_4$-$^1/_2$ teaspoon celery seeds
2 cups fat-free milk
Salt and pepper, to taste

Per Serving
Calories: 212
% Calories from fat: 17
Fat (gm): 4.2
Saturated fat (gm): 0.9
Cholesterol (mg): 1.3
Sodium (mg): 210
Protein (gm): 7.5
Carbohydrate (gm): 37.1
Exchanges
Milk: 0.0
Vegetable: 1.0
Fruit: 0.0
Bread: 2.0
Meat: 0.0
Fat: 1.0

1. Saute onion and celery in margarine in large saucepan until tender, 5 to 8 minutes. Stir in flour; cook over medium-low heat, stirring constantly, 1 minute.

2. Add broth, potatoes, and celery seeds to saucepan; heat to boiling. Reduce heat and simmer, covered, until potatoes are tender, 10 to 15 minutes. Stir in milk; cook over medium heat until hot, 2 to 3 minutes. Season to taste with salt and pepper.

Variation: **Vichyssoise**—Make recipe as above, substituting chopped leek for half the onion and omitting celery and celery seeds. Cool; process soup in food processor or blender until smooth. Refrigerate until chilled. Serve in bowls; sprinkle with minced fresh chives.

HOT CHILI VICHYSSOISE

Potato soup will never be boring if served Tex-Mex style. This version, prepared with chilies, packs a punch!

6 servings (about 1 cup each)

Mesquite-flavored vegetable cooking spray

1 pound small red potatoes, unpeeled, cut into halves

1 medium leek, cut into ³/₄-inch pieces (white part only)

1 large poblano chili, cut into ³/₄-inch pieces

1 medium jalapeño chili, cut into ³/₄-inch pieces

6 cloves garlic, peeled

1¹/₂ teaspoons ground cumin

¹/₂ teaspoon chili powder

¹/₂ teaspoon dried oregano leaves

¹/₂ teaspoon pepper

4 cups reduced-sodium fat-free chicken broth, divided

¹/₂-³/₄ cup fat-free half-and-half *or* fat-free milk

¹/₄ cup minced cilantro
Salt, to taste

Per Serving
Calories: 113
% Calories from fat: 2
Fat (gm): 0.3
Saturated fat (gm): 0
Cholesterol (mg): 0
Sodium (mg): 169
Protein (gm): 6.6
Carbohydrate (gm): 20.9
Exchanges
Milk: 0.0
Vegetable: 1.0
Fruit: 0.0
Bread: 1.0
Meat: 0.0
Fat: 0.0

1. Spray aluminum foil-lined jelly roll pan with cooking spray. Arrange vegetables, chilies, and garlic in single layer on pan; spray generously with cooking spray and sprinkle with herbs and pepper.

2. Roast vegetables at 425 degrees until browned and tender, about 40 minutes, removing garlic when tender, about 20 minutes.

3. Process vegetables and 1 to 2 cups broth in food processor or blender until smooth. Return to saucepan; stir in remaining broth, half-and-half, and cilantro; season with salt. Serve warm, or refrigerate until chilled, 4 to 6 hours, and serve cold.

LIME-SCENTED VEGETABLE SOUP

A soup with a fresh flavor, accented with lime and cilantro. Cubed cooked chicken breast can be added, if you like.

6 servings (about 1¼ cups each)

Vegetable cooking spray
2 cups sliced carrots
1 cup chopped red bell pepper
¾ cup sliced celery
⅓ cup sliced green onions and tops
6 cloves garlic, minced
1 small jalapeño chili, finely chopped
6 cups reduced-sodium fat-free chicken broth
½-¾ cup lime juice
½ teaspoon ground cumin
1 cup chopped tomato
½ cup chopped, seeded cucumber
½ small avocado, peeled, chopped
3-4 tablespoons finely chopped cilantro
1½ cups Herb Croutons (½ recipe) (see p. 655)

Per Serving
Calories: 120
% Calories from fat: 23
Fat (gm): 3.1
Saturated fat (gm): 0.5
Cholesterol (mg): 0
Sodium (mg): 351
Protein (gm): 8.3
Carbohydrate (gm): 15.1
Exchanges
Milk: 0.0
Vegetable: 4.0
Fruit: 0.0
Bread: 0.0
Meat: 0.0
Fat: 0.5

1. Spray large saucepan with cooking spray; heat over medium heat until hot. Saute carrots, bell pepper, celery, green onions, garlic, and jalapeño chili, 5 minutes.

2. Add broth, lime juice, and cumin to saucepan; heat to boiling. Reduce heat and simmer, covered, until vegetables are tender, 10 to 15 minutes.

3. Pour soup into bowls; add tomato, cucumber, and avocado to each bowl. Sprinkle with cilantro and Herb Croutons.

GARDEN HARVEST SOUP

Vary the vegetables according to your garden or greengrocer's bounty.

6 servings (about 1¹/₂ cups each)

2 small onions, sliced
2 cloves garlic, minced
1 tablespoon olive oil
2 carrots, sliced
1 small red bell pepper, sliced
1 small yellow bell pepper, sliced
2 cups whole-kernel corn
5 cups reduced-sodium fat-free chicken broth
1 cup green beans, cut into 1-inch pieces
1 medium zucchini, sliced
1 yellow summer squash, sliced
¹/₂-³/₄ teaspoon dried basil leaves
¹/₂ teaspoon dried oregano leaves
Salt and pepper, to taste
¹/₃ cup fat-free milk, optional
Finely chopped parsley, as garnish

Per Serving
Calories: 136
% Calories from fat: 17
Fat (gm): 2.8
Saturated fat (gm): 0.4
Cholesterol (mg): 0
Sodium (mg): 161
Protein (gm): 8.4
Carbohydrate (gm): 21.3
Exchanges
Milk: 0.0
Vegetable: 4.0
Fruit: 0.0
Bread: 0.0
Meat: 0.0
Fat: 0.5

1. Saute onions and garlic in oil in large saucepan until tender, about 5 minutes. Add carrots, bell peppers, and corn and saute 5 minutes. Add broth, green beans, zucchini, squash, and herbs; heat to boiling. Reduce heat and simmer, covered, until vegetables are tender, about 15 minutes. Season to taste with salt and pepper.

2. Whip milk with immersion blender; stir into soup just before serving. Pour soup into bowls; sprinkle with parsley.

CREAM OF MUSHROOM SOUP

Creamy and rich, this soup resembles the favorite-brand canned soup we remember. For a richer soup, use fat-free half-and-half instead of milk.

4 servings (about 1¼ cups each)

1 pound mushrooms
2 tablespoons margarine, divided
1 cup chopped onion
2½ cups reduced-sodium chicken broth
2½ cups fat-free milk, divided
2 tablespoons plus 2 teaspoons cornstarch
Salt and pepper, to taste
Minced parsley leaves, as garnish

Per Serving
Calories: 183
% Calories from fat: 31
Fat (gm): 6.5
Saturated fat (gm): 1.4
Cholesterol (mg): 2.5
Sodium (mg): 361
Protein (gm): 11
Carbohydrate (gm): 21.8
Exchanges
Milk: 0.5
Vegetable: 3.0
Fruit: 0.0
Bread: 0.0
Meat: 0.0
Fat: 1.5

1. Slice enough mushroom caps to make 2 cups; finely chop stems and remaining mushrooms. Saute sliced mushrooms in 1 tablespoon margarine in large saucepan until browned, about 5 minutes; remove and reserve. Saute onion and chopped mushrooms in remaining 1 tablespoon margarine until onion is tender, about 5 minutes.

2. Add broth and 2 cups milk to saucepan; heat to boiling. Mix remaining ½ cup milk and cornstarch; whisk into boiling mixture. Boil, whisking constantly, until thickened, about 1 minute. Stir in reserved sliced mushrooms. Season to taste with salt and pepper. Serve in bowls; sprinkle with parsley.

BLACK MUSHROOM SOUP

Chinese black mushrooms, also called shiitake mushrooms, add a fragrant, woodsy flavor to this soup.

6 servings (about 1¼ cups each)

1½ ounces dried Chinese black mush-
    rooms (shiitake)
  1 ounce dried cloud ear mushrooms
  2 cups boiling water
    Vegetable cooking spray
 ¼ cup chopped onion
 ¼ cup thinly sliced green onions and tops
  5 cups reduced-sodium fat-free chicken
    broth
  3 cups sliced cremini mushrooms
    Salt and white pepper, to taste
    Finely chopped parsley, as garnish

Per Serving
Calories: 72
% Calories from fat: 3
Fat (gm): 0.3
Saturated fat (gm): 0.1
Cholesterol (mg): 0
Sodium (mg): 145
Protein (gm): 7
Carbohydrate (gm): 11.2
Exchanges
Milk: 0.0
Vegetable: 3.0
Fruit: 0.0
Bread: 0.0
Meat: 0.0
Fat: 0.0

1. Place dried mushrooms in bowl; pour boiling water over. Let stand until mushrooms are softened, about 15 minutes. Drain, reserving liquid. Slice mushrooms, discarding tough stems from black mushrooms.

2. Spray large saucepan with cooking spray; heat over medium heat until hot. Saute onions until tender, about 5 minutes. Add sliced dried mushrooms, reserved liquid, and broth; heat to boiling. Reduce heat and simmer, covered, 20 minutes, adding cremini mushrooms during last 10 minutes. Season to taste with salt and white pepper.

3. Pour soup into bowls; sprinkle with parsley.

SAVORY MUSHROOM AND BARLEY SOUP

Fast and easy to make with quick-cooking barley. Other grains, such as wild rice or oat groats can be substituted for the barley; cook before adding to the soup.

4 servings (about 1¹/₂ cups each)

Vegetable cooking spray
1 cup chopped onion
1 cup sliced celery
²/₃ cup sliced carrots
1 teaspoon dried savory leaves
³/₄ teaspoon fennel seeds, crushed
1 quart water
1 can (16 ounces) reduced-sodium whole tomatoes, undrained, coarsely chopped
¹/₂ cup quick-cooking barley
2 cups sliced cremini, *or* white, mushrooms
Salt and pepper, to taste
Finely chopped parsley, as garnish

Per Serving
Calories: 151
% Calories from fat: 8
Fat (gm): 1.4
Saturated fat (gm): 0.1
Cholesterol (mg): 0
Sodium (mg): 53
Protein (gm): 5.6
Carbohydrate (gm): 32.1
Exchanges
Milk: 0.0
Vegetable: 2.0
Fruit: 0.0
Bread: 1.5
Meat: 0.0
Fat: 0.0

1. Spray large saucepan with cooking spray; heat over medium heat until hot. Saute onion, celery, and carrots until onion is tender, about 5 minutes. Stir in herbs; cook 1 to 2 minutes longer.

2. Add water, tomatoes and liquid, barley, and mushrooms to saucepan; heat to boiling. Cook, covered, until barley is tender, 10 to 15 minutes. Season to taste with salt and pepper.

3. Pour soup into bowls; sprinkle with parsley.

TORTELLINI AND MUSHROOM SOUP

Porcini mushrooms, an Italian delicacy found fresh in Tuscany in fall, are available in dried form year round. Porcini impart a wonderful earthy flavor to recipes. Other dried mushrooms, such as shiitake or Chinese black mushrooms, can be substituted for a similar flavor.

6 servings (about 1 cup each)

2 ounces dried porcini mushrooms
  Vegetable cooking spray
8 ounces fresh white mushrooms, sliced
2 tablespoons finely chopped shallots *or* green onions
2 cloves garlic, minced
1/2 teaspoon dried tarragon, *or* thyme, leaves
2 cans (15 ounces each) reduced-sodium beef broth
1/4 cup dry sherry, optional
1 package (9 ounces) fresh low-fat tomato and cheese tortellini
1/4 teaspoon salt
1/4 teaspoon pepper

Per Serving
Calories: 188
% Calories from fat: 19
Fat (gm): 4.2
Saturated fat (gm): 1.5
Cholesterol (mg): 17.7
Sodium (mg): 235
Protein (gm): 10.1
Carbohydrate (gm): 28.8
Exchanges
Milk: 0.0
Vegetable: 1.0
Fruit: 0.0
Bread: 1.5
Meat: 0.5
Fat: 0.5

1. Place dried mushrooms in bowl; pour hot water over to cover. Let stand until mushrooms are soft, about 15 minutes; drain. Slice mushrooms, discarding any tough parts.

2. Spray large saucepan with cooking spray; heat over medium heat until hot. Saute dried and white mushrooms, shallots, garlic, and tarragon until mushrooms are tender, about 5 minutes.

3. Add beef broth and sherry to vegetables; heat to boiling. Add tortellini; reduce heat and simmer, uncovered, until tortellini are al dente, about 5 minutes. Stir in salt and pepper.

VIDALIA ONION SOUP

The mild sweetness of Vidalia onions makes this soup special, but try it with other flavorful onion varieties too. Half of the soup is pureed, resulting in a wonderful contrast of textures.

8 servings (about 1¹/₄ cups each)

Vegetable cooking spray
6 cups thinly sliced Vidalia onions (1¹/₂ pounds)
2 cloves garlic, minced
1 teaspoon sugar
¹/₃ cup all-purpose flour
6 cups reduced-sodium fat-free chicken, *or* vegetable, broth
1¹/₂ teaspoons dried sage leaves
2 bay leaves
Salt, cayenne, and white pepper, to taste
Snipped chives, as garnish

Per Serving
Calories: 82
% Calories from fat: 2
Fat (gm): 0.2
Saturated fat (gm): 0
Cholesterol (mg): 0
Sodium (mg): 131
Protein (gm): 6.1
Carbohydrate (gm): 12.7
Exchanges
Milk: 0.0
Vegetable: 3.0
Fruit: 0.0
Bread: 0.0
Meat: 0.0
Fat: 0.0

1. Spray Dutch oven with cooking spray; heat over medium heat until hot. Add onions and garlic and cook, covered, over medium-low heat until wilted, 8 to 10 minutes. Stir in sugar and cook, uncovered, over medium-low to low heat until onions are lightly browned, 10 to 15 minutes. Stir in flour; cook 1 to 2 minutes longer.

2. Stir in broth, sage, and bay leaves; heat to boiling. Reduce heat and simmer, covered, 30 minutes. Discard bay leaves.

3. Process half the soup in food processor or blender until smooth; return to pan. Season to taste with salt, cayenne, and white pepper. Serve warm, or refrigerate and serve chilled. Pour soup into bowls; sprinkle with chives.

FRENCH ONION SOUP

This classic soup is topped with bruschetta and fat-free cheese for healthful low-fat dining.

8 servings (about 1¼ cups each)

Vegetable cooking spray

6 cups thinly sliced Spanish onions (1½ pounds)

2 cloves garlic, minced

1 teaspoon sugar

6 cups reduced-sodium fat-free beef broth

2 bay leaves

Salt and white pepper, to taste

8 Bruschetta (²/₃ recipe) (see p. 653)

8 tablespoons (2 ounces) shredded fat-free Swiss, *or* mozzarella, cheese

Per Serving
Calories: 144
% Calories from fat: 6
Fat (gm): 1
Saturated fat (gm): 0.2
Cholesterol (mg): 0
Sodium (mg): 390
Protein (gm): 9
Carbohydrate (gm): 24.3
Exchanges
Milk: 0.0
Vegetable: 3.0
Fruit: 0.0
Bread: 1.0
Meat: 0.0
Fat: 0.0

1. Spray Dutch oven with cooking spray; heat over medium heat until hot. Add onions and garlic and cook, covered, over medium-low heat until wilted, 8 to 10 minutes. Stir in sugar and cook, uncovered, over medium-low to low heat until onions are lightly browned, about 15 minutes.

2. Stir in broth and bay leaves; heat to boiling. Reduce heat and simmer, covered, 30 minutes. Discard bay leaves; season to taste with salt and white pepper.

3. Top each Bruschetta with 1 tablespoon cheese; broil 6 inches from heat source until melted. Pour soup into bowls; top each with a Bruschetta.

THREE-ONION SOUP WITH MUSHROOMS

Mushrooms add flavor and texture interest to this soup.

6 servings (about 1¹/₂ cups each)

3	cups thinly sliced onions
1¹/₂	cups thinly sliced leeks (white part only)
¹/₂	cup chopped shallots *or* green onions and tops
1	tablespoon margarine
1	teaspoon sugar
4	ounces mushrooms, sliced
6¹/₂	cups reduced-sodium fat-free chicken broth
	Salt and pepper, to taste

Per Serving
Calories: 114
% Calories from fat: 18
Fat (gm): 2.2
Saturated fat (gm): 0.4
Cholesterol (mg): 0
Sodium (mg): 218
Protein (gm): 8.5
Carbohydrate (gm): 14.7
Exchanges
Milk: 0.0
Vegetable: 3.0
Fruit: 0.0
Bread: 0.0
Meat: 0.0
Fat: 0.5

1. Cook onions, leeks, and shallots in margarine in large saucepan, covered, over medium-low heat 15 minutes. Stir in sugar; continue cooking, uncovered, until onion mixture is golden, about 10 minutes longer.

2. Stir mushrooms into onion mixture; cook over medium heat until tender, about 5 minutes. Add broth and heat to boiling; reduce heat and simmer, uncovered, 15 minutes. Season to taste with salt and pepper.

ONION AND LEEK SOUP

An Italian-style soup, which combines onions and leeks.

6 servings (about 1¹/₄ cups each)

	Vegetable cooking spray
4	cups sliced onions
2	cups sliced leeks (white part only)
6	cloves garlic, minced
1	teaspoon sugar
7	cups reduced-sodium fat-free chicken broth
	Salt and white pepper, to taste
6	teaspoons grated fat-free Parmesan cheese

Per Serving
Calories: 211
% Calories from fat: 3
Fat (gm): 0.8
Saturated fat (gm): 0.1
Cholesterol (mg): 0
Sodium (mg): 234
Protein (gm): 12.9
Carbohydrate (gm): 37.1
Exchanges
Milk: 0.0
Vegetable: 2.0
Fruit: 0.0
Bread: 2.0
Meat: 0.0
Fat: 0.0

1. Spray large saucepan with cooking spray; heat over medium heat until hot. Add onions, leeks, and garlic and cook, covered, over medium heat until wilted, 5 to 8 minutes. Stir in sugar; cook, uncovered, over medium-low heat until onion mixture is very soft and browned, 15 to 20 minutes.

2. Add broth to saucepan and heat to boiling. Season to taste with salt and white pepper. Pour soup into bowls; sprinkle 1 teaspoon Parmesan cheese over each.

CREAMY PEANUT BUTTER SOUP

This soup will tempt peanut butter lovers! In our low-fat version pureed beans contribute rich texture, without detracting from the peanut flavor.

6 servings (about 1 cup each)

Vegetable cooking spray
- 1/2 cup chopped onion
- 1/2 cup chopped carrot
- 1/2 cup sliced celery
- 1 leek, sliced (white part only)
- 2 cloves garlic, minced
- 3 cups reduced-sodium fat-free chicken broth
- 1 can (15 ounces) Great Northern beans, rinsed, drained
- 1/3-1/2 cup reduced-fat peanut butter
- 1/2 cup fat-free half-and-half *or* fat-free milk
- 1/2 teaspoon curry powder
- 2-3 teaspoons lemon juice
- 1-2 dashes hot pepper sauce
  Salt, cayenne, and black pepper, to taste
  Thinly sliced green onion, as garnish

Per Serving
Calories: 182
% Calories from fat: 26
Fat (gm): 5.5
Saturated fat (gm): 0.9
Cholesterol (mg): 0
Sodium (mg): 452
Protein (gm): 11.8
Carbohydrate (gm): 22.8
Exchanges
Milk: 0.0
Vegetable: 2.0
Fruit: 0.0
Bread: 1.0
Meat: 1.0
Fat: 0.0

1. Spray large saucepan with cooking spray; heat over medium heat until hot. Saute onion, carrot, celery, leek, and garlic 5 minutes. Add broth and beans and heat to boiling; reduce heat and simmer, covered, until vegetables are tender, 10 to 15 minutes.

2. Process soup and peanut butter in food processor or blender until smooth. Return soup to saucepan; stir in half-and-half and curry powder. Heat over medium heat until hot. Season to taste with lemon juice, hot pepper sauce, salt, cayenne, and black pepper.

3. Pour soup into bowls; sprinkle with green onion.

CHICKEN AND CHILIES SOUP

The green chilies add extra zip and give the soup its spicy South-of-the-Border flavor.

6-7 servings

1 medium onion, finely chopped
1 large garlic clove, minced
1 large rib celery, diced
1 teaspoon margarine
1 quart fat-free chicken broth
3/4 cup cubed skinless cooked chicken breast (1/2-inch)
1 can (4 ounces) chopped green chilies, drained
1 1/2 cups small cauliflower florets
1 cup cooked kidney beans
2 tablespoons cornstarch
1/4 cup cold water
1/2 cup (2 ounces) shredded mild Cheddar cheese
1/2 cup (2 ounces) shredded fat-free Cheddar cheese
Chopped chives, as garnish

Per Serving
Calories: 176
% Calories from fat: 25
Fat (gm): 4.9
Saturated fat (gm): 2.4
Cholesterol (mg): 24.8
Sodium (mg): 341
Protein (gm): 18.2
Carbohydrate (gm): 14
Exchanges
Milk: 0.0
Vegetable: 0.0
Fruit: 0.0
Bread: 1.0
Meat: 2.0
Fat: 0.0

1. Saute onion, garlic, and celery in margarine in large saucepan until onion is tender, about 5 minutes. Add chicken broth, chicken, chilies, cauliflower, and beans; heat to boiling. Reduce heat and simmer, covered, 10 minutes.

2. Heat soup to boiling; stir in combined cornstarch and water. Boil, stirring, until thickened, about 1 minute. Reduce heat to low; add cheeses, stirring until melted. Sprinkle each serving with chives.

TWO-SEASON SQUASH SOUP

Winter squash and summer garden zucchini are combined in this perfect soup.

6 servings (about 1 ³/₄ cup each)

1 cup chopped onion
2 cloves garlic, minced
2 teaspoons margarine
3 cups fat-free beef broth
1 medium butternut squash, peeled, seeded, cubed
2 medium zucchini, sliced
1 can (28 ounces) reduced-sodium whole tomatoes, undrained, chopped
1 can (15 ounces) Great Northern beans, drained, rinsed
3 tablespoons minced parsley
1 bay leaf
1 teaspoon very-low-sodium Worcester-shire sauce
1 teaspoon dried marjoram leaves
1/2 teaspoon dried rosemary leaves
Salt and pepper, to taste

Per Serving
Calories: 119
% Calories from fat: 10
Fat (gm): 1.6
Saturated fat (gm): 0.3
Cholesterol (mg): 0
Sodium (mg): 308
Protein (gm): 8.3
Carbohydrate (gm): 23.2
Exchanges
Milk: 0.0
Vegetable: 1.0
Fruit: 0.0
Bread: 1.5
Meat: 0.0
Fat: 0.0

1. Saute onion and garlic in margarine in large saucepan until tender, about 5 minutes. Add remaining ingredients, except salt and pepper, and heat to boiling. Reduce heat and simmer, covered, until squash is tender, about 25 minutes. Discard bay leaf; season to taste with salt and pepper.

CINNAMON-SPICED PUMPKIN SOUP

For convenience, 2 cans of pumpkin can be substituted for the fresh pumpkin. Any yellow winter squash, such as butternut, Hubbard, or acorn, can also be used.

4 servings (about 1¼ cups each)

4	cups cubed, seeded, peeled pumpkin (about 2 pounds)	
2	cups fat-free half-and-half *or* fat-free milk	
1-2	tablespoons light brown sugar	
½	teaspoon ground cinnamon	
¼-½	teaspoon ground nutmeg	
	Snipped chives, as garnish	

Per Serving
Calories: 125
% Calories from fat: 1
Fat (gm): 0.2
Saturated fat (gm): 0.1
Cholesterol (mg): 0
Sodium (mg): 122
Protein (gm): 5.2
Carbohydrate (gm): 23.2
Exchanges
Milk: 1.0
Vegetable: 0.0
Fruit: 0.0
Bread: 0.5
Meat: 0.0
Fat: 0.0

1. Cook pumpkin in medium saucepan, covered, in 1 inch simmering water until tender, about 15 minutes. Drain well. Process pumpkin and half-and-half in food processor or blender; return to saucepan. Stir in brown sugar and spices and heat just to boiling; reduce heat and simmer, uncovered, 5 minutes.

2. Pour soup into bowls; sprinkle with chives.

LIGHTLY CREAMED VEGETABLE SOUP

Fat-free milk, whipped with an immersion blender, lends a wonderful, rich texture to this fragrant creamed soup. If you do not have an immersion blender, just stir the milk into the soup near the end of the cooking time.

6 servings (about 1⅓ cups each)

1	medium onion, sliced
2	medium carrots, sliced
1	medium yellow summer squash, sliced
1	medium green bell pepper, coarsely chopped
1	medium red bell pepper, coarsely chopped
2	ribs celery, sliced
1	clove garlic, minced
1½	tablespoons margarine

Per Serving
Calories: 110
% Calories from fat: 26
Fat (gm): 3.1
Saturated fat (gm): 0.6
Cholesterol (mg): 0.4
Sodium (mg): 182
Protein (gm): 6.5
Carbohydrate (gm): 13.3
Exchanges
Milk: 0.0
Vegetable: 3.0
Fruit: 0.0
Bread: 0.0
Meat: 0.0
Fat: 0.5

4 peppercorns
3 whole cloves
1 bay leaf
4 cups reduced-sodium fat-free chicken broth
1/3 cup all-purpose flour
2/3 cup water
   Salt and pepper, to taste
1/2 cup fat-free milk
   Freshly ground nutmeg, as garnish

1. Saute vegetables in margarine in large saucepan until onion is tender, 8 to 10 minutes. Tie peppercorns, cloves, and bay leaf in cheesecloth bag; add to saucepan with broth and heat to boiling. Simmer, covered, until vegetables are tender, 10 to 15 minutes. Discard bag.

2. Heat soup to boiling. Mix flour and water; stir into soup. Boil, stirring constantly, until thickened, 1 to 2 minutes. Season to taste with salt and pepper.

3. Whip milk with an immersion blender until doubled in volume and stir into soup just before serving. Pour soup into bowls; sprinkle lightly with nutmeg.

ORIENTAL WATERCRESS SOUP

Spinach can be substituted for the watercress in this fragrant Cantonese offering.

6 servings (about 1 cup each)

6 cups reduced-sodium fat-free chicken broth
3 slices gingerroot (scant 1/4 inch thick)
2 large bunches watercress (about 2 cups)
   Salt and white pepper, to taste
2 sliced green onions and tops
2 tablespoons shredded carrot

Per Serving
Calories: 35
% Calories from fat: 1
Fat (gm): 0
Saturated fat (gm): 0
Cholesterol (mg): 0
Sodium (mg): 176
Protein (gm): 6.4
Carbohydrate (gm): 1
Exchanges
Milk: 0.0
Vegetable: 1.0
Fruit: 0.0
Bread: 0.0
Meat: 0.0
Fat: 0.0

1. Heat broth and gingerroot to boiling in large saucepan; reduce heat and simmer, covered, 5 minutes. Remove gingerroot with slotted spoon and discard.

2. Trim stems from watercress and cut into 2-inch lengths. Add to soup and simmer, uncovered, 10 to 15 minutes. Season to taste with salt and white pepper. Pour soup into bowls; sprinkle with green onions and carrot.

WONTON SOUP

Your menu need not be oriental to begin with this soup; it goes well with any simple entrée.

6 servings (about 1 cup each)

24 Five-Spice Potstickers (¹/₂ recipe) (see p. 19)

6 cups reduced-sodium fat-free chicken broth

1 cup sliced spinach

Reduced-sodium tamari soy sauce

Pepper, to taste

1 medium green onion, sliced

Per Serving
Calories: 139
% Calories from fat: 5
Fat (gm): 0.8
Saturated fat (gm): 0.1
Cholesterol (mg): 2.9
Sodium (mg): 426
Protein (gm): 10.7
Carbohydrate (gm): 20.3
Exchanges
Milk: 0.0
Vegetable: 1.0
Fruit: 0.0
Bread: 1.0
Meat: 1.0
Fat: 0.0

1. Make Five-Spice Potstickers through Step 2.

2. Heat broth to boiling in large saucepan; add potstickers and simmer, uncovered, until potstickers rise to the surface, 2 to 3 minutes. Stir in spinach; simmer 2 to 3 minutes longer. Season to taste with soy sauce and pepper.

3. Pour soup into bowls; sprinkle with green onion.

HOT SOUR SOUP

The contrast in hot and sour flavors makes this Mandarin soup a unique offering. The hot chili sesame oil and Sour Sauce are intensely flavored, so use sparingly.

6 servings (about 1 cup each)

1/2 ounce dried Chinese black mushrooms (shiitake)

3/4 cup boiling water

4 cups reduced-sodium fat-free chicken broth

1/2 cup bamboo shoots

1/4 cup white distilled vinegar

2 tablespoons reduced-sodium tamari soy sauce

1 tablespoon finely chopped gingerroot

1 teaspoon sugar

1 tablespoon cornstarch

3 tablespoons water

1½ cups cubed light extra-firm tofu
Salt, cayenne, and black pepper, to taste

1 egg, lightly beaten

1-2 teaspoons dark sesame oil
Sliced green onion, as garnish

12-18 drops hot chili sesame oil *or* Szechwan chili sauce
Sour Sauce (recipe follows)

Per Serving
Calories: 106
% Calories from fat: 20
Fat (gm): 2.3
Saturated fat (gm): 0.4
Cholesterol (mg): 35.3
Sodium (mg): 483
Protein (gm): 10.4
Carbohydrate (gm): 10.6
Exchanges
Milk: 0.0
Vegetable: 2.0
Fruit: 0.0
Bread: 0.0
Meat: 1.0
Fat: 0.0

1. Combine mushrooms and boiling water in small bowl; let stand until mushrooms are softened, 15 to 20 minutes. Drain; reserving liquid. Slice mushrooms, discarding tough stems.

2. Combine broth, mushrooms and reserved liquid, bamboo shoots, vinegar, soy sauce, gingerroot, and sugar in large saucepan; reduce heat and simmer, uncovered, 10 minutes. Heat soup to boiling; mix cornstarch and water and stir into soup. Boil until thickened, about 1 minute, stirring constantly.

3. Stir tofu into soup; simmer, covered, 5 minutes. Season to taste with salt, cayenne, and black pepper. Just before serving, stir egg slowly into soup; stir in sesame oil.

4. Pour soup into bowls; sprinkle with green onion. Pass the hot chili sesame oil and Sour Sauce.

Sour Sauce

makes about 1/3 cup

- 3 tablespoons white distilled vinegar
- 1 tablespoon reduced-sodium tamari soy sauce
- 2 tablespoons sugar

1. Mix all ingredients; refrigerate until serving time.

ORIENTAL SOUP WITH NOODLES AND CHICKEN

The dried chow mein noodles in this soup are not the fried ones we have used with chop suey for many years. Be sure the correct noodles are used.

4 servings (about 3/4 cup each)

- 1 ounce dried cloud ear mushrooms *or* 1/2 ounce dried shiitake mushrooms Olive oil cooking spray
- 1/2 cup julienne carrots
- 2 cans (141/2 ounces each) reduced-sodium chicken broth
- 2 tablespoons dry sherry, optional
- 11/2 teaspoons light soy sauce
- 1/4 teaspoon five-spice powder
- 8 ounces boneless, skinless chicken breast, cooked, shredded
- 2 ounces snow peas, trimmed
- 1/2 cup sliced mushrooms
- 1/2 package (5-ounce size) dried chow mein noodles Salt and pepper, to taste

Per Serving
Calories: 213
% Calories from fat: 30
Fat (gm): 7.6
Saturated fat (gm): 1.2
Cholesterol (mg): 29.2
Sodium (mg): 259
Protein (gm): 16.4
Carbohydrate (gm): 19.7
Exchanges
Milk: 0.0
Vegetable: 0.5
Fruit: 0.0
Bread: 1.0
Meat: 1.5
Fat: 1.0

1. Place dried mushrooms in bowl; pour hot water over to cover. Let stand until mushrooms are soft, about 15 minutes; drain. Slice mushrooms, discarding any tough parts.

2. Spray large saucepan with cooking spray; heat over medium heat until hot. Saute dried mushrooms and carrots 3 to 4 minutes. Add chicken broth, sherry, soy sauce, and five-spice powder. Heat to boiling; reduce heat and simmer, covered, 10 minutes. Stir in chicken, snow peas, and sliced mushrooms; cook until peas are crisp-tender, about 4 minutes.

3. Add noodles to saucepan; cook until noodles are just tender, about 10 minutes. Season to taste with salt and pepper.

SESAME NOODLE SOUP WITH VEGETABLES

Use oriental sesame oil, which is dark in color and concentrated in flavor; light-colored sesame oil is very delicate in flavor. The fresh Chinese-style noodles are sometimes called soup noodles, chow mein noodles, or spaghetti. Caution: Fresh noodles cook very quickly.

4 servings (about 2 cups each)

$^1/_2$ cup sliced green onions and tops

4 cloves garlic, minced

1 tablespoon dark sesame oil

2 cups chopped or thinly sliced napa cabbage

1 cup chopped red bell pepper

$^1/_2$ cup julienne carrots

3 cans (14$^1/_2$ ounces each) reduced-sodium chicken broth

12 ounces boneless, skinless chicken breast, cooked, shredded

1 package (12 ounces) fresh Chinese-style noodles

Salt and pepper, to taste

Per Serving
Calories: 302
% Calories from fat: 19
Fat (gm): 6.5
Saturated fat (gm): 1
Cholesterol (mg): 43.5
Sodium (mg): 144
Protein (gm): 23
Carbohydrate (gm): 37.8
Exchanges
Milk: 0.0
Vegetable: 1.5
Fruit: 0.0
Bread: 2.0
Meat: 2.0
Fat: 0.0

1. Saute green onions and garlic in sesame oil in large saucepan until tender, about 5 minutes. Add cabbage, bell pepper, and carrots; saute until vegetables are crisp-tender, about 5 minutes.

2. Add chicken broth to saucepan; heat to boiling. Stir in chicken and noodles; return to boiling. Reduce heat and simmer, uncovered, until noodles are just tender, 1 to 2 minutes. Season to taste with salt and pepper.

GREEK LEMON-RICE SOUP

Nicely tart; use fresh lemon juice for the best flavor. If making this soup in advance, do not add egg until reheating for serving.

4 servings (about 1 cup each)

3¹/₂	cups reduced-sodium fat-free chicken broth
1/4	cup long-grain rice
2	large cloves garlic, minced
1/4-1/3	cup fresh lemon juice
1	egg, lightly beaten
2	tablespoons finely chopped parsley
	Salt and white pepper, to taste

Per Serving
Calories: 64
% Calories from fat: 19
Fat (gm): 1.3
Saturated fat (gm): 0.4
Cholesterol (mg): 53
Sodium (mg): 166
Protein (gm): 7.3
Carbohydrate (gm): 4.9
Exchanges
Milk: 0.0
Vegetable: 0.0
Fruit: 0.0
Bread: 0.5
Meat: 0.5
Fat: 0.0

1. Heat broth to boiling in medium saucepan; stir in rice and garlic. Reduce heat and simmer, covered, until rice is tender, about 25 minutes. Reduce heat to low.

2. Mix lemon juice and egg; slowly stir mixture into soup. Stir in parsley; season to taste with salt and white pepper. Pour soup into bowls.

SUMMER MINESTRONE

Thick and savory, this traditional Italian soup is always a favorite.

8 servings (about 1 cup each)

	Vegetable cooking spray
2	medium potatoes, cubed
2	medium carrots, thinly sliced
1	small zucchini, cubed
1	cup halved green beans
1	cup thinly sliced, *or* shredded, cabbage
1/2	cup thinly sliced celery
1	medium onion, coarsely chopped
3-4	cloves garlic, minced
2	teaspoons Italian seasoning
1-2	teaspoons dried oregano leaves

Per Serving
Calories: 177
% Calories from fat: 9
Fat (gm): 1.8
Saturated fat (gm): 0.6
Cholesterol (mg): 1.2
Sodium (mg): 256
Protein (gm): 8.1
Carbohydrate (gm): 33.7
Exchanges
Milk: 0.0
Vegetable: 2.0
Fruit: 0.0
Bread: 1.5
Meat: 0.5
Fat: 0.0

2 cans (15 ounces) reduced-sodium
chicken broth

1 can (15 ounces) no-salt-added stewed
tomatoes, undrained

1 can (15 ounces) kidney beans, rinsed,
drained

2 cups water

1¹/₂ cups (4 ounces) mostaccioli (penne),
uncooked

Salt and pepper, to taste

2 tablespoons grated Parmesan, *or*
Romano, cheese

1. Spray bottom of large saucepan with cooking spray; heat over medium heat until hot. Saute fresh vegetables until crisp-tender, 10 to 12 minutes. Stir in Italian seasoning and oregano; cook 1 to 2 minutes more.

2. Add chicken broth, tomatoes and liquid, beans, and water; heat to boiling. Reduce heat and simmer, covered, 10 minutes.

3. Heat soup to boiling; add pasta to saucepan. Reduce heat and simmer, uncovered, until pasta is al dente, 10 to 12 minutes. Season to taste with salt and pepper. Spoon soup into bowls; sprinkle with cheese.

SPINACH AND TORTELLINI SOUP

Pasta soups can be made 2 to 3 days in advance, enhancing flavors. Add pasta to the soup when reheating for serving so that the pasta is fresh and perfectly cooked.

6 servings (about 1 cup each)

Vegetable cooking spray

2 cups sliced carrots

¹/₄ cup sliced green onions and tops

2 cloves garlic, minced

1 teaspoon dried basil leaves

2 cans (15 ounces each) reduced-sodium
chicken broth

1¹/₂ cups water

1 package (9 ounces) fresh low-fat
tomato and cheese tortellini

Per Serving
Calories: 170
% Calories from fat: 18
Fat (gm): 3.5
Saturated fat (gm): 1.6
Cholesterol (mg): 17.7
Sodium (mg): 177
Protein (gm): 8.6
Carbohydrate (gm): 26.9
Exchanges
Milk: 0.0
Vegetable: 1.0
Fruit: 0.0
Bread: 1.5
Meat: 0.0
Fat: 0.5

     3 cups torn spinach leaves
   2-3 teaspoons lemon juice
 1/8-1/4 teaspoon ground nutmeg
   1/8 teaspoon pepper

1. Spray bottom of large saucepan with cooking spray; heat over medium heat until hot. Saute carrots, green onions, garlic, and basil until onions are tender, about 5 minutes.

2. Add chicken broth and water to saucepan; heat to boiling. Reduce heat and simmer, covered, 10 minutes.

3. Heat broth mixture to boiling; stir in tortelloni and spinach. Reduce heat and simmer, uncovered, until tortellini are al dente, about 5 minutes. Stir in lemon juice, nutmeg, and pepper.

MEDITERRANEAN-STYLE SHRIMP VEGETABLE SOUP

A fragrant soup with a citrus accent.

6 servings (about 1 1/2 cups each)

     Olive oil cooking spray
   2 cups sliced mushrooms
   1 medium onion, chopped
 1/2 medium green bell pepper, chopped
   3 cloves garlic, minced
   1 can (16 ounces) reduced-sodium whole tomatoes, undrained, coarsely chopped
   1 can (8 ounces) reduced-sodium tomato sauce
   1 pound peeled, deveined shrimp
 1-2 cups vegetable broth
 1/2 cup dry white wine *or* orange juice
 1/2-1 cup clam juice
   2 strips orange rind (3 x 1/2 inch)
   2 bay leaves
   1 teaspoon dried marjoram leaves
 1/2-3/4 teaspoon dried savory leaves
 1/4 teaspoon fennel seeds, crushed
     Salt and pepper, to taste

Per Serving
Calories: 121
% Calories from fat: 8
Fat (gm): 1.1
Saturated fat (gm): 0.2
Cholesterol (mg): 115.6
Sodium (mg): 211
Protein (gm): 14.8
Carbohydrate (gm): 10.7
Exchanges
Milk: 0.0
Vegetable: 2.0
Fruit: 0.0
Bread: 0.0
Meat: 1.0
Fat: 0.0

1. Spray large saucepan with cooking spray; heat over medium heat until hot. Add mushrooms, onion, bell pepper, and garlic; saute, covered, until vegetables are tender, 8 to 10 minutes. Add remaining ingredients, except salt and pepper; heat to boiling. Reduce heat and simmer, covered, 10 to 15 minutes. Season to taste with salt and pepper.

LIGHT MINESTRONE

Minestrone does not always contain pasta, nor is it always a heavy, hearty soup. Enjoy this light version of an old favorite, selecting vegetables that are freshest and most plentiful.

8 servings (about 1¼ cups each)

1 cup sliced carrots
½ cup chopped onion
½ cup chopped celery
½ cup sliced fennel bulb
2 cloves garlic, minced
1 tablespoon olive oil
5 cups reduced-sodium fat-free beef broth
1 can (19 ounces) garbanzo beans, rinsed, drained
1 cup snap peas
1 small zucchini, sliced
1 cup broccoli florets
¾-1 teaspoon dried basil leaves
¾-1 teaspoon dried oregano leaves
1 cup halved cherry tomatoes
¼ cup finely chopped parsley
Salt and pepper, to taste
1½ cups Parmesan Croutons (½ recipe) (see p. 655)

Per Serving
Calories: 146
% Calories from fat: 21
Fat (gm): 3.5
Saturated fat (gm): 0.6
Cholesterol (mg): 0.5
Sodium (mg): 447
Protein (gm): 8.6
Carbohydrate (gm): 21.3
Exchanges
Milk: 0.0
Vegetable: 1.0
Fruit: 0.0
Bread: 1.0
Meat: 0.0
Fat: 0.5

1. Saute carrots, onion, celery, fennel, and garlic in oil in Dutch oven until onion is tender, 5 to 8 minutes. Add broth, beans, peas, zucchini, broccoli, and herbs; heat to boiling. Reduce heat and simmer, covered, until vegetables are tender, 10 to 15 minutes, adding tomatoes and parsley during last 5 minutes of cooking time. Season to taste with salt and pepper.

2. Pour soup into bowls; sprinkle with Parmesan Croutons.

VEGETABLE SOUP WITH ORZO

Escarole, which lends a unique taste to this hearty soup, is also a flavorful addition to green salads. Spinach leaves can be substituted for the escarole in this recipe, if desired.

4 servings (about 2 cups each)

Olive oil cooking spray
1 medium onion, coarsely chopped
2 medium carrots, sliced
2 medium ribs celery, sliced
3 cloves garlic, minced
2 medium zucchini *or* summer yellow squash, sliced
1 cup sliced mushrooms
1/2 teaspoon dried thyme leaves
1/2 teaspoon dried oregano leaves
5 cups reduced-sodium fat-free chicken broth
1/2 cup (4 ounces) orzo, uncooked
1/2 cup frozen peas
6 medium leaves escarole, sliced or coarsely chopped
1/4 teaspoon salt
1/2 teaspoon pepper
2 tablespoons grated Romano cheese

Per Serving
Calories: 221
% Calories from fat: 8
Fat (gm): 1.9
Saturated fat (gm): 0.8
Cholesterol (mg): 3.7
Sodium (mg): 453
Protein (gm): 15.4
Carbohydrate (gm): 34.9
Exchanges
Milk: 0.0
Vegetable: 4.0
Fruit: 0.0
Bread: 1.0
Meat: 0.0
Fat: 0.5

1. Spray large saucepan with cooking spray; heat over medium heat until hot. Saute onion, carrots, celery, and garlic in saucepan until onion is tender, about 5 minutes. Add zucchini, mushrooms, and herbs; cook, covered, 2 to 3 minutes.

2. Add broth to saucepan; heat to boiling. Stir in orzo, peas, and escarole. Reduce heat and simmer, uncovered, until orzo is al dente, about 7 minutes. Season with salt and pepper. Spoon soup into bowls; sprinkle with cheese.

BEET BORSCHT

Try this delicious beet soup, flavored in the traditional fashion with Polish sausage.

8 servings (about 1¼ cups each)

Per Serving
Calories: 120
% Calories from fat: 25
Fat (gm): 3.7
Saturated fat (gm): 0.4
Cholesterol (mg): 17.2
Sodium (mg): 437
Protein (gm): 10.9
Carbohydrate (gm): 13.1
Exchanges
Milk: 0.0
Vegetable: 3.0
Fruit: 0.0
Bread: 0.0
Meat: 1.0
Fat: 0.0

- 4 medium beets, peeled, cut into julienne strips
- 8 ounces low-fat smoked Polish sausage, sliced
- ½-1 tablespoon margarine
- 6 cups reduced-sodium fat-free beef broth
- 1 small head red cabbage, thinly sliced or shredded
- 2 carrots, cut into julienne strips
- 1 clove garlic, minced
- 1 bay leaf
- 2-3 teaspoons sugar
- 2 tablespoons cider vinegar
  Salt and pepper, to taste
  Finely chopped dill weed *or* parsley, as garnish

1. Saute beets and sausage in margarine in Dutch oven 3 to 4 minutes. Add broth, cabbage, carrots, garlic, bay leaf, sugar, and vinegar; heat to boiling. Reduce heat and simmer, covered, until vegetables are tender, 20 to 30 minutes. Discard bay leaf; season to taste with salt and pepper.

2. Pour soup into bowls; sprinkle with dill weed.

RUSSIAN CABBAGE SOUP

Use red or green cabbage, fresh or canned beets in this savory soup.

8 servings (about 1½ cups each)

2 medium onions, sliced
1 tablespoon margarine
7 cups reduced-sodium fat-free beef broth
1 can (16 ounces) reduced-sodium whole tomatoes, undrained, coarsely chopped
6 cups thinly sliced red cabbage
4 large beets, peeled, cubed
1 tablespoon cider vinegar
2 large carrots, sliced
1 turnip, peeled, cubed
1 large Idaho potato, peeled, cubed
   Salt and pepper, to taste
8 tablespoons fat-free sour cream
   Finely chopped parsley, as garnish

Per Serving
Calories: 121
% Calories from fat: 13
Fat (gm): 1.8
Saturated fat (gm): 0.3
Cholesterol (mg): 0
Sodium (mg): 218
Protein (gm): 8
Carbohydrate (gm): 20.1
Exchanges
Milk: 0.0
Vegetable: 3.0
Fruit: 0.0
Bread: 0.5
Meat: 0.0
Fat: 0.0

1. Saute onions in margarine in Dutch oven until tender, about 5 minutes. Add broth, tomatoes, cabbage, beets, and vinegar; heat to boiling. Reduce heat and simmer, uncovered, 30 minutes; add carrots, turnip, and potato and cook 15 minutes longer. Season to taste with salt and pepper.

2. Pour soup into bowls; spoon 1 tablespoon sour cream into each and sprinkle with parsley.

RAVIOLI SOUP

Wonton wrappers, found in the produce section of your supermarket, make ravioli easy to prepare.

6 servings (about 1¹/₂ cups each)

1/2 cup julienned carrots

1/4 cup sliced green onions and tops

1 teaspoon margarine

2 1/2 quarts fat-free chicken broth

3 cups thinly sliced bok choy *or* Napa cabbage

Chicken Ravioli (recipe follows)

Salt and pepper, to taste

Per Serving
Calories: 252
% Calories from fat: 9
Fat (gm): 2.4
Saturated fat (gm): 0.5
Cholesterol (mg): 27.3
Sodium (mg): 644
Protein (gm): 24
Carbohydrate (gm): 29.7
Exchanges
Milk: 0.0
Vegetable: 0.0
Fruit: 0.0
Bread: 2.0
Meat: 2.0
Fat: 0.0

1. Saute carrots and green onions in margarine in large saucepan until tender, about 5 minutes. Add chicken broth and heat to boiling; reduce heat and simmer, covered, 5 minutes.

2. Stir in bok choy and Chicken Ravioli and heat to boiling; reduce heat and simmer, uncovered, 2 to 3 minutes or until ravioli are tender and rise to top of soup. Season to taste with salt and pepper.

Chicken Ravioli

makes 18 ravioli

8 ounces ground chicken breast

1 tablespoon minced green onion

1 teaspoon minced garlic

1 teaspoon grated gingerroot

1/8 teaspoon salt

1/8 teaspoon pepper

36 wonton wrappers

1. Combine all ingredients, except wonton wrappers, in small bowl. Place rounded teaspoon of chicken mixture in center of each of 18 wonton wrappers. Moisten edges of wrappers with water. Top with remaining wrappers; press edges to seal. Refrigerate, covered, until ready to cook.

CANNELLINI AND CABBAGE SOUP

Tuscany is known for its dishes with white cannellini beans. Cannellini beans are available in specialty sections of supermarkets or in Italian markets; canned Great Northern beans may be substituted.

8 servings (about 1 cup each)

Vegetable cooking spray

3 cups thinly sliced or chopped cabbage

1 small onion, coarsely chopped

3 cloves garlic, minced

1 teaspoon crushed caraway seeds

2 cans (15 ounces each) reduced-sodium chicken broth

1 cup water

1 can (15 ounces) cannellini *or* Great Northern beans, rinsed, drained

1/2 cup (4 ounces) mostaccioli (penne), uncooked

Salt and pepper, to taste

Per Serving
Calories: 107
% Calories from fat: 7
Fat (gm): 1
Saturated fat (gm): 0.1
Cholesterol (mg): 0
Sodium (mg): 175
Protein (gm): 6.9
Carbohydrate (gm): 21.9
Exchanges
Milk: 0.0
Vegetable: 1.0
Fruit: 0.0
Bread: 1.0
Meat: 0.5
Fat: 0.0

1. Spray large saucepan with cooking spray; heat over medium heat until hot. Saute cabbage, onion, garlic, and caraway seeds until cabbage begins to wilt, 8 to 10 minutes.

2. Add chicken broth, water, and beans to saucepan; heat to boiling. Stir in pasta; reduce heat and simmer, uncovered, until pasta is al dente, about 15 minutes. Season to taste with salt and pepper.

BEAN-THICKENED SOUP

This soup is very quick and easy to make. The pureed beans contribute a hearty texture and subtle flavor.

4 servings (about 1¹/₃ cups each)

Vegetable cooking spray
2 carrots, sliced
1 small onion, chopped
2 large cloves garlic, minced
1³/₄ cups vegetable broth
1 can (16 ounces) whole tomatoes, undrained, coarsely chopped
1 can (15 ounces) Great Northern beans, rinsed, drained, pureed
¹/₄-¹/₂ teaspoon dried thyme leaves
¹/₂-³/₄ teaspoon dried sage leaves
Salt and pepper, to taste
Minced parsley, as garnish

Per Serving
Calories: 176
% Calories from fat: 5
Fat (gm): 1
Saturated fat (gm): 0.2
Cholesterol (mg): 0
Sodium (mg): 208
Protein (gm): 9.8
Carbohydrate (gm): 34
Exchanges
Milk: 0.0
Vegetable: 2.0
Fruit: 0.0
Bread: 1.5
Meat: 0.5
Fat: 0.0

1. Spray large saucepan with cooking spray; heat over medium heat until hot. Saute carrots, onion, and garlic until onion is tender, about 5 minutes. Stir in broth, tomatoes and liquid, pureed beans, and herbs. Heat to boiling; reduce heat and simmer, covered, until carrots are tender, about 10 minutes. Season to taste with salt and pepper.

2. Pour soup into bowls; sprinkle with parsley.

COUNTRY LENTIL SOUP

A light soup, yet wholesome in flavor and texture. The soup freezes well, so make extra.

6 servings (about 1¹/₂ cups each)

1¹/₂ cups chopped onions
1 cup sliced celery
1 cup sliced carrots
2 teaspoons minced garlic
1 tablespoon olive oil
3 cups vegetable broth
2 cups water
1 cup dried lentils, washed, sorted
1 can (14¹/₂ ounces) reduced-sodium whole tomatoes, undrained, crushed
2 tablespoons finely chopped parsley
1 teaspoon dried marjoram leaves
¹/₂ teaspoon dried oregano leaves
¹/₄ teaspoon dried thyme leaves
   Salt and pepper, to taste
12 teaspoons grated fat-free Parmesan cheese

Per Serving
Calories: 275
% Calories from fat: 14
Fat (gm): 4.4
Saturated fat (gm): 0.6
Cholesterol (mg): 0
Sodium (mg): 109
Protein (gm): 15.8
Carbohydrate (gm): 42.8
Exchanges
Milk: 0.0
Vegetable: 3.0
Fruit: 0.0
Bread: 2.0
Meat: 0.5
Fat: 0.5

1. Saute onions, celery, carrots, and garlic in oil in Dutch oven 5 to 8 minutes. Add broth, water, lentils, tomatoes, and herbs; heat to boiling. Reduce heat and simmer, covered, until lentils are tender, about 30 minutes. Season to taste with salt and pepper. Pour soup into bowls; sprinkle each with 2 teaspoons Parmesan cheese.

INDIAN LENTIL SOUP

This soup (Dal Shorba) from India is flavored with curry powder and sweet coriander. Red, green, or brown lentils can be used.

8 servings (about 1 cup each)

1/2 cup chopped onion
1 clove garlic, minced
2 teaspoons curry powder
1 teaspoon crushed coriander seeds
1 teaspoon crushed cumin seeds
1/2 teaspoon ground turmeric
1/4 teaspoon crushed red pepper
1 tablespoon olive oil
5 cups reduced-sodium fat-free chicken broth
4 cups water
2 cups dried red or brown lentils, sorted, rinsed
  Salt and pepper, to taste
8 tablespoons plain fat-free yogurt

Per Serving
Calories: 193
% Calories from fat: 11
Fat (gm): 2.4
Saturated fat (gm): 0.3
Cholesterol (mg): 0.3
Sodium (mg): 121
Protein (gm): 16
Carbohydrate (gm): 27.6
Exchanges
Milk: 0.0
Vegetable: 0.0
Fruit: 0.0
Bread: 2.0
Meat: 1.0
Fat: 0.0

1. Saute onion, garlic, and herbs in oil in large saucepan until onion is tender, about 5 minutes, stirring frequently. Add broth, water, and lentils; heat to boiling. Reduce heat and simmer, covered, until lentils are tender, about 30 minutes. Season to taste with salt and pepper.

2. Pour soup into bowls; garnish each with a tablespoon of yogurt.

BLACK BEAN SOUP

Dried beans can also be "quick cooked" rather than soaked overnight before cooking. Place beans in a large saucepan and cover with 2 inches water; heat to boiling and boil 2 minutes. Remove from heat and let stand 1 hour; drain and continue with Step 2 in recipe below. Or, substitute three cans (15 ounces each) rinsed, drained canned black beans for the dried.

4 servings (about 1¼ cups each)

1½ cups dried black beans
　Vegetable cooking spray
1 large onion, chopped
4 cloves garlic, minced
1 tomato, chopped
1 teaspoon dried oregano leaves
½ teaspoon dried thyme leaves
　Salt and pepper, to taste
6 tablespoons fat-free sour cream
　Finely chopped oregano *or* parsley, as garnish

Per Serving
Calories: 200
% Calories from fat: 4
Fat (gm): 0.9
Saturated fat (gm): 0.2
Cholesterol (mg): 0
Sodium (mg): 20
Protein (gm): 13.8
Carbohydrate (gm): 39
Exchanges
Milk: 0.0
Vegetable: 1.0
Fruit: 0.0
Bread: 2.0
Meat: 0.5
Fat: 0.0

1. Wash and sort beans, discarding any stones. Cover beans with 4 inches water in large saucepan; soak overnight and drain.

2. Spray large saucepan with cooking spray; heat over medium heat until hot. Saute onion and garlic 2 to 3 minutes; add tomato and herbs and cook 2 to 3 minutes longer. Add beans to saucepan; cover with 2 inches water and heat to boiling. Reduce heat and simmer, covered, until beans are very tender, 1½ to 2 hours, adding water to cover beans if necessary. Drain mixture, reserving liquid.

3. Process bean mixture in food processor or blender until smooth, adding enough reserved cooking liquid to make desired consistency. Return soup to saucepan; heat over medium heat until hot through, 3 to 4 minutes. Season to taste with salt and pepper.

4. Serve soup in bowls; top each with dollop of sour cream and sprinkle with oregano.

SHRIMP AND BLACK BEAN SOUP

In Mexico, leaves from the avocado tree are used for seasoning in this favorite Oaxacan soup. We've substituted a bay leaf, which is somewhat stronger in flavor.

6 servings (about 1¹/₂ cups each)

Vegetable cooking spray
2 medium onions, chopped
4 cloves garlic, minced
2 medium tomatoes, peeled, cut into wedges
3 cans (14¹/₂ ounces each) reduced-sodium fat-free chicken broth, divided
¹/₂ cup water
3 cups cooked dried black beans *or* 2 cans (15 ounces each) black beans, rinsed, drained
1 teaspoon ground cumin
1 teaspoon dried oregano leaves
1 teaspoon dried thyme leaves
1 bay leaf
8 ounces peeled, deveined shrimp
Salt and pepper, to taste
Finely chopped cilantro, as garnish

Per Serving
Calories: 190
% Calories from fat: 5
Fat (gm): 1.1
Saturated fat (gm): 0.3
Cholesterol (mg): 58.3
Sodium (mg): 136
Protein (gm): 19.1
Carbohydrate (gm): 27
Exchanges
Milk: 0.0
Vegetable: 1.0
Fruit: 0.0
Bread: 1.5
Meat: 1.5
Fat: 0.0

1. Spray large saucepan with cooking spray; heat over medium heat until hot. Saute onions and garlic until tender, about 5 minutes. Process onion mixture, tomatoes, and 1 can chicken broth until smooth; return to saucepan.

2. Add remaining 2 cans broth, water, black beans, and herbs to saucepan; heat to boiling. Reduce heat and simmer, uncovered, 10 minutes, adding shrimp during last 5 minutes; discard bay leaf and season to taste with salt and pepper.

3. Serve soup in bowls; sprinkle with cilantro.

GARBANZO BEAN SOUP

Garbanzo beans are commonly found in the cuisines of central and southern Mexico.

4 servings (about 1¹/₄ cups each)

Vegetable cooking spray
2 medium onions, chopped
2 cloves garlic, minced
2 cans (15¹/₄ ounces each) garbanzo beans, rinsed, drained
2 cans (14¹/₂ ounces each) reduced-sodium fat-free chicken broth, divided
1 teaspoon ground cumin
¹/₂-³/₄ teaspoon dried thyme leaves
Salt and pepper, to taste
¹/₄ cup fat-free sour cream
Paprika *or* chili powder, as garnish

Per Serving
Calories: 264
% Calories from fat: 14
Fat (gm): 4.1
Saturated fat (gm): 0.6
Cholesterol (mg): 0
Sodium (mg): 333
Protein (gm): 16
Carbohydrate (gm): 42.9
Exchanges
Milk: 0.0
Vegetable: 0.0
Fruit: 0.0
Bread: 3.0
Meat: 1.0
Fat: 0.0

1. Spray large saucepan with cooking spray; heat over medium heat until hot. Saute onions and garlic until tender, about 5 minutes. Process onion mixture, garbanzo beans, and 1 can chicken broth in food processor or blender until smooth.

2. Return mixture to saucepan; add remaining broth, cumin, and thyme and heat to boiling. Reduce heat and simmer, covered, 5 minutes. Season to taste with salt and pepper.

3. Serve soup in bowls; top with dollops of sour cream and sprinkle with paprika.

SPLIT PEA SOUP WITH HAM

A perfect main-dish soup for hearty appetites on a crisp autumn or winter day. Serve with thick slices of Garlic Bread (see p. 657).

8 servings (about 1 cup each)

1½ cups chopped onions
1 cup chopped carrots
½ cup sliced celery
1½ cups cubed lean smoked ham (8 ounces), fat trimmed
1 tablespoon vegetable oil
6 cups water
1 can (14½ ounces) reduced-sodium chicken broth
1 pound dried split peas, washed and sorted
1-2 teaspoons beef bouillon crystals
1 teaspoon dried marjoram leaves
Salt and pepper, to taste

Per Serving
Calories: 264
% Calories from fat: 11
Fat (gm): 3.4
Saturated fat (gm): 0.6
Cholesterol (mg): 16.2
Sodium (mg): 513
Protein (gm): 21.6
Carbohydrate (gm): 39.9
Exchanges
Milk: 0.0
Vegetable: 1.0
Fruit: 0.0
Bread: 2.0
Meat: 2.0
Fat: 0.0

1. Saute onions, carrots, celery, and ham in oil in large saucepan until tender, 8 to 10 minutes. Add water, chicken broth, split peas, bouillon crystals, and marjoram; heat to boiling. Reduce heat and simmer, covered, until peas are tender, 1 to 1¼ hours. Season to taste with salt and pepper.

ITALIAN MEATBALL SOUP

Flavorful meatballs for this soup are made with low-fat ground turkey rather than ground beef. Substitute other pastas for the spaghetti, if you like, such as orrechiette (little ears) or conchiglie (shells).

8 servings (about 2 cups each)

1 1/2 pounds ground turkey
2 egg whites
1/4 cup seasoned dry bread crumbs
4 cloves garlic, minced, divided
3 tablespoons Italian seasoning, divided
  Olive oil cooking spray
4 cans (15 ounces each) reduced-sodium chicken broth
3 cups water
2 cups green beans, diagonally cut into 1/2-inch pieces
4 medium carrots, sliced
2 medium onions, coarsely chopped
8 ounces thin spaghetti, uncooked, broken into 2- to 3-inch pieces
2 medium plum tomatoes, coarsely chopped
  Salt and pepper, to taste

Per Serving
Calories: 270
% Calories from fat: 28
Fat (gm): 8.7
Saturated fat (gm): 2
Cholesterol (mg): 31.7
Sodium (mg): 174
Protein (gm): 19
Carbohydrate (gm): 30.2
Exchanges
Milk: 0.0
Vegetable: 1.0
Fruit: 0.0
Bread: 1.5
Meat: 2.0
Fat: 0.5

1. Mix ground turkey, egg whites, bread crumbs, 2 cloves of garlic, and 2 tablespoons of Italian seasoning until well blended; shape mixture into 32 meatballs. Spray large saucepan with cooking spray; heat over medium heat until hot. Cook meatballs until browned on all sides, 5 to 7 minutes.

2. Add chicken broth, water, green beans, carrots, onions, remaining 2 cloves garlic, and remaining 1 tablespoon Italian seasoning to saucepan; heat to boiling. Reduce heat and simmer, covered, until vegetables are almost tender, about 8 minutes.

3. Heat soup to boiling; add pasta and tomatoes. Reduce heat and simmer, uncovered, until pasta is al dente, about 10 minutes. Season to taste with salt and pepper.

BEEF BARLEY AND VEGETABLE SOUP

A hearty, rib-sticking soup that is even better if made a day or so in advance. Leftover soup will thicken, so thin with beef broth or water.

8 servings (about 1 cup each)

Vegetable cooking spray
1 pound lean beef stew meat, fat trimmed, cubed
1 cup chopped onion
2/3 cup sliced celery
2/3 cup chopped carrots
1 clove garlic, minced
1 tablespoon flour
4 cups water
1 can (14¹/2 ounces) reduced-sodium beef broth
1/2 teaspoon dried marjoram leaves
1/2 teaspoon dried thyme leaves
1 bay leaf
1 can (14¹/2 ounces) diced tomatoes, undrained
1 cup cut green beans (1-inch pieces)
1 cup cubed, peeled, parsnips *or* potatoes
1/2 cup frozen peas
1/2 cup quick-cooking barley
Salt and pepper, to taste

Per Serving
Calories: 187
% Calories from fat: 16
Fat (gm): 3.3
Saturated fat (gm): 1.1
Cholesterol (mg): 35.4
Sodium (mg): 153
Protein (gm): 18.8
Carbohydrate (gm): 21.1
Exchanges
Milk: 0.0
Vegetable: 2.0
Fruit: 0.0
Bread: 0.5
Meat: 2.0
Fat: 0.0

1. Spray large Dutch oven with cooking spray; heat over medium heat until hot. Cook beef over medium heat until browned, 8 to 10 minutes. Add onion, celery, carrots, and garlic; cook 5 minutes. Stir in flour; cook l minute.

2. Add water, beef broth, and herbs to Dutch oven; heat to boiling. Reduce heat and simmer, covered, until beef is very tender, 1 to 1¹/2 hours.

3. Add tomatoes and liquid, green beans, and parsnips; simmer, covered, until vegetables are tender, about 10 minutes. Add peas and barley and heat to boiling; reduce heat and simmer, covered, until barley is tender, about 10 minutes. Discard bay leaf; season to taste with salt and pepper.

CHICKEN-VEGETABLE SOUP WITH ORZO

This hearty vegetable soup is perfect for a light supper—just serve with a crusty bread.

4 servings (about 2 cups each)

Olive oil cooking spray
12 ounces boneless, skinless chicken breast, cut into $^1/_2$-inch pieces
1 medium onion, coarsely chopped
2 medium carrots, sliced
2 medium ribs celery, sliced
3 cloves garlic, minced
$^1/_2$ teaspoon dried thyme leaves
$^1/_2$ teaspoon dried oregano leaves
2 cans (15 ounces each) reduced-sodium chicken broth
1 cup water
$^1/_2$ cup (4 ounces) orzo, uncooked
$^1/_2$ cup frozen peas
4 medium leaves escarole, sliced or coarsely chopped
$^1/_4$ teaspoon salt
$^1/_2$ teaspoon pepper
2 tablespoons grated Romano cheese

Per Serving
Calories: 260
% Calories from fat: 15
Fat (gm): 4.1
Saturated fat (gm): 1.3
Cholesterol (mg): 47.1
Sodium (mg): 281
Protein (gm): 24
Carbohydrate (gm): 29.9
Exchanges
Milk: 0.0
Vegetable: 1.5
Fruit: 0.0
Bread: 1.5
Meat: 2.0
Fat: 0.0

1. Spray large saucepan with cooking spray; heat over medium heat until hot. Cook chicken until no longer pink in the center, about 8 minutes; remove from saucepan. Add onion, carrots, celery, garlic, and herbs to saucepan; saute until onion is tender, about 5 minutes. Return chicken to saucepan.

2. Add chicken broth and water to saucepan; heat to boiling. Stir in orzo, peas, and escarole. Reduce heat and simmer, uncovered, until orzo is al dente, about 7 minutes. Stir in salt and pepper. Spoon soup into bowls; sprinkle with cheese.

CHICKEN NOODLE SOUP

A hearty, entrée soup that's quick and easy to make, using reduced-sodium canned chicken broth. If using homemade chicken broth, refrigerate it until chilled, then skim and discard fat before proceeding with the soup.

4 servings (about 1¼ cups each)

Vegetable cooking spray
4 ounces boneless, skinless chicken breast, cut into ³/₄-inch pieces
4 ounces boneless, skinless chicken thighs, fat trimmed, cut into ³/₄-inch pieces
2 cups sliced celery, including some leaves
1 cup sliced carrots
1 cup sliced onion
2 cans (14½ ounces each) reduced-sodium chicken broth
1 teaspoon dried marjoram leaves
1 bay leaf
1 cup uncooked no-yolk broad noodles
1 tablespoon minced parsley leaves
Salt and pepper, to taste

Per Serving
Calories: 307
% Calories from fat: 14
Fat (gm): 5
Saturated fat (gm): 0.8
Cholesterol (mg): 32.9
Sodium (mg): 409
Protein (gm): 22.8
Carbohydrate (gm): 44.3
Exchanges
Milk: 0.0
Vegetable: 1.0
Fruit: 0.0
Bread: 2.5
Meat: 2.0
Fat: 0.0

1. Spray large saucepan with cooking spray; heat over medium heat until hot. Saute chicken until browned, about 5 minutes. Add celery, carrots, and onion and saute until tender, 5 to 7 minutes.

2. Add chicken broth and herbs to saucepan; heat to boiling. Reduce heat and simmer, covered, until chicken and vegetables are tender, 15 to 20 minutes.

3. Heat soup to boiling; add noodles. Cook, uncovered, until noodles are tender, 7 to 10 minutes. Discard bay leaf. Stir in parsley; season to taste with salt and pepper.

TORTILLA SOUP

Add the tortilla strips to the soup just before serving so they are crisp. If desired, the tortilla strips can be baked on a cookie sheet at 350 degrees until browned and crisp, about 5 minutes. The soup should be slightly piquant—add lime juice to taste.

6 servings (about 1 1/2 cups each)

Vegetable cooking spray
3 corn, *or* flour, tortillas, cut into 2 x 1/4-inch strips
1 small onion, chopped
1 cup chopped celery
1 medium tomato, coarsely chopped
1/2 teaspoon dried basil leaves
1/2 teaspoon ground cumin
5 cups reduced-sodium fat-free chicken broth
1 can (15 1/2 ounces) pinto beans, rinsed, drained
6 ounces cooked chicken breast, shredded
2 teaspoons finely chopped cilantro
1-2 teaspoons lime juice
Salt and cayenne pepper, to taste

Per Serving
Calories: 176
% Calories from fat: 10
Fat (gm): 2
Saturated fat (gm): 0.3
Cholesterol (mg): 24.1
Sodium (mg): 386
Protein (gm): 19.1
Carbohydrate (gm): 22.6
Exchanges
Milk: 0.0
Vegetable: 1.0
Fruit: 0.0
Bread: 1.0
Meat: 2.0
Fat: 0.0

1. Spray medium skillet with cooking spray; heat over medium heat until hot. Add tortillas; spray tortillas with cooking spray and cook over medium heat, tossing occasionally, until browned and crisp, about 5 minutes. Reserve.

2. Spray large saucepan with cooking spray; heat over medium heat until hot. Saute onion, celery, tomato, basil, and cumin until onion is tender, 3 to 5 minutes. Add chicken broth, beans, and chicken; heat to boiling. Reduce heat and simmer, uncovered, 3 to 5 minutes. Stir in cilantro; season to taste with lime juice, salt, and pepper.

3. Serve soup in bowls; top with tortilla strips.

POZOLE

Traditionally this soup is made with a pig's head or pork hocks; our version contains lean pork tenderloin and chicken breast instead. The soup always contains hominy and is served with a variety of crisp vegetable garnishes.

6 servings (about 2 cups each)

Per Serving
Calories: 181
% Calories from fat: 16
Fat (gm): 3.2
Saturated fat (gm): 0.9
Cholesterol (mg): 44.8
Sodium (mg): 244
Protein (gm): 21.2
Carbohydrate (gm): 16.7
Exchanges
Milk: 0.0
Vegetable: 1.0
Fruit: 0.0
Bread: 1.0
Meat: 2.5
Fat: 0.0

- 2 ancho chilies, stems, seeds, and veins discarded
- 1 cup boiling water
  Vegetable cooking spray
- 1/2 cup chopped onion
- 1 clove garlic, minced
- 2 cans (14 1/2 ounces each) reduced-sodium fat-free chicken broth
- 8 ounces pork tenderloin, cut into 1-inch pieces
- 8 ounces boneless, skinless chicken breast, cut into l-inch pieces
- 1 can (15 1/2 ounces) hominy, rinsed, drained
- 1 can (14 1/2 ounces) reduced-sodium tomatoes, drained, coarsely chopped
- 1/2 teaspoon dried oregano leaves
- 1/4 teaspoon dried thyme leaves
  Salt and pepper, to taste
- 6 lime wedges
- 1/4 cup each: thinly sliced lettuce, cabbage, green onion, radishes, and shredded carrots

1. Cover chilies with boiling water in small bowl; let stand until softened, about 10 minutes. Process chilies and water in food processor or blender until smooth; reserve.

2. Spray large saucepan with vegetable cooking spray; heat over medium heat until hot. Saute onion and garlic until tender; add chicken broth and meats and heat to boiling. Reduce heat and simmer, covered, until meats are tender, 10 to 15 minutes; strain, returning broth to saucepan. Shred meats with fork.

3. Add reserved chili mixture, meats, hominy, tomatoes, and herbs to saucepan; cook, covered, over low heat 10 to 15 minutes. Season to taste with salt and pepper. Serve soup in bowls; squeeze juice from lime wedge into each bowl. Pass fresh vegetables for each person to add to soup.

CHILI CON CARNE

For a Southwest version of this chili, substitute black or pinto beans for the kidney beans and add 1 minced jalapeño chili. Garnish each serving with a sprinkling of finely chopped cilantro leaves.

8 servings (about 1 cup each)

Vegetable cooking spray
1 pound 95% lean ground beef
1¹/₂ cups chopped onions
1 cup chopped green bell pepper
2 cloves garlic, minced
1-2 tablespoons chili powder
2 teaspoons dried cumin
1 teaspoon dried oregano leaves
¹/₄ teaspoon ground cloves
2 cans (14¹/₂ ounces each) no-salt whole tomatoes, undrained, coarsely chopped
1 can (6 ounces) reduced-sodium tomato paste
³/₄ cup beer *or* reduced-sodium beef broth
1 tablespoon packed light brown sugar
2-3 teaspoons unsweetened cocoa
1 can (15 ounces) red kidney beans, rinsed, drained
Salt and pepper, to taste
¹/₂ cup (2 ounces) shredded fat-free, *or* reduced-fat, Cheddar cheese
¹/₂ cup thinly sliced green onions and tops
¹/₂ cup fat-free sour cream

Per Serving
Calories: 220
% Calories from fat: 13
Fat (gm): 3.6
Saturated fat (gm): 1
Cholesterol (mg): 32.5
Sodium (mg): 224
Protein (gm): 21.9
Carbohydrate (gm): 28.7
Exchanges
Milk: 0.0
Vegetable: 2.0
Fruit: 0.0
Bread: 1.0
Meat: 2.0
Fat: 0.0

1. Spray large saucepan with cooking spray; heat over medium heat until hot. Add ground beef, onions, bell pepper, and garlic; cook over medium heat until meat is brown and vegetables are tender, 5 to 8 minutes. Add chili powder, cumin, oregano, and cloves; cook 1 to 2 minutes longer.

2. Add tomatoes and liquid, tomato paste, beer, brown sugar, and cocoa to beef mixture. Heat to boiling; reduce heat and simmer, covered, 1 hour. Stir in beans and simmer, uncovered, to thicken, if desired. Season to taste with salt and pepper.

3. Spoon chili into bowls; sprinkle each with equal amounts of cheese, green onions, and sour cream.

Variation: **Chili Mac**—In Step 2, add 1 cup uncooked elbow macaroni *or* chili mac pasta and ¹/₂ cup water to chili after 45 minutes cooking time; heat to boiling. Reduce heat and simmer, covered, until macaroni is tender, about 15 minutes; stir in beans and simmer 5 minutes.

THREE

Meats

MUSTARD ROAST BEEF

The spicy coating makes this roast beef extra juicy and flavorful.

8 servings

1/4 cup apricot preserves

2-4 tablespoons spicy brown mustard

2-3 teaspoons reduced-sodium Worcestershire sauce

1 tablespoon light brown sugar

1 tablespoon prepared horseradish

1 teaspoon crushed caraway seeds

1/4 teaspoon ground allspice

1 teaspoon crushed black, *or* mixed, peppercorns

1 boneless beef sirloin tip roast, fat trimmed (about 2 pounds)

Per Serving
Calories: 171
% Calories from fat: 29
Fat (gm): 5.5
Saturated fat (gm): 2.1
Cholesterol (mg): 60.3
Sodium (mg): 118
Protein (gm): 20.7
Carbohydrate (gm): 9
Exchanges
Milk: 0.0
Vegetable: 0.0
Fruit: 0.5
Bread: 0.0
Meat: 3.0
Fat: 0.0

1. Mix all ingredients except beef in medium bowl. Spread on all surfaces of meat. Place meat on rack in roasting pan. Roast at 350 degrees until meat thermometer registers 140 degrees (medium), or 160 degrees (well-done), 30 to 45 minutes.

Variation: **Crumb-Crusted Roast Beef**—Make recipe as above omitting brown sugar, horseradish, caraway seeds, and allspice. Combine 1 cup fresh bread crumbs, 2 teaspoons minced garlic, 1 teaspoon dried basil leaves, 1/2 teaspoon dried oregano leaves, and 1/4 teaspoon dried marjoram leaves with the apricot preserves, mustard, and Worcestershire sauce in medium bowl. Pat crumb mixture onto roast. Roast as above.

VEGETABLE-STUFFED FLANK STEAK

Marinated flank steak, roasted with a flavorful stuffing, makes an impressive entrée. Serve with oven-roasted potatoes and a salad for a well-rounded and delicious meal.

4 servings

1 pound beef flank steak, fat trimmed
1 cup fat-free Italian salad dressing
  Vegetable Stuffing (recipe follows)
  Vegetable cooking spray
1 cup reduced-sodium fat-free beef broth

Per Serving
Calories: 281
% Calories from fat: 29
Fat (gm): 8.8
Saturated fat (gm): 3.6
Cholesterol (mg): 49.8
Sodium (mg): 744
Protein (gm): 33.6
Carbohydrate (gm): 14.4
Exchanges
Milk: 0.0
Vegetable: 0.0
Fruit: 0.0
Bread: 1.0
Meat: 4.0
Fat: 0.0

1. Pound flank steak with meat mallet until even thickness (scant 3/4 inch thick). Using sharp knife, score steak diagonally in diamond pattern on both sides. Place steak in shallow glass baking dish; pour dressing over. Refrigerate, covered, 1 1/2 to 2 hours, turning steak occasionally.

2. Remove steak from marinade; reserve marinade. Spread Vegetable Stuffing on steak, leaving 2-inch margin along sides. Roll up lengthwise, jelly-roll style; secure edge with wooden picks, or tie with kitchen string.

3. Spray large ovenproof skillet with cooking spray; heat over medium-high heat until hot. Add meat and brown on all sides. Add broth to skillet, stirring to dissolve juices from bottom; add reserved marinade. Bake, covered, at 325 degrees until meat thermometer registers 140 degrees (medium) or 160 degrees (well-done), 30 to 45 minutes.

Vegetable Stuffing

makes about 1¹/₄ cups

Vegetable cooking spray
8 ounces sliced mushrooms
¹/₂ cup chopped carrot
¹/₄ cup thinly sliced celery
¹/₄ cup thinly sliced green onions and tops
1 clove garlic, minced
¹/₄ cup unseasoned dry bread crumbs
1¹/₂ teaspoons Italian seasoning
Salt and pepper, to taste

1. Spray large skillet with cooking spray; heat over medium heat until hot. Add mushrooms, carrot, celery, green onions, and garlic and saute until tender, about 5 minutes. Stir in bread crumbs and Italian seasoning; season to taste with salt and pepper. Stir over medium heat until bread crumbs are browned, 2 to 3 minutes.

TOURNEDOS BÉARNAISE

The flavors of the classic, with a fraction of the fat.

4 servings

4 slices Italian, *or* French, bread (³/₄ inch thick)
Vegetable cooking spray
1 clove garlic, cut in half
4 beef tenderloin steaks, fat trimmed (4 ounces each)
Salt and pepper, to taste
Creamy Béarnaise Sauce (recipe follows)

Per Serving
Calories: 335
% Calories from fat: 29
Fat (gm): 10.4
Saturated fat (gm): 3.9
Cholesterol (mg): 76.1
Sodium (mg): 488
Protein (gm): 35.1
Carbohydrate (gm): 22.7
Exchanges
Milk: 0.0
Vegetable: 0.0
Fruit: 0.0
Bread: 1.5
Meat: 4.0
Fat: 0.0

1. Spray bread slices with cooking spray; place on cookie sheet and broil 4 inches from heat source until browned, 1 to 2 minutes on each side. Rub bread slices with garlic.

2. Spray large skillet with cooking spray; heat over medium-high heat until hot. Add steaks and cook to desired degree of doneness (about 3 minutes on each side for medium). Season to taste with salt and pepper.

3. Arrange steaks on bread slices; spoon Creamy Béarnaise Sauce over.

Creamy Béarnaise Sauce

makes about 1¹/₂ cups

> 6 ounces fat-free cream cheese
> ¹/₃ cup fat-free sour cream
> 3-4 tablespoons fat-free milk
> 2 teaspoons minced shallot
> 1-2 teaspoons tarragon vinegar *or* lemon juice
> ¹/₂-1 teaspoon Dijon-style mustard
> 1¹/₂ teaspoons dried tarragon leaves
> ¹/₈ teaspoon ground turmeric
> Salt and white pepper, to taste

1. Heat all ingredients in small saucepan over medium-low to low heat until melted and smooth, stirring constantly. Serve immediately.

FILET MIGNON STROGANOFF

A creamy mushroom sauce makes these steaks very special. Any tender steak may be used in this recipe.

4 servings

> Vegetable cooking spray
> 4 beef tenderloin steaks, fat trimmed (4 ounces each)
> Salt and pepper, to taste
> 3 cups sliced mushrooms
> ³/₄ cup chopped red bell pepper
> ¹/₂ teaspoon dried marjoram leaves
> ¹/₄ teaspoon dried thyme leaves
> 4 tablespoons fat-free cream cheese
> ¹/₃ cup reduced-fat sour cream
> 3 cups cooked rice, warm

Per Serving
Calories: 398
% Calories from fat: 22
Fat (gm): 9.5
Saturated fat (gm): 3.5
Cholesterol (mg): 73.7
Sodium (mg): 157
Protein (gm): 32.6
Carbohydrate (gm): 43.5
Exchanges
Milk: 0.0
Vegetable: 3.0
Fruit: 0.0
Bread: 2.0
Meat: 3.0
Fat: 0.0

1. Spray large skillet with cooking spray; heat over medium heat until hot. Add steaks and saute to desired degree of doneness (about 3 minutes on each side for medium). Season to taste with salt and pepper; remove to serving platter and keep warm.

2. Spray skillet with cooking spray; add mushrooms and bell pepper to skillet and cook over medium heat until mushrooms are tender. Stir in herbs and cream cheese and stir until melted; stir in sour cream and cook until heated through. Season to taste with salt and pepper.

3. Spoon mushroom mixture over steaks; serve with rice.

STEAK AU POIVRE

This elegant special-occasion entrée is made with low-fat beef eye of round steak rather than the traditional higher-fat tenderloin. Beef eye of round steak has less than 30% calories from fat.

4 servings

2 teaspoons crushed black peppercorns
4 beef eye of round steaks (4 ounces each), fat trimmed
Salt, to taste
Vegetable cooking spray
1/3 cup brandy
1/4 cup fat-free sour cream

Per Serving
Calories: 212
% Calories from fat: 20
Fat (gm): 4.5
Saturated fat (gm): 1.6
Cholesterol (mg): 64
Sodium (mg): 68
Protein (gm): 27.7
Carbohydrate (gm): 2.1
Exchanges
Milk: 0.0
Vegetable: 0.0
Fruit: 0.0
Bread: 0.0
Meat: 3.5
Fat: 0.0

1. Press peppercorns into steak, using about 1/4 teaspoon per side; sprinkle lightly with salt. Spray medium skillet with cooking spray; heat over medium to medium-high heat until hot. Add steaks to skillet and cook over medium heat to desired degree of doneness, 3 to 4 minutes on each side for medium. Remove steaks to serving plates.

2. Add brandy to skillet; heat to boiling. Boil, scraping bottom of skillet to loosen cooked particles, until reduced to about 2 tablespoons, 2 to 3 minutes. Stir in sour cream and cook over low heat 1 to 2 minutes. Spoon sauce over steaks.

Note: A mixture of white, pink, green, and black peppercorns can be used.

BEEF STEAKS WITH TOMATILLO AND AVOCADO SAUCE

This sauce has much less avocado than the higher-fat Mexican version of the recipe. We've added a bit of sour cream for richness and subtle flavor. The sauce would also be excellent with grilled or roasted poultry or lean pork.

6 servings

Vegetable cooking spray
1 medium onion, thinly sliced
6 boneless beef eye of round steaks (about 4 ounces each), fat trimmed
Salt and pepper, to taste
1 cup Tomatillo Sauce (¹/₂ recipe) (see p. 203)
2 tablespoons mashed avocado
2 tablespoons fat-free sour cream
6 flour, *or* corn, tortillas, warm

Per Serving
Calories: 271
% Calories from fat: 30
Fat (gm): 8.9
Saturated fat (gm): 3.1
Cholesterol (mg): 56.3
Sodium (mg): 101
Protein (gm): 28.2
Carbohydrate (gm): 19.2
Exchanges
Milk: 0.0
Vegetable: 1.0
Fruit: 0.0
Bread: 1.0
Meat: 3.0
Fat: 0.0

1. Spray large skillet with cooking spray; heat over medium heat until hot. Saute onion 2 to 3 minutes; reduce heat to medium-low and cook until onion is very soft, 5 to 8 minutes. Remove from skillet.

2. Add steaks to skillet; cook over medium heat to desired degree of doneness, 3 to 4 minutes on each side for medium. Season to taste with salt and pepper. Heat Tomatillo Sauce and avocado in small saucepan until hot; stir in sour cream.

3. Arrange steaks on serving platter; top with onions and spoon Tomatillo Sauce over. Serve with tortillas.

BEEF STEAK WITH RED AND GREEN STIR-FRY

If available, use red or rhubarb Swiss chard for its beautiful red and green color.

4 servings

Oriental cooking spray
2 cups sliced red onions
1 cup sliced celery
2 teaspoons minced garlic
1 teaspoon minced gingerroot
6 cups sliced Swiss chard *or* spinach
2 cups sliced red bell pepper
2 cups reduced-sodium fat-free beef broth
2 tablespoons cornstarch
4 teaspoons reduced-sodium tamari soy sauce, divided
1/2-3/4 teaspoon hot chili paste
Salt and pepper, to taste
4 beef eye of round steaks, fat trimmed (4 ounces each)

Per Serving
Calories: 210
% Calories from fat: 17
Fat (gm): 4.1
Saturated fat (gm): 1.4
Cholesterol (mg): 54.9
Sodium (mg): 494
Protein (gm): 26.3
Carbohydrate (gm): 17.1
Exchanges
Milk: 0.0
Vegetable: 2.0
Fruit: 0.0
Bread: 0.0
Meat: 3.0
Fat: 0.0

1. Spray wok or large skillet with cooking spray; heat over medium heat until hot. Stir-fry onions, celery, garlic, and gingerroot 1 to 2 minutes. Add Swiss chard and stir-fry 1 to 2 minutes. Add bell pepper to wok; stir-fry until vegetables are crisp-tender, 2 to 3 minutes.

2. Combine broth, cornstarch, 2 teaspoons tamari, and chili paste; stir into wok. Heat to boiling; boil, stirring constantly, until thickened, about 1 minute. Season to taste with salt and pepper.

3. Spray large skillet with cooking spray; heat over medium heat until hot. Brush beef with remaining 2 teaspoons tamari. Cook in skillet over medium to medium-high heat to desired degree of doneness, 3 to 4 minutes on each side for medium.

4. Arrange beef on serving platter; spoon vegetable mixture over.

CHICKEN-FRIED STEAK

The beef steaks are pounded until thin for faster cooking and tenderness. Use seasoned or unseasoned bread crumbs, as you prefer.

4 servings

- 4 beef eye of round steaks (4 ounces each), fat trimmed
- 2 tablespoons flour
- 2 egg whites *or* 1/4 cup no-cholesterol real egg product
- 1/4 cup fat-free milk
- 1/3 cup seasoned dry bread crumbs
- Vegetable cooking spray
- Salt and pepper, to taste
- Cream Gravy (see p. 144)

Per Serving
Calories: 349
% Calories from fat: **29**
Fat (gm): **11**
Saturated fat (gm): **3**
Cholesterol (mg): 66.2
Sodium (mg): 309
Protein (gm): 36.5
Carbohydrate (gm): 23.8
Exchanges
Milk: 0.5
Vegetable: 0.0
Fruit: 0.0
Bread: 1.5
Meat: 3.5
Fat: 0.0

1. Pound steaks with flat side of mallet to 1/4 inch thickness. Coat steaks lightly with flour; dip in combined egg whites and milk and coat with bread crumbs. Spray both sides of steaks with cooking spray.

2. Spray large skillet generously with cooking spray; heat over medium heat until hot. Cook steaks over medium heat until browned, about 5 minutes on each side. Cover and cook over very low heat until steaks are tender, turning occasionally, 30 to 40 minutes. Season to taste with salt and pepper. Serve with Cream Gravy.

OLD-FASHIONED POT ROAST

Cabbage, turnips, and sweet potatoes are other vegetable choices that can be used in this recipe—use the favorites you remember! Substitute ¹/₂ cup dry red wine for part of the beef broth, if you like.

6 servings

Vegetable cooking spray

2³/₄ pounds beef chuck pot roast, fat trimmed

Salt and pepper, to taste

3 medium onions, cut into wedges, divided

6 cloves garlic, minced

1 cup reduced-sodium beef broth

¹/₂ teaspoon dried thyme leaves

1 bay leaf

1 pound potatoes, unpeeled, cut into 1¹/₂-inch pieces

8 ounces carrots, cut into 1¹/₂-inch pieces

8 ounces peeled rutabaga *or* parsnip, cut into 1¹/₂-inch pieces

¹/₄ cup all-purpose flour

¹/₂ cup water

Per Serving
Calories: 377
% Calories from fat: 15
Fat (gm): 6.4
Saturated fat (gm): 2.2
Cholesterol (mg): 95.6
Sodium (mg): 110
Protein (gm): 37
Carbohydrate (gm): 42.6
Exchanges
Milk: 0.0
Vegetable: 2.0
Fruit: 0.0
Bread: 1.5
Meat: 4.0
Fat: 0.0

1. Spray large Dutch oven with cooking spray; heat over medium heat until hot. Add meat and cook over medium heat until browned, 2 to 3 minutes on each side. Remove from pan and sprinkle lightly with salt and pepper. Add half the onions and all the garlic to the pan; saute 2 to 3 minutes.

2. Return meat to pan. Add beef broth and herbs to pan and heat to boiling. Transfer to oven and bake, covered, at 325 degrees until meat is fork-tender, 2³/₄ to 3 hours. Add remaining onions and vegetables to pan during last hour of cooking time, sprinkling lightly with salt and pepper. Arrange meat and vegetables on serving platter; discard bay leaf.

3. Pour meat juices into glass measure; spoon off and discard fat. Add water to juices, if necessary, to make 2 cups; heat to boiling in Dutch oven. Mix flour and water; stir into boiling juices. Boil, whisking constantly, until thickened, about 1 minute; season to taste with salt and pepper. Serve gravy with pot roast and vegetables.

Variations: **Bourbon Pot Roast**—Make recipe as above, omitting rutabaga, and substituting 2/3 cup tomato juice and 1/3 cup bourbon for the beef broth. Add 1 teaspoon dry mustard and 1/2 teaspoon beef bouillon crystals with the tomato juice in Step 2.

Italian Pot Roast—Make recipe as above, omitting potatoes, carrots, rutabagas, and flour. Substitute 1 cup dry red wine for the beef broth. Add 1 can (15 ounces) roasted garlic diced tomatoes, 1 can (6 ounces) reduced-sodium tomato paste, and 1 teaspoon dried basil leaves in Step 2. Add 1/2 cup chopped carrot, 1/2 cup chopped celery, and 1 cup sliced mushrooms during last hour of cooking time. Serve over Polenta (see p. 458).

COUNTRY BEEF STEW

Simmer this stew for a long time for old-fashioned goodness. Use your family's favorite vegetables, and serve the thick stew over cooked noodles in shallow bowls.

4 servings (about 1 cup each)

Vegetable cooking spray
1 pound lean beef stew meat, fat trimmed, cubed
1/2 cup chopped onion
1/2 cup chopped celery
2 cloves garlic, minced
1 cup reduced-sodium beef broth
1/2 cup dry red wine *or* reduced-sodium beef broth
1 tablespoon tomato paste
1/2 teaspoon dried thyme leaves
1/2 teaspoon dried rosemary leaves
1 bay leaf
1 cup cubed unpeeled potato
1 cup sliced carrots (1-inch pieces)
1/2 cup cubed peeled parsnip *or* turnip
1/2 cup frozen peas
2 tablespoons flour
1/4 cup cold water
Salt and pepper, to taste

Per Serving
Calories: 326
% Calories from fat: 16
Fat (gm): 5.8
Saturated fat (gm): 2
Cholesterol (mg): 70.9
Sodium (mg): 171
Protein (gm): 33.5
Carbohydrate (gm): 29.6
Exchanges
Milk: 0.0
Vegetable: 2.0
Fruit: 0.0
Bread: 1.5
Meat: 3.0
Fat: 0.0

1. Spray large saucepan with cooking spray; heat over medium heat until hot. Add beef and cook until browned, 5 to 8 minutes. Add onion, celery, and garlic; cook until tender, about 5 minutes.

2. Add broth, wine, tomato paste, and herbs to saucepan; heat to boiling. Reduce heat and simmer, covered, until beef is tender, 1¹/₂ to 2 hours. Add remaining vegetables during last 30 minutes of cooking time.

3. Heat stew to boiling. Mix flour and water and stir into stew; boil, stirring constantly, until thickened. Discard bay leaf; season to taste with salt and pepper.

BEEF BRAISED IN RED WINE

The slow simmering gives this dish a rich flavor. A good-quality Chianti works well in this traditional Italian recipe.

6 servings

1¹/₂ pounds boneless beef round steak, cubed

2 tablespoons flour

1 large onion, chopped

1 teaspoon minced garlic

2 cups sliced mushrooms

1 cup reduced-sodium fat-free beef broth, divided

1 tablespoon olive oil

2 large celery stalks, sliced

10 baby carrots

5 medium potatoes, halved

1 can (15 ounces) reduced-sodium tomato sauce

1 cup dry red wine *or* beef broth

1 teaspoon dried thyme leaves

2 large bay leaves

¹/₂ teaspoon dry mustard

¹/₈ teaspoon celery seeds

Salt and pepper, to taste

Per Serving
Calories: 366
% Calories from fat: 18
Fat (gm): 7.4
Saturated fat (gm): 2.2
Cholesterol (mg): 55.9
Sodium (mg): 115
Protein (gm): 31.2
Carbohydrate (gm): 36.9
Exchanges
Milk: 0.0
Vegetable: 2.0
Fruit: 0.0
Bread: 2.0
Meat: 3.0
Fat: 0.0

1. Toss beef with flour in large shallow baking pan. Bake at 350 degrees, stirring occasionally, until browned on all sides, about 25 minutes.

2. Heat onion, garlic, mushrooms, $^1/_4$ cup beef broth, and oil to boiling in large Dutch oven; reduce heat and simmer until onion is tender, about 10 minutes. Stir in browned beef, remaining $^3/_4$ cup broth, and remaining ingredients except salt and pepper. Heat to boiling; place Dutch oven in oven and bake, covered, until beef is tender, about 45 minutes. Season to taste with salt and pepper.

BEEF BOURGUIGNON CÔTE D'OR

Try this French-style stew for special occasions, when ordinary beef stew is not quite fancy enough!

6 servings

1$^1/_2$ pounds beef eye of round steak, fat trimmed, cut into scant 1$^1/_2$-inch cubes

$^1/_4$ cup all-purpose flour

1 tablespoon olive, *or* vegetable, oil

1 cup Burgundy wine *or* reduced-sodium beef broth

1 cup water

1$^1/_2$ cups peeled pearl onions

3 cups cubed, or julienned, carrots

8 ounces small whole mushrooms

1 teaspoon dried marjoram leaves

1 teaspoon dried thyme leaves

2 bay leaves

$^1/_2$ teaspoon salt

$^1/_4$ teaspoon pepper

16 ounces egg noodles, cooked, warm

Per Serving
Calories: 507
% Calories from fat: 16
Fat (gm): 8.8
Saturated fat (gm): 2.1
Cholesterol (mg): 120.2
Sodium (mg): 288
Protein (gm): 34.9
Carbohydrate (gm): 65
Exchanges
Milk: 0.0
Vegetable: 2.0
Fruit: 0.0
Bread: 4.0
Meat: 3.0
Fat: 0.0

1. Coat beef cubes with flour; saute in oil in Dutch oven until browned on all sides, about 10 minutes. Add wine and water; heat to boiling.

2. Transfer Dutch oven to range oven and bake, covered, at 350 degrees until beef is very tender, about 2 hours. Add vegetables, herbs, and salt and pepper during last 30 minutes of baking time. Discard bay leaves. Serve over noodles.

EASY BEEF BOURGUIGNON

12 servings

1 4-pound boneless sirloin roast, cut into 1 1/2-inch cubes

1 cup Burgundy *or* other dry red wine

1 cup water

2 cans (10½ ounces each) reduced-fat cream of mushroom soup

1 package onion soup mix

2 pounds fresh mushrooms, sliced

1 green bell pepper, chopped

1 pound pearl onions, peeled and chopped

½ teaspoon garlic powder

10 grape tomatoes
   Parsley sprigs

6 cups cooked rice

Per Serving
Calories: 392
% Calories from fat: 20
Fat (gm): 8.8
Saturated fat (gm): 3.2
Cholesterol (mg): 84
Sodium (mg): 1429
Protein (gm): 33.1
Carbohydrate (gm): 41.4
Exchanges
Milk: 0.0
Vegetable: 2.0
Fruit: 0.0
Bread: 2.0
Meat: 4.0
Fat: 0.0

1. Preheat oven to 325 degrees. Place beef and mushrooms in 2½-quart casserole dish. Combine wine, water, mushroom soup, and soup mix; stir well, and pour over beef mixture in casserole. Cover and bake for 2 hours. Add remaining ingredients, except the rice, and bake an additional 30 minutes. Garnish with parsley sprigs and serve over rice.

BEEF STROGANOFF

A favorite for buffet entertaining, this dish enjoys well-deserved popularity.

4 servings

1 pound beef eye of round, *or* sirloin, steak, fat trimmed, cut into 1¹/₂ x ¹/₂-inch strips
1 tablespoon margarine
3 cups sliced mushrooms
¹/₂ cup sliced onion
2 cloves garlic, minced
2 tablespoons flour
1¹/₂ cups reduced-sodium beef broth
1 teaspoon Dijon-style mustard
¹/₄ teaspoon dried thyme leaves
¹/₂ cup fat-free sour cream
Salt and pepper, to taste
3 cups cooked no-yolk noodles, warm
Finely chopped parsley leaves, as garnish

Per Serving
Calories: 423
% Calories from fat: 21
Fat (gm): 10
Saturated fat (gm): 2.2
Cholesterol (mg): 64
Sodium (mg): 167
Protein (gm): 39
Carbohydrate (gm): 45.1
Exchanges
Milk: 0.0
Vegetable: 1.0
Fruit: 0.0
Bread: 2.5
Meat: 4.0
Fat: 0.0

1. Saute beef in margarine in large saucepan until browned on all sides, about 5 minutes; remove from pan. Add mushrooms, onion, and garlic; saute until tender, 5 to 8 minutes. Stir in flour and cook, stirring, 1 to 2 minutes.

2. Add beef, beef broth, mustard, and thyme. Heat to boiling; reduce heat and simmer, covered, until beef is tender, 20 to 25 minutes. Reduce heat to low; stir in sour cream and cook 2 to 3 minutes. Season to taste with salt and pepper. Serve over warm noodles; sprinkle with parsley.

BEEF AND ANCHO CHILI STEW

This stew has lots of delicious sauce, so serve with crusty warm rolls or warm tortillas, or serve over a rice dish, such as Black Beans and Rice (see p. 467). Vary the amount of ancho chilies to taste.

8 servings

4-6 ancho chilies, stems, seeds, and veins discarded

2 cups boiling water

4 medium tomatoes, cut into wedges
Vegetable cooking spray

2 pounds boneless beef eye of round, fat trimmed, cut into $3/4$-inch cubes

1 large onion, chopped

2 cloves garlic, minced

1 teaspoon minced serrano, *or* jalapeño, chili

1 teaspoon dried oregano leaves

1 teaspoon crushed cumin seeds

2 tablespoons flour
Salt and pepper, to taste

Per Serving
Calories: 159
% Calories from fat: 23
Fat (gm): 4
Saturated fat (gm): 1.3
Cholesterol (mg): 54.7
Sodium (mg): 56
Protein (gm): 22.1
Carbohydrate (gm): 8.3
Exchanges
Milk: 0.0
Vegetable: 1.0
Fruit: 0.0
Bread: 0.0
Meat: 2.5
Fat: 0.0

1. Place ancho chilies in bowl; pour boiling water over. Let stand until chilies are softened, about 10 minutes. Process chilies and water and tomatoes in food processor or blender until smooth.

2. Spray large saucepan with cooking spray; heat over medium heat until hot. Cook beef until browned on all sides, about 5 minutes. Add onion, garlic, serrano chili, and herbs and cook until onion is tender, about 5 minutes. Stir in flour; cook over medium heat 1 to 2 minutes.

3. Add ancho chili mixture to saucepan; heat to boiling. Reduce heat and simmer, covered, until beef is tender, about 45 minutes. Season to taste with salt and pepper. Serve in shallow bowls.

PEPPER STEAK

Perfect for family meals or for casual buffet-style entertaining. For a colorful variation, use a combination of green, red, and yellow peppers.

6 servings

Vegetable cooking spray
3 cups sliced green bell peppers
2¹/₂ cups sliced onions
4 cloves garlic, minced
1 pound beef eye of round steak *or* sirloin steak, fat trimmed, cut into 3 x ¹/₄-inch strips
2 tablespoons flour
1³/₄ cups reduced-sodium beef broth, divided
¹/₂ cup water
1 tablespoon tomato paste
¹/₂ teaspoon Italian seasoning
2 tablespoons cornstarch
1¹/₂ cups quartered cherry tomatoes
1-2 tablespoons Worcestershire sauce
Salt and pepper, to taste
4¹/₂ cups cooked no-yolk noodles, warm

Per Serving
Calories: 383
% Calories from fat: 13
Fat (gm): 5.8
Saturated fat (gm): 1.2
Cholesterol (mg): 42.6
Sodium (mg): 127
Protein (gm): 28.7
Carbohydrate (gm): 56.2
Exchanges
Milk: 0.0
Vegetable: 3.0
Fruit: 0.0
Bread: 2.5
Meat: 2.5
Fat: 0.0

1. Spray large skillet with cooking spray; heat over medium heat until hot. Saute bell peppers until tender, about 5 minutes; remove from pan and reserve. Add onions and garlic to skillet; saute until tender, 5 to 8 minutes.

2. Coat beef with flour and add to skillet; cook over medium to medium-low heat 3 to 5 minutes, stirring frequently. Add 1¹/₂ cups broth, water, tomato paste, and Italian seasoning; heat to boiling. Reduce heat and simmer, covered, until beef is tender, about 45 minutes, adding reserved peppers during last 10 minutes.

3. Heat pepper steak mixture to boiling. Mix cornstarch and remaining ¹/₄ cup beef broth; stir into boiling mixture. Boil, stirring constantly, until thickened, about 1 minute. Stir in tomatoes and simmer 10 minutes. Season to taste with Worcestershire sauce, salt, and pepper. Serve with noodles.

Variation: **Sweet-Sour Pepper Steak**—Make recipe as above, substituting 1¹/₂ cups snow peas for half of the bell peppers and reduced-sodium soy sauce for the Worcestershire sauce. Stir in ¹/₄ cup apricot preserves, ¹/₂ cup sliced water chestnuts, and 2 to 3 teaspoons cider vinegar at the end of cooking time. Serve over rice.

BEEF AND VEGETABLE LO MEIN

To store leftover gingerroot, place it in a jar, fill with dry sherry, cover, and refrigerate; the gingerroot will last at least 6 months. Gingerroot does not have to be peeled before using.

4 servings

1 package (12 ounces) fresh Chinese-style noodles

4 quarts boiling water

4 Chinese dried black, *or* shiitake, mushrooms

1 tablespoon sesame, *or* vegetable, oil

1 tablespoon finely chopped fresh gingerroot

3 cloves garlic, minced

12 ounces beef eye of round steak, fat trimmed, cut into ¹/₂-inch strips

2 cups broccoli florets

1 cup sliced carrots

¹/₃ cup water

2 tablespoons dry sherry *or* water

2 teaspoons cornstarch

1 tablespoon black bean paste

2 teaspoons light soy sauce

Per Serving
Calories: 300
% Calories from fat: 18
Fat (gm): 6
Saturated fat (gm): 1.4
Cholesterol (mg): 41.2
Sodium (mg): 153
Protein (gm): 22.1
Carbohydrate (gm): 37.9
Exchanges
Milk: 0.0
Vegetable: 1.0
Fruit: 0.0
Bread: 2.0
Meat: 2.5
Fat: 0.0

1. Cook noodles in 4 quarts boiling water until tender, about 2 minutes; drain and reserve. Place dried mushrooms in bowl; pour hot water over to cover. Let stand until mushrooms are soft, about 15 minutes; drain. Slice mushrooms, discarding tough parts.

2. Heat oil in wok or skillet over medium-high heat until hot. Stir-fry mushrooms, gingerroot, and garlic 2 minutes. Add beef; stir-fry until beef is cooked, about 5 minutes. Remove from wok.

3. Add broccoli and carrots to wok; stir-fry until vegetables are crisp-tender, 5 to 8 minutes. Remove from wok.

4. Combine ¹/₃ cup water, sherry, and cornstarch; add to wok and heat to boiling. Boil, stirring constantly, until thickened, about 1 minute. Stir in black bean paste and soy sauce. Return beef and vegetable mixtures to wok; add noodles. Stir-fry over medium heat until hot through, 2 to 3 minutes.

BEEF ORIENTAL WITH RICE

6 servings

1¹/₂ pounds lean round steak
¹/₄ teaspoon minced onion
¹/₄ teaspoon minced garlic
1 tablespoon low-sodium soy sauce
¹/₄ cup water
¹/₈ teaspoon coarsely ground pepper
1 low-sodium beef bouillon cube
1¹/₂ cups hot water
1 package (16 ounces) frozen broccoli florets
1 package (16 ounces) frozen cauliflower florets
¹/₂ cup julienned carrot
2¹/₂ cups sliced fresh mushrooms
¹/₂ cup sliced water chestnuts
¹/₂ cup chopped celery
4 cups cooked white rice

Per Serving
Calories: 349
% Calories from fat: 14
Fat (gm): 5.2
Saturated fat (gm): 1.9
Cholesterol (mg): 55.9
Sodium (mg): 186
Protein (gm): 34
Carbohydrate (gm): 40.8
Exchanges
Milk: 0.0
Vegetable: 2.0
Fruit: 0.0
Bread: 2.0
Meat: 3.0
Fat: 0.0

1. Preheat oven to 350 degrees. Add round steak to baking pan, sprinkle with onion, garlic, soy sauce, ¹/₄ cup water, and pepper; bake for 30 minutes. Remove meat from oven and cut into bite-sized pieces.

2. In a large saucepan, dissolve bouillon cube in 1¹/₂ cups hot water. Add remaining ingredients, except the rice, and heat to boiling; reduce heat and simmer 15 minutes. Add the steak and simmer 15 minutes. Serve over ²/₃ cup rice.

SPICY BEEF AND NOODLES

---

6 servings

1 pound extra-lean round steak, cut into strips

¹/₂ cup sliced onion

1 clove garlic, minced

2 tablespoons low-sodium beef broth

1 can (6 ounces) mushrooms, drained

2 drops hot sauce

1 tablespoon low-sodium Worcestershire sauce

1 tablespoon low-sodium soy sauce

¹/₄ teaspoon pepper

¹/₄ teaspoon paprika

Dash grated nutmeg

1 can (10 ³/₄ ounces) low-sodium, reduced-fat tomato soup

12 ounces yolkless wide noodles, cooked

Per Serving
Calories: 369
% Calories from fat: 11
Fat (gm): 4.6
Saturated fat (gm): 1.4
Cholesterol (mg): 37.3
Sodium (mg): 476
Protein (gm): 28
Carbohydrate (gm): 52.6
Exchanges
Milk: 0.0
Vegetable: 1.0
Fruit: 0.0
Bread: 3.0
Meat: 2.0
Fat: 0.0

1. Saute beef, onion, and garlic in broth in large saucepan until meat is browned. Add remaining ingredients, except the noodles; simmer until beef is tender. Serve over noodles.

CURRIED BEEF STEW WITH CHIVE DUMPLINGS

Part of the beef in this aromatic stew is coarsely chopped, giving the stew an extra-rich texture.

8 servings

2 pounds boneless lean beef, fat trimmed
1-2 tablespoons vegetable oil
1¹/₂ cups chopped onions
3 tablespoons flour
1¹/₂ teaspoons curry powder
2 cups reduced-sodium beef broth
1 large tomato, coarsely chopped
1 bay leaf
1 package (10 ounces) frozen peas
Salt and pepper, to taste
Chive Dumplings (recipe follows)

Per Serving
Calories: 297
% Calories from fat: 22
Fat (gm): 7.3
Saturated fat (gm): 1.9
Cholesterol (mg): 55.3
Sodium (mg): 416
Protein (gm): 27.1
Carbohydrate (gm): 29.4
Exchanges
Milk: 0.0
Vegetable: 0.0
Fruit: 0.0
Bread: 2.0
Meat: 3.0
Fat: 0.0

1. Cut 1 pound beef into scant 1-inch cubes; coarsely chop remaining 1 pound of beef. Cook beef in oil in Dutch oven over medium heat until browned, about 5 minutes; add onions and cook until tender, 5 to 8 minutes. Stir in flour and curry and cook 1 minute longer.

2. Add beef broth, tomato, and bay leaf and heat to boiling; reduce heat and simmer, covered, until beef is tender, about 1 hour, adding peas during last 10 minutes of cooking time. Discard bay leaf; season to taste with salt and pepper.

3. Heat stew to boiling; drop Chive Dumplings dough onto top of stew. Cook, uncovered, 10 minutes; cook, covered, 10 minutes longer or until dumplings are dry.

Chive Dumplings

1²/₃ cups reduced-fat all-purpose baking mix
2 tablespoons finely chopped chives
¹/₄-¹/₂ teaspoon curry powder
²/₃ cup fat-free milk

1. Combine baking mix, chives, and curry powder in bowl; mix in milk, forming a soft dough.

PAPRIKA-SIRLOIN STEW WITH SOUR CREAM

Imagine tender beef, Italian green beans, and red potatoes cloaked in a heavenly paprika-spiked sour cream sauce. And suppose that such a dinner could be ready to eat in about 30 minutes. Daydream no more—here's the real meal!

4 servings

1 cup reduced-sodium fat-free beef broth
2 cups Italian flat green beans
3/4 pound red potatoes, cut into 1/2-inch cubes
2 bay leaves
1 pound boneless beef sirloin steak, fat trimmed, cut into very thin 1-inch-long strips
1 cup pearl onions, peeled
1 can (15 ounces) diced tomatoes, undrained
1 tablespoon paprika
1/2 cup fat-free sour cream
    Salt and pepper, to taste

Per Serving
Calories: 286
% Calories from fat: 17
Fat (gm): 5.4
Saturated fat (gm): 2
Cholesterol (mg): 59.5
Sodium (mg): 768
Protein (gm): 27.4
Carbohydrate (gm): 32.9
Exchanges
Milk: 0.0
Vegetable: 0.0
Fruit: 0.0
Bread: 2.0
Meat: 3.0
Fat: 0.0

1. Heat beef broth, beans, potatoes, and bay leaves to boiling in large saucepan; reduce heat and simmer, covered, until vegetables are tender, about 10 minutes.

2. Saute beef and onions in large skillet until lightly browned; stir into vegetable mixture. Stir in tomatoes and liquid and paprika. Simmer, uncovered, 5 minutes, or until slightly thickened. Stir in sour cream; season to taste with salt and pepper.

QUICK BEEF GOULASH

In Hungary, this paprika-seasoned stew is called "gulyas," and it's often served with dollops of sour cream. This fast version includes beef, mushrooms, tomatoes, onion, and cabbage.

4 servings

12 ounces boneless beef round steak, fat trimmed, cut into 3/4-inch cubes
1 teaspoon olive oil
3 large onions, cut into thin wedges
1 cup chopped portobello mushrooms
1 can (15 ounces) diced tomatoes, undrained
1 tablespoon paprika
1 teaspoon unsweetened cocoa
2 cups coarsely sliced cabbage
1 tablespoon caraway seeds
Salt and pepper, to taste
8 ounces medium egg noodles, cooked, warm

Per Serving
Calories: 407
% Calories from fat: 17
Fat (gm): 7.7
Saturated fat (gm): 2
Cholesterol (mg): 90.9
Sodium (mg): 473
Protein (gm): 29.9
Carbohydrate (gm): 55.2
Exchanges
Milk: 0.0
Vegetable: 2.0
Fruit: 0.0
Bread: 3.0
Meat: 2.0
Fat: 0.5

1. Saute beef in oil in large saucepan until well browned; add onions and mushrooms and saute 5 minutes longer. Add tomatoes and liquid, paprika, and cocoa and heat to boiling; reduce heat and simmer, covered, until meat is tender, about 45 minutes.

2. Stir in cabbage and caraway seeds; cook 5 minutes longer. Season to taste with salt and pepper. Serve over noodles.

HUNGARIAN GOULASH

All the traditional flavors of goulash in an easy-to-assemble casserole.

6 servings

2 pounds beef round steak, fat trimmed, cut into 1/2-inch cubes
1 medium onion, finely chopped
1 teaspoon minced garlic
2 tablespoons flour
1 1/2 teaspoons paprika
1/4 teaspoon dried thyme leaves
1 bay leaf
1 can (14 1/2 ounces) diced tomatoes, undrained
1 container (8 ounces) fat-free sour cream
Salt and pepper, to taste
12 ounces egg, *or* no-yolk, wide noodles, cooked, warm

Per Serving
Calories: 471
% Calories from fat: 17
Fat (gm): 8.7
Saturated fat (gm): 2.9
Cholesterol (mg): 123.5
Sodium (mg): 367
Protein (gm): 44.6
Carbohydrate (gm): 50.5
Exchanges
Milk: 0.0
Vegetable: 1.0
Fruit: 0.0
Bread: 3.0
Meat: 4.0
Fat: 0.0

1. Combine beef, onion, and garlic in lightly greased 2 1/2-quart casserole; sprinkle with flour, paprika, and thyme and toss to coat. Stir in bay leaf and tomatoes and liquid.

2. Bake, covered, at 325 degrees, until beef is tender, about 1 1/2 hours. Stir in sour cream and bake, uncovered, until hot through, about 20 minutes. Season to taste with salt and pepper. Serve over noodles.

Variation: **Three-Meat Goulash**—Make recipe as above, using 3/4 pound each: cubed lean beef, pork, and veal in place of the beef round steak. Add 1 teaspoon caraway seeds and 1/2 teaspoon dried dill weed in Step 1. Add 8 ounces sliced mushrooms with the sour cream in Step 2.

BEEF AND ROASTED PEPPER FAJITAS

The meat in fajitas is often marinated in lime juice. In this recipe the lime is not used because the meat is cooked with the flavorful pasilla chili.

4 servings (2 fajitas each)

Vegetable cooking spray
1 large red bell pepper
1 large green bell pepper
1 large yellow bell pepper
$^1/_2$-1 teaspoon ground cumin
$^1/_4$ teaspoon ground cloves
1 dried pasilla chili, stem, seeds, and veins discarded
1 pound boneless beef eye of round steak, cut into thin strips
3 cloves garlic, minced
$^1/_4$ small jalapeño chili, seeds and veins discarded, minced
Salt, to taste
8 flour, *or* corn, tortillas, warm
2 tablespoons finely chopped cilantro
$^1/_2$ cup fat-free sour cream

Per Serving
Calories: 365
% Calories from fat: 19
Fat (gm): 7.8
Saturated fat (gm): 1.9
Cholesterol (mg): 54.7
Sodium (mg): 355
Protein (gm): 28.9
Carbohydrate (gm): 45
Exchanges
Milk: 0.0
Vegetable: 2.0
Fruit: 0.0
Bread: 2.0
Meat: 3.0
Fat: 0.0

1. Spray aluminum foil-lined jelly roll pan with cooking spray. Cut bell peppers into $^3/_4$-inch pieces; arrange on pan and spray with cooking spray. Bake at 425 degrees until tender and browned, 20 to 25 minutes. Place bell peppers in bowl; toss with cumin and cloves.

2. Cover pasilla chili with hot water in small bowl; let stand until softened, about 15 minutes. Drain and chop.

3. Spray large skillet with cooking spray; heat over medium heat until hot. Cook beef, garlic, and jalapeño and pasilla chilies over medium heat until beef is desired doneness, about 5 minutes for medium. Season to taste with salt.

4. Spoon beef and bell pepper mixtures onto tortillas; sprinkle with cilantro, top with sour cream, and roll up; fold 1 end up to prevent filling from leaking out.

BLACK BEAN AND BEEF BURRITOS

Another favorite that's a Tex-Mex adaptation of Mexican cooking. The large 10-inch flour tortillas are sometimes called "burritos" on the package. Eight small tortillas can be substituted for the larger size.

4 servings

Vegetable cooking spray
1 medium poblano chili, seeds and veins discarded, chopped
1 small onion, chopped
1 clove garlic, minced
1 bay leaf, crumbled
1 can (15 ounces) black beans, rinsed, drained
1 can (8 ounces) no-salt-added tomato sauce
Salt and pepper, to taste
Beef Filling (recipe follows)
4 large flour tortillas (10-inch)
1/2 cup (2 ounces) shredded fat-free Cheddar cheese
1/2 cup fat-free sour cream
2 tablespoons finely chopped cilantro

Per Serving
Calories: 379
% Calories from fat: 14
Fat (gm): 6.5
Saturated fat (gm): 1.4
Cholesterol (mg): 43.6
Sodium (mg): 677
Protein (gm): 35.5
Carbohydrate (gm): 51.8
Exchanges
Milk: 0.0
Vegetable: 2.0
Fruit: 0.0
Bread: 2.5
Meat: 2.5
Fat: 0.0

1. Spray large skillet with cooking spray; heat over medium heat until hot. Saute poblano chili, onion, garlic, and bay leaf until onion is tender, about 5 minutes. Add beans and tomato sauce; heat until hot. Season to taste with salt and pepper.

2. Spoon bean mixture and Beef Filling onto tortillas; top with cheese, sour cream, and cilantro. Roll up; fold 1 end up to prevent filling from leaking out.

Beef Filling

makes about 2 cups

12-16 ounces boneless beef eye of round, fat trimmed
Vegetable cooking spray
2 medium tomatoes, coarsely chopped
1/2 teaspoon ground cinnamon
Salt and pepper, to taste

1. Cut beef into 2-inch cubes and place in saucepan with 2 inches of water. Heat to boiling. Reduce heat and simmer, covered, until beef is tender, 15 to 20 minutes; drain. Cool slightly; shred finely.

2. Spray medium skillet with cooking spray; heat over medium heat until hot. Cook beef until beginning to brown, 3 to 4 minutes. Add tomatoes and cinnamon; cook until tomatoes are wilted. Season to taste with salt and pepper.

BEEF AND VEGETABLE ENCHILADAS

Vary these healthful enchiladas by substituting shredded chicken or pork tenderloin for the beef.

6 servings (2 enchiladas each)

Vegetable cooking spray
2 cups chopped zucchini
1¹/₂ cups chopped tomatoes
³/₄ cup chopped carrots
¹/₄ cup chopped poblano chili *or* green bell pepper
¹/₄ cup thinly sliced green onions and tops
4 cloves garlic, minced
1 teaspoon minced serrano, *or* jalapeño, chili
1 teaspoon dried oregano leaves
1-2 teaspoons ground cumin
1¹/₂ pounds boneless beef eye of round, fat trimmed, cooked, shredded
Salt and pepper, to taste
12 corn, *or* flour, tortillas
Enchilada Sauce (see p. 553)
³/₄ cup (3 ounces) shredded fat-free Cheddar cheese
3 tablespoons finely chopped cilantro

Per Serving
Calories: 305
% Calories from fat: 16
Fat (gm): 5.5
Saturated fat (gm): 1.5
Cholesterol (mg): 57.2
Sodium (mg): 244
Protein (gm): 30.2
Carbohydrate (gm): 34.8
Exchanges
Milk: 0.0
Vegetable: 2.0
Fruit: 0.0
Bread: 1.5
Meat: 3.0
Fat: 0.0

1. Spray large skillet with cooking spray; heat over medium heat until hot. Saute vegetables and herbs until vegetables are tender, about 10 minutes. Add beef; cook over medium heat until no excess juices remain, 5 to 8 minutes. Season to taste with salt and pepper.

2. Dip tortillas in Enchilada Sauce to coat lightly and fill each with about 1/3 cup beef mixture; roll up and place, seam sides down, in large baking pan. Spoon remaining Enchilada Sauce over enchiladas; sprinkle with cheese.

3. Bake enchiladas, uncovered, at 350 degrees 15 to 20 minutes. Sprinkle with cilantro.

BEEF AND PASTA SALAD VINAIGRETTE

Any lean beef or pork can be substituted for the flank steak. Slice meat diagonally, across the grain, into thin slices to maximize tenderness.

4 servings

12 ounces beef flank steak, fat trimmed, broiled *or* grilled to medium doneness
2 medium tomatoes, cut into wedges
1 medium yellow squash *or* zucchini, diagonally sliced
1 medium green bell pepper, sliced
1 large carrot, diagonally sliced
1 small red onion, sliced
3 cups (8 ounces) rotini (corkscrews), cooked, room temperature
Mixed Herb Vinaigrette (recipe follows)
Lettuce leaves, as garnish

Per Serving
Calories: 469
% Calories from fat: 27
Fat (gm): 14
Saturated fat (gm): 4.5
Cholesterol (mg): 57
Sodium (mg): 391
Protein (gm): 32.9
Carbohydrate (gm): 52.1
Exchanges
Milk: 0.0
Vegetable: 2.0
Fruit: 0.0
Bread: 2.5
Meat: 0.0
Fat: 1.5

1. Combine flank steak, tomatoes, squash, bell pepper, carrot, onion, and pasta in large bowl. Pour Mixed Herb Vinaigrette over and toss.

2. Arrange lettuce on salad plates; spoon salad over.

Mixed Herb Vinaigrette

makes about 2/3 cup

1/3 cup red wine vinegar
1/4 cup reduced-sodium beef broth *or* water
1 tablespoon olive oil *or* vegetable oil
2 teaspoons sugar
2 teaspoons Dijon-style mustard
1 teaspoon crushed mustard seeds
3 cloves garlic, minced

1 tablespoon finely chopped fresh, *or*
1 teaspoon dried, marjoram leaves
1 tablespoon finely chopped fresh, *or*
1 teaspoon dried, tarragon leaves
1 tablespoon finely chopped fresh, *or*
$^1/_2$ teaspoon dried, thyme leaves
$^1/_2$ teaspoon salt
$^1/_2$ teaspoon pepper

1. Mix all ingredients; refrigerate until ready to use. Stir before using.

GREEK LENTIL STEW

Lentils are combined with fresh vegetables for flavor contrast.

6 servings (about 1$^1/_2$ cups each)

Vegetable cooking spray
1 cup chopped onion
1 cup chopped green bell pepper
2 teaspoons minced garlic
2 cups cubed Idaho potatoes
1 cup lentils, washed and sorted
1 can (15 ounces) reduced-sodium diced tomatoes, undrained
3 cups reduced-sodium fat-free beef broth
1 teaspoon dried oregano leaves
1 teaspoon dried mint leaves
$^1/_2$ teaspoon ground turmeric
$^1/_2$ teaspoon ground coriander
12 ounces cooked beef eye of round, cubed
1 medium zucchini, sliced
$^1/_2$ pound green beans, trimmed
Salt and pepper, to taste

Per Serving
Calories: 302
% Calories from fat: 7
Fat (gm): 2.6
Saturated fat (gm): 0.8
Cholesterol (mg): 27.5
Sodium (mg): 122
Protein (gm): 25.5
Carbohydrate (gm): 46.7
Exchanges
Milk: 0.0
Vegetable: 3.0
Fruit: 0.0
Bread: 2.0
Meat: 1.5
Fat: 0.0

1. Spray large saucepan with cooking spray; heat over medium heat until hot. Saute onion, bell pepper, and garlic until tender, about 5 minutes. Add potatoes, lentils, tomatoes, broth, and herbs; heat to boiling. Reduce heat and simmer, covered, 15 minutes.

2. Add beef, zucchini, and green beans; simmer, uncovered, until lentils and vegetables are tender and stew is thickened, 10 to 15 minutes. Season to taste with salt and pepper.

ROAST BEEF HASH

Any leftover beef or pork can be used in this recipe as long as it is a lean cut and trimmed of fat; shred or cut into cubes.

4 servings (about 1 cup each)

Vegetable cooking spray
- 1/2 cup chopped onion
- 1/2 cup chopped green bell pepper
- 2 cloves garlic, minced
- 2 cups (8 ounces) shredded *or* cubed cooked lean beef
- 2 cups peeled and cubed cooked potatoes
- 1/2 teaspoon dried marjoram leaves
- 1/4 teaspoon dried thyme leaves
Salt and pepper, to taste

Per Serving
Calories: 244
% Calories from fat: 22
Fat (gm): 6
Saturated fat (gm): 2.3
Cholesterol (mg): 50.7
Sodium (mg): 44
Protein (gm): 19.9
Carbohydrate (gm): 27.5
Exchanges
Milk: 0.0
Vegetable: 1.0
Fruit: 0.0
Bread: 1.5
Meat: 2.0
Fat: 0.0

1. Coat large skillet with cooking spray; heat over medium heat until hot. Saute onion, bell pepper, and garlic until tender.

2. Add beef and potatoes to skillet; sprinkle with herbs. Cook over medium heat until meat and potatoes are browned, about 10 minutes, stirring occasionally. Season to taste with salt and pepper.

Variation: **Corned Beef Hash**—Make recipe as above, substituting corned beef for roast beef. Use only lean parts of the corned beef and trim all fat.

MEXICAN HASH

A wonderful recipe for leftover meats or poultry! Add other vegetables, too, such as sliced zucchini and whole-kernel corn.

4 servings

1 pound boneless beef eye of round, fat trimmed, cut into 1/2-inch cubes
1 quart water
  Vegetable cooking spray
1 large tomato, chopped
2 large poblano chilies, sliced
1 large onion, chopped
1 pound Idaho potatoes, unpeeled, cooked, cut into 1/2-inch cubes
  Chili powder, to taste
  Salt and pepper, to taste

Per Serving
Calories: 242
% Calories from fat: 15
Fat (gm): 4
Saturated fat (gm): 1.3
Cholesterol (mg): 54.7
Sodium (mg): 55
Protein (gm): 23.4
Carbohydrate (gm): 27.90
Exchanges
Milk: 0.0
Vegetable: 1.5
Fruit: 0.0
Bread: 1.0
Meat: 2.5
Fat: 0.0

1. Heat beef cubes and water to boiling in large saucepan; reduce heat and simmer, covered, until beef is tender, 30 to 45 minutes. Drain; shred beef.

2. Spray large skillet with cooking spray; heat over medium heat until hot. Cook beef over medium-high heat until beginning to brown and crisp, about 5 minutes. Add tomato; cook over medium heat 5 minutes. Remove mixture from skillet and reserve.

3. Add poblano chilies and onion to skillet; cook until tender, 5 to 8 minutes. Add potatoes and cook until browned, about 5 minutes. Add reserved meat mixture to skillet; cook until hot, 3 to 4 minutes. Season to taste with chili powder, salt, and pepper.

JUST PLAIN MEAT LOAF

Moist, the way you remember, with plenty of leftovers for sandwiches, too! Add sauteed mushrooms and a teaspoon or two of horseradish, if you like, and serve with Real Mashed Potatoes (see p. 592).

6 servings (2 generous slices each)

1 cup quick-cooking oats

1/2 cup fat-free milk

2 egg whites *or* 1/4 cup no-cholesterol real egg product

1/4 cup catsup *or* chili sauce

1/2 cup chopped onion

1/4 cup chopped green bell pepper

1 clove garlic, minced

1 teaspoon Italian seasoning

1 1/2 pounds ground beef eye of round *or* 95% lean ground beef

3/4 teaspoon salt

1/2 teaspoon pepper

Per Serving
Calories: 241
% Calories from fat: 21
Fat (gm): 5.5
Saturated fat (gm): 1.8
Cholesterol (mg): 64.3
Sodium (mg): 489
Protein (gm): 31.2
Carbohydrate (gm): 15.3
Exchanges
Milk: 0.0
Vegetable: 0.0
Fruit: 0.0
Bread: 1.0
Meat: 3.0
Fat: 0.0

1. Mix oats, milk, egg whites, catsup, onion, bell pepper, garlic, and herbs in medium bowl. Mix in beef, salt, and pepper until blended.

2. Pat mixture into ungreased loaf pan, 9 x 5 inches, or shape into a loaf in baking pan. Bake at 350 degrees until juices run clear and meat thermometer registers 170 degrees, about 1 hour. Let stand in pan 5 minutes; remove to serving plate.

Variations: **Stuffed Green Peppers**—Cut 6 medium green bell peppers lengthwise into halves; discard seeds. Cook peppers in boiling water 3 minutes; drain well on paper toweling. Make meat mixture as above, substituting 1 cup cooked rice for the oats and tomato sauce for the catsup. Fill peppers with beef mixture and place in baking pan. Bake, covered, at 350 degrees until beef mixture is no longer pink in the center, about 45 minutes. Serve with tomato sauce, if desired.

Italian Meat Loaf—Make recipe as above, adding 1/4 cup grated fat-free Parmesan cheese, 1/3 cup shredded reduced-fat mozzarella cheese, and 2 tablespoons chopped pitted ripe olives to mixture in Step 1. After baking, spread meat loaf with 2 tablespoons seasoned tomato sauce and sprinkle with 2 tablespoons each: fat-free Parmesan and shredded reduced-fat mozzarella cheeses. Let stand, loosely covered, 10 minutes.

Savory Cheese Meat Loaf—Make recipe as above, substituting ¹/₂ pound ground lean pork for ¹/₂ pound of the beef, and adding ¹/₂ package (8-ounce size) fat-free cream cheese, ¹/₂ cup shredded reduced-fat Cheddar cheese, and 2 tablespoons Worcestershire sauce to the mixture in Step 1. Spread top of loaf with ¹/₄ cup of catsup before baking. Sprinkle ¹/₄ cup shredded reduced-fat Cheddar cheese on top of meat loaf after baking. Let stand, loosely covered, 10 minutes.

Chutney-Peanut Meat Loaf—Make recipe as above, substituting ¹/₂ cup chopped chutney for the catsup, and adding ¹/₃ cup chopped peanuts, 1 teaspoon curry powder, and ¹/₄ teaspoon ground ginger to the mixture in Step 1.

LEMON MEAT LOAF

Meat loaf takes on a new dimension with lemon flavor and a smooth Egg Lemon Sauce.

6 servings (2 slices each)

1¹/₂ pounds ground beef eye of round *or* 95% lean ground beef

1 cup fresh bread crumbs

2 egg whites *or* ¹/₄ cup no-cholesterol real egg product

¹/₂ cup chopped onion

¹/₄ cup chopped green bell pepper

1 clove garlic, minced

1 tablespoon lemon juice

1 tablespoon grated lemon rind

1 teaspoon Dijon mustard

¹/₂ teaspoon dried savory leaves

³/₄ teaspoon salt

¹/₂ teaspoon pepper

Egg Lemon Sauce (recipe follows)

Per Serving
Calories: 228
% Calories from fat: **29**
Fat (gm): 7.2
Saturated fat (gm): 2.2
Cholesterol (mg): 94.4
Sodium (mg): 463
Protein (gm): 29.4
Carbohydrate (gm): 10.2
Exchanges
Milk: 0.0
Vegetable: 0.0
Fruit: 0.0
Bread: 1.0
Meat: 3.0
Fat: 0.0

1. Mix all ingredients except Egg Lemon Sauce in large bowl until well blended.

2. Pat mixture into ungreased loaf pan, 9 x 5 inches, or shape into a loaf in baking pan. Bake at 350 degrees until juices run clear and meat thermometer registers 170 degrees, about 1 hour. Let stand in pan 5 minutes; remove to serving plate. Serve with Egg Lemon Sauce.

Egg Lemon Sauce

makes about 1¹/₄ cups

> 1 tablespoon margarine
> 2 tablespoons flour
> ¹/₂ cup reduced-sodium fat-free chicken broth
> ¹/₂ cup fat-free milk
> 1 egg, lightly beaten
> 3-4 tablespoons lemon juice
> 1 teaspoon grated lemon rind
> Salt and white pepper, to taste

1. Melt margarine in medium saucepan; whisk in flour and cook, whisking constantly, over medium heat 2 minutes. Whisk in broth and milk and cook over medium heat until mixture boils and thickens, about 3 minutes.

2. Whisk about ¹/₂ the broth mixture into the egg; whisk mixture into saucepan. Whisk constantly over medium heat 1 minute. Add lemon juice and rind; season to taste with salt and white pepper.

Variation: **Sweet-Sour Ham Loaf**—Make recipe as above, substituting ¹/₂ pound ground cooked ham for ¹/₂ pound of the ground beef, and omitting lemon juice, lemon rind, savory, and Egg Lemon Sauce. Add 2 sweet pickles, chopped, ¹/₃ cup coarsely chopped almonds, ¹/₃ cup chopped mixed dried fruit, ¹/₃ cup apricot preserves, 2 tablespoons catsup, 1 tablespoon cider vinegar, and 2 teaspoons soy sauce to the mixture in Step 1.

SALISBURY STEAKS WITH MUSHROOM GRAVY

The rich Mushroom Gravy is a flavorful complement to perfectly cooked, moist Salisbury steaks.

4 servings

1 pound ground beef eye of round *or* 95% lean ground beef

2-4 tablespoons finely chopped onion

3 tablespoons water

$^1/_2$ teaspoon salt

$^1/_4$ teaspoon pepper

Vegetable cooking spray

Mushroom Gravy (recipe follows)

Per Serving
Calories: 184
% Calories from fat: 24
Fat (gm): 4.6
Saturated fat (gm): 1.7
Cholesterol (mg): 64
Sodium (mg): 341
Protein (gm): 28.7
Carbohydrate (gm): 5.2
Exchanges
Milk: 0.0
Vegetable: 1.0
Fruit: 0.0
Bread: 0.0
Meat: 3.0
Fat: 0.0

1. Mix ground beef, onion, water, salt, and pepper in medium bowl just until blended. Shape mixture into four 1-inch-thick oval patties.

2. Spray large skillet with cooking spray; heat over medium heat until hot. Cook Salisbury steaks to desired degree of doneness, 3 to 4 minutes per side for medium. Serve with Mushroom Gravy.

Mushroom Gravy

makes about 1$^1/_4$ cups

1 cup sliced mushrooms

$^1/_4$ cup finely chopped onion

2 tablespoons flour

1 cup reduced-sodium beef broth

Salt and pepper, to taste

1. Saute mushrooms and onion in medium skillet until tender. Stir in flour; cook 1 to 2 minutes longer.

2. Add beef broth and heat to boiling; boil, stirring constantly, until thickened. Season to taste with salt and pepper.

SWEDISH MEATBALLS WITH NOODLES

Serve as a one-dish meal, or just shape the meat mixture into 48 smaller meatballs for appetizer servings for 12 to 16 people.

4 servings

1	pound 95% lean ground beef
1/2	cup finely chopped onion
1/2	cup unseasoned dry bread crumbs
1/3	cup fat-free milk
2	egg whites *or* 1/4 cup no-cholesterol real egg product
1	tablespoon minced parsley leaves
1/2-1	teaspoon dried dill weed
1/4	teaspoon ground allspice
	Pinch ground cardamom
1/2	teaspoon salt
1/8	teaspoon pepper
	Cream Gravy (recipe follows)
	Finely chopped fresh dill weed *or* parsley, as garnish
3	cups cooked no-yolk noodles, warm

Per Serving
Calories: 497
% Calories from fat: 24
Fat (gm): 13
Saturated fat (gm): 3.6
Cholesterol (mg): 67.3
Sodium (mg): 814
Protein (gm): 37.9
Carbohydrate (gm): 56.6
Exchanges
Milk: 0.5
Vegetable: 0.0
Fruit: 0.0
Bread: 3.5
Meat: 3.5
Fat: 0.0

1. Combine ground beef, onion, bread crumbs, milk, egg whites, parsley, dried dill weed, allspice, cardamom, salt, and pepper; shape mixture into 24 meatballs. Bake meatballs in baking pan at 425 degrees until browned and no longer pink in the center, 15 to 20 minutes.

2. Arrange meatballs in serving bowl; pour Cream Gravy over and sprinkle with fresh dill weed. Serve over noodles.

Cream Gravy

makes about 2 cups

2	tablespoons margarine
1/4	cup all-purpose flour
2	cups fat-free milk *or* fat-free half-and-half
1/2	teaspoon beef bouillon crystals
1/4	cup fat-free sour cream
	Salt and pepper, to taste

1. Melt margarine in medium saucepan; stir in flour and cook over medium-low heat 1 minute, stirring constantly. Whisk in milk and bouillon crystals; heat to boiling. Boil, stirring constantly, until thickened, about 1 minute. Stir in sour cream and cook 1 to 2 minutes; season to taste with salt and pepper.

GYROS BURGERS

Delicious burgers of lamb and beef, with Greek accents.

4 servings

1/2 pound lean ground beef
1/2 pound lean ground lamb *or* beef
2 tablespoons chopped onion
2 cloves garlic, minced
1/2 teaspoon dried oregano leaves
1/2 teaspoon dried dill weed
1 teaspoon salt
4 pita breads
Gyros Relish (recipe follows)

Per Serving
Calories: 435
% Calories from fat: 29
Fat (gm): 13.9
Saturated fat (gm): 5
Cholesterol (mg): 87.8
Sodium (mg): 1011
Protein (gm): 34.6
Carbohydrate (gm): 41.2
Exchanges
Milk: 0.0
Vegetable: 0.0
Fruit: 0.0
Bread: 3.0
Meat: 3.0
Fat: 1.0

1. Combine ground beef, ground lamb, onion, garlic, oregano, dill, and salt until blended; shape into 4 patties. Cook in large skillet over medium heat to desired degree of doneness, about 5 minutes on each side for medium.

2. Cut tops of pita breads to form pockets. Place meat patties in bread; spoon Gyros Relish into sandwiches.

Gyros Relish

makes about 2 cups

1 small cucumber, seeded, chopped
1 medium tomato, chopped
1 green onion, sliced
2/3 cup plain fat-free yogurt
1/2 teaspoon dried mint leaves
1/2 teaspoon dried oregano leaves

1. Mix all ingredients.

PORCUPINE PEPPERS

This dish is so named because the rice and meat mixture has an appearance reminiscent of a porcupine—but it isn't prickly, just tasty.

4 servings

1 pound lean ground beef

1 can (14 ounces) diced tomatoes, partially drained

2 cups uncooked instant, *or* boil-in-bag, rice

1/4 teaspoon paprika

1/4 teaspoon celery salt

1/2 teaspoon Worcestershire sauce

4 large green bell peppers, seeded

Per Serving
Calories: 436
% Calories from fat: 32
Fat (gm): 15.2
Saturated fat (gm): 5.9
Cholesterol (mg): 69.9
Sodium (mg): 524
Protein (gm): 25.1
Carbohydrate (gm): 47.9
Exchanges
Milk: 0.0
Vegetable: 1.0
Fruit: 0.0
Bread: 3.0
Meat: 3.0
Fat: 1.0

1. Mix ground beef, tomatoes, rice, paprika, celery salt, and Worcestershire sauce in large bowl until well blended.

2. Cut each pepper lengthwise into 4 or 5 large strips. Place half the peppers on bottom of lightly greased 9-inch square baking dish. Spoon half the beef mixture over, spreading evenly. Repeat with remaining peppers and meat mixture. Bake, covered, at 350 degrees until beef is cooked and peppers are tender, about 45 minutes.

SICILIAN BEEF AND RICE

Instead of serving meat sauce with pasta, try this tasty variation that calls for rice.

4 servings

1 package (16 ounces) frozen pepper and onion blend
1 teaspoon minced garlic
12 ounces ground beef round steak
2 cans (15 ounces each) reduced-sodium tomato sauce
1¹/₂ teaspoons dried basil leaves
1¹/₂ teaspoons dried thyme leaves
Salt and pepper, to taste
3 cups cooked long-grain rice, warm
3 tablespoons grated Parmesan cheese

Per Serving
Calories: 422
% Calories from fat: 11
Fat (gm): 5
Saturated fat (gm): 2.2
Cholesterol (mg): 44.9
Sodium (mg): 186
Protein (gm): 29.3
Carbohydrate (gm): 61.7
Exchanges
Milk: 0.0
Vegetable: 3.0
Fruit: 0.0
Bread: 3.0
Meat: 2.0
Fat: 0.0

1. Cook pepper and onion blend, garlic, and ground beef in large saucepan over medium heat until beef is browned and onions are tender, about 6 minutes. Stir in tomato sauce and herbs; simmer, uncovered, until thickened, about 20 minutes. Season to taste with salt and pepper.

2. Spoon rice into serving bowl. Spoon ¹/₂ the beef mixture over; sprinkle with cheese and toss gently. Serve with remaining beef mixture.

CHILI STEW

A squeeze of lime adds a cooling touch to this spicy favorite.

6 servings (about 1¹/₃ cups each)

1 pound lean ground beef
2 medium onions, cut into 1-inch pieces
2 cups chopped celery
1 red bell pepper, cut into 1-inch pieces
¹/₂ jalapeño chili, finely chopped
2 cloves garlic, minced
2 cups peeled, cubed (1-inch) butternut squash
1 can (15 ounces) reduced-sodium chunky tomato sauce
1 can (15 ounces) red kidney beans, rinsed, drained
3 cups reduced-sodium tomato juice
1 medium zucchini, cubed
1 cup sliced mushrooms
1¹/₂ teaspoons chili powder
1¹/₂ teaspoons ground cumin
Salt and pepper, to taste
6 lime wedges

Per Serving
Calories: 317
% Calories from fat: 30
Fat (gm): 10.8
Saturated fat (gm): 4
Cholesterol (mg): 46.6
Sodium (mg): 357
Protein (gm): 21.2
Carbohydrate (gm): 36.1
Exchanges
Milk: 0.0
Vegetable: 1.0
Fruit: 0.0
Bread: 2.0
Meat: 2.0
Fat: 1.0

1. Cook ground beef in Dutch oven or large saucepan until browned; drain fat. Add onions, celery, bell pepper, jalapeño chili, and garlic. Saute until tender, 8 to 10 minutes.

2. Add remaining ingredients, except salt, pepper, and lime wedges to Dutch oven; heat to boiling. Reduce heat and simmer, uncovered, until vegetables are tender and stew is thickened, 20 to 25 minutes. Season to taste with salt and pepper. Serve stew in bowls; squeeze lime wedge into each.

GOULASH CASSEROLE

This sauerkraut dish, creamy with sour cream and seasoned with caraway, is excellent served with Real Mashed Potatoes (see p. 592).

6 servings (about 1¹/₃ cups each)

Vegetable cooking spray
1 pound ground beef eye of round
2 medium onions, chopped
1 green bell pepper, chopped
1 red bell pepper, chopped
2 cloves garlic, minced
1 tablespoon flour
2 teaspoons paprika
1 teaspoon crushed caraway seeds
¹/₂-³/₄ cup water
1 can (14 ounces) sauerkraut, rinsed, drained
1 large tomato, coarsely chopped
1 cup fat-free sour cream
Salt and pepper, to taste
Minced parsley, as garnish

Per Serving
Calories: 174
% Calories from fat: 15
Fat (gm): 2.8
Saturated fat (gm): 0.9
Cholesterol (mg): 36.6
Sodium (mg): 530
Protein (gm): 17.6
Carbohydrate (gm): 18.1
Exchanges
Milk: 0.0
Vegetable: 3.0
Fruit: 0.0
Bread: 0.0
Meat: 2.0
Fat: 0.0

1. Spray large skillet with cooking spray; heat over medium heat until hot. Add ground beef and cook until browned; add onions, bell peppers, and garlic and cook until tender, 8 to 10 minutes. Stir in flour, paprika, and caraway seeds; cook 1 to 2 minutes longer. Stir in water, sauerkraut, tomato, and sour cream; season to taste with salt and pepper.

2. Spoon mixture into 11 x 7-inch baking dish or 2-quart casserole. Bake, covered, at 350 degrees until hot through, 20 to 30 minutes. Sprinkle with parsley before serving.

MEATBALLS IN TOMATO CHILI SAUCE

The meatballs can be made in advance and frozen; thaw before using. The pasilla chilis are picante—use 2 only if you enjoy a truly hot sauce!

4 servings

¹/₂	pound ground pork tenderloin
¹/₂	pound ground beef rib eye steak
2	egg whites
¹/₄	cup unseasoned dry bread crumbs
¹/₂	cup finely chopped zucchini
¹/₄	cup finely chopped onion
2	cloves garlic, minced
1	teaspoon minced jalapeño chili
¹/₂	teaspoon dried oregano leaves
¹/₄	teaspoon dried thyme leaves
¹/₂	teaspoon salt
¹/₈	teaspoon pepper
	Vegetable cooking spray
1-2	pasilla chilies
1	can (28 ounces) reduced-sodium diced tomatoes, undrained
	Salt and pepper, to taste

Per Serving
Calories: 240
% Calories from fat: 24
Fat (gm): 6.5
Saturated fat (gm): 2.3
Cholesterol (mg): 60.9
Sodium (mg): 435
Protein (gm): 29.3
Carbohydrate (gm): 15.9
Exchanges
Milk: 0.0
Vegetable: 3.0
Fruit: 0.0
Bread: 0.0
Meat: 3.0
Fat: 0.0

1. Mix ground pork and beef, egg whites, bread crumbs, zucchini, onion, garlic, jalapeño chili, oregano, thyme, ¹/₂ teaspoon salt, and ¹/₈ teaspoon pepper. Shape mixture into 16 meatballs.

2. Spray large saucepan with cooking spray; heat over medium heat until hot. Cook pasilla chilies over medium heat until softened; discard stems, seeds, and veins. Process chilies and tomatoes with liquid in blender until smooth.

3. Heat tomato mixture to boiling in large saucepan; add meatballs. Reduce heat and simmer, covered, until meatballs are cooked and no longer pink in the center, about 10 minutes. Season to taste with salt and pepper.

MOCK CHICKEN LEGS

Looking a little like lumpy chicken legs, these kebabs are also known as City Chicken. Use any combination of beef, pork, or veal as long as the cuts are lean and trimmed of all fat.

6 servings

1 pork tenderloin, fat trimmed
8 ounces boneless beef sirloin steak, fat trimmed
¼ cup all-purpose flour
Vegetable cooking spray
Salt and pepper, to taste
Cream Gravy (see p. 144)
4½ cups cooked rice *or* no-yolk noodles, warm

Per Serving
Calories: 397
% Calories from fat: 20
Fat (gm): 8.7
Saturated fat (gm): 2.5
Cholesterol (mg): 66.6
Sodium (mg): 140
Protein (gm): 30.7
Carbohydrate (gm): 46.3
Exchanges
Milk: 0.5
Vegetable: 0.0
Fruit: 0.0
Bread: 2.5
Meat: 3.0
Fat: 0.0

1. Cut meats into 1-inch cubes; assemble on small wooden skewers, alternating kinds of meat. Coat meat with flour; let stand at room temperature 15 minutes.

2. Spray medium skillet with cooking spray; heat over medium heat until hot. Cook kebabs over medium to medium-low heat until well browned on all sides, about 10 minutes.

3. Add ½ inch water to skillet; heat to boiling. Reduce heat and simmer, covered, until meat is fork tender, 15 to 20 minutes. Remove from skillet; season to taste with salt and pepper. Serve with Cream Gravy on rice or noodles.

ROSEMARY ROAST PORK TENDERLOIN

So easy to prepare, you'll make this delicious meat often.

4 servings

1 pork tenderloin (about 16 ounces)
1 clove garlic, cut into 8 to 10 slivers
  Vegetable cooking spray
1 teaspoon crushed dried rosemary leaves
  Salt and pepper

Per Serving
Calories: 139
% Calories from fat: 28
Fat (gm): 4
Saturated fat (gm): 1.4
Cholesterol (mg): 66
Sodium (mg): 47
Protein (gm): 23.5
Carbohydrate (gm): .44
Exchanges
Milk: 0.0
Vegetable: 0.0
Fruit: 0.0
Bread: 0.0
Meat: 3.0
Fat: 0.0

1. Cut small slits in pork and insert garlic slivers. Place pork in small roasting pan and spray lightly with cooking spray. Rub surface of pork with rosemary leaves. Sprinkle lightly with salt and pepper.

2. Roast pork at 425 degrees until meat thermometer inserted in center registers 160 degrees (slightly pink), or 170 degrees (well-done), 20 to 30 minutes.

Note: Pork can be eaten slightly pink; it is safe to eat after the internal temperature has reached 140 degrees.

PORK TENDERLOIN WITH APRICOT STUFFING

This elegant dish is much easier to prepare than the name suggests.

6 servings

1 pound pork tenderloin

1 can (8¹/₂ ounces) apricot halves, undrained

1 stalk celery, finely chopped

1 small onion, finely chopped

¹/₈ teaspoon ground cinnamon

¹/₈ teaspoon ground black pepper

2 cups seasoned croutons

²/₃ cup chicken, *or* vegetable, broth

2 cups instant, *or* boil-in-the-bag, rice, cooked

1¹/₂ teaspoons cornstarch

¹/₈ teaspoon ground nutmeg

Per Serving
Calories: 266
% Calories from fat: 10
Fat (gm): 2.9
Saturated fat (gm): 1
Cholesterol (mg): 43.8
Sodium (mg): 338
Protein (gm): 20
Carbohydrate (gm): 38
Exchanges
Milk: 0.0
Vegetable: 0.0
Fruit: 0.5
Bread: 2.0
Meat: 2.0
Fat: 0.0

1. Slice tenderloin lengthwise, cutting to, but not through, opposite side. Pound meat lightly with meat mallet to rectangle about 10 x 6 inches.

2. Drain apricots, reserving juice. Cut apricots into ¹/₂-inch cubes. Combine apricots, celery, onion, cinnamon, pepper, and croutons in large bowl; pour broth over and toss.

3. Spread stuffing mixture evenly over tenderloin. Roll up jelly-roll style, starting from short side. Secure meat roll with wooden toothpicks or tie with kitchen string at 1-inch intervals. Cut meat roll into six slices.

4. Spread rice in lightly greased 12 x 8-inch baking dish. Arrange meat slices over rice. Combine reserved apricot juice, adding water if necessary to make ³/₄ cup, cornstarch, and nutmeg in small saucepan; whisk over medium heat until mixture boils and thickens, about 3 minutes. Pour over meat and rice. Bake at 325 degrees, covered, until pork is cooked, about 50 minutes.

PORK TENDERLOIN WITH GREMOLATA

Gremolata is a refreshing blend of garlic, lemon peel, and parsley that is often used to flavor osso bucco, an Italian dish of veal shanks and vegetables. Here it perks up a stew of pork, potatoes, and tomatoes.

4 servings

	Per Serving
1 pound pork tenderloin, cut into 1-inch pieces	Calories: 289 % Calories from fat: 17 Fat (gm): 5.5
1 teaspoon olive oil	Saturated fat (gm): 1.6 Cholesterol (mg): 65.7
4 shallots, thinly sliced	Sodium (mg): 523 Protein (gm): 28.6
1 cup reduced-sodium fat-free beef broth	Carbohydrate (gm): 31.2
2 medium potatoes, cut into 1/2-inch cubes	**Exchanges** Milk: 0.0 Vegetable: 0.0
1 can (15 ounces) diced tomatoes, undrained	Fruit: 0.0 Bread: 2.0
Salt and pepper, to taste	Meat: 3.0 Fat: 0.0
Gremolata (recipe follows)	

1. Saute pork in oil in large saucepan until lightly browned. Add shallots and saute until shallots are tender. Stir in broth and heat to boiling; reduce heat and simmer, covered, 10 minutes.

2. Add potatoes and tomatoes and liquid; simmer, covered, until potatoes are tender, about 15 minutes. Season to taste with salt and pepper. Spoon stew into bowls; serve with Gremolata.

Gremolata

makes about 1/2 cup

   1 cup packed parsley sprigs
   1-2 tablespoons grated lemon rind
   4 large cloves garlic, minced

1. Process all ingredients in food processor until finely minced. Refrigerate until ready to use.

SWEET AND SPICY PORK STIR-FRY

Serve half-size portions over steamed rice if desired.

4 servings

8 ounces pork, fat trimmed, cubed
1 carrot, peeled and thinly sliced
2 potatoes, unpeeled, diced
1 small onion, diced
1 cup diced celery
2 cups shredded green cabbage

Sauce

1 tablespoon cornstarch
$^1/_3$ cup cold water
$^1/_4$ cup reduced-sodium soy sauce
$^1/_4$ cup ketchup
2 tablespoons brown sugar

Per Serving
Calories: 243
% Calories from fat: 19
Fat (gm): 5.3
Saturated fat (gm): 1.8
Cholesterol (mg): 26.5
Sodium (mg): 781
Protein (gm): 16.2
Carbohydrate (gm): 33.7
Exchanges
Milk: 0.0
Vegetable: 0.0
Fruit: 0.0
Bread: 2.0
Meat: 2.0
Fat: 0.0

1. Spray large saucepan with cooking spray; add pork and cook over medium-high heat, stirring frequently, until meat is browned. Add carrot and potatoes; cook 5 minutes, stirring often. Add onion, celery, and cabbage; cook 5 minutes or until potato is tender.

2. Combine cornstarch and water in small bowl, whisking until cornstarch is dissolved. Add soy sauce, ketchup, and brown sugar; mix well.

3. Pour sauce over stir-fry and toss to coat. Reduce heat to low and simmer for 10 minutes.

PORK MEDALLIONS WITH SPINACH PASTA AND YOGURT SAUCE

Pork baked with apples and yogurt makes a light, refreshing, and amazingly easy dinner.

4 servings

8 ounces spinach fettuccine *or* linguine

³/4 pound pork tenderloin, cut into
    ¹/2-inch slices

2 medium apples, cut into ¹/2-inch slices

¹/2 cup apple juice

1 small onion, finely chopped

¹/8 teaspoon salt

¹/4 teaspoon rubbed sage

2 tablespoons flour

1 container (8 ounces) plain low-fat
    yogurt

1 tablespoon chopped chives

4 small shallots, halved

Per Serving
Calories: 390
% Calories from fat: 16
Fat (gm): 6.8
Saturated fat (gm): 2.3
Cholesterol (mg): 119.6
Sodium (mg): 220
Protein (gm): 29.1
Carbohydrate (gm): 52.6
Exchanges
Milk: 0.0
Vegetable: 0.0
Fruit: 0.5
Bread: 3.0
Meat: 2.5
Fat: 0.0

1.   Cook fettuccine until almost done, but still al dente; arrange in lightly greased 2¹/2-quart casserole. Place pork slices on top of pasta, overlapping if necessary; arrange apples on top of meat.

2.   Combine apple juice, onion, salt, and sage in small skillet; cook, covered, until onion is tender, about 5 minutes. Whisk flour into yogurt in small bowl; slowly whisk yogurt mixture into skillet, whisking until thickened. Spoon sauce over pork and apples; sprinkle with chives and shallots. Bake at 325 degrees, covered, 1 hour or until bubbly.

PORK TENDERLOIN WITH GREEN PEANUT SAUCE

Although the true Mexican version of Green Peanut Sauce uses a much larger quantity of peanuts, this lower-fat version is very flavorful with a pleasing crunchy texture.

6 servings

Vegetable cooking spray
1 clove garlic, cut in half
1¹/₂ pounds pork tenderloin, fat trimmed, cut into ¹/₄-inch slices
Salt and pepper, to taste
1 cup Tomatillo Sauce (¹/₂ recipe) (see p. 203)
¹/₃ cup chopped light dry-roasted peanuts
4 cups cooked rice, warm

Per Serving
Calories: 347
% Calories from fat: 23
Fat (gm): 8.9
Saturated fat (gm): 2
Cholesterol (mg): 65.4
Sodium (mg): 115
Protein (gm): 28.9
Carbohydrate (gm): 36.6
Exchanges
Milk: 0.0
Vegetable: 1.0
Fruit: 0.0
Bread: 2.0
Meat: 3.0
Fat: 0.0

1. Spray large skillet with cooking spray; heat over medium heat until hot. Rub bottom of skillet with cut sides of garlic. Add pork to skillet and cook over medium to medium-high heat until no longer pink in the center, 3 to 4 minutes on each side. Sprinkle lightly with salt and pepper.

2. Add Tomatillo Sauce to skillet; stir in peanuts and heat until hot. Serve over rice.

PORK WITH PEPPERS AND ONIONS

This dish can also be made with whole pork chops; increase cooking time 10 minutes or longer, according to the thickness of the meat.

4 servings

1 pound pork tenderloin, cut into strips
1 tablespoon olive oil
1 can (15 ounces) reduced-sodium tomato sauce
1 package (16 ounces) frozen pepper and onion blend
2 tablespoons dry sherry, optional
1 teaspoon minced garlic
1 teaspoon dried basil leaves
1 teaspoon dried thyme leaves
Salt and pepper, to taste
8 ounces fusilli, cooked, warm

Per Serving
Calories: 464
% Calories from fat: 17
Fat (gm): 8.4
Saturated fat (gm): 2
Cholesterol (mg): 65.7
Sodium (mg): 99
Protein (gm): 33.9
Carbohydrate (gm): 58.6
Exchanges
Milk: 0.0
Vegetable: 3.0
Fruit: 0.0
Bread: 3.0
Meat: 3.0
Fat: 0.0

1. Cook pork in olive oil in large skillet until browned; add tomato sauce, pepper and onion blend, sherry, garlic, and herbs. Heat to boiling; reduce heat and simmer, covered, until pork is tender, about 12 minutes. Simmer, uncovered, until thickened, 2 to 3 minutes. Season to taste with salt and pepper. Spoon over fusilli in serving bowl.

FETTUCCINE WITH PORK, GREENS, AND CARAMELIZED ONIONS

Cooked chicken breast or shrimp would be delicious alternatives to the pork in this recipe.

4 servings

4 medium onions, sliced
1 tablespoon olive oil
1 teaspoon sugar
2 cans (14¹/₂ ounces each) reduced-sodium fat-free chicken broth
2 cups thinly sliced kale, mustard greens, *or* Swiss chard
2 cups thinly sliced curly endive *or* spinach
¹/₄ teaspoon salt
¹/₄ teaspoon pepper
  Olive oil cooking spray
12 ounces lean pork tenderloin, fat trimmed, cut into ¹/₄-inch slices
8 ounces fettuccine, cooked, warm

Per Serving
Calories: 385
% Calories from fat: 20
Fat (gm): 8.8
Saturated fat (gm): 1.6
Cholesterol (mg): 59.3
Sodium (mg): 354
Protein (gm): 31.2
Carbohydrate (gm): 44.6
Exchanges
Milk: 0.0
Vegetable: 3.0
Fruit: 0.0
Bread: 3.0
Meat: 3.0
Fat: 0.0

1. Cook onions in oil over medium heat in large skillet 5 minutes; reduce heat to low and stir in sugar. Cook until onions are golden in color and very soft, about 20 minutes.

2. Stir chicken broth into onions; heat to boiling. Reduce heat and simmer, uncovered, until broth is reduced by ¹/₃, about 10 minutes. Add kale and endive; simmer, covered, until greens are wilted, 5 to 7 minutes. Simmer, uncovered, until broth is almost absorbed by greens, about 5 minutes. Stir in salt and pepper.

3. Spray large skillet with cooking spray; heat over medium heat until hot. Cook pork slices over medium to medium-high heat until browned and no longer pink in center, about 5 minutes.

4. Spoon onion mixture over pasta and toss; add pork and toss.

TOMATILLO PORK STEW

Tomatillos (Mexican green tomatoes) add a special flavor to this South-of-the-Border version of pork stew.

8 servings

1¹/₂ cups chopped onions
   1 small poblano chili *or* green bell pepper, chopped
   4 cloves garlic, minced
 1-2 tablespoons vegetable oil
   2 pounds boneless lean pork, cut into ³/₄-inch cubes
   2 tablespoons flour
 ³/₄ teaspoon dried oregano leaves
 ¹/₂ teaspoon ground cumin
 ¹/₄ teaspoon dried thyme leaves
 ¹/₂ cup reduced-sodium fat-free chicken broth
   2 large tomatoes, chopped
  12 ounces Mexican green tomatoes (tomatillos), husked, chopped
   1 can (4 ounces) mild, *or* hot, chopped green chilies
 1-2 teaspoons lime juice
      Salt and pepper, to taste
   5 cups cooked rice
      Minced cilantro *or* parsley, as garnish
      Toasted pine nuts *or* almonds, as garnish

Per Serving
Calories: 374
% Calories from fat: 24
Fat (gm): 9.9
Saturated fat (gm): 2.9
Cholesterol (mg): 64.4
Sodium (mg): 118
Protein (gm): 32.1
Carbohydrate (gm): 37.6
Exchanges
Milk: 0.0
Vegetable: 2.0
Fruit: 0.0
Bread: 2.0
Meat: 3.0
Fat: 0.0

1. Saute onions, poblano chili, and garlic in oil in large saucepan 2 to 3 minutes; add pork and saute until browned, about 5 minutes. Stir in flour and herbs and cook 2 minutes longer.

2. Add chicken broth, tomatoes, green tomatoes, and green chilies and heat to boiling; reduce heat and simmer, covered, until pork is tender, 40 to 50 minutes. Season to taste with lime juice, salt, and pepper.

3. Serve stew over rice; sprinkle with cilantro and pine nuts.

PORK LOIN, POTATO, AND CABBAGE STEW

Grated potatoes thicken the sauce in this robust pork stew.

4-5 servings

16 ounces boneless pork loin, fat trimmed, cut into strips

1 pound red potatoes, peeled, grated

1 can (14^1/$_2$ ounces) reduced-sodium stewed tomatoes, undrained

1 can (15 ounces) reduced-sodium tomato sauce

3 cups thinly sliced cabbage

1 large onion, finely chopped

2 cloves garlic, minced

1 tablespoon brown sugar

2 teaspoons balsamic vinegar

2 teaspoons dried thyme leaves

1 bay leaf

Salt and pepper, to taste

Per Serving
Calories: 328
% Calories from fat: 18
Fat (gm): 6.8
Saturated fat (gm): 2.2
Cholesterol (mg): 49.3
Sodium (mg): 101
Protein (gm): 23.4
Carbohydrate (gm): 45.4
Exchanges
Milk: 0.0
Vegetable: 3.0
Fruit: 0.0
Bread: 2.0
Meat: 2.0
Fat: 0.0

1. Combine all ingredients, except salt and pepper, in large saucepan; heat to boiling. Reduce heat and simmer, covered, until meat is tender, about 30 minutes. Discard bay leaf; season to taste with salt and pepper.

SAVORY STEWED PORK AND CHORIZO

A versatile dish, this shredded pork and chorizo "stew" is generally served rolled in a tortilla or used as a topping for tostadas. A less tender cut of meat would typically be used, but pork tenderloin keeps this dish skinny.

6 servings

12	ounces pork tenderloin, fat trimmed, cut into 1-inch cubes
	Vegetable cooking spray
	Chorizo (see p. 166)
1	small onion, sliced
1	clove garlic, minced
2	large tomatoes, chopped
1/4	teaspoon dried oregano leaves
1/4	teaspoon dried thyme leaves
1	bay leaf
2-3	pickled jalapeño chilies, finely chopped
1	tablespoon pickled jalapeño chili juice
	Salt and pepper, to taste
4	cups cooked rice, warm

Per Serving
Calories: 298
% Calories from fat: 15
Fat (gm): 4.7
Saturated fat (gm): 1.5
Cholesterol (mg): 65.7
Sodium (mg): 313
Protein (gm): 27.2
Carbohydrate (gm): 35
Exchanges
Milk: 0.0
Vegetable: 0.0
Fruit: 0.0
Bread: 2.0
Meat: 3.0
Fat: 0.0

1. Cover pork with water in medium saucepan; heat to boiling. Reduce heat and simmer, covered, until tender, 20 to 30 minutes. Cool; drain, reserving 1/2 cup broth. Finely shred pork.

2. Spray large skillet with cooking spray; heat over medium heat until hot. Cook Chorizo over medium heat until done; remove from skillet and crumble. Add onion and garlic to skillet; saute 2 to 3 minutes. Add tomatoes and herbs and cook over medium heat 5 minutes, stirring occasionally.

3. Add pork, Chorizo, 1/2 cup reserved broth, jalapeño chilies, and jalapeño juice to skillet. Cook, uncovered, over medium heat, about 10 minutes, stirring occasionally (mixture should be moist, not dry). Discard bay leaf; season to taste with salt and pepper. Serve over rice.

CHOP SUEY

Chinese bead molasses adds the traditional color and flavor accent to this dish.

4 servings

Per Serving
Calories: 428
% Calories from fat: 18
Fat (gm): 8.4
Saturated fat (gm): 2
Cholesterol (mg): 65.4
Sodium (mg): 467
Protein (gm): 31.8
Carbohydrate (gm): 56.8
Exchanges
Milk: 0.0
Vegetable: 3.0
Fruit: 0.0
Bread: 2.5
Meat: 3.0
Fat: 0.0

- 1 pound pork tenderloin, cut into 1-inch cubes
- 1 tablespoon vegetable oil
- 2 cups thinly sliced Chinese cabbage *or* 1 cup sliced celery
- 1 cup sliced mushrooms
- 1 cup chopped onion
- 1 cup chopped red, *or* green, bell pepper
- 2 cloves garlic, minced
- 1/2 cup oriental broth *or* reduced-sodium chicken broth
- 2 tablespoons cornstarch
- 1/2-1 tablespoon bead molasses
- 2 cups fresh, *or* rinsed, canned, bean sprouts
- 1/2-1 can (8 ounces) bamboo shoots, rinsed, drained
- 1/2-1 can (8 ounces) water chestnuts, rinsed, drained
- Reduced-sodium soy sauce, to taste
- Salt and pepper, to taste
- 3 cups cooked rice *or* 2 cups crisp chow mein noodles

1. Stir-fry pork in hot oil in wok or large skillet until browned, 3 to 5 minutes. Add cabbage, mushrooms, onion, bell pepper, and garlic; stir-fry until vegetables are crisp-tender, 3 to 5 minutes longer.

2. Mix broth, cornstarch, and molasses; stir into wok and heat to boiling. Boil, stirring constantly, until thickened, 1 to 2 minutes. Stir in bean sprouts, bamboo shoots, and water chestnuts; cook until hot through, 1 to 2 minutes. Season to taste with soy sauce, salt, and pepper. Serve over warm rice or crisp chow mein noodles.

MOO SHU PORK

A traditional Mandarin favorite. The Mandarin Pancakes are fabulous and can be made in advance. If short on time, however, flour tortillas can be substituted.

6 servings (2 each)

1½ ounces dry Chinese mushrooms (shiitake)
  Boiling water
2-3 tablespoons reduced-sodium tamari soy sauce
  2 teaspoons sesame oil
  1 tablespoon minced gingerroot
  1 teaspoon sugar
  1 pound pork tenderloin, cut into strips
  Oriental-flavored vegetable cooking spray
  2 eggs, lightly beaten
½ cup water
  2 teaspoons cornstarch
½ cup julienned bamboo shoots
  2 sliced green onions and tops
  Mandarin Pancakes (recipe follows)
½-¾ cup oriental plum sauce
 12 medium green onions

Per Serving
Calories: 278
% Calories from fat: 20
Fat (gm): 6.2
Saturated fat (gm): 1.7
Cholesterol (mg): 114.5
Sodium (mg): 266
Protein (gm): 21.7
Carbohydrate (gm): 33
Exchanges
Milk: 0.0
Vegetable: 4.0
Fruit: 0.0
Bread: 1.0
Meat: 2.0
Fat: 0.0

1. Place mushrooms in bowl; pour boiling water over to cover. Let stand until mushrooms are softened, about 15 minutes. Drain. Slice mushrooms, discarding tough centers.

2. Combine soy sauce, sesame oil, gingerroot, and sugar; pour over pork in bowl. Let stand 30 minutes, stirring occasionally.

3. Spray large skillet with cooking spray; heat over medium heat until hot. Add eggs and cook over low heat until scrambled, breaking into small pieces with a fork; remove from skillet and reserve.

4. Add pork mixture and sliced mushrooms to skillet; cook over medium heat until pork is browned, 3 to 4 minutes, stirring occasionally. Mix water and cornstarch; add to skillet with bamboo shoots and green onions. Heat to boiling; boil, stirring constantly, until thickened, about 1 minute. Stir in reserved egg; cook 1 minute longer.

5. To eat, spread 1 Mandarin Pancake with 2 to 3 teaspoons plum sauce; spoon about 1/3 cup pork mixture onto pancake. Top with a green onion and roll up. Repeat with remaining ingredients.

Mandarin Pancakes

makes 12 pancakes

> 1/3 cup boiling water
> 1 cup all-purpose flour
> Oriental-flavored vegetable cooking spray

1. Stir water into flour in small bowl until crumbly; shape into a ball. Knead on lightly floured surface until smooth and satiny, about 10 minutes. Let stand, covered, 30 minutes.

2. Divide dough into 12 equal pieces; shape into 12 balls. With lightly floured rolling pin, roll 2 balls into 3-inch circles; spray 1 circle lightly with cooking spray and cover with remaining circle. Roll both circles together into a 6-inch circle being careful not to wrinkle dough when rolling.

3. Spray medium skillet with cooking spray; heat over medium heat until hot. Cook dough circle over medium to medium-high heat until pancake blisters and is the color of parchment paper, turning frequently with chop sticks or tongs. Remove from skillet; separate 2 pancakes with pointed knife.

4. Repeat rolling and cooking with remaining dough, making only 1 or 2 dough circles at a time. As pancakes are cooked and separated, they can be covered and kept warm in a 200 degree oven.

Note: Pancakes can be cooled, stacked with plastic wrap, and frozen in a freezer bag or aluminum foil for up to 2 months.

TENDERLOIN CHILI

Treat your taste buds to high-on-the-hog chili: This super-easy, super-fast version sports tender, lean pork and fresh tomatoes and has a superb taste that the usual beef chilies can't match.

4 servings

12 ounces cooked pork tenderloin, shredded

1 can (15 ounces) reduced-sodium fat-
free beef broth

1 pound plum tomatoes, sliced

1 can (15 ounces) pinto beans, rinsed,
drained

2 jalapeño chilies, minced

1 tablespoon chili powder

1 teaspoon cumin seeds, toasted

1 teaspoon Worcestershire sauce

Per Serving
Calories: 274
% Calories from fat: 19
Fat (gm): 5.8
Saturated fat (gm): 1.7
Cholesterol (mg): 67.1
Sodium (mg): 475
Protein (gm): 32.7
Carbohydrate (gm): 23.4
Exchanges
Milk: 0.0
Vegetable: 2.0
Fruit: 0.0
Bread: 1.0
Meat: 3.0
Fat: 0.0

1. Heat all ingredients to boiling in large saucepan; reduce heat and simmer, covered, 15 minutes.

CHORIZO

Chorizo is a well-seasoned Mexican sausage made with pork. The seasonings vary from region to region in Mexico and are often quite hot and spicy. Paprika gives the sausage its traditional red color. The sausage patties can be served with eggs, or the sausage can be cooked and crumbled to serve in quesadillas, nachos, enchiladas, and other dishes.

4 servings

   Vegetable cooking spray

1/4 teaspoon crushed coriander seeds

1/4 teaspoon crushed cumin seeds *or* 1/8
teaspoon ground cumin

1 dried ancho chili

12 ounces pork tenderloin, fat trimmed,
finely chopped *or* ground

2 cloves garlic, minced

1 tablespoon paprika

1/2 teaspoon dried oregano leaves

Per Serving
Calories: 112
% Calories from fat: 27
Fat (gm): 3.3
Saturated fat (gm): 1.1
Cholesterol (mg): 49.1
Sodium (mg): 308
Protein (gm): 17.9
Carbohydrate (gm): 2.1
Exchanges
Milk: 0.0
Vegetable: 0.0
Fruit: 0.0
Bread: 0.0
Meat: 2.0
Fat: 0.0

1/2-3/4 teaspoon salt
    1 tablespoon cider vinegar
    1 tablespoon water

1. Spray small skillet with cooking spray; heat over medium heat until hot. Add coriander and cumin seeds; cook over medium heat, stirring frequently, until toasted. Remove from skillet.

2. Add ancho chili to skillet; cook over medium heat until softened, about 1 minute on each side, turning so that chili does not burn. Remove and discard stem, veins, and seeds. Chop chili finely.

3. Combine pork tenderloin and all ingredients in small bowl, mixing thoroughly. Refrigerate, covered, at least 4 hours or overnight for flavors to blend.

4. Spray small skillet with cooking spray; heat over medium heat until hot. Shape pork mixture into 4 patties; cook over medium heat until cooked through, 4 to 5 minutes on each side.

HAM AND POTATO CASSEROLE AU GRATIN

An old-fashioned casserole modified to meet today's healthy standards, while retaining all that nostalgic flavor.

6 servings

6	large red potatoes, peeled, thinly sliced, divided
12-16	ounces reduced-sodium ham, fat trimmed, cut into 1-inch cubes
1	small green bell pepper, finely chopped
3	scallions, including some tops, chopped
1/2-1	cup (2-4 ounces) shredded reduced-fat Cheddar cheese
	White Sauce (recipe follows)

1/4-1/2 cup unseasoned dry bread crumbs

Per Serving
Calories: 301
% Calories from fat: 30
Fat (gm): 10.4
Saturated fat (gm): 3.6
Cholesterol (mg): 40.5
Sodium (mg): 796
Protein (gm): 20.9
Carbohydrate (gm): 32.9
Exchanges
Milk: 0.0
Vegetable: 0.0
Fruit: 0.0
Bread: 2.0
Meat: 2.0
Fat: 1.0

1. Arrange half the potatoes on bottom of lightly greased 2-quart casserole, overlapping slightly. Sprinkle ham, bell pepper, and scallions over potatoes. Top with remaining potatoes and sprinkle with cheese. Pour White Sauce evenly over cheese.

2. Bake, covered, 45 minutes at 375 degrees. Sprinkle with bread crumbs and bake, uncovered, until potatoes are tender and casserole is golden brown, 20 to 30 minutes.

White Sauce

makes about 2 cups

>   2 tablespoons margarine
>   3 tablespoons flour
>   3/4 teaspoon dry mustard
>   2 cups fat-free milk
>   1/4 teaspoon paprika
>   Salt and pepper, to taste

1. Melt margarine in small saucepan; whisk in flour and dry mustard. Whisk over medium heat 1 minute; gradually whisk in milk and paprika. Heat to boiling, whisking over medium heat until sauce thickens, 3 to 4 minutes. Season to taste with salt and pepper.

MOROCCAN LAMB STEW

Sweet spices season this stew and raisins, almonds, and hard-cooked eggs provide colorful garnish.

8 servings

>   Vegetable cooking spray
>   2 pounds boneless lean lamb, fat trimmed, cut into 3/4-inch cubes
>   1 1/2 cups chopped onions
>   2 large cloves garlic, minced
>   2 teaspoons minced gingerroot
>   1 1/2 cups reduced-sodium fat-free chicken broth
>   1 cup reduced-sodium tomato puree
>   1/2 teaspoon ground cinnamon
>   1/4 teaspoon ground turmeric
>   Generous pinch ground cloves
>   1 bay leaf
>   Salt and pepper, to taste
>   1/3 cup raisins
>   2-4 tablespoons whole almonds, toasted

Per Serving
Calories: 308
% Calories from fat: **20**
Fat (gm): 6.6
Saturated fat (gm): 2
Cholesterol (mg): 101.5
Sodium (mg): 103
Protein (gm): 23.8
Carbohydrate (gm): 37.4
Exchanges
Milk: 0.0
Vegetable: 1.0
Fruit: 0.0
Bread: 2.0
Meat: 2.5
Fat: 0.0

2 hard-cooked eggs, chopped
Finely chopped cilantro, *or* parsley, as
garnish
5 cups cooked couscous *or* rice, warm

1. Spray Dutch oven with cooking spray; heat over medium
heat until hot. Add lamb and saute until browned, 5 to 8 minutes; remove from pan. Add onions, garlic, and gingerroot; saute
until onions are tender, about 5 minutes. Return meat to Dutch
oven.

2. Add chicken broth, tomato puree, and spices; heat to boiling. Reduce heat and simmer, covered, until lamb is tender, 45
to 60 minutes. Simmer, uncovered, until thickened to desired
consistency, about 10 minutes longer. Discard bay leaf; season
with salt and pepper. Stir in raisins.

3. Spoon stew onto rimmed serving platter; sprinkle with almonds, eggs, and cilantro. Serve with couscous.

EASIEST LAMB STEW

*The easiest stew ever—just stir it all together, place in the oven, and put
your feet up with a good book while it cooks.*

6 servings

2 pounds boneless, lean lamb, cut into
1-inch cubes
$1/4$ teaspoon salt
$1/4$ teaspoon pepper
1 bay leaf
4 medium potatoes, peeled and quartered
3 medium carrots, cut into $1/2$-inch slices
2 small onions, thinly sliced
$1/4$ cup quick-cooking tapioca
1 package (10 ounces) frozen peas
2 cups water

Per Serving
Calories: 395
% Calories from fat: 26
Fat (gm): 11.4
Saturated fat (gm): 4.3
Cholesterol (mg): 98.2
Sodium (mg): 230
Protein (gm): 34.7
Carbohydrate (gm): 37.5
Exchanges
Milk: 0.0
Vegetable: 1.0
Fruit: 0.0
Bread: 2.0
Meat: 4.0
Fat: 0.0

1. Combine all ingredients in $2^1/2$-quart casserole; stir well.
Bake, covered, at 325 degrees until lamb is tender, about 2
hours, stirring halfway through cooking time. Discard bay leaf.

HEARTY ROSEMARY LAMB WITH SWEET POTATOES

The pairing of rosemary and lamb is classic, distinctive, and delightful. Here, we offer the two in a robust stew with sweet potatoes and cut green beans.

4 servings

1 pound boneless lamb shoulder, fat trimmed, cut into 3/4-inch cubes

2 tablespoons chopped fresh, *or* 2 teaspoons dried, rosemary leaves

2 tablespoons chopped fresh, *or* 2 teaspoons dried, thyme leaves

1 teaspoon olive oil

1 large onion, cut into thin wedges

3 cups reduced-sodium fat-free beef broth

2 bay leaves

1¼ pounds sweet potatoes, peeled, cut into 3/4-inch cubes

1½ cups cut green beans
Salt and pepper, to taste

Per Serving
Calories: 285
% Calories from fat: 23
Fat (gm): 7.4
Saturated fat (gm): 2.5
Cholesterol (mg): 47.2
Sodium (mg): 171
Protein (gm): 20.6
Carbohydrate (gm): 34.7
Exchanges
Milk: 0.0
Vegetable: 1.0
Fruit: 0.0
Bread: 2.0
Meat: 2.0
Fat: 0.0

1. Toss lamb with herbs; saute in oil in large saucepan until lightly browned. Add onion, broth, and bay leaves. Heat to boiling; reduce heat and simmer, covered, 30 minutes.

2. Stir sweet potatoes and beans into stew. Heat to boiling; reduce heat and simmer, covered, until vegetables are tender, about 10 minutes. Discard bay leaves; season to taste with salt and pepper.

SHEPHERD'S PIE

Usually the recipient of the week's leftovers, this hearty dish may be different each time it is made.

6 servings

1¹/₂ pounds boneless lamb leg steaks, fat trimmed, cut into ¹/₂-inch cubes
1 tablespoon margarine
³/₄ cup chopped onion
³/₄ cup chopped green bell pepper
¹/₂ cup chopped celery
3 cloves garlic, minced
3 tablespoons flour
2¹/₂ cups reduced-sodium beef broth
1¹/₂ cups sliced carrots
1 tablespoon tomato paste
¹/₂ teaspoon dried rosemary leaves
¹/₄-¹/₂ teaspoon dried thyme leaves
1 bay leaf
³/₄ cup frozen peas
Salt and pepper, to taste
2 cups Real Mashed Potatoes (¹/₂ recipe) (see p. 592)

Per Serving
Calories: 274
% Calories from fat: **27**
Fat (gm): 8.4
Saturated fat (gm): 2.3
Cholesterol (mg): 48.5
Sodium (mg): 179
Protein (gm): 21.7
Carbohydrate (gm): 28.5
Exchanges
Milk: 0.0
Vegetable: 2.0
Fruit: 0.0
Bread: 1.0
Meat: 2.5
Fat: 0.5

1. Saute lamb in margarine in large saucepan until browned on all sides, 5 to 8 minutes; remove from pan. Add onion, bell pepper, celery, and garlic; saute until tender, 8 to 10 minutes. Stir in flour; cook over medium heat 1 to 2 minutes, stirring constantly.

2. Return lamb to saucepan; add broth, carrots, tomato paste, and herbs. Heat to boiling; reduce heat and simmer, covered, until lamb is tender, about 25 minutes, adding peas during last 5 minutes cooking time. Discard bay leaf; season to taste with salt and pepper.

3. Pour stew into 1¹/₂-quart casserole. Spoon Real Mashed Potatoes around edge of casserole. Bake at 400 degrees until potatoes are browned, about 10 minutes.

CURRIED LAMB STEW

Known in India as Rogan Josh, this flavorful stew is best prepared 1 to 2 days in advance for flavors to meld; cool stew and refrigerate. Serve with a variety of condiments for flavor and color contrast

12 servings

Per Serving	
Calories: 257	
% Calories from fat: 21	
Fat (gm): 5.9	
Saturated fat (gm): 2	
Cholesterol (mg): 49.9	
Sodium (mg): 82	
Protein (gm): 19.8	
Carbohydrate (gm): 29.4	
Exchanges	
Milk: 0.0	
Vegetable: 0.0	
Fruit: 0.0	
Bread: 2.0	
Meat: 2.0	
Fat: 0.0	

3 pounds boneless leg of lamb, fat trimmed, cut into 1-inch cubes

1¼ cups low-fat plain yogurt

¼ teaspoon crushed red pepper

2 cups chopped onions

1 tablespoon minced gingerroot

2 cloves garlic, minced

2 teasoons coriander seeds, lightly crushed

1 teaspoon cumin seeds, lightly crushed

½ teaspoon cardamom seeds, lightly crushed

1 teaspoon ground turmeric

Generous pinch ground cloves

½ teaspoon pepper

1-2 tablespoons margarine *or* vegetable oil

1 cup reduced-sodium fat-free chicken broth

Salt and pepper, to taste

Turmeric Rice (recipe follows)

Condiments: raisins, toasted slivered almonds, chopped onion and cucumber, finely chopped cilantro *or* parsley (not included in nutritional data)

1. Combine lamb, yogurt, and red pepper in bowl; refrigerate several hours or overnight, stirring occasionally.

2. Saute onions, gingerroot, garlic, and spices in margarine in Dutch oven until onions are tender, 5 to 8 minutes. Stir in lamb mixture and chicken broth; heat to boiling. Reduce heat and simmer, covered, until lamb is tender, 50 to 60 minutes. Season to taste with salt and pepper. Serve stew over Turmeric Rice; pass condiments.

Turmeric Rice

4$^1/_2$ cups water
$^3/_4$ teaspoon turmeric
$^1/_4$ teaspoon salt, optional
2 cups unccoked long-grain rice

1. Heat water to boiling in large saucepan; stir in turmeric and salt. Stir in rice; reduce heat and simmer, covered, until rice is tender, 20 to 25 minutes.

LAMB AND TURNIP STEW WITH CILANTRO

This homespun lamb dish has been updated with fresh sage and cilantro. Serve it with crusty bread to sop up the delicious broth.

4 servings

1 pound boneless lamb shoulder, fat trimmed, cut into 1-inch pieces
1 medium onion, chopped
1 teaspoon olive oil
1 tablespoon minced garlic
$^1/_2$ cup dry red wine *or* beef broth
2$^1/_2$ cups reduced-sodium tomato juice, divided
2 medium potatoes, cut into $^3/_4$-inch cubes
1 large turnip, cut into $^3/_4$-inch cubes
1 tablespoon chopped fresh, *or* 1 teaspoon dried, sage leaves
Salt and pepper, to taste
$^1/_2$ cup chopped cilantro

Per Serving
Calories: 269
% Calories from fat: 24
Fat (gm): 7.3
Saturated fat (gm): 2.4
Cholesterol (mg): 47.2
Sodium (mg): 81
Protein (gm): 17.4
Carbohydrate (gm): 30
Exchanges
Milk: 0.0
Vegetable: 0.0
Fruit: 0.0
Bread: 2.0
Meat: 2.0
Fat: 0.0

1. Saute lamb and onion in oil in 4-quart saucepan until lightly browned; add garlic, wine, and 1$^1/_2$ cups tomato juice and heat to boiling; reduce heat and simmer, covered, 25 minutes.

2. Stir in potatoes, turnip, and remaining 1 cup tomato juice; simmer, covered, until vegetables are tender, about 20 minutes. Stir in sage; season to taste with salt and pepper. Spoon stew into bowls; sprinkle with cilantro.

PASTITSIO

Sweet cinnamon and nutmeg season this Greek favorite.

6 servings

Olive oil cooking spray
1 pound lean ground lamb *or* beef
1 cup chopped onion
1 can (8 ounces) reduced-sodium tomato paste
1/3 cup water
Salt and pepper, to taste
2 cups elbow macaroni, cooked
1/3 cup grated fat-free Parmesan cheese
1/4-1/2 teaspoon ground cinnamon
1/4 teaspoon ground nutmeg
2 1/3 cups fat-free milk
2 tablespoons margarine
2 eggs
1/2 cup no-cholestrol real egg product *or* 4 egg whites
Minced parsley, as garnish

Per Serving
Calories: 361
% Calories from fat: 23
Fat (gm): 9.3
Saturated fat (gm): 2.5
Cholesterol (mg): 104.7
Sodium (mg): 266
Protein (gm): 25.6
Carbohydrate (gm): 42.8
Exchanges
Milk: 0.0
Vegetable: 0.0
Fruit: 0.0
Bread: 3.0
Meat: 3.0
Fat: 0.0

1. Spray large skillet with cooking spray; heat over medium heat until hot. Cook lamb until browned; add onion and cook until tender, 5 to 8 minutes. Drain any fat. Stir in tomato paste and water; cook 2 to 3 minutes longer. Season to taste with salt and pepper.

2. Spoon 1/2 of the macaroni into 13 x 9-inch baking pan; spoon meat mixture over macaroni. Combine cheese and spices; sprinkle over meat. Spoon remaining macaroni over the top.

3. Heat milk and margarine in medium saucepan, stirring until margarine is melted. Beat eggs and egg product in small bowl until blended. Whisk about 1/2 the milk into egg mixture; whisk egg mixture into saucepan. Pour over macaroni.

4. Bake, uncovered, at 350 degrees until casserole is bubbly, 50 to 60 minutes. Sprinkle with parsley.

VEGETABLE MOUSSAKA

Vegetables are added to traditional moussaka to make this delicious casserole.

12 servings

    Olive oil cooking spray
1 large eggplant, unpeeled, sliced
1 pound potatoes, unpeeled, sliced
3 cups chopped onions
8 ounces carrots, sliced
3 cloves garlic, minced
1 teaspoon ground cinnamon
1 teaspoon dried oregano leaves
1/2 teaspoon dried thyme leaves
3/4 cup reduced-sodium fat-free beef broth
2 cups chopped tomatoes
2 cups sliced mushrooms
1 pound ground lean lamb *or* beef, cooked, drained
2 cups cooked barley
1 small zucchini, sliced
    Salt and pepper, to taste
    Custard Topping (recipe follows)
    Ground nutmeg, to taste

Per Serving
Calories: 265
% Calories from fat: 29
Fat (gm): 8.9
Saturated fat (gm): 2.3
Cholesterol (mg): 44.7
Sodium (mg): 152
Protein (gm): 15
Carbohydrate (gm): 32.7
Exchanges
Milk: 0.0
Vegetable: 3.0
Fruit: 0.0
Bread: 1.0
Meat: 1.0
Fat: 1.0

1. Spray aluminum foil-lined jelly roll pan with cooking spray; arrange eggplant on pan and spray with cooking spray. Bake at 350 degrees until eggplant is tender but still firm to touch, about 20 minutes. Arrange eggplant on bottom of 13 x 9-inch baking pan.

2. Heat potatoes, onions, carrots, garlic, cinnamon, oregano, thyme, and broth to boiling in large skillet; reduce heat and simmer, uncovered, 5 minutes. Add tomatoes and mushrooms; simmer, uncovered, until tomatoes are soft. Add lamb, barley, and zucchini; cook, uncovered, until mixture is thick, about 5 minutes. Season to taste with salt and pepper.

3. Spoon vegetable mixture over eggplant. Pour Custard Topping over and sprinkle with nutmeg. Bake at 350 degrees until lightly browned on the top, about 45 minutes. Cool 5 to 10 minutes before cutting.

Custard Topping

1/3 cup margarine
1/2 cup all-purpose flour
  3 cups fat-free milk
  1 egg
  2 egg whites
    Salt and white pepper, to taste

1. Melt margarine in medium saucepan; stir in flour. Cook over medium heat until bubbly, about 2 minutes, stirring constantly. Stir in milk; heat to boiling. Boil, stirring constantly, until thickened, about 1 minute.

2. Beat egg and egg whites in small bowl. Stir about 1 cup milk mixture into eggs; stir egg mixture into saucepan. Cook over low heat until thickened, 2 to 3 minutes. Season to taste with salt and white pepper.

VEAL LADY SHARON

Veal chops are enhanced with a sauce flavored with mushrooms, herbs, and black olives.

4 servings

  4 lean veal chops (about 4 ounces each), fat trimmed
1-3 teaspoons margarine
  2 medium onions, chopped
  1 pound mushrooms, sliced
  1 tablespoon flour
  1 tablespoon tomato paste
3/4 cup reduced-sodium fat-free chicken broth
2/3 cup dry white wine
  1 teaspoon herbes de Provence *or* Italian seasoning
  1 small bay leaf
1/4-1/2 cup sliced black olives
    Salt and pepper, to taste
  2 tablespoons minced parsley

Per Serving
Calories: 302
% Calories from fat: 30
Fat (gm): 10.2
Saturated fat (gm): 2.2
Cholesterol (mg): 100.1
Sodium (mg): 439
Protein (gm): 32
Carbohydrate (gm): 14.5
Exchanges
Milk: 0.0
Vegetable: 3.0
Fruit: 0.0
Bread: 0.0
Meat: 3.0
Fat: 1.0

1. Cook veal chops in margarine in large skillet over high heat until browned on both sides; transfer to shallow baking dish. In same skillet, saute onions and mushrooms until tender; sprinkle with flour and cook 2 to 3 minutes, stirring well. Stir in remaining ingredients, except salt, pepper, and parsley, and heat to boiling. Reduce heat and simmer, covered, 5 minutes. Season to taste with salt and pepper.

2. Pour sauce over veal in dish. Bake, uncovered, at 325 degrees until veal is tender, about 45 minutes. Sprinkle with parsley and serve.

VEAL SAUVIGNON WITH SWISS CHARD

Delight your taste buds with this sophisticated stew. It's a gourmet experience with melt-in-your-mouth veal, tender cauliflower florets, dry white wine, and pasta.

4 servings

1 pound boneless veal cutlets, cut into thin 2-inch-long strips
2 teaspoons olive oil, divided
1 medium onion, thinly sliced
1 teaspoon minced garlic
1 1/2 cups Sauvignon blanc *or* other dry white wine
1 tablespoon tomato paste
3 cups cauliflower florets
1 teaspoon dried marjoram leaves
2 cups torn Swiss chard leaves
Salt and pepper, to taste
8 ounces ziti *or* other pasta, cooked, warm

Per Serving
Calories: 455
% Calories from fat: 16
Fat (gm): 8
Saturated fat (gm): 1.7
Cholesterol (mg): 74.6
Sodium (mg): 148
Protein (gm): 30
Carbohydrate (gm): 51
Exchanges
Milk: 0.0
Vegetable: 1.0
Fruit: 0.0
Bread: 3.0
Meat: 2.0
Fat: 2.0

1. Saute veal in 1 teaspoon oil in large saucepan until lightly browned; remove meat, and keep warm. Saute onion in remaining 1 teaspoon oil in saucepan until tender; stir in garlic and cook 1 minute.

2. Add wine, tomato paste, cauliflower, and marjoram and heat to boiling; reduce heat and simmer, covered, until tender, about 5 minutes. Stir in Swiss chard and veal; heat until hot through, 1 to 2 minutes. Season to taste with salt and pepper. Serve over ziti.

POBLANO VEAL CHILI

Ground veal, a poblano chili, and purchased seasoning mix make this fast-track chili an instant favorite.

4 servings

 1   pound ground lean veal
 1   large onion, chopped
 1   stalk celery, chopped
 1   can (15 ounces) reduced-sodium crushed tomatoes
 1   can (15 ounces) Great Northern beans, rinsed, drained
 ¹/₂-1   package (1¹/₄-ounce size) chili seasoning mix
 1   poblano chili, chopped

Per Serving
Calories: 282
% Calories from fat: 18
Fat (gm): 6.1
Saturated fat (gm): 1.6
Cholesterol (mg): 99.5
Sodium (mg): 659
Protein (gm): 34.2
Carbohydrate (gm): 26.4
Exchanges
Milk: 0.0
Vegetable: 0.0
Fruit: 0.0
Bread: 2.0
Meat: 3.0
Fat: 0.0

1. Cook veal in large saucepan until crumbly and no longer pink, stirring often; drain fat. Add onion and celery and saute until tender.

2. Stir in tomatoes, beans, seasoning mix, and poblano chili. Heat to boiling; simmer, covered, 15 minutes.

FOUR

Poultry

ROAST CHICKEN WITH CORN BREAD STUFFING

Avoid eating the crisp roasted skin on the chicken if you can, as the skin contains many fat calories. We've chosen to bake the stuffing in a casserole; if baked in the chicken, it would absorb unwanted fat from the chicken juices. White or whole wheat bread stuffing mix can be substituted for the corn bread stuffing.

6 servings

1	roasting chicken (about 3 pounds)
	Vegetable cooking spray
1¹/₂	teaspoons dried rosemary leaves, divided
1¹/₂	cups thinly sliced celery
³/₄	cup chopped onion
¹/₄	cup coarsely chopped pecans, optional
³/₄	teaspoon dried sage leaves
¹/₄	teaspoon dried thyme leaves
3	cups corn bread stuffing mix
1¹/₂	cups reduced-sodium chicken broth
	Salt and pepper, to taste
2	egg whites *or* ¹/₄ cup no-cholesterol real egg product

Per Serving
Calories: 258
% Calories from fat: 22
Fat (gm): 6.1
Saturated fat (gm): 1.6
Cholesterol (mg): 57.9
Sodium (mg): 548
Protein (gm): 24.4
Carbohydrate (gm): 25.3
Exchanges
Milk: 0.0
Vegetable: 0.5
Fruit: 0.0
Bread: 1.5
Meat: 2.5
Fat: 0.0

1. Spray chicken with cooking spray; sprinkle with 1 teaspoon rosemary. Roast chicken on rack in roasting pan at 375 degrees until meat thermometer inserted in thickest part of thigh, away from bone, registers 170 degrees (chicken leg will move freely and juices will run clear), about 1¹/₂ hours. Let chicken stand 10 minutes before carving.

2. While chicken is cooking, spray medium skillet with cooking spray; heat over medium heat until hot. Saute celery, onion, and pecans until vegetables are tender, 3 to 5 minutes. Stir in sage, thyme, and remaining ¹/₂ teaspoon rosemary; cook over medium heat 1 to 2 minutes.

3. Add vegetable mixture to stuffing mix in large bowl; add chicken broth and toss. Season to taste with salt and pepper. Mix in egg whites. Spoon stuffing into greased 2-quart casserole. Bake, covered, in oven with chicken during last 30 to 45 minutes roasting time.

Variation: **Pork Chops with Bread Stuffing**—Make stuffing as above in Steps 2 and 3, substituting white or whole wheat stuffing mix for the corn bread mix. Trim fat from 6 loin pork chops (about 5 ounces each); cook in lightly sprayed skillet until well browned, about 5 minutes on each side. Arrange pork chops on top of stuffing in casserole; bake, covered, at 350 degrees until pork chops are tender, 30 to 40 minutes.

GLAZED CORNISH HENS WITH WILD RICE

Cornish hens are marmalade-glazed, roasted to golden perfection, and served with a fruited wild rice mixture for company fare.

4 servings

2 Rock Cornish game hens (1 to 1¹/₄ pounds each)
  Vegetable cooking spray
  Paprika
¹/₃ cup no-sugar-added orange marmalade
¹/₄ cup sliced green onions and tops
¹/₄ cup sliced celery
1 package (6.25 ounces) fast-cooking long-grain white and wild rice, spice packet discarded
1 can (14¹/₂ ounces) reduced-sodium chicken broth
1 can (11 ounces) unsweetened Mandarin orange segments, drained
2 tablespoons raisins
2 tablespoons finely chopped mint, *or* parsley, leaves
  Salt and pepper, to taste
2 tablespoons toasted pecan halves, optional

Per Serving
Calories: 716
% Calories from fat: 7
Fat (gm): 6.2
Saturated fat (gm): 1.2
Cholesterol (mg): 108.5
Sodium (mg): 273
Protein (gm): 41.1
Carbohydrate (gm): 125.8
Exchanges
Milk: 0.0
Vegetable: 0.0
Fruit: 4.0
Bread: 4.0
Meat: 4.0
Fat: 0.0

1. Cut hens into halves with poultry shears and place, cut sides down, on rack in roasting pan. Spray with cooking spray and sprinkle with paprika. Roast at 350 degrees until thickest parts are fork-tender and drumstick meat feels soft when pressed, 1 to 1¹/₄ hours. Baste frequently with marmalade during last 30 minutes of cooking time.

2. Spray medium saucepan with cooking spray; heat over medium heat until hot. Saute green onions and celery until tender, about 5 minutes. Add rice and chicken broth and heat to boiling. Reduce heat and simmer, covered, until rice is tender, about 5 minutes. Stir in orange segments, raisins, and mint; cook 2 to 3 minutes longer. Season to taste with salt and pepper.

3. Spoon rice onto serving platter and sprinkle with pecans; arrange hens on rice.

CRISP OVEN-FRIED CHICKEN

A blend of corn flakes and bread crumbs gives this chicken a perfect crisp coating and golden color. Serve with Real Mashed Potatoes and Cream Gravy, if you like (see pp. 592, 144), substituting chicken bouillon crystals for the beef bouillon in the gravy.

6 servings

- 4 egg whites *or* 1/2 cup no-cholesterol real egg product
- 1/4 cup 2% reduced-fat milk
- 6 skinless chicken breast halves (6 ounces each)
- 1/4 cup all-purpose flour
- 1 1/2 cups finely crushed corn flakes cereal
- 3/4 cup dry unseasoned bread crumbs
- 1/2 teaspoon dried rosemary leaves, crumbled
- 1/4 teaspoon dried thyme leaves
  Butter-flavored vegetable cooking spray
  Salt and pepper, to taste

Per Serving
Calories: 387
% Calories from fat: 13
Fat (gm): 5.4
Saturated fat (gm): 1.5
Cholesterol (mg): 104.2
Sodium (mg): 557
Protein (gm): 44.8
Carbohydrate (gm): 36
Exchanges
Milk: 0.0
Vegetable: 0.0
Fruit: 0.0
Bread: 2.5
Meat: 4.0
Fat: 0.0

1. Beat egg whites and milk in shallow bowl until blended. Coat chicken breasts with flour; dip in egg mixture, then coat generously with combined corn flakes, bread crumbs, and herbs.

2. Spray baking pan with cooking spray. Place chicken, meat sides up, in baking pan; spray generously with cooking spray and sprinkle lightly with salt and pepper. Bake at 350 degrees until chicken is browned and juices run clear, 45 to 60 minutes.

CHICKEN FRICASSEE

Cloves and bay leaf add a flavor update to this dish; more traditional seasonings of rosemary and thyme can be substituted, if desired.

6 servings

Vegetable cooking spray

6 skinless chicken breast halves (6 ounces each)

1 medium onion, cut into wedges

4 medium carrots, cut into 1-inch pieces

4 ribs celery, cut into l-inch pieces

2 cloves garlic, minced

3 tablespoons flour

2 cans (14^1/$_2$ ounces each) reduced-sodium fat-free chicken broth

16 whole cloves

2 bay leaves

1 teaspoon lemon juice

^{1}/$_2$ teaspoon sugar

^{1}/$_2$ teaspoon salt

^{1}/$_4$ teaspoon pepper

12 ounces fettuccine *or* no-yolk noodles, cooked, warm

Minced parsley leaves, as garnish

Per Serving
Calories: 361
% Calories from fat: 13
Fat (gm): 5.1
Saturated fat (gm): 0.9
Cholesterol (mg): 78.6
Sodium (mg): 401
Protein (gm): 35.9
Carbohydrate (gm): 41.5
Exchanges
Milk: 0.0
Vegetable: 2.0
Fruit: 0.0
Bread: 2.0
Meat: 3.0
Fat: 0.0

1. Spray large skillet or Dutch oven with cooking spray; heat over medium heat until hot. Cook chicken until browned, about 8 minutes. Remove from skillet. Add vegetables to skillet; saute 5 minutes. Stir in flour and cook 1 minute, stirring constantly.

2. Return chicken to skillet. Add chicken broth, cloves and bay leaves tied in cheesecloth, lemon juice, and sugar. Heat to boiling; reduce heat and simmer, covered, until chicken is tender, about 20 minutes. Simmer, uncovered, until sauce is thickened to medium consistency, about 10 minutes. Discard spice packet; stir in salt and pepper.

3. Serve chicken and vegetables over pasta; sprinkle with parsley.

TANDOORI CHICKEN WITH ORANGE CILANTRO RICE

Chicken pieces are marinated in a seasoned yogurt mixture for flavor, then grilled or roasted.

4 servings

    1 pound chicken pieces
       Tandoori Marinade (recipe follows)
       Vegetable cooking spray
2$^1/_2$ cups Orange Cilantro Rice
       ($^2/_3$ recipe) (see p. 465)

Per Serving
Calories: 272
% Calories from fat: 12
Fat (gm): 3.6
Saturated fat (gm): 0.9
Cholesterol (mg): 69.3
Sodium (mg): 80
Protein (gm): 29.3
Carbohydrate (gm): 28.7
Exchanges
Milk: 0.0
Vegetable: 2.0
Fruit: 0.0
Bread: 1.0
Meat: 3.0
Fat: 0.0

1. Spread surfaces of chicken with Tandoori Marinade; place in shallow glass baking dish and refrigerate 3 to 4 hours, or overnight.

2. Spray grill rack generously with cooking spray; place chicken on rack over medium hot coals. Grill, covered, until chicken is browned, about 8 minutes on each side. Or, place chicken in greased, aluminum foil-lined baking pan and roast at 350 degrees until juices run clear, 30 to 45 minutes. Serve with Orange Cilantro Rice.

Tandoori Marinade

makes about $^1/_2$ cup

    $^1/_3$ cup plain fat-free yogurt
    1 small jalapeño chili, minced
    1 tablespoon finely chopped coriander *or* parsley
    2 teaspoons minced garlic
    1 teaspoon minced gingerroot
    1 teaspoon grated lime rind
    2 teaspoons paprika
1$^1/_2$ teaspoons ground cumin
    1 teaspoon ground coriander

1. Combine all ingredients; refrigerate until ready to use.

CAJUN CHICKEN

Packaged Cajun seasoning can be purchased, but we particularly like our homemade blend! The spice blend is also delicious on steaks and portobello mushrooms.

4 servings

Butter-flavored vegetable cooking spray
4 boneless, skinless chicken breast halves (4 ounces each)
Cajun Seasoning (recipe follows)

Per Serving
Calories: 144
% Calories from fat: 20
Fat (gm): 3.1
Saturated fat (gm): 0.9
Cholesterol (mg): 69
Sodium (mg): 206
Protein (gm): 25.7
Carbohydrate (gm): 2
Exchanges
Milk: 0.0
Vegetable: 0.0
Fruit: 0.0
Bread: 0.0
Meat: 3.0
Fat: 0.0

1. Lightly spray both sides of chicken pieces with cooking spray; sprinkle with Cajun Seasoning, pressing mixture onto chicken.

2. Grill chicken over medium-hot coals, or broil 6 inches from heat source, until chicken is cooked and juices run clear, about 5 minutes on each side.

Cajun Seasoning

makes about 2 tablespoons

2 teaspoons paprika
1 teaspoon onion powder
1 teaspoon garlic powder
1/2 teaspoon dried thyme leaves
1/2 teaspoon dried oregano leaves
1/2 teaspoon cayenne pepper
1/2 teaspoon black pepper
1/4 teaspoon salt

1. Mix all ingredients; store in airtight container until ready to use.

GINGER CHICKEN WITH ORANGES

8 servings

Vegetable cooking spray
8 boneless, skinless chicken breast halves
   (4 ounces each)
1/8 teaspoon pepper
1 teaspoon ground ginger
1 orange, peeled, sliced
1 cup unsweetened orange juice concentrate, thawed
1 cup unsweetened orange juice
2 tablespoons honey
   Peel of 2 oranges, slivered
1 tablespoon all-purpose flour

Per Serving
Calories: 239
% Calories from fat: 12
Fat (gm): 3.1
Saturated fat (gm): 0.8
Cholesterol (mg): 69
Sodium (mg): 62
Protein (gm): 26.7
Carbohydrate (gm): 25.4
Exchanges
Milk: 0.0
Vegetable: 0.0
Fruit: 1.5
Bread: 0.0
Meat: 3.0
Fat: 0.0

1. Preheat oven to 350 degrees. Spray baking dish with cooking spray; add chicken and sprinkle with pepper, ginger, and orange slices. Brush chicken breasts with half of the orange juice concentrate; cover and bake for 20 minutes. Remove from oven, turn over chicken, and brush on remaining juice concentrate. Return to oven and bake 15 to 20 minutes.

2. Combine remaining ingredients in saucepan and cook until thickened. Serve orange sauce over chicken.

CHICKEN CORDON BLEU

This recipe was once the ultimate in gourmet dining. The ham-and-cheese-stuffed chicken breasts are still delicious in their low-fat form!

6 servings

6 boneless, skinless chicken breast halves
   (4 ounces each)
4 ounces sliced fat-free Swiss cheese
3 .ounces lean smoked ham
   Flour
2 egg whites, beaten
1/3 cup unseasoned dry bread crumbs
   Vegetable cooking spray

Per Serving
Calories: 210
% Calories from fat: 18
Fat (gm): 3.9
Saturated fat (gm): 1.1
Cholesterol (mg): 73.2
Sodium (mg): 540
Protein (gm): 34.6
Carbohydrate (gm): 6.3
Exchanges
Milk: 0.0
Vegetable: 0.0
Fruit: 0.0
Bread: 0.0
Meat: 4.0
Fat: 0.0

1. Pound chicken breasts with flat side of meat mallet until very thin and even in thickness. Layer cheese and ham on chicken breasts, cutting to fit. Roll up chicken and secure with toothpicks.

2. Coat chicken rolls lightly with flour; dip in egg whites and coat in bread crumbs. Spray rolls generously with cooking spray and cook in skillet over medium heat until browned on all sides, 8 to 10 minutes.

3. Place chicken in baking pan. Bake at 350 degrees, uncovered, until cooked through, about 30 minutes.

CHICKEN AND RICE ROLL-UPS

The colors of corn, green peppers, and pimientos make this an attractive dish.

4 servings

1 cup frozen corn, cooked, drained
1 cup finely chopped green bell pepper
3 tablespoons diced pimientos
1/2 cup (2 ounces) shredded Monterey Jack cheese
3 cups cooked long-grain rice
4 boneless, skinless chicken breast halves (4 ounces each)
Salt and pepper, to taste

Per Serving
Calories: 391
% Calories from fat: 18
Fat (gm): 7.8
Saturated fat (gm): 3.7
Cholesterol (mg): 81.6
Sodium (mg): 142
Protein (gm): 33.6
Carbohydrate (gm): 45.6
Exchanges
Milk: 0.0
Vegetable: 0.0
Fruit: 0.0
Bread: 3.0
Meat: 3.0
Fat: 0.0

1. Combine corn, bell pepper, pimientos, cheese, and 1 1/2 cups cooked rice in medium bowl. Pour remaining rice into a lightly greased 11 x 7-inch baking pan.

2. Place chicken breasts between sheets of waxed paper. Pound to about 1/4 inch thickness, using a meat mallet. Remove paper. Spoon 1/4 of the vegetable-rice mixture on each breast, leaving a 1/4-inch border on all sides. Roll each breast, beginning with the short side; secure with toothpicks.

3. Place chicken breasts seam sides down on rice in pan. Sprinkle lightly with salt and pepper. Bake, covered, 30 minutes at 325 degrees. Uncover and bake 15 to 20 minutes longer or until browned. Remove toothpicks from chicken and cut each roll into 1-inch slices. Serve on top of rice.

CHICKEN OSCAR

This dish is easy to prepare, and looks great when served.

6 servings

  6 boneless, skinless chicken breast halves (4 ounces each)

  1 cup unseasoned dry bread crumbs

  2 cups seasoned croutons *or* stuffing mix

  1/2 cup reduced-sodium fat-free chicken broth

 24 stalks asparagus

  6 slices (1/2 ounce each) provolone cheese

Per Serving
Calories: 302
% Calories from fat: 23
Fat (gm): 7.8
Saturated fat (gm): 3.5
Cholesterol (mg): 79.6
Sodium (mg): 447
Protein (gm): 34.7
Carbohydrate (gm): 22.1
Exchanges
Milk: 0.0
Vegetable: 2.0
Fruit: 0.0
Bread: 0.5
Meat: 4.0
Fat: 0.0

1. Place chicken breasts between sheets of waxed paper. Pound to about 1/4 inch thickness with a meat mallet. Remove paper.

2. Coat chicken pieces on both sides with dry bread crumbs; place in lightly greased 13 x 9-inch baking pan. Combine croutons and broth in medium bowl; spoon mixture onto center of each chicken breast.

3. Place 4 asparagus stalks across each chicken breast. Bake, covered, at 350 degrees 30 minutes. Uncover and top each chicken breast with a slice of provolone; bake 10 minutes longer.

DIJON CHICKEN AU GRATIN

For perfect portion control, try the individually packaged chicken breast halves that can be found in the frozen meat section of many supermarkets. You can easily remove and thaw the number of servings you need for your meal.

6 servings

2 cups instant, *or* boil-in-bag, rice

6 boneless, skinless chicken breast halves (4 ounces each)

1 medium zucchini, cut into $1/4$-inch slices

1 large red bell pepper, cut into $1/4$-inch slices

$1/2$ cup Dijon mustard

$1/2$ cup dry white wine *or* reduced-sodium chicken broth

$1/4$ cup water

1 cup unseasoned dry bread crumbs

$1/2$ cup grated Parmesan cheese

2 tablespoons dried tarragon leaves
    Salt and pepper, to taste

Per Serving
Calories: 406
% Calories from fat: **17**
Fat (gm): 7.7
Saturated fat (gm): 2.5
Cholesterol (mg): 74.6
Sodium (mg): 458
Protein (gm): 34.7
Carbohydrate (gm): 44.3
Exchanges
Milk: 0.0
Vegetable: 0.0
Fruit: 0.0
Bread: 3.0
Meat: 3.0
Fat: 0.0

1. Spread uncooked rice in lightly greased 13 x 9-inch baking pan. Place chicken breasts on top of rice. Arrange zucchini and bell pepper on top of chicken.

2. Mix mustard, wine, and water in small bowl until smooth; pour over vegetables and chicken. Combine remaining ingredients, except salt and pepper; sprinkle evenly over entire dish. Bake, covered, at 350 degrees 20 minutes; uncover and bake until rice and chicken are tender and liquid is absorbed, about 25 minutes longer. Sprinkle lightly with salt and pepper.

CHICKEN DIVAN

By using pre-cooked roasted chicken breast from your grocer's meat section, and frozen broccoli, much time is saved without sacrificing flavor in this classic favorite. For added convenience, prepare the casserole ahead of time and refrigerate; simply add 10 minutes to the cooking time.

6 servings

$^1/_2$ cup reduced-fat mayonnaise

$^1/_4$ cup all-purpose flour

$2^1/_2$ cups fat-free milk

1   cup (4 ounces) shredded reduced-fat sharp Cheddar cheese

Salt and pepper, to taste

2   cups instant, *or* boil-in-bag, rice, cooked

1   package (16 ounces) frozen cut broccoli, thawed

$^1/_2$ cup grated fat-free Parmesan cheese, divided

1   pound roasted skinless chicken breast, cut into $^1/_4$-inch slices

Per Serving
Calories: 461
% Calories from fat: 25
Fat (gm): 12.5
Saturated fat (gm): 3.6
Cholesterol (mg): 76.3
Sodium (mg): 612
Protein (gm): 38.9
Carbohydrate (gm): 44.8
Exchanges
Milk: 0.0
Vegetable: 2.0
Fruit: 0.0
Bread: 2.5
Meat: 4.0
Fat: 0.0

1. Whisk mayonnaise and flour in medium saucepan over low heat until smooth. Gradually whisk in milk; whisk constantly over medium-high heat until mixture boils and thickens. Add Cheddar cheese; stir until melted. Season to taste with salt and pepper.

2. Spread rice on bottom of lightly greased 12 x 8-inch baking dish; arrange broccoli over. Spoon half the sauce over; sprinkle with half the Parmesan cheese. Top with chicken, remaining sauce, and remaining Parmesan cheese. Bake, uncovered, at 375 degrees until hot and bubbly, about 35 minutes.

COQ AU VIN

This French classic can be assembled in advance and refrigerated if you like; just increase cooking time by 10 minutes.

6 servings

6 boneless, skinless chicken breast halves (4 ounces each), cut into halves
5 slices reduced-sodium bacon, diced
3 green onions and tops, sliced
5 pearl onions, peeled, halved
8 ounces whole small mushrooms
8 small new potatoes, halved
1 teaspoon minced garlic
1/2 teaspoon dried thyme leaves
1/2 teaspoon salt
1/4 teaspoon pepper
1/2 cup water
1/2 cup Burgundy *or* other dry red wine *or* reduced-sodium chicken broth

Per Serving
Calories: 343
% Calories from fat: 13
Fat (gm): 4.9
Saturated fat (gm): 1.5
Cholesterol (mg): 73.2
Sodium (mg): 357
Protein (gm): 31.2
Carbohydrate (gm): 39.3
Exchanges
Milk: 0.0
Vegetable: 1.0
Fruit: 0.0
Bread: 2.0
Meat: 3.0
Fat: 0.0

1. Place chicken and bacon in 2¹/₂-quart casserole; sprinkle with green onions. Add pearl onions, mushrooms, and potatoes. Sprinkle with combined garlic, thyme, salt, and pepper. Pour water and wine over.

2. Bake, covered, at 325 degrees until chicken and potatoes are tender, about 1¹/₂ hours.

CHICKEN CACCIATORE

Of Italian origin, this "Hunter's Stew" was made from any game brought back from the day's hunting and would vary slightly from kitchen to kitchen.

4 servings

8 ounces boneless, skinless chicken breast
8 ounces boneless, skinless chicken thighs
2 teaspoons dried basil leaves, divided
1/2 teaspoon dried oregano leaves
1/4 teaspoon garlic powder
   Olive oil cooking spray
   Salt and pepper, to taste
1 cup chopped onion
1 cup chopped green bell pepper
6 cloves garlic, minced
3 cups quartered medium mushrooms
2 cans (14 1/2 ounces each) reduced-sodium whole tomatoes, undrained, coarsely chopped
1/2 cup dry red, *or* white, wine
1 bay leaf
4 teaspoons cornstarch
2 tablespoons water
   Salt and pepper, to taste
3 cups cooked no-yolk broad noodles, warm
   Finely chopped basil *or* parsley, as garnish

Per Serving
Calories: 411
% Calories from fat: 15
Fat (gm): 7.2
Saturated fat (gm): 1.7
Cholesterol (mg): 65.5
Sodium (mg): 199
Protein (gm): 30.9
Carbohydrate (gm): 53.7
Exchanges
Milk: 0.0
Vegetable: 4.0
Fruit: 0.0
Bread: 2.0
Meat: 3.0
Fat: 0.0

1. Cut chicken into serving-size pieces; sprinkle with combined 1 teaspoon basil, oregano, and garlic powder. Spray large skillet with cooking spray; heat over medium heat until hot. Cook chicken on medium heat until browned, 5 to 8 minutes; remove from skillet and sprinkle with salt and pepper.

2. Add onion, bell pepper, and garlic to skillet; saute 3 to 4 minutes. Add mushrooms, tomatoes with liquid, wine, remaining 1 teaspoon dried basil, and bay leaf; heat to boiling. Add reserved chicken; reduce heat and simmer, covered, until chicken is tender, 20 to 30 minutes.

3. Heat to boiling; stir in combined cornstarch and water. Boil, stirring constantly, until thickened. Discard bay leaf; season to taste with salt and pepper. Serve chicken and sauce over noodles; sprinkle with basil.

ORANGE CHICKEN AND VEGETABLES

Both orange juice and rind are used to accent this flavorful dish.

6 servings

Vegetable cooking spray
6 boneless, skinless chicken breast halves (4 ounces each)
1 large onion, sliced
2 cloves garlic, chopped
1 tablespoon flour
3 medium tomatoes, chopped
1/2 teaspoon dried marjoram leaves
1/4 teaspoon dried thyme leaves
1 -inch piece cinnamon stick
11/2 cups orange juice
2 teaspoons grated orange rind
3 large carrots, cut into 1-inch pieces
3 medium potatoes, unpeeled, cubed
Salt and pepper, to taste

Per Serving
Calories: 318
% Calories from fat: 10
Fat (gm): 3.5
Saturated fat (gm): 0.9
Cholesterol (mg): 69
Sodium (mg): 87
Protein (gm): 29.4
Carbohydrate (gm): 42.4
Exchanges
Milk: 0.0
Vegetable: 2.0
Fruit: 0.5
Bread: 1.5
Meat: 2.5
Fat: 0.0

1. Spray large skillet with cooking spray; heat over medium heat until hot. Cook chicken over medium heat until browned, about 5 minutes on each side. Arrange chicken in glass baking dish, 12 x 9 inches.

2. Spray skillet with cooking spray; add onion and garlic and saute until tender, 5 to 8 minutes. Stir in flour; cook over medium heat 1 to 2 minutes. Add tomatoes, marjoram, thyme, and cinnamon stick; saute 1 to 2 minutes.

3. Add orange juice and rind to skillet; heat to boiling. Reduce heat and simmer, uncovered, 5 minutes. Arrange carrots and potatoes around chicken; pour orange juice mixture over. Bake, covered, at 350 degrees until chicken is tender, about 30 minutes. Season to taste with salt and pepper.

FETTUCCINE WITH CHICKEN PICCATA

This skinny version of the classic piccata is sure to please.

6 servings

6 small boneless, skinless chicken breast halves (3 ounces each)
Flour
Vegetable cooking spray
1 tablespoon margarine
2 tablespoons flour
1 can (14½ ounces) reduced-sodium chicken broth
½ cup dry white wine *or* chicken broth
2 tablespoons lemon juice
1 tablespoon finely chopped parsley
2 teaspoons drained capers, optional
12 ounces fettuccine, cooked, warm

Per Serving
Calories: 301
% Calories from fat: 18
Fat (gm): 6
Saturated fat (gm): 0.9
Cholesterol (mg): 43.4
Sodium (mg): 175
Protein (gm): 24.3
Carbohydrate (gm): 35
Exchanges
Milk: 0.0
Vegetable: 0.0
Fruit: 0.0
Bread: 2.5
Meat: 2.0
Fat: 0.0

1. Pound chicken with flat side of meat mallet to scant ¼ inch thickness; coat lightly with flour. Spray large skillet with cooking spray; heat over medium heat until hot. Cook chicken over medium to medium-high heat until browned and no longer pink in center, 3 to 5 minutes. Remove chicken from skillet.

2. Melt margarine in skillet; stir in 2 tablespoons flour and cook over medium heat 1 to 2 minutes. Stir in chicken broth, wine, and lemon juice; heat to boiling. Boil, stirring constantly, until slightly thickened, 1 to 2 minutes. Reduce heat and simmer, uncovered, until thickened to a medium sauce consistency, about 15 minutes more. Stir in parsley and capers.

3. Return chicken to sauce; cook over medium-low heat until chicken is hot through, 2 to 3 minutes. Serve chicken and sauce over pasta.

CHICKEN AND FETTUCCINE ALFREDO

An old favorite, updated the low-fat way.

6 servings

6 small boneless, skinless chicken breast halves (3 ounces each)
2 cloves garlic, minced
Paprika
Alfredo Sauce (recipe follows)
1 tablespoon finely chopped fresh, *or* 1 teaspoon dried, basil leaves
12 ounces fettuccine, cooked, warm

Per Serving
Calories: 380
% Calories from fat: 26
Fat (gm): 11
Saturated fat (gm): 2.6
Cholesterol (mg): 48.4
Sodium (mg): 506
Protein (gm): 29.2
Carbohydrate (gm): 41.4
Exchanges
Milk: 0.5
Vegetable: 0.0
Fruit: 0.0
Bread: 2.5
Meat: 2.0
Fat: 1.0

1. Rub chicken with garlic; sprinkle generously with paprika. Place chicken in baking pan and bake at 350 degrees until juices run clear, about 35 minutes.

2. Make Alfredo Sauce, adding basil. Spoon Alfredo Sauce over fettuccine and toss. Top with chicken breasts.

Alfredo Sauce

makes about 2 cups

3 tablespoons margarine
1/4 cup all-purpose flour
2 1/2 cups fat-free milk
1/4 cup grated Parmesan cheese
1/8 teaspoon ground nutmeg
1/2 teaspoon salt
1/4 teaspoon pepper

1. Melt margarine in medium saucepan; stir in flour. Cook over medium heat 1 minute, stirring constantly. Stir in milk; heat to boiling. Boil, stirring constantly, until thickened, about 2 minutes.

2. Reduce heat to low and stir in cheese, nutmeg, salt, and pepper; cook 1 to 2 minutes.

CHICKEN BREASTS WITH ROSEMARY

Easy, yet elegant, this zesty and healthful entrée is good served with a risotto and a simple vegetable or salad.

4 servings

1 tablespoon olive oil, divided
1¹/₂ teaspoons balsamic vinegar
1 teaspoon minced garlic
1 tablespoon grated lemon rind
¹/₄ teaspoon salt
¹/₈ teaspoon pepper
4 boneless, skinless chicken breast halves (4 ounces each)
¹/₃ cup dry white wine *or* reduced-sodium chicken broth
1 teaspoon finely chopped fresh, *or* ¹/₂ teaspoon dried, crumbled rosemary leaves
¹/₂ cup diced, peeled fresh tomato

Per Serving
Calories: 188
% Calories from fat: 31
Fat (gm): 6.4
Saturated fat (gm): 1.3
Cholesterol (mg): 69
Sodium (mg): 209
Protein (gm): 25.6
Carbohydrate (gm): 2.6
Exchanges
Milk: 0.0
Vegetable: 0.5
Fruit: 0.0
Bread: 0.0
Meat: 3.0
Fat: 0.0

1. Whisk 1¹/₂ teaspoons olive oil, vinegar, garlic, lemon rind, salt, and pepper in medium bowl; add chicken and let stand 10 minutes. Drain, reserving marinade.

2. Cook chicken in remaining 1¹/₂ teaspoons olive oil in large skillet over medium-high heat until browned on all sides, adding any remaining marinade after browning. Add wine and rosemary to skillet and heat to boiling; reduce heat and simmer, covered, 10 minutes. Add tomato and simmer, uncovered, until chicken is cooked through, about 6 minutes.

CHICKEN AND BROCCOLI CASSEROLE

6 servings (1 cup each)

1³/₄ cups stuffing mix

   5 tablespoons reduced-calorie margarine, melted

     Vegetable cooking spray

   1 can (10³/₄-ounce) low-fat cream of chicken soup

   2 cups finely chopped cooked chicken breast

   4 ounces non-fat milk

   2 cups frozen chopped broccoli florets, thawed

   1 tablespoon minced onion

 ¹/₈ teaspoon black pepper

Per Serving
Calories: 257
% Calories from fat: **31**
Fat (gm): **9**
Saturated fat (gm): **2**
Cholesterol (mg): **45**
Sodium (mg): 795
Protein (gm): 18
Carbohydrate (gm): 26

Exchanges
Milk: 0.0
Vegetable: 2.0
Fruit: 0.0
Bread: 1.0
Meat: 2.0
Fat: 1.0

1. Pre-heat oven to 425 degrees. Place stuffing mix and melted margarine in a mixing bowl and combine completely. Spread and pat all but ³/₄ cup of the stuffing mixture into the bottom of a 2-quart casserole dish coated with non-stick cooking spray.

2. In a separate bowl, combine remaining ingredients. Pour chicken mixture over stuffing mixture layer. Top with remaining ³/₄ cup of stuffing mixture. Bake 20 to 25 minutes or until golden brown and bubbly. Let stand 5 minutes before serving.

TAGLIATELLE WITH CHICKEN LIVER SAUCE

There are interesting counterpoints of flavor and texture in this savory pasta dish.

6 servings

4	ounces chicken livers, cleaned
	Flour
2	teaspoons olive oil
2	medium onions, sliced
3	cloves garlic, minced
2	teaspoons dried sage leaves
2	cups julienned carrots
2	medium tart apples, cored, sliced
1¹/₂	cups reduced-sodium fat-free chicken broth
¹/₂	cup dry white wine *or* chicken broth
1	tablespoon tomato paste
¹/₄	teaspoon salt
¹/₈	teaspoon pepper
8	ounces fettuccine, cooked, warm

Per Serving
Calories: 245
% Calories from fat: 14
Fat (gm): 3.9
Saturated fat (gm): 0.6
Cholesterol (mg): 73.9
Sodium (mg): 167
Protein (gm): 10.1
Carbohydrate (gm): 40.3
Exchanges
Milk: 0.0
Vegetable: 2.0
Fruit: 0.5
Bread: 2.0
Meat: 0.5
Fat: 0.5

1. Coat chicken livers lightly with flour. Saute in oil in large skillet until tender and no longer pink in center, about 8 minutes. Remove livers from skillet.

2. Add onions, garlic, and sage to skillet; saute until tender, about 5 minutes. Return livers to skillet. Add carrots, apples, chicken broth, and wine. Heat to boiling. Reduce heat and simmer, uncovered, until vegetables are crisp-tender and sauce thickened, about 15 minutes. Stir in tomato paste, salt, and pepper; cook 2 to 3 minutes more.

3. Serve chicken liver mixture over pasta.

SMOKED CHICKEN BREAST AND LINGUINE SALAD

Mesquite and hickory chips are most commonly used for smoking foods on the grill. For subtle flavor, try pecan, cherry, or alder wood when smoking the chicken for this salad. Mesquite-smoked chicken or turkey breast is also available in the deli sections of supermarkets.

4 servings

1	pound boneless, skinless chicken breast
8	ounces linguine, cooked, room temperature
2	cups sliced carrots, cooked until crisp-tender
1/2	can (15-ounce size) artichoke hearts, drained, rinsed, cut into fourths
12	cherry tomatoes, cut into halves
1/4	cup sliced green onions and tops
	Sour Cream Dressing (recipe follows)

Per Serving
Calories: 404
% Calories from fat: 11
Fat (gm): 5.2
Saturated fat (gm): 0.8
Cholesterol (mg): 58
Sodium (mg): 800
Protein (gm): 34.9
Carbohydrate (gm): 58.5
Exchanges
Milk: 0.0
Vegetable: 4.0
Fruit: 0.0
Bread: 2.5
Meat: 2.0
Fat: 0.0

1. Smoke chicken in smoker or on grill, using manufacturer's directions. Cool; refrigerate several hours or overnight to allow flavor to mellow. Cut chicken into strips or pieces.

2. Combine chicken, pasta, and vegetables in bowl; spoon Sour Cream Dressing over and toss.

Sour Cream Dressing

makes about 2/3 cup

1/3	cup fat-free sour cream
1/3	cup fat-free mayonnaise *or* salad dressing
1	tablespoon red wine vinegar
1	clove garlic, minced
1/2	teaspoon dried rosemary leaves, crushed
1/2	teaspoon salt
1/4	teaspoon pepper

1. Mix all ingredients; refrigerate until serving time. Mix again before using.

CHICKEN AND CHEESE RELLENOS

Any lean meat can be substituted for the chicken. Our healthy version of chili rellenos eliminates the customary egg coating and frying in oil.

6 servings

6 large poblano chilies
2-3 quarts water
   Vegetable cooking spray
1 medium onion, chopped
1 carrot, cooked crisp-tender, coarsely chopped
1 clove garlic, chopped
1 pound boneless, skinless chicken breast, cooked, shredded
$1/2$ cup frozen, thawed whole-kernel corn
$1/2$ teaspoon ground cumin
$1/2$ teaspoon dried thyme leaves
$1/2$ cup (2 ounces) shredded reduced-fat Monterey Jack cheese
$1/2$ cup (2 ounces) shredded fat-free Cheddar cheese
   Salt and pepper, to taste
1 tablespoon vegetable oil
   Chili Tomato Sauce (recipe follows)

Per Serving
Calories: 215
% Calories from fat: 26
Fat (gm): 6.4
Saturated fat (gm): 1.9
Cholesterol (mg): 54.4
Sodium (mg): 213
Protein (gm): 25.2
Carbohydrate (gm): 15.1
Exchanges
Milk: 0.0
Vegetable: 2.0
Fruit: 0.0
Bread: 0.5
Meat: 3.0
Fat: 0.0

1.   Cut stems from tops of chilies; remove and discard seeds and veins. Heat water to boiling in large saucepan; add peppers. Reduce heat and simmer, uncovered, 2 to 3 minutes, until peppers are slightly softened. Drain well and cool.

2.   Coat large skillet with cooking spray; heat over medium heat until hot. Saute onion, carrot, and garlic until tender, 3 to 5 minutes. Add chicken, corn, and herbs; cook over medium heat 1 to 2 minutes. Remove from heat; stir in cheeses. Season to taste with salt and pepper.

3.   Stuff peppers with mixture. Heat oil in large skillet until hot; saute peppers over medium to medium-high heat until tender and browned on all sides, 6 to 8 minutes. Serve with Chili Tomato Sauce.

Chili Tomato Sauce

makes 1 cup

   1 cup reduced-sodium tomato sauce
   2 tablespoons water
1-1¹/2 tablespoons chili powder
   1 clove garlic
     Salt and pepper, to taste

1. Combine tomato sauce, water, chili powder, and garlic in small saucepan; heat to boiling. Reduce heat and simmer, uncovered, 2 to 3 minutes. Season to taste with salt and pepper.

CHICKEN FAJITAS

Fajitas are an American interpretation of a soft taco. If grilling fajita ingredients, leave chicken breasts whole and cut peppers in half, then slice before serving.

4 servings (2 each)

   1 pound boneless, skinless chicken breast, cut into 1¹/2 x ¹/2-inch pieces
     Fajita Marinade (recipe follows)
     Vegetable cooking spray
   1 medium red bell pepper, sliced
   1 medium onion, sliced
   1 can (15 ounces) black beans, rinsed, drained
   1 teaspoon ground cumin
¹/2 teaspoon dried marjoram leaves
     Salt and pepper, to taste
   8 flour, *or* corn, tortillas, warm
   2 tablespoons finely chopped cilantro
   1 cup Red Tomato Salsa (¹/2 recipe) (see p. 724)
¹/2 cup fat-free sour cream

Per Serving
Calories: 424
% Calories from fat: 14
Fat (gm): 7.3
Saturated fat (gm): 1.2
Cholesterol (mg): 51.7
Sodium (mg): 645
Protein (gm): 35.9
Carbohydrate (gm): 61.7
Exchanges
Milk: 0.0
Vegetable: 2.0
Fruit: 0.0
Bread: 3.0
Meat: 2.0
Fat: 0.0

1. Place chicken in shallow glass baking dish; brush Fajita Marinade on chicken. Refrigerate, covered, 1 to 2 hours.

2. Spray large skillet with cooking spray; heat over medium heat until hot. Add chicken and cook over medium heat until browned and no longer pink in the center, 5 to 8 minutes; move chicken to side of pan. Add bell pepper and onion; cook over medium heat until tender, about 5 minutes. Add black beans; cook until hot, 2 to 3 minutes. Sprinkle chicken and vegetables with cumin and marjoram; season to taste with salt and pepper.

3. Spoon chicken and vegetable mixture onto tortillas; sprinkle with cilantro, top with Red Tomato Salsa and sour cream, and roll up.

Fajita Marinade

makes about 1/4 cup

> 3 tablespoons lime juice
> 2 cloves garlic
> 3/4 teaspoon dried oregano leaves
> 1/4 teaspoon ground allspice
> 1/4 teaspoon black pepper

1. Mix all ingredients.

CHICKEN FLAUTAS WITH TOMATILLO SAUCE

Flautas are usually deep-fried; these are sauteed to achieve the same crispness.

4 servings (2 each)

> Vegetable cooking spray
> 1 cup chopped tomato
> 1/4 cup chopped onion
> 2-4 tablespoons finely chopped poblano chili
> 1/2 teaspoon ground cumin
> 1/4 teaspoon dried thyme leaves
> 1 pound boneless, skinless chicken breast, cooked, shredded
> 2 tablespoons finely chopped cilantro
> Salt and pepper, to taste
> 8 flour, *or* corn, tortillas

Per Serving
Calories: 388
% Calories from fat: 23
Fat (gm): 9.8
Saturated fat (gm): 1.4
Cholesterol (mg): 75.7
Sodium (mg): 361
Protein (gm): 34
Carbohydrate (gm): 40.6
Exchanges
Milk: 0.0
Vegetable: 2.0
Fruit: 0.0
Bread: 2.0
Meat: 3.5
Fat: 0.0

1 cup Tomatillo Sauce (recipe follows)
4 tablespoons crumbled Mexican white
  cheese *or* farmer's cheese
1/4 cup fat-free sour cream
  Cilantro sprigs, as garnish

1. Spray large skillet with cooking spray; heat over medium heat until hot. Saute tomato, onion, poblano chili, cumin, and thyme until onion is tender, about 5 minutes. Add chicken and cilantro; cook 2 to 3 minutes. Season to taste with salt and pepper.

2. Spoon about 1/3 cup chicken mixture on each tortilla; roll up and fasten with toothpicks. Spray large skillet generously with cooking spray; heat over medium heat until hot. Cook flautas over medium to medium-high heat until browned on all sides, spraying with cooking spray if needed.

3. Arrange flautas on plates; spoon Tomatillo Sauce over. Sprinkle with cheese; top with dollops of sour cream and cilantro.

Tomatillo Sauce

makes about 2 cups

1 1/2 pounds Mexican green tomatoes
  (tomatillos)
1/2 medium onion, chopped
1 clove garlic, minced
1/2 small serrano chili, minced
3 tablespoons finely chopped cilantro
  Vegetable cooking spray
2-3 teaspoons sugar
  Salt and white pepper, to taste

1. Remove and discard husks from tomatoes; simmer tomatoes, covered, in 1 inch water in large saucepan until tender, 5 to 8 minutes. Cool; drain.

2. Process tomatoes, onion, garlic, serrano chili, and cilantro in food processor or blender, using pulse technique, until almost smooth. Spray large skillet with cooking spray; heat over medium heat until hot. Add sauce and "fry" over medium heat until slightly thickened, about 5 minutes; season to taste with sugar, salt, and pepper.

CHICKEN BURRITOS WITH POBLANO CHILI SAUCE

Brushed with sauce and cooked twice for extra flavor, these burritos are a beautiful adobe red color.

4 servings

12-16 ounces boneless, skinless chicken breast
    Salt and pepper, to taste
   3 arbol, *or* New Mexico, chilies, stems, seeds, and veins discarded
    Hot water
    Vegetable cooking spray
   1 small onion, finely chopped
   3 cloves garlic, minced
   2 tablespoons finely chopped cilantro
   1 teaspoon dried marjoram leaves
   1 teaspoon dried oregano leaves
   1 can (15 ounces) pinto beans, rinsed, drained
    Salt, to taste
  1/4 teaspoon cayenne pepper
   4 large flour tortillas (10-inch)
    Poblano Chili Sauce (recipe follows)
  1/2 cup fat-free sour cream
    Medium, *or* hot, prepared salsa
    (not included in nutritional data)

Per Serving
Calories: 385
% Calories from fat: 14
Fat (gm): 6.1
Saturated fat (gm): 1.1
Cholesterol (mg): 51.7
Sodium (mg): 661
Protein (gm): 33.1
Carbohydrate (gm): 52.6
Exchanges
Milk: 0.0
Vegetable: 2.0
Fruit: 0.0
Bread: 3.0
Meat: 2.0
Fat: 0.0

1. Cover chicken with water in small saucepan; heat to boiling. Reduce heat and simmer, covered, until chicken is tender and no longer pink in the center, 8 to 10 minutes. Drain, reserving 1/4 cup cooking liquid. Cool chicken slightly; shred into small pieces. Season lightly with salt and pepper.

2. Cover arbol chilies with hot water in small bowl; let stand until softened, 10 to 15 minutes. Drain; chop finely.

3. Spray medium skillet with cooking spray; heat over medium heat until hot. Saute onion, garlic, and herbs until onion is tender, 3 to 4 minutes. Add beans, ¹/₄ cup reserved cooking liquid, and arbol chilies to skillet; mash coarsely with fork. Cook over medium heat until hot; season to taste with salt and cayenne pepper.

4. Spoon bean mixture and chicken along centers of tortillas; top each with ¹/₄ cup Poblano Chili Sauce. Fold sides of tortillas in, overlapping filling; fold ends in, overlapping to make a square "package"; secure with toothpicks.

5. Spray large skillet with cooking spray; heat over medium heat until hot. Cook burritos until browned on all sides, brushing with remaining Poblano Chili Sauce. Serve hot with sour cream and salsa.

Poblano Chili Sauce

makes about 2 cups

> Vegetable cooking spray
> 2 medium tomatoes, chopped
> ¹/₂ medium poblano chili, stem, seeds and
> veins discarded, chopped
> 1 small onion, chopped
> 2 cloves garlic, minced
> 1-2 tablespoons chili powder
> Salt and pepper, to taste

1. Spray large skillet with cooking spray; heat over medium heat until hot. Cook tomatoes, poblano chili, onion, garlic, and chili powder until chili and onion are very tender, 8 to 10 minutes.

2. Process mixture in food processor or blender until smooth; season to taste with salt and pepper.

CHICKEN MOLE

Mole, the most popular and traditional of all the Mexican sauces, is usually served with turkey or chicken. Picante with chilies and fragrant with sweet spices, the sauce is also flavored with unsweetened chocolate or cocoa. Even this simplified version of the delicious mole is somewhat time consuming to make, so double the recipe and freeze half!

6 servings

Vegetable cooking spray
6 skinless chicken breast halves
   (6 ounces each)
Mole Sauce (recipe follows)
3 tablespoons finely chopped cilantro

Per Serving
Calories: 192
% Calories from fat: 25
Fat (gm): 5.1
Saturated fat (gm): 1
Cholesterol (mg): 68.6
Sodium (mg): 82
Protein (gm): 27.7
Carbohydrate (gm): 6.8
Exchanges
Milk: 0.0
Vegetable: 1.0
Fruit: 0.0
Bread: 0.0
Meat: 3.0
Fat: 0.0

1. Spray large skillet with cooking spray; heat over medium heat until hot. Cook chicken breasts over medium heat until browned, 8 to 10 minutes. Arrange in large baking pan.

2. Spoon Mole Sauce over chicken; bake, loosely covered, until chicken is tender and no longer pink in the center, about 30 minutes. Arrange chicken on serving platter; sprinkle with cilantro.

Mole Sauce

makes about 1¹/₂ cups

Vegetable cooking spray
2 mulato chilies
2 ancho chilies
2 pasilla chilies
Boiling water
1 tablespoon sesame seeds
2 whole peppercorns
2 whole cloves

1/8 teaspoon coriander seeds
1 1/2 -inch piece cinnamon stick
  1 tablespoon raisins
  1 tablespoon slivered almonds
  1 tablespoon pumpkin seeds
1/4 cup chopped onion
  2 cloves garlic, finely chopped
1/2 small corn tortilla
1/2 small tomato, chopped
1/2-3/4 cup reduced-sodium fat-free chicken
    broth
  1 tablespoon unsweetened cocoa
    Salt, to taste

1. Spray medium skillet with cooking spray; heat over medium heat until hot. Cook chilies over medium heat until softened; remove and discard stems, seeds, and veins. (If chilies are already soft, the cooking step can be omitted.) Pour boiling water over chilies to cover in bowl; let stand 10 to 15 minutes. Drain, reserving 3/4 cup liquid.

2. Spray small skillet with cooking spray; heat over medium heat until hot. Add sesame seeds and spices and cook over medium heat until toasted, 1 to 2 minutes, stirring constantly; remove from skillet.

3. Add raisins, almonds, and pumpkin seeds and cook over medium heat until toasted, 1 to 2 minutes, stirring constantly; remove from skillet.

4. Add onion and garlic to skillet; saute until tender, 2 to 3 minutes.

5. Spray tortilla lightly with cooking spray; cook in skillet over medium heat until browned, about 1 minute on each side. Cool tortilla; cut into 1-inch pieces.

6. Process chilies, onion mixture, and tomato in blender until smooth. Add spice mixture, raisin mixture, reserved chili liquid, and tortilla; process, adding enough chicken broth to make smooth, thick mixture.

7. Spray large skillet with cooking spray; heat over medium heat until hot. Add sauce; stir in cocoa and remaining chicken broth. Heat to boiling; reduce heat and simmer, uncovered, 5 minutes, stirring frequently. Season to taste with salt.

CHICKEN ENCHILADAS MOLE

For variation, the enchiladas can also be baked with Tomatillo Sauce (see p. 203). Serve with Jicama Salad (see p. 623) for fresh flavor contrast.

4 servings (2 each)

8 corn, *or* flour, tortillas
1 cup mild, *or* medium, salsa
1 pound boneless, skinless chicken breast, cooked, shredded
1/2 cup (2 ounces) shredded fat-free Cheddar cheese
1/2 cup sliced green onions and tops
4-8 tablespoons fat-free sour cream
1/4 cup finely chopped cilantro
Mole Sauce (see p. 206)

Per Serving
Calories: 333
% Calories from fat: 15
Fat (gm): 5.9
Saturated fat (gm): 1.1
Cholesterol (mg): 69
Sodium (mg): 752
Protein (gm): 39.1
Carbohydrate (gm): 33.1
Exchanges
Milk: 0.0
Vegetable: 1.0
Fruit: 0.0
Bread: 2.0
Meat: 3.0
Fat: 0.0

1. Dip tortillas in salsa to coat lightly. Spoon chicken along centers of tortillas; top with cheese, green onions, sour cream, and cilantro. Roll up and place, seam sides down, in large baking pan. Spoon Mole Sauce over tortillas.

2. Bake, loosely covered, at 350 degrees until enchiladas are hot through, 20 to 30 minutes.

CHICKEN AND VEGETABLE CREPES

These versatile crepes are sauced with a creamy-textured Hollandaise Sauce. Enjoy the sauce with Eggs Benedict and Artichokes with Hollandaise (see pp. 338, 565).

4 servings (2 each)

Vegetable cooking spray
1 pound boneless, skinless chicken breast, cubed
1 1/2 cups thinly sliced cabbage
3/4 cup thinly sliced celery
1/2 medium green bell pepper, thinly sliced
1/2 cup sliced mushrooms
1/3 cup chopped green onions and tops

Per Serving
Calories: 348
% Calories from fat: 21
Fat (gm): 8
Saturated fat (gm): 2.3
Cholesterol (mg): 126.2
Sodium (mg): 581
Protein (gm): 40
Carbohydrate (gm): 26.8
Exchanges
Milk: 0.0
Vegetable: 2.0
Fruit: 0.0
Bread: 1.0
Meat: 4.0
Fat: 0.0

2-3 teaspoons sugar
  2 tablespoons water
2-3 teaspoons lemon juice
    Salt and pepper, to taste
    Crepes (see p. 692), warm
    Mock Hollandaise Sauce (recipe follows)

1. Spray large skillet with cooking spray; heat over medium heat until hot. Add chicken and cook until browned; add cabbage, celery, bell pepper, mushrooms, green onions, sugar, and water. Cook, covered, over medium heat until cabbage and mushrooms are wilted, about 5 minutes. Cook, uncovered, until vegetables are tender, about 5 minutes longer. Season to taste with lemon juice, salt, and pepper.

2. Spoon vegetable mixture along centers of crepes; roll up and arrange, seam sides down, on serving plates. Serve with Mock Hollandaise Sauce.

Mock Hollandaise Sauce

makes about 1¹/₂ cups

    6 ounces fat-free cream cheese
  ¹/₃ cup fat-free sour cream
3-4 tablespoons fat-free milk
1-2 teaspoons lemon juice
¹/₂-1 teaspoon Dijon-style mustard
  ¹/₈ teaspoon ground turmeric

1. Heat all ingredients in small saucepan over low heat until melted and smooth, stirring constantly. Serve immediately.

CHICKEN AND CABBAGE STRUDEL

Fennel adds an aromatic flavor to the strudel. If fresh fennel is not available, substitute sliced celery and add 1/2 teaspoon crushed fennel seeds to the recipe with the anise and caraway seeds.

6 servings

Vegetable cooking spray
1 pound boneless, skinless chicken breast, cubed
3/4 cup onion, chopped
1/2 cup sliced leek (white parts only)
3 cloves garlic, minced
3 cups thinly sliced cabbage
1 cup sliced mushrooms
1/2 cup thinly sliced fennel
1 cup reduced-sodium fat-free chicken broth
1/2 cup dry white wine *or* reduced-sodium chicken broth
1 teaspoon anise seeds, crushed
1/2 teaspoon caraway seeds, crushed
3/4 cup cooked brown rice
1/4 cup dark raisins
Salt and pepper, to taste
6 sheets frozen fillo pastry, thawed
Anise or caraway seeds, to taste
Fresh Tomato and Herb Sauce (recipe follows)

Per Serving
Calories: 318
% Calories from fat: 12
Fat (gm): 4.3
Saturated fat (gm): 0.9
Cholesterol (mg): 46
Sodium (mg): 432
Protein (gm): 23.6
Carbohydrate (gm): 41.9
Exchanges
Milk: 0.0
Vegetable: 4.0
Fruit: 0.0
Bread: 1.5
Meat: 2.0
Fat: 0.0

1. Spray large saucepan with cooking spray; heat over medium heat until hot. Add chicken and cook until browned, about 5 minutes; add onion, leek, and garlic and saute 3 to 5 minutes. Add cabbage, mushrooms, fennel, broth, wine, and anise and caraway seeds; cook, covered, until cabbage wilts, 5 to 10 minutes. Cook, uncovered, over medium heat until cabbage begins to brown, about 10 minutes. Stir in rice and raisins; season to taste with salt and pepper. Cool.

2. Lay 1 sheet fillo on clean surface; cover remaining fillo with damp towel to keep from drying. Spray fillo with cooking spray; top with 2 more sheets fillo, spraying each with cooking spray. Spoon 1/2 the cabbage mixture across dough, 2 inches from short edge; roll up and place, seam-side down, on greased cookie sheet. Flatten roll slightly; spray with cooking spray and sprinkle with anise seeds. Repeat with remaining fillo and cabbage mixture.

3. Bake at 375 degrees until strudels are golden, 35 to 45 minutes. Cool 5 to 10 minutes before cutting. Trim ends of strudels, cutting diagonally. Cut strudels diagonally into serving pieces. Arrange on plates. Serve with Fresh Tomato and Herb Sauce.

Fresh Tomato and Herb Sauce

makes about 4 cups

     5 cups chopped tomatoes
     1 small onion, chopped
     5 cloves garlic, minced
   1/2 cup dry red wine
     2 tablespoons tomato paste
     1 tablespoon sugar
     2 tablespoons finely chopped fresh, *or* 1 1/2
       teaspoons dried, thyme leaves
     2 bay leaves
   3-4 tablespoons finely chopped fresh, *or* 1 1/2
       teaspoons dried, basil leaves
   1/8 teaspoon crushed red pepper
   1/2 teaspoon salt
   1/8 teaspoon pepper

1. Combine all ingredients, except basil, red pepper, and salt and pepper, in large saucepan; heat to boiling. Reduce heat and simmer, covered, 5 minutes. Simmer, uncovered, until sauce is reduced to medium consistency, about 20 minutes.

2. Stir in basil and red pepper and simmer 5 to 10 minutes. Discard bay leaves; season with salt and pepper.

SPAGHETTI SQUASH STUFFED WITH CHICKEN AND VEGETABLES

Jerusalem artichokes, or sun chokes, add extra crunch to the sauteed vegetables.

4 servings

2 medium spaghetti squash (about 2 pounds each), cut lengthwise into halves, seeded

Olive oil cooking spray

12-16 ounces boneless, skinless chicken breast, cubed

2 medium Jerusalem artichokes (about 8 ounces), peeled, cubed

1 medium onion, chopped

2 medium carrots, diagonally sliced

1 1/2 cups quartered mushrooms

1/2 cup sliced celery

2 cloves garlic, minced

2 teaspoons flour

2 medium tomatoes, coarsely chopped

1/2 cup reduced-sodium fat-free chicken broth

3/4-1 teaspoon dried marjoram leaves

Salt and pepper, to taste

2 green onions and tops, thinly sliced

Per Serving
Calories: 243
% Calories from fat: 12
Fat (gm): 3.3
Saturated fat (gm): 0.8
Cholesterol (mg): 51.7
Sodium (mg): 104
Protein (gm): 24.8
Carbohydrate (gm): 30.8
Exchanges
Milk: 0.0
Vegetable: 6.0
Fruit: 0.0
Bread: 0.0
Meat: 2.0
Fat: 0.0

1. Place squash halves, cut sides down, in large baking pan; add 1/2 inch water. Bake, covered, at 350 degrees until squash is tender, 30 to 40 minutes. Scrape pulp into large bowl, separating strands with fork; reserve shells.

2. Spray large skillet with cooking spray; heat over medium heat until hot. Saute chicken, Jerusalem artichokes, onion, carrots, mushrooms, celery, and garlic until chicken is light brown, about 8 minutes. Stir in flour and cook 1 minute longer.

3. Add tomatoes, broth, and marjoram to skillet; heat to boiling. Cook, covered, until vegetables are tender, about 10 minutes. Season to taste with salt and pepper.

4. Toss chicken mixture with spaghetti squash; spoon mixture into reserved squash shells. Sprinkle with green onions.

CHICKEN À LA KING IN TOAST CUPS

Make this comforting dish with 1 cup chicken and 1 cup lean ham if you prefer. Serve in toast cups, over toasted slices of a hearty multi-grain bread, or over fluffy baked potatoes.

4 servings

2¹/₂ tablespoons margarine
¹/₂ cup chopped green bell pepper
1¹/₂ cups sliced mushrooms
¹/₃ cup all-purpose flour
1¹/₄ cups reduced-sodium chicken broth
1¹/₄ cups fat-free milk *or* fat-free half-and-half
2 tablespoons dry sherry, optional
2 cups cubed cooked chicken breast (10-12 ounces)
¹/₂ cup frozen peas, thawed
1 jar (2 ounces) chopped pimiento, rinsed, drained
Salt and pepper, to taste
Toast Cups (recipe follows)
Minced parsley leaves, as garnish

Per Serving
Calories: 386
% Calories from fat: 24
Fat (gm): 11.7
Saturated fat (gm): 2.3
Cholesterol (mg): 55.7
Sodium (mg): 578
Protein (gm): 32.1
Carbohydrate (gm): 39.1
Exchanges
Milk: 0.0
Vegetable: 1.0
Fruit: 0.0
Bread: 2.5
Meat: 3.0
Fat: 0.5

1. Melt margarine in large saucepan; saute bell pepper 2 to 3 minutes. Add mushrooms and saute until tender, 3 to 4 minutes (do not brown). Stir in flour; cook over medium-low heat, stirring constantly, 1 minute.

2. Stir broth, milk, and sherry into saucepan; heat to boiling. Boil, stirring constantly, until thickened, about 1 minute. Stir in chicken, peas, and pimiento; cook until hot through, 3 to 4 minutes. Season to taste with salt and pepper.

3. Arrange Toast Cups on plates; fill each with about ¹/₂ cup chicken mixture. Sprinkle with parsley.

Toast Cups

makes 8 (2 per serving)

> Vegetable cooking spray
> 8 slices whole wheat, *or* white, bread, crusts trimmed

1. Spray 8 muffin cups and 1 side of bread slices with cooking spray. Press bread slices, sprayed sides up, in muffin cups with 4 corners sticking up.

2. Bake at 350 degrees until browned, 10 to 15 minutes. Serve warm.

Variation: **Ham and Eggs à la King**—Make recipe as above, substituting 8 ounces cubed, trimmed lean smoked ham for the chicken; add 2 chopped hard-cooked eggs. Serve over squares of cornbread.

CHICKEN STEW WITH PARSLEY DUMPLINGS

For variation, omit the dumplings and serve this savory stew over noodles or Real Mashed Potatoes (see p. 592).

6 servings

> Vegetable cooking spray
> 1 cup chopped onion
> 3 carrots, cut into $3/4$-inch pieces
> $1/2$ cup sliced celery
> 3 cups reduced-sodium chicken broth, divided
> $1^1/2$ cups cubed boneless, skinless chicken breast
> $1/2$-$3/4$ teaspoon dried sage leaves
> $1/2$ cup frozen peas
> 2 tablespoons finely chopped parsley leaves
> 5 tablespoons flour
> Salt and pepper, to taste
> Parsley Dumplings (recipe follows)

Per Serving
Calories: 233
% Calories from fat: 20
Fat (gm): 5.1
Saturated fat (gm): 1.4
Cholesterol (mg): 35.5
Sodium (mg): 383
Protein (gm): 19.2
Carbohydrate (gm): 26.7
Exchanges
Milk: 0.0
Vegetable: 2.0
Fruit: 0.0
Bread: 1.0
Meat: 1.5
Fat: 0.5

1. Spray large saucepan with cooking spray; heat over medium heat until hot. Saute onion, carrots, and celery 5 minutes. Add 2¹/₂ cups chicken broth, chicken, and sage; heat to boiling. Reduce heat and simmer, covered, until chicken is cooked and vegetables are tender, 10 to 15 minutes.

2. Stir peas and parsley into stew; heat to boiling. Mix flour and remaining ¹/₂ cup chicken broth; stir into stew. Boil, stirring constantly, until thickened, 1 to 2 minutes. Season to taste with salt and pepper.

3. Spoon dumpling dough into 6 mounds on top of boiling chicken and vegetables (do not drop directly into liquid). Reduce heat and simmer, covered, 10 minutes. Simmer, uncovered, 10 minutes longer.

Parsley Dumplings

> ³/₄ cup all-purpose flour
> 1 teaspoon baking powder
> ¹/₄ teaspoon salt
> 1¹/₂ tablespoons vegetable shortening
> ¹/₃ cup 2% reduced-fat milk
> 1 tablespoon finely chopped parsley

1. Combine flour, baking powder, and salt in small bowl. Cut in shortening with pastry blender until mixture resembles coarse crumbs. Stir in milk to make a soft dough; stir in parsley.

CHICKEN PAPRIKASH

Lean veal can be used in this recipe instead of chicken.

4 servings

1 pound boneless, skinless chicken breast, cut into scant 1-inch cubes
1 tablespoon margarine
1 cup chopped onion
4 cloves garlic, minced
1/2 cup reduced-sodium chicken broth
1/4 cup dry white wine
1 cup chopped tomato
1 teaspoon paprika
2 tablespoons flour
1/4 cup cold water
1/2 cup fat-free sour cream
   Salt and white pepper, to taste
3 cups cooked no-yolk noodles, warm
   Finely chopped parsley leaves, as garnish

Per Serving
Calories: 416
% Calories from fat: 18
Fat (gm): 8.4
Saturated fat (gm): 1.4
Cholesterol (mg): 69
Sodium (mg): 139
Protein (gm): 35.9
Carbohydrate (gm): 47.9
Exchanges
Milk: 0.0
Vegetable: 1.0
Fruit: 0.0
Bread: 3.0
Meat: 3.0
Fat: 0.0

1. Saute chicken in margarine in large saucepan until browned. Add onion and garlic and saute until tender, about 5 minutes. Add chicken broth, wine, tomato, and paprika and heat to boiling; reduce heat and simmer, covered, until chicken is tender, 15 to 20 minutes.

2. Heat mixture to boiling. Mix flour and water; stir into boiling stew. Boil, stirring constantly, until thickened, about 1 minute. Reduce heat to low; stir in sour cream and cook 2 to 3 minutes. Season to taste with salt and white pepper. Serve over noodles; sprinkle with parsley.

CHICKEN-PASTA SKILLET WITH SUN-DRIED TOMATOES AND OLIVES

Sun-dried tomatoes and black olives lend a rich, earthy flavor to this colorful one-dish meal.

4 servings

4 ounces rigatoni

$^1/_2$ cup chopped onion

$^1/_2$ cup chopped green bell pepper

1 tablespoon olive oil

1 pound boneless, skinless chicken breast, cut into 1-inch cubes

1 large zucchini, cubed

1 can ($15^1/_2$ ounces) Italian-seasoned diced tomatoes, undrained

1 teaspoon dried marjoram leaves

3 tablespoons chopped sun-dried tomatoes

2 tablespoons chopped, pitted, oil-cured black, *or* Greek, olives

Salt and pepper, to taste

Per Serving
Calories: 330
% Calories from fat: 25
Fat (gm): 9.1
Saturated fat (gm): 1.6
Cholesterol (mg): 69
Sodium (mg): 761
Protein (gm): 30.9
Carbohydrate (gm): 30.7
Exchanges
Milk: 0.0
Vegetable: 1.0
Fruit: 0.0
Bread: 2.0
Meat: 3.0
Fat: 0.0

1. Cook rigatoni according to package directions, just until barely al dente; drain.

2. In large skillet, saute onion and bell pepper in olive oil until tender; add chicken and cook, stirring, about 5 minutes. Stir in zucchini, tomatoes and liquid, marjoram, sun-dried tomatoes, olives, and cooked pasta. Heat to boiling; reduce heat and simmer, uncovered, until thickened, about 10 minutes.

CHICKEN RISOTTO

While the risotto is cooking, prepare the chicken and vegetables, and dinner will be ready in no time!

4 servings

Microwave Risotto (see p. 476)

12 ounces boneless, skinless chicken breast, cubed

1 tablespoon olive oil

2 cups frozen stir-fry pepper blend

1/4 cup reduced-sodium fat-free chicken broth

1/4 cup dry white wine *or* dry sherry *or* reduced-sodium chicken broth

1 teaspoon dried thyme leaves

1/2 teaspoon dried oregano leaves

Salt and pepper, to taste

Per Serving
Calories: 391
% Calories from fat: 19
Fat (gm): 7.9
Saturated fat (gm): 2.4
Cholesterol (mg): 57
Sodium (mg): 330
Protein (gm): 30.9
Carbohydrate (gm): 42.8
Exchanges
Milk: 0.0
Vegetable: 3.0
Fruit: 0.0
Bread: 2.0
Meat: 3.0
Fat: 0.0

1. Make Microwave Risotto, omitting Parmesan cheese.

2. Cook chicken in olive oil in large skillet until lightly browned. Add remaining ingredients except salt and pepper. Heat to boiling; reduce heat and simmer, covered, until chicken is tender, about 10 minutes. Stir chicken mixture into risotto; season to taste with salt and pepper.

SPICY CHICKEN AND SPANISH RICE

You'll get a taste of the Southwest from this casserole!

4 servings

2 cups instant, *or* boil-in-bag, rice

1 pound boneless, skinless chicken breast, cut into 2-inch cubes

1 can (14 1/2 ounces) diced tomatoes, undrained

1 can (8 ounces) tomato sauce

1 package (10 ounces) frozen corn

3 tablespoons diced pimiento

1 can (4 ounces) diced green chilies, drained

Per Serving
Calories: 415
% Calories from fat: 7
Fat (gm): 3.6
Saturated fat (gm): 0.9
Cholesterol (mg): 69
Sodium (mg): 773
Protein (gm): 32.8
Carbohydrate (gm): 63.2
Exchanges
Milk: 0.0
Vegetable: 1.0
Fruit: 0.0
Bread: 3.0
Meat: 3.0
Fat: 0.0

1/4 teaspoon chili powder
1/4 teaspoon ground cumin
1/8 teaspoon cayenne pepper

1. Combine all ingredients in 2¹/₂-quart casserole. Bake, covered, at 350 degrees until rice and chicken are tender and liquid is absorbed, 50 to 60 minutes.

CHICKEN AND PORK STEW WITH FRUIT

A luscious stew with flavor accents of tropical fruit, sweet cinnamon, and piquant ancho chili.

6 servings

Vegetable cooking spray
12 ounces pork tenderloin, cut into 1¹/₂-inch cubes
12 ounces boneless, skinless chicken breast, cut into 1¹/₂-inch cubes
2 tablespoons slivered almonds
1 tablespoon sesame seeds
1 -inch piece cinnamon stick
3 ancho chilies, stems, seeds, and veins discarded
2 medium tomatoes, cut into 1-inch pieces
1 can (14¹/₂ ounces) reduced-sodium fat-free chicken broth, divided
1 cup cubed jicama
1 cup cubed pineapple *or* 1 can (8 ounces) unsweetened pineapple chunks, drained
1 small ripe plantain, cut into ¹/₂-inch pieces
Salt and pepper, to taste
4 cups cooked rice, warm, optional

Per Serving
Calories: 239
% Calories from fat: 22
Fat (gm): 5.9
Saturated fat (gm): 1.4
Cholesterol (mg): 67.2
Sodium (mg): 81
Protein (gm): 28.1
Carbohydrate (gm): 19.6
Exchanges
Milk: 0.0
Vegetable: 1.0
Fruit: 1.0
Bread: 0.0
Meat: 3.0
Fat: 0.0

1. Spray large skillet with cooking spray; heat over medium heat until hot. Cook pork and chicken over medium heat until browned, about 5 minutes. Remove from skillet.

2. Add almonds, sesame seeds, and cinnamon to skillet. Cook over medium heat until almonds and sesame seeds are toasted, 3 to 4 minutes; transfer mixture to blender container. Add chilies and tomatoes to skillet and cook over medium heat until tomatoes are soft, 1 to 2 minutes; transfer to blender. Add 1 cup broth to blender and process until mixture is smooth.

3. Spray medium saucepan with cooking spray; heat over medium heat until hot. Cook chili mixture over medium heat until slightly thickened, 4 to 5 minutes. Add meat mixture, remaining broth, jicama, and fruit; heat to boiling. Reduce heat and simmer, covered, until meats are tender, about 30 minutes. Season to taste with salt and pepper. Serve over rice.

CHICKEN VERONIQUE

Breast of chicken is cooked in a sauce with mushrooms, capers, white grapes, and wine.

4 servings

2   tablespoons vegetable oil
1   cup sliced mushrooms
3   tablespoons sliced green onions and tops
1   pound boneless, skinless chicken breast, cubed
1   tablespoon flour
1   cup reduced-sodium fat-free chicken broth
1/4   cup dry white wine *or* reduced-sodium chicken broth
1   cup seedless green grapes, halved
1   tablespoon drained capers
    Salt and pepper, to taste
2   cups cooked rice, warm

Per Serving
Calories: 341
% Calories from fat: 27
Fat (gm): 10.1
Saturated fat (gm): 1.8
Cholesterol (mg): 69
Sodium (mg): 184
Protein (gm): 29.6
Carbohydrate (gm): 28.8
Exchanges
Milk: 0.0
Vegetable: 0.0
Fruit: 0.5
Bread: 1.5
Meat: 3.0
Fat: 0.5

1. Saute mushrooms and green onions in oil in large skillet until tender; add chicken and saute 5 minutes or until browned. Sprinkle with flour and cook, stirring, 2 to 3 minutes. Stir in broth and white wine. Heat to boiling; reduce heat and simmer, covered, until chicken is cooked, 5 to 8 minutes.

2. Stir in grapes and capers; season to taste with salt and pepper. Serve over rice.

CHICKEN ATHENOS

Cinnamon and lemon pair up to give this tomato-based stew the signature flavors of Greek cooking. Crumbly feta cheese tops the dish off with an unexpected salty tang.

4 servings

1 pound boneless, skinless chicken breast, cut into 3/4-inch pieces

1 teaspoon olive oil

1 can (14 ounces) reduced-sodium stewed tomatoes, undrained

1 tablespoon lemon juice

2 teaspoons minced garlic

1 cinnamon stick

1 bay leaf

1/4 cup dry sherry *or* reduced-sodium chicken broth

Salt and pepper, to taste

8 ounces medium egg noodles, cooked, warm

1/4 cup crumbled feta cheese

Per Serving
Calories: 412
% Calories from fat: 17
Fat (gm): 7.9
Saturated fat (gm): 2.5
Cholesterol (mg): 124.2
Sodium (mg): 370
Protein (gm): 34.4
Carbohydrate (gm): 46
Exchanges
Milk: 0.0
Vegetable: 2.0
Fruit: 0.0
Bread: 2.0
Meat: 4.0
Fat: 0.0

1. Saute chicken in oil in large saucepan until lightly browned. Add tomatoes and liquid, lemon juice, garlic, cinnamon stick, bay leaf, and sherry. Heat to boiling; reduce heat and simmer, covered, until chicken is cooked through, about 15 minutes. Season to taste with salt and pepper; discard bay leaf and cinnamon stick.

2. Toss chicken mixture with noodles in large serving bowl. Sprinkle with cheese.

CHICKEN AND PASTA STEW WITH MUSHROOMS

The orange-scented tomato sauce, subtly seasoned with herbs and wine, benefits from day-ahead preparation, giving flavors an opportunity to meld.

6 servings

6 small boneless, skinless chicken breast halves (3 ounces each)
Flour
1 tablespoon olive oil
1 small onion, chopped
3 cloves garlic, minced
1 can (14^1/2 ounces) reduced-sodium chicken broth
^{1}/2 cup dry white wine *or* reduced-sodium chicken broth
3 tablespoons tomato paste
2 tablespoons grated orange peel
1 teaspoon dried tarragon leaves
1 teaspoon dried thyme leaves
2 cups sliced mushrooms
^{1}/4 teaspoon salt, optional
^{1}/4 teaspoon pepper
12 ounces pappardelle *or* other wide, flat pasta, cooked, warm

Per Serving
Calories: 343
% Calories from fat: 16
Fat (gm): 6.1
Saturated fat (gm): 1.1
Cholesterol (mg): 43.5
Sodium (mg): 133
Protein (gm): 25.4
Carbohydrate (gm): 42.7
Exchanges
Milk: 0.0
Vegetable: 1.0
Fruit: 0.0
Bread: 2.5
Meat: 2.5
Fat: 0.0

1. Coat chicken breasts lightly with flour. Saute in oil in Dutch oven until browned, about 4 minutes each side. Remove chicken. Add onion and garlic to Dutch oven; saute until tender, 3 to 4 minutes.

2. Add chicken broth, wine, tomato paste, orange rind, and herbs to Dutch oven; heat to boiling. Add chicken and bake, loosely covered, at 350 degrees until chicken is tender, 45 to 60 minutes, adding mushrooms during last 15 to 20 minutes of cooking time. Stir in salt and pepper. Serve over pasta in bowls, topping each serving with a chicken breast.

HUNTER'S STEW

Any game brought back from the hunt was used in this stew of Italian origin.

5 servings

1¹/₃ pound boneless, skinless chicken breast, cut into 1-inch cubes

¹/₄ cup all-purpose flour

1¹/₂ tablespoons olive oil

2 medium onions, chopped

1 medium carrot, coarsely diced

1 cup diced red bell pepper

2 large cloves garlic, minced

1 can (14¹/₂ ounces) reduced-sodium Italian-style chopped tomatoes, undrained

1¹/₂-2 cups reduced-sodium fat-free chicken broth

³/₄ teaspoon dried thyme leaves

³/₄ teaspoon dried marjoram leaves

¹/₄ cup tomato paste

¹/₄ cup water

Salt and pepper, to taste

Per Serving
Calories: 291
% Calories from fat: 24
Fat (gm): 7.9
Saturated fat (gm): 1.5
Cholesterol (mg): 73.6
Sodium (mg): 393
Protein (gm): 32.1
Carbohydrate (gm): 23.8
Exchanges
Milk: 0.0
Vegetable: 3.0
Fruit: 0.0
Bread: 0.5
Meat: 3.5
Fat: 0.0

1. Coat chicken with flour; saute in oil in Dutch oven until browned, about 8 minutes. Stir in onions, carrot, bell peppers, and garlic; saute until vegetables begin to brown, about 5 minutes.

2. Add remaining ingredients, except tomato paste, water, salt, and pepper; heat to boiling. Reduce heat and simmer, covered, until chicken is tender, about 25 minutes. Add tomato paste and water and simmer 5 minutes longer; season to taste with salt and pepper.

CHICKEN AND VEGETABLE CURRY

A variety of spices and herbs are combined to make the fragrant curry that seasons this dish.

4 servings

Vegetable cooking spray
12-16 ounces boneless, skinless chicken breast, cubed
$1/2$ cup chopped onion
2 cloves garlic
1 medium head cauliflower, cut into florets
2 medium potatoes, peeled, cut into $1/2$-inch cubes
2 large carrots, cut into $1/2$-inch slices
$1^1/2$ cups reduced-sodium fat-free chicken broth
$3/4$ teaspoon ground turmeric
$1/4$ teaspoon dry mustard
$1/4$ teaspoon ground cumin
$1/4$ teaspoon ground coriander
1 tablespoon flour
2 tablespoons cold water
1 large tomato, chopped
2 tablespoons finely chopped parsley
1-2 tablespoons lemon juice
Salt, cayenne, and black pepper, to taste

Per Serving
Calories: 250
% Calories from fat: 11
Fat (gm): 3.1
Saturated fat (gm): 0.7
Cholesterol (mg): 51.7
Sodium (mg): 203
Protein (gm): 28.4
Carbohydrate (gm): 29
Exchanges
Milk: 0.0
Vegetable: 2.0
Fruit: 0.0
Bread: 1.0
Meat: 2.0
Fat: 0.0

1. Spray large saucepan with cooking spray; heat over medium heat until hot. Saute chicken, onion, and garlic until chicken is browned, 5 to 6 minutes. Add cauliflower, potatoes, carrots, broth, and herbs to saucepan; heat to boiling. Reduce heat and simmer, covered, until chicken and vegetables are tender, 10 to 15 minutes.

2. Heat mixture to boiling. Mix flour and water; stir into boiling mixture. Cook, stirring constantly, until thickened. Stir in tomato, parsley, and lemon juice; simmer 2 to 3 minutes longer. Season to taste with salt, cayenne, and black pepper.

THAI-SPICED CHICKEN AND CARROTS

Peanut sauce, gingerroot, and sesame oil put plenty of Asian-style pizzazz into this dish. And it's a breeze to make!

4 servings

1 pound boneless, skinless chicken breast, cut into 1/2-inch cubes

4 carrots, thinly sliced on the diagonal

1 tablespoon minced gingerroot

1 tablespoon minced garlic

1 can (14 1/2 ounces) reduced-sodium fat-free chicken broth

1 tablespoon reduced-sodium soy sauce

3/4 cup sliced scallions

1 tablespoon Thai peanut sauce *or* 1 tablespoon peanut butter and 1/2 teaspoon crushed red pepper

1 teaspoon sugar

1/2 teaspoon dark sesame oil

3 cups cooked rice, warm

Per Serving
Calories: 358
% Calories from fat: 11
Fat (gm): 4.3
Saturated fat (gm): 1.3
Cholesterol (mg): 69
Sodium (mg): 371
Protein (gm): 32.8
Carbohydrate (gm): 44.4
Exchanges
Milk: 0.0
Vegetable: 2.0
Fruit: 0.0
Bread: 2.0
Meat: 3.0
Fat: 0.0

1. Combine chicken, carrots, gingerroot, garlic, broth, and soy sauce in large saucepan. Heat to boiling; reduce heat and simmer, covered, until chicken is cooked through and carrots are tender, about 15 minutes.

2. Stir scallions, peanut sauce, sugar, and sesame oil into chicken mixture; cook 5 minutes longer. Serve over rice.

CHICKEN STEW WITH RED WINE

Serve this stew with rice or noodles to soak up the delicious broth.

4 servings

4 boneless, skinless chicken breast halves
2 teaspoons olive oil
1 medium onion, chopped
2 large cloves garlic, minced
1 tablespoon flour
3/4 cup reduced-sodium fat-free chicken broth
3/4 cup dry red wine *or* reduced-sodium fat-free chicken broth
1 bay leaf
1 1/2 teaspoons dried oregano leaves
1/2 teaspoon dried thyme leaves
1/4 teaspoon black pepper
    Salt, to taste

Per Serving
Calories: 207
% Calories from fat: 24
Fat (gm): 5.3
Saturated fat (gm): 1.2
Cholesterol (mg): 69
Sodium (mg): 152
Protein (gm): 26.8
Carbohydrate (gm): 4.7
Exchanges
Milk: 0.0
Vegetable: 1.0
Fruit: 0.0
Bread: 0.0
Meat: 3.0
Fat: 0.0

1. Cook chicken in oil in large skillet until browned on both sides, about 8 minutes. Stir in onion and garlic and saute until tender, about 5 minutes; sprinkle with flour and cook 1 to 2 minutes longer.

2. Add remaining ingredients, except salt; heat to boiling. Reduce heat and simmer, uncovered, until chicken is tender, about 15 minutes; simmer, uncovered, until thickened to desired consistency, 5 to 10 minutes. Discard bay leaf; season to taste with salt.

CALI-FLORIDA CHILI

With this chili, experience a regional "fusion" cuisine that traces its heritage right to the good old U.S.A.

6 servings

1 teaspoon crushed mixed peppercorns, divided

1 pound boneless, skinless chicken breast, cut into 1-inch cubes

4 cups sliced plum tomatoes

1 cup diced sun-dried tomatoes (not in oil)

1 cup Zinfandel *or* other dry red wine *or* reduced-sodium chicken broth

2 dried California chilies, chopped

4 teaspoons chili powder

1 avocado, chopped

2 tablespoons sunflower seeds, toasted
Salt, to taste

6 tablespoons finely chopped fresh purple basil

Per Serving
Calories: 258
% Calories from fat: 30
Fat (gm): 9.2
Saturated fat (gm): 1.8
Cholesterol (mg): 46
Sodium (mg): 272
Protein (gm): 21.5
Carbohydrate (gm): 19.7
Exchanges
Milk: 0.0
Vegetable: 4.0
Fruit: 0.0
Bread: 0.0
Meat: 2.0
Fat: 1.0

1. Sprinkle ¹/₂ teaspoon peppercorns in a medium non-stick skillet; add chicken and saute until pieces are lightly browned.

2. Combine fresh and dried tomatoes, wine, chilies, and chili powder in large saucepan; stir in chicken. Heat to boiling; reduce heat and simmer, covered, 6 minutes. Uncover and simmer until slightly thickened, about 5 minutes.

3. Stir in avocado, sunflower seeds, and remaining ¹/₂ teaspoon peppercorns. Season to taste with salt. Spoon into bowls; sprinkle with basil.

MESQUITE CHICKEN CHILI

Looking for a differently delicious Tex-Mex dish that will appeal to adventurous and not-so-adventurous palates alike? This fast chili will fit the bill. It gets its unique essence from mesquite flavoring and tomatillos.

4 servings

12 ounces boneless, skinless chicken breast, cut into 1/2-inch cubes

1 teaspoon olive oil

1 large onion, chopped

1 can (28 ounces) reduced-sodium crushed tomatoes

1/2 pound tomatillos, husked and coarsely chopped

1 can (15 ounces) red beans, rinsed, drained

1 poblano chili, chopped

2 tablespoons chili powder

2 teaspoons minced garlic

1 teaspoon mesquite smoke flavoring
Salt and pepper, to taste

Per Serving
Calories: 293
% Calories from fat: 15
Fat (gm): 5.3
Saturated fat (gm): 1.1
Cholesterol (mg): 51.7
Sodium (mg): 469
Protein (gm): 28.1
Carbohydrate (gm): 36.3
Exchanges
Milk: 0.0
Vegetable: 2.0
Fruit: 0.0
Bread: 2.0
Meat: 2.0
Fat: 0.0

1.   Saute chicken in oil in large saucepan until lightly browned; add onion and cook until tender. Add tomatoes, tomatillos, beans, poblano chili, chili powder, and garlic. Heat to boiling; reduce heat and simmer, covered, 10 minutes. Stir in smoke flavoring; season to taste with salt and pepper.

CHICKEN CHOWDER HISPANIOLA

Caribbean "fusion" cuisine is hot! And so is this enticing chowder that boasts sofrito, a popular Cuban seasoning, and Spanish favorites like chicken, almonds, and olive oil.

4 servings

12	ounces boneless, skinless chicken breast, cut into $3/4$-inch cubes
1	teaspoon olive oil
1	onion, chopped
1	can (15 ounces) garbanzo beans, rinsed, drained
1	can ($14^{1}/_{2}$ ounces) reduced-sodium fat-free chicken broth
1	can (15 ounces) reduced-sodium diced tomatoes, undrained
2	cups packed fresh spinach leaves
2	tablespoons sofrito sauce, optional
	Salt and pepper, to taste
$1/4$	cup slivered almonds, toasted

Per Serving
Calories: 346
% Calories from fat: 29
Fat (gm): 10.5
Saturated fat (gm): 1.9
Cholesterol (mg): 54.3
Sodium (mg): 639
Protein (gm): 30.5
Carbohydrate (gm): 28.2
Exchanges
Milk: 0.0
Vegetable: 3.0
Fruit: 0.0
Bread: 1.0
Meat: 3.0
Fat: 1.0

1. Saute chicken in oil in large saucepan until lightly browned. Add onion; saute until tender.

2. Add beans, broth, and tomatoes and liquid. Heat to boiling; reduce heat and simmer, covered, 10 minutes. Stir in spinach and sofrito, and simmer 10 minutes longer; season to taste with salt and pepper.

3. Spoon chowder into bowls; sprinkle with almonds.

CHICKEN CORN CHOWDER WITH SWEET PEPPERS

Bright red bell peppers and a few tablespoons of picante sauce are all it takes to transform an ordinary corn chowder into an extra special dish like this one.

6 servings

1 pound boneless, skinless chicken breast, cut into ¹/₂-inch pieces
1 teaspoon olive oil
1 onion, chopped
2 teaspoons minced garlic
2 cups cubed, peeled potatoes
¹/₂ cup reduced-sodium fat-free chicken broth
2 cans (15 ounces each) cream-style corn
1 red bell pepper, chopped
5 tablespoons mild picante sauce
Salt and pepper, to taste
Chopped black olives, as garnish

Per Serving
Calories: 291
% Calories from fat: 17
Fat (gm): 3.9
Saturated fat (gm): 0.7
Cholesterol (mg): 46
Sodium (mg): 536
Protein (gm): 22
Carbohydrate (gm): 45.6
Exchanges
Milk: 0.0
Vegetable: 0.0
Fruit: 0.0
Bread: 2.5
Meat: 2.0
Fat: 0.0

1. Saute chicken in oil in large saucepan until lightly browned; add onion and garlic and saute until tender. Stir in potatoes and broth. Heat to boiling; reduce heat and simmer, covered, until potatoes are tender, about 15 minutes.

2. Stir in corn, bell pepper, and picante sauce. Cook, covered, until hot and slightly thickened, about 10 minutes. Season to taste with salt and pepper. Serve soup in large bowls; sprinkle with olives.

TURKEY CUTLETS WITH SAGE

Sage is delicious paired with turkey—it adds a robust flavor and aroma to this dish.

4 servings

4 teaspoons red wine vinegar
2 teaspoons minced garlic
2 teaspoons dried sage leaves
1 pound turkey breast cutlets
Salt and pepper, to taste
1/4 cup all-purpose flour
2 teaspoons olive oil
1/2 cup reduced-sodium fat-free chicken broth
1 tablespoon lemon juice

Per Serving
Calories: 158
% Calories from fat: 26
Fat (gm): 4.5
Saturated fat (gm): 1
Cholesterol (mg): 44.7
Sodium (mg): 63
Protein (gm): 21.1
Carbohydrate (gm): 7
Exchanges
Milk: 0.0
Vegetable: 0.0
Fruit: 0.0
Bread: 0.5
Meat: 3.0
Fat: 0.0

1. Lay a large sheet of plastic wrap on counter; sprinkle with half the combined vinegar, garlic, and sage. Place cutlets on plastic wrap; sprinkle with remaining vinegar mixture. Sprinkle lightly with salt and pepper. Cover cutlets with second sheet of plastic wrap. Using kitchen mallet or bottom of heavy pan, pound cutlets to flatten. Let stand 5 minutes.

2. Sprinkle both sides of cutlets with flour. Heat oil in large skillet over medium-high heat; add half the cutlets and cook until browned on bottom, about 1 1/2 minutes. Turn and cook on second side until cooked through, about 3 minutes. Remove cutlets to oven-proof serving platter; keep warm. Repeat with remaining cutlets.

3. Heat broth and lemon juice to boiling in skillet; cook until reduced by half. Pour mixture over cutlets; serve immediately.

HOME-STYLE TURKEY STEW

Here's a "thymely" stew that's loaded with tasty vegetables and ready to serve in less than 30 minutes of cooking.

4 servings

12 ounces boneless, skinless turkey breast, cut into ³/₄-inch cubes
2 medium onions, cut into thin wedges
4 ounces mushrooms, halved
2 teaspoons olive oil
2 carrots, sliced
2 potatoes, cut into ³/₄-inch cubes
1 can (14¹/₂ ounces) reduced-sodium fat-free chicken broth
³/₄ teaspoon celery seeds
1¹/₄ teaspoons dried thyme leaves
1 cup frozen peas
Salt and pepper, to taste

Per Serving
Calories: 246
% Calories from fat: 16
Fat (gm): 4.4
Saturated fat (gm): 0.9
Cholesterol (mg): 33.5
Sodium (mg): 158
Protein (gm): 22.1
Carbohydrate (gm): 29.8
Exchanges
Milk: 0.0
Vegetable: 2.0
Fruit: 0.0
Bread: 1.0
Meat: 2.0
Fat: 0.0

1. Saute turkey, onions, and mushrooms in oil in 4-quart saucepan until onions are tender, about 8 minutes. Add remaining ingredients, except peas, salt, and pepper, and heat to boiling. Reduce heat and simmer, covered, until turkey and vegetables are tender, about 15 minutes.

2. Stir in peas; cook 3 to 4 minutes. Season to taste with salt and pepper.

TURKEY-WILD RICE STEW

Get ready to dine on the wild side—the wild side of rice, that is. Actually wild rice isn't really rice at all. It is a long-grain marsh grass that grows in the northern Great Lakes region. In this recipe, we've combined wild rice with another native American food, turkey, to create a super stick-to-your-ribs supper.

4 servings

1 pound boneless, skinless turkey breast, cut into ¹/₂-inch cubes

1 teaspoon olive oil

1 onion, chopped

3 cups reduced-sodium fat-free chicken broth

¹/₂ cup wild rice

2 carrots, thinly sliced

2 cups chopped broccoli florets

1 tablespoon chopped fresh, *or* 1 teaspoon dried, sage leaves

Salt and pepper, to taste

Per Serving
Calories: 250
% Calories from fat: 13
Fat (gm): 3.8
Saturated fat (gm): 0.9
Cholesterol (mg): 44.7
Sodium (mg): 196
Protein (gm): 29
Carbohydrate (gm): 24.6
Exchanges
Milk: 0.0
Vegetable: 1.0
Fruit: 0.0
Bread: 1.0
Meat: 3.0
Fat: 0.0

1. Saute turkey in oil in large saucepan until lightly browned. Add onion and cook until tender. Stir in broth, wild rice, and carrots. Heat to boiling; reduce heat and simmer, covered, until rice is tender, about 45 minutes.

2. Stir in broccoli and sage; simmer until broccoli is tender, about 5 minutes. Season to taste with salt and pepper.

TURKEY SANCOCHE

Sancoche is a hearty stew of meats, fish, vegetables, and seasonings that hails from Latin America. Our one-pot version features turkey, winter vegetables, and black beans, topped with toasted cashews.

4 servings

1 pound boneless, skinless turkey breast, cut into ³/₄-inch cubes

1 sweet potato, peeled, cut into ³/₄-inch cubes

1 white potato, peeled, cut into ³/₄-inch cubes

1 small butternut squash, peeled, cut into ³/₄-inch cubes

1 onion, chopped

1 can (15 ounces) black beans, rinsed, drained

1 can (14¹/₂ ounces) reduced-sodium fat-free chicken broth

1 jalapeño chili, minced

1 teaspoon annatto seeds

1 teaspoon cumin seeds, toasted

Salt and pepper, to taste

¹/₄ cup coarsely chopped cashews, toasted

Per Serving
Calories: 324
% Calories from fat: 18
Fat (gm): 7.2
Saturated fat (gm): 1.5
Cholesterol (mg): 44.7
Sodium (mg): 652
Protein (gm): 29.6
Carbohydrate (gm): 43.7
Exchanges
Milk: 0.0
Vegetable: 0.0
Fruit: 0.0
Bread: 2.5
Meat: 2.0
Fat: 0.0

1. Combine all ingredients, except salt, pepper, and cashews, in 4-quart saucepan. Heat to boiling; reduce heat and simmer, covered, until turkey and vegetables are tender, about 20 minutes. Season to taste with salt and pepper. Spoon into serving bowls and sprinkle with cashews.

TURKEY DIVAN

For real convenience, assemble this casserole in advance and refrigerate up to 24 hours. Then sprinkle with bread crumbs and bake until bubbly, about 40 minutes.

4 servings

1¹/₂ cups cubed cooked turkey, *or* chicken, breast (12 ounces)

  2 cups broccoli florets, cooked until crisp-tender

¹/₃ cup chopped onion

  1 tablespoon margarine

¹/₃ cup all-purpose flour

³/₄ cup reduced-sodium chicken broth

³/₄ cup fat-free half-and-half *or* fat-free milk

¹/₄ cup dry white wine *or* fat-free milk

¹/₄-¹/₂ teaspoon dried savory leaves

¹/₄ teaspoon dried marjoram leaves

2-3 pinches ground nutmeg

  1 cup (4 ounces) shredded fat-free Swiss cheese

Salt, cayenne, and white pepper, to taste

3-4 tablespoons unseasoned dry bread crumbs

Per Serving
Calories: 300
% Calories from fat: **13**
Fat (gm): 4.2
Saturated fat (gm): 0.9
Cholesterol (mg): 70.9
Sodium (mg): 566
Protein (gm): 37.4
Carbohydrate (gm): 22.9
Exchanges
Milk: 0.5
Vegetable: 1.0
Fruit: 0.0
Bread: 1.0
Meat: 3.0
Fat: 0.0

1. Arrange turkey and broccoli in 10 x 6-inch baking dish.

2. Saute onion in margarine in medium saucepan until tender, 2 to 3 minutes. Mix flour and chicken broth until smooth; stir into saucepan with half-and-half and wine. Heat to boiling; boil, whisking constantly, until thickened, about 1 minute. Reduce heat to low; add herbs and cheese, whisking until cheese is melted. Season to taste with salt, cayenne, and white pepper.

3. Pour sauce over turkey and broccoli in baking dish; sprinkle with bread crumbs. Bake at 350 degrees until bubbly, about 25 minutes.

TURKEY POT PIE

So tasty, your family will never realize you're disguising the leftovers from Thanksgiving dinner! Vary the vegetables for this versatile dish according to your family's preferences.

6 servings

Vegetable cooking spray
1 cup chopped onion
1/2 cup chopped green bell pepper
2 1/2 cups reduced-sodium chicken broth
1 cup cubed potato, turnip, *or* parsnip
1 cup sliced carrots
1 cup broccoli florets
3/4 cup small mushrooms
1/2 cup frozen whole-kernel corn
1/2 cup frozen peas
1 pound cooked turkey breast, cubed
1/2-3/4 teaspoon dried rosemary leaves
1/4 teaspoon dried thyme leaves
6 tablespoons all-purpose flour
1/2 cup fat-free half-and-half *or* fat-free milk
Salt and pepper, to taste
Pot Pie Pastry (recipe follows)
Fat-free milk
1 tablespoon grated Parmesan cheese

Per Serving
Calories: 380
% Calories from fat: 17
Fat (gm): 7.1
Saturated fat (gm): 2.1
Cholesterol (mg): 65.5
Sodium (mg): 284
Protein (gm): 32.8
Carbohydrate (gm): 45.1
Exchanges
Milk: 0.0
Vegetable: 0.0
Fruit: 0.0
Bread: 3.0
Meat: 3.0
Fat: 0.0

1. Spray large saucepan with cooking spray; heat over medium heat until hot. Saute onion and bell pepper until tender, about 5 minutes. Add chicken broth, remaining vegetables, turkey, and herbs. Heat to boiling; reduce heat and simmer, covered, until vegetables are tender, about 10 minutes.

2. Heat mixture to boiling. Mix flour and half-and-half; stir into boiling mixture. Boil, stirring constantly, until thickened, 1 to 2 minutes. Season to taste with salt and pepper. Pour into 2-quart casserole or soufflé dish.

3. Roll pastry on floured surface to fit top of casserole; place on casserole, trim, and flute. Cut steam vents in top of pastry. Bake at 425 degrees for 20 minutes. Brush with milk and sprinkle with cheese; bake until golden, 5 to 10 minutes longer. Cool 5 to 10 minutes before serving.

Pot Pie Pastry

> 1   cup all-purpose flour
> 2   tablespoons grated Parmesan cheese
> 2¹/₂-3   tablespoons vegetable shortening
> 3-4   tablespoons ice water

1. Combine flour and Parmesan cheese in medium bowl. Cut in shortening with pastry blender until mixture resembles coarse crumbs. Add water, a tablespoon at a time, mixing with fork just until dough holds together. Refrigerate until ready to use.

TURKEY SAUSAGE-STUFFED ACORN SQUASH

Easy to make, delicious to eat!

4 servings

> 2   acorn squash (about 1 pound each)
>   Vegetable cooking spray
> 1   small onion, chopped
> 1   clove garlic, minced
> 8   ounces Italian-style turkey sausage,
>   casing removed
> ¹/₂   cup chopped tomato
> ¹/₄   cup water
> ¹/₂   cup cooked rice
> ¹/₂   teaspoon dried sage leaves
> ¹/₂   teaspoon dried thyme leaves
>   Salt and pepper, to taste
>   Minced parsley, as garnish

Per Serving
Calories: 263
% Calories from fat: 21
Fat (gm): 6.6
Saturated fat (gm): 1.8
Cholesterol (mg): 30.4
Sodium (mg): 472
Protein (gm): 13.7
Carbohydrate (gm): 43.4
Exchanges
Milk: 0.0
Vegetable: 0.0
Fruit: 0.0
Bread: 3.0
Meat: 1.0
Fat: 0.0

1. Cut squash into quarters and scoop out seeds. Place squash, cut sides down, in baking pan; add ¹/₂ inch water. Bake, covered, at 400 degrees until flesh is fork-tender, about 30 minutes. Drain.

2. Spray large skillet with cooking spray; heat over medium heat until hot. Saute onion, garlic, and sausage until browned, about 5 minutes. Add tomato, water, rice, sage, and thyme. Cook over medium to medium-high heat until mixture is almost dry, about 5 minutes, stirring occasionally. Season to taste with salt and pepper.

3. Spoon mixture over squash quarters and sprinkle with parsley.

JAMBALAYA

This Louisiana favorite can't get much easier to prepare while retaining all that Cajun flavor.

8 servings

2 cups long-grain rice
1-1¹/₂ pounds smoked turkey sausage, sliced
1 pound mushrooms, halved
2 large green bell peppers, chopped
1 large onion, chopped
3 ribs celery, chopped
1 package (10 ounces) frozen sliced okra
1 jar (4 ounces) diced pimientos, undrained
2 cans (14¹/₂ ounces each) reduced-sodium diced tomatoes, undrained
¹/₂ teaspoon cayenne pepper
¹/₂ cup water
1 teaspoon paprika
Salt, to taste

Per Serving
Calories: 324
% Calories from fat: 16
Fat (gm): 6
Saturated fat (gm): 0.5
Cholesterol (mg): 30.9
Sodium (mg): 645
Protein (gm): 15.3
Carbohydrate (gm): 54
Exchanges
Milk: 0.0
Vegetable: 2.0
Fruit: 0.0
Bread: 3.0
Meat: 1.0
Fat: 0.0

1. Pour rice into lightly greased 2¹/₂-quart casserole. Combine remaining ingredients, except water, paprika, and salt, and spoon over rice. Pour water over and sprinkle with paprika and salt. Bake, covered, at 325 degrees until rice is tender and liquid is absorbed, 1 to 1¹/₂ hours.

ITALIAN-STYLE TURKEY SAUSAGE AND FENNEL STEW

A perennial favorite—sweet Italian sausage—perks up this stew of squash, parsnips, and Brussels sprouts. To spice things up a bit more, replace the sweet sausage with the hot variety.

4 servings

Vegetable cooking spray

12 ounces Italian turkey sausage

1 medium onion, cut into thin wedges

1 can (15 ounces) reduced-sodium diced tomatoes, undrained

1 cup reduced-sodium fat-free chicken broth

1 pound butternut squash, peeled, cut into ³/₄-inch cubes

2 parsnips, peeled, sliced

1 fennel bulb, trimmed, cut into ¹/₂-inch slices

12 Brussels sprouts, halved

¹/₂ teaspoon crushed red pepper

1 teaspoon Italian seasoning

Salt and pepper, to taste

Per Serving
Calories: 310
% Calories from fat: 26
Fat (gm): 9.7
Saturated fat (gm): 2.6
Cholesterol (mg): 45.6
Sodium (mg): 780
Protein (gm): 21.8
Carbohydrate (gm): 39.4
Exchanges
Milk: 0.0
Vegetable: 2.0
Fruit: 0.0
Bread: 2.0
Meat: 2.0
Fat: 0.0

1. Spray large saucepan with cooking spray; heat over medium heat until hot. Add sausage and cook until browned, about 10 minutes; remove sausage and slice. Add onion to saucepan; saute until tender, about 5 minutes.

2. Stir in tomatoes and liquid, broth, squash, parsnips, fennel, and sliced sausage. Heat to boiling; reduce heat and simmer, covered, 10 minutes. Stir in Brussels sprouts, crushed red pepper, and Italian seasoning. Simmer until Brussels sprouts are tender, 10-15 minutes. Season to taste with salt and pepper.

RIGATONI WITH TURKEY SAUSAGE AND FENNEL PESTO

Italian and smoked sausages are now being made with "skinnier" ground turkey.

6 servings

1 pound Italian-style turkey sausage
1¹/2 cups thinly sliced fennel bulb *or* celery
1 cup chopped onion
2 cloves garlic, minced
1 can (8 ounces) low-sodium whole tomatoes, drained, chopped
Fennel Pesto (recipe follows)
12 ounces rigatoni *or* other tube pasta, cooked, warm

Per Serving
Calories: 406
% Calories from fat: 29
Fat (gm): 13
Saturated fat (gm): 2.9
Cholesterol (mg): 48.2
Sodium (mg): 711
Protein (gm): 24.6
Carbohydrate (gm): 48.3
Exchanges
Milk: 0.0
Vegetable: 1.0
Fruit: 0.0
Bread: 2.5
Meat: 2.0
Fat: 2.0

1. Cook sausage in large skillet over medium heat until browned, 8 to 10 minutes. Remove sausage from skillet and drain on paper toweling; drain excess fat from skillet. Slice sausage into ¹/2-inch pieces.

2. Add fennel, onion, and garlic to skillet; saute until onion is transparent. Stir in tomatoes and sausage; stir in Fennel Pesto. Heat to boiling; reduce heat and simmer, covered, about 15 minutes.

3. Spoon sauce mixture over pasta and toss.

Fennel Pesto

makes about 1¹/3 cups

1 tablespoon fennel seeds
1 cup chopped fennel bulb *or* celery
¹/2 cup loosely packed parsley leaves
2 cloves garlic
14 walnut halves (about 1 ounce)
3 tablespoons water
1 tablespoon olive oil
¹/4 cup grated Parmesan cheese

1. Place fennel seeds in small bowl; pour hot water over to cover. Let stand 10 minutes; drain.

2. Process fennel, fennel seeds, parsley, and garlic in food processor or blender until finely chopped. Add walnuts, 3 tablespoons water, and oil; process until walnuts are finely chopped. Stir in Parmesan cheese.

ROASTED VEGETABLES, TURKEY SAUSAGE, AND MUSHROOM TORTELLINI

A medley of roasted vegetables and sausage complement pasta in this colorful dish. Substitute ravioli or a shaped pasta for the tortellini if you wish.

4 servings

Vegetable cooking spray
3 medium Italian plum tomatoes
8 ounces small okra, ends trimmed
4 ounces small mushrooms, halved
1 medium zucchini, cut into 1/4-inch slices
1 medium yellow summer squash, cut into 1/4-inch slices
4 ounces broccoli rabe, rinsed, dried, cut into 3-inch pieces *or* broccoli, cut into small florets
12 ounces low-fat smoked turkey sausage, cut into 1/2-inch slices
1 1/2 teaspoons Italian seasoning
Salt and pepper, to taste
1 package (9 ounces) fresh mushroom, *or* herb, tortellini, cooked, warm
1-2 tablespoons olive oil, optional

Per Serving
Calories: 386
% Calories from fat: 30
Fat (gm): 13.5
Saturated fat (gm): 4.1
Cholesterol (mg): 89.1
Sodium (mg): 959
Protein (gm): 28.7
Carbohydrate (gm): 42.2
Exchanges
Milk: 0.0
Vegetable: 3.0
Fruit: 0.0
Bread: 2.0
Meat: 2.0
Fat: 1.0

1. Line large jelly roll pan with aluminum foil; spray with cooking spray.

2. Cut each tomato into 6 wedges; cut wedges in half. Arrange tomatoes, remaining vegetables, and sausage on jelly roll pan; spray generously with cooking spray. Sprinkle with Italian seasoning; sprinkle lightly with salt and pepper.

3. Roast vegetables and sausage at 425 degrees until tender and browned, about 40 minutes, removing broccoli rabe and sausage after about 20 minutes. Combine vegetables, sausage, and tortellini in serving bowl; drizzle with olive oil, if using, and toss.

FIVE

Fish

AND

Seafood

NEW ENGLAND CLAM CHOWDER

Fresh clams can be used in this fragrant clam chowder. Soak 3 dozen clams in cold water to cover for 30 minutes. Heat clams to boiling in a covered skillet with 1/2 cup water; boil until clams have opened, 2 to 4 minutes. Remove clams from shells and add to chowder; discard any that did not open. Strain broth through a double layer of cheesecloth and add to chowder.

6 servings

2 slices bacon
1 cup chopped onion
1 cup chopped celery
1/4 cup all-purpose flour
2 cups clam juice
2 cans (6 1/2 ounces each) diced clams, undrained
1 can (6 1/2 ounces) whole clams, undrained
1 3/4 cups peeled, cubed russet potatoes
1 teaspoon dried thyme leaves
1 bay leaf
1 1/2-2 cups fat-free half-and-half *or* fat-free milk
Salt and pepper, to taste

Per Serving
Calories: 195
% Calories from fat: 11
Fat (gm): 2.3
Saturated fat (gm): 0.6
Cholesterol (mg): 59.2
Sodium (mg): 261
Protein (gm): 13.4
Carbohydrate (gm): 30.3
Exchanges
Milk: 0.0
Vegetable: 0.0
Fruit: 0.0
Bread: 1.5
Meat: 1.0
Fat: 0.0

1. Fry bacon in large saucepan until crisp; drain well, crumble, and reserve. Drain all fat from pan; add onion and celery and saute until tender, 5 to 8 minutes. Stir in flour; cook over medium-low heat, stirring constantly, 1 minute.

2. Stir in clam juice, undrained clams, potatoes, reserved bacon, and herbs; heat to boiling. Reduce heat and simmer, covered, until potatoes are tender, about 15 minutes. Stir in half-and-half; cook over medium heat until hot through, about 5 minutes. Discard bay leaf; season to taste with salt and pepper.

EASY MANHATTAN CLAM CHOWDER

Here's a quick version of the always-popular clam chowder. Marjoram replaces the usual thyme, and gives a subtle flavor twist.

4 servings

2 slices turkey bacon, diced

2 medium onions, chopped

2 potatoes, peeled, cut into 1/2-inch cubes

1 carrot, thinly sliced

1 can (15 ounces) reduced-sodium diced tomatoes, undrained

1 cup clam juice

1 can (6 ounces) minced clams, und-rained

1/2 teaspoon dried marjoram leaves

1/4 teaspoon black pepper

Per Serving
Calories: 187
% Calories from fat: 11
Fat (gm): 2.4
Saturated fat (gm): 0.4
Cholesterol (mg): 33.4
Sodium (mg): 305
Protein (gm): 14.9
Carbohydrate (gm): 27.5
Exchanges
Milk: 0.0
Vegetable: 2.0
Fruit: 0.0
Bread: 1.0
Meat: 1.0
Fat: 0.0

1. Cook bacon over medium-high heat in 4-quart pot until lightly browned. Add onions and saute until tender, about 5 minutes.

2. Add potatoes, carrot, tomatoes and liquid, and clam juice. Heat to boiling; reduce heat and simmer, covered, until carrot and potatoes are tender, 15 to 20 minutes. Stir in remaining ingredients and simmer 5 minutes longer.

CREAMY CLAM AND BROCCOLI CHOWDER

An unforgettable chowder with a smooth, pureed white bean base. Cooking time is less than 10 minutes.

4 servings

2 cups cooked navy, *or* other white, beans, divided

1 can (14 ounces) reduced-sodium fat-free chicken broth, divided

4 teaspoons minced garlic

1 teaspoon olive oil

1¹/₂ cups broccoli florets

2 cans (6¹/₂ ounces each) minced clams, rinsed, drained

4 plum tomatoes, coarsely chopped

2 tablespoons dry white wine

2 tablespoons 2% reduced-fat milk

2 tablespoons snipped fresh dill weed

Salt and pepper, to taste

Per Serving
Calories: 336
% Calories from fat: 11
Fat (gm): 4.1
Saturated fat (gm): 0.6
Cholesterol (mg): 62.2
Sodium (mg): 199
Protein (gm): 36.4
Carbohydrate (gm): 37.6
Exchanges
Milk: 0.0
Vegetable: 1.0
Fruit: 0.0
Bread: 2.0
Meat: 3.0
Fat: 0.0

1. Process 1 cup beans with ¹/₂ cup broth in food processor or blender until smooth.

2. Saute garlic in oil in large saucepan 1 minute. Stir in pureed bean mixture, remaining 1 cup beans, remaining broth, and broccoli. Heat to boiling; reduce heat and simmer until broccoli is crisp-tender, about 4 minutes. Stir in clams, tomatoes, wine, milk, and dill weed. Heat just until hot through, 3 to 4 minutes; season to taste with salt and pepper.

SPICY CRAB AND SCALLOP CHOWDER

Ladle up some fare with flair! The flavor kick in this seafood chowder comes from pickling spice, which is readily available in supermarkets.

4 servings

1 medium onion, chopped
1 stalk celery, chopped
1 tablespoon margarine
1¹/₂ cups clam juice
1 can (14 ounces) reduced-sodium stewed tomatoes, undrained
2 teaspoons pickling spice
1 can (4 ounces) lump crabmeat, drained
¹/₂ pound bay scallops
¹/₄ cup 2% reduced-fat milk
Salt and pepper, to taste

Per Serving
Calories: 144
% Calories from fat: 26
Fat (gm): 4.3
Saturated fat (gm): 0.8
Cholesterol (mg): 50.4
Sodium (mg): 485
Protein (gm): 18.2
Carbohydrate (gm): 8.9
Exchanges
Milk: 0.0
Vegetable: 1.0
Fruit: 0.0
Bread: 0.0
Meat: 2.0
Fat: 0.0

1. Saute onion and celery in margarine in large saucepan until softened. Add clam juice and stewed tomatoes and liquid. Place pickling spice in a mesh tea ball or tie in cheesecloth; add to mixture. Heat to boiling; simmer 2 minutes.

2. Stir in crabmeat and scallops; simmer until scallops are tender and opaque, about 3 minutes. Discard pickling spice. Stir in milk; heat until hot (do not boil). Season to taste with salt and pepper.

CRAB CHOWDER WITH SNOW PEAS

This classy chowder gets its sensual, perfumy essence from jasmine rice, gingerroot, and sorrel. The crabmeat is canned, eliminating the need to pick meat from shells.

4 servings

2 cups clam juice
2½ cups water
½ cup jasmine, *or* long-grain, rice
2 scallions, sliced
1 tablespoon minced gingerroot
2 cans (4 ounces each) lump crabmeat
2 cups snow peas, halved crosswise
1 tablespoon dry sherry
½ cup 2% reduced-fat milk
2 cups torn sorrel leaves
Salt and pepper, to taste

Per Serving
Calories: 209
% Calories from fat: 8
Fat (gm): 1.9
Saturated fat (gm): 0.5
Cholesterol (mg): 52.7
Sodium (mg): 491
Protein (gm): 17.6
Carbohydrate (gm): 28.8
Exchanges
Milk: 0.0
Vegetable: 1.0
Fruit: 0.0
Bread: 1.0
Meat: 2.0
Fat: 0.0

1. Heat clam juice and water to boiling in large saucepan. Stir in rice, scallions, and gingerroot; reduce heat and simmer, covered, until rice is tender, about 20 minutes.

2. Stir in crabmeat and snow peas; simmer for 1 minute. Stir in sherry, milk, and sorrel. Season to taste with salt and pepper.

LOBSTER AND SHRIMP CHOWDER

This chowder is elegant enough for a special dinner party, easy enough for a casual supper, and fast enough for a week-night meal. Cooked lobster and shrimp can be purchased in the seafood department of many supermarkets.

4 servings

2 large Yukon gold potatoes, peeled, cut into 1/2-inch cubes

1 Spanish onion, chopped

1 can (15 ounces) reduced-sodium diced tomatoes, undrained

1 bottle (11 ounces) clam juice

8 ounces cooked lobster meat, cut into small chunks

4 ounces cooked small shrimp

1 teaspoon dried tarragon leaves

1 cup 1% low-fat milk

1/4 cup chopped parsley
   Salt and pepper, to taste

Per Serving
Calories: 210
% Calories from fat: 9
Fat (gm): 2.1
Saturated fat (gm): 0.9
Cholesterol (mg): 100.7
Sodium (mg): 519
Protein (gm): 22.4
Carbohydrate (gm): 25.7
Exchanges
Milk: 0.0
Vegetable: 1.0
Fruit: 0.0
Bread: 1.0
Meat: 2.0
Fat: 0.0

1. Combine potatoes, onion, tomatoes and liquid, and clam juice in large saucepan. Heat to boiling; reduce heat and simmer, covered, until potatoes are tender, about 12 minutes.

2. Add remaining ingredients, except salt and pepper, and simmer 5 minutes. Season to taste with salt and pepper.

CURRIED SCALLOPS AND POTATO CHOWDER

Create a stir with this sensational soup. It's got a lively curry flavor and bright yellow color, and takes less than half an hour to cook.

4 servings

1 bottle (11 ounces) clam juice

1/2 cup dry white wine *or* water

1 pound potatoes, peeled, cut into 1/2-inch cubes

1 teaspoon curry powder

1/2 teaspoon minced garlic

1 pound sea scallops

1 cup frozen peas

1/4 cup 1% low-fat milk

Salt and pepper, to taste

Per Serving
Calories: 251
% Calories from fat: 7
Fat (gm): 1.8
Saturated fat (gm): 0.2
Cholesterol (mg): 49.3
Sodium (mg): 482
Protein (gm): 25.6
Carbohydrate (gm): 29.4

1. Heat clam juice, wine, potatoes, curry powder, and garlic to boiling in large saucepan; reduce heat and simmer, covered, 10 minutes. Add scallops; simmer until scallops are cooked and opaque, 5 to 10 minutes. Remove about half the potatoes and scallops to a large bowl with slotted spoon; keep warm.

2. Process remaining mixture in food processor or blender until smooth. Return mixture to pan. Stir in peas, milk, and reserved potatoes and scallops. Heat until peas are tender and chowder is hot through, about 5 minutes. Do not boil. Season to taste with salt and pepper.

SHRIMP AND SAUSAGE GUMBO

Okra plays a dual role in this fast-to-make version of the bayou favorite, gumbo. It thickens the stew while giving it a characteristic Creole flavor.

4 servings

4 ounces turkey smoked sausage, halved, thinly sliced
1 teaspoon margarine
2 cloves garlic, minced
1 red bell pepper, chopped
8 ounces fresh, *or* frozen, thawed, okra, sliced
2 cans (14 ounces each) reduced-sodium stewed tomatoes, undrained
1 dried cayenne pepper, minced *or* 1/2 teaspoon crushed red pepper
8 ounces medium shrimp, peeled, deveined
   Salt, to taste
3 cups cooked rice, warm

Per Serving
Calories: 316
% Calories from fat: **14**
Fat (gm): 5
Saturated fat (gm): 1.2
Cholesterol (mg): 104.4
Sodium (mg): 395
Protein (gm): 19.9
Carbohydrate (gm): 48.9
Exchanges
Milk: 0.0
Vegetable: 3.0
Fruit: 0.0
Bread: 2.0
Meat: 2.0
Fat: 0.0

1. Saute sausage in margarine in large saucepan until browned; add garlic and saute 1 minute. Stir in bell pepper, okra, tomatoes and liquid, cayenne pepper, and shrimp. Heat to boiling; reduce heat and simmer, covered, until shrimp is cooked through, about 10 minutes. Season to taste with salt. Serve over rice in bowls.

CIOPPINO

Our version of this classic Italian soup is made with shellfish. Clams in their shells are traditionally used, but canned whole clams may be substituted, if you prefer.

6 servings

1 large onion, thinly sliced
1 green bell pepper, diced
1 cup sliced green onions and tops
3 cloves garlic, minced
1 tablespoon olive oil
1 can (14¹/₂ ounces) reduced-sodium diced tomatoes, undrained
1 cup dry white wine *or* clam juice
1 cup water
1 teaspoon dried tarragon leaves
1 teaspoon dried thyme leaves
¹/₄ teaspoon dried rosemary leaves, crumbled
1 bay leaf
1 cup diced fresh tomato
1 pound crabmeat, flaked *or* firm white fish, cubed
8-12 ounces shrimp, peeled, deveined
16 clams in shells, cleaned
Salt and pepper, to taste

Per Serving
Calories: 210
% Calories from fat: 19
Fat (gm): 4.3
Saturated fat (gm): 0.6
Cholesterol (mg): 130.6
Sodium (mg): 276
Protein (gm): 24.1
Carbohydrate (gm): 10.2
Exchanges
Milk: 0.0
Vegetable: 2.0
Fruit: 0.0
Bread: 0.0
Meat: 3.0
Fat: 0.0

1. Saute onion, bell pepper, green onions, and garlic in oil in large saucepan, over low heat, until tender, stirring frequently. Add canned tomatoes and liquid, wine, water, and herbs. Heat to boiling; reduce heat and simmer, covered, 1 hour.

2. Add fresh tomato, crabmeat, shrimp, and clams; heat to boiling. Reduce heat and simmer until shrimp are cooked and clams have opened, about 8 minutes. Discard bay leaf and any clams that have not opened. Season to taste with salt and pepper.

EASY ITALIAN FISH SOUP

A surprisingly simple combination of ingredients yields savory results in this healthful, hurry-up meal. Chicken or vegetable broth can be substituted for the clam juice, although the flavor of the soup will be quite different.

4 servings

1 large onion, chopped
1 large rib celery, chopped
1/2 teaspoon minced garlic
1 tablespoon olive oil
1 can (14 1/2 ounces) reduced-sodium diced tomatoes, undrained
1 bottle (8 ounces) clam juice
1/4 cup dry white wine *or* clam juice
1/4 cup plus 2 tablespoons chopped parsley, divided
1/4 teaspoon dried marjoram leaves
1 pound halibut steaks *or* other lean, firm fish, cut into 1-inch pieces
Salt and pepper, to taste

Per Serving
Calories: 206
% Calories from fat: 27
Fat (gm): 6.3
Saturated fat (gm): **0.9**
Cholesterol (mg): **36.1**
Sodium (mg): 242
Protein (gm): 25.4
Carbohydrate (gm): **9.7**
Exchanges
Milk: 0.0
Vegetable: 2.0
Fruit: 0.0
Bread: 0.0
Meat: 3.0
Fat: 0.0

1. Saute onion, celery, and garlic in oil in large saucepan over medium heat until tender and lightly browned, about 5 minutes. Stir in tomatoes and liquid, clam juice, wine, 1/4 cup parsley, and marjoram. Heat to boiling; reduce heat and simmer, uncovered, 20 minutes.

2. Add halibut; simmer 3 to 5 minutes longer, until fish is tender and flakes with a fork. Season to taste with salt and pepper. Sprinkle with remaining 2 tablespoons parsley.

SEAFOOD SAMPLER

Can't decide whether to buy haddock, scallops, or shrimp? Then get some of each and simmer up this sensibly seasoned chowder. Wonderful with croutons or a chunk of crusty bread.

4 servings

1   yellow bell pepper, chopped
1   medium onion, cut into thin wedges
1   teaspoon olive oil
1   can (15 ounces) reduced-sodium diced tomatoes undrained
2   medium potatoes, cut into 1/2-inch cubes
1/2 cup dry white wine *or* clam juice
8   ounces haddock, cut into 1-inch cubes
4   ounces bay scallops
4   ounces shrimp, peeled, deveined
1   teaspoon herbes de Provence *or* Italian seasoning
1/2 teaspoon celery seeds
1   teaspoon hot pepper sauce
    Salt, to taste

Per Serving
Calories: 231
% Calories from fat: 10
Fat (gm): 2.5
Saturated fat (gm): 0.4
Cholesterol (mg): 88
Sodium (mg): 172
Protein (gm): 23.7
Carbohydrate (gm): 24.7
Exchanges
Milk: 0.0
Vegetable: 1.0
Fruit: 0.0
Bread: 1.0
Meat: 3.0
Fat: 0.0

1.   Saute pepper and onion in oil in large saucepan until lightly browned. Add tomatoes and liquid, potatoes, and wine. Heat to boiling; reduce heat and simmer, covered, 10 minutes. Add seafood, herbes de Provence, and celery seeds. Simmer until fish is tender and flakes with a fork, 10 to 15 minutes. Stir in hot pepper sauce; season to taste with salt.

HALIBUT AND POTATO CHOWDER

This chunky chowder has a thick, flavorful base of pureed vegetables. For a fun change of pace, serve the chowder in a bread bowl—start with a large round loaf of crusty bread, then cut off the top and hollow it out.

4 servings

2	slices turkey bacon
1	large onion, chopped
1	rib celery, chopped
1¹/₂	cups clam juice
4	cups cubed, peeled potatoes
1	teaspoon ground savory
1-2	teaspoons hot pepper sauce
1	carrot, shredded
1	pound halibut, cut into ³/₄-inch pieces
1	cup 1% low-fat milk
	Salt, to taste

Per Serving
Calories: 394
% Calories from fat: 12
Fat (gm): 5.4
Saturated fat (gm): 1.4
Cholesterol (mg): 45.7
Sodium (mg): 430
Protein (gm): 31.4
Carbohydrate (gm): 55.4
Exchanges
Milk: 0.0
Vegetable: 1.0
Fruit: 0.0
Bread: 3.0
Meat: 3.0
Fat: 0.0

1. Cook bacon over medium-high heat in 4-quart saucepan until crisp. Drain on paper towels; crumble bacon and reserve.

2. Add onion and celery to saucepan; saute vegetables until tender, about 5 minutes. Stir in clam juice and potatoes. Heat to boiling; reduce heat and simmer, covered, until tender, about 15 minutes. Using a slotted spoon, transfer half the vegetables to a bowl; keep warm.

3. Using a potato masher or immersion blender, puree the vegetables in the saucepan. Return reserved vegetables to pan; stir in savory and hot pepper sauce.

4. Heat to boiling; add carrot and halibut. Reduce heat and simmer, covered, until halibut is tender and flakes with a fork, 3 to 5 minutes. Stir in milk; heat until hot. Season to taste with salt. Serve chowder in bowls; sprinkle each serving with reserved bacon.

MONKFISH-CHEDDAR CHOWDER

One nibble and you'll be hooked on this rich-tasting, creamy chowder with monkfish, potatoes, and carrots.

4 servings

1 medium onion, chopped

2 teaspoons margarine

1 pound potatoes, peeled, cut into $^1/_2$-inch cubes

2 carrots, thinly sliced

1 can (14 ounces) reduced-sodium fat-free chicken broth

1 pound monkfish, membrane removed, cut into $^3/_4$-inch cubes

$^1/_2$ cup fat-free milk

$^1/_2$ cup (2 ounces)shredded reduced-sodium Cheddar cheese

1 teaspoon hot pepper sauce

Salt, to taste

1 tablespoon chopped fresh chives

Per Serving
Calories: 274
% Calories from fat: 19
Fat (gm): 5.9
Saturated fat (gm): 1.8
Cholesterol (mg): 35.4
Sodium (mg): 344
Protein (gm): 24.9
Carbohydrate (gm): 29.5
Exchanges
Milk: 0.0
Vegetable: 0.0
Fruit: 0.0
Bread: 1.5
Meat: 3.0
Fat: 0.0

1. Saute onion in margarine in large saucepan until softened; add potatoes, carrots, and broth. Heat to boiling; reduce heat and simmer, covered, until vegetables are tender, about 12 minutes. Using a slotted spoon, remove 2 cups vegetables to a bowl; reserve.

2. Process remaining vegetable mixture in blender or food processor until smooth; return to pan. Add fish; heat to boiling. Reduce heat and simmer, covered, until fish is tender and flakes with a fork, 5 to 10 minutes. Stir in milk, cheese, hot pepper sauce, and reserved vegetables. Stir over medium heat until hot, 2 to 3 minutes. Season to taste with salt. Serve in bowls; sprinkle with chives.

SALMON AND ROASTED PEPPER CHOWDER

Salmon aficionados take note—in this recipe, salmon is paired with corn and seasoned with jalapeño chilies, cumin, and oregano for a fast and fabulous feast.

4 servings

2 cups frozen corn

2 medium potatoes, peeled, cut into
¹/₂-inch cubes

2 cups reduced-sodium vegetable broth

2 jalapeño chilies, minced

2 teaspoons minced garlic

1 teaspoon cumin seeds

1 teaspoon dried oregano leaves

12 ounces salmon steaks, cut into 1¹/₂-inch cubes

1 cup chopped roasted red pepper
Salt and pepper, to taste

1 tablespoon chopped parsley

Per Serving
Calories: 259
% Calories from fat: 12
Fat (gm): 3.4
Saturated fat (gm): 0.5
Cholesterol (mg): 42.8
Sodium (mg): 197
Protein (gm): 20.5
Carbohydrate (gm): 36.4
Exchanges
Milk: 0.0
Vegetable: 0.0
Fruit: 0.0
Bread: 2.0
Meat: 2.0
Fat: 0.0

1. Combine all ingredients, except salmon, roasted red pepper, salt, pepper, and parsley, in large saucepan. Heat to boiling; reduce heat and simmer, covered, 10 minutes. Add salmon and simmer until potatoes are tender and salmon flakes with a fork, about 10 minutes. Stir in roasted red pepper; season to taste with salt and pepper. Serve in bowls; sprinkle with parsley.

PASTA AND CRABMEAT SALAD WITH FRUIT VINAIGRETTE

Any firm-textured fish, such as halibut or haddock, can be substituted for the crab meat; surimi (imitation crabmeat) can also be used.

4 servings

6 ounces crabmeat, flaked into ¹/₂-inch pieces

1 small cucumber, peeled, seeded, chopped

1 medium tomato, seeded, chopped

1 cup cooked peas

8 ounces farfalle (bow ties), cooked, room temperature

Fruit Vinaigrette (recipe follows)

Per Serving
Calories: 330
% Calories from fat: 16
Fat (gm): 6.1
Saturated fat (gm): 0.9
Cholesterol (mg): 42.5
Sodium (mg): 267
Protein (gm): 19.4
Carbohydrate (gm): 50.1
Exchanges
Milk: 0.0
Vegetable: 1.0
Fruit: 0.0
Bread: 3.0
Meat: 1.0
Fat: 0.5

1. Combine crabmeat, cucumber, tomato, peas, and pasta in salad bowl. Pour Fruit Vinaigrette over and toss.

Fruit Vinaigrette

makes about ²/₃ cup

¹/₄ cup orange juice

3 tablespoons raspberry red wine vinegar

2 tablespoons lime juice

1 tablespoon olive oil

1 clove garlic, minced

2 tablespoons finely chopped cilantro, tarragon, *or* parsley

1 teaspoon grated lime rind

¹/₄ teaspoon ground nutmeg

¹/₄ teaspoon salt

¹/₈ teaspoon cayenne pepper

¹/₈ teaspoon ground black pepper

1. Mix all ingredients; refrigerate until serving time. Mix again before using.

NIÇOISE PLATTER

Flaked tuna and a garden of vegetables are drizzled with vinaigrette and served with garlic-spiked aioli.

6 servings

12 small red potatoes (about 1¹/₄ pounds)
12 ounces green beans, ends trimmed
 2 large beets
 4 Braised Whole Artichokes (see p. 564)
1-2 hard-cooked eggs, halved
 2 medium tomatoes, cut into wedges
 2 cans (6¹/₈ ounces each) no-salt tuna in oil, well drained
 3 cups mixed salad greens, torn into bite-size pieces
1¹/₂-2 tablespoons sliced ripe olives
 4 teaspoons drained capers
 ¹/₂ cup salt-free, fat-free Italian dressing with herbs
 1 small shallot, minced
 1 clove garlic, minced
 Salt and pepper, to taste
 Aioli (recipe follows)

Per Serving
Calories: 319
% Calories from fat: 23
Fat (gm): 8.3
Saturated fat (gm): 1.5
Cholesterol (mg): 45.7
Sodium (mg): 531
Protein (gm): 24.2
Carbohydrate (gm): 39.6
Exchanges
Milk: 0.0
Vegetable: 2.0
Fruit: 0.0
Bread: 2.0
Meat: 2.0
Fat: 0.3

1. Steam potatoes, green beans, and beets until tender. Cut potatoes into fourths; peel and slice or cube beets. Cool to room temperature. Arrange cooked vegetables, Braised Whole Artichokes, eggs, tomatoes, and tuna on plates lined with salad greens. Sprinkle with olives and capers.

2. Combine Italian dressing, shallot, and garlic; drizzle over vegetables and sprinkle lightly with salt and pepper. Serve with Aioli.

Aioli

makes about 3/4 cup

- 3/4 cup fat-free mayonnaise
- 1 teaspoon tarragon vinegar
- 1 teaspoon lemon juice
- 1/2-1 teaspoon Dijon-style mustard
- 3 cloves garlic, minced
  Salt and white pepper, to taste

1. Mix all ingredients, except salt and pepper; season to taste with salt and pepper.

2. Refrigerate, covered, until ready to use.

TUNA PASTA SALAD

This Italian salad, with artichoke hearts, black olives, and pasta, is a delicious change from the traditional tuna salad. Purchased low-fat dressing may be substituted for the Italian Dressing in the recipe.

6 servings

- 12 ounces penne *or* mostaccioli, cooked, cooled
- 1 can (15 ounces) artichoke hearts, drained, quartered
- 4 Italian plum tomatoes, cubed
- 1 1/2 cups cubed zucchini
- 1/4 cup sliced green onion tops
- 1/4 cup sliced black olives
  Italian Dressing (recipe follows)
- 2 cans (6 1/8 ounces each) solid white tuna in water, drained, flaked
  Salt and pepper, to taste

Per Serving
Calories: 435
% Calories from fat: 29
Fat (gm): 14.1
Saturated fat (gm): 2.1
Cholesterol (mg): 24.3
Sodium (mg): 590
Protein (gm): 23.9
Carbohydrate (gm): 52.7
Exchanges
Milk: 0.0
Vegetable: 3.0
Fruit: 0.0
Bread: 2.0
Meat: 2.0
Fat: 2.0

1. Combine all ingredients, except salt and pepper, in large bowl, tossing until well mixed. Season to taste with salt and pepper. Serve at room temperature, or refrigerate several hours, up to 24 hours, before serving.

Italian Dressing

makes about 1/2 *cup*

- 1/4 cup olive oil
- 1 tablespoon lemon juice
- 1 tablespoon red wine vinegar
- 1 tablespoon water
- 1/2 teaspoon minced garlic
- 1/2 teaspoon dry mustard
- 1/2 teaspoon dried oregano leaves
- 1/2 teaspoon dried thyme leaves
- 1/2 teaspoon sugar

1. Whisk all ingredients in small bowl.

TUNA, FENNEL, AND PASTA SALAD WITH ORANGE VINAIGRETTE

Use the freshest fish possible; haddock, halibut, or salmon are alternatives to the tuna. The orange segments and fennel are fresh-flavor counterpoints to the fish.

6 servings

- 1 pound tuna steaks, grilled *or* broiled, warm
- 1 1/2 cups (6 ounces) conchiglie (shells), cooked, room temperature
- 3 cups torn leaf lettuce
- 2 medium heads Belgium endive, torn into bite-size pieces
- 2 oranges, cut into segments
- 1/2 cup very thinly sliced fennel bulb *or* celery
- 1 small red bell pepper, sliced
  Orange Vinaigrette (recipe follows)

Per Serving
Calories: 296
% Calories from fat: 26
Fat (gm): 8.6
Saturated fat (gm): 1.2
Cholesterol (mg): 33.9
Sodium (mg): 140
Protein (gm): 23.4
Carbohydrate (gm): 31.6
Exchanges
Milk: 0.0
Vegetable: 1.0
Fruit: 0.5
Bread: 1.5
Meat: 2.0
Fat: 0.5

1. Remove skin and any bones from fish and discard; break fish into large chunks.

2. Combine pasta shells, greens, orange segments, fennel, and bell pepper in salad bowl. Pour Orange Vinaigrette over and toss. Add warm fish and toss.

Orange Vinaigrette

makes about 2/3 cup

1/4 cup orange juice
3 tablespoons olive oil
3 tablespoons balsamic vinegar *or* red wine vinegar
2 tablespoons finely chopped shallots *or* red onion
2 cloves garlic, minced
1 teaspoon dried rosemary leaves
1/2 teaspoon fennel seeds, crushed
1/4 teaspoon salt
1/8 teaspoon white pepper

1. Mix all ingredients; refrigerate until serving time. Mix again before using.

SHRIMP DE JONGHE

For an elegant presentation, assemble and bake the shrimp in individual shell dishes.

4 servings

2 tablespoons finely chopped shallots *or* onion
4 cloves garlic, minced
3 tablespoons margarine
2 tablespoons dry sherry, optional
1 tablespoon lemon juice
1/4 teaspoon dried marjoram leaves
1/4 teaspoon dried tarragon leaves
Pinch ground nutmeg
Pinch cayenne pepper
1 cup fresh white bread crumbs
1/4 cup finely chopped parsley leaves
Salt and pepper, to taste
1 pound peeled, deveined shrimp
3 cups cooked rice

Per Serving
Calories: 370
% Calories from fat: 27
Fat (gm): 10.8
Saturated fat (gm): 2.1
Cholesterol (mg): 129.1
Sodium (mg): 287
Protein (gm): 22
Carbohydrate (gm): 42.8
Exchanges
Milk: 0.0
Vegetable: 1.0
Fruit: 0.0
Bread: 2.5
Meat: 2.0
Fat: 1.0

1. Saute shallots and garlic in margarine in medium skillet until tender, 2 to 3 minutes. Stir in sherry, lemon juice, marjoram, tarragon, nutmeg, and cayenne pepper. Pour mixture over combined bread crumbs and parsley in bowl and toss. Season to taste with salt and pepper.

2. Arrange shrimp in single layer in shell dishes or in 10 x 7-inch baking dish; top with crumb mixture. Bake at 450 degrees until shrimp are cooked, about 10 minutes. Serve with rice.

SHRIMP DIANE

This dish of shrimp with white wine, artichoke hearts, and mushrooms is lovely served over rice, couscous, or angel hair pasta.

4 servings

$^1/_2$	cup sliced mushrooms
2	tablespoons minced shallots
1	tablespoon margarine
$^1/_4$	cup dry white wine *or* fat-free chicken broth
1	can (15$^1/_2$ ounces) artichoke hearts, drained, quartered
$^1/_4$	cup chopped chives
$^1/_4$	cup chopped pimiento
12-16	ounces peeled, deveined shrimp
	Salt and pepper, to taste
	Chopped parsley, as garnish

Per Serving
Calories: 149
% Calories from fat: 23
Fat (gm): 3.6
Saturated fat (gm): 0.8
Cholesterol (mg): 130
Sodium (mg): 460
Protein (gm): 17.2
Carbohydrate (gm): 8.2
Exchanges
Milk: 0.0
Vegetable: 1.0
Fruit: 0.0
Bread: 0.0
Meat: 2.0
Fat: 0.0

1. Saute mushrooms and shallots in margarine in large skillet until tender; stir in wine, artichoke hearts, chives, and pimiento. Heat to boiling; reduce heat and simmer, covered, 2 minutes.

2. Stir in shrimp and simmer, covered, until shrimp are tender and pink, 3 to 5 minutes. Season to taste with salt and pepper. Sprinkle with parsley.

SHRIMP WITH GARLIC

The secret to this garlic sauce is to cook the garlic very slowly. The sauce is also excellent served over grilled or baked fish fillets or steaks.

4 servings

1 pound peeled, deveined shrimp
2-3 tablespoons lime juice
1 large head garlic
2 tablespoons olive, *or* vegetable, oil
Salt and pepper, to taste
2 tablespoons finely chopped cilantro
Yellow Salsa Rice (see p. 465)
4 corn, *or* flour, tortillas

Per Serving
Calories: 388
% Calories from fat: 20
Fat (gm): 8.5
Saturated fat (gm): 1.3
Cholesterol (mg): 131.6
Sodium (mg): 340
Protein (gm): 21.7
Carbohydrate (gm): 55.1
Exchanges
Milk: 0.0
Vegetable: 0.0
Fruit: 0.0
Bread: 3.5
Meat: 2.5
Fat: 0.0

1. Arrange shrimp in glass dish; sprinkle with lime juice and refrigerate, covered, 30 minutes.

2. Peel garlic cloves and cut into halves. Heat oil in medium skillet until hot; add garlic and cook over low heat until garlic is soft and golden, 15 to 20 minutes. Remove garlic from skillet with slotted spoon and reserve.

3. Add shrimp to skillet; cook over medium to medium-high heat until shrimp are tender and pink, about 5 minutes. Return garlic to skillet; cook and stir over low heat 1 to 2 minutes. Season to taste with salt and pepper; sprinkle with cilantro. Serve with Yellow Salsa Rice and tortillas.

SPRING VEGETABLE AND SHRIMP STIR-FRY

The best of spring's bounty, seasoned with fresh ginger, sesame oil, and tamari soy sauce.

4 servings

Oriental-flavored vegetable cooking spray

1 medium onion, sliced

4-6 small red potatoes, cut into $1/4$-inch slices

1 cup sliced mushrooms

1 pound asparagus, cut into $1^1/2$-inch pieces

$1/2$ cup chopped red bell pepper

2 cloves garlic, minced

2-4 teaspoons minced gingerroot

$1/2$ cup reduced-sodium fat-free chicken broth

12-16 ounces peeled deveined shrimp

4 teaspoons cornstarch

$1/4$ cup cold water

1-2 tablespoons reduced-sodium tamari soy sauce

1-2 teaspoons dark sesame oil

Salt and pepper, to taste

3 cups cooked brown and wild rice

1 teaspoon toasted sesame seeds

Per Serving
Calories: 310
% Calories from fat: 10
Fat (gm): 3.5
Saturated fat (gm): 0.5
Cholesterol (mg): 130
Sodium (mg): 537
Protein (gm): 23
Carbohydrate (gm): 48.9
Exchanges
Milk: 0.0
Vegetable: 3.0
Fruit: 0.0
Bread: 2.0
Meat: 2.0
Fat: 0.0

1. Spray wok or large skillet with cooking spray; heat over medium heat until hot. Stir-fry onion, potatoes, and mushrooms 3 to 5 minutes. Add asparagus, bell pepper, garlic, and gingerroot to wok; stir-fry 5 minutes.

2. Add broth to wok and heat to boiling; add shrimp. Reduce heat and simmer, covered, until vegetables are crisp-tender, and shrimp are cooked, 3 to 5 minutes. Heat to boiling; stir in combined cornstarch and water. Boil, stirring constantly, until thickened, about 1 minute. Stir in soy sauce and sesame oil; season to taste with salt and pepper.

3. Spoon mixture over rice on serving platter; sprinkle with sesame seeds.

SHRIMP AND CHEESE ROTOLI WITH MANY-CLOVES GARLIC SAUCE

Some people prefer cutting the lasagne noodles into halves before filling, as they are easier to handle in eating. If cut, spread each noodle half with ¹/₂ to 2 tablespoons of the cheese mixture.

6 servings

1	pound peeled, deveined shrimp, cooked, chopped
1¹/₄	cups reduced-fat ricotta cheese
3-4	cloves garlic, minced
³/₄	teaspoon dried marjoram leaves
¹/₂	teaspoon dried thyme leaves
¹/₂	teaspoon salt
¹/₄	teaspoon pepper
12	lasagne noodles (10 ounces), cooked, room temperature
	Many-Cloves Garlic Sauce (see p. 23)

Per Serving
Calories: 323
% Calories from fat: 16
Fat (gm): 5.9
Saturated fat (gm): 1.7
Cholesterol (mg): 128.1
Sodium (mg): 403
Protein (gm): 25
Carbohydrate (gm): 40
Exchanges
Milk: 0.0
Vegetable: 0.0
Fruit: 0.0
Bread: 2.0
Meat: 3.0
Fat: 0.0

1. Mix shrimp, cheese, garlic, herbs, salt, and pepper. Spread 3 to 4 tablespoons of mixture evenly on each noodle; roll up and place in baking dish.

2. Spoon Many Cloves Garlic Sauce over rotoli. Bake, loosely covered with aluminum foil, at 350 degrees until rotoli are hot through and sauce is bubbly, 20 to 30 minutes.

SHRIMP TOSTADAS

A perfect brunch or lunch entrée, South-of-the-Border style! Serve with Zucchini from Puebla, Yellow Salsa Rice, or Refried Beans (see pp. 609, 465, 447).

4 servings

Vegetable cooking spray
4 corn tortillas
12-16 ounces peeled, deveined medium shrimp
1 small onion, chopped
1/2 serrano chili, seeds and veins discarded, finely chopped
1 cup Chili Tomato Sauce (see p. 201), warm
2 cups chopped romaine lettuce
1 medium tomato, chopped
1/4 cup crumbled fat-free feta, *or* Mexican white, cheese
1/3 cup Guacamole (1/2 recipe) (see p. 36)

Per Serving
Calories: 216
% Calories from fat: 19
Fat (gm): 4.7
Saturated fat (gm): 0.4
Cholesterol (mg): 130
Sodium (mg): 292
Protein (gm): 21.5
Carbohydrate (gm): 24.3
Exchanges
Milk: 0.0
Vegetable: 1.0
Fruit: 0.0
Bread: 1.0
Meat: 2.0
Fat: 0.0

1. Spray medium skillet with cooking spray; heat over medium heat until hot. Cook tortillas until crisp and browned, about 1 minute on each side. Place tortillas on serving plates.

2. Leave 4 shrimp whole for garnish; cut remaining shrimp into halves or thirds. Spray medium saucepan with cooking spray; heat over medium heat until hot. Cook whole and cut-up shrimp, onion, and serrano chili until shrimp are cooked and pink, 3 to 5 minutes. Remove the 4 whole shrimp and reserve. Stir Chili Tomato Sauce into remaining shrimp mixture.

3. Top tortillas with chopped lettuce and tomato; spoon shrimp mixture over. Sprinkle with crumbled cheese; top each with a large dollop of Guacamole and a whole shrimp.

SHRIMP AND CRAB ENCHILADAS WITH PASILLA CHILI SAUCE

The rich Pasilla Chili Sauce is creamy in texture, slightly smoky in flavor; it would be excellent served with grilled chicken breast or lean pork.

4 servings (2 enchiladas each)

8	ounces peeled, deveined shrimp, cooked, coarsely chopped
4	ounces Alaskan King crabmeat *or* peeled, deveined shrimp
	Pasilla Chili Sauce (recipe follows)
8	flour tortillas
1/2	cup (2 ounces) shredded fat-free Cheddar cheese
1/4	cup finely chopped cilantro

Per Serving
Calories: 318
% Calories from fat: 13
Fat (gm): 4.5
Saturated fat (gm): 0.7
Cholesterol (mg): 101.9
Sodium (mg): 722
Protein (gm): 28.3
Carbohydrate (gm): 41.2
Exchanges
Milk: 0.0
Vegetable: 0.5
Fruit: 0.0
Bread: 2.0
Meat: 3.0
Fat: 0.0

1. Combine shrimp, crabmeat, and 3/4 cup Pasilla Chili Sauce. Divide mixture on tortillas and roll up. Place tortillas, seam sides down, in lightly greased glass baking dish, 11 x 7 inches. Spoon remaining Pasilla Chili Sauce over enchiladas; sprinkle with cheese.

2. Bake enchiladas, uncovered, at 350 degrees until hot through, about 20 minutes. Sprinkle with cilantro.

Pasilla Chili Sauce

makes about 2 cups

	Vegetable cooking spray
3	pasilla chilies
2	medium tomatoes, coarsely chopped
1	small onion, coarsely chopped
1/2	teaspoon sugar
1	cup fat-free sour cream
	Salt and pepper, to taste

1. Spray small skillet with cooking spray; heat over medium heat until hot. Cook chilies over medium heat until soft; remove and discard stems, seeds, and veins. Process chilies, tomatoes, onion, and sugar in blender until smooth.

2. Spray large skillet with cooking spray; heat over medium heat until hot. Cook chili mixture over medium heat, stirring occasionally, until thickened, about 5 minutes. Reduce heat to low; stir in sour cream and cook until hot through. Season to taste with salt and pepper.

SEAFOOD NEWBURG

Any shellfish or lean white fish can be used in this classic Newburg.

4 servings

- 8 ounces peeled, deveined shrimp
- 8 ounces bay scallops
- 1/2 cup water
- 1/4 cup finely chopped shallots *or* onion
- 2 tablespoons margarine
- 1/4 cup all-purpose flour
- 1 1/2 cups fat-free half-and-half *or* fat-free milk
- 1 egg yolk
- 1-2 tablespoons dry sherry, optional
  Pinch ground nutmeg
  Pinch cayenne pepper
  Salt and white pepper, to taste
- 4 slices toast, cut diagonally into halves
  Finely chopped parsley, as garnish

Per Serving
Calories: 326
% Calories from fat: 26
Fat (gm): 9.1
Saturated fat (gm): 1.8
Cholesterol (mg): 164.8
Sodium (mg): 495
Protein (gm): 26.7
Carbohydrate (gm): 29.9
Exchanges
Milk: 0.8
Vegetable: 0.0
Fruit: 0.0
Bread: 2.0
Meat: 3.0
Fat: 0.5

1. Simmer shrimp and scallops in 1/2 cup water in small saucepan, covered, until cooked, 3 to 5 minutes. Drain, reserving liquid.

2. Saute shallots in margarine in medium saucepan until tender, 2 to 3 minutes. Mix in flour and cook 1 to 2 minutes. Whisk in half-and-half and reserved cooking liquid; heat to boiling. Boil, whisking constantly, until thickened, about 1 minute. Whisk about half the mixture into egg yolk in small bowl; whisk egg mixture into saucepan. Cook over very low heat, whisking constantly, 30 seconds.

3. Stir in shrimp, scallops, sherry, nutmeg, and cayenne pepper; cook 2 to 3 minutes. Season to taste with salt and white pepper.

4. Arrange toast points on serving plates; spoon mixture over and sprinkle with parsley.

SCALLOPS WITH APPLES AND PEA PODS

This delicious and elegant entrée can be cooked in less than 15 minutes! Serve over steamed rice, rice noodles, or Chinese egg noodles.

4 servings

3 small apples, unpeeled, thinly sliced
1 medium onion, chopped
1 medium red bell pepper, chopped
3 ounces snow peas, trimmed
2 tablespoons vegetable oil, divided
12 ounces scallops
1/4 cup apple cider
2 teaspoons cornstarch
1 tablespoon reduced-sodium soy sauce
   Salt and pepper, to taste

Per Serving
Calories: 238
% Calories from fat: 30
Fat (gm): 8.3
Saturated fat (gm): 1
Cholesterol (mg): 36.2
Sodium (mg): 315
Protein (gm): 17.5
Carbohydrate (gm): 26
Exchanges
Milk: 0.0
Vegetable: 0.0
Fruit: 1.5
Bread: 0.0
Meat: 2.0
Fat: 1.0

1. Stir-fry apples, onion, bell pepper, and pea pods in 1 tablespoon oil in wok or large skillet over medium-high heat until crisp-tender, about 3 minutes. Remove from wok.

2. Stir-fry scallops in wok in remaining 1 tablespoon oil until cooked and opaque, about 4 minutes. Stir in combined cider, cornstarch, and soy sauce, and cook until mixture boils and thickens, 1 to 2 minutes. Stir in apple mixture; heat to boiling. Season to taste with salt and pepper.

CRAB CAKES WITH POBLANO CHILI SAUCE

Shrimp or imitation crabmeat can easily be substituted for all or part of the crab.

4 servings

12 ounces Alaskan king crabmeat *or* peeled, deveined, cooked shrimp, finely chopped

$^1/_2$ small onion, finely chopped

$^1/_2$ medium tomato, finely chopped

$^1/_2$ small jalapeño chili, seeds and veins discarded, minced

1 egg white

2-4 tablespoons unseasoned dry bread crumbs

$^1/_2$ teaspoon dried oregano leaves

$^1/_2$ teaspoon salt, optional

Flour or unseasoned dry bread crumbs

Vegetable Cooking Spray

$^1/_2$ cup Poblano Chili Sauce ($^1/_4$ recipe) (see p. 205)

Per Serving
Calories: 133
% Calories from fat: 10
Fat (gm): 1.4
Saturated fat (gm): 0.2
Cholesterol (mg): 35.7
Sodium (mg): 793
Protein (gm): 18.6
Carbohydrate (gm): 12.1
Exchanges
Milk: 0.0
Vegetable: 2.0
Fruit: 0.0
Bread: 0.0
Meat: 2.0
Fat: 0.0

1. Combine crabmeat, onion, tomato, jalapeño chili, and egg white in small bowl; mix in bread crumbs, oregano, and salt. Form mixture into 4 patties about $^1/_2$ inch thick; coat lightly with flour or bread crumbs.

2. Spray large skillet with cooking spray; heat over medium heat until hot. Cook patties over medium heat until cooked through and lightly browned, 3 to 4 minutes on each side.

3. Arrange crab cakes on serving dish; spoon Poblano Chili Sauce over.

POACHED SALMON WITH HOLLANDAISE SAUCE

This delicious offering can be served warm or cold depending upon the occasion and the season of the year.

6 servings

³/4 cup dry white wine *or* clam juice
¹/2 cup water
   2 thin slices onion
   4 dill, *or* parsley, sprigs
¹/4 teaspoon dried thyme leaves
¹/4 teaspoon dried tarragon leaves
   1 bay leaf
   4 peppercorns
¹/2 teaspoon salt
   4 small salmon steaks (3¹/2-4 ounces each)
     Mock Hollandaise Sauce (see p. 209)
     Finely chopped parsley leaves, as garnish
   4 lemon wedges

Per Serving
Calories: 195
% Calories from fat: 30
Fat (gm): 6.2
Saturated fat (gm): 0.9
Cholesterol (mg): 53.3
Sodium (mg): 351
Protein (gm): 26.9
Carbohydrate (gm): 4.2
Exchanges
Milk: 0.5
Vegetable: 0.0
Fruit: 0.0
Bread: 0.0
Meat: 3.0
Fat: 0.0

1.   Heat wine, water, onion, herbs, and salt to boiling in medium skillet. Reduce heat and simmer, covered, 5 minutes.

2.   Add salmon to skillet; simmer, covered, until fish is cooked and flakes with a fork, 6 to 10 minutes, depending upon thickness of fish. Carefully remove fish from skillet with slotted pancake turner.

3.   Arrange salmon on serving platter and spoon Mock Hollandaise Sauce over; sprinkle with parsley. Serve with lemon wedges.

FLOUNDER EN PAPILLOTE

A lovely presentation, yet very simple to prepare. This recipe, traditionally made with a lean white fish, is also very delicious with other fish, such as salmon or tuna.

6 servings

6 flounder, sole, *or* other lean white fish fillets (1¹/₂ pounds)
Salt and pepper, to taste
1 cup julienned, *or* shredded, carrots
1 cup sliced mushrooms
¹/₄ cup finely chopped shallots *or* onion
2 cloves garlic, minced
¹/₂ teaspoon dried tarragon leaves
2 teaspoons margarine
¹/₂ cup dry white wine *or* water
¹/₄ cup finely chopped parsley leaves
6 lemon wedges

Per Serving
Calories: 149
% Calories from fat: 17
Fat (gm): 2.8
Saturated fat (gm): 0.6
Cholesterol (mg): 59.8
Sodium (mg): 118
Protein (gm): 22.3
Carbohydrate (gm): 5.7
Exchanges
Milk: 0.0
Vegetable: 1.0
Fruit: 0.0
Bread: 0.0
Meat: 2.5
Fat: 0.0

1. Cut six 12-inch squares of parchment paper. Fold in half, and cut each into a large heart shape. Open hearts and place 1 fish fillet on each; sprinkle lightly with salt and pepper.

2. Saute carrots, mushrooms, shallots, garlic, and tarragon in margarine in large skillet until carrots are crisp-tender, about 5 minutes. Stir in wine and parsley; season to taste with salt and pepper.

3. Spoon vegetable mixture over fish. Fold heart packets in half, bringing edges together. Crimp edges tightly to seal. Place packets on jelly roll pan, and bake at 425 degrees until packets puff, 10 to 12 minutes. Serve with lemon wedges.

Note: Aluminum foil can be used in place of parchment paper; bake fish 15 minutes.

TUNA STEAKS WITH SWEET-AND-SOUR TOMATO-BASIL RELISH

Spicy tomato relish nicely complements grilled tuna in this easy but elegant recipe.

4 servings

   2 teaspoons olive oil
   1 teaspoon minced garlic
   1 teaspoon lemon juice
 1/2 teaspoon dried basil leaves
 1/2 teaspoon dried thyme leaves
   4 tuna steaks (about 4 ounces each)
    Salt and pepper, to taste
    Sweet-and-Sour Tomato-Basil Relish
    (recipe follows)

Per Serving
Calories: 182
% Calories from fat: 23
Fat (gm): 4.6
Saturated fat (gm): 0.7
Cholesterol (mg): 49.4
Sodium (mg): 108
Protein (gm): 26.2
Carbohydrate (gm): 8.4
Exchanges
Milk: 0.0
Vegetable: 1.0
Fruit: 0.0
Bread: 0.0
Meat: 3.0
Fat: 0.0

1. Combine olive oil, garlic, lemon juice, and herbs in small bowl.

2. Broil fish 5 inches from heat source 10 minutes; turn. Brush with oil mixture; sprinkle lightly with salt and pepper. Broil until fish is tender and flakes with a fork, 6 to 10 minutes. Serve with Sweet-and-Sour Tomato-Basil Relish.

Sweet-and-Sour Tomato-Basil Relish

makes about 1 cup

   2 tablespoons tomato paste
1 1/2 tablespoons red wine vinegar
 1/2 tablespoon water
1 1/2 tablespoons sugar
   1 teaspoon olive oil
 1/4 teaspoon dried basil leaves
 1/4 teaspoon dried thyme leaves
    Olive oil cooking spray
   1 large tomato, seeded, cubed

1. Whisk tomato paste, vinegar, and water in small bowl until smooth. Whisk in sugar, olive oil, and herbs. Reserve.

2. Just before fish is cooked, spray small skillet with cooking spray; heat pan over medium-high heat. Add tomato and stir briefly until seared. Stir into reserved tomato paste mixture.

FRIED HALIBUT WITH SOUR CREAM AND POBLANO SAUCE

The versatile Sour Cream and Poblano Sauce is also excellent served with shredded chicken breast or lean pork in soft tacos, or served over favorite enchiladas.

4 servings

1 pound halibut steaks
3 tablespoons lime juice
1 clove garlic, minced
1-2 tablespoons flour
Vegetable cooking spray
Salt and pepper, to taste
Sour Cream and Poblano Sauce (recipe follows)
Finely chopped cilantro, as garnish
4 lime wedges

Per Serving
Calories: 184
% Calories from fat: 13
Fat (gm): 2.7
Saturated fat (gm): 0.4
Cholesterol (mg): 36.4
Sodium (mg): 101
Protein (gm): 28.2
Carbohydrate (gm): 11.9
Exchanges
Milk: 0.0
Vegetable: 1.0
Fruit: 0.0
Bread: 0.0
Meat: 3.0
Fat: 0.0

1. Place fish in glass baking dish. Combine lime juice and garlic; brush over fish. Refrigerate, covered, 1 hour.

2. Pat fish dry; coat lightly with flour. Generously spray large skillet with cooking spray; heat over medium heat until hot. Cook over medium heat until fish is lightly browned and flakes with a fork, 4 to 5 minutes on each side. Season lightly with salt and pepper.

3. Arrange fish on serving platter; spoon Sour Cream and Poblano Sauce over. Sprinkle with cilantro; serve with lime wedges.

Sour Cream and Poblano Sauce

makes about 1 cup

Vegetable cooking spray
1 large poblano chili, veins and seeds discarded, thinly sliced
1 small onion, finely chopped
2 cloves garlic, minced
1 cup fat-free sour cream
1/4 teaspoon ground cumin
Salt and pepper, to taste

1. Spray small saucepan with cooking spray; heat over medium heat until hot. Saute poblano chili, onion, and garlic until very tender, about 5 minutes. Stir in sour cream and cumin; cook over low heat until hot through, 2 to 3 minutes. Season to taste with salt and pepper.

GRILLED FISH WITH CHILI PASTE

Dried ancho and pasilla chilies and vinegar combine to create a piquant seasoning for the fish.

4 servings

1 pound fish fillets (red snapper, tuna, *or* any firm-fleshed fish)
  Chili Paste (recipe follows)
1 green onion and top, sliced
4 lime wedges

Per Serving
Calories: 133
% Calories from fat: 11
Fat (gm): 1.5
Saturated fat (gm): 0.3
Cholesterol (mg): 41.6
Sodium (mg): 377
Protein (gm): 23.4
Carbohydrate (gm): 4.6
Exchanges
Milk: 0.0
Vegetable: 0.5
Fruit: 0.0
Bread: 0.0
Meat: 2.5
Fat: 0.0

1. Spread top of fish with Chili Paste. Grill over medium-hot coals or broil 6 inches from heat source until fish is tender and flakes with a fork, 10 to 15 minutes, depending upon thickness of fish.

2. Arrange fish on serving platter; sprinkle with green onion. Serve with lime wedges.

Chili Paste

makes about 1/4 cup

    Vegetable cooking spray
1 ancho chili
1 pasilla chili
2 cloves garlic
1/2 teaspoon salt
1 tablespoon white wine vinegar
    Water

1. Spray medium skillet with cooking spray; heat over medium heat until hot. Cook chilies over medium heat until softened, 1 to 2 minutes. Remove and discard stems, seeds, and veins.

2. Process chilies, garlic, salt, and vinegar in food processor or blender, adding very small amount of water, if necessary to make smooth paste.

RED SNAPPER BAKED WITH CILANTRO

Tuna, salmon, cod, or any firm-fleshed white fish can be used in this recipe.

6 servings

1 1/2 pounds red snapper fillets *or* steaks
1/3 cup lime juice
1 1/2 tablespoons pickled jalapeño chili juice
1 teaspoon ground cumin
1 medium onion, thinly sliced
2 pickled jalapeño chilies, minced
2 cloves garlic, minced
1 cup coarsely chopped cilantro
Salt and pepper, to taste
Thinly sliced green onion and top, as garnish
6 lime wedges

Per Serving
Calories: 135
% Calories from fat: 12
Fat (gm): 1.7
Saturated fat (gm): 0.3
Cholesterol (mg): 41.6
Sodium (mg): 169
Protein (gm): 24
Carbohydrate (gm): 5
Exchanges
Milk: 0.0
Vegetable: 0.0
Fruit: 0.0
Bread: 0.0
Meat: 3.0
Fat: 0.0

1. Arrange fish in glass baking dish. Combine lime juice, jalapeño juice, and cumin; pour over fish. Arrange onion, jalapeño chilies, garlic, and cilantro over fish. Refrigerate, covered, 2 hours, turning fish once.

2. Bake, uncovered, at 400 degrees until fish is tender and flakes with a fork, about 10 minutes. Sprinkle fish lightly with salt and pepper. Arrange fish on serving platter; sprinkle with green onion and serve with lime wedges.

RED SNAPPER VERACRUZ

In this famous dish from Veracruz, Mexico, red snapper is baked in a full-flavored tomato sauce with olives and capers. The fish can also be grilled or baked, then topped with the sauce.

6 servings

1 whole red snapper, dressed (about 2 pounds)
2 tablespoons lime juice
2 cloves garlic, minced
  Veracruz Sauce (recipe follows)
6 lime wedges

Per Serving
Calories: 198
% Calories from fat: 15
Fat (gm): 3.3
Saturated fat (gm): 0.6
Cholesterol (mg): 55.5
Sodium (mg): 311
Protein (gm): 32.6
Carbohydrate (gm): 9.2
Exchanges
Milk: 0.0
Vegetable: 2.0
Fruit: 0.0
Bread: 0.0
Meat: 3.0
Fat: 0.0

1. Pierce surfaces of fish with long-tined fork; rub with lime juice and garlic. Refrigerate, covered, in large glass baking dish 2 hours.

2. Spoon Veracruz Sauce over fish. Bake, uncovered, at 400 degrees until fish is tender and flakes with a fork, 25 to 35 minutes. Place fish on serving plate; garnish with lime wedges.

Veracruz Sauce

makes about 2 cups

  Vegetable cooking spray
1 cup chopped onion
3 cloves garlic, minced
1 pickled jalapeño chili, minced
1-2 -inch piece cinnamon stick
1 bay leaf
1/2 teaspoon dried oregano leaves
1/4 teaspoon dried thyme leaves
1/4 teaspoon ground cumin
3 cups chopped tomatoes
1/4 cup sliced pitted green olives
1-2 tablespoons drained capers
  Salt and pepper, to taste

1. Spray large skillet with cooking spray; heat over medium heat until hot. Saute onion, garlic, jalapeño chili, cinnamon, and herbs until onion is tender, 5 to 8 minutes.

2. Add tomatoes, olives, and capers; cook, covered, over medium-high heat until tomatoes release juice. Reduce heat and simmer, uncovered, until sauce is a medium consistency, about 10 minutes. Discard bay leaf; season to taste with salt and pepper.

GRILLED RED SNAPPER WITH TROPICAL SALSA

New trendy salsas are appearing in many restaurants, even in Mexico. You'll enjoy our fruit and black bean version.

6 servings

1 whole red snapper, dressed (about 2 pounds)
3 tablespoons lime juice
2 cloves garlic, minced
Tropical Salsa (recipe follows)
Lime wedges, as garnish
Cilantro *or* parsley sprigs, as garnish

Per Serving
Calories: 189
% Calories from fat: 11
Fat (gm): 2.2
Saturated fat (gm): 0.5
Cholesterol (mg): 55.5
Sodium (mg): 75
Protein (gm): 32.1
Carbohydrate (gm): 9
Exchanges
Milk: 0.0
Vegetable: 0.0
Fruit: 0.0
Bread: 0.0
Meat: 3.0
Fat: 0.0

1. Pierce surfaces of fish with long-tined fork; rub with lime juice and garlic. Refrigerate, covered, in large glass baking dish 2 hours.

2. Grill fish over medium-hot coals, or bake, uncovered, at 400 degrees, until fish is tender and flakes with a fork, 20 to 25 minutes.

3. Arrange fish on serving platter; spoon Tropical Salsa around fish. Garnish with lime wedges and cilantro.

Tropical Salsa

makes about 1 1/2 cups

1/2 cup cubed papaya *or* mango
1/2 cup cubed pineapple
1/2 cup chopped tomato
1/4 cup chopped, seeded cucumber
1/4 cup cooked black beans
1/2 teaspoon minced jalapeño chili
 2   tablespoons finely chopped cilantro
1/4 cup orange juice
 1   tablespoon lime juice
2-3 teaspoons sugar

1. Combine papaya, pineapple, tomato, cucumber, black beans, jalapeño chili, and cilantro in small bowl; add combined orange and lime juice and sugar and toss. Refrigerate until serving time.

SPICY SHRIMP AND RICE STEW

This full-bodied shrimp and rice stew is seasoned with a creative combination of spices.

6 servings

 1 large onion, chopped
 2 large garlic cloves, minced
 2 teaspoons olive oil
 3 cups reduced-sodium fat-free chicken broth
 2 ribs celery, diced
 1 large carrot, peeled, diced
 1 large green bell pepper, seeded, chopped
 1 can (14 1/2 ounces) reduced-sodium diced tomatoes, undrained
 1 large bay leaf
1 1/2 teaspoons dried thyme leaves
 3/4 teaspoon paprika
 1 cup uncooked long-grain white rice
 1 pound medium shrimp, peeled, deveined
    Salt, cayenne, and black pepper, to taste

Per Serving
Calories: 217
% Calories from fat: 9
Fat (gm): 2.1
Saturated fat (gm): 0.4
Cholesterol (mg): 87.5
Sodium (mg): 217
Protein (gm): 14.2
Carbohydrate (gm): 34.6
Exchanges
Milk: 0.0
Vegetable: 1.0
Fruit: 0.0
Bread: 2.0
Meat: 1.0
Fat: 0.0

1. Saute onion and garlic in oil in large saucepan until onion is tender, about 5 minutes. Add remaining ingredients, except rice, shrimp, salt, cayenne, and black pepper, and heat to boiling. Reduce heat and simmer, covered, 15 minutes.

2. Heat to boiling and add rice; reduce heat and simmer, covered, until rice is tender, about 20 minutes. Add shrimp; simmer, covered, until shrimp and cooked and pink. Discard bay leaf; season to taste with salt, cayenne, and black pepper.

CARIBBEAN-STYLE FLOUNDER

Here's our version of an ideal island fisherman's feast—a fuss-free, flavorful dish of flounder, sweet potatoes, and tomatoes that's cooked to perfection in less than 30 minutes.

4 servings

2 teaspoons peanut oil

1 tablespoon annatto seeds

1 medium onion, thinly sliced

2 cups reduced-sodium fat-free chicken broth

1 sweet potato, peeled, cut into $1/2$-inch cubes

1 can (14 ounces) reduced-sodium whole tomatoes, undrained, cut up

1 teaspoon dried thyme leaves

1 cup frozen peas

1 pound flounder fillets, cut into $3/4$-inch cubes

4 teaspoons lemon juice
   Salt and pepper, to taste

Per Serving
Calories: 240
% Calories from fat: 16
Fat (gm): 4.2
Saturated fat (gm): 0.8
Cholesterol (mg): 60.1
Sodium (mg): 227
Protein (gm): 28.5
Carbohydrate (gm): 21.4
Exchanges
Milk: 0.0
Vegetable: 0.0
Fruit: 0.0
Bread: 1.0
Meat: 3.0
Fat: 0.0

1. Heat oil in large saucepan over medium-high heat; add annatto seeds and saute for 3 minutes. Remove seeds with slotted spoon and discard. Add onion to saucepan; saute 2 minutes.

2. Add broth, potato, tomatoes and liquid, and thyme. Heat to boiling; reduce heat and simmer, covered, until potato is tender, about 10 minutes. Using potato masher or kitchen fork, coarsely mash mixture in pan.

3. Add peas and flounder; simmer until fish is tender and flakes with a fork, about 10 minutes. Stir in lemon juice; season to taste with salt and pepper.

BRAISED FISH WITH SUN-DRIED TOMATO SAUCE

The combination of tomato sauce and sun-dried tomatoes gives this dish rich color and flavor. Red snapper or other firm-fleshed white fish can be substituted for the halibut.

4 servings

1 large onion, chopped

1 teaspoon minced garlic

1 tablespoon olive oil

1 cup clam juice *or* reduced-fat chicken broth

3 tablespoons chopped oil-packed sun-dried tomatoes

1 teaspoon dried marjoram leaves

1/2 teaspoon dried oregano leaves

4 halibut steaks (about 4 ounces each)

1 can (8 ounces) reduced-sodium tomato sauce

Salt and pepper, to taste

Per Serving
Calories: 204
% Calories from fat: 30
Fat (gm): 6.8
Saturated fat (gm): 0.9
Cholesterol (mg): 36.1
Sodium (mg): 232
Protein (gm): 25.4
Carbohydrate (gm): 9.6
Exchanges
Milk: 0.0
Vegetable: 2.0
Fruit: 0.0
Bread: 0.0
Meat: 3.0
Fat: 0.0

1. Saute onion and garlic in oil in large skillet until tender and well-browned. Stir in clam juice, sun-dried tomatoes, and herbs. Heat to boiling; boil, uncovered, stirring frequently until liquid is almost evaporated, about 5 minutes.

2. Add fish and tomato sauce; simmer gently until fish is tender and flakes with a fork, 3 to 5 minutes. Season to taste with salt and pepper.

FISH STEW MARSALA

Marsala wine adds a distinctive, appealing note to this simple Italian fish stew. Substitute any lean white fish you prefer.

4 servings

1 large onion, chopped

1 cup chopped mixed red and green bell peppers

$^1/_2$ cup chopped celery

1 teaspoon minced garlic

$1^1/_2$ tablespoons olive oil

$2^1/_4$ cups reduced-sodium fat-free chicken broth

$^1/_3$ cup dry Marsala wine *or* fat-free chicken broth

1 teaspoon dried thyme leaves

$^1/_4$ cup reduced-sodium tomato paste

$^1/_4$ cup water

2 tablespoons lemon juice

2 cups medium pasta shells, cooked, warm

1 pound haddock steaks, cut into large chunks

Salt and pepper, to taste

Chopped parsley, as garnish

Per Serving
Calories: 409
% Calories from fat: 15
Fat (gm): 7
Saturated fat (gm): 1
Cholesterol (mg): 65.2
Sodium (mg): 206
Protein (gm): 33
Carbohydrate (gm): 49
Exchanges
Milk: 0.0
Vegetable: 1.0
Fruit: 0.0
Bread: 3.0
Meat: 3.0
Fat: 0.0

1. Saute onion, bell peppers, celery, and garlic in oil in large skillet until tender and lightly browned, about 5 minutes. Add broth, Marsala, and thyme. Heat to boiling; reduce heat and simmer, uncovered, 10 minutes.

2. Combine tomato paste and water; stir into broth mixture in skillet. Stir in lemon juice, pasta, and fish and simmer until fish flakes with a fork, about 5 minutes. Season to taste with salt and pepper. Serve stew in large soup plates or bowls. Sprinkle with parsley.

SOLE, MEDITERRANEAN STYLE

This fast and flavorful fish dinner features sole, but any lean, mild-flavored white fish, such as flounder, halibut, or turbot, can be substituted.

4 servings

1/2 cup sun-dried tomatoes (not in oil)

1 package (16 ounces) frozen stir-fry pepper blend

1/2 cup reduced-sodium fat-free chicken broth

2 teaspoons olive oil

1 teaspoon minced garlic

1 teaspoon dried basil leaves

Salt and pepper, to taste

8 ounces penne *or* mostaccioli, cooked, warm

1/4 cup grated Parmesan cheese

Vegetable cooking spray

12-16 ounces skinless sole fillets

Chopped parsley, as garnish

Per Serving
Calories: 387
% Calories from fat: 14
Fat (gm): 6
Saturated fat (gm): 1.7
Cholesterol (mg): 49
Sodium (mg): 347
Protein (gm): 28.3
Carbohydrate (gm): 53.3
Exchanges
Milk: 0.0
Vegetable: 2.0
Fruit: 0.0
Bread: 3.0
Meat: 2.0
Fat: 0.0

1. Place sun-dried tomatoes in small bowl; cover with hot water and let stand until softened, about 10 minutes. Drain, discarding water, and chop.

2. Combine tomatoes, stir-fry blend, broth, olive oil, garlic, and basil in large skillet; heat to boiling. Reduce heat and simmer, stirring frequently, until vegetables are very tender, about 5 minutes; season to taste with salt and pepper. Toss with penne and Parmesan in large bowl; keep warm.

3. Spray large skillet with cooking spray; heat over medium heat until hot. Add sole to skillet and cook until browned on the bottom, 3 to 4 minutes; turn and cook until fish is tender and flakes with fork, 3 to 4 minutes longer. Sprinkle lightly with salt and pepper. Spoon pasta mixture onto serving platter; top with fish. Sprinkle with chopped parsley.

CIOPPINO PASTA

Feel free to substitute other kinds of fresh fish, according to season, availability, and price. The seafood is added to the sauce toward the end of the cooking time to avoid overcooking. Serve pasta in bowls to accommodate the generous amount of sauce.

8 servings (about 1 cup each)

1 cup chopped green bell pepper
1 cup chopped onion
1 cup sliced mushrooms
4 cloves garlic, minced
1 tablespoon olive oil
3 cups chopped tomatoes
1/2 cup dry white wine *or* clam juice
1 tablespoon tomato paste
2 tablespoons finely chopped parsley
2 teaspoons dried oregano leaves
2 teaspoons dried basil leaves
1 teaspoon ground turmeric
8 ounces sea scallops
8 ounces crabmeat, flaked into 1/2-inch pieces
1 halibut, *or* haddock, steak (4 ounces), cut into 1-inch pieces
12 mussels in the shell, scrubbed
1/2 teaspoon salt
1/4 teaspoon pepper
12 ounces fettuccine, cooked, warm

Per Serving
Calories: 387
% Calories from fat: **24**
Fat (gm): **10.2**
Saturated fat (gm): **2.1**
Cholesterol (mg): **80.9**
Sodium (mg): 514
Protein (gm): 24.5
Carbohydrate (gm): **47**
Exchanges
Milk: 0.0
Vegetable: 2.0
Fruit: 0.0
Bread: 2.0
Meat: 2.0
Fat: 0.75

1. Saute bell pepper, onion, mushrooms, and garlic in oil in large saucepan until onion is tender, about 5 minutes. Stir in tomatoes, wine, tomato paste, and herbs; heat to boiling. Reduce heat and simmer, covered, 5 minutes. Simmer, uncovered, 20 minutes more, until mixture is thickened to desired consistency, adding seafood during last 10 to 15 minutes of cooking time.

2. Discard any mussels that have not opened. Stir in salt and pepper. Toss with fettuccine in serving bowl.

WHITE FISH AND LINGUINE WITH LEMON-CAPER SAUCE

Any white-fleshed fish, such as cod, halibut, haddock, or orange roughy, can be used.

6 servings

6	small white fish fillets (about 3 ounces each)	
1	tablespoon Dijon-style mustard	
2	cloves garlic, minced	
1	teaspoon dried tarragon leaves	
2-3	tablespoons margarine	
3	tablespoons flour	
1	can (14½ ounces) reduced-sodium fat-free chicken broth	
2-3	teaspoons lemon juice	
3	tablespoons drained capers	
¼	teaspoon salt	
⅛	teaspoon white pepper	
12	ounces linguine, cooked, warm	

Per Serving
Calories: 326
% Calories from fat: 28
Fat (gm): 10
Saturated fat (gm): 1.5
Cholesterol (mg): 49.3
Sodium (mg): 505
Protein (gm): 23.7
Carbohydrate (gm): 35.4
Exchanges
Milk: 0.0
Vegetable: 0.0
Fruit: 0.0
Bread: 2.5
Meat: 2.0
Fat: 1.0

1. Brush tops of fish fillets with combined mustard, garlic, and tarragon. Place in baking pan; bake at 350 degrees until fish is tender and flakes with fork, 10 to 12 minutes.

2. Melt margarine in small saucepan; stir in flour. Cook over medium heat, stirring constantly, 1 to 2 minutes. Stir in chicken broth and lemon juice; heat to boiling. Boil, stirring constantly, until thickened, 1 to 2 minutes. Stir in capers, salt, and white pepper.

3. Arrange fish on linguine on serving platter; spoon sauce over fish.

SALMON WITH CILANTRO PESTO FETTUCCINE

Tuna or halibut substitute nicely for the salmon.

6 servings

6 salmon steaks (about 4 ounces each)
2-3 teaspoons Dijon-style mustard
12 ounces spinach fettuccine, cooked, warm
Cilantro Pesto (recipe follows)

Per Serving
Calories: 372
% Calories from fat: 30
Fat (gm): 12.3
Saturated fat (gm): 2.6
Cholesterol (mg): 126.7
Sodium (mg): 319
Protein (gm): 32.7
Carbohydrate (gm): 31.1
Exchanges
Milk: 0.0
Vegetable: 0.0
Fruit: 0.0
Bread: 2.0
Meat: 3.0
Fat: 1.0

1. Brush salmon with mustard; place on broiler pan. Broil, 6 inches from heat source, until salmon is tender and flakes with fork, 10 to 15 minutes, turning once.

2. Toss fettuccine with Cilantro Pesto; arrange around salmon on serving platter.

Cilantro Pesto

makes about ³/₄ cup

1¹/₂ cups packed cilantro leaves
¹/₂ cup packed parsley
1 clove garlic, minced
¹/₄ cup grated Parmesan cheese
3 tablespoons pine nuts *or* walnuts
1 tablespoon olive oil
1 tablespoon lemon juice
¹/₄ teaspoon salt
¹/₄ teaspoon pepper

1. Combine herbs, garlic, Parmesan cheese, and pine nuts in food processor or blender. Process, adding oil and lemon juice gradually, until mixture is very finely chopped. Stir in salt and pepper.

FLORENTINE FISH DINNER

Pasta, spinach, and fish fillets combine in this quick and complete dinner. Any mild-flavored white fish can be used.

4 servings

1 can (14 ounces) reduced-sodium diced tomatoes, undrained

2 cups frozen chopped spinach, thawed

1 tablespoon olive oil

1/2 teaspoon minced garlic

Salt and pepper, to taste

Vegetable cooking spray

1 pound skinless flounder fillets

8 ounces linguine, cooked, warm

3 tablespoons grated Parmesan cheese

Per Serving
Calories: 353
% Calories from fat: 18
Fat (gm): 7.5
Saturated fat (gm): 1.6
Cholesterol (mg): 63.1
Sodium (mg): 355
Protein (gm): 32.6
Carbohydrate (gm): 41.7
Exchanges
Milk: 0.0
Vegetable: 2.0
Fruit: 0.0
Bread: 2.0
Meat: 3.0
Fat: 0.0

1. Combine tomatoes and liquid, spinach, olive oil, and garlic in medium saucepan; heat to boiling. Reduce heat and simmer until thickened to desired consistency, about 10 minutes; season to taste with salt and pepper.

2. Spray large skillet with cooking spray; heat over medium heat until hot. Sprinkle flounder lightly with salt and pepper; add to skillet and cook 3 to 4 minutes on each side or until fish is tender and flakes with a fork.

3. Place linguine on serving platter; top with tomato sauce mixture and flounder. Sprinkle with Parmesan cheese.

SALMON RISOTTO

This rich and flavorful entrée makes a wonderful centerpiece for a company meal. It's a real time-saver because you prepare the salmon and sauce while the risotto is cooking in the microwave oven.

6 servings

1 cup arborio rice

2 teaspoons olive oil

3¹/₂ cups reduced-sodium fat-free chicken broth

12-16 ounces salmon steaks

³/₄ cup sliced green onions and tops

¹/₄ cup dry sherry *or* reduced-fat chicken broth

1 cup reduced-fat sour cream

¹/₂ cup 1% low-fat milk

2 teaspoons dried, *or* 1 tablespoon chopped fresh, dill weed

Salt and pepper, to taste

Dill and parsley sprigs, as garnish

Per Serving
Calories: 291
% Calories from fat: 23
Fat (gm): 7.1
Saturated fat (gm): 3.4
Cholesterol (mg): 42.7
Sodium (mg): 175
Protein (gm): 20
Carbohydrate (gm): 31.2
Exchanges
Milk: 0.0
Vegetable: 0.0
Fruit: 0.0
Bread: 2.0
Meat: 2.0
Fat: 0.5

1. Combine rice and olive oil in 3-quart microwave-safe casserole dish; microwave on high, uncovered, 60 seconds. Add broth and stir well; cover and microwave on high 20 to 25 minutes, stirring every 8 minutes, until most of the liquid is absorbed and rice is al dente. Let stand 2 to 3 minutes.

2. While rice is cooking, cook salmon in large greased nonstick skillet until fish flakes with fork, about 10 minutes. Remove fish from pan; remove skin, flake fish, and set aside.

3. In same skillet, cook green onions and sherry over medium heat, stirring frequently, until tender. Stir in sour cream, milk, and dill weed; add salmon and stir over low heat 2 to 3 minutes. Do not boil.

4. Stir salmon mixture into cooked risotto; season to taste with salt and pepper. Garnish with dill and parsley sprigs.

FISH BAKED WITH STUFFING

Fish fillets are cooked on a bed of mushroom-bread stuffing in this dish. Just add a salad or vegetable, and dinner is served!

4 servings

1	large onion, chopped
1/2	teaspoon minced garlic
6	ounces mushrooms, sliced
2	tablespoons reduced-sodium fat-free chicken, *or* vegetable, broth
1 1/2	cups crumb-type seasoned stuffing mix
3	tablespoons grated Parmesan cheese
1	pound lean white fish fillets
1/4	teaspoon dried basil leaves
	Salt and pepper, to taste
1/4	cup dry white wine *or* chicken broth

Per Serving
Calories: 241
% Calories from fat: 13
Fat (gm): 3.5
Saturated fat (gm): 1.1
Cholesterol (mg): 63.1
Sodium (mg): 584
Protein (gm): 27.5
Carbohydrate (gm): 22.4
Exchanges
Milk: 0.0
Vegetable: 0.0
Fruit: 0.0
Bread: 1.5
Meat: 3.0
Fat: 0.0

1. Combine onion, garlic, mushrooms, and chicken broth in large skillet; cook over medium heat, covered, until onion is tender, stirring occasionally. Stir in stuffing mix and Parmesan cheese; spoon stuffing into large baking dish.

2. Sprinkle fish with basil, salt, and pepper; arrange on top of stuffing in dish, overlapping slightly, if necessary. Pour wine over fish. Cover tightly with aluminum foil, and bake at 375 degrees until fish flakes easily with a fork, about 25 minutes.

ASPARAGUS-ROUGHY AU GRATIN

Orange roughy is a light-flavored fish with a nice, firm texture—delicious baked with asparagus.

6 servings

2 cups instant, *or* boil-in-bag, rice
1 pound fresh asparagus, cut into 1-inch pieces
6 orange roughy fillets (6 ounces each)
3 tablespoons margarine
1 medium onion, finely chopped
1/3 cup all-purpose flour
1 cup fat-free milk
1 cup (4 ounces) shredded reduced-fat Cheddar cheese
1/4 teaspoon salt
1/4 teaspoon pepper
1 cup unseasoned dry bread crumbs

Per Serving
Calories: 468
% Calories from fat: 22
Fat (gm): 11.2
Saturated fat (gm): 2.8
Cholesterol (mg): 44
Sodium (mg): 712
Protein (gm): 37.2
Carbohydrate (gm): 51.3
Exchanges
Milk: 0.0
Vegetable: 1.0
Fruit: 0.0
Bread: 3.0
Meat: 4.0
Fat: 0.0

1. Cook rice according to package directions; spread over bottom of 13 x 9-inch baking dish. Arrange asparagus over rice; top with fish fillets, overlapping slightly if necessary.

2. Melt margarine in medium saucepan over medium heat; add onion and cook, stirring, 3 to 5 minutes. Stir in flour and cook 1 to 2 minutes. Whisk in milk; heat to boiling, whisking until thickened, about 1 minute. Whisk in cheese, salt, and pepper.

3. Spoon sauce over fish; sprinkle with bread crumbs. Bake, covered, at 350 degrees until sauce is bubbly, about 35 minutes. Uncover and bake until top is browned, about 10 minutes. Let stand 10 minutes before serving.

TUNA CASSEROLE

Just like Mom used to make, but with fewer calories and less fat. No-yolk noodles can be used for a further reduction in fat and cholesterol.

8 servings

12 ounces thin egg noodles

2 cans (12 ounces each) solid white tuna in water, drained, flaked

1 jar (2½ ounces) diced pimientos, drained

8 ounces mushrooms, sliced

1 can (10½ ounces) reduced-fat cream of mushroom soup

1 can (10½ ounces) reduced-fat cream of celery soup

1 cup water

½ cup dry bread crumbs

Per Serving
Calories: 364
% Calories from fat: 15
Fat (gm): 5.6
Saturated fat (gm): 1.3
Cholesterol (mg): 77.7
Sodium (mg): 684
Protein (gm): 28.5
Carbohydrate (gm): 44.2
Exchanges
Milk: 0.0
Vegetable: 0.0
Fruit: 0.0
Bread: 3.0
Meat: 2.0
Fat: 0.0

1. Place half the uncooked noodles in 2½-quart casserole. Layer half the tuna, pimientos, and mushrooms on noodles. Repeat layers with remaining noodles, tuna, pimientos, and mushrooms.

2. Mix soups and water until smooth. Pour evenly over casserole; top with breadcrumbs. Bake, covered, 25 minutes at 375 degrees. Uncover and bake until brown and bubbly, about 15 minutes.

SALMON CASSEROLE

This light and flavorful casserole is great for brunch, lunch, or dinner.

8 servings

2 cans (14³/4 ounces each) salmon, drained, flaked, bones removed

1/4 teaspoon ground black pepper

1/2 teaspoon ground nutmeg

1 pound mushrooms, coarsely chopped

1 shallot, finely chopped

1-2 tablespoons margarine

2 tablespoons flour

1¹/2 cups fat-free milk

2 whole cloves

1 bay leaf

1/2 cup unseasoned dry bread crumbs

4 potatoes, peeled, boiled, mashed

1 teaspoon paprika

Per Serving
Calories: 297
% Calories from fat: 30
Fat (gm): 9.9
Saturated fat (gm): 2.2
Cholesterol (mg): 46.7
Sodium (mg): 667
Protein (gm): 26.4
Carbohydrate (gm): 25.1
Exchanges
Milk: 0.0
Vegetable: 0.0
Fruit: 0.0
Bread: 1.5
Meat: 3.0
Fat: 0.0

1. Combine salmon, pepper, nutmeg, and mushrooms in 12 x 8-inch baking dish.

2. Saute shallot in margarine in small saucepan 1 minute over low heat. Whisk in flour; cook over low heat 1 to 2 minutes, whisking constantly. Whisk in milk; add cloves and bay leaf. Heat to boiling; boil, whisking until thickened, about 1 minute. Remove cloves and bay leaf; pour sauce over salmon mixture in baking dish.

3. Sprinkle sauce evenly with bread crumbs. Spoon mashed potatoes around edge of dish, forming a border; sprinkle with paprika. Bake, uncovered, at 375 degrees until top is lightly browned, about 35 minutes.

TUNA PATTIES WITH CREAMED PEA SAUCE

These generous patties can also be served in buns, or pack the mixture into a small loaf pan and bake as a loaf.

4 servings

2 cans (6¹/₈ ounces each) light tuna packed in water, drained

³/₄ cup dry unseasoned bread crumbs, divided

¹/₄ cup finely chopped onion

¹/₄ cup finely chopped celery

2 tablespoons chopped red, *or* green, bell pepper

2-3 tablespoons fat-free mayonnaise

1-2 teaspoons Worcestershire sauce
Salt and cayenne pepper, to taste

1 egg
Vegetable cooking spray
Creamed Pea Sauce (recipe follows)

Per Serving
Calories: 325
% Calories from fat: 25
Fat (gm): 8.9
Saturated fat (gm): 2
Cholesterol (mg): 79.2
Sodium (mg): 726
Protein (gm): 30
Carbohydrate (gm): 28.6
Exchanges
Milk: 0.5
Vegetable: 1.0
Fruit: 0.0
Bread: 1.0
Meat: 3.5
Fat: 0.0

1. Combine tuna, ¹/₂ cup bread crumbs, onion, celery, bell pepper, mayonnaise, and Worcestershire sauce in medium bowl; season to taste with salt and cayenne pepper. Add egg, mixing until ingredients are well blended. Shape into 4 patties, each a generous ¹/₂ inch thick.

2. Spray a large skillet with cooking spray; heat over medium heat until hot. Coat patties with remaining ¹/₄ cup bread crumbs; spray patties lightly with cooking spray. Cook over medium-low heat until browned, about 5 minutes on each side. Serve with Creamed Pea Sauce.

Creamed Pea Sauce

makes about 1 cup

> 2 tablespoons margarine
> 2 tablespoons flour
> 1/2 cup fat-free milk
> 1/2 cup fat-free half-and-half *or* fat-free milk
> 1/2 cup frozen, thawed peas
> Salt and pepper, to taste

1. Melt margarine in small saucepan. Stir in flour and cook, stirring constantly, over medium-low heat 1 minute. Whisk in milk and half-and-half; heat to boiling. Boil, whisking constantly, until thickened, about 1 minute. Stir in peas; cook over low heat 2 to 3 minutes. Season to taste with salt and pepper. Serve hot.

SALMON SOUFFLÉ

This casserole takes a little care in preparation, but the results are well worth it.

6 servings

> 1 small green bell pepper, coarsely chopped
> 1 small red bell pepper, coarsely chopped
> 1 tablespoon margarine
> 1/4 cup all-purpose flour
> 1 1/2 cups fat-free milk
> 1 package (10 ounces) frozen whole-kernel corn
> 3/4 teaspoon dried dill weed
> 1/4 teaspoon salt
> 1/8 teaspoon white pepper
> 2-3 egg yolks, lightly beaten
> 1 can (6 1/2 ounces) salmon, drained, flaked, bones removed
> 5 egg whites
> Pinch cream of tartar

Per Serving
Calories: 183
% Calories from fat: 30
Fat (gm): 6.2
Saturated fat (gm): 1.5
Cholesterol (mg): 85.6
Sodium (mg): 367
Protein (gm): 14.3
Carbohydrate (gm): 18.2
Exchanges
Milk: 0.0
Vegetable: 0.0
Fruit: 0.0
Bread: 1.0
Meat: 2.0
Fat: 0.0

1. Saute bell peppers in margarine in large saucepan until tender, about 5 minutes. Stir in flour and cook over medium heat 1 to 2 minutes. Gradually blend in milk, corn, dill weed, salt, and pepper; heat to boiling over medium heat. Remove from heat.

2. Gradually stir a small amount of vegetable mixture into egg yolks; stir yolks into vegetable mixture. Mix in salmon.

3. Beat egg whites and cream of tartar in large bowl to stiff peaks. Fold into salmon mixture. Pour into lightly greased 2-quart soufflé dish. Bake, uncovered, at 350 degrees until golden brown and knife inserted near center comes out clean, about 45 minutes. Serve immediately.

SIX

Vegetarian Entrées

BEAN AND BARLEY SOUP

A soup that can be easily increased to serve a crowd; make it a day ahead of time for best flavor.

6 servings

  1 cup chopped onion
  ³/4 cup chopped red, *or* green, bell pepper
  2 teaspoons minced roasted garlic
  2 tablespoons olive oil
  1 tablespoon flour
1¹/2 teaspoons Italian seasoning
  7 cups salt-free vegetable broth
  2 cans (15 ounces each) cannellini, *or* Great Northern, beans, rinsed, drained
  2 tablespoons reduced-sodium tomato paste
 ¹/2 cup quick-cooking barley
  1 large Idaho potato, unpeeled, cut into ¹/2-inch pieces
  1 cup sliced carrots
  1 cup packed baby spinach leaves
    Salt and pepper, to taste

Per Serving
Calories: 297
% Calories from fat: 17
Fat (gm): 5.6
Saturated fat (gm): 0.7
Cholesterol (mg): 0
Sodium (mg): 325
Protein (gm): 10
Carbohydrate (gm): 52.1
Exchanges
Milk: 0.0
Vegetable: 1.0
Fruit: 0.0
Bread: 3.0
Meat: 0.0
Fat: 1.0

1. Saute onion, bell pepper, and garlic in oil in Dutch oven 5 minutes. Add flour and Italian seasoning; cook 1 to 2 minutes longer.

2. Add remaining ingredients, except spinach, salt, and pepper, to Dutch oven; heat to boiling. Reduce heat and simmer, uncovered, 20 to 25 minutes, adding spinach during last 5 minutes of cooking time. Season to taste with salt and pepper.

MONTEREY CHILI ACINI DE PEPE

Some vegetarian chilies call for bulgur or cracked wheat. This fuss-free and satisfying recipe uses acini de pepe, a tiny pasta that is readily available.

4 servings

1 medium onion, chopped

1 green bell pepper, chopped

1 teaspoon olive oil

1 can (15 ounces) pinto beans, rinsed, drained

1 can (14 ounces) reduced-sodium diced tomatoes, undrained

1 tablespoon chili powder

1 teaspoon dried oregano leaves

1 teaspoon unsweetened cocoa

1/2 cup acini de pepe, cooked, warm

1/4 cup chopped cilantro

Salt and pepper, to taste

3/4 cup (3 ounces) shredded Monterey Jack cheese

Per Serving
Calories: 275
% Calories from fat: 29
Fat (gm): 9.2
Saturated fat (gm): 4.5
Cholesterol (mg): 18.9
Sodium (mg): 461
Protein (gm): 14
Carbohydrate (gm): 36
Exchanges
Milk: 0.0
Vegetable: 1.0
Fruit: 0.0
Bread: 2.0
Meat: 1.0
Fat: 1.0

1. Saute onion and bell pepper in oil in large saucepan until tender. Stir in beans, tomatoes and liquid, chili powder, oregano, and cocoa. Heat to boiling; reduce heat and simmer, covered, 10 minutes. Stir in acini de pepe and cilantro; season to taste with salt and pepper. Serve in bowls; top with cheese.

SHIITAKE-PORTOBELLO CHOWDER

Celebrate a rich combination of distinctive mushrooms! The chowder features a rich broth that combines the flavors of Gruyère cheese and Marsala wine.

4 servings

 4 shallots, thinly sliced
 2 teaspoons margarine, divided
 2 large potatoes, cut into $1/4$-inch cubes
 3 cups reduced-sodium vegetable broth
 4 ounces shiitake mushroom caps
 2 cups cubed portobello mushrooms
 $1/4$ cup (1 ounce) shredded Gruyère, *or* Swiss, cheese
 2 tablespoons Marsala wine
 Salt and white pepper, to taste

Per Serving
Calories: 162
% Calories from fat: 26
Fat (gm): 5
Saturated fat (gm): 1.8
Cholesterol (mg): 7.8
Sodium (mg): 114
Protein (gm): 5.6
Carbohydrate (gm): 24.7
Exchanges
Milk: 0.0
Vegetable: 2.0
Fruit: 0.0
Bread: 1.0
Meat: 0.0
Fat: 1.0

1. Saute shallots in 1 teaspoon margarine in large saucepan until tender. Add potatoes and broth. Heat to boiling; reduce heat and simmer, covered, until potatoes are tender, about 15 minutes. Process mixture in blender or food processor until smooth; return to saucepan.

2. Saute mushrooms in remaining 1 teaspoon margarine in large skillet until wilted and golden brown, about 8 minutes; stir into potato mixture. Heat to boiling; remove from heat and add cheese and wine, stirring until cheese is melted. Season to taste with salt and white pepper.

MEATLESS SLOPPY JOES

A sandwich for kids of all ages! Serve with lots of pickles and fresh vegetable relishes.

4 servings

1/2	cup chopped onion
1/2	cup chopped green, *or* red, bell pepper
1	teaspoon minced garlic
1-2	tablespoons vegetable oil
1/2	cup catsup
2/3	cup water
2	tablespoons light brown sugar
1	tablespoon prepared mustard
1/2	teaspoon chili powder
2/3	cup textured vegetable protein *or* 1 1/2-2 cups frozen pre-browned all-vegetable protein crumbles
	Salt and pepper, to taste
4	whole wheat hamburger buns, toasted

Per Serving
Calories: 239
% Calories from fat: **23**
Fat (gm): 6.4
Saturated fat (gm): **1.1**
Cholesterol (mg): 0
Sodium (mg): 675
Protein (gm): 8.6
Carbohydrate (gm): 38.9
Exchanges
Milk: 0.0
Vegetable: 0.0
Fruit: 0.0
Bread: 2.5
Meat: 0.0
Fat: 1.0

1. Saute onion, bell pepper, and garlic in oil in medium saucepan 5 minutes. Stir in catsup, water, brown sugar, mustard, chili powder, and vegetable protein; heat to boiling. Reduce heat and simmer, covered, 10 minutes. Season to taste with salt and pepper. Spoon sandwich mixture into buns.

FALAFEL PATTIES

The falafel mixture can also be shaped into 1-inch balls and cooked as the recipe directs; serve with Yogurt Cucumber Sauce as appetizers, or in pitas for sandwiches.

4 servings (2 each)

  1 package (6 ounces) falafel mix
 1/2 cup shredded carrots
 1/4 cup sunflower kernels
  2 tablespoons thinly sliced green onions and tops
    Vegetable cooking spray
    Yogurt Cucumber Sauce (recipe follows)

Per Serving
Calories: 255
% Calories from fat: 30
Fat (gm): 7.7
Saturated fat (gm): 0.5
Cholesterol (mg): 1
Sodium (mg): 586
Protein (gm): 11.7
Carbohydrate (gm): 28.6
Exchanges
Milk: 0.0
Vegetable: 0.0
Fruit: 0.0
Bread: 2.0
Meat: 1.0
Fat: 1.0

1. Prepare falafel mix with water according to package directions; mix in carrots, sunflower kernels, and green onions. Shape mixture into 8 patties about 1/2 inch thick.

2. Spray large skillet with cooking spray; heat over medium heat until hot. Place patties in skillet and spray tops with cooking spray; cook until browned, 4 to 5 minutes on each side.

3. Serve with Yogurt Cucumber Sauce.

Yogurt Cucumber Sauce

makes about 1 1/3 cups

  1 cup plain fat-free yogurt
  1 cup shredded, *or* chopped, cucumber
 1/2 teaspoon dried dill weed
 1/2 teaspoon dried mint leaves
    Salt and white pepper, to taste

1. Mix yogurt, cucumber, and herbs. Season to taste with salt and white pepper.

SWEET POTATO AND TEMPEH PATTIES

Use cornbread stuffing crumbs in this recipe if you can, as they add great flavor and texture to the patties.

4 servings

1/2	cup chopped onion
1/2	cup chopped red bell pepper
1/2	jalapeño chili, minced
2	teaspoons minced garlic
1-2	teaspoons vegetable oil
1	package (8 ounces) tempeh, crumbled
1	can (15 ounces) sweet potatoes, drained, mashed (1 1/2 cups)
2	tablespoons sugar-free apricot preserves
1	cup cornbread stuffing crumbs
	Salt and pepper, to taste
1/2	cup applesauce
1/2	cup reduced-fat sour cream

Per Serving
Calories: 336
% Calories from fat: 23
Fat (gm): 8.8
Saturated fat (gm): 3
Cholesterol (mg): 10
Sodium (mg): 224
Protein (gm): 17.2
Carbohydrate (gm): 48.9
Exchanges
Milk: 0.0
Vegetable: 1.0
Fruit: 0.0
Bread: 3.0
Meat: 1.0
Fat: 1.0

1. Saute onion, bell pepper, jalapeño chili, and garlic in oil in large skillet 2 to 3 minutes. Add tempeh to skillet; cook until vegetables are tender, 5 to 8 minutes. Remove from heat; stir in sweet potatoes and apricot preserves.

2. Crush stuffing crumbs with rolling pin to make fine crumbs; stir 2/3 cup crumbs into vegetable mixture, reserving remaining crumbs. Season to taste with salt and pepper. Shape mixture into 4 patties; coat with reserved crumbs.

3. Cook patties over medium heat in greased large skillet until browned, about 5 minutes on each side. Serve patties warm with applesauce and sour cream.

FALAFEL DINNER LOAF

Dried fruit provides a marvelous sweet accent in this easy-to-make loaf. We think it's also terrific cold for warm-weather dining.

4 servings

1 package (6 ounces) falafel mix
1/2 cup shredded zucchini
1/2 cup dried fruit bits *or* chopped mixed dried fruit
3 tablespoons coarsely chopped toasted pecans
2 tablespoons thinly sliced green onions and tops
2 eggs *or* 1/2 cup no-cholesterol real egg product
3/4 cup plain fat-free yogurt

Per Serving
Calories: 311
% Calories from fat: 29
Fat (gm): 9.5
Saturated fat (gm): 1.1
Cholesterol (mg): 106.8
Sodium (mg): 603
Protein (gm): 12.9
Carbohydrate (gm): 38.3
Exchanges
Milk: 0.0
Vegetable: 0.0
Fruit: 0.5
Bread: 2.0
Meat: 0.0
Fat: 2.0

1. Prepare falafel mix with water according to package directions; mix in remaining ingredients, except yogurt. Pack mixture into lightly greased 7¹/₂ x 3¹/₂-inch loaf pan.

2. Bake at 350 degrees until mixture is set, about 30 minutes. Invert loaf onto serving plate; slice and serve with dollops of yogurt.

HASH BROWN LOAF WITH EGGS

Served with fried or poached eggs, this loaf is a perfect entrée for brunch or a light supper.

4 servings

3/4 cup textured vegetable protein
3/4 cup vegetable broth
    Vegetable cooking spray
1 cup shredded carrots
1 small onion, finely chopped
1/4 cup chopped red bell pepper
2 cloves garlic, minced
3/4 cup shredded Idaho potatoes

Per Serving
Calories: 310
% Calories from fat: 21
Fat (gm): 7.4
Saturated fat (gm): 2
Cholesterol (mg): 211
Sodium (mg): 493
Protein (gm): 36.2
Carbohydrate (gm): 26
Exchanges
Milk: 0.0
Vegetable: 2.0
Fruit: 0.0
Bread: 1.0
Meat: 3.0
Fat: 0.0

$1^1/2$ teaspoons dried thyme leaves
  1 teaspoon dried chives
    Salt and pepper, to taste
  1 cup no-cholesterol real egg product
  1 cup (4 ounces) fat-free Cheddar cheese, divided
  4 fried, *or* poached, eggs

1. Combine vegetable protein and broth in medium bowl; let stand until broth is absorbed, 5 to 10 minutes.

2. Spray medium skillet with cooking spray; heat over medium heat until hot. Saute carrots, onion, bell pepper, and garlic until tender, about 5 minutes. Stir in potatoes and herbs; season to taste with salt and pepper. Mix in egg product and $3/4$ cup cheese.

3. Pack mixture into greased $7^1/2$ x $3^3/4$-inch loaf pan. Bake, loosely covered, at 350 degrees 45 minutes; uncover and sprinkle with remaining $1/4$ cup cheese. Bake until loaf is set and cheese melted, about 15 minutes longer. Let stand 10 minutes before serving.

4. Loosen sides of loaf with sharp knife; unmold onto serving plate. Slice loaf and arrange slices on serving plates; serve eggs on top or alongside loaf.

ROASTED VEGETABLE FAJITAS

A colorful and flavorful vegetarian entrée, although chicken breast, lean beef, or pork can be added if you like. The vegetables can be grilled over mesquite chips for a smoky accent; cut vegetables in large enough pieces so they don't fall through the grill rack!

4 servings (2 fajitas each)

    Vegetable cooking spray
  2 medium red bell peppers, cut into $3/4$-inch strips
  2 medium poblano chilies *or* green bell peppers, cut into $3/4$-inch strips
  2 medium onions, cut into wedges
  2 medium carrots, cut into $1/2$-inch slices
  1 large tomato, cut into wedges

Per Serving
Calories: 300
% Calories from fat: 30
Fat (gm): 11.5
Saturated fat (gm): 1.6
Cholesterol (mg): 0
Sodium (mg): 264
Protein (gm): 8.8
Carbohydrate (gm): 51.7
Exchanges
Milk: 0.0
Vegetable: 4.0
Fruit: 0.0
Bread: 2.0
Meat: 0.0
Fat: 2.0

1 medium zucchini, cut into 1-inch
pieces
1 large chayote squash, unpeeled, seeded,
cut into 1-inch pieces
8 ounces large mushrooms, cut into
halves
2 teaspoons ground cumin
2 teaspoons dried oregano leaves
Fajita Dressing (recipe follows)
Salt and pepper, to taste
8 flour, *or* corn, tortillas, warm

1. Line large jelly roll pan with aluminum foil; spray with cooking spray. Arrange vegetables in pan; spray generously with cooking spray and sprinkle with cumin and oregano.

2. Bake vegetables at 425 degrees until tender and browned, 30 to 40 minutes. Spoon vegetables into serving bowl; drizzle with Fajita Dressing and toss. Season to taste with salt and pepper.

3. Spoon vegetable mixture onto tortillas and roll up.

Fajita Dressing

makes about 1/4 cup

2 tablespoons olive oil
1 tablespoon lime juice
2-3 teaspoons cider vinegar
2-3 cloves garlic, minced

1. Mix all ingredients.

TEMPEH FAJITAS

Fajitas are an American interpretation of soft tacos. They can include any combination of vegetables you want.

6 servings (2 fajitas each)

8 ounces tempeh, cut into 2 x $^1/_2$ x $^1/_2$-inch strips

$^1/_3$ cup lime juice

1 tablespoon vegetable oil

1$^1/_2$ cups frozen stir-fry pepper blend

1 teaspoon minced garlic

1$^1/_2$ teaspoons ground cumin

1$^1/_2$ teaspoons dried oregano leaves

1 can (15 ounces) black beans, rinsed, drained

Salt and pepper, to taste

12 flour, *or* corn, tortillas, warm

3 tablespoons finely chopped cilantro

$^1/_2$ cup mild, *or* medium, salsa

$^3/_4$ cup fat-free sour cream

Per Serving
Calories: 416
% Calories from fat: 22
Fat (gm): 11
Saturated fat (gm): 1.6
Cholesterol (mg): 0
Sodium (mg): 771
Protein (gm): 19.7
Carbohydrate (gm): 65.4
Exchanges
Milk: 0.0
Vegetable: 1.0
Fruit: 0.0
Bread: 4.0
Meat: 1.0
Fat: 1.0

1. Place tempeh in shallow glass baking dish; pour lime juice over. Let stand 20 minutes; drain.

2. Saute tempeh in oil in large skillet until browned, about 5 minutes; move tempeh to side of pan. Add pepper blend, garlic, and herbs; cook over medium heat until tender, about 5 minutes. Add beans; cook until hot, 2 to 3 minutes. Season to taste with salt and pepper.

3. Spoon mixture onto tortillas; sprinkle with cilantro, top with salsa and sour cream, and roll up.

MEXICAN-STYLE VEGETABLES AND RICE

These cheesy vegetables can also make a delicious filling for soft tacos.

6 servings

1½ cups frozen stir-fry pepper blend
1½ teaspoons minced garlic
 1 jalapeño chili, finely chopped
 1 tablespoon vegetable oil
 2 medium chayote squash, peeled, seeded, cubed
 2 cups halved small cremini mushrooms
 1 cup frozen, *or* canned, drained whole-kernel corn
¾ teaspoon dried oregano leaves
½ teaspoon ground cumin
½ teaspoon chili powder
 4 cups cooked white, *or* brown, rice
    Salt and pepper, to taste
¾ cup (3 ounces) shredded reduced-fat Monterey Jack cheese
 6 tablespoons reduced-fat sour cream
 2 green onions and tops, sliced

Per Serving
Calories: 272
% Calories from fat: 22
Fat (gm): 6.7
Saturated fat (gm): 3.2
Cholesterol (mg): 15.1
Sodium (mg): 141
Protein (gm): 11.2
Carbohydrate (gm): 42.3
Exchanges
Milk: 0.0
Vegetable: 3.0
Fruit: 0.0
Bread: 2.0
Meat: 0.0
Fat: 1.0

1. Saute pepper blend, garlic, and jalapeño chili in oil in large skillet over medium heat 5 minutes; add squash, mushrooms, corn, oregano, cumin, and chili powder. Cook, covered, over medium heat until squash and mushrooms are tender, 8 to 10 minutes, stirring occasionally. Stir in rice; season to taste with salt and pepper.

2. Sprinkle cheese over vegetable mixture; cook, covered, until cheese melts, 3 to 5 minutes. Garnish with sour cream and green onions.

WHEAT AND BARLEY BOWL

Grains and greens are cooked together, then combined with tomatoes and toasted nuts.

4 servings (about 1 cup each)

Vegetable cooking spray
3/4 cup barley
2 1/2 cups reduced-sodium vegetable broth
1/4 cup bulgur
1/2 teaspoon dried thyme leaves
6 ounces thinly sliced turnip greens, kale, *or* spinach
1/2 cup thinly sliced green onions and tops
1/4 cup finely chopped parsley
1 large tomato, coarsely chopped
1/4-1/2 cup coarsely chopped walnuts, toasted
1-2 tablespoons lemon juice
Salt and pepper, to taste

Per Serving
Calories: 257
% Calories from fat: 20
Fat (gm): 6
Saturated fat (gm): 0.6
Cholesterol (mg): 0
Sodium (mg): 66
Protein (gm): 8.6
Carbohydrate (gm): 41.7
Exchanges
Milk: 0.0
Vegetable: 1.0
Fruit: 0.0
Bread: 2.5
Meat: 0.0
Fat: 1.0

1. Spray large saucepan with cooking spray; heat over medium heat until hot. Add barley to saucepan; spray lightly with cooking spray. Cook over medium heat, stirring occasionally, until barley is golden, 5 to 8 minutes.

2. Add stock to saucepan; heat to boiling. Reduce heat and simmer, covered, 40 minutes. Stir in bulgur and thyme; simmer, covered, 15 minutes. Stir in greens, green onions, and parsley; cook, covered, until all liquid is absorbed, about 10 minutes. Stir in tomato, walnuts and lemon juice; cook 5 minutes longer. Season to taste with salt and pepper.

STUFFED CABBAGE WITH CHILI TOMATO SAUCE

The cabbage can be served as a vegetarian entrée, or a cooked shredded meat such as pork or beef can be added to the rice.

6 servings

1 large green cabbage
1 large onion, chopped
1 clove garlic, minced
1/4-1/2 jalapeño chili, seeds and veins discarded, minced
1 tablespoon vegetable oil
3/4 teaspoon dried oregano leaves
1/2 teaspoon dried thyme leaves
1 can (15 ounces) black beans, rinsed, drained
2 medium tomatoes, chopped
1 cup cooked rice
1/2 cup raisins
2 tablespoons finely chopped cilantro
Salt and pepper, to taste
2 cups Chili Tomato Sauce (double recipe) (see p. 201)

Per Serving
Calories: 228
% Calories from fat: 13
Fat (gm): 4
Saturated fat (gm): 0.4
Cholesterol (mg): 0
Sodium (mg): 441
Protein (gm): 9.3
Carbohydrate (gm): 48.4
Exchanges
Milk: 0.0
Vegetable: 3.0
Fruit: 0.0
Bread: 2.0
Meat: 0.0
Fat: 0.5

1. Trim cabbage, discarding any wilted outside leaves. Place cabbage in large saucepan with water to cover; heat to boiling. Reduce heat and simmer, covered, 10 minutes. Drain cabbage; cool until warm enough to handle.

2. Saute onion, garlic, and jalapeño chili in oil until tender in large skillet, about 5 minutes. Add oregano and thyme; cook 1 minute longer.

3. Add beans and tomatoes to skillet; cook over medium heat, lightly mashing beans with a fork, and cooking until tomatoes release liquid, about 10 minutes. Stir in rice, raisins, and cilantro; season to taste with salt and pepper.

4. Place cabbage on large square of double-thickness cheesecloth. Spread outer cabbage leaves as flat as possible without breaking them off. Cut out inner part of cabbage, chop finely, and add to bean mixture; remove and discard core of cabbage.

5. Pack bean mixture into ball in center of the cabbage; fold outer leaves over mixture, reshaping cabbage. Gather up cheesecloth and tie with string. Place cabbage in large saucepan and add water to cover; heat to boiling. Reduce heat and simmer, covered, 1 hour. Lift cabbage from saucepan and remove cheesecloth.

6. Place cabbage on serving plate; cut into wedges. Serve with Chili Tomato Sauce.

CURRIED COUSCOUS WITH SMOKED TOFU

A delicious combination of flavors and textures. Serve with a green salad and crusty bread.

6 servings (about 1 cup each)

¹/₂	cup finely chopped onion
¹/₂	cup finely chopped red, *or* green, bell pepper
1¹/₂	teaspoons minced garlic
1	tablespoon olive oil
1¹/₂	teaspoons curry powder
1¹/₄	cups vegetable broth
1	package (10 ounces) couscous
2	packages (6 ounces each) smoked tofu, cubed
1	can (11 ounces) Mandarin orange segments, drained
	Salt and pepper, to taste
6	tablespoons (1¹/₂ ounces) crumbled reduced-fat feta cheese

Per Serving
Calories: 328
% Calories from fat: 23
Fat (gm): 8.8
Saturated fat (gm): 1.7
Cholesterol (mg): 2.5
Sodium (mg): 318
Protein (gm): 17.3
Carbohydrate (gm): 46.8
Exchanges
Milk: 0.0
Vegetable: 0.0
Fruit: 0.0
Bread: 3.0
Meat: 1.0
Fat: 1.0

1. Saute onion, bell pepper, and garlic in oil in large saucepan until tender, about 5 minutes. Stir in curry powder; cook 1 to 2 minutes longer, stirring constantly. Add broth to saucepan; heat to boiling.

2. Stir in couscous, discarding spice packet, and tofu; remove from heat and let stand, covered, 5 minutes. Stir in orange segments; season to taste with salt and pepper. Spoon couscous mixture into individual serving bowls; sprinkle each portion with cheese.

VIETNAMESE CURRIED VEGETABLE AND COCONUT STEW

Rice stick noodles, made with rice flour, can be round or flat. Angel hair pasta can be substituted.

6 servings (about 1¹/2 cups each)

Vegetable cooking spray
2 cups frozen stir-fry pepper blend
2 tablespoons minced gingerroot
1 tablespoon minced garlic
3-4 tablespoons curry powder
3¹/2 cups vegetable broth
3 cups reduced-fat coconut milk
1 tablespoon grated lime rind
1 teaspoon oriental chili paste
1 cup broccoli florets
1 cup cubed, peeled, seeded acorn, *or* butternut, squash
¹/2 package (8-ounce size) rice stick noodles
¹/4 cup all-purpose flour
¹/4 cup cold water
¹/4 cup lime juice
Salt, to taste
Finely chopped cilantro, as garnish

Per Serving
Calories: 218
% Calories from fat: 28
Fat (gm): 7.2
Saturated fat (gm): 0.1
Cholesterol (mg): 0
Sodium (mg): 627
Protein (gm): 4.1
Carbohydrate (gm): 37.1
Exchanges
Milk: 0.0
Vegetable: 1.0
Fruit: 0.0
Bread: 2.0
Meat: 0.0
Fat: 1.0

1. Spray large saucepan with cooking spray; heat over medium heat until hot. Saute pepper blend, gingerroot, and garlic 5 minutes. Stir in curry powder and cook 1 minute longer.

2. Add broth, coconut milk, lime rind, and chili paste to saucepan; heat to boiling. Add vegetables; reduce heat and simmer, covered, until vegetables are tender, about 15 minutes.

3. While stew is cooking, place noodles in large bowl; pour cold water over to cover. Let stand until noodles are separate and soft, about 5 minutes. Stir noodles into 4 quarts boiling water in large saucepan. Reduce heat and simmer, uncovered, until tender, about 5 minutes; drain.

4. Heat stew to boiling. Mix flour, cold water, and lime juice; stir into boiling stew. Boil, stirring constantly, until thickened, about 1 minute. Season to taste with salt. Serve stew over noodles in shallow bowls; sprinkle generously with cilantro.

ROASTED STUFFED PORTOBELLO MUSHROOMS WITH SPINACH-CILANTRO PESTO

Serve one mushroom as an appetizer or first course. The vegetable stuffing can also be used to fill large white mushroom caps.

4 servings

8 large portobello mushrooms (5-6 inches diameter)
  Vegetable cooking spray
1 cup finely chopped zucchini
1 cup shredded carrots
3 green onions and tops, thinly sliced
4 tablespoons dry unseasoned bread-crumbs
  Spinach-Cilantro Pesto (recipe follows)
  Salt and pepper, to taste
1/2 cup (2 ounces) shredded reduced-fat mozzarella cheese

Per Serving
Calories: 185
% Calories from fat: 20
Fat (gm): 3.9
Saturated fat (gm): 1.8
Cholesterol (mg): 7.6
Sodium (mg): 206
Protein (gm): 16
Carbohydrate (gm): 19.1
Exchanges
Milk: 0.0
Vegetable: 4.0
Fruit: 0.0
Bread: 0.5
Meat: 1.0
Fat: 0.0

1. Remove and chop mushroom stems. Spray large skillet with cooking spray; heat over medium heat until hot. Saute mushroom stems, zucchini, carrots, and green onions until crisp-tender, 8 to 10 minutes. Stir in breadcrumbs and pesto. Season to taste with salt and pepper. Spoon vegetable mixture onto mushrooms.

2. Spray aluminum-foil-lined jelly roll pan with cooking spray; arrange mushrooms on pan. Roast mushrooms at 425 degrees until mushrooms are tender, about 20 minutes, sprinkling with cheese the last 5 minutes of roasting time.

Spinach-Cilantro Pesto

makes about 1/2 cup

  1   cup loosely packed spinach leaves
 1/4 cup finely chopped cilantro
  3   cloves garlic
 1/4 teaspoon ground cumin
  1   tablespoon grated fat-free Parmesan
      cheese
 1-2 teaspoons olive oil
 1-2 teaspoons lime juice
 1-2 teaspoons water
      Salt and pepper, to taste

1. Process all ingredients, except water, salt, and pepper, in food processor or blender until smooth; add water if necessary for consistency. Season to taste with salt and pepper. Serve at room temperature.

GINGER COCONUT RICE AND SWEET POTATOES

Jasmine rice, scented with lemon grass and coconut, enhances this Asian-inspired entrée offering.

4 servings

          Vegetable cooking spray
   1/2   cup finely chopped onion
 11/2-2   tablespoons minced gingerroot
 1-11/2   tablespoons minced lemon grass
    1   teaspoon minced garlic
  11/4   cups water
  11/4   cups reduced-fat coconut milk
    1   cup jasmine, *or* long-grain, rice
    1   sweet potato, peeled, quartered, cut
          into 1/4-inch slices
    2   cups frozen stir-fry vegetable blend with
          asparagus
   1/4   cup finely chopped cilantro
  1-2   tablespoons lime juice
          Salt and pepper, to taste

Per Serving
Calories: 270
% Calories from fat: 13
Fat (gm): 3.9
Saturated fat (gm): 0
Cholesterol (mg): 0
Sodium (mg): 12
Protein (gm): 4.8
Carbohydrate (gm): 52.8
Exchanges
Milk: 0.0
Vegetable: 1.0
Fruit: 0.0
Bread: 3.0
Meat: 0.0
Fat: 0.5

1. Spray large saucepan with cooking spray; heat over medium heat until hot. Saute onion, gingerroot, lemon grass, and garlic until onion is tender, about 5 minutes. Stir in water, coconut milk, rice, and sweet potato; heat to boiling. Reduce heat and simmer, covered, 10 minutes.

2. Mix in stir-fry blend; cook, covered, until vegetables are tender and liquid absorbed, 8 to 10 minutes. Stir in cilantro; season to taste with lime juice, salt, and pepper.

TEMPEH STEAK WITH RED AND GREEN STIR-FRY

If available, use red or rhubarb Swiss chard for its beautiful red and green color.

6 servings

2 cups sliced red onions
1 cup sliced celery
2 teaspoons minced garlic
1 teaspoon minced gingerroot
2-3 teaspoons peanut oil
6 cups thinly sliced red, *or* green, Swiss chard *or* spinach
2 cups sliced red, *or* green, bell peppers
2 cups vegetable broth
2 tablespoons cornstarch
4 teaspoons reduced-sodium tamari soy sauce, divided
1/2-3/4 teaspoon hot chili paste
3 packages (8 ounces each) tempeh, cut into halves

Per Serving
Calories: 315
% Calories from fat: 29
Fat (gm): 11.1
Saturated fat (gm): 1.8
Cholesterol (mg): 0
Sodium (mg): 731
Protein (gm): 28.4
Carbohydrate (gm): 31.2
Exchanges
Milk: 0.0
Vegetable: 3.0
Fruit: 0.0
Bread: 1.0
Meat: 2.0
Fat: 1.0

1. Stir-fry onions, celery, garlic, and gingerroot in oil in wok or large skillet 1 to 2 minutes. Add Swiss chard and stir-fry 1 to 2 minutes. Add bell peppers to wok; stir-fry until vegetables are crisp-tender, 2 to 3 minutes.

2. Combine broth, cornstarch, 2 teaspoons soy sauce, and chili paste; stir into wok. Heat to boiling; boil, stirring constantly, until thickened, about 1 minute.

3. Brush tempeh with remaining 2 teaspoons soy sauce. Cook tempeh in greased large skillet over medium heat until browned, 2 to 3 minutes on each side. Arrange tempeh on serving platter; spoon vegetable mixture over.

GREEN ON GREEN STIR-FRY WITH TOFU

The variety of green vegetables creates a beautiful presentation.

6 servings

Oriental-flavored vegetable cooking spray
3 cups sliced leeks
1 cup sliced celery
1 teaspoon minced garlic
1 teaspoon minced gingerroot
1/2 teaspoon crushed red pepper
4 cups sliced bok choy
4 cups snow peas, trimmed
1 cup chopped green bell pepper
2 cups vegetable broth
2 tablespoons cornstarch
2 teaspoons reduced-sodium tamari soy sauce
1 package (10 ounces) firm light tofu, cubed
Salt and pepper, to taste
4 cups cooked rice, warm

Per Serving
Calories: 275
% Calories from fat: 5
Fat (gm): 1.5
Saturated fat (gm): 0.2
Cholesterol (mg): 0
Sodium (mg): 194
Protein (gm): 11.9
Carbohydrate (gm): 54
Exchanges
Milk: 0.0
Vegetable: 3.0
Fruit: 0.0
Bread: 2.0
Meat: 1.0
Fat: 0.0

1. Spray wok or large skillet with cooking spray; heat over medium heat until hot. Stir-fry leeks, celery, garlic, gingerroot, and crushed red pepper 2 to 3 minutes. Add bok choy and stir-fry 1 minute; add snow peas and bell pepper and stir-fry 2 to 3 minutes longer.

2. Combine broth, cornstarch, and soy sauce; stir into wok and heat to boiling. Boil, stirring constantly until thickened, about 1 minute. Gently stir in tofu; cook 1 to 2 minutes longer. Season to taste with salt and pepper. Serve over rice.

ASIAN FRIED RICE

The combination of wild and white rice adds a new dimension to an Asian favorite. Lightly scrambled egg is a traditional addition to many fried rice recipes; it can be omitted, if desired.

4 servings (about 1 1/2 cups each)

1 package (6 1/4 ounces) quick-cooking long-grain and wild rice
2 cups broccoli florets
2 ounces snow peas, cut into halves
2 medium carrots, sliced
3/4 cup bean sprouts
3/4 cup sliced shiitake, *or* white, mushrooms
1/2 cup chopped red, *or* green, bell pepper
1 teaspoon minced garlic
1 teaspoon finely chopped gingerroot
2 tablespoons vegetable oil
1/2 cup vegetable broth
2 tablespoons reduced-sodium soy sauce
1 egg, lightly scrambled, crumbled

Per Serving
Calories: 305
% Calories from fat: **25**
Fat (gm): 8.9
Saturated fat (gm): **1.4**
Cholesterol (mg): **53**
Sodium (mg): 435
Protein (gm): 10.6
Carbohydrate (gm): **48.3**
Exchanges
Milk: 0.0
Vegetable: 3.0
Fruit: 0.0
Bread: 2.0
Meat: 0.0
Fat: 2.0

1. Cook rice according to package directions, discarding seasoning packet.

2. Stir-fry vegetables, garlic, and gingerroot in oil in wok over medium-high heat until crisp-tender, 5 to 8 minutes.

3. Add broth and soy sauce to wok; stir in rice and scrambled egg and cook 2 to 3 minutes more.

STIR-FRIED RICE NOODLES WITH VEGETABLES

Rice noodles are also called cellophane noodles, or "bihon."

4 servings

Per Serving
Calories: 250
% Calories from fat: 14
Fat (gm): 4
Saturated fat (gm): 0.5
Cholesterol (mg): 0
Sodium (mg): 691
Protein (gm): 7.5
Carbohydrate (gm): 47.6
Exchanges
Milk: 0.0
Vegetable: 3.0
Fruit: 0.0
Bread: 2.0
Meat: 0.0
Fat: 0.5

    1 package (8 ounces) rice noodles
       Cold water
    1 tablespoon vegetable oil
    1 cup halved green beans
    1 cup cubed yellow summer squash
  1/2 cup sliced red, *or* green, bell pepper
    4 green onions and tops, thinly sliced
    1 tablespoon finely chopped fresh
       gingerroot
    2 cups thinly sliced napa cabbage
    1 cup vegetable broth
  2-3 teaspoons soy sauce
1/2-1 teaspoon Szechwan chili sauce

1. Place noodles in large bowl; pour cold water over to cover. Let stand until noodles separate and are soft, about 15 minutes; drain.

2. Heat oil in wok or skillet over medium-high heat until hot. Add green beans, squash, bell pepper, green onions, and gingerroot. Stir-fry until vegetables are tender, 8 to 10 minutes.

3. Add cabbage to wok; stir-fry just until cabbage turns bright in color, about 1 minute. Stir in drained noodles, broth, soy sauce, and chili sauce. Heat to boiling; reduce heat and simmer, uncovered, until noodles have absorbed all liquid, about 5 minutes.

BUCATINI WITH BRUSSELS SPROUTS AND WALNUTS

This dish provides an interesting contrast of textures and hot and cold ingredients.

4 servings

12 ounces Brussels sprouts, cut into halves

2 teaspoons minced garlic

2 teaspoons olive oil

8 ounces bucatini *or* spaghetti, cooked, warm

2 cups chopped, seeded Italian plum tomatoes

2/3 cup minced parsley

1/4 cup plain bread crumbs, toasted

1/2 cup chopped walnuts

2-4 tablespoons shredded Parmesan cheese

Salt and pepper, to taste

Per Serving
Calories: 415
% Calories from fat: 29
Fat (gm): 13.9
Saturated fat (gm): 1.7
Cholesterol (mg): 2.3
Sodium (mg): 125
Protein (gm): 16
Carbohydrate (gm): 60.6
Exchanges
Milk: 0.0
Vegetable: 3.0
Fruit: 0.0
Bread: 3.0
Meat: 0.0
Fat: 2.5

1. Cook Brussels sprouts in 2 inches simmering water until crisp-tender, about 8 minutes; drain.

2. Saute garlic in oil in medium skillet 1 to 2 minutes; add Brussels sprouts and cook 2 to 3 minutes longer.

3. Toss pasta with sprouts mixture, tomatoes, parsley, bread crumbs, walnuts, and Parmesan cheese in serving bowl; season to taste with salt and pepper.

FETTUCCINE WITH EGGPLANT PERSILLADE

"Persillade" is a French term meaning "with lots of parsley," which this fragrant dish does have.

4 servings

Olive oil cooking spray
1 medium onion, chopped
1 green bell pepper, chopped
1 red bell pepper, chopped
1 small eggplant, unpeeled, cut into 1/2-inch cubes
2 teaspoons minced roasted garlic
1/2 cup canned reduced-sodium vegetable broth
Salt and pepper, to taste
1/2 cup finely chopped parsley
8 ounces whole wheat fettuccine, cooked, warm
2-4 tablespoons grated fat-free Parmesan cheese

Per Serving
Calories: 246
% Calories from fat: 9
Fat (gm): 2.5
Saturated fat (gm): 0.1
Cholesterol (mg): 0
Sodium (mg): 136
Protein (gm): 11
Carbohydrate (gm): 48.7
Exchanges
Milk: 0.0
Vegetable: 3.0
Fruit: 0.0
Bread: 2.0
Meat: 0.5
Fat: 0.0

1. Spray large skillet with cooking spray; heat over medium heat until hot. Saute onion, bell peppers, eggplant, and garlic 5 minutes, stirring occasionally. Add broth and heat to boiling; reduce heat and simmer, covered, until eggplant is tender and broth absorbed, about 5 minutes. Season to taste with salt and pepper. Add parsley and toss.

2. Toss vegetable mixture with pasta and spoon onto plates; sprinkle lightly with cheese.

FETTUCCINE WITH GREENS AND CARAMELIZED ONIONS

4 servings

Per Serving
Calories: 281
% Calories from fat: 18
Fat (gm): 5.8
Saturated fat (gm): 0.5
Cholesterol (mg): 0
Sodium (mg): 151
Protein (gm): 10.3
Carbohydrate (gm): 49.9
Exchanges
Milk: 0.0
Vegetable: 2.0
Fruit: 0.0
Bread: 2.5
Meat: 0.0
Fat: 1.0

    4 medium onions, sliced
    1 tablespoon olive oil
    1 teaspoon sugar
    1 can (14$^{1}/_{2}$ ounces) reduced-sodium vegetable broth
1$^{1}/_{2}$ cups water
    2 cups thinly sliced kale *or* mustard greens *or* Swiss chard
    2 cups thinly sliced curly endive *or* spinach
      Salt and pepper, to taste
    8 ounces fettuccine, cooked, warm

1. Cook onions in oil over medium heat in large skillet 5 minutes; reduce heat to low and stir in sugar. Cook until onions are golden in color and very soft, about 20 minutes.

2. Stir broth and water into onions; heat to boiling. Reduce heat and simmer, uncovered, until broth is reduced by $^{1}/_{3}$, about 10 minutes. Add greens; simmer, covered, until greens are wilted, 5 to 7 minutes. Simmer, uncovered, until broth is almost absorbed, about 5 minutes. Season to taste with salt and pepper.

3. Spoon onion mixture over pasta and toss.

POTATO GNOCCHI WITH SAGE CREAM

A rich, creamy sauce flavors the gnocchi in this dish.

6 servings

2 cups whole milk
1 teaspoon dried sage leaves
1 cup chopped onion
2-3 teaspoons margarine
4 cups small broccoflower, *or* broccoli, florets
1/2 cup water, divided
1 package (16 ounces) potato gnocchi
2 tablespoons all-purpose flour
1/2 teaspoon ground nutmeg
Salt and pepper, to taste
Shredded Parmesan cheese, as garnish

Per Serving
Calories: 254
% Calories from fat: 18
Fat (gm): 5.4
Saturated fat (gm): 2.6
Cholesterol (mg): 16.6
Sodium (mg): 403
Protein (gm): 10
Carbohydrate (gm): 42.3
Exchanges
Milk: 0.0
Vegetable: 0.0
Fruit: 0.0
Bread: 3.0
Meat: 0.0
Fat: 1.0

1. Heat milk and sage leaves to boiling in medium saucepan; reduce heat and simmer 10 minutes.

2. Saute onion in margarine in large skillet 2 to 3 minutes; add broccoflower and 1/4 cup water and heat to boiling. Reduce heat and simmer, covered, until broccoflower is tender and water gone, 5 to 8 minutes.

3. Cook gnocchi according to package directions; add to vegetables in skillet.

4. Heat milk mixture to boiling. Mix flour, nutmeg, and remaining 1/4 cup water; whisk into milk. Boil, whisking constantly, until thickened, about 1 minute. Pour sauce over vegetables and gnocchi in skillet; season to taste with salt and pepper. Spoon into serving bowl; sprinkle with Parmesan cheese.

TUSCAN BEAN BAKE

Easy to combine and bake, the beans are lemon-scented and seasoned with sun-dried tomatoes, garlic, and herbs. Any white beans, such as garbanzo beans, soy beans, or navy beans can be used.

4 servings (about 1 cup each)

1 cup chopped onion
2 teaspoons minced garlic, divided
1/2 cup chopped red, *or* green, bell pepper
1 tablespoon olive oil
1 large tomato, chopped
6 sun-dried tomatoes (not in oil), sliced
2-3 teaspoons grated lemon rind
1 teaspoon dried sage leaves
1 teaspoon dried rosemary leaves
2 cans (15 ounces each) cannellini, *or* Great Northern, beans, rinsed, drained
Salt and pepper, to taste
1 cup fresh whole wheat bread crumbs
1/4 cup minced parsley

Per Serving
Calories: 311
% Calories from fat: 14
Fat (gm): 5.1
Saturated fat (gm): 0.7
Cholesterol (mg): 0
Sodium (mg): 400
Protein (gm): 12.7
Carbohydrate (gm): 55.8
Exchanges
Milk: 0.0
Vegetable: 2.0
Fruit: 0.0
Bread: 3.0
Meat: 0.0
Fat: 1.0

1. Saute onion, 1 teaspoon garlic, and bell pepper in oil in large skillet 5 minutes. Add tomato, sun-dried tomatoes, lemon rind, and herbs and saute 2-3 minutes longer. Stir in beans and season to taste with salt and pepper; pour into 1 1/2-quart casserole.

2. Combine bread crumbs, parsley, and remaining 1 teaspoon garlic; sprinkle over top of bean mixture and press lightly onto beans to moisten bread crumbs. Bake, uncovered, at 350 degrees until liquid has evaporated and bread crumbs are browned, 25 to 30 minutes.

EGGPLANT POLENTA STACK

Purchase packaged flavored polenta in the produce section; choose any favorite flavor for this dish.

4 servings

8 slices (³/₄ inch) eggplant (about 1 pound)
2 egg whites, lightly beaten *or* ¹/₄ cup no-cholesterol real egg product
¹/₂ cup Italian-seasoned dry bread crumbs
¹/₄ cup grated Parmesan cheese
Olive oil cooking spray
1 package (16 ounces) prepared Italian-herb polenta, cut into 8 slices
8 slices (¹/₂ inch) tomato
Salt and pepper, to taste
2-4 ounces reduced-fat feta, *or* goat, cheese, crumbled

Per Serving
Calories: 222
% Calories from fat: 18
Fat (gm): 4.5
Saturated fat (gm): 2.4
Cholesterol (mg): 9
Sodium (mg): 624
Protein (gm): 10.9
Carbohydrate (gm): 35
Exchanges
Milk: 0.0
Vegetable: 1.0
Fruit: 0.0
Bread: 2.0
Meat: 0.0
Fat: 1.0

1. Dip eggplant slices in egg whites and coat with combined bread crumbs and Parmesan cheese. Spray large skillet with cooking spray and heat over medium heat until hot. Cook eggplant until browned on the bottom, about 10 minutes; spray tops of slices with cooking spray and turn. Cook until eggplant is tender and browned on other side, about 10 minutes longer.

2. Arrange eggplant in baking pan; top each slice with a slice of polenta and tomato. Sprinkle tomatoes with salt and pepper; sprinkle stack with feta cheese.

3. Bake at 450 degrees until tomatoes are hot and cheese lightly browned, about 10 minutes.

VEGETABLES MARENGO

A delicious dish that picks up the colors and flavors of the Mediterranean.

4 servings

1 package (10^1/$_2$ ounces) light tofu, cut into scant 1-inch cubes
2 tablespoons olive oil
2 medium onions, cut into wedges
2 medium zucchini, cubed
1 cup small mushrooms
1 teaspoon minced garlic
1 tablespoon flour
1 can (14^1/$_2$ ounces) diced tomatoes, undrained
3/4 cup vegetable broth
1 strip orange rind (3 x 1 inch)
1/2 teaspoon dried thyme leaves
1/2 teaspoon dried oregano leaves
    Salt and pepper, to taste
3 cups cooked couscous *or* rice, warm

Per Serving
Calories: 349
% Calories from fat: 27
Fat (gm): 10.8
Saturated fat (gm): 1
Cholesterol (mg): 0
Sodium (mg): 608
Protein (gm): 16.7
Carbohydrate (gm): 48.4
Exchanges
Milk: 0.0
Vegetable: 3.0
Fruit: 0.0
Bread: 2.0
Meat: 1.0
Fat: 1.5

1. Cook tofu in oil in large saucepan over medium heat until browned on all sides, about 5 minutes. Remove from pan and reserve.

2. Add onions, zucchini, mushrooms, and garlic to saucepan; saute 5 minutes. Stir in flour and cook 1 to 2 minutes longer. Add tomatoes, broth, orange rind, herbs, and reserved tofu; heat to boiling. Reduce heat and simmer, covered, until vegetables are tender, 10 to 15 minutes. Season to taste with salt and pepper. Serve mixture over couscous in shallow bowls.

MARINATED TORTELLINI AND VEGETABLE KABOBS

The vegetables are served uncooked on these kabobs. Cook other vegetables, such as eggplant, broccoli, cauliflower, etc., until crisp-tender before marinating.

4 servings

1 large red bell pepper, cut into 1-inch pieces

1 small yellow summer squash, cut into 1/2-inch slices

1 small zucchini, cut into 1/2-inch slices

1 small cucumber, cut into 1/2-inch slices

24 cherry tomatoes

24 medium mushroom caps

16 pitted Greek, *or* ripe, olives

4 ounces fat-free mozzarella cheese, cut into cubes

4 ounces fat-free Cheddar cheese, cut into cubes

1/2 package (9-ounce size) mushroom, *or* cheese, tortellini, cooked

1 1/4-1 1/2 cups fat-free, sodium-free Italian salad dressing

3 cloves garlic, minced

2 tablespoons grated fat-free Parmesan cheese

4 cups torn salad greens

Per Serving
Calories: 362
% Calories from fat: 16
Fat (gm): 6.2
Saturated fat (gm): 1.6
Cholesterol (mg): 13.3
Sodium (mg): 606
Protein (gm): 30.6
Carbohydrate (gm): 44.3
Exchanges
Milk: 0.0
Vegetable: 5.0
Fruit: 0.0
Bread: 1.5
Meat: 2.5
Fat: 0.0

1. Arrange vegetables, olives, cubed cheese, and tortellini on wooden skewers and place in large baking dish or plastic bag.

2. Mix salad dressing, garlic, and Parmesan cheese; pour over kabobs. Refrigerate 4 to 6 hours, turning kabobs occasionally.

3. Drain kabobs; reserving 3/4 cup marinade. Arrange kabobs on lettuce on plates; drizzle each with 2 to 3 tablespoons of marinade.

GARDEN VEGETABLE AND TEMPEH SAUTE

Vary the vegetables according to season and availability. Serve over rice, fresh Chinese-style noodles, or pasta, if desired.

4 servings

2 cups frozen stir-fry pepper blend

1 teaspoon minced garlic

1-2 teaspoons olive oil

1 package (8 ounces) tempeh, cut into ¹/₂-inch cubes

1 cup tomato juice

2 tablespoons tamari soy sauce

1 medium zucchini, sliced

2 cups (4 ounces) sliced mushrooms

1 teaspoon dried basil leaves

1 teaspoon dried oregano leaves

¹/₄ teaspoon cayenne pepper

2 medium tomatoes, cut into wedges

Salt, to taste

Per Serving
Calories: 180
% Calories from fat: 28
Fat (gm): 6.1
Saturated fat (gm): 1
Cholesterol (mg): 0
Sodium (mg): 732
Protein (gm): 15.6
Carbohydrate (gm): 19.2
Exchanges
Milk: 0.0
Vegetable: 1.0
Fruit: 0.0
Bread: 1.0
Meat: 1.0
Fat: 0.5

1. Saute pepper blend and garlic in oil in large skillet 2 to 3 minutes. Add tempeh and cook 5 minutes. Stir in remaining ingredients, except tomatoes and salt; heat to boiling. Reduce heat and simmer, covered, until vegetables are tender, about 5 minutes.

2. Add tomato wedges; cook, covered, until softened, about 5 minutes. Season to taste with salt.

ROASTED VEGETABLES AND BEANS WITH PORTOBELLO MUSHROOMS

Roasting vegetables intensifies their natural flavor and sweetness; roasting time is cut in half with a frozen roasted vegetable blend. Complement this full-flavored entrée with warm garlic bread.

6 servings

Vegetable cooking spray

1 package (1 pound, 10 ounces) frozen Parmesan-herb oven-roasted vegetables

1 can (15 ounces) pinto beans, rinsed, drained

1 can (15 ounces) dark kidney beans, rinsed, drained

1 red, *or* green, bell pepper, cut into ¹/₂-inch strips

1 small onion, cut into thin wedges

2 tablespoons olive, *or* vegetable, oil, divided

4 large portobello mushrooms, stems removed (3 ounces each)

Per Serving
Calories: 299
% Calories from fat: 18
Fat (gm): 5.5
Saturated fat (gm): 0.8
Cholesterol (mg): 3.3
Sodium (mg): 764
Protein (gm): 9.8
Carbohydrate (gm): 47.2
Exchanges
Milk: 0.0
Vegetable: 2.0
Fruit: 0.0
Bread: 3.0
Meat: 0.0
Fat: 2.0

1. Line large jelly roll pan with aluminum foil; spray with cooking spray. Combine oven-roasted vegetables, beans, bell pepper, and onion on pan; drizzle with 1 tablespoon oil and toss.

2. Chop mushroom stems and add to vegetable mixture; sprinkle vegetables with seasoning packet. Brush mushroom caps with remaining 1 tablespoon oil and place at end of pan.

3. Bake at 450 degrees until browned, about 30 minutes, stirring mixed vegetables halfway through baking time. Arrange mushrooms on plates; spoon vegetables over.

CABBAGE RAGOUT WITH MASHED POTATOES

Fresh fennel, gingerroot, and apple lend aromatic flavor highlights to this cabbage stew. If fresh fennel is not available, substitute celery and increase the amount of fennel seeds to 1¹/₂ teaspoons.

6 servings (about 1¹/₃ cups each)

1 medium eggplant (about 1¹/₄ pounds), unpeeled, cut into ¹/₂-inch cubes
1 cup chopped onion
¹/₂ cup thinly sliced fennel bulb
2 teaspoons minced garlic
4 teaspoons minced gingerroot
1 teaspoon fennel seeds, crushed
1-2 tablespoons vegetable oil
8 cups thinly sliced cabbage
2 cups vegetable broth
2 medium unpeeled apples, cored, cubed
1 cup fat-free sour cream
Salt and pepper, to taste
³/₄ package (22-ounce size) frozen mashed potatoes

Per Serving
Calories: 244
% Calories from fat: 21
Fat (gm): 5.9
Saturated fat (gm): 0.8
Cholesterol (mg): 0.2
Sodium (mg): 518
Protein (gm): 7.3
Carbohydrate (gm): 43.6
Exchanges
Milk: 0.0
Vegetable: 5.0
Fruit: 0.0
Bread: 1.0
Meat: 0.0
Fat: 1.0

1. Saute eggplant, onion, fennel, garlic, gingerroot, and fennel seeds in oil in large saucepan until vegetables are tender and beginning to brown, about 10 minutes, stirring occasionally.

2. Add cabbage and broth; heat to boiling. Reduce heat and simmer, covered, until cabbage is wilted and crisp-tender, about 5 minutes. Stir apples into cabbage mixture; cook, covered, until apples are tender, about 5 minutes. Stir in sour cream; cook over medium heat until hot through, 3 to 4 minutes. Season to taste with salt and pepper.

3. While ragout is cooking, prepare mashed potatoes according to package directions. Serve ragout over potatoes.

Tip: 1¹/₂ packages (16-ounce size) of cabbage slaw mix can be used in place of the 8 cups of sliced cabbage.

BARBECUED TEMPEH AND PEPPERS

Serve in toasted multigrain buns for fabulous sandwiches, too!

4 servings (generous 1 cup each)

1   package (8 ounces) tempeh
     Tamari Marinade (recipe follows)
     Vegetable cooking spray
1   cup sliced onion
2   medium red, *or* green, bell peppers,
     sliced
1   teaspoon minced garlic
1   cup water
¼   cup reduced-sodium tomato paste
1-2 tablespoons unsulphured molasses
1-2 tablespoons brown sugar
2   teaspoons prepared mustard
2   teaspoons cider vinegar
1   teaspoon chili powder
     Salt and pepper, to taste
3   cups cooked brown basmati rice, warm

Per Serving
Calories: 371
% Calories from fat: 15
Fat (gm): 6.4
Saturated fat (gm): 0.8
Cholesterol (mg): 0
Sodium (mg): 394
Protein (gm): 20.1
Carbohydrate (gm): 64.1
Exchanges
Milk: 0.5
Vegetable: 3.0
Fruit: 0.0
Bread: 3.0
Meat: 1.0
Fat: 0.5

1.   Place tempeh in shallow glass bowl; pour Tamari Marinade over. Refrigerate, covered, several hours or overnight, turning occasionally. Drain; reserve marinade. Cut tempeh into ½-inch cubes.

2.   Spray large skillet with cooking spray; heat over medium heat until hot. Saute onion, bell peppers, and garlic until tender, 5 to 8 minutes.

3.   Add reserved marinade and remaining ingredients, except salt and pepper and rice, to skillet; heat to boiling. Reduce heat and simmer, uncovered, until mixture is thickened, mashing cubes of tempeh slightly with a fork. Season to taste with salt and pepper; serve over rice.

Tamari Marinade

makes about 4 tablespoons

       2 tablespoons reduced-sodium tamari soy
          sauce
       2 tablespoons cider vinegar
    1¹/₂ teaspoons minced garlic
    ¹/₂-1 teaspoon chili powder

1. Mix all ingredients; refrigerate until ready to use.

VEGETABLE STRUDEL WITH CHEESE

A special dish for festive occasions that's easy enough for family dinners, too.

4 servings

    1¹/₂ cups cubed, peeled, seeded butternut, *or*
          acorn, squash
    1¹/₂ cups small broccoli florets
       2 packages (1.25 ounces each) cheese
          sauce mix
       1 cup sliced shiitake, *or* cremini, mush-
          rooms
    ¹/₂ cup chopped red, *or* green, bell pepper
    ¹/₂ cup chopped yellow, *or* green, bell
          pepper
    ¹/₄ cup chopped shallots
       1 teaspoon minced garlic
       2 teaspoons margarine
    ³/₄ cup (3 ounces) shredded reduced-fat
          brick, *or* Swiss, cheese
          Salt and pepper, to taste
       5 sheets frozen, thawed fillo pastry
          Vegetable cooking spray

Per Serving
Calories: 245
% Calories from fat: 25
Fat (gm): 7.7
Saturated fat (gm): 3.3
Cholesterol (mg): 11.1
Sodium (mg): 724
Protein (gm): 12.1
Carbohydrate (gm): 38.6
Exchanges
Milk: 0.0
Vegetable: 1.0
Fruit: 0.0
Bread: 2.0
Meat: 1.0
Fat: 0.5

1. Cook squash and broccoli, covered, in 1-inch simmering water until tender, about 10 minutes; drain. Make cheese sauce according to package directions.

2. Saute mushrooms, bell peppers, shallots, and garlic in margarine in large skillet 5 minutes. Stir in squash, broccoli, and half the cheese sauce. Remove from heat and stir in shredded cheese; season to taste with salt and pepper.

3. Lay 1 sheet fillo on clean towel on table; spray generously with cooking spray. Cover with second sheet fillo and spray generously with cooking spray; repeat with remaining fillo.

4. Spoon vegetable mixture along long edge of fillo, 3 to 4 inches from the edge. Fold edge of fillo over filling and roll up, using towel to help lift and roll; place seam side down on greased cookie sheet. Spray top of fillo generously with cooking spray.

5. Bake at 400 degrees until golden, about 20 minutes. Let stand 5 minutes before cutting. Trim ends; cut strudel into 4 pieces and arrange on plates. Serve with remaining cheese sauce.

SPINACH CHEESE CREPES

For variation, saute ¹/₂ cup chopped portobello mushrooms and add to the spinach-cheese mixture.

4 servings (2 each)

Vegetable cooking spray
¹/₄ cup chopped onion
1 package (10 ounces) frozen chopped spinach, thawed, well drained
1 cup fat-free cottage cheese
¹/₄ teaspoon dried thyme leaves
2-3 pinches ground nutmeg
Salt and pepper, to taste
8 slices (¹/₂-³/₄ ounces each) fat-free mozzarella, *or* Swiss, cheese
Crepes (see p. 692), warm
2 cups Fresh Tomato and Herb Sauce (¹/₂ recipe) (see p. 211)

Per Serving
Calories: 277
% Calories from fat: 25
Fat (gm): 7.9
Saturated fat (gm): 1.7
Cholesterol (mg): 107
Sodium (mg): 684
Protein (gm): 26.3
Carbohydrate (gm): 27.3
Exchanges
Milk: 0.0
Vegetable: 2.5
Fruit: 0.0
Bread: 1.0
Meat: 2.5
Fat: 0.0

1. Spray medium skillet with cooking spray; heat over medium heat until hot. Saute onion until tender, 3 to 4 minutes. Add spinach to skillet; cook until spinach is very dry, about 5 minutes. Remove from heat and mix in cottage cheese, thyme, and nutmeg; season to taste with salt and pepper.

2. Place cheese slices on crepes; spoon spinach-cheese mixture along centers of crepes. Roll up crepes and place, seam sides down, in lightly greased baking dish. Bake, loosely covered, at 325 degrees until filling is hot and cheese melted, about 10 minutes.

3. Transfer crepes to serving plates; spoon Fresh Tomato and Herb Sauce over.

BLACK BEAN AND SMOKED TOFU SALAD

The smoky flavor of the tofu is a pleasant contrast to the picante chili, fresh-flavored cilantro, and mustard-honey dressing.

6 servings

- 2 cans (15 ounces each) black beans, rinsed, drained
- 3 packages (6 ounces each) smoked tofu, cubed
- 1 large tomato, seeded, chopped
- 1 medium red, *or* green, bell pepper, chopped
- 1/2 cup thinly sliced red onion
- 1/4 cup finely chopped cilantro
- 1/4 cup finely chopped parsley
- 1 jalapeño chili, finely chopped
- 2 teaspoons minced roasted garlic
- 1/2 cup prepared fat-free honey-Dijon dressing
  Lettuce leaves

Per Serving
Calories: 179
% Calories from fat: 15
Fat (gm): 3.8
Saturated fat (gm): 0
Cholesterol (mg): 0
Sodium (mg): 712
Protein (gm): 12.7
Carbohydrate (gm): 35.2
Exchanges
Milk: 0.0
Vegetable: 0.0
Fruit: 0.0
Bread: 2.0
Meat: 1.0
Fat: 0.0

1. Combine all ingredients, except honey-Dijon dressing and lettuce, in salad bowl; pour dressing over and toss. Serve on lettuce-lined plates.

VEGETABLE SALAD WITH MILLET

Finely chop the vegetables by hand or in a food processor. Serve the salad in bowls, in beefsteak tomato halves, or use it as a filling for warm pita breads.

6 servings (about 1¹/₃ cups each)

1¹/₄ cups millet
3¹/₃ cups water
¹/₂ cup sliced celery
¹/₂ medium red, *or* green, bell pepper, sliced
  4 green onions and tops, sliced
  1 medium carrot, sliced
  4 tablespoons finely chopped fresh basil *or* 2 teaspoons dried basil leaves
¹/₂ head iceberg lettuce, sliced
  1 medium tomato, coarsely chopped
    Oregano Vinaigrette (recipe follows)
    Salt and pepper, to taste
    Spinach, *or* lettuce, leaves
  4 pita breads

Per Serving
Calories: 348
% Calories from fat: 23
Fat (gm): 9.2
Saturated fat (gm): 1.3
Cholesterol (mg): 0
Sodium (mg): 236
Protein (gm): 9.3
Carbohydrate (gm): 57.1
Exchanges
Milk: 0.0
Vegetable: 2.0
Fruit: 0.0
Bread: 3.0
Meat: 0.0
Fat: 2.0

1. Cook millet in large saucepan over medium heat until toasted, 2 to 3 minutes. Add water and heat to boiling; reduce heat and simmer, covered, until millet is tender and liquid absorbed, 15 to 20 minutes. Cool.

2. Combine celery, bell pepper, green onions, carrot, and basil in food processor; process, using pulse technique, until finely chopped. Transfer mixture to large bowl.

3. Add lettuce to food processor; process, using pulse technique, until finely chopped. Add to bowl with vegetables.

4. Add tomato and millet to vegetable mixture and toss; drizzle with Oregano Vinaigrette and toss. Season to taste with salt and pepper. Spoon salad into spinach-lined salad bowls; serve with pita breads.

Oregano Vinaigrette

makes about 1/3 cup

3-4 tablespoons olive oil

3 tablespoons white wine vinegar

1 teaspoon dried oregano leaves

1. Mix all ingredients; refrigerate until ready to serve.

SEVEN

Eggs

AND

Cheese

EGGS BENEDICT

A hollandaise sauce that is almost too good to be true brings a popular brunch dish back to the table in healthy style. Six slices of English Muffin Bread (see p. 673) can be substituted for the English muffins.

6 servings

6 ounces sliced lean Canadian bacon
3 English muffins, halved, toasted
6 poached eggs
   Mock Hollandaise Sauce (see p. 209)
   Paprika, as garnish
   Finely chopped parsley leaves, as garnish

Per Serving
Calories: 204
% Calories from fat: 27
Fat (gm): 5.6
Saturated fat (gm): 1.7
Cholesterol (mg): 228.3
Sodium (mg): 786
Protein (gm): 19
Carbohydrate (gm): 17
Exchanges
Milk: 0.0
Vegetable: 0.0
Fruit: 0.0
Bread: 1.0
Meat: 2.5
Fat: 0.0

1. Heat Canadian bacon in small skillet until hot and lightly browned. Arrange Canadian bacon on muffin halves and top with poached eggs.

2. Spoon Mock Hollandaise Sauce over eggs; sprinkle with paprika and parsley

EGGS IN A CUMULUS CLOUD

Delicious flavors in a unique presentation.

4 servings

2 pumpernickel bagels, split, toasted
8 tablespoons fat-free cream cheese
4 eggs, separated
   Salt and pepper, to taste
   Parsley sprigs, as garnish
   Paprika, as garnish

Per Serving
Calories: 188
% Calories from fat: 26
Fat (gm): 6.4
Saturated fat (gm): 1.8
Cholesterol (mg): 214.4
Sodium (mg): 332
Protein (gm): 15.1
Carbohydrate (gm): 26.4
Exchanges
Milk: 0.0
Vegetable: 0.0
Fruit: 0.0
Bread: 1.5
Meat: 1.0
Fat: 0.5

1. Spread toasted bagel halves with cream cheese. Beat egg whites to stiff peaks; spoon completely over bagel halves, covering hole. Make a well in center of egg white and place 1 yolk in each well.

2. Broil 6 inches from heat source until egg white is lightly browned and yolks are set, 2 to 3 minutes. Sprinkle lightly with salt and pepper. Garnish with parsley and paprika.

EGGS IN HELL

Here is a hair of the dog that may have bitten you—a hangover remedy that is perfect for a late-night breakfast.

4 servings

1¹/₂ cups reduced-sodium vegetable juice cocktail

6-8 drops hot pepper sauce

2 teaspoons yeast extract, such as Vegemite, *or* 2 teaspoons Worcestershire sauce

4 eggs

¹/₃ cup light beer

4 slices whole wheat bread, toasted
Chopped parsley *or* cilantro, as garnish

Per Serving
Calories: 169
% Calories from fat: 32
Fat (gm): 6.1
Saturated fat (gm): 1.8
Cholesterol (mg): 212
Sodium (mg): 323
Protein (gm): 9.6
Carbohydrate (gm): 17.5
Exchanges
Milk: 0.0
Vegetable: 1.0
Fruit: 0.0
Bread: 1.0
Meat: 1.0
Fat: 0.5

1. Heat vegetable juice, hot pepper sauce, and yeast extract to boiling in small skillet; reduce heat to medium-low. Break eggs into a saucer, and slip them into juice mixture. Simmer gently, spooning juice mixture over eggs as they cook. When eggs are done, pour beer over; heat just until warm.

2. Remove eggs from skillet with slotted spoon; drain. Place on toast; garnish with parsley.

NEW MEXICO EGG TOSTADAS

These easy tostadas are baked and served with a simple chili sauce.

4 servings

4 whole wheat tortillas
  Vegetable cooking spray
2 cups fat-free refried beans
2 green onions, thinly sliced
4 eggs
  Fresh cilantro leaves, as garnish
  Red Sauce (recipe follows)
4 tablespoons fat-free sour cream

Per Serving
Calories: 251
% Calories from fat: 18
Fat (gm): 5.1
Saturated fat (gm): 1.6
Cholesterol (mg): 212
Sodium (mg): 715
Protein (gm): 15.2
Carbohydrate (gm): 35.1
Exchanges
Milk: 0.0
Vegetable: 0.0
Fruit: 0.0
Bread: 2.5
Meat: 1.0
Fat: 0.5

1. To crisp tortillas, quickly immerse in water and drain. Bake tortillas on lightly greased cookie sheet at 450 degrees 2 to 3 minutes or until lightly browned.

2. Spoon a ring of refried beans around outer edge of each tortilla. Sprinkle green onions evenly over beans. Break an egg into center of each tortilla. Bake at 350 degrees until eggs are set, 15 to 20 minutes.

3. Carefully loosen tortillas from pan with wide spatula and place on serving plates. Garnish with cilantro; serve with Red Sauce and sour cream.

Red Sauce

makes about 3/4 cup

1/4 cup chopped onion
1/2 cup reduced-sodium fat-free beef broth
1/4 cup crushed New Mexico chilies, seeds
  and stems discarded

1. Heat onion and broth to boiling in small saucepan; reduce heat and simmer, covered, until onion is soft, about 5 minutes. Add chilies and cook 2 to 3 minutes to soften. Puree mixture in blender or food processor until smooth.

HUEVOS RANCHEROS

Everyone loves "huevos rancheros"—Mexican country-style eggs. They're perfect for a hearty breakfast, brunch, or light supper.

6 servings

6 corn tortillas
Vegetable cooking spray
6 eggs
Salt and pepper, to taste
Serrano Tomato Sauce (recipe follows)
Refried Beans (see p. 447)

Per Serving
Calories: 252
% Calories from fat: **22**
Fat (gm): 6.2
Saturated fat (gm): **1.7**
Cholesterol (mg): 213
Sodium (mg): 109
Protein (gm): 14.3
Carbohydrate (gm): **35.6**
Exchanges
Milk: 0.0
Vegetable: 1.0
Fruit: 0.0
Bread: 2.0
Meat: 1.5
Fat: 0.0

1. Spray tortillas lightly with cooking spray; cook in large skillet until browned, about 1 minute on each side.

2. Spray large skillet with cooking spray; heat over medium heat until hot. Add eggs; reduce heat to medium-low and cook, covered, until eggs are glazed on top, 3 to 4 minutes. Season to taste with salt and pepper.

3. Arrange tortillas on serving plates; place eggs on tortillas and spoon Serrano Tomato Sauce over. Serve with Refried Beans.

Serrano Tomato Sauce

makes about 2 cups

2 large tomatoes, cut into wedges
Vegetable cooking spray
1 small onion, finely chopped
1 serrano chili, seeds and veins discarded, minced
1 clove garlic, minced
Salt, to taste

1. Process tomatoes in food processor or blender until almost smooth.

2. Spray medium skillet with cooking spray; heat over medium heat until hot. Saute onion, serrano chili, and garlic until tender, 3 to 4 minutes. Add tomatoes and heat to boiling; cook over medium to medium-high heat until mixture thickens to a medium sauce consistency. Season to taste with salt; serve warm.

COUNTRY STYLE POTATO KUGEL

This hash brown kugel owes its light texture to beaten egg whites. It can be served with a tomato sauce.

6 servings

2 packages (5¹/₂ ounces each) hash brown potato mix with onions
3 cups boiling water
6 egg yolks
1¹/₂ cups cool water
1 teaspoon baking powder
1 teaspoon dried basil
¹/₂ teaspoon dried oregano
2 tablespoons snipped chives
1 teaspoon salt
¹/₂ teaspoon pepper
6 egg whites, beaten to stiff peaks
Vegetable cooking spray

Per Serving
Calories: 123
% Calories from fat: 28
Fat (gm): 3.9
Saturated fat (gm): 1.2
Cholesterol (mg): 159.8
Sodium (mg): 559
Protein (gm): 6.3
Carbohydrate (gm): 15.8
Exchanges
Milk: 0.0
Vegetable: 0.0
Fruit: 0.0
Bread: 1.0
Meat: 1.0
Fat: 0.0

1. Place potato mix in large bowl; pour boiling water over. Let stand 20 to 25 minutes, stirring occasionally.

2. Process egg yolks, 1¹/₂ cups water, baking powder, basil, and oregano in food processor or blender until smooth. Mix yolk mixture, chives, salt, and pepper into potatoes. Fold potato mixture into egg whites.

3. Spray 11 x 7-inch baking dish with cooking spray; place in oven at 300 degrees until hot. Pour kugel mixture into dish; bake until browned and set, about 60 minutes.

MEXICAN SCRAMBLED EGGS WITH CHORIZO

In this recipe, the Chorizo is crumbled, rather than being made into patties as the chorizo recipe directs.

6 servings

Vegetable cooking spray

1 large tomato, chopped

1/2 cup sliced green onions and tops

2-3 teaspoons finely chopped serrano, *or* jalapeño, chilies

2 small cloves garlic, minced

Chorizo (see p. 166), crumbled

6 eggs

6 egg whites *or* 3/4 cup no-cholesterol real egg product

3 tablespoons fat-free milk

Salt and pepper, to taste

Tomatillo Sauce, warm (see p. 203)

6 corn, *or* flour, tortillas

Per Serving
Calories: 327
% Calories from fat: 24
Fat (gm): 8.9
Saturated fat (gm): 2.2
Cholesterol (mg): 284.1
Sodium (mg): 628
Protein (gm): 28.7
Carbohydrate (gm): 34.4
Exchanges
Milk: 0.0
Vegetable: 3.5
Fruit: 0.0
Bread: 1.0
Meat: 3.0
Fat: 0.0

1. Spray large skillet with cooking spray; heat over medium heat until hot. Saute tomato, green onions, chilies, and garlic until tender, about 5 minutes. Add Chorizo and cook 3 to 4 minutes.

2. Beat eggs, egg whites, and milk until foamy; add to skillet. Cook over medium to medium-low heat until eggs are cooked, stirring occasionally; season to taste with salt and pepper. Serve with Tomatillo Sauce and tortillas.

MEXICAN SCRAMBLED EGGS WITH SHRIMP

Crabmeat can be substituted for the shrimp in this recipe if you prefer.

4 servings

Vegetable cooking spray
1 medium tomato, chopped
1/4 cup sliced green onions and tops
1-2 teaspoons finely chopped serrano, *or* jalapeño, chili
1 small clove garlic, minced
8 ounces peeled deveined shrimp
4 eggs
4 egg whites *or* 1/2 cup no-cholesterol real egg product
2 tablespoons fat-free milk
Salt and pepper, to taste
1 cup Tomatillo Sauce, warm (see p. 203)

Per Serving
Calories: 243
% Calories from fat: 26
Fat (gm): 7.1
Saturated fat (gm): 1.8
Cholesterol (mg): 300.6
Sodium (mg): 268
Protein (gm): 22.3
Carbohydrate (gm): 22.5
Exchanges
Milk: 0.0
Vegetable: 1.0
Fruit: 0.0
Bread: 1.0
Meat: 2.5
Fat: 0.0

1. Spray large skillet with cooking spray; heat over medium heat until hot. Saute tomato, green onions, serrano chili, and garlic until tender, about 5 minutes. Add shrimp and cook over medium heat until shrimp are pink and cooked, 3 to 4 minutes.

2. Beat eggs, egg whites, and milk until foamy; add to skillet. Cook over medium to medium-low heat until eggs are cooked, stirring occasionally; season to taste with salt and pepper. Serve with Tomatillo Sauce.

EGGS SCRAMBLED WITH CRISP TORTILLA STRIPS

This is a good recipe to use with day-old or slightly stale tortillas. Complement this hearty egg dish with Refried Beans and Chorizo (see pp. 447, 166).

6 servings

6 corn tortillas, cut into 2 x $^1/_2$-inch strips
Vegetable cooking spray

6 eggs

6 egg whites *or* $^3/_4$ cup no-cholesterol real egg product

3 tablespoons fat-free milk
Salt and pepper, to taste

3 tablespoons crumbled Mexican white cheese *or* farmer's cheese

3 tablespoons finely chopped cilantro
Poblano Chili Sauce, warm (see p. 205)
Black Beans and Rice (see p. 467)

Per Serving
Calories: 367
% Calories from fat: 18
Fat (gm): 7.7
Saturated fat (gm): 2.2
Cholesterol (mg): 215.7
Sodium (mg): 480
Protein (gm): 22.9
Carbohydrate (gm): 55.9
Exchanges
Milk: 0.0
Vegetable: 1.0
Fruit: 0.0
Bread: 3.0
Meat: 2.5
Fat: 0.0

1. Spray tortilla strips lightly with cooking spray; cook in skillet over medium to medium-high heat until browned and crisp.

2. Beat eggs, egg whites, and milk until foamy; pour over tortilla strips in skillet. Cook over medium to medium-low heat until eggs are cooked, stirring occasionally. Season to taste with salt and pepper; sprinkle with cheese and cilantro. Spoon Poblano Chili Sauce over eggs; serve with Black Beans and Rice.

EGGS SCRAMBLED WITH CACTUS

Cactus paddles, or "nopales," are available canned as well as fresh; the canned cactus do not have to be cooked. Poblano chilies or sweet green or red peppers can be substituted, if preferred.

4 servings

1 quart boiling water
8 ounces cactus paddles, sliced
1 teaspoon salt
1/4 teaspoon baking soda
Vegetable cooking spray
1 small tomato, chopped
1/4 cup chopped onion
1 teaspoon finely chopped jalapeño chili
4 eggs
4 egg whites *or* 1/2 cup no-cholesterol real egg product
2 tablespoons fat-free milk
Salt and pepper, to taste
4 corn, *or* flour, tortillas, warm

Per Serving
Calories: 367
% Calories from fat: 18
Fat (gm): 7.7
Saturated fat (gm): 2.2
Cholesterol (mg): 215.7
Sodium (mg): 480
Protein (gm): 22.9
Carbohydrate (gm): 55.9
Exchanges
Milk: 0.0
Vegetable: 1.0
Fruit: 0.0
Bread: 3.0
Meat: 2.5
Fat: 0.0

1. Heat water to boiling in medium saucepan; add cactus, 1 teaspoon salt, and baking soda. Reduce heat and simmer, uncovered, until cactus is crisp-tender, about 20 minutes. Rinse well in cold water and drain.

2. Spray large skillet with cooking spray; heat over medium heat until hot. Saute cactus, tomato, onion, and jalapeño chili until onion is tender, 3 to 4 minutes.

3. Beat eggs, egg whites, and milk until foamy; add to skillet. Cook over medium to medium-low heat until eggs are cooked, stirring occasionally. Season to taste with salt and pepper. Serve with tortillas.

MESQUITE HASH AND EGGS

You'll enjoy the unusual smoky mesquite flavor of this vegetable hash.

4 servings

Mesquite-flavored vegetable cooking spray

1 cup chopped onions

1/2 package (16-ounce size) refrigerated cubed potatoes

1 cup frozen peas

1 cup fresh, *or* canned, drained whole-kernel corn

1/4-1/2 teaspoon dried thyme leaves

Salt and pepper, to taste

4 eggs

Per Serving
Calories: 203
% Calories from fat: 24
Fat (gm): 5.4
Saturated fat (gm): 1.6
Cholesterol (mg): 212
Sodium (mg): 103
Protein (gm): 11
Carbohydrate (gm): 29.3
Exchanges
Milk: 0.0
Vegetable: 0.0
Fruit: 0.0
Bread: 3.0
Meat: 1.0
Fat: 0.0

1. Spray large skillet with cooking spray; heat over medium heat until hot. Saute onions 2 minutes; add potatoes and spray generously with cooking spray. Cook over medium heat until potatoes are browned, 8 to 10 minutes, stirring frequently. Add peas, corn, and thyme; cook 2 to 3 minutes longer. Season to taste with salt and pepper.

2. Move hash to sides of skillet; add eggs to center of skillet. Cook, covered, over low heat until eggs are cooked, 3 to 4 minutes; season to taste with salt and pepper.

SWEET POTATO HASH WITH POACHED EGGS

A colorful hash dish that's perfect for a hearty breakfast, brunch, or light supper.

4 servings

2	cups cubed peeled sweet potatoes (¹/₂-inch cubes)
2	cups cubed unpeeled Idaho potatoes (¹/₂-inch cubes)
¹/₂	cup chopped onion
¹/₂	cup chopped red, *or* green, bell pepper
1	teaspoon dried rosemary leaves
¹/₂	teaspoon dried thyme leaves
1-2	tablespoons margarine
	Salt and pepper, to taste
4	eggs

Per Serving
Calories: 310
% Calories from fat: 21
Fat (gm): 8.2
Saturated fat (gm): 2.2
Cholesterol (mg): 212
Sodium (mg): 186
Protein (gm): 10.5
Carbohydrate (gm): 49.4
Exchanges
Milk: 0.0
Vegetable: 2.0
Fruit: 0.0
Bread: 1.0
Meat: 3.0
Fat: 0.0

1. Cook vegetables and herbs in margarine in large skillet, covered, over medium heat 10 minutes; uncover and cook over medium-high heat until vegetables are browned and tender, about 5 minutes, stirring occasionally. Season to taste with salt and pepper.

2. While potatoes are cooking, fry eggs in lightly greased medium skillet over medium heat. Spoon hash onto plates; top each serving with an egg.

CHIPOTLE POTATO AND EGG BAKE

Perfect for brunch, this recipe boasts the convenience of frozen vegetable products. One-half cup each of sliced red, yellow, and green bell peppers and onion can be substituted for the frozen stir-fry pepper blend.

4 servings

Vegetable cooking spray
2 cups frozen stir-fry pepper blend
1-2 teaspoons minced garlic
1/2-1 small canned chipotle chili in adobo sauce, chopped
1 1/3 cups fat-free milk
2 2/3 cups frozen mashed potatoes
Salt, to taste
4 eggs
1/2-3/4 cup (2-3 ounces) shredded reduced-fat Cheddar cheese

Per Serving
Calories: 242
% Calories from fat: 27
Fat (gm): 7.2
Saturated fat (gm): 2.2
Cholesterol (mg): 213.6
Sodium (mg): 452
Protein (gm): 16.5
Carbohydrate (gm): 27.1
Exchanges
Milk: 0.0
Vegetable: 2.0
Fruit: 0.0
Bread: 1.0
Meat: 2.0
Fat: 0.5

1. Spray medium saucepan with cooking spray; heat over medium heat until hot. Saute pepper blend and garlic until liquid is evaporated and peppers begin to brown, about 5 minutes. Add chipotle chili and milk; heat until milk is steaming. Stir potatoes into milk mixture; cook over medium heat, stirring frequently, until potatoes are thickened, 4 to 5 minutes. Season to taste with salt.

2. Spread potato mixture in 8-inch square or round baking pan, or 4 individual gratin dishes. Make 4 indentations in potatoes with back of spoon; break eggs into indentations. Sprinkle cheese over potatoes and eggs.

3. Bake at 350 degrees until eggs are desired doneness, 13 to 15 minutes.

Tip: For a serving variation, potato mixture can be spooned onto serving plates and topped with poached or fried eggs.

PASTA FRITTATA

A pasta frittata is a delicious way to use leftover linguine, fettuccine, or spaghetti. Vary the vegetables in the topping according to season and availability.

4 servings

2 medium carrots, sliced
8 ounces cauliflower florets
1 cup sliced red bell pepper
1/3 cup sliced green onions and tops
2 cloves garlic, minced
1 tablespoon olive oil *or* vegetable oil
1 medium zucchini, sliced
1 medium tomato, chopped
1 teaspoon dried basil leaves
3/4 teaspoon dried oregano leaves
3/4 teaspoon dried marjoram leaves
4 ounces thin spaghetti, cooked
4 egg whites
2 tablespoons grated Parmesan cheese
1/2 teaspoon salt
1/4 teaspoon pepper
   Olive oil cooking spray
   Minced parsley, as garnish

Per Serving
Calories: 249
% Calories from fat: 19
Fat (gm): 5.4
Saturated fat (gm): 1.2
Cholesterol (mg): 2.5
Sodium (mg): 416
Protein (gm): 12
Carbohydrate (gm): 39.5
Exchanges
Milk: 0.0
Vegetable: 3.0
Fruit: 0.0
Bread: 2.0
Meat: 0.0
Fat: 0.5

1. Saute carrots, cauliflower, bell pepper, onions, and garlic in oil in medium skillet until carrots are crisp-tender, 5 to 7 minutes. Stir in zucchini, tomato, and herbs; saute until vegetables are tender, about 5 minutes more.

2. Mix spaghetti, egg whites, cheese, salt, and pepper in large bowl. Spray medium skillet with cooking spray; heat over medium heat until hot. Add pasta mixture, spreading it evenly. Cook, uncovered, over medium to medium-low heat until browned on the bottom, about 5 minutes. Turn and cook until browned on other side, about 5 minutes. Slide frittata onto serving platter; spoon vegetable mixture over and sprinkle with parsley.

VEGETABLE FRITTATA WITH PARMESAN TOAST

An Italian-style vegetable omelet that is quick and easy to prepare, delicious to eat!

4 servings

Vegetable cooking spray
1 medium poblano chili, sliced
1 medium onion, sliced
2 cups sliced mushrooms
2 cloves garlic, minced
2 tablespoons finely chopped lovage, *or* parsley, leaves
1/2 cup vegetable, *or* chicken, broth
1 1/2 cups no-cholesterol real egg product *or* 6 eggs
1/4 cup fat-free milk
1/2 cup cooked brown rice
1/2 cup (2 ounces) shredded fat-free Cheddar cheese
1/4 teaspoon salt
1/8 teaspoon pepper
4 slices Italian, *or* French, bread
4 teaspoons grated Parmesan cheese

Per Serving
Calories: 212
% Calories from fat: 9
Fat (gm): 2.2
Saturated fat (gm): 0.8
Cholesterol (mg): 4.4
Sodium (mg): 590
Protein (gm): 18.4
Carbohydrate (gm): 30
Exchanges
Milk: 0.0
Vegetable: 1.5
Fruit: 0.0
Bread: 1.5
Meat: 1.5
Fat: 0.0

1. Spray medium oven-proof skillet with cooking spray; heat over medium heat until hot. Saute vegetables 5 minutes; add lovage and broth. Cook, covered, over medium heat until vegetables are tender and liquid is absorbed, about 5 minutes.

2. Beat egg product and milk; mix in cooked rice, Cheddar cheese, salt, and pepper. Pour mixture over vegetables in skillet; cook without stirring, uncovered, over medium-low heat until egg is set and lightly browned on bottom, 15 to 20 minutes.

3. Broil frittata 6 inches from heat source until cooked on top, 3 to 4 minutes; invert frittata onto plate, slide back into skillet, and cook until lightly browned, 3 to 5 minutes.

4. Sprinkle bread with Parmesan cheese; broil 6 inches from heat source until browned, 2 to 3 minutes. Slide frittata onto serving plate; cut into wedges. Serve with Parmesan toast.

SAUSAGE AND EGG PIZZA

Tempting for brunch, lunch, or healthy snacking.

6 servings

Olive oil cooking spray

2 large poblano chilies, sliced

1 cup chopped onion

1 clove garlic, minced

6 eggs

4 egg whites *or* 1/2 cup no-cholesterol real egg product

1/4 cup fat-free milk

4 ounces Italian-style turkey sausage, cooked, drained, crumbled

Salt and pepper, to taste

Potato Pizza Crust (recipe follows)

1/2-1 cup (2-4 ounces) shredded fat-free mozzarella cheese

Per Serving
Calories: 294
% Calories from fat: 25
Fat (gm): 8.1
Saturated fat (gm): 2.4
Cholesterol (mg): 257.6
Sodium (mg): 449
Protein (gm): 20.2
Carbohydrate (gm): 35.8
Exchanges
Milk: 0.0
Vegetable: 1.0
Fruit: 0.0
Bread: 2.0
Meat: 2.0
Fat: 0.5

1. Spray large skillet with cooking spray; heat over medium heat until hot. Add chilies, onion, and garlic; cook over medium to medium-low heat until chilies are very soft, 20 to 30 minutes. Remove from skillet and reserve.

2. Beat eggs, egg whites, and milk; pour into skillet. Cook eggs until just set, stirring occasionally. Gently stir sausage and reserved chili mixture into eggs; season to taste with salt and pepper. Spoon egg mixture into baked Potato Pizza Crust and sprinkle with cheese.

3. Bake pizza at 400 degrees until cheese is melted, about 5 minutes.

Potato Pizza Crust

makes 1 crust

1 package (11/4 pounds) refrigerated shredded potatoes for hash browns

1/3 cup finely chopped onion

1 egg

1 egg white

$^1/_4$ teaspoon salt
$^1/_4$ teaspoon pepper
Butter-flavored vegetable cooking spray

1. Drain potatoes well on paper toweling. Mix potatoes, onion, egg, egg white, salt, and pepper.

2. Spray 12-inch skillet with cooking spray; press potato mixture evenly on bottom and 1 inch up side of skillet. Spray potatoes with cooking spray. Bake at 400 degrees until browned, about 20 minutes.

OMELET PUFF WITH VEGETABLE MÉLANGE

Made with beaten egg whites, this oven-baked omelet soars to new heights. Do not overbeat the whites!

2 servings

5 egg whites
$^1/_4$ cup water
$^1/_3$ cup no-cholesterol real egg product
$^1/_4$ teaspoon dried tarragon leaves
$^1/_4$ teaspoon salt
$^1/_4$ teaspoon pepper
Vegetable cooking spray
Vegetable Mélange (recipe follows)
2 slices crusty Italian bread, warm

Per Serving
Calories: 264
% Calories from fat: 7
Fat (gm): 2.1
Saturated fat (gm): 0.4
Cholesterol (mg): 0
Sodium (mg): 662
Protein (gm): 20.5
Carbohydrate (gm): 43.9
Exchanges
Milk: 0.0
Vegetable: 4.0
Fruit: 0.0
Bread: 1.5
Meat: 1.5
Fat: 0.0

1. Beat egg whites in large bowl until foamy; mix in water and beat until stiff peaks form. Beat egg product, tarragon, salt, and pepper in small bowl until thick and lemon colored, 2 to 3 minutes. Fold egg white mixture into egg product mixture.

2. Spray 10-inch oven-proof skillet with cooking spray; heat over medium heat until hot. Pour egg mixture into skillet; cook over medium to medium-low heat until bottom of omelet is light brown, about 5 minutes.

3. Bake at 325 degrees, uncovered, until omelet is puffed and light brown. Loosen edge of omelet with spatula; slide onto serving platter, carefully folding omelet in half. Spoon Vegetable Mélange over omelet. Serve with bread.

Vegetable Mélange

makes about 3 cups

    Vegetable cooking spray
2 medium zucchini, sliced
2 medium onions, sliced
2 medium tomatoes, cut into wedges
4 ounces fresh, *or* frozen thawed, whole okra
1 medium green bell pepper, sliced
2 tablespoons vegetable broth *or* water

1. Spray large skillet with cooking spray; heat over medium heat until hot. Saute vegetables until crisp-tender, 3 to 5 minutes. Add broth; cook, covered, over medium-low heat 5 minutes.

PANCAKE PUFF WITH EGGS PIPERADE

A puffed Dutch Pancake is a wonderful serving bowl for chili-inspired scrambled eggs.

4 servings

    Dutch Pancake (recipe follows)
    Vegetable cooking spray
2 cups frozen stir-fry pepper blend
1/2-1 jalapeño chili, minced
1 teaspoon minced garlic
1 small tomato, chopped
4 eggs
8 egg whites *or* 1 cup no-cholesterol real egg product
2 tablespoons fat-free milk
    Salt and pepper, to taste
    Minced parsley *or* chives, as garnish

Per Serving
Calories: 314
% Calories from fat: 29
Fat (gm): 9.8
Saturated fat (gm): 2.8
Cholesterol (mg): 319
Sodium (mg): 460
Protein (gm): 24.5
Carbohydrate (gm): 29.9
Exchanges
Milk: 0.0
Vegetable: 0.0
Fruit: 0.0
Bread: 2.0
Meat: 2.0
Fat: 0.5

1. Make Dutch Pancake.

2. Spray large skillet with cooking spray; heat over medium heat until hot. Saute stir-fry blend, jalapeño chili, and garlic until tender, 5 to 8 minutes; stir in tomato.

3. Whisk eggs, egg whites, and milk until well blended. Add eggs to skillet and cook over medium heat until set, stirring frequently. Sprinkle lightly with salt and pepper. Spoon into hot Dutch Pancake to serve. Garnish with parsley.

Dutch Pancake

makes 1 pancake

- 2 eggs
- 1/2 cup no-cholesterol real egg product *or* 4 egg whites
- 3/4 cup fat-free milk
- 3/4 cup all-purpose flour
- 1 tablespoon sugar
- 1/4 teaspoon salt
- 2 teaspoons margarine

1. Whisk all ingredients, except margarine, in large bowl until almost smooth (batter will be slightly lumpy).

2. Heat margarine in large skillet with oven-proof handle until melted and bubbly; pour in batter. Bake, uncovered, at 425 degrees until pancake is puffed and browned, 20 to 25 minutes (do not open door during first 15 minutes). Serve immediately.

EGG AND BROCCOLI CASSEROLE

This delicious casserole can be assembled up to 1 day ahead and refrigerated until you are ready to bake. Just add 10 minutes to the baking time.

4 servings

- 2 packages (10 ounces each) frozen chopped broccoli, cooked, well drained
- 4 hard-cooked eggs, peeled, thinly sliced
- 1 cup fat-free sour cream
- 1/2 cup fat-free mayonnaise
- 2 tablespoons tarragon vinegar *or* white wine vinegar and 1/2 tablespoon dried tarragon leaves
- 1/4 teaspoon paprika

Per Serving
Calories: 205
% Calories from fat: 23
Fat (gm): 5.2
Saturated fat (gm): 1.6
Cholesterol (mg): 212
Sodium (mg): 357
Protein (gm): 14.7
Carbohydrate (gm): 24.3
Exchanges
Milk: 0.0
Vegetable: 2.0
Fruit: 0.0
Bread: 1.0
Meat: 1.0
Fat: 0.5

1. Arrange broccoli in lightly greased 13 x 9-inch baking dish. Top with egg slices.

2. Combine sour cream, mayonnaise, and vinegar in small saucepan. Heat over low heat, stirring constantly until warm, about 4 minutes. Pour over broccoli and eggs; sprinkle with paprika. Bake, uncovered, at 325 degrees 15 to 20 minutes.

VEGETABLE PUFF

Perfect for brunch or lunch, vegetables are baked with an egg custard.

6 servings

Vegetable cooking spray
4 ounces mushrooms, sliced
$1/2$ cup chopped red bell pepper
$1/2$ cup finely chopped shallots
2 cloves garlic, minced
1 pound broccoflower, cooked, coarsely chopped
1 cup finely shredded carrots, cooked
$2/3$ cup frozen corn, thawed
2 teaspoons lemon juice
$3/4$ teaspoon dried thyme leaves
$1/2$ teaspoon salt
$1/2$ teaspoon pepper
1 cup fat-free half-and-half *or* fat-free milk
2 tablespoons flour
1 cup no-cholesterol real egg product
5 large egg whites
$1/2$ teaspoon cream of tartar

Per Serving
Calories: 133
% Calories from fat: 3
Fat (gm): 0.5
Saturated fat (gm): 0.1
Cholesterol (mg): 0
Sodium (mg): 359
Protein (gm): 11.8
Carbohydrate (gm): 21.2
Exchanges
Milk: 0.0
Vegetable: 2.0
Fruit: 0.0
Bread: 0.5
Meat: 1.0
Fat: 0.0

1. Spray large skillet with cooking spray; heat over medium heat until hot. Saute mushrooms, bell pepper, shallots, and garlic until tender, about 4 minutes. Stir in broccoflower, carrots, corn, lemon juice, and thyme; saute 5 minutes. Transfer mixture to large bowl and stir in salt and pepper.

2. Whisk half-and-half and flour until smooth in small saucepan. Heat to boiling; boil, whisking constantly, until thickened, about 1 minute. Whisk about half the mixture into egg product; whisk egg mixture back into half-and-half. Stir into vegetable mixture.

3. Beat egg whites in large bowl until foamy. Add cream of tartar and continue beating until stiff peaks form; fold into vegetable mixture. Transfer mixture to a lightly greased $1^{1/2}$-quart casserole. Place casserole in a large roasting pan on center rack of oven; add 2 inches hot water to pan.

4. Bake, uncovered, at 375 degrees 35 minutes or until casserole is puffed and lightly browned on top. Serve immediately.

EASY CHEESE PUFF

A delicious and fast casserole that tastes like cheese blintzes, but requires much less time and effort to prepare. Serve this dish as a brunch entrée or a dessert. Blueberry Syrup (see p. 691) would be a delicious finishing touch.

8 servings

4 eggs *or* 1 cup no-cholesterol real-egg product
1¼ cups fat-free milk
2 tablespoons fat-free sour cream *or* plain yogurt
2 tablespoons margarine, melted
1 teaspoon vanilla
1⅓ cups all-purpose flour
1 tablespoon sugar
1 tablespoon baking powder
Sweet Cheese Filling (recipe follows)
Powdered sugar, cinnamon, as garnish
2 cups sliced strawberries

Per Serving
Calories: 293
% Calories from fat: 26
Fat (gm): 8.4
Saturated fat (gm): 3
Cholesterol (mg): 125.3
Sodium (mg): 454
Protein (gm): 20.7
Carbohydrate (gm): 32.1
Exchanges
Milk: 0.0
Vegetable: 0.0
Fruit: 0.0
Bread: 2.0
Meat: 2.0
Fat: 0.5

1. Combine eggs, milk, sour cream, margarine, vanilla, flour, sugar, and baking powder in large mixing bowl. Beat with mixer until very smooth. Pour 1½ cups batter into lightly greased 13 x 9-inch baking dish. Bake at 350 degrees until set, about 10 minutes.

2. Spread Sweet Cheese Filling over baked puff. Whisk remaining puff batter to combine; pour over cheese, covering it completely. Bake at 350 degrees until top is puffed and browned, about 45 minutes. Sprinkle with powdered sugar and cinnamon. Cut into serving pieces and top with strawberries.

Sweet Cheese Filling

makes about 3¹/₂ cups

- 1 pound reduced-fat farmer's cheese *or* ricotta cheese
- 1 container (15 ounces) fat-free ricotta
- 4 egg whites *or* ¹/₂ cup no-cholesterol real-egg product
- 2 tablespoons sugar
- 2 tablespoons lemon juice

1. Combine all ingredients in large bowl, mixing well.

FRENCH TOAST CASSEROLE

Your favorite fruit, such as bananas, blueberries, strawberries, or golden raisins, can be used instead of raspberries.

6 servings

- 2 cups fat-free milk
- 3 eggs, lightly beaten
- 12 slices whole-grain bread, cut into halves, divided
- 2 tablespoons margarine, melted, divided
- ¹/₂ cup powdered sugar, divided
- 2 cups fresh, *or* frozen, thawed, drained, raspberries, divided
- 2-3 teaspoons ground cinnamon

Per Serving
Calories: 301
% Calories from fat: 20
Fat (gm): 7.7
Saturated fat (gm): 1.6
Cholesterol (mg): 107.5
Sodium (mg): 258
Protein (gm): 15.4
Carbohydrate (gm): 52.6
Exchanges
Milk: 0.0
Vegetable: 0.0
Fruit: 1.5
Bread: 2.0
Meat: 1.0
Fat: 0.5

1. In shallow bowl or pie plate, beat milk and eggs lightly to blend. Dip bread halves into egg mixture to coat well. Layer 8 bread halves in lightly greased 9-inch square baking dish. Drizzle about 2 teaspoons margarine over bread; sprinkle with 3 tablespoons sugar and 1 cup raspberries. Top with 8 more bread halves, arranging them in opposite direction from bottom layer. Drizzle with 2 teaspoons margarine, 3 tablespoons sugar, and remaining 1 cup raspberries. Top with remaining 8 bread halves, 2 teaspoons margarine, and 2 tablespoons sugar. Sprinkle with cinnamon.

2. Bake, covered, 25 minutes at 400 degrees; uncover and bake until browned, about 10 minutes longer.

CRUNCHY FRENCH TOAST SANDWICH

A new twist on French toast—crushed corn flakes add a crunchy texture.

2 servings

 2 egg whites *or* ¹/₄ cup no-cholesterol real egg product
³/₄ cup fat-free milk
 1 teaspoon vanilla
 1 cup corn flakes, crushed
 1 teaspoon ground cinnamon
 2 teaspoons granulated sugar
¹/₄ cup fresh, *or* frozen, blueberries
 2 teaspoons grated lemon rind
²/₃ cup fat-free cottage cheese
 4 slices day-old, reduced-calorie white bread

Per Serving
Calories: 290
% Calories from fat: 4
Fat (gm): 1.4
Saturated fat (gm): 0.4
Cholesterol (mg): 1.7
Sodium (mg): 723
Protein (gm): 21.9
Carbohydrate (gm): 49.5
Exchanges
Milk: 0.0
Vegetable: 0.0
Fruit: 0.0
Bread: 3.0
Meat: 1.0
Fat: 0.0

1. Beat egg whites, milk, and vanilla in shallow bowl or pie plate. Combine corn flakes, cinnamon, and granulated sugar on sheet of waxed paper.

2. Stir blueberries and lemon rind into cottage cheese. Spread cheese mixture on 2 slices of bread; cover with remaining bread slices. Dip both sides of sandwiches into egg mixture, then lightly into crumb mixture, coating both sides. Place sandwiches on lightly greased cookie sheet.

3. Bake at 450 degrees until crisp and lightly browned, about 10 minutes on each side.

CINNAMON-SPRINKLED FRENCH TOAST

This is a super way to use day-old or slightly stale bread. Top with your favorite light syrup or fresh berries.

4 servings

1   egg plus 2 egg whites
$1/2$ cup fat-free milk
$1/4$ teaspoon vanilla extract
$1/8$ teaspoon cinnamon
8   slices bread
   Butter-flavored cooking spray

Per Serving
Calories: 172
% Calories from fat: 17
Fat (gm): 3.1
Saturated fat (gm): 0.8
Cholesterol (mg): 54.1
Sodium (mg): 327
Protein (gm): 8.5
Carbohydrate (gm): 26.8
Exchanges
Milk: 0.0
Vegetable: 0.0
Fruit: 0.0
Bread: 2.0
Meat: 0.0
Fat: 0.5

1. Whisk together egg, egg whites, milk, vanilla, and cinnamon. Coat both sides of bread slices with egg mixture.

2. Spray large skillet with cooking spray; heat over medium heat until hot. Place bread slices in skillet and cook until golden; turn slices and cook until golden. If cooking French toast in 2 batches, re-coat skillet with cooking spray between batches.

3. Place 2 slices of toast on each serving plate; garnish with cinnamon.

FRUIT, WINE, AND CHEESE SOUFFLÉ SANDWICH

For a variation on this sandwich, substitute mushrooms for the cherries, and spread bread with Dijon mustard.

2 servings

4   slices white, *or* wheat, bread
$1/2$ cup (2 ounces) shredded reduced-fat Swiss cheese
$1/2$ cup chopped, pitted sweet cherries
4   egg whites *or* $1/2$ cup no-cholesterol real egg product
$1/2$ cup fat-free evaporated milk
$1/3$ cup dry white wine *or* evaporated milk

Per Serving
Calories: 331
% Calories from fat: 20
Fat (gm): 7.2
Saturated fat (gm): 3.7
Cholesterol (mg): 21.4
Sodium (mg): 468
Protein (gm): 23.1
Carbohydrate (gm): 37.3
Exchanges
Milk: 0.0
Vegetable: 0.0
Fruit: 0.5
Bread: 2.0
Meat: 2.0
Fat: 1.0

1. Place 2 bread slices in lightly greased small baking dish. Sprinkle with cheese; top with cherries and remaining bread slices.

2. Beat egg whites, evaporated milk, and wine until foamy; pour over sandwiches. Bake at 375 degrees until puffed, and knife inserted in center comes out clean, about 25 minutes.

BREAKFAST BURRITOS

Not limited to breakfast, these chunky burritos are perfect for brunch, lunch, or supper.

6 servings (1 burrito each)

1	package (1¹/₄ pounds) refrigerated potato wedges
1¹/₂	cups cubed zucchini
1	cup chopped red, *or* green, bell pepper
¹/₂	cup sliced green onions and tops
2	teaspoons minced garlic
1	tablespoon margarine
8	eggs, lightly beaten
³/₄	teaspoon dried oregano leaves
	Salt and pepper, to taste
6	flour tortillas (10-inch)
1	cup (4 ounces) shredded reduced-fat mozzarella, *or* Cheddar, cheese
1¹/₂	cups mild, *or* hot, prepared salsa

Per Serving
Calories: 363
% Calories from fat: 24
Fat (gm): 14.5
Saturated fat (gm): 4.8
Cholesterol (mg): 292.7
Sodium (mg): 929
Protein (gm): 22.5
Carbohydrate (gm): 40
Exchanges
Milk: 0.0
Vegetable: 1.0
Fruit: 0.0
Bread: 3.0
Meat: 2.0
Fat: 1.0

1. Saute potatoes, zucchini, bell pepper, green onions, and garlic in margarine in large skillet until potatoes are browned and peppers and onions are tender, about 10 minutes.

2. Add eggs and oregano to skillet and cook until eggs are set, stirring occasionally. Season to taste with salt and pepper.

3. Spoon mixture onto tortillas; sprinkle with cheese. Fold 2 sides of each tortilla in about 2 inches, then roll up from other side to enclose filling. Serve with salsa.

TOMATO, SPINACH, AND CHEESE BURRITOS

A Neapolitan burrito!

4 servings

  1 cup fat-free ricotta cheese
  1 cup reduced-fat ricotta cheese
  1 teaspoon grated Parmesan cheese
 3/4 teaspoon chili powder
 1/2 teaspoon crushed red pepper
 1/2 teaspoon ground cumin
  8 ounces fresh spinach leaves, divided
  4 flour tortillas (8-inch)
  1 large tomato, chopped
     Olive oil cooking spray
 1/2 cup prepared salsa
 1/2 cup fat-free sour cream

Per Serving
Calories: 285
% Calories from fat: 16
Fat (gm): 5.3
Saturated fat (gm): 1.9
Cholesterol (mg): 16.9
Sodium (mg): 712
Protein (gm): 26.6
Carbohydrate (gm): 34.7
Exchanges
Milk: 0.0
Vegetable: 2.0
Fruit: 0.0
Bread: 1.0
Meat: 3.0
Fat: 0.0

1. Process cheeses, chili powder, red pepper, and cumin in food processor, or beat in large mixing bowl, until smooth. Coarsely shred half the spinach leaves.

2. Layer shredded spinach, cheese mixture, and tomato in center of each tortilla. Fold opposite sides of tortilla over filling, then roll tortilla. Lay burritos, seam sides down, in lightly greased baking pan. Spray lightly with cooking spray.

3. Bake at 400 degrees until golden brown, about 25 minutes. Divide remaining spinach leaves among 4 plates; arrange burritos on spinach. Serve with salsa and sour cream.

GOAT CHEESE PILLOWS

Perfect as a light lunch, or cut into wedges and serve as an appetizer. Serve with Tropical Salsa (p. 280) and use blue corn tortillas for a different look.

2 servings

- ²/₃ cup fat-free cottage cheese
- 4 ounces reduced-fat goat cheese
- 4 tablespoons chopped, softened sun-dried tomatoes (not in oil)
  Olive oil cooking spray
- 4 corn, *or* flour, tortillas
- 2 tablespoons chopped mint leaves
  Alfalfa sprouts, as garnish

Per Serving
Calories: 259
% Calories from fat: 26
Fat (gm): 7.6
Saturated fat (gm): 4.3
Cholesterol (mg): 10.3
Sodium (mg): 770
Protein (gm): 17.3
Carbohydrate (gm): 32.1
Exchanges
Milk: 0.0
Vegetable: 0.0
Fruit: 0.0
Bread: 2.0
Meat: 2.0
Fat: 0.0

1. Combine cheeses and sun-dried tomatoes in small bowl. Spray large skillet with cooking spray; heat over medium heat until hot. Heat each tortilla in skillet to soften, 30 to 60 seconds on each side.

2. Spread cheese mixture over half of each tortilla; sprinkle with mint. Press alfalfa sprouts into cheese mixture. Fold tortillas over to close, forming half circles. Spray with cooking spray and cook, covered, in large skillet over medium heat until browned, 1 to 2 minutes per side. Serve immediately.

HOT CHEESE BAVARIAN

A little German mustard would set this Bavarian off to perfection!

2 servings

2 slices rye bread, toasted
2 teaspoons margarine
1/4 cup sauerkraut, well rinsed, drained
1/4 cup thinly sliced cabbage *or* rinsed, drained sauerkraut
1/2 medium tomato, sliced
4 ounces sliced reduced-fat mozzarella cheese

Per Serving
Calories: 218
% Calories from fat: 21
Fat (gm): 5
Saturated fat (gm): 1
Cholesterol (mg): 0
Sodium (mg): 765
Protein (gm): 21.2
Carbohydrate (gm): 21.9
Exchanges
Milk: 0.0
Vegetable: 1.0
Fruit: 0.0
Bread: 1.0
Meat: 2.0
Fat: 0.0

1. Spread bread with margarine. Top with combined sauerkraut, cabbage, sliced tomato, and cheese. Broil 6 inches from heat source until golden and bubbly, 3 to 4 minutes.

BEER-CHEESE PUFF

Just a touch of beer flavors the cheese topping on this open-faced sandwich.

2 servings

3/4 cup fat-free cottage cheese
1/2 cup (2 ounces) shredded reduced-fat Cheddar cheese
1 tablespoon grated Parmesan cheese
1/4 cup non-alcoholic beer
1/3 cup minced green onion
Dash Worcestershire sauce
Dash hot pepper sauce
2 large slices pumpernickel bread, toasted

Per Serving
Calories: 226
% Calories from fat: 24
Fat (gm): 6.3
Saturated fat (gm): 3.7
Cholesterol (mg): 12.1
Sodium (mg): 782
Protein (gm): 22.6
Carbohydrate (gm): 19.9
Exchanges
Milk: 0.0
Vegetable: 0.0
Fruit: 0.0
Bread: 1.0
Meat: 3.0
Fat: 0.0

1. Combine all ingredients, except pumpernickel bread, in medium bowl. Spread half the cheese mixture on each slice of bread. Broil 6 inches from heat source until bubbly, 3 to 4 minutes.

WELSH RAREBIT

Perhaps you know this dish as Welsh Rabbit. Whatever the name, the distinctively seasoned sauce is rich and flavorful. Rarebit is also delicious served over sliced ham or chicken breast and asparagus spears on toast.

6 servings (about 1/2 cup sauce each)

1/4	cup very finely chopped onion
2	tablespoons margarine
1/4	cup all-purpose flour
2	cups fat-free milk
1/2	cup white wine *or* fat-free milk
2	ounces light pasteurized process cheese product, cubed
1/2	cup (2 ounces) reduced-fat sharp Cheddar cheese
1/4-1/2	teaspoon dry mustard
1/2	teaspoon Worcestershire sauce
	White and cayenne pepper, to taste
6	slices sourdough, *or* multi-grain, bread
	Butter-flavored vegetable cooking spray
6	thick slices tomato
	Finely chopped parsley leaves, as garnish

Per Serving
Calories: 219
% Calories from fat: 31
Fat (gm): 7.6
Saturated fat (gm): 3.4
Cholesterol (mg): 11.5
Sodium (mg): 502
Protein (gm): 9.9
Carbohydrate (gm): 24.1
Exchanges
Milk: 0.0
Vegetable: 0.0
Fruit: 0.0
Bread: 1.5
Meat: 1.0
Fat: 1.0

1. Saute onion in margarine in medium saucepan until tender, 2 to 3 minutes. Stir in flour and cook over medium-low heat, stirring constantly, 1 minute. Whisk in milk and wine; heat to boiling. Boil, whisking constantly, until thickened, about 1 minute.

2. Stir in cheeses, dry mustard, and Worcestershire sauce; cook over low heat until cheeses are melted. Season to taste with white and cayenne pepper.

3. Spray both sides of bread with cooking spray; cook over medium heat in large skillet until browned, 2 to 3 minutes on each side. Broil tomato slices 4 inches from heat source until hot through. Arrange bread on plates; top with tomato slices, and spoon cheese sauce over. Sprinkle with parsley.

CHEESE AND VEGETABLE RAREBIT

For variation, serve this melty mixture in pita breads, or roll in flour tortillas, tucking up one end to contain the filling.

6 servings

Vegetable cooking spray
2/3 cup small broccoli florets
2/3 cup chopped portobello mushrooms
2/3 cup chopped yellow summer squash
1/3 cup chopped onion
2-3 tablespoons water
1/2 teaspoon dried marjoram leaves
1/2 teaspoon dried savory leaves
1/4 teaspoon dried thyme leaves
2 tablespoons margarine
1/4 cup all-purpose flour
2 cups fat-free milk
1/2 cup (2 ounces) shredded, *or* cubed,
       light American cheese
1/2-1 teaspoon white Worcestershire sauce
       Salt and pepper, to taste
6 slices sourdough bread, toasted
2 green onions and tops, sliced

Per Serving
Calories: 185
% Calories from fat: 30
Fat (gm): 6.2
Saturated fat (gm): 2
Cholesterol (mg): 6.4
Sodium (mg): 387
Protein (gm): 8.3
Carbohydrate (gm): 24.1
Exchanges
Milk: 0.0
Vegetable: 1.0
Fruit: 0.0
Bread: 1.5
Meat: 0.0
Fat: 1.0

1. Spray large skillet with cooking spray; heat over medium heat until hot. Saute broccoli, mushrooms, squash, and chopped onion 3 to 4 minutes; stir in water and herbs. Reduce heat and cook, covered, until vegetables are tender, 5 to 8 minutes.

2. Heat margarine in medium saucepan until melted; stir in flour and cook over medium-low heat, stirring constantly, 1 minute. Whisk in milk and heat to boiling, whisking until thickened, about 1 minute. Remove from heat; add cheese and Worcestershire sauce, whisking until cheese is melted.

3. Stir vegetables into cheese sauce; season to taste with salt and pepper. Spoon vegetable mixture over toast on plates; sprinkle with green onions.

CHEDDAR CHEESE SOUFFLÉ

This spectacular soufflé soars above the soufflé dish!

4 servings

Vegetable cooking spray

1-2 tablespoons grated fat-free Parmesan cheese

1 cup fat-free milk

3 tablespoons flour

$^1/_2$ teaspoon dry mustard

$^1/_2$ teaspoon snipped fresh chives

$^1/_2$ teaspoon dried marjoram leaves

$^1/_4$ teaspoon cayenne pepper

1-2 pinches ground nutmeg

3 egg yolks, lightly beaten

1$^1/_4$ cups (5 ounces) shredded fat-free Cheddar cheese

Salt and white pepper, to taste

3 egg whites

$^1/_4$ teaspoon cream of tartar

Per Serving
Calories: 162
% Calories from fat: 23
Fat (gm): 4.1
Saturated fat (gm): 1.3
Cholesterol (mg): 160.8
Sodium (mg): 340
Protein (gm): 19.3
Carbohydrate (gm): 11.2
Exchanges
Milk: 0.0
Vegetable: 0.0
Fruit: 0.0
Bread: 0.5
Meat: 2.5
Fat: 0.0

1. Spray 1-quart soufflé dish with cooking spray and coat with Parmesan cheese. Attach an aluminum foil collar to dish, extending foil 3 inches above top of dish; spray inside of collar with cooking spray.

2. Mix milk and flour until smooth in small saucepan; mix in mustard, chives, marjoram, cayenne, and nutmeg. Heat to boiling, whisking constantly; boil until thickened, about 1 minute, whisking constantly.

3. Whisk about $^1/_2$ cup milk mixture into egg yolks; whisk egg mixture into saucepan. Add cheese; whisk over low heat until melted. Season to taste with salt and white pepper.

4. Beat egg whites in medium bowl until foamy; add cream of tartar and beat to stiff, but not dry, peaks. Stir about $^1/_3$ of egg whites into cheese mixture; fold cheese mixture into remaining whites. Spoon into prepared soufflé dish. Bake at 350 degrees until soufflé is puffed, browned, and just set in the center, 35 to 40 minutes. Serve immediately.

SPINACH SOUFFLÉ

Any cooked vegetable can be substituted for the spinach in this recipe. Just be sure it's very well drained before chopping and measuring so the sauce will remain thick.

4 servings

1 small onion, minced
1 teaspoon margarine
3 tablespoons flour
1/2 teaspoon ground nutmeg
1/2 cup fat-free milk
1/2 cup reduced-sodium fat-free beef, *or* vegetable, broth
2 egg yolks, lightly beaten
1 package (10 ounces) frozen chopped spinach, thawed, well drained
Pinch white pepper
4 egg whites
Pinch cream of tartar

Per Serving
Calories: 118
% Calories from fat: 28
Fat (gm): 3.9
Saturated fat (gm): 1.1
Cholesterol (mg): 107.1
Sodium (mg): 167
Protein (gm): 9.7
Carbohydrate (gm): 12.1
Exchanges
Milk: 0.0
Vegetable: 1.0
Fruit: 0.0
Bread: 0.5
Meat: 1.0
Fat: 0.0

1. Saute onion in margarine in medium saucepan until tender; stir in flour and nutmeg and cook 1 to 2 minutes. Whisk in milk and broth and heat to boiling, whisking until thickened. Whisk about half the sauce into egg yolks; whisk yolk mixture into saucepan. Mix in spinach and white pepper.

2. Beat egg whites and cream of tartar in large bowl to stiff, but not dry, peaks; fold into spinach mixture and spoon into soufflé dish. Bake, uncovered, at 350 degrees until puffed and browned, about 40 minutes. Serve immediately.

CHEESE FONDUE

Flavorful with wine and a hint of garlic, this creamy fondue is made entirely with fat-free cheese!

8 servings (about ¹/₄ cup each)

1¹/₂ cups dry white wine

2-3 large cloves garlic, peeled

1 package (8 ounces) fat-free cream cheese

2 cups (8 ounces) shredded fat-free Swiss cheese

1 tablespoon flour

Salt, cayenne, and black pepper, to taste

French, *or* Italian, bread, cubed, for dipping

Per Serving
Calories: 100
% Calories from fat: 0
Fat (gm): 0
Saturated fat (gm): 0
Cholesterol (mg): 0
Sodium (mg): 547
Protein (gm): 10.8
Carbohydrate (gm): 5
Exchanges
Milk: 0.0
Vegetable: 0.0
Fruit: 0.0
Bread: 0.0
Meat: 1.5
Fat: 0.0

1. Heat wine and garlic cloves to boiling in medium saucepan; reduce heat and boil gently until reduced to ³/₄ cup. Discard garlic.

2. Add cream cheese and cook over low heat, stirring until melted and smooth. Toss shredded cheese with flour; add to saucepan and cook, stirring constantly, until melted. Season to taste with salt, cayenne, and black pepper.

3. Serve in fondue pot or bowl with bread cubes (not included in nutritional data) for dipping.

Notes: If fondue becomes too thick, it can be thinned with white wine, fat-free milk, or water.

Three-fourths cup fat-free milk can be substituted for the wine. Simmer with garlic 5 minutes, then proceed with recipe as above.

QUICHE LORRAINE

Enjoy the rich texture and flavor of this classic quiche, modified to low-fat goodness by using a combination of fat-free and evaporated fat-free milk. For Spinach Quiche, see the variation following the recipe.

6 servings

Reduced-Fat Pie Pastry (recipe follows)
Vegetable cooking spray
$^1/_4$ cup finely chopped onion
$^3/_4$ cup fat-free milk
$^1/_2$ can (12-ounce size) fat-free evaporated milk
1 egg
2 egg whites
$^1/_4$ cup fat-free sour cream
$^1/_4$ teaspoon salt
$^1/_8$ teaspoon cayenne pepper
$^1/_8$ teaspoon ground nutmeg
1 cup (4 ounces) shredded fat-free Swiss cheese
1 tablespoon flour
2 slices bacon, cooked, well drained, crumbled

Per Serving
Calories: 276
% Calories from fat: 26
Fat (gm): 7.9
Saturated fat (gm): 2.1
Cholesterol (mg): 38.7
Sodium (mg): 562
Protein (gm): 14.4
Carbohydrate (gm): 34.7
Exchanges
Milk: 0.0
Vegetable: 0.0
Fruit: 0.0
Bread: 2.0
Meat: 2.0
Fat: 0.5

1. Roll pastry on floured surface into circle 1 inch larger than inverted 8-inch pie pan. Ease pastry into pan; trim and flute. Line bottom of pastry with aluminum foil and fill with a single layer of pie weights or dried beans. Bake at 425 degrees for 7 minutes; remove pie weights and foil. Bake 3 to 5 minutes longer or until crust is light golden brown. Cool on wire rack.

2. Spray small skillet with cooking spray; place over medium heat until hot. Saute onion until tender, 3 to 5 minutes.

3. Mix milk and evaporated milk, egg, egg whites, sour cream, salt, cayenne pepper, and nutmeg in medium bowl until smooth. Toss cheese with flour; stir into milk mixture. Stir in bacon and onion and pour into baked pie crust.

4. Bake quiche at 350 degrees until set in the center and a sharp knife inserted near center comes out clean, about 40 minutes. Cover edge of pie crust with aluminum foil if becoming too brown. Cool quiche on wire rack 5 minutes before cutting.

Reduced-Fat Pie Pastry

one 8- or 9-inch pie crust

  1¼ cups all-purpose flour
  ¼ teaspoon salt
  3 tablespoons cold margarine *or* vegetable
      shortening, cut into pieces
  3-4 tablespoons ice water

1. Combine flour and salt in medium bowl; cut in margarine with pastry blender until mixture forms coarse crumbs. Sprinkle with ice water, 1 tablespoon at a time, mixing with fork until dough holds together. Refrigerate, covered, 30 minutes before using.

Variation: **Spinach Quiche**—Make Step 1 as above. Replace Step 2 as follows: Spray medium skillet with vegetable cooking spray; heat over medium heat until hot. Saute ¼ cup finely chopped onion until tender, 3 to 5 minutes. Drain ½ package (10-ounce size) frozen thawed spinach between paper toweling. Add spinach to skillet, cooking over medium to medium-low heat until mixture is quite dry, 3 to 4 minutes. Complete recipe as above, stirring spinach mixture into milk mixture in Step 3.

BLACK BEAN CHEESECAKE WITH SALSA

This savory cheesecake can also be served in smaller pieces as an appetizer or first course. It can also be served at room temperature, rather than heating as the recipe directs. Make it a day in advance, as overnight chilling is essential.

8 servings

- 4 flour tortillas
- 3 packages (8 ounces each) reduced-fat cream cheese, room temperature
- 6 eggs *or* 1¹/₂ cups no-cholesterol real egg product
- 1 can (15 ounces) black beans, rinsed, drained
- ¹/₂ jalapeño chili, finely chopped
- 3 teaspoons minced garlic
- 2 teaspoons Worcestershire sauce
- 2 teaspoons ground cumin
- ¹/₂ teaspoon dried oregano leaves
- ¹/₂ teaspoon salt
- ¹/₂ teaspoon cayenne pepper
  Mild, *or* medium, salsa, as garnish

Per Serving
Calories: 229
% Calories from fat: 25
Fat (gm): 6.7
Saturated fat (gm): 2.1
Cholesterol (mg): 165.8
Sodium (mg): 793
Protein (gm): 20.8
Carbohydrate (gm): 24.5
Exchanges
Milk: 0.0
Vegetable: 0.0
Fruit: 0.0
Bread: 1.5
Meat: 2.0
Fat: 0.0

1. Lightly grease 9-inch springform pan and line with overlapping tortillas.

2. Beat cream cheese in large bowl until smooth; beat in eggs. Mix in remaining ingredients, except salsa. Transfer mixture to prepared springform pan.

3. Bake at 300 degrees until center is set and sharp knife inserted halfway between center and edge of cheesecake comes out almost clean, 1³/₄ to 2 hours. Cool to room temperature on wire rack. Refrigerate overnight.

4. Remove side of pan. Cut cheesecake into 8 wedges. Cook wedges of cheesecake in lightly greased large skillet over medium-low heat until browned on both sides. Garnish each wedge with small dollop of salsa.

BEAN AND CHEESE CHILI RELLENOS

Authentic chili rellenos are made with poblano peppers. Green bell peppers can be substituted and the rellenos will be delicious, but the flavor of the pepper is not the same. Chili rellenos are normally coated with a beaten egg white mixture and fried in deep oil; our skinny version omits this fat-laden step.

6 servings

6 large poblano chilies

2-3 quarts water

Vegetable cooking spray

1/2 small jalapeño chili, seeds and veins discarded, minced

4 cloves garlic, minced

1 teaspoon dried oregano leaves

2 packages (8 ounces each) fat-free cream cheese, room temperature

1/2 cup (2 ounces) Mexican white cheese (*queso blanco*) *or* farmer's cheese, crumbled

1 1/2 cups cooked pinto beans *or* 1 can (15 ounces) pinto beans, rinsed, drained

1 tablespoon vegetable oil

Per Serving
Calories: 204
% Calories from fat: 25
Fat (gm): 5.5
Saturated fat (gm): 0.4
Cholesterol (mg): 22.3
Sodium (mg): 520
Protein (gm): 17.2
Carbohydrate (gm): 19.4
Exchanges
Milk: 0.0
Vegetable: 1.0
Fruit: 0.0
Bread: 1.0
Meat: 1.5
Fat: 0.5

1. Cut stems from tops of poblano chilies; remove and discard seeds and veins. Heat water to boiling in large saucepan; add poblano chilies. Reduce heat and simmer, uncovered, 2 to 3 minutes, until chilies are slightly softened. Drain well and cool.

2. Spray small skillet with cooking spray; heat over medium heat until hot. Saute jalalpeño chili, garlic, and oregano until chili is tender, 2 to 3 minutes.

3. Mix cream cheese, white cheese, beans, and jalapeño chili mixture; stuff poblano chilies with mixture. Heat oil in medium skillet until hot; saute chillies over medium to medium-high heat until tender and browned on all sides, 6 to 8 minutes. Serve hot.

EIGHT

Pasta

HOMEMADE PASTA

Fresh pasta dough is not difficult to make. A pasta machine provides a very simple and expedient way of kneading, rolling, and cutting the dough, producing a high-quality pasta. Rolling and cutting the dough by hand is somewhat more difficult, requiring practice to make thin, delicate pasta. Follow cooking directions in Step 5 carefully. Fresh pasta cooks very quickly—much more quickly than purchased fresh or dried pasta.

4 servings

1¹/₂ cups all-purpose flour
   2 large eggs

Per Serving
Calories: 208
% Calories from fat: 13
Fat (gm): 3
Saturated fat (gm): 0.8
Cholesterol (mg): 106.5
Sodium (mg): 32
Protein (gm): 8
Carbohydrate (gm): 36.1
Exchanges
Milk: 0.0
Vegetable: 0.0
Fruit: 0.0
Bread: 2.5
Meat: 0.0
Fat: 0.5

1. Mound flour on cutting board, making a well in center. Drop eggs into center of well.

2. Break egg yolks and mix eggs with fork. While mixing eggs, gradually start to incorporate flour into the eggs. As flour is incorporated, it will be necessary to move the mound of flour toward the center, using your hands. Continue mixing until all or almost all flour has been incorporated, forming a soft, but not sticky, ball of dough.

3. Knead and cut pasta, using pasta machine, or by hand, as described below.

4. Pasta can be cooked fresh, or it can be frozen or dried to be cooked later. To freeze pasta, place in heavy plastic freezer bag and freeze. To dry pasta, let stand on floured surface (or hang over rack) until completely dried. (Be sure pasta is completely dried or it will turn moldy in storage.) Store at room temperature in airtight container.

5. To cook fresh, frozen, or dried pasta, heat 4 to 5 quarts lightly salted water to boiling. Add pasta and begin testing for doneness as soon as water returns to boiling. Cooking time will vary from 10 seconds to 2 minutes once water has returned to boiling.

Machine Kneading and Cutting

To knead dough using a pasta machine, set machine rollers on widest setting. Cut dough into 2 equal pieces and process both as follows. Lightly flour outside of 1 piece, and pass it through machine. Fold piece of dough into thirds; pass it through machine again, inserting open edges (not the fold) of dough first. Repeat folding and rolling 8 to 12 times or until dough feels smooth and satiny; lightly flour dough only if it begins to feel sticky.

Move machine rollers to next widest setting. Pass dough through rollers (do not fold dough), beginning to roll out and stretch dough. Move machine rollers to next widest setting; pass dough through rollers. Continue process until pasta is as thin as desired. (Often the narrowest setting on machine makes pasta too thin; 1 or 2 settings from the end is usually best.) Lightly flour dough if it begins to feel even slightly sticky at any time.

To cut dough, set cutting rollers for width of pasta desired; pass dough through cutters. Arrange cut pasta in single layer on lightly floured surface.

Hand Kneading and Cutting

To knead dough by hand, knead on lightly floured surface until dough is smooth and satiny, about 10 minutes. Cover dough lightly with damp towel and let rest 10 minutes.

Place dough on lightly floured surface. Starting in center of dough, roll with rolling pin from center to edge. Continue rolling, always from center to edge (to keep dough as round as possible) until dough is about $1/16$ inch thick. Lightly flour dough if it begins to feel even slightly sticky at any time.

To cut dough, flour top of dough lightly and roll up. Cut into desired width with sharp knife. Immediately unroll cut pasta to keep noodles from sticking together, and arrange in single layer on lightly floured surface.

PASTA BOLOGNESE

Bolognese Sauce is most often served with spaghetti, but a shaped pasta such as farfalle (bow ties) or ruote (wheels) can also be used.

6 servings

1 pound ground beef eye of round *or* turkey

1 small onion, finely chopped

1/4 cup thinly sliced carrot

1/4 cup thinly sliced celery

3 cloves garlic, minced

1/2 teaspoon dried oregano leaves

1/2 teaspoon dried tarragon leaves

1/2 teaspoon dried thyme leaves

1/8 teaspoon ground nutmeg

1 can (8 ounces) reduced-sodium tomato sauce

1 can (8 ounces) reduced-sodium whole tomatoes, drained, chopped

1/4 cup tomato juice

1/2 teaspoon salt

1/4 teaspoon pepper

8 ounces spaghetti, cooked, warm

Per Serving
Calories: 307
% Calories from fat: 12
Fat (gm): 4.1
Saturated fat (gm): 1.3
Cholesterol (mg): 37.2
Sodium (mg): 245
Protein (gm): 24.1
Carbohydrate (gm): 40.7
Exchanges
Milk: 0.0
Vegetable: 2.0
Fruit: 0.0
Bread: 2.0
Meat: 2.0
Fat: 0.0

1. Cook ground beef in medium saucepan over medium heat until browned, 5 to 8 minutes; drain well and crumble.

2. Add onion, carrot, celery, and garlic to saucepan; saute until crisp-tender, about 5 minutes. Stir in herbs; cook 1 minute. Add tomato sauce, tomatoes, and wine; heat to boiling. Reduce heat and simmer, uncovered, until thick sauce consistency, about 15 minutes. Stir in salt and pepper. Serve over spaghetti.

PASTA WITH TOMATO AND MEATBALL SAUCE

You'll savor the full-bodied herb flavors in this updated version of a traditional meatball sauce. Serve with traditional spaghetti or one of the more unusually shaped pastas such as cappelletti (little hats) or gnocchi.

8 servings

1 cup chopped onion
3 cloves garlic, minced
1 tablespoon olive oil
1 can (16 ounces) reduced-sodium whole tomatoes, drained, chopped
1 can (8 ounces) reduced-sodium tomato sauce
1 tablespoon tomato paste
1 teaspoon dried basil leaves
1/2 teaspoon dried tarragon leaves
1/2 teaspoon dried oregano leaves
1/8 teaspoon crushed red pepper
1/2 teaspoon salt
1/4 teaspoon pepper
Herb-Seasoned Meatballs (recipe follows)
12 ounces spaghetti, cooked, warm

Per Serving
Calories: 355
% Calories from fat: 21
Fat (gm): 8.4
Saturated fat (gm): 1.9
Cholesterol (mg): 42.3
Sodium (mg): 405
Protein (gm): 20.2
Carbohydrate (gm): 48.8
Exchanges
Milk: 0.0
Vegetable: 3.0
Fruit: 0.0
Bread: 2.0
Meat: 1.5
Fat: 1.0

1. Saute onion and garlic in oil in large saucepan 2 to 3 minutes. Stir in tomatoes, tomato sauce, tomato paste, herbs, and red pepper; heat to boiling. Reduce heat and simmer, uncovered, 10 minutes; stir in salt and pepper.

2. Add Herb-Seasoned Meatballs to tomato mixture. Simmer, uncovered, until medium sauce consistency, 10 to 15 minutes. Serve over spaghetti.

Herb-Seasoned Meatballs

makes 6 servings (3 meatballs each)

1	pound ground turkey
1/3	cup unseasoned dry bread crumbs
1	egg white
3	cloves garlic, minced
2	tablespoons minced parsley
3/4	teaspoon dried basil leaves
3/4	teaspoon dried oregano leaves
1/4	teaspoon dried thyme leaves
1/2	teaspoon salt
1/4	teaspoon pepper

1. Mix ground turkey and remaining ingredients; shape into 18 meatballs. Cook meatballs over medium heat in skillet until browned on all sides and no longer pink in the center, 8 to 10 minutes. Drain well.

PASTA PUTTANESCA

This spicy sauce is also wonderful over shaped pasta such as penne, farfalle, etc.

8 servings

3	large onions, chopped
2	teaspoons minced garlic
2¹/2	tablespoons olive oil
1	cup diced lean ham *or* Canadian bacon
2	cans (28 ounces each) reduced-sodium tomatoes, undrained, chopped
1/4	cup sliced green olives
2	teaspoons dried basil leaves
1/8-1/4	teaspoon crushed red pepper flakes
	Salt and pepper, to taste
12	ounces spaghetti, cooked, warm

Per Serving
Calories: 316
% Calories from fat: 19
Fat (gm): 6.9
Saturated fat (gm): 1.1
Cholesterol (mg): 5.3
Sodium (mg): 332
Protein (gm): 13
Carbohydrate (gm): 52
Exchanges
Milk: 0.0
Vegetable: 4.0
Fruit: 0.0
Bread: 2.0
Meat: 0.0
Fat: 1.5

1. Saute onions and garlic in olive oil in large saucepan until tender and golden brown, stirring frequently. Add remaining ingredients, except salt, pepper, and spaghetti, and heat to boiling. Reduce heat and simmer, uncovered, until thickened, about 20 minutes. Season to taste with salt and pepper. Serve over spaghetti.

PASTA PEPERONATA

Italian peperonata, a slow-cooked mixture of sweet peppers, onions, and garlic, is also wonderful served in pita breads.

6 servings

5 large bell peppers, assorted colors, sliced
4 medium onions, sliced
4 teaspoons minced garlic
3 tablespoons olive oil
3 tablespoons water
1 teaspoon sugar
Salt and pepper, to taste
8 ounces spaghetti, cooked, warm
1/4 cup shredded Parmesan cheese

Per Serving
Calories: 294
% Calories from fat: 27
Fat (gm): 8.8
Saturated fat (gm): 1.2
Cholesterol (mg): 2
Sodium (mg): 67
Protein (gm): 8.6
Carbohydrate (gm): 45
Exchanges
Milk: 0.0
Vegetable: 2.0
Fruit: 0.0
Bread: 3.0
Meat: 0.0
Fat: 1.5

1. Saute peppers, onions, and garlic in oil in large skillet 2 to 3 minutes. Add water; cook, covered, over medium to medium-high heat until soft, 2 to 3 minutes.

2. Stir sugar into pepper mixture; cook, uncovered, over medium-low heat until mixture is very soft and browned, about 20 minutes. Season to taste with salt and pepper. Toss with spaghetti and sprinkle with cheese.

FETTUCCINE WITH ROASTED GARLIC, ONIONS, AND PEPPERS

A dish that is deceptively simple to make, incredibly delicious to eat.

8 side-dish servings

2   bulbs garlic
    Olive oil cooking spray
3   medium onions, cut into wedges
2   large red bell peppers, cut into 1/2-inch slices
2   tablespoons olive oil *or* vegetable oil
2   tablespoons lemon juice
2   tablespoons finely chopped parsley
1/2 teaspoon salt
1/4 teaspoon pepper
8   ounces fettuccine, cooked, warm

Per Serving
Calories: 151
% Calories from fat: 26
Fat (gm): 4.5
Saturated fat (gm): 0.5
Cholesterol (mg): 0
Sodium (mg): 184
Protein (gm): 5
Carbohydrate (gm): 24.4
Exchanges
Milk: 0.0
Vegetable: 1.5
Fruit: 0.0
Bread: 1.0
Meat: 0.0
Fat: 1.0

1.   Heat oven to 400 degrees. Cut a scant 1/2 inch off tops of garlic bulbs, exposing ends of cloves. Wrap garlic cloves loosely in aluminum foil. Spray jelly roll pan with cooking spray. Arrange garlic, onions, and bell peppers on pan. Bake vegetables, uncovered, until garlic is very soft and vegetables are tender, 15 to 20 minutes.

2.   Cool garlic slightly; squeeze pulp into small bowl. Stir in oil, lemon juice, parsley, salt, and pepper. Spoon garlic mixture over pasta and toss; add onions and peppers and toss. Serve warm.

LINGUINE WITH MIXED HERB PESTO

Packaged fresh herbs are readily available in most supermarkets. Each ¹/₂-ounce package yields about ¹/₄ cup of packed herb leaves. Serve pesto sauces at room temperature, mixing with hot pasta.

4 servings

¹/₂ cup packed fresh, *or* 2 tablespoons dried, basil leaves

¹/₂ cup packed fresh parsley leaves

¹/₄ cup packed fresh, *or* 2 tablespoons dried, oregano leaves

3 cloves garlic, minced

3-4 tablespoons grated fat-free Parmesan cheese

1 ounce walnuts (about 14 medium)

1 tablespoon olive oil

2 teaspoons lemon juice

2-4 tablespoons reduced-sodium fat-free chicken broth *or* water

¹/₂ teaspoon salt

¹/₄ teaspoon pepper

8 ounces linguine, cooked, warm

Per Serving
Calories: 253
% Calories from fat: 30
Fat (gm): 8.8
Saturated fat (gm): 0.7
Cholesterol (mg): 0
Sodium (mg): 447
Protein (gm): 9.7
Carbohydrate (gm): 36
Exchanges
Milk: 0.0
Vegetable: 1.0
Fruit: 0.0
Bread: 2.0
Meat: 0.0
Fat: 1.5

1. Combine herbs, garlic, Parmesan cheese, and walnuts in food processor or blender. Process, adding oil and lemon juice gradually, until mixture is very finely chopped; continue processing, adding enough broth to make a smooth, spoonable consistency. Stir in salt and pepper. Spoon mixture over linguine and toss.

GRILLED SUMMER VEGETABLES IN PASTA NESTS

For an attractive presentation, the linguine is shaped into small nests to contain the medley of roasted vegetables.

6 servings

3 tablespoons olive oil, divided

2 tablespoons balsamic vinegar *or* red wine vinegar

1 teaspoon lemon juice

3 cloves garlic, minced, divided

2 teaspoons crushed caraway seeds

1/4 teaspoon salt

1/4 teaspoon pepper

1 medium eggplant, peeled, cut into 1-inch pieces

1 medium zucchini, sliced

1 medium red, *or* green, bell pepper, cut into 1-inch pieces

1 small red onion, cut into 1-inch wedges

Vegetable cooking spray

12 ounces linguine, cooked, warm

1 tablespoon minced parsley

Per Serving
Calories: 263
% Calories from fat: 30
Fat (gm): 9.1
Saturated fat (gm): 1.1
Cholesterol (mg): 0
Sodium (mg): 184
Protein (gm): 8.5
Carbohydrate (gm): 38.8
Exchanges
Milk: 0.0
Vegetable: 2.0
Fruit: 0.0
Bread: 2.0
Meat: 0.0
Fat: 1.5

1. Mix 2 tablespoons of oil, vinegar, lemon juice, 2 cloves of garlic, caraway seeds, salt, and pepper; pour over combined vegetables in shallow glass baking dish. Let stand, covered, 30 to 60 minutes.

2. Spray 2 aluminum foil-lined jelly roll pans with cooking spray; arrange vegetables on pans. Spray vegetables generously with cooking spray and toss. Bake at 425 degrees until vegetables are browned and just tender, 30 to 40 minutes.

3. Toss linguine with remaining 1 tablespoon oil, parsley, and remaining 1 clove garlic. Shape linguine into 8 small nests; spoon vegetables into nests.

FETTUCCINE PAPRIKASH

Suit your preference of hot or sweet paprika in this recipe. Reduced-fat sour cream adds a wonderful creamy texture and richness to the sauce. Serve over any kind of pasta.

6 servings

- 1 medium red bell pepper, sliced
- 1 medium green bell pepper, sliced
- 1 large onion, sliced
- 1 tablespoon margarine
- 2 tablespoons flour
- 1 tablespoon sweet Hungarian paprika
- $1/2$ teaspoon salt
- $1/4$ teaspoon pepper
- 1 can (8 ounces) reduced-sodium tomato sauce
- $1/2$ cup reduced-sodium fat-free chicken broth
- $1/2$ cup dry white wine *or* chicken broth
- $1/2$ cup reduced-fat sour cream
- 12 ounces fettuccine, cooked, warm

Per Serving
Calories: 264
% Calories from fat: 20
Fat (gm): 5.8
Saturated fat (gm): 1.7
Cholesterol (mg): 16.7
Sodium (mg): 267
Protein (gm): 9.5
Carbohydrate (gm): 41
Exchanges
Milk: 0.0
Vegetable: 2.0
Fruit: 0.0
Bread: 2.0
Meat: 0.0
Fat: 1.5

1. Cook bell peppers and onion in margarine in large skillet over medium heat until peppers are very soft, 10 to 15 minutes. Stir in flour, paprika, salt, and pepper; cook 1 to 2 minutes, stirring occasionally.

2. Stir in tomato sauce, chicken broth, and wine; heat to boiling. Reduce heat and simmer, uncovered, until sauce is thickened, 5 to 7 minutes; stir in sour cream. Serve over fettuccine.

FETTUCCINE WITH GORGONZOLA SAUCE

Although higher in fat content than some of the other blue cheeses, Gorgonzola lends richness of flavor to this creamy sauce.

6 servings

- 2 cups fat-free milk
- 1/4 cup dry white wine *or* milk
- 1/4 cup all-purpose flour
- 3 ounces Gorgonzola cheese, crumbled
- 2 tablespoons margarine
- 1/4 teaspoon pepper
- 12 ounces fettuccine, cooked, warm

Per Serving
Calories: 298
% Calories from fat: 230
Fat (gm): 10
Saturated fat (gm): 3.5
Cholesterol (mg): 22.1
Sodium (mg): 295
Protein (gm): 12.4
Carbohydrate (gm): 38.4
Exchanges
Milk: 0.0
Vegetable: 2.0
Fruit: 0.0
Bread: 2.0
Meat: 0.0
Fat: 2.0

1. Whisk milk, wine, and flour in medium saucepan until smooth; heat to boiling. Boil, whisking constantly, until thickened, 1 to 2 minutes.

2. Reduce heat to low, and stir in cheese, margarine, and pepper; cook 1 to 2 minutes. Serve over fettuccine.

LINGUINE WITH WHITE CLAM SAUCE

One of Italy's most treasured dishes!

4 servings

- 3 cloves garlic, minced
- 1 tablespoon olive oil
- 2 tablespoons cornstarch
- 2 cups clam juice
- 1 pound shucked clams *or* 2 cans (7½ ounces each) baby clams, undrained
- 1 tablespoon lemon juice
- 1 tablespoon finely chopped parsley
- 1-2 teaspoons dried basil leaves
- 1/8 teaspoon ground white pepper
- 8 ounces linguine, cooked, warm

Per Serving
Calories: 319
% Calories from fat: 18
Fat (gm): 6.5
Saturated fat (gm): 0.6
Cholesterol (mg): 38.6
Sodium (mg): 305
Protein (gm): 23.5
Carbohydrate (gm): 39.1
Exchanges
Milk: 0.0
Vegetable: 0.5
Fruit: 0.0
Bread: 2.5
Meat: 2.0
Fat: 0.5

1. Saute garlic in oil in medium saucepan, 1 to 2 minutes. Mix cornstarch and clam juice; stir into saucepan. Stir in wine and heat to boiling; boil, stirring constantly, until thickened, about 1 minute.

2. Add undrained clams and remaining ingredients, except linguine, to juice mixture. Simmer, covered, until clams are cooked, 5 to 7 minutes. Serve over linguine.

LINGUINE WITH RED CLAM SAUCE

This light tomato sauce is rich with succulent clams. If you prefer white clam sauce, try Linguine with White Clam Sauce (see p. 386).

4 servings

2 cloves garlic, minced
1 tablespoon olive oil
1 can (28 ounces) Italian tomatoes, undrained, coarsely chopped
2 teaspoons dried oregano leaves
1 pound shucked baby clams *or* 2 cans (7^1/$_2$ ounces each) baby clams, undrained
^{1}/$_4$ cup clam juice
1 tablespoon lemon juice
^{1}/$_8$-^{1}/$_4$ teaspoon cayenne pepper
^{1}/$_4$ teaspoon black pepper
8 ounces linguine, cooked, warm

Per Serving
Calories: 332
% Calories from fat: 16
Fat (gm): 5.8
Saturated fat (gm): 0.6
Cholesterol (mg): 38.1
Sodium (mg): 590
Protein (gm): 22.3
Carbohydrate (gm): 43.8
Exchanges
Milk: 0.0
Vegetable: 2.0
Fruit: 0.0
Bread: 2.0
Meat: 2.0
Fat: 0.5

1. Saute garlic in oil in medium saucepan until tender. Stir in tomatoes with liquid and oregano; heat to boiling. Reduce heat and simmer, uncovered, until mixture is medium sauce consistency, about 10 minutes.

2. Stir in undrained clams, wine, lemon juice, cayenne and black pepper. Simmer, covered, until clams are cooked, 5 to 7 minutes. Serve over linguine.

JERK CHICKEN AND SHRIMP WITH LINGUINE

Enjoy the highly seasoned flavors of the Caribbean in this pasta dish!

4 servings

8 ounces chicken tenders

4 ounces peeled, deveined shrimp
Jerk Sauce (recipe follows)

1 can (14¹/₂ ounces) reduced-sodium chicken broth

2 teaspoons lime juice

1 pound broccoli florets, steamed until crisp-tender

8 ounces linguine, cooked, warm

Per Serving
Calories: 332
% Calories from fat: 13
Fat (gm): 4.9
Saturated fat (gm): 0.6
Cholesterol (mg): 73
Sodium (mg): 232
Protein (gm): 28
Carbohydrate (gm): 47
Exchanges
Milk: 0.0
Vegetable: 2.0
Fruit: 0.0
Bread: 2.5
Meat: 2.0
Fat: 0.0

1. Place chicken and shrimp in shallow glass baking dish. Spoon Jerk Sauce over and toss to coat chicken and shrimp. Refrigerate, covered, 30 minutes.

2. Transfer undrained chicken and shrimp to large skillet. Cook over medium-high heat until chicken and shrimp are cooked, about 5 minutes. Stir remaining ingredients, except linguine, into skillet; heat to boiling. Reduce heat and simmer, uncovered, until liquid is thin sauce consistency, 5 to 7 minutes. Spoon over linguine on rimmed serving platter.

Jerk Sauce

makes about ¹/₃ cup

3 tablespoons water

2 tablespoons finely chopped cilantro

2 tablespoons minced gingerroot

2 cloves garlic, minced

2 tablespoons packed brown sugar

1 tablespoon ground allspice

2 teaspoons black peppercorns

¹/₄-¹/₂ teaspoon crushed red pepper

¹/₄ teaspoon ground coriander

¹/₄ teaspoon ground mace

1. Process all ingredients in food processor or blender until coarse paste is formed. Refrigerate until ready to use.

FUSILLI WITH TOMATOES AND CORN

A perfect salad, especially when homegrown tomatoes, corn, and basil are available!

8 side-dish servings

2 cups chopped plum tomatoes
1 cup fresh, *or* frozen, whole-kernel corn, cooked
$^1/_2$ cup sliced green onions and tops
$2^2/_3$ cups (6 ounces) fusilli (spirals), *or* corkscrews, cooked, room temperature
Fresh Basil Dressing (recipe follows)

Per Serving
Calories: 135
% Calories from fat: 26
Fat (gm): 4
Saturated fat (gm): 0.6
Cholesterol (mg): 0
Sodium (mg): 141
Protein (gm): 4.1
Carbohydrate (gm): 21.8
Exchanges
Milk: 0.0
Vegetable: 1.0
Fruit: 0.0
Bread: 1.0
Meat: 0.0
Fat: 1.0

1. Combine tomatoes, corn, green onions, and pasta in salad bowl; pour Fresh Basil Dressing over and toss.

Fresh Basil Dressing

makes about $^1/_4$ cup

$^1/_3$ cup red wine vinegar
2 tablespoons olive oil *or* vegetable oil
3 tablespoons finely chopped fresh basil
2 cloves garlic, minced
$^1/_2$ teaspoon salt
$^1/_4$ teaspoon pepper

1. Mix all ingredients; refrigerate until serving time. Stir before using.

PASTA WITH GREENS, RAISINS, AND PINE NUTS

Radicchio, escarole, curly endive, or mustard greens can be substituted for the kale in this sweet-and-bitter Italian favorite.

8 servings

3-4 medium onions, sliced
2 teaspoons minced garlic
1 tablespoon olive oil
1 teaspoon sugar
12 ounces kale leaves, sliced
1/3 cup dark raisins
1/2 cup vegetable broth
Salt and pepper, to taste
12 ounces spaghetti *or* linguine, cooked, warm
1/4 cup pine nuts *or* slivered almonds

Per Serving
Calories: 225
% Calories from fat: 21
Fat (gm): 5.2
Saturated fat (gm): 0.8
Cholesterol (mg): 0
Sodium (mg): 78
Protein (gm): 7.3
Carbohydrate (gm): 38.4
Exchanges
Milk: 0.0
Vegetable: 1.5
Fruit: 0.0
Bread: 2.0
Meat: 2.0
Fat: 0.5

1. Saute onions and garlic in oil in large skillet 5 minutes. Stir in sugar; cook over low heat until onions are golden, 10 to 15 minutes, stirring occasionally.

2. Stir kale, raisins, and broth into onion mixture; cook, covered, over low heat until kale is wilted, about 10 minutes. Season to taste with salt and pepper. Spoon mixture over spaghetti and toss; sprinkle with pine nuts.

TAGLIATELLE WITH CHILI-MUSHROOM STROGANOFF SAUCE

Shiitake mushrooms and dried ancho chilies add unique flavors to this aromatic pasta sauce. The chilies can be quite hot, so adjust amount according to your taste.

8 servings

1 package (1³/₄ ounces) dried shiitake mushrooms
1-2 dried ancho chilies
3 cups boiling water, divided
2 cups vegetable broth, divided
1 cup chopped onion
8 ounces white mushrooms, halved or quartered
2 tablespoons margarine
¹/₄ cup all-purpose flour
¹/₂ teaspoon dried thyme leaves
1 cup reduced-fat sour cream
1 teaspoon Dijon-style mustard
Salt and pepper, to taste
12 ounces tagliatelle (flat pasta) *or* fettuccine, cooked, warm
Minced parsley, as garnish

Per Serving
Calories: 278
% Calories from fat: 22
Fat (gm): 6.7
Saturated fat (gm): 2.7
Cholesterol (mg): 10
Sodium (mg): 314
Protein (gm): 9.8
Carbohydrate (gm): 45.6
Exchanges
Milk: 0.0
Vegetable: 2.0
Fruit: 0.0
Bread: 2.0
Meat: 0.0
Fat: 0.0

1. Place shiitake mushrooms and chilies in separate bowls; pour 2 cups boiling water over the mushrooms and 1 cup over the chilies. Let stand until vegetables are softened, about 10 minutes.

2. Drain mushrooms, reserving liquid. Slice mushrooms, discarding tough centers. Drain chilies, discarding liquid. Process chilies and 1 cup broth in blender or food processor until smooth.

3. Saute onion, shiitake, and white mushrooms in margarine in large skillet until wilted, about 5 minutes. Stir in flour; cook 1 minute longer, stirring frequently. Stir in reserved mushroom liquid, chili mixture, remaining 1 cup broth, and thyme. Heat to boiling; reduce heat and simmer, covered, until shiitake mushrooms are tender, 10 to 15 minutes. Simmer uncovered, if necessary, until thickened.

4. Stir in sour cream and mustard; cook until hot through, 2 to 3 minutes. Season to taste with salt and pepper. Toss pasta with sauce in serving bowl; sprinkle generously with parsley.

PASTA WITH GOAT CHEESE AND ONION CONFIT

Try this recipe with flavored specialty pastas such as dried mushroom, herb, or black pepper.

6 servings

Olive oil cooking spray
4 cups thinly sliced onions
1 teaspoon minced garlic
$^{1}/_{2}$ teaspoon dried sage leaves
$^{1}/_{2}$ teaspoon dried rosemary leaves
1 teaspoon sugar
$^{1}/_{2}$ fat-free milk
2 ounces fat-free cream cheese
2-3 ounces goat cheese
Salt and white pepper, to taste
8 ounces whole wheat, *or* plain, thin spaghetti
$^{1}/_{4}$ cup coarsely chopped walnuts

Per Serving
Calories: 249
% Calories from fat: 24
Fat (gm): 6.6
Saturated fat (gm): 2.3
Cholesterol (mg): 8.2
Sodium (mg): 107
Protein (gm): 10.9
Carbohydrate (gm): 36.5
Exchanges
Milk: 0.0
Vegetable: 1.5
Fruit: 0.0
Bread: 2.5
Meat: 0.0
Fat: 0.0

1. Spray large skillet with cooking spray; heat over medium heat until hot. Add onions; cook, covered, over medium-low to low heat until onions are very soft, about 20 minutes.

2. Stir garlic, sage, rosemary, and sugar into onions; cook, uncovered, over medium-low to low heat until onions are caramelized and brown, 10 to 15 minutes. Stir in wine; simmer 2 to 3 minutes longer. Stir in cream cheese and goat cheese; cook over low heat, stirring, until melted. Season to taste with salt and white pepper.

3. Toss pasta and onion mixture on serving platter; sprinkle with walnuts.

PASTA WITH THREE-ONION SAUCE

The vegetables for this sauce are cooked very slowly until the onions are caramelized and golden.

6 servings

1½ cups sliced leeks, white parts only
1½ cups chopped red onions
  6 shallots, sliced
  3 tablespoons olive oil
¼ cup all-purpose flour
  1 can (14½ ounces) reduced-sodium fat-free chicken broth
¼ teaspoon dried thyme leaves
½ teaspoon salt
¼ teaspoon pepper
  8 ounces mafalde *or* other flat pasta, cooked, warm

Per Serving
Calories: 236
% Calories from fat: 26
Fat (gm): 7.6
Saturated fat (gm): 1.1
Cholesterol (mg): 0
Sodium (mg): 251
Protein (gm): 7.9
Carbohydrate (gm): 40
Exchanges
Milk: 0.0
Vegetable: 2.0
Fruit: 0.0
Bread: 2.0
Meat: 0.0
Fat: 1.5

1. Saute leeks, onions, and shallots in oil in medium saucepan 2 to 3 minutes. Reduce heat to medium-low and cook slowly until mixture is golden brown, about 15 minutes. Stir in flour; cook over medium heat 1 to 2 minutes more.

2. Stir chicken broth, thyme, salt, and pepper into leek mixture; heat to boiling. Boil, stirring constantly, until thickened, 1 to 2 minutes. Serve over mafalde.

FUSILLI WITH ARTICHOKE SAUCE

Minced jalapeño chilis add a hint of piquancy to this sauce.

4 servings

1 cup sliced onion

2 cloves garlic, minced

1 tablespoon olive oil

1 can (14 ounces) artichoke hearts, drained, rinsed, sliced

1/4 teaspoon minced, seeded jalapeño chili

2 tablespoons flour

1 cup reduced-sodium fat-free chicken broth

1/4 cup grated Parmesan cheese

2 tablespoons finely chopped parsley

1/4 teaspoon salt

1/4 teaspoon pepper

8 ounces fusilli (spirals), cooked, warm

Per Serving
Calories: 339
% Calories from fat: 16
Fat (gm): 6
Saturated fat (gm): 1.6
Cholesterol (mg): 3.9
Sodium (mg): 533
Protein (gm): 14.2
Carbohydrate (gm): 55.6
Exchanges
Milk: 0.0
Vegetable: 2.0
Fruit: 0.0
Bread: 3.0
Meat: 0.0
Fat: 1.5

1. Saute onion and garlic in oil in medium saucepan until tender, about 5 minutes. Stir in artichoke hearts and jalapeño chili; cook over medium heat 10 minutes. Stir in flour; cook 1 to 2 minutes more.

2. Stir chicken broth into artichoke mixture; heat to boiling. Boil, stirring constantly, until thickened, 1 to 2 minutes.

3. Reduce heat to low, and stir in Parmesan cheese, parsley, salt, and pepper; cook 1 to 2 minutes. Serve over fusilli.

PASTA WITH CABBAGE AND POTATOES

A nourishing meatless entrée. For those who prefer heartier fare, 12 ounces of cubed lean ham can be sauteed in olive oil cooking spray and added.

8 servings

6 cups thinly sliced cabbage

4 cloves garlic, minced

1/3 cup reduced-sodium chicken broth

4 medium Idaho potatoes, peeled, cooked, cut into 1/2-inch cubes

1 teaspoon dried rosemary leaves

1 teaspoon dried sage leaves

1/2 teaspoon salt

1/4 teaspoon pepper

12 ounces pappardelle *or* other wide, flat pasta, cooked, warm

1/4 cup grated Parmesan cheese

1 tablespoon finely chopped parsley

Per Serving
Calories: 241
% Calories from fat: 9
Fat (gm): 2.3
Saturated fat (gm): 0.8
Cholesterol (mg): 25
Sodium (mg): 212
Protein (gm): 9
Carbohydrate (gm): 45
Exchanges
Milk: 0.0
Vegetable: 1.5
Fruit: 0.0
Bread: 2.5
Meat: 0.0
Fat: 0.5

1. Combine cabbage, garlic, and broth in large skillet; heat to boiling. Cook, covered, over medium-high heat until cabbage is wilted, about 5 minutes; cook, uncovered, 5 minutes more.

2. Stir potatoes, herbs, salt, and pepper into cabbage mixture. Cook over medium to medium-high heat until excess liquid is gone, about 10 minutes.

3. Spoon mixture over pasta and toss; sprinkle with Parmesan cheese and toss. Sprinkle with parsley.

CREAMY TOMATO-PEPPER SAUCE WITH PENNE

Quick, easy, and delicious—this sauce is so creamy you'd swear it's high in fat, but it is really quite low.

6 servings

1   medium onion, chopped
¹/₂   teaspoon minced garlic
1   tablespoon olive oil
2   tablespoons chicken broth
1   can (15 ounces) Italian-seasoned tomato sauce
¹/₃   cup chopped roasted red peppers
2   teaspoons sugar
¹/₄   cup reduced-fat sour cream
    Salt and pepper, to taste
8   ounces penne, cooked, warm

Per Serving
Calories: 213
% Calories from fat: 16
Fat (gm): 3.8
Saturated fat (gm): 1.1
Cholesterol (mg): 3.3
Sodium (mg): 402
Protein (gm): 6.8
Carbohydrate (gm): 37.3
Exchanges
Milk: 0.0
Vegetable: 1.5
Fruit: 0.0
Bread: 2.0
Meat: 0.0
Fat: 0.5

1. Saute onion and garlic in oil in large saucepan until softened, about 5 minutes. Stir in sherry, tomato sauce, roasted peppers, and sugar. Heat to boiling; reduce heat and simmer 10 to 15 minutes or until lightly thickened. Stir in sour cream; season to taste with salt and pepper. Serve sauce over penne.

ROTINI AND BEANS NIÇOISE

Tarragon lends a fresh herb flavor to this pasta and bean combination. Garbanzo or kidney beans can be substituted for any of the beans used.

6 servings

¹/₂   cup chopped shallots
2   cups chopped Italian plum tomatoes
1   teaspoon minced garlic
2   teaspoons margarine
2   tablespoons drained capers
¹/₂   teaspoon dried tarragon leaves
2   cups diagonally sliced Italian, *or* regular, green beans, cooked
1   can (13¹/₄ ounces) baby lima beans, rinsed, drained

Per Serving
Calories: 265
% Calories from fat: 7
Fat (gm): 2.4
Saturated fat (gm): 0.4
Cholesterol (mg): 0
Sodium (mg): 430
Protein (gm): 13.8
Carbohydrate (gm): 53.9
Exchanges
Milk: 0.0
Vegetable: 2.0
Fruit: 0.0
Bread: 3.0
Meat: 0.0
Fat: 0.0

1 can (15 ounces) cannellini beans,
  rinsed, drained
4 cups cooked rotini *or* other shaped
  pasta, warm
  Salt and pepper, to taste
  Grated fat-free Parmesan cheese,
  as garnish

1. Saute shallots, tomatoes, and garlic in margarine in large skillet 2 to 3 minutes; cook, covered, over medium heat until tomatoes are wilted, 3 to 5 minutes. Stir in capers and tarragon and cook 1 to 2 minutes longer.

2. Stir beans into skillet; cook, covered, over medium-low heat until hot through, about 5 minutes. Stir in rotini and season to taste with salt and pepper. Spoon mixture into serving bowl; sprinkle lightly with Parmesan cheese.

PASTA FROM PESCIA

I have fond memories of this hearty dish from the Tuscany region of Italy. To save preparation time, use cabbage slaw mix to replace the sliced cabbage in the recipe.

8 servings

8 small new potatoes
3 cups thinly sliced cabbage
1½ cups halved Brussels sprouts
2 medium carrots, diagonally sliced
1 teaspoon minced garlic
½ teaspoon dried sage leaves
⅓ cup vegetable broth
⅓ cup shredded Parmesan cheese
1 tablespoon minced parsley
  Salt and pepper, to taste
8 ounces rigatoni *or* ziti, cooked, warm

Per Serving
Calories: 200
% Calories from fat: 8
Fat (gm): 1.8
Saturated fat (gm): 0.8
Cholesterol (mg): 2.6
Sodium (mg): 128
Protein (gm): 8
Carbohydrate (gm): 39.4
Exchanges
Milk: 0.0
Vegetable: 1.5
Fruit: 0.0
Bread: 3.0
Meat: 0.0
Fat: 0.0

1. Cook potatoes in 2 inches simmering water until tender, about 10 minutes; drain. Heat cabbage, Brussels sprouts, carrots, garlic, sage, and broth to boiling in large skillet. Reduce heat and simmer, covered, until cabbage is wilted, about 5 minutes. Add potatoes and cook, uncovered, until liquid is gone and cabbage is lightly browned, about 5 minutes.

2. Stir cheese and parsley into vegetables; season to taste with salt and pepper. Spoon mixture over pasta on serving platter and toss.

PEASANT-STYLE PASTA WITH BEANS, TOMATOES, AND SAGE

Hearty and chunky with 2 types of beans, this sauce is excellent served over any of the shaped pastas such as ziti, rotini, or rigatoni.

8 servings

1   can (15½ ounces) red kidney beans, rinsed, drained
1   can (15 ounces) cannellini, *or* Great Northern, beans, rinsed, drained
½   cup chopped onion
½   cup chopped celery
2   cloves garlic, minced
1   can (16 ounces) plum tomatoes, drained, chopped
1   can (14½ ounces) reduced-sodium fat-free chicken broth
1   teaspoon dried sage leaves
    Salt and pepper, to taste
8   ounces mostaccioli, cooked, warm

Per Serving
Calories: 214
% Calories from fat: 4
Fat (gm): 1
Saturated fat (gm): 0.1
Cholesterol (mg): 0
Sodium (mg): 341
Protein (gm): 11
Carbohydrate (gm): 40
Exchanges
Milk: 0.0
Vegetable: 0.0
Fruit: 0.0
Bread: 2.5
Meat: 0.5
Fat: 0.0

1. Heat beans, onion, celery, and garlic to boiling in large saucepan. Reduce heat and simmer, covered, 5 minutes.

2. Stir in tomatoes, chicken broth, and sage; heat to boiling. Reduce heat and simmer, uncovered, until mixture is desired sauce consistency, about 20 minutes. Season to taste with salt and pepper. Serve over mostaccioli.

CREOLE PASTA

Creole flavors accent this substantial sauce. If you enjoy okra, it would be an excellent addition.

8 servings

1¹/₂ cups sliced green bell peppers
³/₄ cup sliced carrots
¹/₂ cup sliced onion
¹/₂ cup sliced celery
3 cloves garlic, minced
2 tablespoons olive oil
1 medium tomato, chopped
1 teaspoon dried basil leaves
1 teaspoon dried oregano leaves
1 teaspoon paprika
¹/₂ teaspoon gumbo file powder, optional
¹/₂ teaspoon dried thyme leaves
1 bay leaf
¹/₄ teaspoon cayenne pepper
¹/₂ teaspoon salt
1 can (14¹/₂ ounces) reduced-sodium fat-free chicken broth
1 can (8 ounces) reduced-sodium tomato sauce
16 ounces ziti *or* rigatoni, cooked, warm

Per Serving
Calories: 285
% Calories from fat: 14
Fat (gm): 4.6
Saturated fat (gm): 0.6
Cholesterol (mg): 0
Sodium (mg): 204
Protein (gm): 9.8
Carbohydrate (gm): 50.9
Exchanges
Milk: 0.0
Vegetable: 1.0
Fruit: 0.0
Bread: 3.0
Meat: 0.0
Fat: 1.0

1. Saute bell peppers, carrots, onion, celery, and garlic in oil until peppers are tender, 8 to 10 minutes. Stir in tomato, herbs, cayenne pepper, and salt. Cook over medium heat 2 to 3 minutes, stirring frequently.

2. Add chicken broth and tomato sauce; heat to boiling. Reduce heat and simmer, uncovered, until vegetables are tender and sauce is thickened to desired consistency, about 20 minutes. Discard bay leaf. Serve over ziti.

PASTA SANTA FE

Enjoy flavors of the Southwest, picante with poblano chilies. If poblanos are not available, substitute green bell peppers and add a finely chopped jalapeño chili to the onions when sauteing.

4 servings

1 medium onion, sliced
3 cloves garlic, minced
2 tablespoons vegetable oil
2 medium zucchini, sliced
2 medium tomatoes, cut into wedges
2 poblano chilies, sliced
1 cup fresh, *or* frozen, thawed, whole-kernel corn
2 tablespoons chili powder
1 teaspoon dried oregano leaves
1/2 teaspoon ground cumin
2 tablespoons minced cilantro *or* parsley
1/2 teaspoon salt
1/4 teaspoon pepper
8 ounces trio maliano (combination of corkscrews, shells, and rigatoni), cooked, warm

Per Serving
Calories: 350
% Calories from fat: 24
Fat (gm): 9.6
Saturated fat (gm): 1.2
Cholesterol (mg): 0
Sodium (mg): 327
Protein (gm): 11.6
Carbohydrate (gm): 58
Exchanges
Milk: 0.0
Vegetable: 2.0
Fruit: 0.0
Bread: 3.0
Meat: 0.0
Fat: 2.0

1. Saute onion and garlic in oil in large skillet until tender, about 5 minutes. Add remaining vegetables, chili powder, oregano, and cumin. Cook, uncovered, over medium to medium-low heat until vegetables are crisp-tender, 12 to 15 minutes. Stir in cilantro, salt, and pepper.

2. Spoon vegetable mixture over pasta and toss.

STIR-FRIED RICE NOODLES WITH SHRIMP

This Asian-inspired dish can also be made with cooked angel hair pasta.

4 servings

1 package (8 ounces) rice noodles
1 tablespoon vegetable oil
8 ounces peeled, deveined shrimp
4 green onions and tops, thinly sliced
1 tablespoon finely chopped fresh gingerroot
2 cups shredded napa cabbage
1 cup reduced-sodium chicken broth
2 tablespoons dry sherry, optional
2-3 teaspoons light soy sauce
1/2-1 teaspoon Szechwan chili sauce

Per Serving
Calories: 292
% Calories from fat: 13
Fat (gm): 4.2
Saturated fat (gm): 0.6
Cholesterol (mg): 87.1
Sodium (mg): 223
Protein (gm): 17.1
Carbohydrate (gm): 46.6
Exchanges
Milk: 0.0
Vegetable: 1.0
Fruit: 0.0
Bread: 3.0
Meat: 1.0
Fat: 0.0

1. Place noodles in large bowl; pour cold water over to cover. Let stand until noodles separate and are soft, about 15 minutes; drain.

2. Heat oil in wok or skillet over medium-high heat until hot. Add shrimp, green onions, and gingerroot. Stir-fry until shrimp are pink and cooked; remove from wok.

3. Add cabbage to wok; stir-fry just until cabbage turns bright in color, about 1 minute. Stir in drained noodles and shrimp mixture; add chicken broth, sherry, soy sauce, and chili sauce. Heat to boiling; reduce heat and simmer, uncovered, until noodles have absorbed all liquid, about 5 minutes.

CURRIED TORTELLINI WITH BEANS AND SQUASH

Coconut milk adds a subtle Asian accent to this colorful pasta combination.

6 servings

1¹/₃ cups chopped onions

²/₃ cup chopped red, *or* green, bell pepper

2 teaspoons minced garlic

1 tablespoon vegetable oil

1 teaspoon curry powder

2 cups halved Italian, *or* regular, green beans

2 cups cubed (¹/₂ inch) peeled, seeded butternut, *or* acorn, squash

¹/₄ cup water

1 cup reduced-fat coconut milk

2 packages (9 ounces each) fresh mushroom, *or* herb, tortellini, cooked, warm

Salt and pepper, to taste

3 tablespoons finely chopped cilantro

Per Serving
Calories: 275
% Calories from fat: 25
Fat (gm): 8.5
Saturated fat (gm): 2
Cholesterol (mg): 13.3
Sodium (mg): 277
Protein (gm): 10.7
Carbohydrate (gm): 42
Exchanges
Milk: 0.0
Vegetable: 2.0
Fruit: 0.0
Bread: 2.0
Meat: 0.0
Fat: 1.5

1. Saute onions, bell pepper, and garlic in oil in large skillet 4 minutes. Stir in curry powder; cook 1 to 2 minutes longer.

2. Add beans, squash, and water to skillet; heat to boiling. Reduce heat and simmer, covered, until vegetables are tender and water gone, 10 to 12 minutes. Stir in coconut milk and cook over medium heat until hot, 2 to 3 minutes. Stir in tortellini. Season to taste with salt and pepper.

3. Spoon pasta mixture into serving bowl; sprinkle plentifully with cilantro.

SPINACH GNOCCHI AND CHICKEN PRIMAVERA

Gnocchi, or dumplings, are often made from potatoes. This spinach version is a delicious variation.

6 servings

Vegetable cooking spray
1/2 cup chopped onion
2 cloves garlic, minced
3 packages (10 ounces each) frozen chopped spinach, thawed
2/3 cup plus 1/4 cup all-purpose flour, divided
1 cup reduced-fat ricotta cheese
1/2 cup grated Parmesan cheese
1 egg
1/4 teaspoon ground nutmeg
1/2 teaspoon salt, optional
1/2 teaspoon pepper
11/4 pounds boneless, skinless chicken breasts, baked, sliced
Primavera Sauce (recipe follows)

Per Serving
Calories: 464
% Calories from fat: 30
Fat (gm): 15.8
Saturated fat (gm): 5.5
Cholesterol (mg): 105.2
Sodium (mg): 664
Protein (gm): 40
Carbohydrate (gm): 41.6
Exchanges
Milk: 0.0
Vegetable: 4.0
Fruit: 0.0
Bread: 1.5
Meat: 4.0
Fat: 1.0

1. Spray large skillet with cooking spray; heat over medium heat until hot. Saute onion and garlic until tender, about 5 minutes. Stir in spinach. Cook over medium heat until spinach mixture is quite dry, about 8 minutes, stirring frequently.

2. Stir 2/3 cup flour into spinach. Stir in cheeses, egg, nutmeg, salt, and pepper; cool. Drop 2 tablespoons spinach mixture into remaining 1/4 cup flour; roll into ball. Repeat with remaining spinach mixture, making 18 gnocchi.

3. Heat 3 quarts water to boiling in large saucepan. Add gnocchi to saucepan. Reduce heat and simmer, uncovered, until gnocchi float to surface, about 10 minutes.

4. Arrange chicken and gnocchi on serving platter; spoon Primavera Sauce over.

Primavera Sauce

makes about 3 cups

> 3 tablespoons margarine
> 1/4 cup all-purpose flour
> 2 cups 2% reduced-fat milk
> 1/4 cup dry white wine *or* reduced-sodium chicken broth
> 2 cups broccoli florets, steamed until crisp-tender
> 2 cups cauliflower florets, steamed until crisp-tender
> 1 cup diagonally sliced carrots, steamed until crisp-tender
> 1 medium bell pepper, sliced
> 1/4 cup grated Parmesan cheese
> 1/4-1/2 teaspoon ground nutmeg
> 1/4 teaspoon salt
> 1/4 teaspoon pepper

1. Melt margarine in large saucepan; stir in flour. Cook over medium heat 1 minute, stirring constantly. Stir in milk and wine; heat to boiling. Boil, stirring constantly until thickened, 1 to 2 minutes.

2. Stir in vegetables and cook over medium heat until hot through, 2 to 3 minutes. Reduce heat to low; stir in cheese, nutmeg, salt, and pepper and cook 1 to 2 minutes longer.

QUICK GNOCCHI CHOWDER WITH SMOKED TURKEY

Gnocchi, Italian for "dumplings," are usually topped with butter and Parmesan cheese and served as a side dish. Here, they're the main attraction in a stew that's loaded with broccoli, cauliflower, and smoked deli turkey as well. Magnifico!

6 servings

1 cup reduced-sodium fat-free chicken broth

1 can (15 ounces) reduced-sodium crushed tomatoes, undrained

10 ounces smoked deli turkey, cut into 1/2-inch cubes

12 ounces frozen gnocchi

1 teaspoon poultry seasoning

2 cups broccoli florets

2 cups cauliflower florets

1/2 cup chopped fresh basil

1/4 cup (1 ounce) shredded provolone cheese

Salt and pepper, to taste

Per Serving
Calories: 221
% Calories from fat: 17
Fat (gm): 4.2
Saturated fat (gm): 2.1
Cholesterol (mg): 24.3
Sodium (mg): 745
Protein (gm): 16.8
Carbohydrate (gm): 30
Exchanges
Milk: 0.0
Vegetable: 1.0
Fruit: 0.0
Bread: 1.5
Meat: 2.0
Fat: 0.0

1. Combine chicken broth, tomatoes and liquid, turkey, gnocchi, and poultry seasoning in large saucepan. Heat to boiling; reduce heat and simmer, covered, 5 minutes. Stir in broccoli and cauliflower; simmer 5 minutes longer. Add basil and cheese, stirring until cheese is melted. Season to taste with salt and pepper.

CHEESE RAVIOLI WITH BASIL

Love ravioli? In the mood for a stew? This dish offers both, and it's packed with fresh vegetables—squash, tomatoes, carrots, and escarole, too. Don't overcook the stew or the ravioli will become soggy.

4 servings

2 cans (14 ounces each) reduced-sodium vegetable broth
2 carrots, cut into thin 2-inch-long strips
1¼ cups chopped yellow summer squash
3 plum tomatoes, coarsely chopped
1 package (20 ounces) frozen small cheese ravioli
½ teaspoon crushed red pepper
2 cups torn escarole
½ cup chopped fresh basil
Salt, to taste

Per Serving
Calories: 331
% Calories from fat: 19
Fat (gm): 7.2
Saturated fat (gm): 3.9
Cholesterol (mg): 38.6
Sodium (mg): 416
Protein (gm): 16.5
Carbohydrate (gm): 51.8
Exchanges
Milk: 0.0
Vegetable: 4.0
Fruit: 0.0
Bread: 2.0
Meat: 0.0
Fat: 1.5

1. Combine broth and carrots in large saucepan. Heat to boiling; reduce heat and simmer, covered, until carrots are tender, about 10 minutes. Add squash, tomatoes, and ravioli; simmer until squash is tender and ravioli are hot, about 10 minutes.

2. Stir in crushed red pepper, escarole, and basil; simmer 1 minute. Season to taste with salt.

EGGPLANT RAVIOLI

The ravioli are easily made with wonton wrappers. Assemble 2 to 3 hours ahead for convenience, and refrigerate in a single layer, covered, with plastic wrap.

6 servings (4 ravioli each)

Eggplant Filling (recipe follows)
48 wonton wrappers
Fresh Tomato and Herb Sauce (see p. 211)

Per Serving
Calories: 306
% Calories from fat: 10
Fat (gm): 3.6
Saturated fat (gm): 0.6
Cholesterol (mg): 8
Sodium (mg): 493
Protein (gm): 15.9
Carbohydrate (gm): 54.6
Exchanges
Milk: 0.0
Vegetable: 3.0
Fruit: 0.0
Bread: 2.5
Meat: 1.0
Fat: 0.0

1. Place scant 1¹/₂ tablespoons eggplant mixture on wonton wrapper; brush edges of wrapper with water. Top with second wonton wrapper and press edges together to seal. Repeat with remaining wonton wrappers and eggplant mixture.

2. Heat about 2 quarts water to boiling in large saucepan; add 4 to 6 ravioli. Reduce heat and simmer, uncovered, until ravioli float to the surface and are al dente, 3 to 4 minutes. Remove with slotted spoon; repeat cooking procedure with remaining ravioli. Serve with Fresh Tomato and Herb Sauce.

Eggplant Filling

makes about 2 cups

Olive oil cooking spray
¹/₂ cup minced onion
¹/₂ cup minced green bell pepper
2 teaspoons minced garlic
1 small eggplant, peeled, cubed (¹/₂-inch)
1 teaspoon dried oregano leaves
1 teaspoon dried basil leaves
1 teaspoon dried marjoram leaves
¹/₂ cup water
1-2 teaspoons light brown sugar
1 teaspoon balsamic vinegar
¹/₂ cup (2 ounces) shredded fat-free mozzarella cheese
¹/₂ cup fat-free ricotta cheese
¹/₄ cup grated fat-free Parmesan cheese
Salt and pepper, to taste

1. Spray large skillet with cooking spray; heat over medium heat until hot. Saute onion, bell pepper, and garlic until tender, about 5 minutes.

2. Stir eggplant into skillet and saute 1 to 2 minutes. Stir in herbs and water; heat to boiling. Reduce heat and simmer, covered, until vegetables are tender, about 10 minutes. Stir in sugar and vinegar; cook, uncovered, until liquid is almost gone, about 5 minutes.

3. Remove skillet from heat and cool to room temperature; stir in cheeses. Season to taste with salt and pepper.

20-MINUTE RAVIOLI

Use any favorite flavor of refrigerated fresh ravioli with this quick and nutritious bean sauce.

4 servings

1 package (9 ounces) fresh sun-dried tomato ravioli
3/4 cup chopped onion
2 teaspoons minced garlic
1 tablespoon olive oil
3/4 cup canned kidney beans, rinsed, drained
1 large tomato, cubed
1/2 teaspoon dried thyme leaves
Salt and pepper, to taste

Per Serving
Calories: 234
% Calories from fat: 35
Fat (gm): 9.4
Saturated fat (gm): 3.8
Cholesterol (mg): 32.8
Sodium (mg): 320
Protein (gm): 9.5
Carbohydrate (gm): 29.1
Exchanges
Milk: 0.0
Vegetable: 0.0
Fruit: 0.0
Bread: 2.0
Meat: 1.0
Fat: 1.0

1. Cook ravioli according to package directions.

2. Saute onion and garlic in oil in large skillet until tender, about 5 minutes. Stir in beans, tomato, and thyme; cook 2 to 3 minutes longer. Season to taste with salt and pepper.

SHRIMP AND ARTICHOKE RAVIOLI WITH TARRAGON SAUCE

Fresh Tomato and Herb Sauce (see p. 211) would also be a flavorful sauce selection for these ravioli.

4 servings (4 ravioli each)

Olive oil cooking spray
8 ounces finely chopped, peeled, deveined shrimp
1 can (14 ounces) artichoke hearts, drained, rinsed, finely chopped
1 clove garlic, minced
1/4 teaspoon ground nutmeg
3 tablespoons water
32 wonton wrappers
Tarragon Sauce (recipe follows)

Per Serving
Calories: 289
% Calories from fat: 5
Fat (gm): 1.5
Saturated fat (gm): 0.3
Cholesterol (mg): 92.4
Sodium (mg): 923
Protein (gm): 20.6
Carbohydrate (gm): 45.2
Exchanges
Milk: 0.0
Vegetable: 0.0
Fruit: 0.0
Bread: 3.0
Meat: 1.0
Fat: 0.0

1. Spray large skillet with cooking spray; heat over medium heat until hot. Add shrimp, artichoke hearts, garlic, nutmeg, and water. Cook over medium heat until shrimp are cooked and liquid is gone, about 5 minutes. Cool.

2. Place about 2 teaspoons shrimp mixture on wonton wrapper; brush edges of wrapper with water. Top with second wonton wrapper and press edges together to seal. Repeat with remaining wonton wrappers and shrimp mixture.

3. Heat about 2 quarts water to boiling in large saucepan; add 4 to 6 ravioli. Reduce heat and simmer, uncovered, until ravioli float to surface and are al dente, 3 to 4 minutes. Remove ravioli with slotted spoon; repeat with remaining ravioli. Serve with Tarragon Sauce.

Tarragon Sauce

makes about 1 cup

- 2 medium shallots, finely chopped
- 1 tablespoon finely chopped fresh, *or* 1/2 teaspoon dried, tarragon leaves
- 1 1/2 cups reduced-sodium chicken broth, divided
- 1 tablespoon flour
- 1/4 teaspoon salt
- 1/8 teaspoon white pepper

1. Heat shallots, tarragon, and 1/2 cup chicken broth to boiling in small saucepan; reduce heat and simmer, uncovered, until mixture is reduced to 1/4 cup.

2. Add 1/2 cup chicken broth; heat to boiling. Mix flour and remaining 1/2 cup chicken broth; stir into boiling mixture. Boil until thickened (sauce will be thin), stirring constantly. Stir in salt and white pepper.

CHICKEN AND SWEET POTATO RAVIOLI WITH CURRY SAUCE

The light curry-flavored sauce is a delicate accompaniment to these unusual ravioli.

4 servings (4 ravioli each)

8 ounces boneless, skinless chicken breast, cooked, shredded

1 cup mashed sweet potatoes

2 small cloves garlic, minced

1/2-3/4 teaspoon ground ginger

1/4 teaspoon salt

1/4 teaspoon white pepper

32 wonton wrappers

Curry Sauce (recipe follows)

Per Serving
Calories: 383
% Calories from fat: 13
Fat (gm): 5.5
Saturated fat (gm): 1.1
Cholesterol (mg): 37.2
Sodium (mg): 587
Protein (gm): 19.8
Carbohydrate (gm): 62.4
Exchanges
Milk: 0.0
Vegetable: 0.5
Fruit: 0.0
Bread: 4.0
Meat: 1.5
Fat: 0.0

1. Mix chicken, sweet potatoes, garlic, ginger, salt, and white pepper. Spoon about 2 teaspoons chicken mixture onto wonton wrapper; brush edges of wrapper with water. Top with second wonton wrapper and press edges together to seal. Repeat with remaining wonton wrappers and chicken mixture.

2. Heat about 2 quarts water to boiling in large saucepan; add 4 to 6 ravioli. Reduce heat and simmer, uncovered, until ravioli float to surface and are al dente, 3 to 4 minutes. Remove ravioli with slotted spoon; repeat with remaining ravioli. Serve with Curry Sauce.

Curry Sauce

makes about 1 cup

2 tablespoons finely chopped onion

2 cloves garlic, minced

1 tablespoon margarine

1 tablespoon flour

2 teaspoons curry powder

1/8 teaspoon cayenne pepper

1 cup reduced-sodium chicken broth

2-4 tablespoons dry white wine, optional

1. Saute onion and garlic in margarine in small saucepan 2 to 3 minutes; stir in flour, curry powder, and cayenne pepper. Cook 1 minute more, stirring constantly.

2. Stir chicken broth and wine into saucepan; heat to boiling. Boil until sauce is thickened (sauce will be thin), stirring constantly.

TURKEY AND HERBED-CHEESE RAVIOLI WITH WILD MUSHROOM SAUCE

Reduced-fat turkey Italian sausage can be substituted nicely in these ravioli.

4 servings (4 ravioli each)

    Olive oil cooking spray
  8 ounces ground turkey
  1 small onion, minced
  2 cloves garlic, minced
  1 cup reduced-fat ricotta cheese
  1 teaspoon dried rosemary leaves
32 wonton wrappers
    Wild Mushroom Sauce (recipe follows)

Per Serving
Calories: 360
% Calories from fat: 18
Fat (gm): 7.2
Saturated fat (gm): 1.4
Cholesterol (mg): 37
Sodium (mg): 593
Protein (gm): 22
Carbohydrate (gm): 53
Exchanges
Milk: 0.0
Vegetable: 1.5
Fruit: 0.0
Bread: 3.0
Meat: 1.5
Fat: 0.5

1. Spray small skillet with cooking spray; heat over medium heat until hot. Cook turkey over medium heat until browned, about 5 minutes; drain on paper toweling. Discard excess fat. Add onion and garlic to skillet and saute until onion is tender, about 5 minutes. Mix in ricotta cheese and rosemary; mix in turkey.

2. Place about 2 teaspoons mixture on wonton wrapper; brush edges of wrapper with water. Top with a second wonton wrapper and press edges together to seal. Repeat with remaining wonton wrappers and turkey mixture.

3. Heat about 2 quarts water to boiling in large saucepan; add 4 to 6 ravioli. Reduce heat and simmer, uncovered, until ravioli float to surface and are al dente, 3 to 4 minutes. Repeat with remaining ravioli. Serve with Wild Mushroom Sauce.

Wild Mushroom Sauce

makes about 2¹/₂ cups

Olive oil cooking spray
¹/₄ cup finely chopped shallot
2 cloves garlic, minced
2 cups chopped, *or* sliced, wild mushrooms
   (portobello, shiitake, cremini, etc.)
¹/₃ cup dry sherry *or* reduced-sodium
   vegetable broth
2-3 tablespoons lemon juice
¹/₄-¹/₂ teaspoon dried thyme leaves
2 cups reduced-sodium vegetable broth
2 tablespoons cornstarch
Salt and pepper, to taste

1. Spray medium saucepan with cooking spray; heat over medium heat until hot. Saute shallot and garlic until tender, 3 to 4 minutes. Stir in mushrooms; cook, covered, over medium-low heat until mushrooms are wilted, about 5 minutes. Stir in sherry, lemon juice, and thyme; heat to boiling. Reduce heat and simmer, uncovered, until mushrooms are tender and liquid is evaporated, about 5 minutes.

2. Mix broth and cornstarch; stir into saucepan and heat to boiling. Boil, stirring constantly, until thickened, about 1 minute. Season to taste with salt and pepper.

MUSHROOM RAVIOLI WITH RED PEPPER SALSA

Ravioli are very easy to make using purchased wonton wrappers (found in the produce or refrigerated sections of supermarkets). Colorful Red Pepper Salsa is a perfect complement to the mushroom-filled pasta.

4 servings (6 ravioli each)

Vegetable cooking spray
2 cups sliced mushrooms
4 tablespoons chopped shallots *or* green
   onions
2 cloves garlic, minced
2 tablespoons finely chopped parsley
¹/₄ teaspoon salt

Per Serving
Calories: 364
% Calories from fat: 20
Fat (gm): 8
Saturated fat (gm): 1.4
Cholesterol (mg): 67.6
Sodium (mg): 430
Protein (gm): 12
Carbohydrate (gm): 62
Exchanges
Milk: 0.0
Vegetable: 2.0
Fruit: 0.0
Bread: 3.0
Meat: 0.0
Fat: 2.0

1/4 teaspoon pepper
48 wonton wrappers
    Red Pepper Salsa (recipe follows)

1. Spray large skillet with cooking spray; heat over medium heat until hot. Saute mushrooms, shallots, and garlic until tender, about 7 minutes; stir in parsley, salt, and pepper. Transfer mixture to food processor or blender; process until finely chopped but not smooth.

2. Spoon about 2 teaspoons mushroom mixture in center of 1 wonton wrapper; brush edges of wrapper with water. Top with a second wonton wrapper, and press edges together to seal. Repeat with remaining wonton wrappers and mushroom mixture.

3. Heat about 2 quarts water to boiling in large saucepan; add 4 to 6 wonton ravioli. Reduce heat and simmer, uncovered, until ravioli float to surface and are al dente, 3 to 4 minutes. Remove ravioli with slotted spoon; repeat cooking procedure with remaining ravioli. Serve with Red Pepper Salsa.

Red Pepper Salsa

makes about 2 cups

    2 large red bell peppers, finely chopped
    2 medium tomatoes, chopped
    4 cloves garlic, minced
1/2-1 teaspoon minced, seeded jalapeño
      pepper
    2 tablespoons finely chopped fresh, *or* 1
      teaspoon dried, basil leaves
    2 tablespoons finely chopped fresh, *or* 1
      teaspoon dried, cilantro leaves
    4 teaspoons olive oil
    4 teaspoons red wine vinegar
  1/2 teaspoon salt
  1/2 teaspoon pepper

1. Mix all ingredients; refrigerate 3 to 4 hours for flavors to blend.

SQUASH AND MUSHROOM LASAGNE

A white sauce and tomato sauce are combined in this delicate lasagne.

8 servings

Olive oil spray
1 cup sliced onion
1 tablespoon minced garlic
1 pound portobello, *or* white, mushrooms, sliced
1/2 cup dry white wine *or* vegetable broth
Salt and pepper, to taste
1/4 cup finely chopped shallots *or* green onions and tops
2 teaspoons margarine
1/4 cup all-purpose flour
1 teaspoon dried rosemary leaves
1/2 teaspoon dried thyme leaves
2 cups fat-free milk
2 cups prepared reduced-sodium spaghetti sauce
1/2 package (8-ounce size) fat-free cream cheese, cubed
3/4 cup grated fat-free Parmesan cheese, divided
12 lasagne noodles (10 ounces), cooked
1 pound winter yellow squash (acorn, butternut, Hubbard, etc.), peeled, thinly sliced

Per Serving
Calories: 280
% Calories from fat: 18
Fat (gm): 5.6
Saturated fat (gm): 1.5
Cholesterol (mg): 3.8
Sodium (mg): 236
Protein (gm): 14.2
Carbohydrate (gm): 39.3
Exchanges
Milk: 0.0
Vegetable: 2.0
Fruit: 0.0
Bread: 2.0
Meat: 1.0
Fat: 0.5

1. Spray large skillet with cooking spray; heat over medium heat until hot. Saute onion and garlic 3 to 4 minutes; add mushrooms and saute 5 minutes. Add wine to skillet and heat to boiling. Cook over medium heat until mixture is dry, about 5 minutes, stirring occasionally. Season to taste with salt and pepper.

2. Saute shallots in margarine in medium saucepan until tender, 2 to 3 minutes. Stir in flour and herbs; cook 1 to 2 minutes, stirring constantly. Whisk in milk and heat to boiling; boil, whisking constantly, until thickened, about 1 minute. Mix in spaghetti sauce, cream cheese, and 1/2 cup Parmesan cheese;

cook, stirring frequently, until sauce is hot and cream cheese melted, 5 to 7 minutes. Season to taste with salt and pepper.

3. Stir 1 cup sauce into mushroom mixture. Spread about 1/2 cup remaining sauce in bottom of 13 x 9-inch baking pan; arrange 4 noodles in pan, overlapping edges. Spoon 1/2 the mushroom mixture and 1/2 the squash slices over noodles and spread with generous 1 cup sauce. Repeat layers, ending with layer of noodles and generous 1 cup sauce. Sprinkle with remaining 1/4 cup Parmesan cheese.

4. Bake lasagne, loosely covered, at 350 degrees until noodles and squash are tender, 50 to 60 minutes. Let stand 10 minutes before serving.

ROASTED RED PEPPER AND SPINACH LASAGNE

For convenience, the recipe uses jarred roasted red peppers; you can roast your own using the method in Roasted Red Pepper Sauce (see p. 45).

8 servings

Olive oil cooking spray
1 cup chopped onion
2 teaspoons minced roasted garlic
1 teaspoon dried marjoram leaves
1/2-3/4 teaspoon dried oregano leaves
3 cups fat-free milk, divided
1/4 cup plus 2 tablespoons all-purpose flour
1 cup grated fat-free Parmesan cheese
1/2 package (8-ounce size) fat-free cream cheese, cubed
2/3 cup finely chopped parsley
Salt and pepper, to taste
2 packages (10 ounces each) frozen, thawed chopped spinach, very well drained
2/3 cup fat-free ricotta cheese
12 lasagne noodles (10 ounces), cooked
1 jar (15 ounces) roasted red peppers, drained, cut into 1-inch slices
1 cup (4 ounces) reduced-fat mozzarella cheese

Per Serving
Calories: 261
% Calories from fat: 13
Fat (gm): 3.8
Saturated fat (gm): 1.7
Cholesterol (mg): 9.1
Sodium (mg): 386
Protein (gm): 21.4
Carbohydrate (gm): 36.8
Exchanges
Milk: 0.5
Vegetable: 2.0
Fruit: 0.0
Bread: 1.5
Meat: 1.0
Fat: 0.0

1. Spray large saucepan with cooking spray; heat over medium heat until hot. Saute onion and garlic until tender, 5 to 8 minutes; stir in marjoram and oregano and cook 1 to 2 minutes longer.

2. Add 2 cups milk to saucepan; heat to boiling. Mix remaining 1 cup milk and flour; whisk into boiling milk mixture. Boil, whisking constantly, until thickened, about 1 minute. Remove from heat; mix in Parmesan and cream cheese, stirring until cream cheese is melted. Stir in parsley; season to taste with salt and pepper.

3. Mix spinach and ricotta cheese; season to taste with salt and pepper.

4. Spread 1/2 cup sauce in bottom of 13 x 9-inch baking pan. Arrange 4 noodles in pan, overlapping edges. Top with 1/2 the spinach mixture and 1/2 the red pepper slices; spread with generous 1 cup sauce. Repeat layers 2 more times. Place remaining 4 noodles on top of lasagne and spread with remaining 1¹/4 cups sauce. Sprinkle with mozzarella cheese.

5. Bake lasagne at 350 degrees, loosely covered, until hot through, about 45 minutes. Let stand 10 minutes before serving.

ARTICHOKE LASAGNE

The lasagne can be assembled up to a day in advance and refrigerated, covered. Then bake as directed below, increasing baking time by 15 to 20 minutes.

8 servings

Olive oil cooking spray
1¹/2 cups sliced shiitake, *or* white, mushrooms
1¹/2 cups chopped onions
1 cup chopped red bell peppers
2 teaspoons minced garlic
8 cups loosely packed spinach, torn into bite-size pieces
2 packages (9 ounces each) frozen, thawed artichoke hearts, cut into bite-size pieces
Salt and pepper, to taste

Per Serving
Calories: 278
% Calories from fat: 7
Fat (gm): 2.1
Saturated fat (gm): 0.2
Cholesterol (mg): 1.5
Sodium (mg): 438
Protein (gm): 22.5
Carbohydrate (gm): 46.4
Exchanges
Milk: 0.0
Vegetable: 3.0
Fruit: 0.0
Bread: 2.0
Meat: 1.0
Fat: 0.0

  3 cups fat-free milk, divided
 1/4 cup plus 2 tablespoons flour
  1 cup (4 ounces) grated fat-free Parmesan
      cheese
 1/2 package (8-ounce size) fat-free cream
      cheese, cubed
 2/3 cup finely chopped parsley
 1/2 teaspoon dried thyme leaves
  1 teaspoon lemon juice
 12 lasagne noodles (10 ounces), cooked
  1 cup (4 ounces) shredded reduced-fat
      mozzarella cheese

1. Spray large skillet with cooking spray; heat over medium heat until hot. Saute mushrooms, onions, bell peppers, and garlic 3 minutes; add spinach and artichoke hearts. Cook, covered, over medium heat until spinach is wilted, about 5 minutes. Cook, uncovered, until mixture is dry. Remove from heat; season to taste with salt and pepper.

2. Heat 2 cups milk to boiling in large saucepan. Mix remaining 1 cup milk and flour; whisk into boiling milk. Boil, whisking constantly, until thickened, about 1 minute. Remove from heat; mix in Parmesan and cream cheese, parsley, thyme, and lemon juice, stirring until cream cheese is melted. Season to taste with salt and pepper.

3. Spread 1/2 cup sauce mixture in bottom of 13 x 9-inch baking pan; arrange 4 noodles in pan, overlapping edges. Spoon 1/2 the artichoke mixture over noodles and spread with generous 1 cup sauce. Repeat layers 2 times, ending with layer of noodles and generous 1 cup sauce. Sprinkle with mozzarella cheese.

4. Bake lasagne at 350 degrees, loosely covered, until hot through, about 45 minutes. Let stand 10 minutes before cutting.

RICOTTA-STUFFED SHELLS WITH SPINACH PESTO

Pesto sauces are traditionally served at room temperature. Spinach Pesto can be made up to 1 week in advance and refrigerated. Before serving, let it stand until room temperature, or microwave in glass bowl at medium setting until softened, about 30 seconds.

4 servings (6 shells each)

Vegetable cooking spray
1/2 cup finely chopped onion
4-6 cloves garlic, minced
1 teaspoon dried basil leaves
1 cup chopped fresh spinach
1 1/2 cups low-fat ricotta cheese
1/2 teaspoon ground nutmeg
1/2 teaspoon salt
1/2 teaspoon pepper
24 conchiglie (jumbo pasta shells), about 8 ounces, cooked
Spinach Pesto (recipe follows)
4 tablespoons chopped red, *or* green, bell pepper, roasted *or* raw
Basil sprigs, as garnish

Per Serving
Calories: 356
% Calories from fat: 24
Fat (gm): 9.4
Saturated fat (gm): 1.6
Cholesterol (mg): 14.4
Sodium (mg): 432
Protein (gm): 19
Carbohydrate (gm): 49.2
Exchanges
Milk: 0.0
Vegetable: 2.0
Fruit: 0.0
Bread: 3.0
Meat: 1.0
Fat: 1.0

1. Spray medium skillet with cooking spray; saute onion, garlic, and dried basil until onion is tender, 3 to 4 minutes. Add spinach; cook over medium heat until spinach is wilted, about 5 minutes.

2. Mix spinach mixture and cheese, nutmeg, salt, and pepper. Stuff mixture into shells; place in baking pan. Bake at 350 degrees, covered, until hot through, about 20 minutes.

3. Arrange shells on small serving plates; spoon Spinach Pesto over shells or serve on the side. Sprinkle with bell pepper; garnish with basil sprigs.

Spinach Pesto

makes about 1 cup

- 2 cups fresh spinach, loosely packed
- 6 tablespoons finely chopped fresh, *or 2* tablespoons dried, basil leaves
- 2-4 cloves garlic, minced
- 2 tablespoons grated Parmesan cheese
- 4 teaspoons olive oil
- 2-4 teaspoons lemon juice

1. Process all ingredients, except lemon juice, in food processor or blender until smooth. Season to taste with lemon juice.

2. Let stand 2 to 3 hours for flavors to blend, or refrigerate until serving time. Serve at room temperature.

MOLDED CAPELLINI CARBONARA

Thin spaghetti or linguine can be substituted for the capellini (angel hair pasta).

4 servings

Olive oil cooking spray
- 1/4 cup minced shallots
- 1 teaspoon minced garlic
- 1 cup seeded, chopped Italian plum tomatoes
- 1/4 teaspoon crushed red pepper
- 1/2 teaspoon dried oregano leaves
- 2 tablespoons crumbled crisp bacon
  Salt and pepper, to taste
- 8 ounces capellini (angel hair pasta), cooked
- 3 eggs, beaten

Per Serving
Calories: 249
% Calories from fat: 24
Fat (gm): 6.9
Saturated fat (gm): 2.2
Cholesterol (mg): 224.1
Sodium (mg): 99
Protein (gm): 12.8
Carbohydrate (gm): 34.1
Exchanges
Milk: 0.0
Vegetable: 1.0
Fruit: 0.0
Bread: 2.0
Meat: 1.0
Fat: 0.5

1. Spray skillet with cooking spray; heat over medium heat until hot. Saute shallots and garlic until tender, 3 to 4 minutes. Add tomatoes, crushed red pepper, and oregano. Cook, covered, over medium heat, until tomatoes soften, about 5 minutes. Stir in bacon; season to taste with salt and pepper.

2. Combine tomato mixture, pasta, and eggs; spoon into greased 6-cup ring mold. Bake, uncovered, at 350 degrees until set, about 20 minutes. Invert onto serving plate.

NOODLES FLORENTINE

Cut into generous squares and serve with a tossed vegetable salad and thick slices of warm multi-grain bread.

4 servings

    Vegetable cooking spray
1 cup finely chopped red onion
1 medium red bell pepper, chopped
2 cloves garlic, minced
2 teaspoons sugar
1/2 teaspoon ground nutmeg
    Salt and pepper, to taste
1 cup no-cholesterol real egg product
4 packages (10 ounces each) frozen chopped spinach, thawed and drained
2 cups cooked spinach noodles, drained
1 cup fresh whole wheat bread crumbs
2 slices (2 ounces) reduced-fat Swiss cheese, cut diagonally in half

Per Serving
Calories: 307
% Calories from fat: 14
Fat (gm): 5
Saturated fat (gm): 2
Cholesterol (mg): 36.1
Sodium (mg): 372
Protein (gm): 22.6
Carbohydrate (gm): 47
Exchanges
Milk: 0.0
Vegetable: 3.5
Fruit: 0.0
Bread: 2.0
Meat: 1.5
Fat: 0.0

1. Spray large saucepan with cooking spray; heat over medium heat until hot. Saute onion, bell pepper, and garlic until softened, about 4 minutes. Stir in sugar and nutmeg; season to taste with salt and pepper.

2. Transfer onion mixture to large bowl and cool to room temperature; stir in egg product, spinach, noodles, and bread crumbs.

3. Spoon mixture into lightly greased 11 x 7-inch baking dish. Bake, uncovered, at 325 degrees 30 minutes. Top with cheese; bake 10 minutes longer or until sharp knife inserted near center comes out clean. Cool on wire rack 5 minutes before serving.

VEGGIE KUGEL

This kugel, with lots of veggies, uses no-cholesterol real egg product and fat-free evaporated milk to keep fat and calories in line.

8 servings

3/4 cup chopped red bell pepper

3/4 cup finely chopped onion

2 tablespoons margarine

8 ounces Brussels sprouts, halved, cooked

8 ounces cubed, peeled sweet potatoes *or* sliced carrots, cooked

3/4 teaspoon dried thyme leaves

1/2 teaspoon dried marjoram leaves

2 tablespoons flour

1 can (12 ounces) fat-free evaporated milk

1 cup no-cholesterol real egg product

2 packages (10 ounces each) frozen chopped spinach, thawed, well drained

1/2 teaspoon salt

1/2 teaspoon pepper

12 ounces no-yolk noodles, cooked

Per Serving
Calories: 289
% Calories from fat: 10
Fat (gm): 3.5
Saturated fat (gm): 0.7
Cholesterol (mg): 1.4
Sodium (mg): 319
Protein (gm): 12.6
Carbohydrate (gm): 54
Exchanges
Milk: 0.5
Vegetable: 1.5
Fruit: 0.0
Bread: 2.5
Meat: 0.5
Fat: 0.5

1. Saute bell pepper and onion in margarine in large saucepan until tender, about 5 minutes; add Brussels sprouts, sweet potatoes, thyme, and marjoram and cook 3 to 4 minutes longer.

2. Mix flour and evaporated milk; add to saucepan and heat to boiling; boil, stirring constantly, until thickened, about 1 minute. Remove from heat and cool to room temperature; stir in egg product, spinach, salt, and pepper. Stir in noodles.

3. Spoon mixture into greased 13 x 9-inch baking dish. Bake at 350 degrees 35 minutes or until sharp knife inserted near center comes out clean. Cool on wire rack 5 minutes; cut into squares.

ARTICHOKE TORTELLINI BAKE

Refrigerated fresh tortellini and ravioli are convenient to have on hand for speedy meal preparation—use any favorite kind in this dish.

4 servings

1 package (9 ounces) mozzarella-garlic tortellini
Vegetable cooking spray
2 cups (4 ounces) sliced mushrooms
1 small onion, sliced
1 teaspoon minced garlic
2 tablespoons flour
1 cup fat-free milk
Salt and cayenne pepper, to taste
1 can (14 ounces) artichoke hearts, drained
1/2-1 cup (2-4 ounces) shredded reduced-fat Italian 6-cheese blend, divided
1-2 tablespoons seasoned dry bread crumbs

Per Serving
Calories: 249
% Calories from fat: 15
Fat (gm): 4.1
Saturated fat (gm): 1.9
Cholesterol (mg): 13.1
Sodium (mg): 619
Protein (gm): 16.6
Carbohydrate (gm): 37.1
Exchanges
Milk: 0.0
Vegetable: 2.0
Fruit: 0.0
Bread: 2.0
Meat: 1.0
Fat: 0.0

1. Cook tortellini according to package directions.

2. Spray large saucepan with cooking spray; heat over medium heat until hot. Saute mushrooms, onion, and garlic until tender, about 5 minutes. Stir in flour; cook 1 to 2 minutes. Add milk and heat to boiling; boil, stirring constantly, until thickened, 1 to 2 minutes. Season to taste with salt and cayenne pepper.

3. Stir in artichokes, tortellini, and all but 2 tablespoons of the cheese. Pour into greased 1 1/2-quart casserole; sprinkle with bread crumbs and remaining 2 tablespoons cheese. Bake at 350 degrees until bubbly and browned on the top, about 20 minutes.

BOW TIE BLACK BEAN PASTA

5 servings

4	ounces dried black beans
1/2	tablespoon canola oil
1/2	cup chopped onions
1/2	cup chopped red bell pepper
1/2	tablespoon crushed garlic
1/2	cup cooking sherry
2	cups vegetable stock
3	quarts water
1/2	teaspoon salt
4	ounces tiny bow tie pasta, uncooked
2	teaspoons fresh oregano
1	teaspoon fresh basil
1/2	tablespoon minced fresh thyme
1/2	teaspoon chopped fresh rosemary
	Salt and pepper, to taste
2	green onions, chopped, as garnish

Per Serving
Calories: 201
% Calories from fat: 9
Fat (gm): 2
Saturated fat (gm): 0
Cholesterol (mg): 0
Sodium (mg): 380
Protein (gm): 8
Carbohydrate (gm): 33
Exchanges
Milk: 0.0
Vegetable: 0.5
Fruit: 0.0
Bread: 2.0
Meat: 0.0
Fat: 0.5

1. Soak black beans overnight. Drain.

2. Heat canola oil in large saucepan over medium heat. Add onions, bell pepper, and garlic. Cook until onions are clear and tender. Add sherry and simmer until most liquid is absorbed. Add vegetable stock and black beans. Bring to a boil, simmer, and cook 1 1/2 hours or until beans are tender.

3. Bring water to a boil. Add salt and pasta. Stir occasionally to prevent pasta from sticking. Cook 10 to 12 minutes or to desired tenderness.

4. Add pasta to black bean mixture. Add spices and return pan to a simmer. Season with salt and pepper to taste. Garnish with chopped green onions.

PASTA NIÇOISE

A pasta salad with the flavors of the traditional salad Niçoise. Use Niçoise or Greek olives for the most authentic flavor.

4 servings

   3 cups cooked small shell pasta, room temperature

12-16 ripe olives, pitted, sliced

   2 cups fresh green beans, steamed, cooled

   ¹/4 cup sliced green onions and tops

   1 tomato, diced

   1 can (6 ounces) solid white tuna in water, drained

     Niçoise Dressing (recipe follows)

     Salt and pepper, to taste

Per Serving
Calories: 251
% Calories from fat: 25
Fat (gm): 7.2
Saturated fat (gm): 1.1
Cholesterol (mg): 17.9
Sodium (mg): 289
Protein (gm): 15.8
Carbohydrate (gm): 32.4
Exchanges
Milk: 0.0
Vegetable: 0.0
Fruit: 0.0
Bread: 2.0
Meat: 1.0
Fat: 1.0

1. Toss pasta, vegetables, tuna, and Niçoise Dressing in large salad bowl; season to taste with salt and pepper. Serve immediately, or refrigerate up to 3 hours.

Niçoise Dressing

makes about ³/4 cup

   ¹/2 cup loosely packed parsley leaves

   ¹/4 cup tarragon wine vinegar

   ¹/4 cup water

 1-2 tablespoons extra-virgin olive oil

   1 large clove garlic

   ¹/2 teaspoon Dijon mustard

   1 teaspoon dried oregano leaves

1. Process all ingredients in blender until almost smooth.

TORTELLINI WITH TUNA

A great dish for lunch, picnics, or a light supper.

8 servings

12 ounces cheese tortellini, cooked, room temperature
1 cup fresh, *or* frozen, thawed, peas
1/2 green bell pepper, chopped
1/2 cup sliced green onions and tops
1 can (14 ounces) artichoke hearts, drained, quartered
1 can (6 ounces) solid white tuna in water, drained
1/2 cup chopped fresh parsley
1/4 cup chopped fresh basil
Tomato Vinaigrette (recipe follows)
Salt and pepper, to taste

Per Serving
Calories: 246
% Calories from fat: 27
Fat (gm): 7.3
Saturated fat (gm): 1.9
Cholesterol (mg): 31.5
Sodium (mg): 430
Protein (gm): 15.5
Carbohydrate (gm): 29.5
Exchanges
Milk: 0.0
Vegetable: 3.0
Fruit: 0.0
Bread: 1.0
Meat: 1.0
Fat: 1.0

1. Toss tortellini, vegetables, tuna, herbs, and Tomato Vinaigrette in large salad bowl; season to taste with salt and pepper. Serve immediately, or refrigerate up to 3 hours.

Tomato Vinaigrette

makes about 1 cup

2 tomatoes, diced
2 tablespoons white wine vinegar
2 tablespoons extra-virgin olive oil
2 teaspoons Dijon mustard
1 clove garlic
3 tablespoons sliced green onions and tops
1 teaspoon dried oregano leaves
1 teaspoon dried basil leaves
1/4 cup grated fat-free Parmesan cheese

1. Process all ingredients in blender until smooth.

NINE

Rice, Grains
AND
Beans

EGGPLANT AND BEAN CURRY STEW

*The flavorful curry seasoning is created by making a simple paste of on-
ion, garlic, and herbs.*

4 servings (about 1 cup each)

2 medium red potatoes, peeled, cut into
  $^3/_4$-inch cubes

1 tablespoon olive oil

1 small eggplant, cut into $^3/_4$-inch cubes

$^1/_2$ medium onion, chopped

1 teaspoon minced garlic

1 teaspoon ground coriander

$^1/_2$ teaspoon ground cumin

$^1/_4$ teaspoon crushed red pepper

$^1/_8$ teaspoon ground turmeric

1 tablespoon water

1 can (16 ounces) reduced-sodium whole
  tomatoes, undrained, coarsely chopped

1 can (15 ounces) garbanzo beans,
  rinsed, drained

$^1/_2$ cup water
  Salt and pepper, to taste

$^1/_4$ cup finely chopped cilantro

Per Serving
Calories: 242
% Calories from fat: 21
Fat (gm): 6
Saturated fat (gm): 0.8
Cholesterol (mg): 0
Sodium (mg): 446
Protein (gm): 8.2
Carbohydrate (gm): 41.8
Exchanges
Milk: 0.0
Vegetable: 2.0
Fruit: 0.0
Bread: 2.0
Meat: 0.0
Fat: 1.0

1. Saute potatoes in oil in large saucepan until browned; remove and reserve. Add eggplant to saucepan; cook over medium
to medium-low heat until lightly browned, stirring frequently.
Remove eggplant and reserve.

2. Process onion, garlic, herbs, and 1 tablespoon water in food
processor until a smooth paste. Add to saucepan and cook over
medium-low heat, 3 to 4 minutes, stirring frequently to prevent
burning. Add reserved potatoes and eggplant, tomatoes with liquid, beans, and $^1/_2$ cup water to saucepan; heat to boiling. Reduce heat and simmer, covered, until eggplant is tender, 20 to 25
minutes. Season to taste with salt and pepper; stir in cilantro.

TWO-BEAN MINESTRONE

Cannellini beans and chickpeas enrich this soup with protein, fiber, and vitamins.

8 to 10 servings

  2 cloves garlic, minced
  1/2 cup chopped onion
  2 tablespoons olive oil
  3 large carrots, sliced
  2 medium potatoes, diced
  1 medium leek, white part only, thinly sliced
  3 ribs celery, sliced
  1 cup chopped parsley, divided
1 1/2 quarts water
  1 can (14 ounces) plum tomatoes, undrained, chopped
  1 cup dry red wine
  1 tablespoon dried oregano leaves
  1 tablespoon dried basil leaves
  1/2 cup uncooked small elbow macaroni
  1 can (15 ounces) cannellini, *or* Great Northern, beans, rinsed, drained
  1 can (15 ounces) chickpeas, rinsed, drained
  2 zucchini, sliced
  2 cups shredded cabbage
    Salt and pepper, to taste
  8 teaspoons grated Parmesan cheese

Per Serving
Calories: 267
% Calories from fat: 17
Fat (gm): 5.3
Saturated fat (gm): 0.9
Cholesterol (mg): 1.3
Sodium (mg): 331
Protein (gm): 9
Carbohydrate (gm): 43.1
Exchanges
Milk: 0.0
Vegetable: 2.0
Fruit: 0.0
Bread: 2.0
Meat: 0.0
Fat: 1.5

1. Saute garlic and onion in olive oil in large saucepan until onion is tender. Add carrots, potatoes, leek, celery, 1/2 of the parsley, water, plum tomatoes with liquid, red wine, and herbs; heat to boiling. Reduce heat and simmer, covered, until vegetables are almost tender, about 15 minutes.

2. Heat to boiling; stir in macaroni. Reduce heat and simmer, uncovered, 7 minutes. Add remaining ingredients, except salt, pepper, and Parmesan cheese, and simmer until pasta is al dente, about 5 minutes. Season to taste with salt and pepper. Ladle soup into bowls and top with 1 teaspoon Parmesan and remaining parsley.

TUSCAN BEAN SOUP

A hearty bean soup, savory with sage, rosemary, and thyme.

8 servings (about 1 1/2 cups each)

1	cup chopped onion
1/2	cup sliced celery
1/2	cup chopped green bell pepper
2	teaspoons minced roasted garlic
2	tablespoons olive oil
1	tablespoon flour
3/4-1	teaspoon dried rosemary leaves
1/2	teaspoon dried sage leaves
1/4	teaspoon dried thyme leaves
2	bay leaves
7	cups reduced-sodium fat-free beef broth
2	cans (15 ounces each) cannellini, *or* Great Northern, beans, rinsed, drained
2	tablespoons reduced-sodium tomato paste
1/2	cup quick-cooking barley
1	large Idaho potato, unpeeled, cut into 1/2-inch pieces
1	cup sliced carrots
1	cup packed sliced spinach leaves
	Salt and pepper, to taste

Per Serving
Calories: 213
% Calories from fat: 18
Fat (gm): 4.3
Saturated fat (gm): 0.6
Cholesterol (mg): 0
Sodium (mg): 319
Protein (gm): 11.3
Carbohydrate (gm): 33.1
Exchanges
Milk: 0.0
Vegetable: 1.0
Fruit: 0.0
Bread: 2.0
Meat: 0.0
Fat: 1.0

1. Saute onion, celery, bell pepper, and garlic in oil in Dutch oven until tender, about 5 minutes. Add flour and herbs; cook 1 to 2 minutes longer.

2. Add broth, beans, and tomato paste to pan; heat to boiling. Reduce heat and simmer, uncovered, 20 to 25 minutes, adding barley, potato, carrots, and spinach during last 10 minutes of cooking time. Discard bay leaves. Season to taste with salt and pepper.

CURRIED BEAN SOUP

Use any white bean, such as cannellini, navy, soy, lima, or garbanzo, in this rich, aromatic soup.

4 servings (about 1¹/₂ cups each)

1 cup chopped onion
1 cup sliced leeks (white part only)
1 tablespoon minced garlic
1 tablespoon curry powder
2 tablespoons margarine
2 cans (15¹/₂ ounces each) Great Northern beans, rinsed, drained
3¹/₂ cups reduced-sodium chicken broth
¹/₂ cup 2% reduced-fat milk
Salt and pepper, to taste
6 tablespoons reduced-fat sour cream *or* plain yogurt
3 tablespoons finely chopped cilantro
2 tablespoons finely chopped red, *or* green, bell pepper

Per Serving
Calories: 288
% Calories from fat: 29
Fat (gm): 10.7
Saturated fat (gm): 3.9
Cholesterol (mg): 9.8
Sodium (mg): 735
Protein (gm): 16.1
Carbohydrate (gm): 42.3
Exchanges
Milk: 0.0
Vegetable: 0.0
Fruit: 0.0
Bread: 3.0
Meat: 0.0
Fat: 1.5

1. Saute onion, leeks, garlic, and curry powder in margarine in large saucepan 5 minutes. Add beans and broth to saucepan; heat to boiling. Reduce heat and simmer, covered, 5 minutes.

2. Process bean mixture in food processor or blender until smooth; return to saucepan. Stir in milk; cook over medium heat until hot, 2 to 3 minutes. Season to taste with salt and pepper.

3. Serve soup in bowls; top each with a dollop of sour cream. Sprinkle with cilantro and bell pepper.

NAVY BEAN SOUP WITH HAM

A quick-soak method is used for the beans. If you prefer soaking the beans overnight, omit Step 1 and proceed with Step 2 in the recipe.

6 servings (about 1¼ cups each)

8 ounces dried navy, *or* Great Northern, beans, washed and sorted
1½ cups cubed lean smoked ham (8 ounces), fat trimmed
⅔ cup chopped onion
⅔ cup chopped carrot
1 rib celery, thinly sliced
2 cloves garlic, minced
1 tablespoon vegetable oil
1 tablespoon flour
4 cups reduced-sodium chicken broth
1 cup water
¼ teaspoon dried thyme leaves
1 bay leaf
Salt and pepper, to taste

Per Serving
Calories: 223
% Calories from fat: 16
Fat (gm): 4.0
Saturated fat (gm): 0.9
Cholesterol (mg): 21.6
Sodium (mg): 639
Protein (gm): 20.1
Carbohydrate (gm): 29.5
Exchanges
Milk: 0.0
Vegetable: 0.0
Fruit: 0.0
Bread: 2.0
Meat: 2.0
Fat: 0.0

1. Cover beans with 2 inches of water in large saucepan; heat to boiling and boil, uncovered, 2 minutes. Remove from heat and let stand, covered, 1 hour; drain.

2. Saute ham, onion, carrot, celery, and garlic in oil in large saucepan until vegetables are tender, 5 to 8 minutes. Stir in flour; cook over medium heat 1 minute.

3. Add beans, broth, water, and herbs to saucepan; heat to boiling. Reduce heat and simmer, covered, until beans are tender, 1¼ to 1½ hours. Discard bay leaf; season to taste with salt and pepper.

TWO-BEAN AND PASTA SOUP

This substantial soup thickens upon standing; thin with additional chicken broth or water, if necessary.

6 servings (about 2 cups each)

Vegetable cooking spray
1¹/2 cups cubed carrots
1 medium green bell pepper, chopped
¹/2 cup sliced green onions and tops
3 cloves garlic, minced
2 teaspoons dried basil leaves
2 teaspoons dried oregano leaves
2 cans (15 ounces each) reduced-sodium chicken broth
1 cup water
1 can (15 ounces) no-salt-added stewed tomatoes
1 can (15 ounces) cannellini, *or* Great Northern, beans, rinsed, drained
1 can (15 ounces) fava beans *or* pinto beans, rinsed, drained
1¹/2 cups (4 ounces) rigatoni, uncooked
2-3 teaspoons lemon juice
¹/4 teaspoon salt
¹/2 teaspoon pepper

Per Serving
Calories: 222
% Calories from fat: 7
Fat (gm): 2
Saturated fat (gm): 0.1
Cholesterol (mg): 0
Sodium (mg): 534
Protein (gm): 14.3
Carbohydrate (gm): 43.8
Exchanges
Milk: 0.0
Vegetable: 2.0
Fruit: 0.0
Bread: 2.0
Meat: 0.5
Fat: 0.0

1. Spray large saucepan with cooking spray; saute carrots, bell pepper, onions, and garlic until vegetables are tender, about 7 minutes. Stir in basil and oregano; cook 1 to 2 minutes.

2. Add chicken broth, water, tomatoes, and both beans to saucepan; heat to boiling. Reduce heat and simmer, covered, 10 minutes.

3. Heat soup to boiling; add pasta to saucepan. Reduce heat and simmer, uncovered, until pasta is al dente, 12 to 15 minutes. Season with lemon juice, salt, and pepper. Serve immediately.

CHICKPEA AND PASTA SOUP

Many fresh garden vegetables can be substituted for the zucchini and celery in this soup—carrots, cauliflower, broccoli florets, mushrooms, peas, and green beans are possible choices.

4 servings (about 1³/₄ cups each)

Olive oil cooking spray
1 small zucchini, cubed
2 ribs celery, thinly sliced
1 medium onion, chopped
3-4 cloves garlic, minced
1 teaspoon dried rosemary leaves
1 teaspoon dried thyme leaves
¹/₈ teaspoon crushed red pepper
1 can (15 ounces) reduced-sodium chicken broth
1 can (15 ounces) no-salt-added stewed tomatoes
1 can (15 ounces) chickpeas, rinsed, drained
2 cups water
1 cup (4 ounces) farfalle (bow ties), uncooked
2 tablespoons finely chopped parsley
2-3 teaspoons lemon juice
Salt and pepper, to taste

Per Serving
Calories: 259
% Calories from fat: 7
Fat (gm): 2.3
Saturated fat (gm): 0.2
Cholesterol (mg): 0
Sodium (mg): 224
Protein (gm): 15
Carbohydrate (gm): 51.1
Exchanges
Milk: 0.0
Vegetable: 2.0
Fruit: 0.0
Bread: 2.5
Meat: 0.5
Fat: 0.0

1. Spray bottom of large saucepan with cooking spray; heat over medium heat until hot. Saute zucchini, celery, onion, and garlic until zucchini is crisp-tender, about 8 minutes. Stir in herbs and red pepper; cook 1 to 2 minutes.

2. Add chicken broth, tomatoes, chickpeas, and water; heat to boiling. Reduce heat and simmer, covered, 10 minutes.

3. Heat soup to boiling; add pasta to saucepan. Reduce heat and simmer, uncovered, until pasta is al dente, about 8 minutes. Stir in parsley; season with lemon juice, salt, and pepper.

BLACK AND WHITE BEAN CHILI

Made with black and white beans, this chili is uniquely accented in flavor and color with sun-dried tomatoes.

4 servings (about 1¼ cups each)

- ¼ cup sun-dried tomatoes (not in oil)
- ½ cup boiling water
  Garlic-flavored vegetable cooking spray
- 12 ounces 95% lean ground beef
- 1 cup chopped onion
- ½ cup chopped green bell pepper
- 1 medium jalapeño chili, finely chopped
- 2 teaspoons minced garlic
- 2-3 tablespoons chili powder
- 1-1½ teaspoons ground cumin
- 1 teaspoon dried oregano leaves
- 1 bay leaf
- 2 cans (16 ounces each) reduced-sodium whole tomatoes, undrained, coarsely chopped
- 1 can (15½ ounces) Great Northern beans, rinsed, drained
- 1 can (15 ounces) black beans, rinsed, drained
  Salt and pepper, to taste
- 4 tablespoons finely chopped cilantro

Per Serving
Calories: 305
% Calories from fat: 12
Fat (gm): 4.9
Saturated fat (gm): 1.2
Cholesterol (mg): 41.2
Sodium (mg): 770
Protein (gm): 28.9
Carbohydrate (gm): 52.4
Exchanges
Milk: 0.0
Vegetable: 2.0
Fruit: 0.0
Bread: 2.0
Meat: 2.0
Fat: 0.0

1. Cover sun-dried tomatoes with boiling water in small bowl; let stand until softened, about 10 minutes. Drain; reserve liquid. Chop tomatoes.

2. Spray large saucepan with cooking spray; heat over medium heat until hot. Cook ground beef, onion, bell pepper, jalapeño chili, and garlic until beef is browned and vegetables are tender, 8 to 10 minutes. Stir in chili powder and herbs; cook 1 to 2 minutes longer.

3. Stir in sun-dried tomatoes and reserved liquid, and remaining ingredients, except salt, pepper, and cilantro. Heat to boiling; reduce heat and simmer, covered, 30 minutes. Discard bay leaf; season to taste with salt and pepper. Stir in cilantro.

MEXI-BEANS AND GREENS

The chilies and cayenne pepper in this heartily spiced dish can be decreased if less hotness is desired. Four cans (15 ounces each) pinto beans, rinsed, and drained, can be substituted for the dried beans; omit Step 1 in recipe.

8 servings

2 cups dry pinto beans
1 medium onion, coarsely chopped
1 medium poblano chili, chopped
1 medium red bell pepper, chopped
4 cloves garlic, minced
1 tablespoon finely chopped gingerroot
2 serrano chilies, finely chopped
2 tablespoons olive oil
2-3 teaspoons chili powder
2 teaspoons dried oregano leaves
1 teaspoon ground cumin
1/2 teaspoon cayenne pepper
3 cups water
1 can (15 ounces) diced tomatoes, undrained
2 cups coarsely chopped turnip, *or* mustard, greens
Salt, to taste
Cilantro, finely chopped, as garnish

Per Serving
Calories: 228
% Calories from fat: 16
Fat (gm): 4.4
Saturated fat (gm): 0.6
Cholesterol (mg): 0
Sodium (mg): 233
Protein (gm): 11.7
Carbohydrate (gm): 37.9
Exchanges
Milk: 0.0
Vegetable: 2.0
Fruit: 0.0
Bread: 2.0
Meat: 0.0
Fat: 1.0

1. Sort and rinse beans, discarding any stones. Cover beans with 2 inches water in large saucepan; heat to boiling and boil, uncovered, 2 minutes. Remove from heat and let stand, covered, 1 hour; drain.

2. Saute onion, poblano chili, bell pepper, garlic, gingerroot, and serrano chilies in oil in large saucepan until tender, 8 to 10 minutes. Stir in chili powder, herbs, and cayenne pepper; cook 1 to 2 minutes longer.

3. Add 3 cups water and sauted vegetables to beans; heat to boiling. Reduce heat and simmer, covered, until beans are tender, 1 to 1¹/₄ hours, adding water if necessary. Stir in tomatoes and turnip greens; simmer, uncovered, until mixture is desired thickness, 15 to 30 minutes. Season to taste with salt. Spoon into bowls; sprinkle generously with cilantro.

HOPPING JOHN

Be sure to eat your portion of Hopping John before noon on January 1 to guarantee a new year of good luck!

6 servings (about 1 cup each)

Mesquite-flavored vegetable cooking spray
1³/₄ cups chopped onions, divided
¹/₂ cup chopped celery
3 cloves garlic, minced
4 ounces lean ham, cubed
1 cup long-grain white rice
3 cups reduced-sodium vegetable broth
1 teaspoon dried oregano leaves
1 bay leaf
2 cans (15 ounces each) black-eyed peas, rinsed, drained
2-3 dashes liquid smoke, optional
2-3 dashes red pepper sauce
Salt and pepper, to taste

Per Serving
Calories: 287
% Calories from fat: 6
Fat (gm): 2
Saturated fat (gm): 0.6
Cholesterol (mg): 5.7
Sodium (mg): 565
Protein (gm): 14.1
Carbohydrate (gm): 53.1
Exchanges
Milk: 0.0
Vegetable: 1.0
Fruit: 0.0
Bread: 3.0
Meat: 1.0
Fat: 0.0

1. Spray large saucepan with cooking spray; heat over medium heat until hot. Saute 1¹/₂ cups onions, celery, garlic, and ham until onions are tender, 5 to 8 minutes. Add rice, broth, oregano, and bay leaf; heat to boiling. Reduce heat and simmer, covered, until rice is tender, about 25 minutes.

2. Stir black-eyed peas into rice mixture; season to taste with liquid smoke, red pepper sauce, salt, and pepper. Cook, covered, over medium-low heat 5 minutes. Discard bay leaf.

3. Spoon into serving bowl; sprinkle with remaining ¹/₄ cup onions.

WINTER STEW STROGANOFF

A warming stew for cold winter evenings. Substitute turnips, parsnips, or rutabagas for one of the potatoes, if you like.

6 servings

1 pound Idaho potatoes, peeled, cubed
1 pound sweet potatoes, peeled, cubed
3 medium onions, thinly sliced
8 ounces mushrooms, halved
3 tablespoons margarine
1 cup frozen peas
1¹/₃ cups boiling water
2 vegetable bouillon cubes
1 tablespoon dry mustard
1 tablespoon sugar
1 cup fat-free sour cream
¹/₄ cup coarsely chopped parsley
Salt and pepper, to taste
4¹/₂ cups cooked wide noodles, warm

Per Serving
Calories: 414
% Calories from fat: 13
Fat (gm): 6.1
Saturated fat (gm): 1
Cholesterol (mg): 39.8
Sodium (mg): 653
Protein (gm): 14.4
Carbohydrate (gm): 78.9
Exchanges
Milk: 0.0
Vegetable: 2.0
Fruit: 0.0
Bread: 4.5
Meat: 0.0
Fat: 1.0

1. Simmer Idaho and sweet potatoes in 2 inches water in large saucepan until tender, 8 to 10 minutes; drain and reserve.

2. Saute onions and mushrooms in margarine in large saucepan until onions are tender. Stir in reserved potatoes, peas, water, and bouillon cubes; heat to boiling. Reduce heat and simmer 5 minutes.

3. Stir in combined dry mustard, sugar, and sour cream; simmer until hot, 3 to 4 minutes. Stir in parsley; season to taste with salt and pepper. Serve over noodles.

ITALIAN-STYLE BEANS AND VEGETABLES WITH POLENTA

This colorful mélange can also be served over pasta, rice, or squares of warm cornbread.

6 servings (about 1¹/₄ cups each)

12 ounces Italian-style turkey sausage, casings removed

1¹/₂ cups chopped onions

1¹/₂ cups portobello mushrooms

4 cloves garlic, minced

2 tablespoons olive oil

2 cups broccoli florets and sliced stems

1 cup sliced yellow summer squash

1 can (15 ounces) garbanzo beans, rinsed, drained

1 can (15 ounces) red kidney beans, rinsed, drained

1 can (14¹/₂ ounces) reduced-sodium whole tomatoes, undrained, coarsely chopped

1 teaspoon dried basil leaves

¹/₂ teaspoon dried oregano leaves

¹/₄ teaspoon dried thyme leaves

¹/₄-¹/₂ teaspoon crushed red pepper

Salt and pepper, to taste

Herbed Polenta (see p. 459)

Per Serving
Calories: 367
% Calories from fat: 30
Fat (gm): 12.9
Saturated fat (gm): 2.6
Cholesterol (mg): 30.4
Sodium (mg): 828
Protein (gm): 21.3
Carbohydrate (gm): 45.5
Exchanges
Milk: 0.0
Vegetable: 2.0
Fruit: 0.0
Bread: 2.0
Meat: 2.0
Fat: 1.0

1. Saute sausage, onions, mushrooms, and garlic in oil in large saucepan until onions are tender, about 10 minutes; drain excess fat. Add broccoli and squash; cook, covered, over medium heat 5 minutes.

2. Stir in beans, tomatoes with liquid, herbs, and crushed red pepper; heat to boiling. Reduce heat and simmer, covered, until broccoli is tender, 5 to 8 minutes. Season to taste with salt and pepper.

3. Serve bean mixture over polenta wedges.

THREE-BEAN STEW WITH POLENTA

Use any kind of canned or cooked dried beans that you like; one 15-ounce can of drained beans yields 1 1/2 cups beans. Many flavors of prepared polenta are now available in the produce department, and can be substituted for the Polenta used in this recipe.

6 servings (about 1 cup each)

1 cup chopped onion
1/2 cup chopped red, *or* green, bell pepper
1-2 tablespoons olive oil
1 tablespoon flour
1 can (15 ounces) black-eyed peas, rinsed, drained
1 can (15 ounces) black beans, rinsed, drained
1 can (15 ounces) red beans, rinsed, drained
1 can (14 1/2 ounces) reduced-sodium diced tomatoes, undrained
1 tablespoon minced roasted garlic
3/4 teaspoon dried sage leaves
1/2 teaspoon dried rosemary leaves
1 cup reduced-sodium vegetable broth
Salt and pepper, to taste
Polenta (see p. 458)

Per Serving
Calories: 267
% Calories from fat: 13
Fat (gm): 4.2
Saturated fat (gm): 0.6
Cholesterol (mg): 0
Sodium (mg): 590
Protein (gm): 12.5
Carbohydrate (gm): 52.2
Exchanges
Milk: 0.0
Vegetable: 1.0
Fruit: 0.0
Bread: 3.0
Meat: 0.0
Fat: 0.5

1. Saute onion and bell pepper in oil in large saucepan until tender, about 5 minutes. Stir in flour; cook 1 minute longer.

2. Add beans, tomatoes and liquid, garlic, herbs, and broth to saucepan; heat to boiling. Reduce heat and simmer, covered, 10 minutes. Season to taste with salt and pepper.

3. Spoon Polenta into shallow bowls; spoon stew over.

WINTER BEAN AND VEGETABLE STEW

Root vegetables and beans combine in this satisfying stew, perfect for cold-weather meals. Serve with crusty Italian bread.

6 servings (about 1¹/₃ cups each)

1 cup chopped onion

1 medium Idaho potato, unpeeled, cut into 1-inch cubes

1 large sweet potato, peeled, cut into 1-inch cubes

³/₄ cup chopped green bell pepper

1 teaspoon minced garlic

2 tablespoons olive oil

1 tablespoon flour

1¹/₂ cups reduced-sodium vegetable broth

1 can (15 ounces) black beans, rinsed, drained

1 can (13¹/₄ ounces) baby lima beans, rinsed, drained

1 can (16 ounces) tomato wedges, undrained

³/₄ teaspoon dried sage leaves

Salt and pepper, to taste

Per Serving
Calories: 209
% Calories from fat: 21
Fat (gm): 5.5
Saturated fat (gm): 0.7
Cholesterol (mg): 0
Sodium (mg): 493
Protein (gm): 7.7
Carbohydrate (gm): 39.2
Exchanges
Milk: 0.0
Vegetable: 1.0
Fruit: 0.0
Bread: 2.0
Meat: 0.0
Fat: 1.0

1. Saute onion, potato, sweet potato, bell pepper, and garlic in oil in large saucepan 5 minutes; stir in flour and cook 1 to 2 minutes longer. Add remaining ingredients, except salt and pepper, to saucepan; heat to boiling. Reduce heat and simmer, covered, until vegetables are tender, 15 to 20 minutes. Season to taste with salt and pepper.

CASSOULET À LA CRAIG

This version of the French classic includes the traditional beans and meats of the original, but cuts out much of the fat and sodium.

8 servings (about ¹/₂ cup each)

1   pound lean pork loin, fat trimmed, cut into 1-inch cubes

8   ounces lean lamb, cut into 1-inch cubes

4   ounces turkey smoked sausage, cut into 1-inch pieces

3   slices low-sodium bacon, cut into 1-inch pieces

3   cans (15¹/₂ ounces each) Great Northern beans, rinsed, drained
    Salt and pepper, to taste

4   shallots *or* pearl onions, cut into halves

2   teaspoons minced garlic

2   cans (14¹/₂ ounces each) reduced-sodium diced tomatoes, undrained

2   cans (6 ounces each) reduced-sodium tomato paste

1   rib celery, coarsely chopped

1   bay leaf

1   teaspoon dried parsley leaves

1   teaspoon dried thyme leaves

1   cup unseasoned dry bread crumbs

Per Serving
Calories: 370
% Calories from fat: 23
Fat (gm): 10.4
Saturated fat (gm): 3.5
Cholesterol (mg): 57.1
Sodium (mg): 793
Protein (gm): 32.6
Carbohydrate (gm): 45.1
Exchanges
Milk: 0.0
Vegetable: 0.0
Fruit: 0.0
Bread: 3.0
Meat: 3.0
Fat: 0.0

1.   Combine pork, lamb, sausage, bacon, and beans in roasting pan or Dutch oven; sprinkle lightly with salt and pepper. Place shallot halves on top and sprinkle with garlic. Mix tomatoes and liquid, tomato paste, celery, and herbs in large bowl; pour over meat and bean mixture. Sprinkle bread crumbs over tomato mixture.

2.   Bake, covered, 2 hours at 325 degrees; uncover and bake until meats are tender and sauce thickened, about 30 minutes. With a large spoon, remove any fat that rises to the surface; discard bay leaf.

BLACK-EYED PEAS AND GREENS

Oriental foods and flavors combine in this sesame-accented meatless main course. Cooked shrimp or cubed chicken can be added with the black-eyed peas in Step 2, if you like.

12 servings (about ½ cup each)

8 ounces snow peas, diagonally cut into halves

¹/₃ cup chopped onion

1 small red, *or* green, bell pepper, sliced

1 tablespoon finely chopped gingerroot

2 teaspoons minced garlic

1 serrano, *or* jalapeño, chili, finely chopped

1 tablespoon sesame oil

3 cups thinly sliced bok choy *or* Chinese cabbage

2 cans (15 ounces each) black-eyed peas, rinsed, drained

1-2 tablespoons reduced-sodium tamari soy sauce

1-2 teaspoons black bean, *or* hoisin, sauce

1 package (16 ounces) Chinese-style egg noodles *or* 4 cups cooked rice, cooked

2 teaspoons toasted sesame seeds

Per Serving
Calories: 217
% Calories from fat: 8
Fat (gm): 2
Saturated fat (gm): 0.3
Cholesterol (mg): 0
Sodium (mg): 211
Protein (gm): 7.7
Carbohydrate (gm): 42.5
Exchanges
Milk: 0.0
Vegetable: 1.0
Fruit: 0.0
Bread: 2.5
Meat: 0.0
Fat: 0.5

1. Stir-fry snow peas, onion, bell pepper, gingerroot, garlic, and serrano chili in sesame oil in wok or large skillet, 5 to 8 minutes. Stir in bok choy; cook, covered, over medium heat until wilted, 2 to 3 minutes.

2. Stir black-eyed peas into wok; stir-fry until hot, about 5 minutes. Stir in soy sauce and black bean sauce. Serve mixture over noodles or rice; sprinkle with sesame seeds.

SANTA FE BAKED BEANS

These baked beans boast flavors of the great Southwest.

10 servings (about ½ cup each)

1 cup chopped onion
½ cup chopped poblano chili *or* green bell pepper
½-1 serrano, *or* jalapeño, chili, finely chopped
1 tablespoon olive oil
2 cans (15 ounces each) pinto beans, rinsed, drained
2 cups frozen, *or* canned, drained, whole-kernel corn
6 sun-dried tomatoes (not in oil), cut into fourths
2-3 tablespoons honey
½-1 teaspoon ground cumin
½ teaspoon dried thyme leaves
½ cup (2 ounces) crumbled Mexican white, *or* farmer's, cheese
¼ cup finely chopped cilantro

Per Serving
Calories: 167
% Calories from fat: 21
Fat (gm): 4.1
Saturated fat (gm): 1.4
Cholesterol (mg): 5.4
Sodium (mg): 432
Protein (gm): 7.4
Carbohydrate (gm): 27.9
Exchanges
Milk: 0.0
Vegetable: 1.0
Fruit: 0.0
Bread: 1.5
Meat: 0.0
Fat: 1.0

1. Saute onion and chilies in oil in small skillet until tender, about 5 minutes. Combine all ingredients, except cheese and cilantro, in 1½-quart casserole; sprinkle cheese on top.

2. Bake, covered, at 350 degrees until bean mixture is hot, about 30 minutes. Sprinkle top of casserole with cilantro before serving.

RED HOT PINTO BEANS

Keep the water close for this firestarter! A good recipe to use with your leftover ham.

13 servings

1	pound dried pinto beans, sorted, rinsed
15	cups water, divided
1	cup chopped lean ham (about 5 ounces)
1	large onion, chopped
1	can (4 ¹/₂ ounces) chopped green chilies
1	tablespoon ground cumin
1	tablespoon chili powder
1	teaspoon salt
¹/₄	teaspoon pepper

Per Serving
Calories: 146
% Calories from fat: 7
Fat (gm): 1.2
Saturated fat (gm): 0.3
Cholesterol (mg): 6
Sodium (mg): 370
Protein (gm): 10.3
Carbohydrate (gm): 24
Exchanges
Milk: 0.0
Vegetable: 0.0
Fruit: 0.0
Bread: 2.0
Meat: 0.0
Fat: 0.0

1. Combine beans, 10 cups water, ham, and onion in a stock-pot; cover and heat to boiling over high heat. Reduce heat and simmer, covered, for 2 hours, stirring occasionally. Add remaining ingredients, including remaining 5 cups water, and simmer, covered, 30 minutes or until beans are tender, stirring occasionally. If a thicker "soup" is desired, mash some of the beans with a spoon during this last 30 minutes of cooking.

JUST PEACHY BEAN POT

Peaches and nectar, dried fruit, and mango chutney add special flavor to this bean combo. Mango and mango nectar may be substituted for the peach and peach nectar.

12 servings (about ²/₃ cup each)

    1 cup chopped onion
    1 clove garlic, minced
    1 tablespoon margarine
1-1¹/₂ teaspoons curry powder
¹/₂-³/₄ teaspoon ground allspice
¹/₄-¹/₂ teaspoon crushed red pepper
    2 cans (15 ounces each) red kidney beans, rinsed, drained
    1 can (15 ounces) navy beans, rinsed, drained
 1¹/₂ cups diced, peeled peaches
  ¹/₂ cup coarsely chopped mixed dried fruit
  ¹/₂ cup mango chutney
¹/₂-³/₄ cup peach nectar
    3 tablespoons cider vinegar

Per Serving
Calories: 170
% Calories from fat: 7
Fat (gm): 1.4
Saturated fat (gm): 0.3
Cholesterol (mg): 0
Sodium (mg): 299
Protein (gm): 6.9
Carbohydrate (gm): 34.2
Exchanges
Milk: 0.0
Vegetable: 0.0
Fruit: 0.5
Bread: 2.0
Meat: 0.0
Fat: 0.0

1. Saute onion and garlic in margarine in small skillet until tender, about 5 minutes. Stir in curry powder, allspice, and crushed red pepper; cook 1 to 2 minutes longer.

2. Mix all ingredients in 2¹/₂-quart casserole. Bake, covered, at 350 degrees 30 minutes; bake, uncovered, if thicker consistency is desired, about 15 minutes.

SEASONED MASHED BLACK BEANS

Black beans at their flavorful best—quick and easy too!

6 servings (about ²/₃ cup each)

    Vegetable cooking spray
2 medium onions, chopped
4 cloves garlic, minced
1-2 small jalapeño chilies, minced
2 cans (15 ounces each) black beans, rinsed, drained
2 cups reduced-sodium vegetable broth
³/₄-1 teaspoon dried cumin
¹/₃ cup finely chopped cilantro leaves
    Salt and pepper, to taste

Per Serving
Calories: 158
% Calories from fat: 8
Fat (gm): 1.7
Saturated fat (gm): 0.1
Cholesterol (mg): 0
Sodium (mg): 476
Protein (gm): 12.5
Carbohydrate (gm): 31.2
Exchanges
Milk: 0.0
Vegetable: 1.0
Fruit: 0.0
Bread: 2.0
Meat: 0.0
Fat: 0.0

1. Spray medium skillet with cooking spray; heat over medium heat until hot. Saute onions, garlic, and jalapeño chili until tender, 3 to 4 minutes.

2. Add beans and broth to skillet; cook over medium heat, coarsely mashing beans with fork. Stir in cumin and cilantro. Season to taste with salt and pepper.

REFRIED BEANS

Two cans (15 ounces each) pinto beans, rinsed and drained, can be substituted for the dried beans. Make the recipe beginning with Step 2, substituting 1 can (14½ ounces) reduced-sodium fat-free chicken broth for the bean cooking liquid.

6 servings (about ½ cup each)

1¹/₄ cups dried pinto beans
    Vegetable cooking spray
1 medium onion, coarsely chopped
    Salt and pepper, to taste

Per Serving
Calories: 106
% Calories from fat: 3
Fat (gm): 0.4
Saturated fat (gm): 0.1
Cholesterol (mg): 0
Sodium (mg): 2
Protein (gm): 6.1
Carbohydrate (gm): 20
Exchanges
Milk: 0.0
Vegetable: 0.0
Fruit: 0.0
Bread: 1.5
Meat: 0.0
Fat: 0.0

1. Wash and sort beans, discarding any stones. Cover beans with 2 inches water in large saucepan; heat to boiling and boil, uncovered, 2 minutes. Remove from heat; let stand, covered, 1 hour. Drain beans; cover with 2 inches water and heat to boiling. Reduce heat and simmer, covered, until beans are tender, 1¹/2 to 2 hours. Drain, reserving 2 cups liquid.

2. Spray large skillet with cooking spray; heat over medium heat until hot. Saute onion until tender, 3 to 5 minutes. Add 1 cup beans and 1 cup reserved liquid to skillet; cook over high heat, mashing beans until almost smooth with end of meat mallet or potato masher. Add half the remaining beans and liquid; continue cooking, mashing beans. Repeat with remaining beans and liquid. Season to taste with salt and pepper.

FRIED LENTILS

Fried lentils (dal) are a staple of Indian cooking. Normally cooked in a large quantity of clarified, browned butter (ghee), we have substituted a small amount of vegetable oil to keep the dish low in fat.

8 servings (about ¹/2 cup each)

1¹/2 cups dried red lentils
1 cup chopped onion
1 teaspoon ground turmeric
1 teaspoon crushed cumin seeds
¹/4 teaspoon crushed red pepper
2 tablespoons vegetable oil
¹/2 cup chopped cilantro *or* parsley
Salt, to taste
2 teaspoons grated lemon rind

Per Serving
Calories: 171
% Calories from fat: 20
Fat (gm): 4
Saturated fat (gm): 0.5
Cholesterol (mg): 0
Sodium (mg): 4.4
Protein (gm): 10.5
Carbohydrate (gm): 24.6
Exchanges
Milk: 0.0
Vegetable: 1.0
Fruit: 0.0
Bread: 1.5
Meat: 0.0
Fat: 1.0

1. Wash and sort lentils, discarding any stones. Cover lentils with 2 inches water and heat to boiling; reduce heat and simmer, covered, until very soft, 30 to 40 minutes. Drain well.

2. Saute onion, turmeric, cumin seeds, and crushed red pepper in oil in large skillet until onions are tender, 5 to 8 minutes. Reserve ¹/4 cup onion mixture.

3. Stir lentils into skillet; cook over low heat, stirring frequently to prevent burning, until mixture is thickened, 10 to 20 minutes. Stir in cilantro; season to taste with salt.

4. Spoon lentils into serving bowl; sprinkle with reserved ¹/₄ cup onion mixture and lemon rind.

WHEAT BERRY AND LENTIL STEW WITH DUMPLINGS

Wheat berries have a wonderful, nutty texture. They can be readily purchased at health food stores; barley or another grain can be substituted.

10 servings (about 1 cup each)

1	cup wheat berries
	Vegetable cooking spray
2	medium onions, chopped
¹/₂	cup chopped celery
4	cloves garlic, minced
1	teaspoon dried savory leaves
3	cups reduced-sodium vegetable broth
2	pounds russet potatoes, unpeeled, cubed
2	medium carrots, sliced
1¹/₂	cups lentils
	Salt and pepper, to taste
	Herb Dumplings (recipe follows)

Per Serving
Calories: 248
% Calories from fat: 10
Fat (gm): 2.8
Saturated fat (gm): 0.4
Cholesterol (mg): 0.2
Sodium (mg): 155
Protein (gm): 10
Carbohydrate (gm): 47.2
Exchanges
Milk: 0.0
Vegetable: 0.5
Fruit: 0.0
Bread: 3.0
Meat: 0.0
Fat: 0.5

1. Cover wheat berries with 2 to 3 inches water in saucepan; let stand overnight. Heat to boiling; reduce heat and simmer, covered, until wheat berries are tender, 45 to 55 minutes. Drain.

2. Spray large saucepan with cooking spray; heat over medium heat until hot. Saute onions, celery, garlic, and savory until onions are tender, 3 to 5 minutes. Add broth, potatoes, carrots, and lentils and heat to boiling; reduce heat and simmer, covered, until vegetables are just tender, 10 to 15 minutes. Stir in wheat berries. Season to taste with salt and pepper.

3. Spoon dumpling mixture into 10 mounds on top of stew; cook, uncovered, 5 minutes. Cook, covered, until dumplings are dry, 5 to 10 minutes longer.

Herb Dumplings

$1/2$ cup all-purpose flour
$1/2$ cup yellow cornmeal
$1^1/2$ teaspoons baking powder
$1/2$ teaspoon dried sage leaves
$1/4$ teaspoon dried thyme leaves
$1/2$ teaspoon salt
  2 tablespoons vegetable shortening
$1/2$ cup fat-free milk

1. Combine flour, cornmeal, baking powder, sage, thyme, and salt in medium bowl. Cut in shortening with pastry blender or 2 knives until mixture resembles coarse crumbs. Stir in milk.

WHEAT BERRY AND GARDEN TOMATO SALAD

The "toothsome" texture of wheat berries is a perfect complement to crisp cucumbers and sun-ripened tomatoes. Kamut is an excellent grain to substitute for the wheat berries.

8 servings (about $3/4$ cup each)

  3 cups cooked wheat berries
  4 cups coarsely chopped ripe tomatoes
$1^1/2$ cups cubed, seeded cucumber
$1/2$ cup sliced green onions and tops
$1/4$ cup finely chopped parsley
$1/2$ cup (2 ounces) crumbled reduced-fat feta cheese
Roasted Garlic Vinaigrette (recipe follows)
Salt and pepper, to taste
Curly endive *or* escarole, as garnish

Per Serving
Calories: 140
% Calories from fat: 30
Fat (gm): 5
Saturated fat (gm): 1.2
Cholesterol (mg): 2.6
Sodium (mg): 111
Protein (gm): 4.7
Carbohydrate (gm): 21.4
Exchanges
Milk: 0.0
Vegetable: 1.0
Fruit: 0.0
Bread: 1.0
Meat: 0.0
Fat: 1.0

1. Combine wheat berries, vegetables, parsley, and cheese in salad bowl; pour Roasted Garlic Vinaigrette over and toss. Season to taste with salt and pepper. Serve on endive-lined plates.

Roasted Garlic Vinaigrette

makes about ¹/₂ cup

- 2-4 tablespoons olive oil
- ¹/₄ cup balsamic vinegar
- 2 teaspoons minced roasted garlic
- 1 teaspoon dried mint leaves
- 1 teaspoon dried oregano leaves

1. Mix all ingredients; refrigerate until serving time. Mix again before using.

BULGUR AND BARLEY WITH LEMON GREENS

Grains and greens are cooked together, then combined with tomatoes and toasted nuts.

8 servings (about ¹/₂ cup each)

- Vegetable cooking spray
- ³/₄ cup barley
- 2¹/₂ cups reduced-sodium vegetable broth
- ¹/₄ cup bulgur
- ¹/₂ teaspoon dried thyme leaves
- 6 ounces thinly sliced turnip greens, kale, *or* spinach
- ¹/₂ cup thinly sliced green onions and tops
- ¹/₄ cup finely chopped parsley
- 1 large tomato, coarsely chopped
- ¹/₄-¹/₂ cup coarsely chopped walnuts, toasted
- 1-2 tablespoons lemon juice
- Salt and pepper, to taste

Per Serving
Calories: 129
% Calories from fat: 20
Fat (gm): 3
Saturated fat (gm): 0.3
Cholesterol (mg): 0
Sodium (mg): 33
Protein (gm): 4.3
Carbohydrate (gm): 20.9
Exchanges
Milk: 0.0
Vegetable: 0.5
Fruit: 0.0
Bread: 1.0
Meat: 0.0
Fat: 0.5

1. Spray large saucepan with cooking spray; heat over medium heat until hot. Add barley to saucepan; spray lightly with cooking spray. Cook over medium heat, stirring occasionally, until barley is golden, 5 to 8 minutes.

2. Add broth to saucepan; heat to boiling. Reduce heat and simmer, covered, 40 minutes. Stir in bulgur and thyme; simmer, covered, 15 minutes. Stir in greens, green onions, and parsley; cook, covered, until all liquid is absorbed, about 10 minutes. Stir in tomato and walnuts; cook 5 minutes longer. Season to taste with lemon juice, salt, and pepper.

BARLEY WITH PEPPERS AND POTATOES

Here's a variation on the delicious Mexican "rajas con papas." If poblano chilies are not available, substitute green bell peppers and 1 to 2 teaspoons of minced jalapeño chili.

6 servings (about 1/2 cup each)

3	large poblano chilies, sliced
1	medium onion, chopped
1	tablespoon olive oil *or* vegetable oil
12	ounces russet potatoes, unpeeled, cooked, cubed
2	cups cooked barley
2	tablespoons finely chopped cilantro leaves
1/2	teaspoon dried cumin
	Salt and cayenne pepper, to taste

Per Serving
Calories: 147
% Calories from fat: 16
Fat (gm): 2.8
Saturated fat (gm): 0.4
Cholesterol (mg): 0
Sodium (mg): 6
Protein (gm): 2.7
Carbohydrate (gm): 29.3
Exchanges
Milk: 0.0
Vegetable: 2.0
Fruit: 0.0
Bread: 1.0
Meat: 0.0
Fat: 0.5

1. Saute chilies and onion in oil in large skillet until crisp-tender, about 5 minutes. Add potatoes; saute until browned, 5 to 8 minutes.

2. Add barley to skillet; cook over medium heat until hot through, 3 to 4 minutes. Stir in cilantro and cumin. Season to taste with salt and cayenne pepper.

TABBOULEH

Always a favorite—this tabbouleh version includes finely chopped mint, as well as parsley.

8 servings (about 1/2 cup each)

	Boiling water
3/4	cup bulgur
1 1/2	cups coarsely chopped seeded tomatoes
3/4	cup thinly sliced green onions and tops
3/4	cup finely chopped parsley
1/4	cup finely chopped mint
1/3-2/3	cup plain fat-free yogurt
1/4-1/3	cup lemon juice
1 1/2-2	tablespoons olive oil
	Salt and pepper, to taste

Per Serving
Calories: 88
% Calories from fat: 28
Fat (gm): 3.0
Saturated fat (gm): 0.4
Cholesterol (mg): 0.2
Sodium (mg): 17
Protein (gm): 29
Carbohydrate (gm): 14.1
Exchanges
Milk: 0.0
Vegetable: 0.5
Fruit: 0.0
Bread: 0.5
Meat: 0.0
Fat: 0.5

1. Pour boiling water over bulgur to cover; let stand 15 minutes or until bulgur is tender but slightly chewy. Drain well.

2. Mix bulgur, tomatoes, green onions, parsley, and mint; stir in yogurt, lemon juice, and oil. Season to taste with salt and pepper. Refrigerate 1 to 2 hours for flavors to blend.

SWEET BULGUR PILAF

A pilaf with sweet accents of yellow squash, currants, and cinnamon.

4 servings (about 1 cup each)

2/3 cup thinly sliced green onions and tops
1 teaspoon minced garlic
1 cup bulgur
1-2 tablespoons olive oil
2¹/4 cups reduced-sodium fat-free chicken broth
1/2-³/4 teaspoon ground cinnamon
2 cups cubed, peeled, seeded butternut, *or* acorn, squash
¹/4 cup currants *or* raisins
¹/4 cup pine nuts, toasted
¹/4 cup finely chopped parsley
Salt and pepper, to taste

Per Serving
Calories: 295
% Calories from fat: 26
Fat (gm): 9.1
Saturated fat (gm): 1.3
Cholesterol (mg): 0
Sodium (mg): 110
Protein (gm): 11.7
Carbohydrate (gm): 46.7
Exchanges
Milk: 0.0
Vegetable: 0.0
Fruit: 0.0
Bread: 3.0
Meat: 0.0
Fat: 2.0

1. Saute green onions, garlic, and bulgur in oil in large saucepan over medium heat until onions are tender, about 5 minutes. Stir in broth and cinnamon and heat to boiling; reduce heat and simmer, covered, 10 minutes.

2. Stir squash and currants into bulgur mixture; simmer, covered, until squash is tender, about 15 minutes. Stir in pine nuts and parsley; season to taste with salt and pepper.

MUSHROOM AND ASPARAGUS PILAF

The dried Chinese black, or shiitake, mushrooms impart a hearty, woodsy flavor to the pilaf. The mushrooms are available in large supermarkets or oriental groceries.

8 servings (about 1¹/₄ cups each)

3¹/₃ cups reduced-sodium vegetable broth, divided

2 cups dried Chinese mushrooms
   Vegetable cooking spray

1¹/₂ cups chopped onions

2 teaspoons minced garlic

2 teaspoons bouquet garni

1¹/₂ pounds asparagus, cut into 1¹/₂-inch pieces

¹/₄ cup dry sherry *or* water

2 packages (6 ounces each) tabbouleh wheat salad mix

¹/₄ teaspoon hot pepper sauce
   Salt and pepper, to taste

4 green onions and tops, thinly sliced

¹/₄ cup toasted pecan halves

Per Serving
Calories: 248
% Calories from fat: 12
Fat (gm): 3.4
Saturated fat (gm): 0.3
Cholesterol (mg): 0
Sodium (mg): 537
Protein (gm): 7.5
Carbohydrate (gm): 45.8
Exchanges
Milk: 0.0
Vegetable: 3.0
Fruit: 0.0
Bread: 2.0
Meat: 0.0
Fat: 0.5

1. Heat 2 cups broth to boiling; pour over mushrooms in bowl and let stand until mushrooms are softened, about 10 minutes. Drain, reserving broth. Slice mushrooms, discarding tough stems.

2. Spray large skillet with cooking spray; heat over medium heat until hot. Saute mushrooms, onions, garlic, and herbs until onions are tender, about 5 minutes. Add asparagus; saute 5 minutes more.

3. Add sherry, reserved broth from mushrooms, and remaining 1¹/₃ cups broth to skillet; heat to boiling. Stir in wheat salad mix (discard spice packet). Reduce heat and simmer, covered, until broth is absorbed and pilaf is tender, 3 to 5 minutes. Stir in hot pepper sauce; season to taste with salt and pepper. Spoon into serving bowl; sprinkle with green onions and pecans.

QUINOA WITH ROASTED EGGPLANT AND SQUASH

Grain recipes are versatile, as almost any grain can be used in them. Couscous, millet, or kasha would be excellent choices in this recipe.

4 servings (about 1½ cups each)

Garlic-flavored vegetable cooking spray
1 small butternut squash, peeled, seeded, cubed
1 medium eggplant, unpeeled, cubed
2 medium onions, cut into wedges
2 large red, *or* green, bell peppers, cored, cut into thick slices
1 teaspoon dried rosemary leaves
½ teaspoon dried savory leaves
½ teaspoon dried thyme leaves
2 cups reduced-sodium vegetable broth
1 cup quinoa
Salt and pepper, to taste

Per Serving
Calories: 261
% Calories from fat: 10
Fat (gm): 3
Saturated fat (gm): 0.4
Cholesterol (mg): 0
Sodium (mg): 58
Protein (gm): 8.4
Carbohydrate (gm): 53.6
Exchanges
Milk: 0.0
Vegetable: 2.0
Fruit: 0.0
Bread: 3.0
Meat: 0.0
Fat: 0.0

1. Spray aluminum foil-lined jelly roll pan with cooking spray; arrange vegetables in single layer on pan. Spray vegetables generously with cooking spray; sprinkle with herbs. Roast at 450 degrees until vegetables are tender, about 30 minutes.

2. While vegetables are roasting, heat broth to boiling in medium saucepan; add quinoa. Reduce heat and simmer, covered, until quinoa is tender and broth absorbed, about 15 minutes. Combine quinoa and warm vegetables in serving bowl; season to taste with salt and pepper.

KASHA WITH GREEN VEGGIES

Kasha is buckwheat groats that have been roasted. Traditionally, kasha is mixed with raw egg and cooked in a skillet until dry, which keeps the grains separate while cooking.

4 servings

1¹/2 cups kasha
1 egg, beaten
1 large green bell pepper, chopped
¹/2 cup sliced green onions and tops
1 teaspoon minced garlic
1 tablespoon olive oil
4 cups reduced-sodium fat-free chicken broth
¹/2 teaspoon dried marjoram leaves
¹/4 teaspoon dried thyme leaves
12 ounces broccoli rabe, cut into 1-inch pieces
Salt and pepper, to taste

Per Serving
Calories: 323
% Calories from fat: 17
Fat (gm): 6.7
Saturated fat (gm): 1.3
Cholesterol (mg): 53
Sodium (mg): 217
Protein (gm): 17.6
Carbohydrate (gm): 52.7
Exchanges
Milk: 0.0
Vegetable: 0.0
Fruit: 0.0
Bread: 3.5
Meat: 0.0
Fat: 1.5

1. Mix kasha and egg in bowl; transfer to large skillet and cook over medium heat until kasha is dry and grains are separated, 3 to 4 minutes.

2. Saute bell pepper, green onions, and garlic in oil in large saucepan until tender, about 5 minutes. Add kasha, broth, and herbs to saucepan; heat to boiling. Reduce heat and simmer, covered, until kasha is tender and liquid absorbed, 25 to 30 minutes.

3. Cook broccoli rabe in 1 inch simmering water until crisp-tender; drain. Stir into kasha mixture; season to taste with salt and pepper.

CURRIED COUSCOUS WITH VEGETABLES

Couscous, a staple in Mediterranean countries, is one of the fastest, easiest grains to cook. Serve this dish with a selection of condiments so that the dish can be enjoyed with a variety of flavor accents.

4 servings (about 1¹/₂ cups each)

8 ounces fresh, *or* frozen, thawed, whole okra

1 cup chopped onion

1 teaspoon minced garlic

2 tablespoons vegetable oil

1 cup frozen, *or* canned, drained, whole-kernel corn

1 cup sliced mushrooms

2 medium carrots, sliced

1¹/₂ teaspoons curry powder

1 cup reduced-sodium vegetable, *or* chicken, broth

²/₃ cup couscous

1 medium tomato, chopped

Salt and pepper, to taste

Condiments: plain reduced-fat yogurt, chopped cucumber, chopped peanuts, raisins (not included in nutritional data)

Per Serving
Calories: 280
% Calories from fat: 24
Fat (gm): 7.7
Saturated fat (gm): 1
Cholesterol (mg): 0
Sodium (mg): 46
Protein (gm): 7.9
Carbohydrate (gm): 47.8
Exchanges
Milk: 0.0
Vegetable: 3.0
Fruit: 0.0
Bread: 2.0
Meat: 0.0
Fat: 1.5

1. Saute okra, onion, and garlic in oil in large saucepan 5 minutes. Stir in corn, mushrooms, carrots, and curry powder; cook 2 minutes.

2. Add broth to saucepan and heat to boiling; reduce heat and simmer, covered, until vegetables are tender, 8 to 10 minutes. Stir in couscous (discard spice packet) and tomato. Remove from heat and let stand, covered, until couscous is tender and broth absorbed, about 5 minutes. Season to taste with salt and pepper.

3. Spoon couscous mixture into serving bowl; serve with condiments.

SUN-DRIED TOMATO COUSCOUS WITH CHICKEN AND MUSHROOMS

Couscous, the national dish of Morocco, is made easy with the many new mixes now available. With the addition of chicken and mushrooms, we have an easy and delicious light meal.

4 servings

1 package (6 ounces) sun-dried tomato couscous
4 boneless, skinless chicken breast halves
1 pound mushrooms, cut into halves
1 tablespoon olive oil
1¹/₂ cups water

Per Serving
Calories: 362
% Calories from fat: 20
Fat (gm): 8.3
Saturated fat (gm): 1.3
Cholesterol (mg): 71.5
Sodium (mg): 525
Protein (gm): 34.6
Carbohydrate (gm): 39.3
Exchanges
Milk: 0.0
Vegetable: 2.0
Fruit: 0.0
Bread: 2.0
Meat: 3.0
Fat: 0.0

1. Combine couscous and seasoning packet in 11 x 7-inch baking dish. Arrange chicken on couscous; sprinkle mushrooms on top of chicken. Drizzle olive oil over mushrooms, and pour water over all. Bake, covered, at 350 degrees until chicken is cooked, about 35 minutes.

POLENTA

This basic recipe can be varied to your taste by adding sauteed onion and garlic, cheese, herbs, etc. Note the variations below.

6 servings (about 1 cup each)

3 cups water
³/₄ cup yellow cornmeal
Salt and pepper, to taste

Per Serving
Calories: 55
% Calories from fat: 9
Fat (gm): 0.5
Saturated fat (gm): 0.1
Cholesterol (mg): 0
Sodium (mg): 5
Protein (gm): 1.2
Carbohydrate (gm): 11.7
Exchanges
Milk: 0.0
Vegetable: 0.0
Fruit: 0.0
Bread: 1.0
Meat: 0.0
Fat: 0.0

1. Heat water to boiling in medium saucepan; gradually stir in cornmeal. Cook over medium to medium-low heat, stirring constantly, until polenta thickens enough to hold its shape but is still soft, 5 to 8 minutes. Season to taste with salt and pepper.

Variations: **Blue Cheese Polenta**—Stir $1/2$ cup (2 ounces) crumbled blue cheese or other blue-veined cheese into the cooked polenta.

Goat Cheese Polenta—Stir $1/4$ to $1/2$ cup (1 to 2 ounces) crumbled goat cheese into the cooked polenta.

Garlic Polenta—Saute $1/4$ cup finely chopped onion and 4 to 6 cloves minced garlic in 1 tablespoon olive oil in medium saucepan; add water, as above, and complete recipe.

HERBED POLENTA

Gently seasoned with onions, garlic, and basil, the polenta can be served immediately after cooking, or cooled in a pan as the recipe directs.

4 to 6 servings

Olive oil cooking spray
2 green onions and tops, sliced
1 clove garlic, minced
1 teaspoon dried basil leaves
$2^1/2$ cups reduced-sodium vegetable, *or* chicken, broth
$3/4$ cup yellow cornmeal
$1/2$ teaspoon salt

Per Serving
Calories: 124
% Calories from fat: 9
Fat (gm): 1.3
Saturated fat (gm): 0.2
Cholesterol (mg): 0
Sodium (mg): 309
Protein (gm): 2.5
Carbohydrate (gm): 22.4
Exchanges
Milk: 0.0
Vegetable: 0.0
Fruit: 0.0
Bread: 1.5
Meat: 0.0
Fat: 0.5

1. Spray large saucepan with cooking spray; heat over medium heat until hot. Saute onions, garlic, and basil until tender, about 5 minutes. Add broth and heat to boiling; gradually stir in cornmeal and salt. Cook over low heat, stirring constantly, until thickened, about 10 minutes.

2. Pour polenta into lightly greased 8-inch cake pan; cool to room temperature. Refrigerate, lightly covered, until polenta is firm, 3 to 4 hours.

3. Spray large skillet with cooking spray; heat over medium heat until hot. Cut polenta into wedges; cook in skillet over medium heat until browned, 3 to 4 minutes on each side.

OLD-FASHIONED COUNTRY-STYLE CORN BREAD

9 servings

1³/4 cups self-rising white cornmeal mix
 1/4 cup all-purpose flour
   1 egg
   2 teaspoons corn oil
1¹/2 cups low-fat buttermilk
      Vegetable cooking spray

Per Serving
Calories: 142
% Calories from fat: 16
Fat (gm): 2.4
Saturated fat (gm): 0.6
Cholesterol (mg): 25
Sodium (mg): 412
Protein (gm): 4.7
Carbohydrate (gm): 24.7
Exchanges
Milk: 0.0
Vegetable: 0.0
Fruit: 0.0
Bread: 1.5
Meat: 0.0
Fat: 0.5

1. Preheat oven to 450 degrees. Combine all ingredients in large mixing bowl. Generously spray 8 x 8-inch baking pan with cooking spray; add batter and bake 20 to 25 minutes or until corn bread is golden brown.

BEST BREAKFAST CEREAL

Delicious, and nutritious! Although we all appreciate a breakfast that is fast to make, this cereal is even more delicious made with steel-cut oats which take about 30 minutes to cook. Treat yourself!

6 servings (about 1 cup each)

   3 cups water
 1/16 teaspoon salt
1¹/2 cups quick-cooking oats
1¹/2 cups cooked wheat berries *or* brown rice
 1/4 cup chopped toasted pecans *or* walnuts
 1/2 cup dried fruit bits *or* raisins
1/4-1/2 cup packed dark brown sugar
   1 cup fat-free milk

Per Serving
Calories: 209
% Calories from fat: 13
Fat (gm): 3.3
Saturated fat (gm): 0.4
Cholesterol (mg): 0.5
Sodium (mg): 37
Protein (gm): 6.5
Carbohydrate (gm): 40.9
Exchanges
Milk: 0.0
Vegetable: 0.0
Fruit: 0.5
Bread: 2.5
Meat: 0.0
Fat: 0.5

1. Heat water and salt to boiling in medium saucepan; stir in oats, wheat berries, pecans, and dried fruit bits. Reduce heat and simmer until oatmeal is cooked to desired consistency, about 5 minutes.

2. Stir brown sugar into cereal, or spoon cereal into bowls and sprinkle with sugar. Serve with milk.

WILD RICE SOUFFLÉ

When you're in the mood for something new and different, try this great soufflé!

4 servings

1/3 cup wild rice
1 cup reduced-sodium vegetable broth
1 cup fat-free milk
1/4 cup all-purpose flour
1/2 cup (2 ounces) shredded reduced-fat Cheddar cheese
2 tablespoons finely chopped onion
1/4 cup finely chopped parsley
1/2 teaspoon paprika
1/4-1/2 teaspoon dried savory leaves
1/4-1/2 teaspoon dried thyme leaves
White pepper, to taste
3 egg yolks
3 egg whites, beaten to stiff peaks

Per Serving
Calories: 210
% Calories from fat: 28
Fat (gm): 6.5
Saturated fat (gm): 2.4
Cholesterol (mg): 168.3
Sodium (mg): 288
Protein (gm): 13
Carbohydrate (gm): 23
Exchanges
Milk: 0.0
Vegetable: 0.0
Fruit: 0.0
Bread: 1.5
Meat: 1.5
Fat: 0.5

1. Rinse rice under cold water and drain. Heat rice and broth to boiling in small saucepan; reduce heat and simmer, covered, until rice is tender and stock absorbed, 45 to 55 minutes.

2. Mix milk and flour in medium saucepan; heat over medium-high heat, whisking constantly, to boiling. Boil, whisking constantly, until thickened. Remove from heat; add cheese and whisk until cheese is melted (sauce will be very thick). Cool slightly; stir in onion and herbs. Season to taste with white pepper.

3. Beat egg yolks in small bowl until thick and lemon colored, about 5 minutes; whisk into cheese mixture. Stir about 1/4 the beaten egg whites into cheese mixture; fold cheese mixture into remaining egg whites. Fold in rice.

4. Pour mixture into lightly greased 1-quart soufflé dish. Bake at 350 degrees until knife inserted halfway between center and edge comes out clean, 45 to 55 minutes. Serve immediately.

FRUIT PILAF

A simple pilaf with dried fruit and nuts that is simply delicious.

8 servings (about 1/2 cup each)

2/3 cup brown rice

1/3 cup wild rice

1/2 cup sliced green onions and tops

1/4 cup thinly sliced celery

1-2 tablespoons margarine

2 1/2 cups reduced-sodium vegetable broth

1/2 teaspoon dried sage *or* marjoram leaves

1/4 teaspoon dried thyme leaves

1 large tart, *or* sweet, apple, peeled, cored, cubed

1/3 cup chopped dried apricots

1/3 cup chopped dried pears

4-6 tablespoons pecan *or* walnut halves, toasted

Salt and pepper, to taste

Per Serving
Calories: 177
% Calories from fat: 23
Fat (gm): 4.6
Saturated fat (gm): 0.6
Cholesterol (mg): 0
Sodium (mg): 40
Protein (gm): 3.2
Carbohydrate (gm): 30.5
Exchanges
Milk: 0.0
Vegetable: 0.0
Fruit: 0.5
Bread: 1.5
Meat: 0.0
Fat: 1.0

1. Saute brown and wild rice, green onions, and celery in margarine in large saucepan until onions are tender, about 5 minutes. Add broth and herbs and heat to boiling; reduce heat and simmer, covered, 45 minutes.

2. Stir apple, apricots, and pears into rice mixture; simmer, covered, until rice is tender and stock absorbed, about 10 minutes. Stir in pecans; season to taste with salt and pepper.

ORIENTAL PILAF

Snow peas, water chestnuts, oriental seasonings and a combination of brown rice and millet make this pilaf a favorite.

8 servings (about ²/₃ cups each)

¹/₂	cup brown rice
¹/₂	cup millet
¹/₂	cup finely chopped onion
¹/₄	cup chopped celery
2-3	teaspoons finely chopped gingerroot
2	cloves minced garlic
1	tablespoon dark sesame, *or* vegetable, oil
2¹/₂	cups oriental broth
1¹/₂	cups halved snow peas
¹/₂	can (6-ounce size) sliced water chestnuts, rinsed, drained
¹/₂	cup thinly sliced green onions and tops
2-3	tablespoons reduced-sodium tamari soy sauce
	Salt and pepper, to taste

Per Serving
Calories: 137
% Calories from fat: 18
Fat (gm): 2.7
Saturated fat (gm): 0.4
Cholesterol (mg): 0
Sodium (mg): 194
Protein (gm): 4.1
Carbohydrate (gm): 24
Exchanges
Milk: 0.0
Vegetable: 0.5
Fruit: 0.0
Bread: 1.5
Meat: 0.0
Fat: 0.0

1. Saute rice, millet, onion, celery, gingerroot, and garlic in sesame oil in large saucepan until onion is tender, about 10 minutes. Add broth and heat to boiling; reduce heat and simmer, covered, 15 minutes.

2. Stir snow peas, water chestnuts, and green onions into grain mixture; simmer, covered, until grains and snow peas are tender and broth absorbed, about 10 minutes. Stir in soy sauce; season to taste with salt and pepper.

SPICY RICE

An aromatic spiced dish of east Indian origins that will complement many meals. The turmeric lends a beautiful yellow color to the rice.

6 servings (about ²/₃ cup each)

1   medium onion, sliced
1   clove garlic, minced
1   tablespoon olive oil
1   cup uncooked basmati, *or* other aromatic, rice
¹/₂   cup plain reduced-fat yogurt
1-2   cardamom pods, crushed
¹/₄   teaspoon ground turmeric
¹/₄   teaspoon ground ginger
¹/₈   teaspoon crushed red pepper
2   cups reduced-sodium vegetable, *or* chicken, broth
Salt and pepper, to taste
1   small tomato, cut into 6 wedges
1   tablespoon finely chopped cilantro

Per Serving
Calories: 166
% Calories from fat: 19
Fat (gm): 3.6
Saturated fat (gm): 0.5
Cholesterol (mg): 1.2
Sodium (mg): 54
Protein (gm): 4.4
Carbohydrate (gm): 27.9
Exchanges
Milk: 0.0
Vegetable: 1.0
Fruit: 0.0
Bread: 1.5
Meat: 0.0
Fat: 0.5

1.   Saute onion and garlic in oil in large saucepan until tender, about 8 minutes. Stir in rice; cook over medium heat, stirring frequently, 5 minutes. Stir in yogurt, herbs, and crushed red pepper; cook over medium-high to high heat 5 minutes, stirring frequently.

2.   Add broth to saucepan and heat to boiling; reduce heat and simmer, covered, until rice is tender, about 25 minutes. Season to taste with salt and pepper.

3.   Spoon rice mixture into serving bowl; arrange tomato wedges on top and sprinkle with cilantro.

YELLOW SALSA RICE

Ground turmeric contributes subtle flavor and attractive yellow color to the rice.

6 servings (about ²/₃ cup each)

1 can (14¹/₂ ounces) reduced-sodium fat-free chicken broth
¹/₃ cup water
¹/₂ teaspoon ground turmeric
1 cup converted rice
¹/₄ cup prepared medium, *or* hot, salsa
1 medium tomato, chopped
Salt and pepper, to taste
Finely chopped cilantro *or* parsley, as garnish

Per Serving
Calories: 126
% Calories from fat: 2
Fat (gm): 0.3
Saturated fat (gm): 0.1
Cholesterol (mg): 0.3
Sodium (mg): 99
Protein (gm): 3.8
Carbohydrate (gm): 26.6
Exchanges
Milk: 0.0
Vegetable: 1.0
Fruit: 0.0
Bread: 1.5
Meat: 0.0
Fat: 0.0

1. Heat chicken broth, water, and turmeric to boiling in medium saucepan; stir in rice and salsa. Reduce heat and simmer, covered, until rice is tender and liquid absorbed, 20 to 25 minutes; stir in tomato during last 5 minutes of cooking time. Season to taste with salt and pepper.

2. Spoon rice into serving bowl; sprinkle with cilantro.

ORANGE CILANTRO RICE

A perfect accompaniment to grilled or roasted lean meats or poultry.

6 servings (about ²/₃ cup each)

Vegetable cooking spray
¹/₂ cup sliced green onions and tops
1 cup converted rice
Grated rind of 1 small orange
2¹/₄ cups water
2 tablespoons finely chopped cilantro
Salt and pepper, to taste

Per Serving
Calories: 118
% Calories from fat: 1
Fat (gm): 0.2
Saturated fat (gm): 0
Cholesterol (mg): 0
Sodium (mg): 2
Protein (gm): 2.3
Carbohydrate (gm): 26
Exchanges
Milk: 0.0
Vegetable: 0.0
Fruit: 0.0
Bread: 1.5
Meat: 0.0
Fat: 0.0

1. Spray medium saucepan with cooking spray; heat over medium heat until hot. Saute green onions until tender, 3 to 5 minutes. Add rice and orange rind to saucepan; cook over medium heat until rice is lightly browned, 2 to 3 minutes, stirring frequently.

2. Add water to saucepan and heat to boiling; reduce heat and simmer, covered, until rice is tender, 20 to 25 minutes. Stir in cilantro; season to taste with salt and pepper.

MEXICAN RED RICE

The tomatoes are pureed in the traditional version of this recipe. We've chosen to chop the tomatoes for enhanced color and flavor.

6 servings (about 2/3 cup each)

Vegetable cooking spray
1 large tomato, chopped
1/2 cup chopped onion
1 clove garlic, minced
1/2 teaspoon dried oregano leaves
1/4 teaspoon ground cumin
1 cup converted rice
1 can (14 1/2 ounces) reduced-sodium fat-free chicken broth
1/3 cup water
1 carrot, cooked, diced
1/2 cup frozen, thawed peas
   Salt and pepper, to taste

Per Serving
Calories: 146
% Calories from fat: 2
Fat (gm): 0.4
Saturated fat (gm): 0.1
Cholesterol (mg): 0
Sodium (mg): 41
Protein (gm): 4.7
Carbohydrate (gm): 30.7
Exchanges
Milk: 0.0
Vegetable: 0.0
Fruit: 0.0
Bread: 2.0
Meat: 0.0
Fat: 0.0

1. Spray large saucepan with cooking spray; heat over medium heat until hot. Saute tomato, onion, garlic, and herbs until onion is tender, 3 to 5 minutes. Add rice; cook over medium heat until rice is lightly browned, 2 to 3 minutes, stirring frequently.

2. Add broth and water to saucepan; heat to boiling. Reduce heat and simmer, covered, until rice is tender, about 25 minutes, adding carrot and peas during last 5 minutes. Season to taste with salt and pepper.

BLACK BEANS AND RICE

Serve this hearty rice with grilled lean meats or poultry, or with stews, such as Beef and Ancho Chili Stew (see p. 124).

6 servings (about ²/₃ cup each)

> Vegetable cooking spray
> ¹/₄ cup chopped onion
> ¹/₄ cup sliced green onions and tops
> 4 cloves garlic, minced
> 1 cup converted rice
> 2¹/₂ cups reduced-sodium fat-free chicken broth
> 1 can (15 ounces) black beans, rinsed, drained
> 2 tablespoons finely chopped cilantro
> Salt and pepper, to taste

Per Serving
Calories: 186
% Calories from fat: 4
Fat (gm): 0.8
Saturated fat (gm): 0.1
Cholesterol (mg): 0
Sodium (mg): 253
Protein (gm): 10.1
Carbohydrate (gm): 38.8
Exchanges
Milk: 0.0
Vegetable: 0.0
Fruit: 0.0
Bread: 2.5
Meat: 0.0
Fat: 0.0

1. Spray medium saucepan with cooking spray; heat over medium heat until hot. Saute onion, green onions, and garlic until tender, about 5 minutes. Add rice; cook over medium heat until rice is lightly browned, 2 to 3 minutes, stirring frequently.

2. Add chicken broth to saucepan and heat to boiling; reduce heat and simmer, covered, until rice is tender, 20 to 25 minutes, adding beans during last 5 minutes. Stir in cilantro; season to taste with salt and pepper.

ITALIAN RICE SALAD

This hearty rice salad can also be served as a side dish or as part of a salad buffet.

4 servings

1 cup long-grain rice, cooked
4 ounces Italian-style turkey sausage, cooked, drained, crumbled
1 large red, *or* yellow, bell pepper, cubed
1 cup shredded cabbage
8-12 large black olives, pitted, sliced
1/4 cup minced chives *or* thinly sliced green onions
1/2-3/4 cup fat-free Italian salad dressing
Salt and pepper, to taste

Per Serving
Calories: 250
% Calories from fat: 16
Fat (gm): 4.6
Saturated fat (gm): 1.1
Cholesterol (mg): 15.2
Sodium (mg): 675
Protein (gm): 9
Carbohydrate (gm): 42.9
Exchanges
Milk: 0.0
Vegetable: 0.0
Fruit: 0.0
Bread: 2.5
Meat: 1.0
Fat: 0.5

1. Combine all ingredients, except salad dressing, salt, and pepper, in large bowl; pour dressing over and toss. Season to taste with salt and pepper.

WINTER RISOTTO

Arborio rice, a short-grain rice grown in the Arborio region of Italy, can be purchased in Italian groceries and in many supermarkets with ethnic food sections. This rice is especially suited for making risotto, as it cooks to a wonderful creaminess. Other longer-grained rices can be used, but the texture of the risotto will be less creamy.

8 servings (about 2/3 cup each)

Olive oil cooking spray
1 small onion, chopped
3 cloves garlic, minced
1 cup sliced cremini, *or* white, mushrooms
1 teaspoon dried rosemary leaves
1 teaspoon dried thyme leaves
1 1/2 cups arborio rice
6 cups reduced-sodium fat-free chicken broth

Per Serving
Calories: 232
% Calories from fat: 5
Fat (gm): 1.2
Saturated fat (gm): 0.6
Cholesterol (mg): 2
Sodium (mg): 190
Protein (gm): 10.1
Carbohydrate (gm): 43.7
Exchanges
Milk: 0.0
Vegetable: 1.5
Fruit: 0.0
Bread: 2.5
Meat: 0.0
Fat: 0.5

   1 cup halved Brussels sprouts, cooked
     until crisp-tender
   1 cup cubed peeled sweet potato, cooked
     until crisp-tender
 1/4 cup grated Parmesan cheese
     Salt and pepper, to taste
     Parsley, minced, as garnish

1. Spray large saucepan with cooking spray; heat over medium heat until hot. Saute onion and garlic until tender, about 5 minutes. Add mushrooms and herbs; cook until tender, 5 to 7 minutes. Stir in rice; cook over medium heat until rice begins to brown, 2 to 3 minutes, stirring frequently.

2. Heat broth just to boiling in medium saucepan; reduce heat to medium-low to keep broth hot. Add broth to rice mixture, 1/2 cup at a time, stirring constantly until broth is absorbed before adding next 1/2 cup. Continue process until rice is al dente and mixture is creamy, 20 to 25 minutes, adding Brussels sprouts and sweet potato during last 10 minutes of cooking time. Stir in cheese; season to taste with salt and pepper.

3. Serve risotto in bowls; sprinkle with parsley.

SHRIMP AND MUSHROOM RISOTTO

White wine can be substituted for part of the broth in the recipe.

6 servings (about 3/4 cup each)

     Olive oil cooking spray
   1 small onion, chopped
   3 cloves garlic, minced
   2 cups sliced mushrooms
   1 teaspoon dried rosemary leaves
   1 teaspoon dried thyme leaves
1 1/2 cups arborio rice
1 1/2 quarts reduced-sodium chicken broth
   8 ounces peeled, deveined shrimp
 1/4 teaspoon pepper
   2 tablespoons grated Parmesan cheese

Per Serving
Calories: 252
% Calories from fat: 8
Fat (gm): 2.1
Saturated fat (gm): 0.6
Cholesterol (mg): 59.6
Sodium (mg): 172
Protein (gm): 13.4
Carbohydrate (gm): 43.4
Exchanges
Milk: 0.0
Vegetable: 0.5
Fruit: 0.0
Bread: 2.5
Meat: 0.5
Fat: 0.0

1. Spray large saucepan with cooking spray; heat over medium heat until hot. Saute onion and garlic until tender, about 5 minutes. Add mushrooms and herbs; cook until tender, 5 to 7 minutes. Stir in rice; cook over medium heat until rice begins to brown, 2 to 3 minutes, stirring frequently.

2. Heat chicken broth just to boiling in medium saucepan; reduce heat to medium-low to keep broth hot. Add broth to rice mixture, 1/2 cup at a time, stirring constantly until broth is absorbed before adding next 1/2 cup. Continue process until rice is al dente and mixture is creamy, 20 to 25 minutes.

3. Stir shrimp and pepper into mixture during last 10 to 15 minutes of cooking time. Serve in bowls; sprinkle with cheese.

ITALIAN SAUSAGE AND BROCCOLI RISOTTO

This risotto is enhanced with the addition of homemade Italian sausage, made with ground turkey and abundantly seasoned with spices and herbs.

6 servings (about 1 1/2 cups each)

12	ounces ground turkey
1	teaspoon fennel seeds, crushed
1	teaspoon dried sage leaves
1	teaspoon dried thyme leaves
1/2	teaspoon dried oregano leaves
1/4	teaspoon ground allspice
1/8	teaspoon ground mace
1/2	teaspoon salt, optional
1	small onion, chopped
2	cloves garlic, minced
1 1/2	cups arborio rice
1 1/2	quarts reduced-sodium chicken broth
2	cups broccoli florets, steamed
1/2	cup raisins
2	tablespoons grated Parmesan cheese, optional

Per Serving
Calories: 322
% Calories from fat: 16
Fat (gm): 5.6
Saturated fat (gm): 1.3
Cholesterol (mg): 21.1
Sodium (mg): 101
Protein (gm): 14.6
Carbohydrate (gm): 53.4
Exchanges
Milk: 0.0
Vegetable: 1.0
Fruit: 0.5
Bread: 2.5
Meat: 1.0
Fat: 0.5

1. Mix turkey, herbs, spices, and salt; refrigerate 1 to 2 hours. Cook turkey mixture in large saucepan until browned; remove from saucepan and drain. Discard fat from saucepan. Reserve turkey mixture.

2. Add onion and garlic to saucepan; saute until tender, about 5 minutes. Stir in rice; cook over medium heat until rice begins to brown, 2 to 3 minutes, stirring frequently.

3. Heat chicken broth to boiling in medium saucepan; reduce heat to medium-low to keep broth hot. Add broth to rice mixture, 1/2 cup at a time, stirring constantly until broth is absorbed before adding another 1/2 cup. Continue process until rice is al dente, 20 to 25 minutes.

4. Add reserved turkey mixture, broccoli, and raisins to risotto during last 10 minutes of cooking time. Serve in bowls; sprinkle with Parmesan cheese.

SUMMER SQUASH RISOTTO

A perfect risotto for summer, when squash and tomatoes are garden-fresh.

6 servings

1 small zucchini, sliced
1 small yellow squash, sliced
2 teaspoons olive oil
1 small onion, chopped
2 cloves garlic, minced
4 Italian plum tomatoes, cut into fourths
1 teaspoon dried oregano leaves
3/4 cup arborio rice
3 cups reduced-sodium chicken broth
2 tablespoons grated Romano cheese
1/4 teaspoon pepper

Per Serving
Calories: 152
% Calories from fat: 18
Fat (gm): 3.1
Saturated fat (gm): 0.7
Cholesterol (mg): 2.4
Sodium (mg): 70
Protein (gm): 4.8
Carbohydrate (gm): 27
Exchanges
Milk: 0.0
Vegetable: 1.0
Fruit: 0.0
Bread: 1.5
Meat: 0.0
Fat: 0.5

1. Saute zucchini and yellow squash in oil in large saucepan until crisp-tender, 5 to 7 minutes; remove from saucepan and reserve.

2. Add onion and garlic to saucepan; saute until tender, about 5 minutes. Add tomatoes and oregano; cook until tomatoes are soft, about 3 minutes. Add rice; cook over medium heat until rice begins to brown, 2 to 3 minutes.

3. Heat chicken broth to boiling in small saucepan; reduce heat to medium-low to keep broth hot. Add broth to rice mixture, $1/2$ cup at a time, stirring constantly until broth is absorbed before adding another $1/2$ cup. Continue process until rice is al dente, 20 to 25 minutes.

4. Add reserved squash to risotto during last few minutes of cooking time. Stir in Romano cheese and pepper.

ALL-SEASON RISOTTO

A blending of summer and winter squash provides color and flavor to this creamy risotto dish. If preferred, the reserved vegetable mixture can be heated and served to the side rather than mixing it into the risotto.

6 servings (about $2/3$ cup each)

1 cup peeled, cubed winter yellow squash (acorn, butternut, Hubbard, etc.)

1 small zucchini, sliced

$3/4$ cup sliced cremini, *or* white, mushrooms

1 small red bell pepper, chopped

3 plum tomatoes, cut into fourths

1 teaspoon dried oregano leaves

2 tablespoons olive oil *or* vegetable oil, divided

$1/2$ cup chopped onion

1 clove garlic, minced

$3/4$ cup arborio rice

1 can ($14^{1}/2$ ounces each) reduced-sodium vegetable, *or* chicken, broth

1 cup water

2 tablespoons grated fat-free Parmesan cheese

$3/4$ cup canned black beans, rinsed, drained

$1/4$ cup frozen peas, thawed

Salt and pepper, to taste

Per Serving
Calories: 196
% Calories from fat: 13
Fat (gm): 3.1
Saturated fat (gm): 0.4
Cholesterol (mg): 0
Sodium (mg): 164
Protein (gm): 7.4
Carbohydrate (gm): 38
Exchanges
Milk: 0.0
Vegetable: 1.0
Fruit: 0.0
Bread: 2.0
Meat: 0.0
Fat: 0.5

1. Saute squash, mushrooms, bell pepper, tomatoes, and oregano in 1 tablespoon oil in large skillet until tender; remove from heat and reserve.

2. Heat remaining 1 tablespoon oil until hot in large saucepan; add onion and garlic and saute until tender, 3 to 4 minutes. Add rice; cook 2 to 3 minutes, stirring occasionally.

3. Heat broth and water to simmering in medium saucepan; reduce heat to low and keep warm. Add broth to rice mixture, $1/2$ cup at a time, stirring constantly until broth is absorbed before adding next $1/2$ cup. Continue process until rice is al dente and mixture is creamy, 20 to 25 minutes.

4. Stir cheese, beans, and peas into rice mixture. Stir in reserved vegetables and heat until hot. Season to taste with salt and pepper. Serve with additional grated cheese if desired.

PORCINI RISOTTO

Use dried shiitake, or Chinese black, mushrooms if the porcini are not available.

8 servings (about $1/2$ cup each)

$1/4$-$1/2$ ounce dried porcini mushrooms
    Olive oil cooking spray
  1 small onion, chopped
  3 cloves garlic, minced
  1 small tomato, seeded, chopped
  1 teaspoon dried sage leaves
$1/4$ teaspoon dried thyme leaves
$1^{1}/2$ cups arborio rice
$1^{1}/2$ quarts reduced-sodium vegetable, *or* chicken, broth
$1/4$ cup grated Parmesan cheese
    Salt and pepper, to taste
  2 tablespoons pine nuts *or* slivered almonds, toasted
  2 tablespoons finely chopped fresh sage *or* parsley

Per Serving
Calories: 195
% Calories from fat: 13
Fat (gm): 3.0
Saturated fat (gm): 1.0
Cholesterol (mg): 2.5
Sodium (mg): 68
Protein (gm): 5.1
Carbohydrate (gm): 34
Exchanges
Milk: 0.0
Vegetable: 1.0
Fruit: 0.0
Bread: 2.0
Meat: 0.0
Fat: 0.5

1. Place mushrooms in bowl; pour hot water over to cover. Let stand until mushrooms are soft, about 15 minutes; drain, reserving liquid. Slice mushrooms, discarding any tough parts.

2. Spray large saucepan with cooking spray; heat over medium heat until hot. Saute mushrooms, onion, and garlic until tender, about 5 minutes. Stir in tomato, sage, and thyme; cook 2 to 3 minutes more. Stir in rice. Cook over medium heat until rice begins to brown, 2 to 3 minutes, stirring frequently.

3. Heat broth and reserved porcini liquid to boiling in medium saucepan; reduce heat to medium-low to keep broth hot. Add broth to rice mixture, 1/2 cup at a time, stirring constantly until broth is absorbed before adding another 1/2 cup. Continue process until rice is al dente and mixture is creamy, 20 to 25 minutes. Stir in cheese; season to taste with salt and pepper.

4. Serve risotto in bowls; sprinkle with pine nuts and sage.

TWO-CHEESE RISOTTO

This flavorful risotto is quickly prepared with a simplified method that requires little stirring. Serve with a salad and steamed green vegetable for a simple but elegant meal.

4 servings (about 1 cup each)

Vegetable cooking spray
1/2 cup finely chopped onion
1 cup arborio rice
2 1/2 cups reduced-sodium vegetable broth
1/2 cup dry white wine
1 cup (4 ounces) shredded Parmesan cheese
1/4-1/2 cup (1-2 ounces) crumbled blue cheese
2-3 tablespoons chopped chives *or* Italian parsley
Salt and pepper, to taste

Per Serving
Calories: 383
% Calories from fat: 26
Fat (gm): 10.9
Saturated fat (gm): 6.8
Cholesterol (mg): 27.7
Sodium (mg): 681
Protein (gm): 17.4
Carbohydrate (gm): 47.6
Exchanges
Milk: 0.0
Vegetable: 0.0
Fruit: 0.0
Bread: 3.0
Meat: 1.0
Fat: 2.5

1. Spray large saucepan with cooking spray; heat over medium heat until hot. Add onion and saute until tender, 3 to 4 minutes. Add rice to saucepan; cook over medium heat until beginning to brown, 3 to 4 minutes.

2. Add vegetable broth and wine to saucepan; heat to boiling. Reduce heat and simmer, covered, until rice is tender and liquid absorbed, 25 to 30 minutes, stirring occasionally. Remove from heat; stir in cheeses and chives. Season to taste with salt and pepper.

RISI BISI

Opinions vary as to whether Risi Bisi is a risotto or a thick soup. If you agree with the latter definition, use an additional ¹/₂ to ₁ cup of broth to make the mixture a thick soup consistency.

8 servings (about ¹/₂ cup each)

Olive oil cooking spray
1 small onion, chopped
3 cloves garlic, minced
1¹/₂ cups arborio rice
2 teaspoons dried basil leaves
1¹/₂ quarts reduced-sodium chicken broth
8 ounces frozen, thawed tiny peas
¹/₄ cup grated Parmesan cheese
Salt and pepper, to taste

Per Serving
Calories: 192
% Calories from fat: **9**
Fat (gm): **1.8**
Saturated fat (gm): **0.7**
Cholesterol (mg): **2.5**
Sodium (mg): **132**
Protein (gm): **7.1**
Carbohydrate (gm): **35.8**
Exchanges
Milk: 0.0
Vegetable: 0.5
Fruit: 0.0
Bread: 2.5
Meat: 0.0
Fat: 0.0

1. Spray large saucepan with cooking spray; heat over medium heat until hot. Saute onion and garlic until tender, about 5 minutes. Stir in rice and basil. Cook over medium heat until rice begins to brown, 2 to 3 minutes, stirring frequently.

2. Heat chicken broth to boiling in medium saucepan; reduce heat to medium-low to keep broth hot. Add broth to rice mixture, ¹/₂ cup at a time, stirring constantly until broth is absorbed before adding another ¹/₂ cup. Continue process until rice is al dente and mixture is creamy, 20 to 25 minutes.

3. Stir peas into risotto during last 10 minutes of cooking time. Stir in Parmesan cheese; season to taste with salt and pepper.

MICROWAVE RISOTTO

This is the easiest possible way to make risotto. Use of the microwave eliminates the constant stirring usually required for this dish.

4 servings

1 cup arborio rice
3¹/3 cups reduced-sodium fat-free chicken broth, divided
¹/4 teaspoon white pepper
¹/3 cup grated Parmesan cheese

Per Serving
Calories: 235
% Calories from fat: 9
Fat (gm): 2.3
Saturated fat (gm): 1.3
Cholesterol (mg): 2.5
Sodium (mg): 266
Protein (gm): 11
Carbohydrate (gm): 39.9
Exchanges
Milk: 0.0
Vegetable: 0.0
Fruit: 0.0
Bread: 2.5
Meat: 1.0
Fat: 0.0

1. Combine rice and 3 tablespoons broth in 3-quart microwave-safe casserole. Microwave, uncovered, on high power 60 seconds; stir well. Add remaining broth and white pepper and stir well. Microwave on high power, covered, 9 minutes; stir well.

2. Microwave on high power, uncovered, 12 to 15 minutes until rice is tender but still al dente. Let stand 2 to 3 minutes for rice to absorb any remaining liquid. Stir in Parmesan cheese.

CHEESE AND ARTICHOKE RISOTTO PANCAKES

A perfect recipe for using leftover risotto. Top each serving with a poached or fried egg for a hearty brunch or light supper.

4 servings

Vegetable cooking spray
¹/2 cup chopped onion
1 cup arborio rice
2¹/2 cups reduced-sodium vegetable broth
¹/2 cup dry white wine
³/4 cup (3 ounces) shredded Parmesan cheese
¹/4-¹/2 cup (1-2 ounces) crumbled blue cheese
4 egg whites *or* ¹/2 cup no-cholesterol real egg product

Per Serving
Calories: 392
% Calories from fat: 21
Fat (gm): 8.7
Saturated fat (gm): 5.5
Cholesterol (mg): 22.1
Sodium (mg): 764
Protein (gm): 18.9
Carbohydrate (gm): 51.1
Exchanges
Milk: 0.0
Vegetable: 1.0
Fruit: 0.0
Bread: 3.0
Meat: 2.0
Fat: 1.0

6 canned artichoke hearts, coarsely
chopped
1/4 cup coarsely chopped roasted red
pepper
Salt and pepper, to taste
Finely chopped parsley, as garnish

1. Spray large saucepan with cooking spray; heat over medium heat until hot. Add onion and saute 2 minutes. Add rice to saucepan; cook over medium heat until beginning to brown, 3 to 4 minutes.

2. Add vegetable broth and wine to saucepan; heat to boiling. Reduce heat and simmer, covered, until rice is tender and liquid absorbed, 20 to 25 minutes, stirring occasionally. Remove from heat; stir in cheeses, egg whites, artichoke hearts, and red pepper. Season to taste with salt and pepper.

3. Spray two 10-inch skillets generously with cooking spray; heat over medium heat until hot. Spoon half the risotto mixture into each skillet, shaping into large pancakes. Cook over medium heat until lightly browned on the bottoms, 5 to 8 minutes. Invert pancakes onto plates; slide back into skillets and cook until lightly browned on the bottoms, 5 to 8 minutes. Cut pancakes in half; slide onto serving plates and sprinkle with parsley.

RISOTTO-VEGETABLE CAKES

This makes a perfect side dish with any grilled meat or fish.

8 servings

Olive oil cooking spray
1 medium onion, finely chopped
2 cloves garlic, minced
2 teaspoons dried oregano leaves, divided
1 cup arborio rice
4 cups reduced-sodium vegetable, *or* chicken, broth
1/4 cup (1 ounce) shredded reduced-fat Cheddar, *or* Monterey Jack, cheese
5 tablespoons grated fat-free Parmesan cheese, divided
1 medium zucchini, chopped

Per Serving
Calories: 208
% Calories from fat: 9
Fat (gm): 2.1
Saturated fat (gm): 0.5
Cholesterol (mg): 1.9
Sodium (mg): 307
Protein (gm): 8.5
Carbohydrate (gm): 43.8
Exchanges
Milk: 0.0
Vegetable: 2.0
Fruit: 0.0
Bread: 2.0
Meat: 0.0
Fat: 0.0

2 medium carrots, chopped
1 medium red bell pepper, chopped
1/2 cup chopped celery
2 egg whites
2/3 cup Italian-seasoned bread crumbs
8 beefsteak tomatoes, sliced 1/2 inch thick
Salt and pepper, to taste

1. Spray medium saucepan with cooking spray; heat over medium heat until hot. Saute onion, garlic, and 1 teaspoon oregano until tender, about 3 minutes. Add rice; cook 2 to 3 minutes.

2. Heat broth to simmering in medium saucepan; reduce heat to low to keep broth warm. Add broth to rice mixture, 1/2 cup at a time, stirring constantly until broth is absorbed before adding next 1/2 cup. Continue process until rice is al dente and mixture is creamy, 20 to 25 minutes. Stir in Cheddar cheese and 4 tablespoons Parmesan cheese. Cool to room temperature.

3. Spray large skillet with cooking spray; heat over medium heat until hot. Saute zucchini, carrots, bell pepper, and celery until tender, 5 to 8 minutes. Stir vegetables, egg whites, and bread crumbs into rice mixture.

4. Form rice mixture into 8 patties, each a scant 3/4 inch thick. Broil on lightly greased broiler pan, 6 inches from heat source, until browned, 2 to 4 minutes each side. Top each patty with tomato slice; sprinkle with remaining 1 teaspoon oregano and remaining 1 tablespoon Parmesan cheese. Sprinkle lightly with salt and pepper. Broil until browned on top, 2 to 3 minutes.

TEN

45-Minute
Entrées

HEARTY CORN AND POTATO CHOWDER

Cut corn fresh from the cob for this soup, or for convenience, use frozen, thawed whole-kernel corn.

6 servings (about 1¹/₃ cups each)

2 cups fresh, *or* frozen, thawed whole-kernel corn

1 medium onion, chopped

1 tablespoon vegetable oil

2 cups reduced-sodium fat-free chicken broth

2 cups cubed unpeeled Idaho potatoes

¹/₂ cup sliced celery

¹/₂ teaspoon dried thyme leaves

1³/₄ cups fat-free half-and-half *or* fat-free milk

Salt and pepper, to taste

Finely chopped parsley and chives, as garnishes

Per Serving
Calories: 201
% Calories from fat: 11
Fat (gm): 2.6
Saturated fat (gm): 0.4
Cholesterol (mg): 0
Sodium (mg): 143
Protein (gm): 7.8
Carbohydrate (gm): 36.2
Exchanges
Milk: 0.0
Vegetable: 0.0
Fruit: 0.0
Bread: 2.5
Meat: 0.0
Fat: 0.5

1. Saute corn and onion in oil in large saucepan until onion is tender, 5 to 8 minutes. Process ¹/₂ the vegetable mixture and the broth in food processor or blender until finely chopped, using pulse technique. Return mixture to saucepan.

2. Add potatoes, celery, and thyme to saucepan; heat to boiling. Reduce heat and simmer, covered, until vegetables are tender, 10 to 15 minutes. Stir in half-and-half; cook until hot, 2 to 3 minutes. Season to taste with salt and pepper.

3. Pour soup into bowls; sprinkle with parsley and chives.

Note: If a thicker soup is desired, mix 2 to 3 tablespoons flour with ¹/₃ cup water. Heat soup to boiling; stir in flour mixture and boil, stirring constantly, until thickened, about 1 minute.

FLORIDA AVOCADO AND TOMATO CHOWDER

In this easy recipe, corn, tomatoes, avocado, and smoked turkey create a kaleidoscope of fresh colors and flavors. Bacon, lime, and thyme complete the sensory experience.

4 servings

3 large potatoes, peeled, cut into ¹/₂-inch cubes

1 can (14 ounces) reduced-sodium fat-free chicken broth

1 teaspoon ground thyme

¹/₂ pound smoked turkey breast, cut into ¹/₂-inch cubes

1 cup frozen corn

4 plum tomatoes, coarsely chopped

1 avocado, peeled, cut into ¹/₂-inch cubes

Juice of 1 lime

3 slices bacon, cooked, crumbled

Salt and pepper, to taste

Per Serving
Calories: 333
% Calories from fat: 26
Fat (gm): 10.2
Saturated fat (gm): 2.4
Cholesterol (mg): 51.1
Sodium (mg): 765
Protein (gm): 21
Carbohydrate (gm): 44.7
Exchanges
Milk: 0.0
Vegetable: 2.0
Fruit: 0.0
Bread: 2.0
Meat: 2.0
Fat: 1.5

1. Heat potatoes, broth, and thyme to boiling in medium saucepan; reduce heat and simmer, covered, until potatoes are tender, about 15 minutes. Using slotted spoon, transfer ¹/₂ the potatoes to a medium bowl.

2. Process remaining broth mixture in food processor or blender until smooth; return to saucepan. Add turkey, corn, and reserved potatoes. Heat to boiling; reduce heat and simmer 5 minutes. Stir in tomatoes, avocado, lime juice, and bacon. Season to taste with salt and pepper.

MEATBALL SOUP

*A great favorite in Mexico, this soup is traditionally seasoned with mint;
we've offered oregano as an addition or alternative, if you like.*

4 servings

Vegetable cooking spray
1/4 cup chopped onion
2 cloves garlic, minced
1 small jalapeño chili, seeds and veins
   discarded, minced
1 tablespoon flour
2 cups reduced-sodium tomato juice
2 cups water
2 cans (14 1/2 ounces each) reduced-
   sodium fat-free chicken broth
3 medium carrots, sliced
2 medium zucchini, sliced
1/2 teaspoon dried mint leaves *and/or* 1 1/2-2
   teaspoons dried oregano leaves
   Meatballs (recipe follows)
   Salt and pepper, to taste

Per Serving
Calories: 227
% Calories from fat: 16
Fat (gm): 4.1
Saturated fat (gm): 1.4
Cholesterol (mg): 54.7
Sodium (mg): 426
Protein (gm): 28
Carbohydrate (gm): 20.2
Exchanges
Milk: 0.0
Vegetable: 3.0
Fruit: 0.0
Bread: 0.0
Meat: 3.0
Fat: 0.0

1. Spray large saucepan with cooking spray; heat over medium
heat until hot. Saute onion, garlic, and jalapeño chili until tender, about 5 minutes. Stir in flour; cook over medium heat 1 to 2
minutes.

2. Add tomato juice, water, chicken broth, carrots, zucchini,
and mint to saucepan; heat to boiling. Add Meatballs; reduce
heat and simmer, covered, until vegetables are tender and Meatballs are cooked, 10 to 15 minutes. Season to taste with salt and
pepper. Serve in bowls.

Meatballs

makes 24

1 pound ground beef eye of round
1/4 cup cooked rice
1/3 cup finely chopped onion
1 clove garlic, minced

1/2 teaspoon dried mint leaves
1/4 teaspoon dried oregano leaves
1/4 teaspoon ground cumin
1/2 teaspoon salt
1/4 teaspoon pepper

1. Mix all ingredients; form into 24 small meatballs. Refrigerate, covered, until ready to cook (no longer than 8 hours).

BOURBON STREET RED BEANS AND RICE

Our low-fat version of a New Orleans favorite!

6 servings (about 3/4 cup each)

5	ounces low-fat smoked sausage, sliced
1	cup chopped onion
1	cup chopped green bell peppers
1	cup chopped celery
1/2-1	jalapeño chili, finely chopped
1	tablespoon vegetable oil
2	cans (15 ounces each) red beans, rinsed, drained
3/4	cup reduced-sodium vegetable, *or* chicken, broth
1 1/2	teaspoons dried thyme leaves
1	teaspoon dried oregano leaves
1/2	teaspoon dried sage leaves
1/4-1/2	teaspoon ground cumin
1/4-1/2	teaspoon hot pepper sauce
4-6	drops liquid smoke, optional
	Salt, to taste
3	cups cooked rice, warm

Per Serving
Calories: 305
% Calories from fat: 12
Fat (gm): 4.1
Saturated fat (gm): 0.8
Cholesterol (mg): 11
Sodium (mg): 521
Protein (gm): 14
Carbohydrate (gm): 60
Exchanges
Milk: 0.0
Vegetable: 2.0
Fruit: 0.0
Bread: 2.5
Meat: 0.5
Fat: 0.5

1. Saute sausage, onion, bell peppers, celery, and jalapeño chili in oil in large saucepan 8 minutes. Add beans, broth, and herbs, and cook, covered, over medium heat 10 minutes. Simmer, uncovered, until thickened, 5 to 10 minutes.

2. Stir red pepper sauce and liquid smoke into beans; season to taste with salt. Serve bean mixture over rice in shallow bowls.

BLACK BEAN AND OKRA GUMBO

Lightly spiked with chili powder, the gumbo is delicious served over corn bread.

8 servings (about 1¹/₃ cups each)

Vegetable cooking spray
8-12 ounces reduced-sodium smoked turkey sausage, sliced
2 cups coarsely chopped onions
2 cups sliced carrots
1 cup chopped green bell pepper
1 cup chopped red bell pepper
4 teaspoons chili powder
1 teaspoon gumbo file powder
3 cups reduced-sodium fat-free chicken broth
2 cans (15¹/₂ ounces each) black beans, rinsed, drained
2 cups fresh, *or* frozen, cut okra
Salt and pepper, to taste
5 cups cooked rice, warm

Per Serving
Calories: 288
% Calories from fat: 11
Fat (gm): 4.1
Saturated fat (gm): 0.9
Cholesterol (mg): 17.7
Sodium (mg): 713
Protein (gm): 15.4
Carbohydrate (gm): 56.8
Exchanges
Milk: 0.0
Vegetable: 2.0
Fruit: 0.0
Bread: 3.0
Meat: 0.0
Fat: 0.5

1. Spray large skillet with cooking spray; heat over medium heat until hot. Add sausage, onions, carrots, and bell peppers and cook, covered, over medium heat until lightly browned, 5 to 8 minutes. Stir in chili powder and file powder; cook 2 to 3 minutes.

2. Add broth, beans, and okra; heat to boiling. Reduce heat and simmer, uncovered, until vegetables are tender and broth thickened, 8 to 10 minutes. Season to taste with salt and pepper.

3. Serve stew over rice in shallow bowls.

SPICED BEAN CHILI WITH FUSILLI

Use any favorite beans or shaped pasta in this versatile chili.

8 servings (about 1¼ cups each)

1 pound lean ground beef
2 cups chopped onions
½ cup sliced celery
1 cup sliced mushrooms
1-2 tablespoons vegetable oil
2 cans (14½ ounces each) diced tomatoes with roasted garlic
1 can (15½ ounces) garbanzo beans, rinsed, drained
1 can (15 ounces) dark red kidney beans, rinsed, drained
1-2 tablespoons chili powder
1-2 teaspoons ground cumin
¾ teaspoon dried oregano leaves
8 ounces fusilli, cooked, warm
  Salt and pepper, to taste
3-4 tablespoons sliced green, *or* ripe, olives, optional

Per Serving
Calories: 367
% Calories from fat: 26
Fat (gm): 10.6
Saturated fat (gm): 3.2
Cholesterol (mg): 35.2
Sodium (mg): 759
Protein (gm): 21.3
Carbohydrate (gm): 47.3
Exchanges
Milk: 0.0
Vegetable: 1.0
Fruit: 0.0
Bread: 3.0
Meat: 1.0
Fat: 1.5

1. Cook ground beef, onions, celery, and mushrooms in oil in large saucepan until beef is browned, about 8 minutes; drain well. Add tomatoes, beans, chili powder, and herbs. Heat to boiling. Reduce heat and simmer, covered, until vegetables are tender, about 10 minutes.

2. Stir in pasta. Season to taste with salt and pepper. Serve stew in bowls; sprinkle with olives.

YELLOW SQUASH AND WHITE BEAN CHILI

Add a minced jalapeño chili, if you like your chili hot!

4 servings (about 1¹/₂ cups each)

1 pound lean ground pork
2 cups chopped onions
1 cup chopped yellow bell pepper
2 teaspoons minced garlic
2 teaspoons cumin seeds
1-2 tablespoons olive oil
1 medium yellow summer squash, cubed
2 cans (15 ounces each) Great Northern beans, rinsed, drained
2 cups reduced-sodium fat-free chicken broth
¹/₂ cup dry white wine, optional
1 teaspoon dried oregano leaves
¹/₂ teaspoon ground cinnamon
2 teaspoons chili powder
Salt and pepper, to taste
Finely chopped tomato and cilantro, as garnishes

Per Serving
Calories: 350
% Calories from fat: 23
Fat (gm): 10
Saturated fat (gm): 2.7
Cholesterol (mg): 49.3
Sodium (mg): 719
Protein (gm): 32.7
Carbohydrate (gm): 41.2
Exchanges
Milk: 0.0
Vegetable: 2.0
Fruit: 0.0
Bread: 2.0
Meat: 3.0
Fat: 0.0

1. Cook pork over medium heat in medium skillet until browned, about 10 minutes; drain well.

2. Saute onions, bell pepper, garlic, and cumin seeds in oil in large saucepan 5 minutes. Add pork and remaining ingredients, except salt, pepper, and garnishes, to saucepan; heat to boiling. Reduce heat and simmer, covered, until vegetables are tender, about 15 minutes. Simmer, uncovered, until thickened, 5 to 10 minutes. Season to taste with salt and pepper.

3. Serve chili in bowls; sprinkle with tomato and cilantro.

SWEET POTATO CHIPOTLE CHILI

Chipotle chilies are dried smoked jalapeño chilies. They are often canned in adobo sauce, which is made with ground chilies and spices. They add a distinctive smoky flavor to this robust chili; taste before adding a second chili, as they can be fiercely hot in flavor!

6 servings (about 1 cup each)

2 cups frozen stir-fry pepper blend
1 teaspoon minced garlic
1-2 teaspoons minced gingerroot
1 teaspoon cumin seeds
1-2 tablespoons peanut, *or* vegetable, oil
3 cups cubed, peeled sweet potatoes ($1/2$-inch)
1 can ($14^1/2$ ounces) reduced-sodium diced tomatoes, undrained
2 cans (15 ounces each) black beans, rinsed, drained
1-2 chipotle chilies in adobo sauce, chopped
1 cup water *or* vegetable broth
2-3 teaspoons chili powder
$1/2$-1 teaspoon ground cumin
Salt, to taste

Per Serving
Calories: 213
% Calories from fat: 13
Fat (gm): 3.9
Saturated fat (gm): 0.5
Cholesterol (mg): 0
Sodium (mg): 521
Protein (gm): 8.3
Carbohydrate (gm): 48.6
Exchanges
Milk: 0.0
Vegetable: 1.5
Fruit: 0.0
Bread: 2.0
Meat: 0.0
Fat: 1.0

1. Saute pepper blend, garlic, gingerroot, and cumin seeds in oil in large saucepan until tender, about 5 minutes.

2. Add remaining ingredients, except salt, to saucepan; heat to boiling. Reduce heat and simmer, covered, until potatoes are tender, about 15 minutes. Season to taste with salt.

SCOTCH BONNET CHILI

A true "hot-heads" delight, this chili gets its firepower from the redoubt-able habanero chili, often called the Scotch bonnet. Substitute jalapeño chili for a milder flavor.

4 servings

1 large onion, chopped
1 medium green bell pepper, chopped
1 habanero chili, chopped
1/4 pound smoked turkey sausage, halved lengthwise, sliced
1 teaspoon olive oil
1 can (14 1/2 ounces) reduced-sodium whole tomatoes, undrained, cut up
2 cups refried beans
1 tablespoon chili powder
1 teaspoon ground cumin
  Salt, to taste
1 cup fat-free sour cream

Per Serving
Calories: 293
% Calories from fat: 18
Fat (gm): 5.9
Saturated fat (gm): 1
Cholesterol (mg): 25.6
Sodium (mg): 767
Protein (gm): 17.1
Carbohydrate (gm): 43.8
Exchanges
Milk: 0.0
Vegetable: 0.0
Fruit: 0.0
Bread: 3.0
Meat: 1.0
Fat: 0.5

1. Saute onion, bell pepper, habanero chili, and sausage in oil in large saucepan until onions are tender. Stir in tomatoes and liquid, beans, chili powder, and cumin. Heat to boiling; reduce heat and simmer, uncovered, until slightly thickened, about 15 minutes. Season to taste with salt. Ladle into bowls; top with sour cream.

PRAIRIE CHILI WITH CHICKEN

Few dishes have snappier flavor or are simpler to prepare than this six-minute chili. Sporting ancho chilies and a mild picante sauce, it ranks low on the Scoville heat scale. Looking for a fiery punch? Just double the red pepper and use hot picante sauce.

4 servings

12 ounces cooked chicken breast, shredded

1 can (14 ounces) reduced-sodium stewed tomatoes, undrained

1 can (15^1/$_2$ ounces) pinto beans, rinsed, drained

^{3}/$_4$ cup mild picante sauce

2 ancho chiles, softened, chopped

2 tablespoons dried onion flakes

^{1}/$_2$ teaspoon crushed red pepper

1 teaspoon paprika

1 teaspoon dried parsley

1 cup fresh, *or* canned, rinsed, drained, bean sprouts

Salt, to taste

Per Serving
Calories: 352
% Calories from fat: 29
Fat (gm): 11.5
Saturated fat (gm): 2.9
Cholesterol (mg): 70.5
Sodium (mg): 689
Protein (gm): 34.2
Carbohydrate (gm): 28.8
Exchanges
Milk: 0.0
Vegetable: 3.0
Fruit: 0.0
Bread: 1.0
Meat: 4.0
Fat: 0.0

1. Combine all ingredients except parsley, bean sprouts, and salt, in large saucepan. Heat to boiling; reduce heat and simmer, covered, 5 minutes. Add parsley and bean sprouts. Season to taste with salt.

SOUTHERN STEWED BLACK-EYED PEAS, CHICKPEAS, AND HAM

A hearty stew that can be made in 20 minutes with pantry staples. Serve with warm biscuits or cornbread.

6 servings (about 1¹/₄ cups each)

10	ounces reduced-sodium ham, cubed
1¹/₂	cups chopped onions
1	teaspoon minced garlic
1	tablespoon olive oil
1	can (28 ounces) reduced-sodium diced tomatoes, undrained
1	can (15¹/₂ ounces) chickpeas, rinsed, drained
1	can (15¹/₂ ounces) black-eyed peas, rinsed, drained
1	package (10 ounces) frozen spinach
2	cups fresh, *or* frozen, okra, cut into 1-inch pieces
1	teaspoon dried marjoram leaves
³/₄	teaspoon dried thyme leaves
¹/₄	teaspoon hot pepper sauce
	Salt and pepper, to taste

Per Serving
Calories: 282
% Calories from fat: 16
Fat (gm): 5.2
Saturated fat (gm): 1
Cholesterol (mg): 21.9
Sodium (mg): 776
Protein (gm): 18.9
Carbohydrate (gm): 42.8
Exchanges
Milk: 0.0
Vegetable: 3.0
Fruit: 0.0
Bread: 2.0
Meat: 1.0
Fat: 0.0

1. Saute ham, onions, and garlic in oil in large saucepan until onions are tender, about 5 minutes. Stir in remaining ingredients, except salt and pepper; heat to boiling. Reduce heat and simmer, covered, until okra is tender, about 10 minutes. Season to taste with salt and pepper.

CREAMY FETTUCCINE PRIMAVERA

The sauce for this dish should be somewhat thin, as it thickens once it is removed from the heat. Purchase your mushrooms and broccoflower already cut to minimize preparation time.

4 servings

Vegetable cooking spray
2 cups sliced mushrooms
2 cups broccoflower, *or* cauliflower, florets
1/2 cup chopped red, *or* green, bell pepper
1/2 cup water
1 package (8 ounces) fat-free cream cheese
2/3-1 cup fat-free milk, divided
1/4 cup sliced green onions and tops
1/2 teaspoon Italian seasoning
2 tablespoons grated Parmesan cheese
Salt and white pepper, to taste
8 ounces fettuccine *or* linguine, cooked, warm

Per Serving
Calories: 270
% Calories from fat: 13
Fat (gm): 4
Saturated fat (gm): 1.1
Cholesterol (mg): 17.2
Sodium (mg): 401
Protein (gm): 19
Carbohydrate (gm): 41.4
Exchanges
Milk: 0.0
Vegetable: 2.0
Fruit: 0.0
Bread: 2.0
Meat: 1.0
Fat: 0.5

1. Spray large skillet with cooking spray; heat over medium heat until hot. Saute mushrooms, broccoflower, and bell pepper 3 to 4 minutes. Add water and heat to boiling. Reduce heat and simmer, covered, until broccoflower is tender and water absorbed, about 8 minutes.

2. Heat cream cheese, 2/3 cup milk, green onions, and Italian seasoning in small saucepan over low heat until cream cheese is melted, stirring frequently. Stir in Parmesan cheese and enough remaining milk to make a thin consistency (sauce will thicken when removed from heat). Season to taste with salt and pepper. Pour sauce over fettuccine in serving bowl and toss; add vegetable mixture and toss gently.

ANGEL HAIR WITH VEGETABLES AND GOAT CHEESE

Goat cheese adds a creamy texture and piquant accent to this flavorful pasta dish.

6 servings

Vegetable cooking spray

8	ounces snow peas
8	ounces mushrooms, sliced
3	medium carrots, julienned
4	large plum tomatoes, sliced
2	teaspoons dried oregano leaves
1	teaspoon dried tarragon leaves
1/2	cup reduced-sodium chicken broth
1/2	cup fat-free milk
2	teaspoons tomato paste
1/4	teaspoon salt
1/4	teaspoon pepper
3	ounces goat cheese *or* reduced-fat cream cheese
12	ounces capellini (angel hair) *or* thin spaghetti, cooked, warm

Per Serving
Calories: 293
% Calories from fat: 13
Fat (gm): 4.3
Saturated fat (gm): 2.5
Cholesterol (mg): 12.9
Sodium (mg): 190
Protein (gm): 13.2
Carbohydrate (gm): 50.7
Exchanges
Milk: 0.0
Vegetable: 2.5
Fruit: 0.0
Bread: 2.5
Meat: 0.0
Fat: 0.5

1. Spray large skillet with cooking spray; heat over medium heat until hot. Saute vegetables until snow peas are crisp-tender, 6 to 8 minutes. Stir in herbs; cook 1 minute.

2. Stir in chicken broth, milk, and tomato paste; heat to boiling. Reduce heat and simmer, uncovered, until thickened to sauce consistency, about 10 minutes, stirring occasionally. Stir in salt and pepper.

3. Stir goat cheese into warm pasta until melted; add vegetable mixture and toss.

PASTA WITH OYSTER MUSHROOMS

A wide variety of wild or exotic mushrooms are now readily available in supermarkets: oyster, shiitake, enoki, cremini, morel, portobello, etc. Although this recipe specifies oyster mushrooms, feel free to substitute any other type.

6 servings

16 ounces oyster mushrooms

1-2 tablespoons minced garlic

4 tablespoons margarine

2 tablespoons flour

2 cups fat-free milk

1/2 cup reduced-sodium chicken, *or* vegetable, broth

2 teaspoons lemon juice

1 cup chopped, seeded tomato

1/2 teaspoon salt

1/2 teaspoon pepper

12 ounces fettuccine, cooked, warm

2 tablespoons grated Parmesan cheese

Per Serving
Calories: 328
% Calories from fat: 30
Fat (gm): 11.0
Saturated fat (gm): 2
Cholesterol (mg): 3.0
Sodium (mg): 454
Protein (gm): 15.0
Carbohydrate (gm): 44.4
Exchanges
Milk: 0.0
Vegetable: 3.0
Fruit: 0.0
Bread: 2.0
Meat: 0.0
Fat: 2.0

1. Separate oyster mushrooms into pieces. Saute mushrooms and garlic in margarine in large skillet until soft, about 5 minutes. Stir in flour; cook 1 minute.

2. Add milk, broth, and lemon juice to skillet; heat to boiling. Reduce heat and simmer, uncovered, until liquid is reduced by half. Stir in tomato, salt, and pepper; cook over medium heat until hot. Spoon sauce over pasta; sprinkle with Parmesan cheese.

SHRIMP WITH ARTICHOKES AND PEPPERS

This skillet supper is quick, easy, and brimming with flavor.

6 servings

2 cups frozen stir-fry pepper blend
1 teaspoon minced garlic
1 tablespoon olive oil
1 can (15 ounces) reduced-sodium chunky tomato sauce
1 can (14 ounces) artichoke hearts, drained, quartered
3 tablespoons dry sherry *or* chicken broth
2 teaspoons Italian seasoning
12 ounces medium shrimp, peeled, deveined
  Salt and pepper, to taste
8 ounces penne, cooked, warm
  Chopped parsley, as garnish

Per Serving
Calories: 277
% Calories from fat: 11
Fat (gm): 3.4
Saturated fat (gm): 0.5
Cholesterol (mg): 87
Sodium (mg): 292
Protein (gm): 17.4
Carbohydrate (gm): 40.5
Exchanges
Milk: 0.0
Vegetable: 2.0
Fruit: 0.0
Bread: 2.0
Meat: 1.5
Fat: 0.0

1. Saute pepper blend and garlic in oil in large skillet until tender; add tomato sauce, artichoke hearts, and sherry. Heat to boiling; reduce heat and simmer, covered, 6 to 7 minutes.

2. Stir in Italian seasoning and shrimp and simmer 4 to 5 minutes, until shrimp are cooked and pink. Season to taste with salt and pepper. Spoon over penne in large serving bowl; sprinkle with parsley.

TUNA STEAKS WITH GARLIC PASTA

Slow-cooking gives a sweet, mellow flavor to the garlic. Prepared peeled garlic can be found in jars in the produce section of most supermarkets.

4 servings

8 ounces (2 cups) orrechiette *or* cappelletti

1 cup frozen peas

4 tuna steaks (4 ounces each)

1/3 cup slivered (1/4-inch pieces), *or* thinly sliced, garlic

2-3 teaspoons olive oil

2 tablespoons minced parsley

1 tablespoon minced fresh rosemary *or* 1 teaspoon crushed dried rosemary leaves

1/4-1/3 cup freshly grated Parmesan cheese
Salt and pepper, to taste

Per Serving
Calories: 430
% Calories from fat: 13
Fat (gm): 6
Saturated fat (gm): 1.7
Cholesterol (mg): 53.4
Sodium (mg): 173
Protein (gm): 37.9
Carbohydrate (gm): 54.1
Exchanges
Milk: 0.0
Vegetable: 2.0
Fruit: 0.0
Bread: 3.0
Meat: 3.0
Fat: 0.0

1. Cook pasta according to package directions, adding peas 1 minute before end of cooking time; drain.

2. Broil tuna steaks 6 inches from heat source until fish is tender and flakes with a fork, 4 to 5 minutes on each side.

3. While fish is cooking, cook garlic over very low heat in oil in small skillet until very tender but not browned, about 10 minutes. Add herbs; toss with pasta mixture and cheese in serving bowl. Season to taste with salt and pepper; serve with tuna.

FETTUCCINE WITH FENNEL, SPROUTS, AND HAM

Crispy ham strips accent the many flavors in this dish.

4 servings

Olive oil cooking spray
4 ounces sliced reduced-sodium ham, cut into thin strips
1 fennel bulb, thinly sliced
1 medium onion, thinly sliced
8 ounces small Brussels sprouts, halved
1/4 cup water *or* chicken broth
1 tablespoon lemon juice
Salt and pepper, to taste
8 ounces spinach fettuccine, cooked, warm
1-2 ounces shredded, *or* shaved, Parmesan cheese
2-4 tablespoons toasted pine nuts *or* slivered almonds

Per Serving
Calories: 307
% Calories from fat: 24
Fat (gm): 8.4
Saturated fat (gm): 2.7
Cholesterol (mg): 85.6
Sodium (mg): 474
Protein (gm): 18.7
Carbohydrate (gm): 41.2
Exchanges
Milk: 0.0
Vegetable: 2.0
Fruit: 0.0
Bread: 2.0
Meat: 1.0
Fat: 1.0

1. Spray large skillet with cooking spray; heat over medium heat until hot. Add ham and cook over medium heat until crisp; reserve.

2. Spray skillet with cooking spray; heat over medium heat until hot. Add fennel and onion to skillet and saute 3 to 4 minutes. Add Brussels sprouts and water and heat to boiling; reduce heat and simmer, covered, until sprouts are crisp-tender, 5 to 8 minutes. Stir in lemon juice; season to taste with salt and pepper.

3. Spoon fennel and sprouts mixture over pasta on serving platter; sprinkle with ham, Parmesan cheese, and pine nuts.

ROASTED EGGPLANT WITH PASTA

Cook the eggplant on a charcoal grill to get a wonderful smoky flavor. The eggplant can be roasted or grilled up to 2 days in advance; refrigerate it in a plastic bag.

6 servings

- 2 medium eggplant (³/₄ pound each)
- 6 ounces smoked turkey, cut into thin strips
- 2 large tomatoes, seeded, coarsely chopped
- 8 green onions and tops, sliced
- 4 tablespoons balsamic vinegar *or* red wine vinegar
- 2 tablespoons olive oil
- 2-3 teaspoons lemon juice
- 2 tablespoons finely chopped parsley
- 3 cups (12 ounces) fusilli *or* rotini (spirals or corkscrews), cooked, room temperature

Per Serving
Calories: 338
% Calories from fat: 19
Fat (gm): 7.3
Saturated fat (gm): 1.2
Cholesterol (mg): 15.6
Sodium (mg): 367
Protein (gm): 12.9
Carbohydrate (gm): 55.7
Exchanges
Milk: 0.0
Vegetable: 2.0
Fruit: 0.0
Bread: 3.0
Meat: 1.0
Fat: 0.5

1. Pierce eggplant 6 to 8 times with fork; place in baking pan. Bake, uncovered, at 425 degrees until tender, about 30 minutes. Cool until warm enough to handle easily. Cut eggplant in half; scoop out pulp with large spoon, and cut into ³/₄-inch pieces.

2. Combine eggplant, turkey, tomatoes, and onions in bowl; stir in vinegar, oil, lemon juice, and parsley. Spoon over pasta and toss.

ROASTED EGGPLANT, TOMATOES, AND SAUSAGE WITH ZITI

Canned diced tomatoes replace winter's less-than-flavorful tomatoes. Enjoy with any pasta, soft polenta, or in a warm pita.

6 servings

Olive oil cooking spray
1 medium eggplant, unpeeled, cut into
   $1/2$-inch slices
3 medium onions, cut into $1/2$-inch
   wedges
$1/2$ teaspoon dried thyme leaves
$1/2$ teaspoon dried marjoram leaves
$1/2$ teaspoon dried savory leaves
   Salt and pepper, to taste
12 ounces Italian-style turkey sausage,
   casings removed
1 can ($14^{1}/_{2}$ ounces) reduced-sodium
   diced tomatoes, undrained
1 tablespoon roasted garlic
8 ounces ziti, cooked, warm

Per Serving
Calories: 298
% Calories from fat: 21
Fat (gm): 7.1
Saturated fat (gm): 1.9
Cholesterol (mg): 30.4
Sodium (mg): 473
Protein (gm): 17.1
Carbohydrate (gm): 44.1
Exchanges
Milk: 0.0
Vegetable: 2.0
Fruit: 0.0
Bread: 2.0
Meat: 2.0
Fat: 0.0

1. Line jelly roll pan with aluminum foil and spray with cooking spray. Cut eggplant slices into fourths; arrange on jelly roll pan with onions. Spray vegetables with cooking spray; sprinkle with herbs, salt, and pepper. Roast vegetables at 450 degrees until tender, about 20 minutes.

2. Cook sausage in medium skillet until browned, about 8 minutes; drain well and crumble. Spoon sausage, tomatoes and liquid, and garlic over vegetables and roast until eggplant is tender, 5 to 10 minutes longer. Serve over ziti.

BUTTER BEANS, MOSTACCIOLI, AND HAM

This extra-easy recipe has three great things going for it—it's fast to pre-pare, has a wonderfully subtle anchovy flavor, and is delightfully rich tasting, thanks to Romano cheese.

4 servings

1¹/₂ cups frozen, thawed small butter beans
2 cans (14 ounces each) reduced-sodium fat-free chicken broth
4 ounces mostaccioli
4 ounces lean reduced-sodium ham, diced
¹/₂ can (2-ounce size) anchovies, rinsed, drained, mashed
2 teaspoons garlic
1 small mild chili pepper, chopped
¹/₂ cup sliced scallions
¹/₄ cup grated Romano cheese

Per Serving
Calories: 289
% Calories from fat: 16
Fat (gm): 4.9
Saturated fat (gm): 2
Cholesterol (mg): 28.4
Sodium (mg): 783
Protein (gm): 23.5
Carbohydrate (gm): 36
Exchanges
Milk: 0.0
Vegetable: 0.0
Fruit: 0.0
Bread: 2.5
Meat: 2.0
Fat: 0.0

1. Combine beans, broth, mostaccioli, ham, anchovies, and garlic in large saucepan. Heat to boiling; reduce heat and sim-mer, covered, until pasta is tender, about 7 minutes. Add re-maining ingredients; cook 1 minute.

CORNED BEEF AND RED CABBAGE DINNER

Don't wait until St. Patrick's Day to enjoy this luck-of-the-Irish stew. It's fast. It's easy. It's delicious.

4 servings

8-12 ounces deli corned beef, cut into ¹/₂-inch cubes
6 medium red potatoes, cut into ¹/₂-inch cubes
1¹/₂ cups sliced carrots
1 cup cubed, peeled turnips
1 can (14 ounces) reduced-sodium fat-free chicken broth
1 tablespoon apple cider vinegar
1 teaspoon pickling spice
1 pound red cabbage, coarsely sliced

Per Serving
Calories: 259
% Calories from fat: 29
Fat (gm): 8.5
Saturated fat (gm): 2.8
Cholesterol (mg): 42.3
Sodium (mg): 646
Protein (gm): 13.6
Carbohydrate (gm): 34.1
Exchanges
Milk: 0.0
Vegetable: 1.0
Fruit: 0.0
Bread: 2.0
Meat: 1.0
Fat: 1.0

1. Combine corned beef, potatoes, carrots, turnips, broth, vinegar, and pickling spice in large saucepan. Heat to boiling; reduce heat and simmer, covered, 12 minutes.

2. Add cabbage; simmer until cabbage is tender, about 5 minutes.

PORK AND SQUASH RAGOUT

Stews don't have to be long cooked to be good—this delicious stew is simmered to savory goodness in less than 30 minutes. Serve with Garlic Bread (see p. 657).

6 servings (about 1¼ cups each)

Olive oil cooking spray
1 pound pork tenderloin, cubed
1½ cups chopped onions
1½ cups coarsely chopped green bell peppers
2 teaspoons minced roasted garlic
1 tablespoon flour
2 cups cubed, peeled, butternut, *or* acorn, squash (½-inch cubes)
2 cans (16 ounces each) reduced-sodium diced tomatoes, undrained
1 can (15 ounces) red kidney beans, rinsed, drained
½-¾ teaspoon Italian seasoning
Salt and pepper, to taste

Per Serving
Calories: 241
% Calories from fat: 12
Fat (gm): 3.3
Saturated fat (gm): 1
Cholesterol (mg): 43.8
Sodium (mg): 223
Protein (gm): 22.5
Carbohydrate (gm): 32.8
Exchanges
Milk: 0.0
Vegetable: 0.0
Fruit: 0.0
Bread: 2.0
Meat: 2.0
Fat: 0.0

1. Spray large saucepan with cooking spray; heat over medium heat until hot. Add pork and cook until browned, 8 to 10 minutes; remove from skillet. Add onions, bell peppers, and garlic to skillet and saute until tender, about 8 minutes. Stir in flour; cook 1 minute longer.

2. Add pork and remaining ingredients, except salt and pepper, to saucepan; heat to boiling. Reduce heat and simmer 10 to 15 minutes. Season to taste with salt and pepper.

VEGETABLE AND BEEF STROGANOFF

Fat-free half-and-half and sour cream contribute wonderful rich flavor and creamy texture.

8 servings (about 1 cup each)

1½ pounds lean ground beef

2 medium onions, thinly sliced

12 ounces mixed wild mushrooms (shiitake, oyster, enoki, or cremini), sliced

2 cloves garlic, minced

¼ cup dry red wine *or* beef broth

12 ounces broccoli florets and sliced stalks

1 cup fat-free half-and-half *or* fat-free milk

2 tablespoons flour

1½ teaspoons Dijon-style mustard

1 cup fat-free sour cream

½ teaspoon dried dill weed

Salt and white pepper, to taste

16 ounces no-yolk noodles, cooked, warm

Per Serving
Calories: 467
% Calories from fat: 22
Fat (gm): 11.3
Saturated fat (gm): 4.1
Cholesterol (mg): 52.9
Sodium (mg): 468
Protein (gm): 27.7
Carbohydrate (gm): 61.5
Exchanges
Milk: 0.0
Vegetable: 3.0
Fruit: 0.0
Bread: 3.0
Meat: 2.0
Fat: 1.0

1. Cook ground beef in large skillet until browned, about 10 minutes; drain well. Add onions, mushrooms, and garlic to skillet and saute until softened, about 5 minutes. Add wine and broccoli; heat to boiling. Reduce heat and simmer, covered, until broccoli is tender, 8 to 10 minutes.

2. Mix half-and-half, flour, and mustard; stir into skillet. Heat to boiling; boil, stirring constantly, until thickened. Reduce heat to low; stir in sour cream and dill weed and cook 1 to 2 minutes longer. Season to taste with salt and white pepper. Serve over noodles.

VEAL AND VEGETABLE PAPRIKASH

Your preference of hot or sweet paprika can be used in this recipe. Serve over any flat pasta or rice.

6 servings

Vegetable cooking spray

1¼ pounds veal scallopine, cut into 1-inch pieces

3 cups packaged coleslaw mix

1 cup chopped onion

1 medium zucchini, sliced

1½ cups sliced mushrooms

1 medium tomato, chopped

¼ cup all-purpose flour

1 tablespoon paprika

1 cup chicken broth

½-¾ cup reduced-fat sour cream

Salt and pepper, to taste

12 ounces egg noodles, cooked, warm

Per Serving
Calories: 419
% Calories from fat: 20
Fat (gm): 9.1
Saturated fat (gm): 3.2
Cholesterol (mg): 138.5
Sodium (mg): 264
Protein (gm): 33.5
Carbohydrate (gm): 49.8
Exchanges
Milk: 0.0
Vegetable: 2.0
Fruit: 0.0
Bread: 3.0
Meat: 3.0
Fat: 0.0

1. Spray large skillet with cooking spray and heat over medium heat until hot. Cook veal until browned, 3 to 5 minutes; add coleslaw, onion, and zucchini, and cook, covered, 5 to 8 minutes. Add mushrooms and tomato. Cook over medium heat, covered, until mushrooms and tomato are wilted, about 2 minutes.

2. Stir in flour and paprika; cook 1 to 2 minutes, stirring constantly. Stir in broth; heat to boiling. Boil, stirring constantly, until sauce thickens, about 1 minute. Stir in sour cream; season to taste with salt and pepper. Serve over noodles.

GARDEN STEW WITH CHICKEN AND COUSCOUS

Take advantage of your garden's bounty with this quick and easy stew, substituting vegetables you have in abundance.

8 servings (about 1 cup each)

Garlic-flavored vegetable cooking spray
4 boneless, skinless chicken breast halves (4 ounces each)
Salt and pepper, to taste
2 medium onions, cut into 1-inch pieces
8 ounces shiitake, *or* white, mushrooms, sliced
1 small jalapeño chili, finely chopped
1 tablespoon flour
2 cups reduced-sodium fat-free chicken broth
2 medium zucchini, sliced
1 medium turnip, cut into 1/4-inch cubes
8 ounces baby carrots, halved
4 medium tomatoes, coarsely chopped
1/2 cup loosely packed cilantro leaves
2 packages (5.9 ounces each) couscous, spice packets discarded, cooked, warm

Per Serving
Calories: 298
% Calories from fat: 6
Fat (gm): 2
Saturated fat (gm): 0.5
Cholesterol (mg): 35
Sodium (mg): 106
Protein (gm): 21.8
Carbohydrate (gm): 47.3
Exchanges
Milk: 0.0
Vegetable: 2.0
Fruit: 0.0
Bread: 2.0
Meat: 1.5
Fat: 0.0

1. Spray large skillet with cooking spray; heat over medium heat until hot. Cook chicken over medium heat until no longer pink in the center, 15 to 20 minutes, turning to brown both sides. Season to taste with salt and pepper. Remove from skillet; keep warm.

2. Add onions, mushrooms, and jalapeño chili to skillet; saute 5 minutes. Stir in flour; cook 1 minute longer.

3. Add broth, zucchini, turnip, and carrots to skillet; heat to boiling. Reduce heat and simmer, covered, until vegetables are tender, 10 to 12 minutes. Add tomatoes and cilantro to stew; season to taste with salt and pepper. Spoon stew over couscous in bowls; top with chicken breasts.

WINE-GLAZED CHICKEN WITH RAVIOLI AND ASPARAGUS

A reduction of broth, white wine, and orange juice creates an elegant and fragrant sauce for chicken and flavorful pasta.

4 servings

4 boneless, skinless chicken breast halves (4 ounces each)
   Salt and pepper, to taste
2 cups reduced-sodium fat-free chicken broth
1 cup dry white wine
1 cup orange juice
1/4 teaspoon crushed red pepper
1 pound asparagus, cut into 1-inch pieces
2 tablespoons margarine
1 package (9 ounces) fresh mushroom ravioli, cooked, warm

Per Serving
Calories: 340
% Calories from fat: **34**
Fat (gm): 12.5
Saturated fat (gm): 2
Cholesterol (mg): 76.9
Sodium (mg): 454
Protein (gm): 33
Carbohydrate (gm): 11.7
Exchanges
Milk: 0.0
Vegetable: 1.0
Fruit: 0.0
Bread: 2.0
Meat: 3.0
Fat: 0.5

1. Spray medium skillet with cooking spray; heat over medium heat until hot. Cook chicken over medium heat until chicken is no longer pink in center, 15 to 20 minutes, turning to brown both sides. Sprinkle lightly with salt and pepper.

2. Heat broth, white wine, orange juice, and crushed red pepper to boiling in large skillet; boil, uncovered, 10 minutes, or until liquid is reduced to about 1/2 cup.

3. Add asparagus to skillet; cook, covered, over medium heat until crisp-tender, 3 to 4 minutes. Add chicken, margarine, and ravioli; cook 1 to 2 minutes longer. Season to taste with salt and pepper.

CHICKEN WITH ONIONS AND PEPPERS

Serve this Italian dish over rice or your favorite pasta.

4 servings

- 1 pound boneless, skinless chicken breast, cut into 1-inch cubes
- 1/2 teaspoon minced garlic
- 1 tablespoon olive oil
- 2 cups frozen stir-fry pepper blend
- 1 can (15 ounces) chunky Italian-seasoned tomato sauce
  Salt and pepper, to taste
- 2 tablespoons grated Parmesan cheese

Per Serving
Calories: 215
% Calories from fat: 29
Fat (gm): 7
Saturated fat (gm): 1.8
Cholesterol (mg): 71
Sodium (mg): 674
Protein (gm): 28.5
Carbohydrate (gm): 9.7
Exchanges
Milk: 0.0
Vegetable: 2.0
Fruit: 0.0
Bread: 0.0
Meat: 3.0
Fat: 0.0

1. Saute chicken and garlic in oil in large skillet until lightly browned. Push chicken to side of pan; add stir-fry pepper blend and cook until softened, 3 to 4 minutes. Stir in tomato sauce. Heat to boiling; reduce heat and simmer, covered, until chicken is cooked through, about 10 minutes. Season to taste with salt and pepper; sprinkle with Parmesan cheese.

QUICK CHICKEN AND VEGETABLE STEW

Pureed beans provide a perfect thickening for the stew, and canned vegetables make it extra quick.

8 servings (about 3/4 cup each)

- Vegetable cooking spray
- 1 pound chicken tenders, cut into 1/2-inch pieces
- 3 carrots, sliced
- 3/4 cup chopped onion
- 2 teaspoons minced garlic
- 1 can (15 ounces) navy beans, rinsed, drained
- 2 cups reduced-sodium fat-free chicken broth, divided
- 1 can (16 ounces) Italian-style zucchini with mushrooms in tomato sauce

Per Serving
Calories: 326
% Calories from fat: 9
Fat (gm): 3.4
Saturated fat (gm): 0.8
Cholesterol (mg): 59
Sodium (mg): 607
Protein (gm): 26
Carbohydrate (gm): 47.5
Exchanges
Milk: 0.0
Vegetable: 1.0
Fruit: 0.0
Bread: 3.0
Meat: 1.5
Fat: 0.0

1 can (15 ounces) black beans, rinsed, drained
1 cup frozen peas
1¹/2 teaspoons Italian seasoning
Salt and pepper, to taste
8 ounces egg noodles, cooked, warm

1. Spray large saucepan with cooking spray; heat over medium heat until hot. Saute chicken, carrots, onion, and garlic until chicken is browned, about 8 minutes. Puree navy beans with half the broth in blender; add to chicken and vegetables in saucepan. Add remaining broth, zucchini, black beans, peas, and Italian seasoning.

2. Heat to boiling. Reduce heat and simmer, uncovered, until vegetables are tender, about 10 minutes. Season to taste with salt and pepper. Spoon stew over noodles in shallow bowls.

ISLAND STEW, SWEET-AND-SOUR

Sweet-and-sour flavors team with chicken, pineapple, and beans for this island-inspired dish—delicious with jasmine rice or couscous.

6 servings (about 1¹/4 cups each)

1¹/2 pounds chicken tenders
1 tablespoon vegetable oil
3 cups frozen stir-fry pepper blend
2 teaspoons minced garlic
2 teaspoons minced gingerroot
1-2 jalapeño chilies, finely chopped
3 cups reduced-sodium fat-free chicken broth
1 can (20 ounces) unsweetened pineapple chunks in juice, drained, juice reserved
2 tablespoons light brown sugar
2-3 teaspoons curry powder
2-3 tablespoons apple cider vinegar
2 tablespoons cornstarch
1 can (15 ounces) black beans, rinsed, drained

Per Serving
Calories: 288
% Calories from fat: 12
Fat (gm): 3.9
Saturated fat (gm): 0.3
Cholesterol (mg): 48.2
Sodium (mg): 537
Protein (gm): 29.7
Carbohydrate (gm): 34.7
Exchanges
Milk: 0.0
Vegetable: 1.0
Fruit: 0.5
Bread: 1.0
Meat: 3.0
Fat: 0.0

1. Cook chicken in oil in large skillet over medium heat until browned, about 8 minutes. Remove from skillet.

2. Add pepper blend, garlic, gingerroot, and jalapeño chilies to skillet; saute 5 minutes. Stir in broth, pineapple (reserve juice), sugar, curry powder, vinegar, and chicken; heat to boiling. Reduce heat and simmer, uncovered, 5 minutes.

3. Heat mixture to boiling. Mix cornstarch and reserved pineapple juice; stir into boiling mixture. Boil, stirring frequently, until mixture is thickened, about 1 minute. Stir in beans; cook over medium heat 2 to 3 minutes longer.

SPEEDY CHICKEN AND RAVIOLI

Use any favorite flavor of refrigerated fresh ravioli with this quick and nutritious bean sauce.

4 servings

Vegetable cooking spray
1 pound chicken tenders, cut into 1/2-inch pieces
3/4 cup chopped onion
2 teaspoons minced garlic
3/4 cup canned kidney beans, rinsed, drained
1 large tomato, cubed
1/2 teaspoon dried thyme leaves
1 package (9 ounces) fresh sun-dried tomato ravioli, cooked, warm
Salt and pepper, to taste

Per Serving
Calories: 262
% Calories from fat: 17
Fat (gm): 5.1
Saturated fat (gm): 2.3
Cholesterol (mg): 63.5
Sodium (mg): 626
Protein (gm): 29.8
Carbohydrate (gm): 25.2
Exchanges
Milk: 0.0
Vegetable: 0.0
Fruit: 0.0
Bread: 1.5
Meat: 3.0
Fat: 0.0

1. Spray large skillet with cooking spray; heat over medium heat until hot. Cook chicken, onion, and garlic until browned, 5 to 8 minutes. Stir in beans, tomato, and thyme; cook 2-3 minutes. Stir in ravioli and cook 2-3 minutes longer. Season to taste with salt and pepper.

CHICKEN TORTELLINI WITH SHERRIED VEGETABLE SAUCE

Dry sherry and thyme accent the richly textured and seasoned sauce.

6 servings

Vegetable cooking spray
1/2 cup chopped onion
2 small leeks (white parts only), very thinly sliced
1/3 cup chopped shallots
8 large mushrooms, chopped
1/2 cup dry sherry *or* reduced-sodium chicken broth
1/2 teaspoon salt
1/2 teaspoon pepper
2 cups reduced-sodium chicken broth
2 medium tomatoes, chopped
3-4 teaspoons dried thyme leaves
3 bay leaves
2 packages (9 ounces each) fresh chicken tortellini, cooked, warm
4 tablespoons drained capers, optional

Per Serving
Calories: 334
% Calories from fat: 16
Fat (gm): 6.2
Saturated fat (gm): 3.0
Cholesterol (mg): 40.4
Sodium (mg): 438
Protein (gm): 17.4
Carbohydrate (gm): 51.6
Exchanges
Milk: 0.0
Vegetable: 2.0
Fruit: 0.0
Bread: 3.0
Meat: 0.0
Fat: 1.0

1.   Spray medium saucepan with cooking spray; heat over medium heat until hot. Saute onion, leeks, shallots, and mushrooms until very soft, 7 to 10 minutes. Add sherry; cook over high heat until liquid is almost absorbed, 2 to 3 minutes. Stir in salt and pepper.

2.   Add chicken broth, tomatoes, thyme, and bay leaves to saucepan; heat to boiling. Reduce heat and simmer, uncovered, until tomato is very soft, about 15 minutes; discard bay leaves. Process mixture in food processor or blender until smooth. Return to saucepan; cook over medium heat until hot.

3.   Spoon sauce over tortellini; sprinkle with capers.

CHICKEN, VEGETABLE, AND GOAT CHEESE CASSEROLE

Delicious, with a generous amount of melty cheese.

4 servings

1¹/₂ cups cut asparagus (1¹/₂-inch pieces)

1 package (9 ounces) unsalted frozen artichoke hearts

1 package (6¹/₄ ounces) fast-cooking long-grain and wild rice

12 ounces cooked chicken breast, cubed

3 ounces fat-free cream cheese, cubed

³/₄ cup (3 ounces) shredded reduced-fat mozzarella cheese

3-4 ounces reduced-fat goat cheese, crumbled

Salt and pepper, to taste

Per Serving
Calories: 445
% Calories from fat: 20
Fat (gm): 10
Saturated fat (gm): 4.8
Cholesterol (mg): 84.1
Sodium (mg): 804
Protein (gm): 44.2
Carbohydrate (gm): 45.1
Exchanges
Milk: 0.0
Vegetable: 3.0
Fruit: 0.0
Bread: 2.0
Meat: 4.0
Fat: 0.0

1. Cook asparagus and artichoke hearts in boiling water to cover, 4 minutes. Drain well.

2. Cook rice according to package directions, using ¹/₂ the spice packet. Mix rice, chicken, vegetables, and cheeses; season to taste with salt and pepper. Spoon into 1¹/₂-quart casserole.

3. Bake, covered, at 375 degrees until casserole is hot and cheese is melted, about 20 to 30 minutes.

QUICK CHICKEN AND STUFFING

If you are really rushed, or for a change of pace, frozen mixed vegetables can be substituted for the carrot, celery, and onions. Thaw and drain the frozen vegetables before using.

6 servings

- 3 cups croutons
- 1 cup reduced-sodium fat-free chicken broth
- 2 large carrots, coarsely chopped
- 1 rib celery, coarsely chopped
- 1 small onion, finely chopped
- 1 teaspoon dried marjoram leaves
- 1/2 teaspoon dried thyme leaves
- 1 can (10 1/2 ounces) cream of mushroom soup
- 1/2 cup fat-free milk
- 1 teaspoon dried parsley leaves
- 1/8 teaspoon black pepper
- 6 boneless, skinless chicken breast halves (4 ounces each)
  Paprika, as garnish

Per Serving
Calories: 276
% Calories from fat: 29
Fat (gm): 7.8
Saturated fat (gm): 2.1
Cholesterol (mg): 69.9
Sodium (mg): 562
Protein (gm): 30
Carbohydrate (gm): 19.7
Exchanges
Milk: 0.0
Vegetable: 0.0
Fruit: 0.0
Bread: 1.5
Meat: 3.0
Fat: 0.0

1. In a large bowl, combine croutons, broth, carrots, celery, onion, and herbs. Spoon stuffing mixture down center of a 13 x 9-inch baking dish.

2. Mix soup, milk, parsley, and pepper in medium bowl; spoon 1/2 the soup mixture on each side of stuffing. Place chicken breasts over soup, overlapping if necessary. Pour remaining soup mixture over chicken. Sprinkle with paprika.

3. Bake, covered, 20 minutes at 400 degrees; uncover and bake 10 minutes longer.

FAST HAM AND CHICKEN BAKE

Use meat from the deli case to prepare this casserole; smoked turkey would also be delicious.

6 servings

8 ounces lean ham, cut into 1/2-inch cubes

8 ounces cooked chicken breast, cut into 1/2-inch cubes

1 small onion, finely chopped

1 small red bell pepper, finely chopped

1 can (15 ounces) cream-style corn

1 package (10 ounces) frozen whole-kernel corn

1/2 cup fat-free milk

1-2 cups croutons

3 tablespoons margarine, melted

1-2 teaspoons Worcestershire sauce

1 1/2 teaspoon bouquet garni

Per Serving
Calories: 283
% Calories from fat: 28
Fat (gm): 9
Saturated fat (gm): 1.9
Cholesterol (mg): 47
Sodium (mg): 676
Protein (gm): 21.5
Carbohydrate (gm): 31.4
Exchanges
Milk: 0.0
Vegetable: 0.0
Fruit: 0.0
Bread: 2.0
Meat: 2.0
Fat: 0.5

1. Combine ham, chicken, onion, bell pepper, corn, and milk in lightly greased 2-quart casserole. Spread croutons over the top. Drizzle with combined margarine and Worcestershire sauce; sprinkle with herbs. Bake, uncovered, at 350 degrees until brown and bubbly, about 35 minutes.

EASIEST SPAGHETTI BAKE

This very easy casserole can be made ahead of time and refrigerated, or even frozen, if you need some kid-friendly dinners on hand. Thaw in the refrigerator overnight, if frozen, and bake according to directions, increasing baking time by 5 to 10 minutes.

6 servings

8 ounces ground beef eye of round, cooked, drained

8 ounces spaghetti, cooked al dente

1 jar (28 ounces) no-salt-added spaghetti sauce

1/2-1 cup (2-4 ounces) shredded reduced-fat Cheddar cheese

Per Serving
Calories: 351
% Calories from fat: 26
Fat (gm): 10
Saturated fat (gm): 2.9
Cholesterol (mg): 23.4
Sodium (mg): 172
Protein (gm): 16.8
Carbohydrate (gm): 46.2
Exchanges
Milk: 0.0
Vegetable: 2.0
Fruit: 0.0
Bread: 4.0
Meat: 2.0
Fat: 2.0

1. Combine beef, spaghetti, and sauce in large bowl; transfer to 13 x 9-inch baking dish and sprinkle with cheese. Bake at 350 degrees, uncovered, 30 minutes.

LAZY LASAGNE

One of the quickest, easiest lasagnes ever, thanks to no-boil lasagne noodles. Roasted garlic is available in jars in the produce section of the supermarket.

4 to 6 servings

6 no-boil lasagne noodles (4 ounces)

1 can (15 ounces) cannellini, *or* Great Northern, beans, rinsed, drained, slightly mashed

1 cup reduced-fat cottage cheese

1-1 1/2 cups (4-6 ounces) shredded Italian 6-cheese blend, divided

1 can (14 1/2 ounces) reduced-sodium diced tomatoes

1 tablespoon roasted minced garlic

Per Serving
Calories: 347
% Calories from fat: 23
Fat (gm): 9.2
Saturated fat (gm): 4.7
Cholesterol (mg): 24.8
Sodium (mg): 575
Protein (gm): 24
Carbohydrate (gm): 42.3
Exchanges
Milk: 0.0
Vegetable: 2.0
Fruit: 0.0
Bread: 2.0
Meat: 2.0
Fat: 1.0

1. Place 2 lasagne noodles in lightly greased 8-inch square baking pan. Top with $1/2$ the beans, $1/2$ the cottage cheese, and $1/3$ cup shredded cheese. Repeat layers, ending with 2 lasagne noodles. Spoon combined diced tomatoes and roasted garlic over top of lasagne.

2. Bake, covered with aluminum foil, at 375 degrees until noodles are fork-tender, about 30 minutes. Uncover and sprinkle with remaining $1/3$ cup cheese; let stand 5 to 10 minutes before serving.

Tip: Any kind of beans can be substituted for the cannellini beans.

MEXI-CAN LASAGNE

This simple South-of-the-Border lasagne is one you'll say "ole" to!

4 to 6 servings

> 6 no-boil lasagne noodles
> 1 can (15 ounces) no-salt, low-fat refried beans
> 1 can (11 ounces) nacho cheese soup
> $1/3$ cup fat-free milk
> 1 tablespoon minced jalapeño chili
> 1 teaspoon ground cumin, divided
> 1 cup frozen, *or* canned, drained, whole-kernel corn
> 1 can ($14^1/2$ ounces) reduced-sodium stewed tomatoes
> 2 teaspoons chili powder
> $1/2$ teaspoon dried oregano leaves
> $1/2$-$3/4$ cup (2-3 ounces) shredded reduced-fat Monterey Jack, *or* Cheddar, cheese

Per Serving
Calories: 393
% Calories from fat: 24
Fat (gm): 11.3
Saturated fat (gm): 4.5
Cholesterol (mg): 20.2
Sodium (mg): 686
Protein (gm): 20.8
Carbohydrate (gm): 58.6
Exchanges
Milk: 0.0
Vegetable: 2.0
Fruit: 0.0
Bread: 3.0
Meat: 2.0
Fat: 0.5

1. Place 2 lasagne noodles in lightly greased 8-inch square baking pan; top with $1/2$ the refried beans. Mix cheese soup, milk, jalapeño chili, and $1/2$ teaspoon cumin. Spoon $1/2$ the cheese sauce over the beans and sprinkle with $1/2$ the corn. Repeat layers, ending with 2 noodles. Mix tomatoes, chili powder, remaining $1/2$ teaspoon cumin, and oregano; spoon over top of lasagne.

2. Bake, covered with aluminum foil, at 375 degrees until noodles are fork-tender, about 30 minutes. Uncover and sprinkle with shredded cheese; let stand 5 to 10 minutes before serving.

PIZZA WITH CARAMELIZED ONIONS AND SMOKED TURKEY

Caramelized onions and smoked turkey make a wonderful pizza topping. Use a purchased ready-made crust or one from the dairy case, or try it with your own homemade dough.

4 servings

2 cups thinly sliced onions
2 teaspoons sugar
1 1/2 tablespoons margarine
3 ounces deli reduced-fat smoked turkey, cut into thin strips
1 large unbaked pizza crust
2/3 cup pizza sauce
1/2-1 cup (2-4 ounces) shredded reduced-fat mozzarella cheese

Per Serving
Calories: 332
% Calories from fat: 26
Fat (gm): 9.7
Saturated fat (gm): 2.9
Cholesterol (mg): 7.5
Sodium (mg): 719
Protein (gm): 16.7
Carbohydrate (gm): 45.3
Exchanges
Milk: 0.0
Vegetable: 3.0
Fruit: 0.0
Bread: 2.0
Meat: 2.0
Fat: 0.0

1. Saute onions and sugar in margarine in large skillet over medium heat, stirring frequently, until very tender and well browned, about 15 minutes. Add turkey and cook 2 to 3 minutes.

2. Place crust on large cookie sheet; spread with pizza sauce and sprinkle with cheese. Spoon onion mixture over cheese. Bake at 450 degrees until edges and bottom of crust are browned, about 12 minutes.

THAI FRIED RICE

Although packaged coconut ginger rice is delicious, 1¹/₂ cups of any kind of cooked rice can be used.

2 servings

1 package (16 ounces) frozen stir-fry vegetable blend with sugar snap peas

6 green onions and tops, sliced, divided

4 ounces pork tenderloin, finely chopped

¹/₂-1 teaspoon hot chili sesame oil

2 eggs, lightly beaten

1 package (6.4 ounces) Thai coconut ginger rice, cooked, warm

1-2 tablespoons reduced-sodium tamari soy sauce

1 tablespoon reduced-fat peanut butter

¹/₂ teaspoon minced gingerroot

Per Serving
Calories: 407
% Calories from fat: 25
Fat (gm): 11.2
Saturated fat (gm): 3
Cholesterol (mg): 244.8
Sodium (mg): 777
Protein (gm): 27
Carbohydrate (gm): 47
Exchanges
Milk: 0.0
Vegetable: 3.0
Fruit: 0.0
Bread: 2.0
Meat: 3.0
Fat: 0.5

1. Stir-fry frozen vegetables, 4 green onions, and pork in sesame oil in large skillet until tender, 3 to 4 minutes. Move mixture to side of skillet.

2. Add eggs to skillet; cook over medium heat until set, stirring occasionally, about 2 minutes. Break up eggs with spatula and mix with vegetables; stir in rice and combined soy sauce, peanut butter, and gingerroot. Spoon rice mixture into serving dish and sprinkle with remaining 2 green onions.

THAI STIR-FRY

An aromatic rice, such as basmati or jasmine, can be substituted for the Thai rice; cook with light coconut milk, if desired, or sprinkle with flaked coconut when serving.

4 servings

Oriental-flavored vegetable cooking spray

1 pound round steak, fat trimmed, cut into strips

8 green onions and tops, sliced

8 ounces broccoli florets

8 ounces carrots, thinly sliced

1/3-2/3 cup Thai peanut sauce

1/2 cup reduced-sodium fat-free beef broth

2 teaspoons cornstarch

1 package (6.4 ounces) Thai coconut ginger rice, cooked, warm

1/4 cup finely chopped cilantro

1/4 cup dry roasted peanuts, optional

Per Serving
Calories: 289
% Calories from fat: 19
Fat (gm): 6.2
Saturated fat (gm): 1.7
Cholesterol (mg): 55
Sodium (mg): 788
Protein (gm): 28
Carbohydrate (gm): 30.1
Exchanges
Milk: 0.0
Vegetable: 3.0
Fruit: 0.0
Bread: 1.0
Meat: 3.0
Fat: 0.0

1. Spray large skillet with cooking spray; heat over medium heat until hot. Saute beef until browned, about 5 minutes; remove from skillet. Add onions, broccoli, and carrots and saute until crisp-tender, 4 to 5 minutes. Stir in peanut sauce; stir in combined broth and cornstarch; heat to boiling. Boil until thickened, about 1 minute; stir in beef.

2. Serve mixture over rice; sprinkle with cilantro and peanuts.

SESAME CHICKEN AND ASPARAGUS STIR-FRY

Check the Asian section of your supermarket for the interesting selection of sauces available for noodles and rice.

6 servings (about ²/₃ cup each)

Oriental, *or* plain, vegetable cooking spray

1 pound boneless, skinless chicken breast, cut into ³/₄-inch pieces

8 ounces asparagus, cut into 1-inch pieces

¹/₄ teaspoon crushed red pepper

1 can (15 ounces) black beans, rinsed, drained

¹/₂ jar (14-ounce size) Mandarin sesame sauce for noodles and rice

1 small tomato, coarsely chopped

1 package (8 ounces) Chinese egg noodles, cooked, warm

Per Serving
Calories: 285
% Calories from fat: 8
Fat (gm): 2.9
Saturated fat (gm): 0.6
Cholesterol (mg): 46
Sodium (mg): 295
Protein (gm): 24
Carbohydrate (gm): 45.7
Exchanges
Milk: 0.0
Vegetable: 1.5
Fruit: 0.5
Bread: 1.5
Meat: 2.0
Fat: 0.0

1. Spray wok or medium skillet with cooking spray; heat over medium heat until hot. Stir-fry chicken until browned, about 5 minutes; remove from wok. Add asparagus to wok; stir fry 3 to 4 minutes or until browned. Add red pepper; cook 1 minute longer.

2. Stir chicken, beans, and Mandarin sesame sauce into wok and cook 2 to 3 minutes; stir in tomato. Serve over noodles.

CHINESE NOODLES WITH CHICKEN STIR-FRY

Fresh Chinese noodles and oriental ingredients make this pasta dish special.

8 servings

Oriental-flavored vegetable cooking spray

1 pound boneless, skinless chicken breast, cut into strips

2 cups cubed, peeled sweet potatoes (1/2-inch cubes)

3/4 cup diagonally sliced green onions and tops

3 teaspoons minced garlic

1-2 teaspoons minced gingerroot

2 cups halved snow peas

1/2 cup chopped red, *or* green, bell pepper

3/4 cup reduced-sodium fat-free chicken broth

1-2 teaspoons tamari soy sauce

1 1/2 teaspoons cornstarch

Salt and pepper, to taste

1-2 teaspoons toasted sesame seeds

1 package (8 ounces) fresh Chinese egg noodles, cooked, warm

Per Serving
Calories: 237
% Calories from fat: 7
Fat (gm): 1.8
Saturated fat (gm): 0.5
Cholesterol (mg): 35
Sodium (mg): 95
Protein (gm): 17.6
Carbohydrate (gm): 36.9
Exchanges
Milk: 0.0
Vegetable: 1.0
Fruit: 0.0
Bread: 2.0
Meat: 1.5
Fat: 0.0

1. Spray wok or large skillet with cooking spray; heat over medium heat until hot. Stir-fry chicken until browned; remove from wok. Add potatoes, green onions, garlic, and gingerroot to wok; stir-fry 2 to 3 minutes. Cook, covered, over low heat until potatoes are almost tender, 10 to 12 minutes, stirring occasionally.

2. Add snow peas and bell pepper to wok; stir-fry over medium heat until peas are crisp-tender, about 5 minutes. Stir in chicken. Combine broth, soy sauce, and cornstarch; add to wok and heat to boiling. Boil, stirring constantly, until thickened, about 1 minute. Season to taste with salt and pepper.

3. Spoon mixture into serving bowl; sprinkle with sesame seeds. Serve over noodles.

LIGHT SUMMER PASTA

The fragrant aroma and flavor of fresh herbs and garlic accent summer ripe tomatoes in this salad.

4 servings

8 ounces spaghetti, cooked, cooled
1 pound Italian plum tomatoes, chopped
1/2-3/4 cup (2-3 ounces) cubed (1/4-inch) reduced-fat mozzarella cheese
3 tablespoons finely chopped fresh basil leaves *or* 2 teaspoons dried basil
2 tablespoons finely chopped parsley
Garlic Vinaigrette (recipe follows)

Per Serving
Calories: 379
% Calories from fat: 26
Fat (gm): 10.9
Saturated fat (gm): 2.7
Cholesterol (mg): 7.5
Sodium (mg): 264
Protein (gm): 14.2
Carbohydrate (gm): 56.8
Exchanges
Milk: 0.0
Vegetable: 2.0
Fruit: 0.0
Bread: 3.0
Meat: 0.0
Fat: 2.0

1. Combine spaghetti, tomatoes, cheese, and herbs in serving bowl; pour Garlic Vinaigrette over and toss.

Garlic Vinaigrette

makes about 1/3 cup

3 tablespoons red wine vinegar
2 tablespoons olive oil
2 teaspoons minced garlic
1/4 teaspoon salt
1/8 teaspoon pepper

1. Mix all ingredients.

PASTA, PORK, AND PORTOBELLO MUSHROOM SALAD

Strips of warm sauteed pork and mushrooms are tossed with vegetables and pasta to make a refreshing summer supper. For picnics or pot-luck, make the salad early in the day and allow it to marinate in the refrigerator. Arrange on lettuce at serving time.

4 servings

12	ounces pork tenderloin, cut into $1/2$-inch slices
1	tablespoon olive oil
12	ounces portobello mushrooms, sliced
2	medium tomatoes, cut into wedges
1	medium yellow squash *or* zucchini, sliced
1	medium green bell pepper, sliced
1	large carrot, sliced
1	small red onion, sliced
8	ounces rotini, cooked, cooled
$1/2$-$3/4$	cup reduced-fat Italian dressing
	Lettuce leaves, as garnish

Per Serving
Calories: 312
% Calories from fat: 29
Fat (gm): 10
Saturated fat (gm): 1.9
Cholesterol (mg): 51.1
Sodium (mg): 300
Protein (gm): 24.8
Carbohydrate (gm): 29.9
Exchanges
Milk: 0.0
Vegetable: 3.0
Fruit: 0.0
Bread: 1.0
Meat: 3.0
Fat: 0.0

1. Cut pork slices into $1/4$-inch strips; cook in oil in large skillet 2 to 3 minutes. Add mushrooms and cook until tender, about 5 minutes.

2. Combine pork mixture, vegetables, and pasta in bowl; pour Italian dressing over and toss. Arrange lettuce on salad plates; spoon salad over.

MAFALDE WITH GARBANZO BEANS, TOMATOES, AND CROUTONS

This warm salad has many flavor and color contrasts. Serve with Italian-style turkey sausage, if you like.

8 servings

1/2 cup chopped poblano chili *or* green bell pepper

1/3 cup chopped onion

1 teaspoon minced garlic

2 teaspoons olive oil

1 can (15 ounces) garbanzo beans, rinsed, drained

2 cups seeded, chopped Italian plum tomatoes

1/4 cup loosely packed chopped basil leaves

1/4 cup reduced-fat Italian salad dressing

8 ounces mafalde *or* other flat pasta, cooked, warm

1 1/2 cups herb, *or* Parmesan, croutons
Shredded Parmesan cheese, as garnish

Per Serving
Calories: 210
% Calories from fat: 15
Fat (gm): 3.5
Saturated fat (gm): 0.5
Cholesterol (mg): 0.5
Sodium (mg): 253
Protein (gm): 7.5
Carbohydrate (gm): 38
Exchanges
Milk: 0.0
Vegetable: 1.5
Fruit: 0.0
Bread: 2.0
Meat: 0.0
Fat: 0.5

1. Saute poblano chili, onion, and garlic in oil in medium skillet until tender, 5 to 8 minutes. Add beans and cook, covered, over medium heat until hot, 2 to 3 minutes. Remove from heat and stir in tomatoes, basil, and salad dressing.

2. Toss pasta and bean mixture in serving bowl; add croutons and toss. Sprinkle with Parmesan cheese.

MIXED VEGETABLE FETTUCCINE

Roasting is an effortless way to cook many vegetables at the same time, also enhancing their natural flavors.

6 servings

Olive oil cooking spray

2 sweet potatoes, peeled, cut into scant
  $1/2$-inch slices

1 yellow summer squash, sliced

1 large tomato, cut into 8 wedges

1 green bell pepper, cut into $3/4$-inch
  slices

4 green onions and tops, very thinly
  sliced

$1/4$ cup cider vinegar

2 tablespoons olive oil *or* vegetable oil

1 teaspoon lemon juice

1 tablespoon finely chopped parsley

1 tablespoon finely chopped fresh, *or*
  1 teaspoon dried, oregano leaves

1 tablespoon finely chopped fresh, *or*
  1 teaspoon dried, tarragon leaves

8 ounces fettuccine, cooked, room
  temperature

1 tablespoon grated Parmesan cheese

Per Serving
Calories: 267
% Calories from fat: 26
Fat (gm): 8.5
Saturated fat (gm): 1.1
Cholesterol (mg): 1.1
Sodium (mg): 119
Protein (gm): 9.1
Carbohydrate (gm): 46.4
Exchanges
Milk: 0.0
Vegetable: 1.5
Fruit: 0.0
Bread: 2.5
Meat: 0.0
Fat: 1.5

1. Spray aluminum foil-lined jelly roll pan with cooking spray. Arrange vegetables on pan; spray generously with cooking spray and toss. Bake at 400 degrees until vegetables are browned and just tender, 20 to 25 minutes.

2. Mix vinegar, olive oil, lemon juice, and herbs; drizzle over warm roasted vegetables and toss. Spoon over pasta and toss; sprinkle with Parmesan cheese.

ELEVEN

Casseroles

STUFFED ARTICHOKE CASSEROLE

The flavor of stuffed artichokes, with far less work! Microwave cooking speeds preparation, but if you prefer, cook vegetables in a saucepan, combine the ingredients, then bake the casserole in the oven at 375 degrees, 20 to 25 minutes.

5 servings

1   large onion, chopped

1/2   teaspoon chopped garlic

1   tablespoon olive oil

2/3   cup reduced-sodium fat-free chicken broth, divided

1/2   teaspoon dried oregano leaves

1   can (14 ounces) artichoke hearts, drained, sliced

2   cups seasoned stuffing cubes
   Salt and pepper, to taste

Per Serving
Calories: 145
% Calories from fat: 22
Fat (gm): 3.6
Saturated fat (gm): 0.4
Cholesterol (mg): 0
Sodium (mg): 505
Protein (gm): 5.3
Carbohydrate (gm): 22.8
Exchanges
Milk: 0.0
Vegetable: 0.0
Fruit: 0.0
Bread: 1.5
Meat: 0.0
Fat: 0.5

1.   Combine onion, garlic, oil, and 3 tablespoons chicken broth in 2-quart glass casserole. Microwave on high power, covered, **3** to **4** minutes, until onion is tender. Stir in remaining ingredients, except salt and pepper, mixing well. Cover and microwave on high until stuffing is heated through, about 5 minutes. Season to taste with salt and pepper.

VEGETABLE AND MIXED RICE CASSEROLE

Fast-cooking rice is a kitchen lifesaver when cooking minutes count; any preferred rice can be substituted. however.

8 servings

1 package (6.25 ounces) fast-cooking long-grain and wild rice

1¹/2 cups sliced shiitake *or* cremini mushrooms

1 cup sliced zucchini

¹/2 cup chopped onion

¹/2 cup chopped green bell pepper

¹/2 cup chopped red, *or* green, bell pepper

1 teaspoon dried thyme leaves

1-2 teaspoons vegetable oil

1 cup frozen, *or* canned, drained whole-kernel corn

1 cup fat-free sour cream

1 cup (4 ounces) shredded reduced-fat Cheddar cheese, divided

Salt and pepper, to taste

Per Serving
Calories: 203
% Calories from fat: 15
Fat (gm): 3.5
Saturated fat (gm): 1.9
Cholesterol (mg): 10.1
Sodium (mg): 141
Protein (gm): 10.5
Carbohydrate (gm): 33.7
Exchanges
Milk: 0.0
Vegetable: 1.0
Fruit: 0.0
Bread: 2.0
Meat: 0.0
Fat: 0.5

1. Cook rice according to package directions, discarding spice packet. Cook mushrooms, zucchini, onion, bell peppers, and thyme in oil in medium skillet, covered, over medium heat until vegetables are tender, 8 to 10 minutes. Combine rice, cooked vegetable mixture, corn, sour cream, and ¹/2 cup cheese; season to taste with salt and pepper.

2. Spoon mixture into 2-quart casserole; sprinkle with remaining ¹/2 cup cheese. Bake, uncovered, at 350 degrees until hot through, about 30 minutes.

ASPARAGUS POLENTA BAKE

This dish can be prepared a day in advance, then baked before serving; increase baking time 5 to 10 minutes. It is delicious with any roasted or grilled meats.

6 servings

6 ounces portobello mushrooms, thinly sliced

8 ounces asparagus, cut into 1-inch pieces

1-2 teaspoons olive oil

1 package (16 ounces) prepared Italian-Herb polenta

1 cup water

1 ounce sun-dried tomatoes (not in oil) (about 8 halves), sliced

1/4-1/2 cup (1-2 ounces) shredded Parmesan cheese

Per Serving
Calories: 110
% Calories from fat: 18
Fat (gm): 2.2
Saturated fat (gm): 1
Cholesterol (mg): 4.2
Sodium (mg): 94
Protein (gm): 5.4
Carbohydrate (gm): 16.7
Exchanges
Milk: 0.0
Vegetable: 2.0
Fruit: 0.0
Bread: 0.5
Meat: 0.0
Fat: 0.5

1. Saute mushrooms and asparagus in oil in large skillet 2 to 3 minutes; cook, covered, until asparagus is crisp-tender, about 5 minutes.

2. Mash polenta in medium saucepan; mix in water and cook over medium heat, whisking until smooth and hot, about 5 minutes. Stir in mushrooms and asparagus, and sun-dried tomatoes. Spoon mixture into 4 ramekins or a shallow casserole or quiche dish; sprinkle with Parmesan cheese.

3. Bake at 425 degrees until cheese is browned and polenta puffed, about 20 minutes.

Tip: If sun-dried tomatoes need to be softened, soak in hot water to cover, 5 to 10 minutes.

VEGGIE PIE

In this version of a family favorite, savory, herb-seasoned vegetables are topped with toasted bread crumbs and baked. A perfect pot-luck side dish!

6 servings

Vegetable cooking spray
1 cup sliced leek (white part only)
1 large red, *or* green, bell pepper, sliced
2 teaspoons minced garlic
3 tablespoons flour
1¹/₂ teaspoons bouquet garni
2 cups reduced-sodium vegetable broth
2 medium russet potatoes, peeled, cubed
2 medium yellow summer squash, sliced
1 cup halved green beans
¹/₂ cup cauliflower florets
¹/₂ cup frozen peas
Salt and pepper, to taste
³/₄ cup fresh bread crumbs
2 tablespoons margarine, melted

Per Serving
Calories: 158
% Calories from fat: 24
Fat (gm): 4.3
Saturated fat (gm): 0.9
Cholesterol (mg): 0
Sodium (mg): 129
Protein (gm): 4.3
Carbohydrate (gm): 26.4
Exchanges
Milk: 0.0
Vegetable: 2.0
Fruit: 0.0
Bread: 1.0
Meat: 0.0
Fat: 1.0

1. Spray large saucepan with cooking spray; heat over medium heat until hot. Saute leek, bell pepper, and garlic 5 minutes; stir in flour and bouquet garni and cook 1 minute longer. Add broth and remaining vegetables; heat to boiling. Reduce heat and simmer, covered, until vegetables are tender, about 10 minutes. Season to taste with salt and pepper. Pour mixture into 1¹/₂-quart soufflé dish or casserole.

2. Toss bread crumbs with margarine; sprinkle over top of casserole. Bake pie at 425 degrees until crumbs are browned, about 20 minutes. Cool on wire rack 5 minutes before serving.

SPINACH TORTELLINI WITH MUSHROOMS

This hearty casserole is a snap to make—it uses mostly prepared ingredients. Use your favorite flavor of sauce, such as roasted garlic, garden vegetable, or even olive, to add interest.

6 servings

1 pound frozen spinach tortellini, thawed
1 pound whole mushrooms
1 medium red bell pepper, chopped
1 cup frozen peas
3/4 cup (3 ounces) shredded reduced-fat mozzarella cheese
1 jar (28 ounces) no-salt-added spaghetti sauce

Per Serving
Calories: 260
% Calories from fat: 30
Fat (gm): 8.7
Saturated fat (gm): 2.3
Cholesterol (mg): 4.2
Sodium (mg): 390
Protein (gm): 12.6
Carbohydrate (gm): 33.6
Exchanges
Milk: 0.0
Vegetable: 0.0
Fruit: 0.0
Bread: 2.0
Meat: 1.0
Fat: 1.0

1. Combine tortellini, mushrooms, pepper, peas, and cheese in 2½-quart casserole. Pour sauce evenly over casserole. Bake, covered, at 350 degrees until hot, about 40 minutes.

BAKED FUSILLI AND CHEESE PRIMAVERA

Asparagus spears, broccoli florets, sliced zucchini, carrots, and mushrooms are other vegetable choices for this cheesy casserole.

6 servings

1 cup sliced cremini, *or* white, mushrooms
3/4 cup chopped onion
1/2 cup chopped red, *or* green, bell pepper
1 teaspoon minced garlic
2 tablespoons margarine
3 cups fat-free milk
1/3 cup all-purpose flour
3 ounces light pasteurized processed cheese product, cubed
1/2 cup (2 ounces) shredded reduced-fat sharp, *or* mild, Cheddar cheese

Per Serving
Calories: 369
% Calories from fat: 19
Fat (gm): 7.9
Saturated fat (gm): 2.9
Cholesterol (mg): 14
Sodium (mg): 231
Protein (gm): 19.6
Carbohydrate (gm): 54.1
Exchanges
Milk: 0.0
Vegetable: 2.0
Fruit: 0.0
Bread: 3.0
Meat: 1.0
Fat: 1.0

1 teaspoon Dijon-style mustard
10 ounces fusilli *or* rotini, cooked .
³/₄ cup frozen peas
 Salt and pepper, to taste
2 tablespoons unseasoned dry bread
 crumbs

1. Saute mushrooms, onion, bell pepper, and garlic in margarine in large saucepan until tender, 5 to 8 minutes. Mix milk and flour until blended; stir into saucepan and heat to boiling, stirring constantly. Boil, stirring constantly, until thickened, about 1 minute.

2. Reduce heat to low; stir in cheeses and mustard, stirring until cheeses are melted. Combine sauce mixture, fusilli, and peas in 2-quart casserole; season to taste with salt and pepper. Sprinkle with bread crumbs. Bake, uncovered, at 375 degrees until bubbly, 20 to 25 minutes.

VEGETARIAN TETRAZZINI

A versatile dish—use any vegetable or pasta you care to substitute.

8 servings

8 ounces sliced mushrooms
1 medium zucchini, sliced
1 cup broccoli florets
1 cup sliced red, *or* green, bell pepper
¹/₂ cup chopped onion
1-2 tablespoons margarine
2 tablespoons flour
1³/₄ cups reduced-sodium vegetable broth
1 cup fat-free milk
¹/₂ cup dry white wine *or* fat-free milk
16 ounces thin spaghetti, cooked
¹/₄ cup grated Parmesan cheese
¹/₄ teaspoon ground nutmeg
 Salt and pepper, to taste

Per Serving
Calories: 333
% Calories from fat: 10
Fat (gm): 3.7
Saturated fat (gm): 1
Cholesterol (mg): 2.5
Sodium (mg): 105
Protein (gm): 12.4
Carbohydrate (gm): 60.1
Exchanges
Milk: 0.0
Vegetable: 3.0
Fruit: 0.0
Bread: 3.0
Meat: 0.0
Fat: 1.0

1. Saute vegetables in margarine in large saucepan 5 minutes. Sprinkle vegetables with flour and cook 1 to 2 minutes longer. Add broth, milk, and wine; heat to boiling. Boil, stirring constantly, until thickened, about 1 minute (sauce will be very thin). Stir in spaghetti, Parmesan cheese, and nutmeg; season to taste with salt and pepper.

2. Spoon mixture into 2-quart casserole or baking dish. Bake, uncovered, at 375 degrees until lightly browned and bubbly, about 30 minutes.

FETTUCCINE FLORENTINE TIMBALE

An impressive side dish for entertaining or special family meals. The casserole can be assembled several hours in advance and refrigerated.

10 servings

Vegetable cooking spray
3 tablespoons dry unseasoned bread crumbs
1 package (1.8 ounces) white sauce mix
2¼ cups fat-free milk
1¼ cups (5 ounces) shredded reduced-fat Italian 6-cheese blend, divided
12 ounces florentine, *or* spinach, fettuccine, cooked
1 package (10 ounces) frozen chopped spinach, thawed, well drained
1 cup fat-free cottage cheese
Salt and pepper, to taste
½ cup roasted red peppers, drained

Per Serving
Calories: 190
% Calories from fat: 14
Fat (gm): 2.9
Saturated fat (gm): 1.2
Cholesterol (mg): 43.1
Sodium (mg): 399
Protein (gm): 14.4
Carbohydrate (gm): 26.4
Exchanges
Milk: 0.0
Vegetable: 1.0
Fruit: 0.0
Bread: 1.5
Meat: 1.0
Fat: 0.0

1. Spray 9-inch springform pan with cooking spray; coat with bread crumbs. Make white sauce mix in large saucepan according to package directions, using milk; stir in ½ cup shredded cheese. Stir in fettuccine; spoon ½ the fettuccine mixture into prepared pan.

2. Mix spinach, ¹/₂ cup shredded cheese, and cottage cheese; season to taste with salt and pepper. Spoon spinach mixture evenly over pasta in pan. Arrange red peppers over spinach mixture; top with remaining pasta mixture.

3. Bake, uncovered, at 375 degrees until golden, 55 to 60 minutes, sprinkling with remaining ¹/₄ cup shredded cheese during last 10 minutes of baking time. Let stand 10 minutes; loosen side of pan with sharp knife and remove. Cut into wedges.

ONE-DISH CHICKEN AND RICE

Just mix and bake this delicious casserole—perfect for a quick dinner.

4 servings

1 can (10¹/₂ ounces) reduced-fat cream of mushroom soup
³/₄ cup fat-free milk
³/₄ cup long-grain rice
¹/₄ teaspoon paprika, divided
¹/₄ teaspoon ground white pepper, divided
¹/₂ teaspoon dried tarragon leaves
1 package (10 ounces) frozen cut green beans
4 boneless, skinless chicken breast halves (4 ounces each)
Salt, to taste

Per Serving
Calories: 342
% Calories from fat: 14
Fat (gm): 5.5
Saturated fat (gm): 1.3
Cholesterol (mg): 72.9
Sodium (mg): 675
Protein (gm): 31
Carbohydrate (gm): 41
Exchanges
Milk: 0.0
Vegetable: 2.0
Fruit: 0.0
Bread: 2.0
Meat: 3.0
Fat: 0.0

1. Combine soup, milk, rice, ¹/₈ teaspoon paprika, ¹/₈ teaspoon pepper, tarragon, and beans in 2-quart shallow baking dish. Place chicken over rice mixture; sprinkle with remaining ¹/₈ teaspoon each of paprika and pepper. Sprinkle lightly with salt. Bake, covered, at 375 degrees 45 minutes.

CHICKEN AND NOODLES

A "comfort" casserole you may remember from your childhood. It's still delicious!

4 servings

3 tablespoons margarine

1/3 cup all-purpose flour

1/4 teaspoon dried sage leaves

1/4 teaspoon dried marjoram leaves

1 can (13³/4 ounces) reduced-sodium fat-free chicken broth

1/4 cup fat-free milk

3 tablespoons diced pimientos

1/4 teaspoon black pepper

1 package (10 ounces) frozen mixed vegetables, thawed, drained

1 pound boneless, skinless chicken breast, cut into 1-inch pieces

8 ounces thin egg noodles, cooked al dente

1/4 cup unseasoned dry bread crumbs, optional

Per Serving
Calories: 507
% Calories from fat: 25
Fat (gm): 13.9
Saturated fat (gm): 3
Cholesterol (mg): 118.2
Sodium (mg): 273
Protein (gm): 38.6
Carbohydrate (gm): 55.5
Exchanges
Milk: 0.0
Vegetable: 3.0
Fruit: 0.0
Bread: 3.0
Meat: 3.0
Fat: 1.0

1. Melt margarine in large saucepan over medium heat; whisk in flour, sage, and marjoram and cook, whisking constantly, 1 to 2 minutes. Whisk in broth and milk; whisk until boiling and thickened. Add pimientos and pepper.

2. Combine vegetables, chicken, and noodles in 2-quart casserole. Pour sauce evenly over top; sprinkle with bread crumbs, if using. Bake, uncovered, at 350 degrees until browned and bubbly, about 30 minutes.

CAPER CHICKEN WITH TOMATO-BASIL LINGUINE

Lemon and capers add a distinctive flavor to this light dish. If you cannot find tomato-basil linguine, any other flavor or plain linguine can be used.

4 servings

1 can (13³/₄ ounces) reduced-sodium fat-free chicken broth
2 tablespoons arrowroot *or* cornstarch
3 tablespoons lemon juice
2¹/₂ tablespoons diced pimientos
2 tablespoons drained capers
8 ounces mushrooms, sliced
1 package (10 ounces) frozen cut broccoli
1 can (8 ounces) sliced water chestnuts, drained
8 ounces tomato-basil linguine
1 pound boneless, skinless chicken breast, cut into 1-inch strips
Salt and pepper, to taste

Per Serving
Calories: 382
% Calories from fat: 11
Fat (gm): 4.7
Saturated fat (gm): 0.9
Cholesterol (mg): 69
Sodium (mg): 415
Protein (gm): 37.3
Carbohydrate (gm): 49.8
Exchanges
Milk: 0.0
Vegetable: 1.0
Fruit: 0.0
Bread: 3.0
Meat: 3.0
Fat: 0.0

1. Combine broth and arrowroot in small saucepan; whisk over medium-high heat until thickened. Remove from heat; stir in lemon juice, pimientos, and capers.

2. Combine mushrooms, broccoli, and water chestnuts in large bowl. Place uncooked linguine in lightly greased 13 x 9-inch baking dish. Place chicken strips on top of linguine; sprinkle with salt and pepper to taste. Spread vegetables over chicken and pour sauce evenly over vegetables. Bake, covered, at 350 degrees until linguine and chicken are tender, about 40 minutes.

TURKEY BOW-TIE PASTA AU GRATIN

The flavors of a favorite pasta salad are recreated in this cold-weather casserole.

8 servings

16 ounces bow-tie pasta (farfalle), cooked al dente

1 pound cooked turkey breast, cut into 1-inch pieces

1 package (10 ounces) frozen cut broccoli, thawed, well drained

1 rib celery, finely chopped

1/2 cup reduced-sodium fat-free chicken broth

1/2 cup fat-free sour cream

1 tablespoon dried dill weed

1 teaspoon black pepper

1 cup (4 ounces) shredded reduced-fat mozzarella cheese

1/4 cup unseasoned dry bread crumbs

Per Serving
Calories: 396
% Calories from fat: 18
Fat (gm): 7.6
Saturated fat (gm): 2.6
Cholesterol (mg): 111.8
Sodium (mg): 217
Protein (gm): 32.6
Carbohydrate (gm): 46.4
Exchanges
Milk: 0.0
Vegetable: 2.0
Fruit: 0.0
Bread: 2.0
Meat: 3.0
Fat: 0.0

1. Combine pasta, turkey, broccoli, and celery in 2 1/2-quart casserole. Mix broth, sour cream, dill, and pepper in medium bowl; stir into pasta mixture. Sprinkle with cheese and bread crumbs. Bake, covered, at 350 degrees 30 minutes; uncover and bake 15 minutes longer.

TURKEY TETRAZZINI

This dish was named for the famous Italian opera singer, Lucia Tetrazzini, who claimed it as her favorite.

8 servings

- 8 ounces mushrooms, sliced
- 2 tablespoons margarine
- 2 tablespoons flour
- 1 can (14½ ounces) reduced-sodium chicken broth
- 1½ cups fat-free milk
- 16 ounces spaghettini (thin spaghetti) cooked
- 12 ounces boneless, skinless turkey, *or* chicken, breast, cooked, cubed
- ¼ cup grated Parmesan cheese
- ¼ teaspoon ground nutmeg
- ¼ teaspoon salt
- ¼ teaspoon pepper

Per Serving
Calories: 370
% Calories from fat: 16
Fat (gm): 6.5
Saturated fat (gm): 1.7
Cholesterol (mg): 35.7
Sodium (mg): 218
Protein (gm): 23.6
Carbohydrate (gm): 50.3
Exchanges
Milk: 0.0
Vegetable: 1.0
Fruit: 0.0
Bread: 3.0
Meat: 2.0
Fat: 0.5

1. Saute mushrooms in margarine in large saucepan until tender, about 5 minutes. Stir in flour; cook over medium heat 1 to 2 minutes more. Stir in chicken broth and milk and heat to boiling. Boil, stirring constantly, until thickened, 1 to 2 minutes (sauce will be very thin). Stir in pasta, turkey, Parmesan cheese, nutmeg, salt, and pepper.

2. Spoon pasta mixture into 2-quart casserole or baking dish. Bake, uncovered, at 350 degrees until lightly browned on top and bubbly, about 45 minutes.

CHICKEN AND CHEESE ROTOLI WITH MANY-CLOVES GARLIC SAUCE

Some people prefer cutting lasagne noodles into halves before filling, as they are easier to handle in eating. If cut, spread each noodle half with 1¹/₂ to 2 tablespoons of the cheese mixture.

6 servings

1 pound boneless, skinless chicken breast, cooked, shredded

1¹/₄ cups reduced-fat ricotta cheese

3-4 cloves garlic, minced

³/₄ teaspoon dried marjoram leaves

¹/₂ teaspoon dried thyme leaves

¹/₂ teaspoon salt

¹/₄ teaspoon pepper

12 lasagne noodles (10 ounces), cooked, room temperature

Many-Cloves Garlic Sauce (see p.23)

Per Serving
Calories: 295
% Calories from fat: 28
Fat (gm): 9.4
Saturated fat (gm): 1.1
Cholesterol (mg): 45.1
Sodium (mg): 315
Protein (gm): 23.3
Carbohydrate (gm): 28.1
Exchanges
Milk: 0.0
Vegetable: 1.0
Fruit: 0.0
Bread: 1.5
Meat: 2.5
Fat: 0.5

1. Mix chicken, cheese, garlic, herbs, salt, and pepper. Spread 3 to 4 tablespoons of mixture evenly on each noodle; roll up and place in baking dish.

2. Spoon Many-Cloves Garlic Sauce over rotoli. Bake, loosely covered with aluminum foil, at 350 degrees until rotoli are hot through and sauce is bubbly, 20 to 30 minutes.

SPINACH-MUSHROOM ROTOLI WITH MARINARA SAUCE

No-boil lasagne noodles can be used in this recipe. Soak them in warm water until softened, about 8 minutes, before using.

6 servings

Olive oil cooking spray
2 cups sliced mushrooms
1 package (10 ounces) fresh spinach, cleaned, chopped
2 cloves garlic, minced
1 teaspoon dried basil leaves
1 teaspoon dried tarragon leaves
1/2 package (8-ounce size) reduced-fat cream cheese, room temperature
1/2 cup fat-free ricotta cheese
1/4 teaspoon salt
1/4 teaspoon pepper
12 lasagne noodles, cooked, room temperature
Marinara Sauce (recipe follows)

Per Serving
Calories: 286
% Calories from fat: 30
Fat (gm): 10.3
Saturated fat (gm): 2.7
Cholesterol (mg): 8.7
Sodium (mg): 686
Protein (gm): 12.5
Carbohydrate (gm): 38
Exchanges
Milk: 0.0
Vegetable: 3.0
Fruit: 0.0
Bread: 1.5
Meat: 0.0
Fat: 2.0

1. Spray large skillet with cooking spray; heat over medium heat until hot. Cook mushrooms, covered, until they release juices, 3 to 5 minutes. Add spinach, garlic, and herbs to skillet; cook, covered, until spinach is wilted, 2 to 3 minutes. Cook, uncovered, over medium to medium-high heat until liquid is gone, about 10 minutes; cool.

2. Combine cheeses, salt, and pepper in large bowl; stir in mushroom mixture. Spread 3 to 4 tablespoons cheese mixture on each noodle; roll up and place, seam side down, in baking dish.

3. Spoon Marinara Sauce over rotoli. Bake, loosely covered with aluminum foil, at 350 degrees until rotoli are hot through and sauce is bubbly, 20 to 30 minutes.

Marinara Sauce

makes about 4 cups

    2 medium onions, chopped
  6-8 cloves garlic, minced
    2 tablespoons olive oil
    2 cans (16 ounces each) plum tomatoes,
         drained, chopped
  1/2 cup dry white wine *or* tomato juice
  1/4 cup tomato paste
  2-3 tablespoons lemon juice
  1/2 teaspoon salt
  1/4 teaspoon pepper

1. Saute onions and garlic in oil in large saucepan until tender, about 5 minutes. Stir in tomatoes, wine, and tomato paste; heat to boiling. Reduce heat and simmer, uncovered, until mixture is medium sauce consistency, about 20 minutes. Stir in lemon juice, salt, and pepper.

EASY EGGPLANT ROTOLI

Incredibly simple to prepare, thanks to no-boil lasagne noodles!

4 servings (2 each)

    8 no-boil lasagne noodles
    4 cups frozen stir-fry pepper blend
    2 teaspoons minced garlic
    1 tablespoon olive oil
    1 small eggplant (about 1 pound),
         unpeeled, cut into 1/2-inch cubes
  1-2 teaspoons Italian seasoning
    2 cups fat-free ricotta cheese
       Salt and pepper, to taste
    2 cans (16 ounces each) no-salt-added
         spaghetti sauce
  1/4 cup grated fat-free Parmesan cheese *or* 1
         cup (4 ounces) shredded reduced-fat
         mozzarella cheese

Per Serving
Calories: 512
% Calories from fat: 29
Fat (gm): 16.3
Saturated fat (gm): 3.8
Cholesterol (mg): 11.4
Sodium (mg): 370
Protein (gm): 28.8
Carbohydrate (gm): 60.8
Exchanges
Milk: 0.0
Vegetable: 3.0
Fruit: 0.0
Bread: 3.0
Meat: 2.0
Fat: 2.0

1. Arrange noodles in flat baking dish or pan and cover with warm water; let stand until noodles are softened, about 8 minutes. Drain well.

2. Saute pepper blend and garlic in oil in large skillet 3 to 4 minutes. Add eggplant and Italian seasoning and cook, covered, until eggplant is tender, about 10 minutes, stirring occasionally. Remove from heat and stir in ricotta cheese; season to taste with salt and pepper.

3. Spread 1/2 cup cheese mixture on each noodle and roll up. Arrange rotoli, seam sides down, in 13 x 9-inch baking pan. Pour spaghetti sauce over and sprinkle with Parmesan cheese. Bake, uncovered, until hot through, about 20 minutes.

CHICKEN-STUFFED SHELLS WITH WHITE SAUCE

Purchased ground chicken or turkey breast can be used in this dish, though the texture of the filling is better if prepared according to the recipe. Cook the shells for the minimum time indicated so they are al dente.

6 servings (5 shells each)

1	pound boneless, skinless chicken breast
1	cup fat-free milk
1	egg white
1 1/2-2	tablespoons fennel seeds, crushed
3	cloves garlic, minced
1	teaspoon dried rosemary leaves
1/4	teaspoon ground nutmeg
1/4	teaspoon salt
1/4	teaspoon pepper
3-4	dashes hot pepper sauce
30	jumbo shells (9 ounces), cooked, room temperature
	White Sauce (recipe follows)
	Parsley, finely chopped, as garnish

Per Serving
Calories: 321
% Calories from fat: 18
Fat (gm): 6.5
Saturated fat (gm): 2
Cholesterol (mg): 43.8
Sodium (mg): 302
Protein (gm): 27
Carbohydrate (gm): 37.4
Exchanges
Milk: 0.5
Vegetable: 0.0
Fruit: 0.0
Bread: 2.0
Meat: 2.5
Fat: 0.0

1. Process chicken breast in the food processor, using pulse technique, until very finely chopped. Add remaining ingredients, except pasta, White Sauce, and parsley; process just until blended.

2. Spoon mixture into shells and arrange in lightly greased baking pan; spoon White Sauce over shells. Bake, loosely covered, at 350 degrees until filling is cooked and begins to pull away from edges of shells, 30 to 35 minutes. Sprinkle with parsley.

White Sauce

makes about 2 cups

1 tablespoon margarine
2 tablespoons flour
2 cups fat-free milk
$^1/_4$ cup grated Parmesan cheese
$^1/_8$ teaspoon ground white pepper

1. Melt margarine in medium saucepan; stir in flour. Cook over medium heat, stirring constantly, 1 to 2 minutes.

2. Add milk to saucepan; heat to boiling, stirring frequently. Boil, stirring constantly, until thickened, 1 to 2 minutes (sauce will be very thin).

3. Remove saucepan from heat; stir in cheese and pepper.

CHICKEN-VEGETABLE MANICOTTI WITH CREAMED SPINACH SAUCE

Tomato Sauce with Mushrooms and Sherry (see p. 543) is also an excellent accompaniment for the manicotti.

6 servings (2 manicotti each)

Olive oil cooking spray
$^1/_2$ cup chopped onion
3 cloves garlic, minced
2 cups spinach leaves, chopped
$^1/_2$ cup chopped zucchini
$^1/_2$ cup chopped yellow summer squash
1 teaspoon dried basil leaves
1 teaspoon dried oregano leaves
8 ounces boneless, skinless chicken, cooked, finely shredded
$^1/_2$ cup reduced-fat ricotta cheese
$^1/_4$ teaspoon salt
$^1/_4$ teaspoon pepper
1 package (8 ounces) manicotti, cooked, room temperature
Creamed Spinach Sauce (recipe follows)

Per Serving
Calories: 340
% Calories from fat: 24
Fat (gm): 2.7
Saturated fat (gm): 2.5
Cholesterol (mg): 31
Sodium (mg): 427
Protein (gm): 23
Carbohydrate (gm): 435
Exchanges
Milk: 0.5
Vegetable: 2.0
Fruit: 0.0
Bread: 2.0
Meat: 1.0
Fat: 1.5

1. Spray large skillet with cooking spray; heat over medium heat until hot. Saute onion and garlic until tender, about 3 minutes. Add remaining vegetables; saute until tender, 5 to 8 minutes. Stir in herbs and cook 2 minutes more. Stir in chicken, cheese, salt, and pepper.

2. Spoon about 3 tablespoons chicken-vegetable mixture into each manicotti; arrange in baking pan. Spoon Creamed Spinach Sauce over manicotti. Bake, loosely covered with aluminum foil, at 350 degrees until manicotti are hot and sauce is bubbly, 35 to 40 minutes.

Creamed Spinach Sauce

makes about 3 cups

>   2 cloves garlic, minced
>   2 tablespoons margarine
>   1/4 cup all-purpose flour
>   3 cups 2% reduced-fat milk
>   1 1/2 pounds fresh spinach, cleaned, chopped
>   2 teaspoons dried basil leaves
>   1/8-1/4 teaspoon ground nutmeg
>   4-6 dashes hot pepper sauce
>   1/4-1/2 teaspoon salt

1. Saute garlic in margarine in large saucepan 1 to 2 minutes. Stir in flour and cook over medium heat 1 to 2 minutes more. Stir in milk; heat to boiling. Boil, stirring constantly, until thickened, 1 to 2 minutes.

2. Stir spinach and remaining ingredients into sauce. Cook, uncovered, over medium heat until spinach is cooked, 5 to 7 minutes.

MUSHROOM-BROCCOLI MANICOTTI

Any pasta that is going to be filled and baked should be cooked only until al dente so that the completed dish is not overcooked.

6 servings (2 manicotti each)

Olive oil cooking spray

4   shallots *or* green onions, chopped

3   cloves garlic, minced

2   cups sliced mushrooms

2   cups finely chopped, cooked broccoli

2   teaspoons dried basil leaves

1   teaspoon dried marjoram leaves

1   cup reduced-fat ricotta cheese

1/4   teaspoon salt

1/4   teaspoon pepper

1   package (8 ounces) manicotti, cooked, room temperature

Tomato Sauce with Mushrooms and Sherry (recipe follows)

Per Serving
Calories: 263
% Calories from fat: 17
Fat (gm): 5.2
Saturated fat (gm): 0.5
Cholesterol (mg): 5.3
Sodium (mg): 443
Protein (gm): 12.8
Carbohydrate (gm): 42.3
Exchanges
Milk: 0.0
Vegetable: 2.5
Fruit: 0.0
Bread: 2.0
Meat: 0.0
Fat: 1.0

1. Spray large skillet with cooking spray; heat over medium heat until hot. Saute shallots and garlic until tender, 2 to 3 minutes. Add mushrooms; cook, covered, until mushrooms release juices, 3 to 5 minutes. Cook, uncovered, over medium to medium-high heat, until liquid is gone, about 10 minutes. Stir in broccoli, basil, and marjoram; cook 2 to 3 minutes. Stir in cheese, salt, and pepper.

2. Spoon about 3 tablespoons vegetable-cheese mixture into each manicotti; arrange in baking pan. Spoon Tomato Sauce with Mushrooms and Sherry over manicotti. Bake, loosely covered with aluminum foil, at 350 degrees until manicotti are hot and sauce is bubbly, 30 to 35 minutes.

Tomato Sauce with Mushrooms and Sherry

makes about 2 cups

  1 small onion, finely chopped
  2 cloves garlic, minced
  1 tablespoon olive oil
  4 cups sliced mushrooms
  3 tablespoons dry sherry *or* water
  1 can (28 ounces) crushed tomatoes, undrained
  2 tablespoons finely chopped parsley
$^1/_2$ teaspoon dried rosemary leaves, crushed
$^1/_2$ teaspoon dried oregano leaves
  1 teaspoon sugar
$^1/_4$ teaspoon salt
$^1/_4$ teaspoon pepper

1. Saute onion and garlic in oil in medium saucepan 2 to 3 minutes. Add mushrooms and sherry; cook, covered, over medium-high heat until mushrooms are wilted and release liquid. Reduce heat and cook, uncovered, until mushrooms are soft and have darkened, stirring occasionally.

2. Stir in tomatoes and liquid, herbs, and sugar; heat to boiling. Reduce heat and simmer, covered, 10 to 15 minutes. Stir in salt and pepper.

VEGGIE LASAGNE WITH EGGPLANT SAUCE

The hearty Eggplant Sauce is also wonderful served over shaped or tube pastas, such as corkscrews or ziti, or over cheese or chicken tortellini.

8 servings

Olive oil cooking spray
1 medium onion, sliced
1 medium zucchini, sliced
1 medium red bell pepper, sliced
1 cup sliced mushrooms
3 cloves garlic, minced
2 cups fat-free ricotta cheese
1/4 cup grated Parmesan cheese
Eggplant Sauce (recipe follows)
12 lasagne noodles (10 ounces), cooked, room temperature
2 medium sweet potatoes, sliced, cooked until crisp-tender
2 cups (8 ounces) shredded reduced-fat mozzarella cheese

Per Serving
Calories: 375
% Calories from fat: 24
Fat (gm): 10.4
Saturated fat (gm): 4.2
Cholesterol (mg): 23.7
Sodium (mg): 685
Protein (gm): 24.1
Carbohydrate (gm): 47
Exchanges
Milk: 0.0
Vegetable: 3.0
Fruit: 0.0
Bread: 2.0
Meat: 2.5
Fat: 0.5

1. Spray large skillet with cooking spray; heat over medium heat until hot. Saute onion, zucchini, bell pepper, mushrooms, and garlic until tender, about 10 minutes. Mix ricotta and Parmesan cheese in small bowl.

2. Spread about 1/2 cup Eggplant Sauce in bottom of 13 x 9-inch baking pan; top with 4 lasagne noodles, overlapping slightly. Spoon 1/3 of ricotta cheese mixture over noodles, spreading lightly with rubber spatula. Top with 1/3 of the sweet potatoes and 1/3 of the sauteed vegetables. Spoon 1/3 of the Eggplant Sauce over vegetables; sprinkle with 1/3 of the mozzarella cheese. Repeat layers 2 times.

3. Bake lasagne, loosely covered with aluminum foil, at 350 degrees until sauce is bubbly, about 1 hour.

Eggplant Sauce

makes about 6 cups

- 1 pound unpeeled eggplant, cut into 1^1/$_2$-inch pieces
- 1 cup chopped onion
- ^{1}/$_2$ cup chopped green bell pepper
- 6 cloves garlic, minced
- 2 tablespoons olive oil
- 3 cups chopped tomatoes
- ^{3}/$_4$ teaspoon dried tarragon leaves
- ^{3}/$_4$ teaspoon dried thyme leaves
- 1 can (28 ounces) crushed tomatoes, undrained
- ^{1}/$_2$ cup dry red wine
- 2 tablespoons drained capers
- 2 teaspoons sugar
- ^{1}/$_2$ teaspoon salt
- ^{1}/$_4$ teaspoon pepper

1. Saute eggplant, onion, bell pepper, and garlic in oil in large saucepan 5 minutes. Add chopped tomatoes and herbs, and saute until onions are crisp-tender, 5 to 7 minutes.

2. Stir canned tomatoes and liquid, wine, capers, and sugar into vegetable mixture; heat to boiling. Reduce heat and simmer, covered, until eggplant is tender, about 20 minutes. Simmer, uncovered, until desired sauce consistency, about 10 minutes more. Stir in salt and pepper.

SAUSAGE LASAGNE

The traditional lasagne we all love, with a low-fat rendering.

8 servings

2 cups fat-free ricotta cheese

1/4 cup grated Parmesan cheese

3 cups (12 ounces) shredded reduced-fat mozzarella cheese

Tomato Sauce with Italian Sausage (recipe follows)

12 lasagne noodles (10 ounces), cooked, room temperature

Per Serving
Calories: 375
% Calories from fat: 30
Fat (gm): 12.9
Saturated fat (gm): 6
Cholesterol (mg): 47.3
Sodium (mg): 679
Protein (gm): 31.3
Carbohydrate (gm): 33.9
Exchanges
Milk: 0.0
Vegetable: 2.5
Fruit: 0.0
Bread: 1.5
Meat: 3.5
Fat: 0.5

1. Combine cheeses in bowl. Spread 1 cup Tomato Sauce with Italian Sausage on bottom of 13 x 9-inch baking pan; top with 4 lasagne noodles, overlapping slightly. Spoon 1/3 of cheese mixture over noodles, spreading lightly with rubber spatula. Top with 1 cup sauce. Repeat layers 2 times, ending with layer of noodles, cheese, and remaining sauce.

2. Bake lasagne, loosely covered with aluminum foil, at 350 degrees until sauce is bubbly, about 1 hour.

Tomato Sauce with Italian Sausage

makes about 4¹/₂ cups

Olive oil cooking spray

2 cups chopped onions

3 cloves garlic, minced

1 teaspoon dried basil leaves

1 teaspoon dried tarragon leaves

1 teaspoon dried thyme leaves

2 cans (16 ounces each) reduced-sodium whole tomatoes, undrained, coarsely chopped

2 cans (8 ounces each) reduced-sodium tomato sauce

1 cup water

1-2 teaspoons sugar

8 ounces Italian-style turkey sausage, cooked, well drained

1/4 teaspoon salt

1/4 teaspoon pepper

1. Spray large saucepan with cooking spray; heat over medium heat until hot. Saute onions and garlic until tender, about 5 minutes; stir in herbs and cook 1 to 2 minutes more.

2. Add tomatoes and liquid, tomato sauce, and water; heat to boiling. Reduce heat and simmer, uncovered, until sauce is reduced to about 4 1/2 cups, 15 to 20 minutes. Stir in sugar; stir in sausage, salt, and pepper.

MEXICAN-STYLE LASAGNE

A lasagne with a difference!

8 servings

2 cups fat-free ricotta cheese

2 cups (8 ounces) shredded reduced-fat Monterey Jack cheese

1 can (15 ounces) pinto beans, rinsed, drained

1 can (15 ounces) black beans, rinsed, drained

Chili-Tomato Sauce (recipe follows)

12 lasagne noodles (10 ounces), cooked, room temperature

1/4 cup finely chopped cilantro *or* parsley

Per Serving
Calories: 360
% Calories from fat: 18
Fat (gm): 8
Saturated fat (gm): 3.1
Cholesterol (mg): 26.3
Sodium (mg): 748
Protein (gm): 30.7
Carbohydrate (gm): 51
Exchanges
Milk: 0.0
Vegetable: 3.0
Fruit: 0.0
Bread: 2.0
Meat: 2.5
Fat: 0.5

1. Combine ricotta and Monterey Jack cheese. Combine pinto and black beans. Spread 1 1/2 cups Chili-Tomato Sauce on bottom of 13 x 9-inch baking pan; top with 4 lasagne noodles, overlapping slightly. Spoon 1/3 of the cheese mixture over noodles, spreading lightly with rubber spatula; top with 1/3 of the beans and 1 cup sauce. Repeat layers 2 times, ending with remaining 1 1/2 cups sauce.

2. Bake lasagne, loosely covered with aluminum foil, at 350 degrees until sauce is bubbly, about 1 hour. Sprinkle with cilantro before serving.

Chili-Tomato Sauce

makes about 5 cups

Olive oil cooking spray
2 cups chopped onions
3 cloves garlic, minced
2-3 teaspoons minced jalapeño chilies
2 cans (14¹/₂ ounces each) reduced-sodium stewed tomatoes
2 cans (8 ounces each) reduced-sodium tomato sauce
2 tablespoons chili powder
2 teaspoons ground cumin
1 teaspoon dried oregano leaves
¹/₄-¹/₂ teaspoon salt

1. Spray large saucepan with cooking spray; heat over medium heat until hot. Saute onions, garlic, and jalapeño chilies until the onions are tender, 5 to 8 minutes.

2. Stir in remaining ingredients, except salt; heat to boiling. Reduce heat and simmer, uncovered, until sauce is reduced to 5 cups, about 20 minutes. Stir in salt.

SPAGHETTI AND EGGPLANT PARMESAN

Baked in a springform pan, the presentation of this dish is unusual and quite attractive.

8 servings

Olive oil cooking spray
1 large eggplant (about 3 pounds), sliced ¹/₄ inch thick
1 small onion, very finely chopped
3 cloves garlic, minced
1 tablespoon olive oil
2 cans (8 ounces each) reduced-sodium tomato sauce
8 medium plum tomatoes, chopped
¹/₈ teaspoon crushed red pepper
3 tablespoons finely chopped fresh, *or* 2 teaspoons dried, basil leaves

Per Serving
Calories: 279
% Calories from fat: 13
Fat (gm): 4.1
Saturated fat (gm): 1.1
Cholesterol (mg): 2.5
Sodium (mg): 104
Protein (gm): 10.1
Carbohydrate (gm): 52.5
Exchanges
Milk: 0.0
Vegetable: 2.0
Fruit: 0.0
Bread: 2.5
Meat: 0.0
Fat: 1.0

12 ounces spaghetti, cooked, room temperature

1/4 cup grated Parmesan cheese

2-3 tablespoons dry unseasoned bread crumbs

1. Spray large skillet with cooking spray; heat over medium heat until hot. Cook eggplant slices until browned, about 4 minutes on each side. Set aside.

2. Saute onion and garlic in oil in same large skillet until tender, 3 to 5 minutes. Add tomato sauce, tomatoes, and red pepper to skillet; heat to boiling. Reduce heat and simmer, uncovered, until mixture is medium sauce consistency, about 15 minutes. Remove from heat; stir in basil. Pour sauce over spaghetti and toss; stir in Parmesan cheese.

3. Heat oven to 350 degrees. Spray 9-inch springform pan with cooking spray; coat with bread crumbs. Line bottom and side of pan with 3/4 of the eggplant slices, overlapping slices and allowing those on sides to extend 1 to 1 1/2 inches above top of pan. Spoon spaghetti mixture into pan; press into pan firmly. Fold eggplant slices at top of pan over spaghetti mixture. Overlap remaining eggplant slices on top, pressing firmly into place.

4. Bake, uncovered, until hot through, about 30 minutes. Remove side of pan. Cut into wedges.

LASAGNE CASSEROLE

The flavors of lasagne, made with macaroni rather than lasagne noodles. Try any shape of small pasta that you like. The casserole can also be cooked in the microwave; cook covered, on high power for about 10 minutes or until bubbly.

6 servings

  2 cans (15 ounces each) reduced-sodium tomato sauce
  1 bag (16 ounces) frozen stir-fry pepper blend, slightly thawed
  1 teaspoon minced garlic
  1 tablespoon Italian seasoning
     Salt and pepper, to taste
 10 ounces macaroni, cooked, warm
  1 carton (15 ounces) reduced-fat ricotta cheese
  2 cups (8 ounces) shredded reduced-fat mozzarella, divided
 1/2 cup grated Parmesan cheese, divided

Per Serving
Calories: 467
% Calories from fat: 25
Fat (gm): 12.8
Saturated fat (gm): 7.4
Cholesterol (mg): 41.4
Sodium (mg): 641
Protein (gm): 32.9
Carbohydrate (gm): 55
Exchanges
Milk: 0.0
Vegetable: 3.0
Fruit: 0.0
Bread: 3.0
Meat: 2.0
Fat: 1.5

1. Combine tomato sauce, pepper blend, garlic, and Italian seasoning in medium bowl; season to taste with salt and pepper. Spoon 1/3 of the macaroni into a 3-quart casserole dish. Mix ricotta with 1 3/4 cups mozzarella; spoon half the cheese mixture over macaroni in dish, smoothing with spoon. Sprinkle with 2 tablespoons Parmesan. Spoon 1/3 of the sauce mixture over cheese. Top with another 1/3 of the macaroni, the remaining cheese mixture, and sprinkle with 2 tablespoons Parmesan. Spoon half the remaining sauce mixture over; top with remaining macaroni and remaining sauce.

2. Bake, uncovered, at 375 degrees until bubbly, about 40 minutes, sprinkling casserole with remaining Parmesan and 1/4 cup mozzarella during last 5 minutes of baking time.

CHILIQUILES

Leftovers, Mexican-style! Chiliquiles is a family-style casserole dish usually made with stale tortillas and leftover cooked meats. Vary this casserole with ingredients you have on hand!

8 servings

8 corn, *or* flour, tortillas
Vegetable cooking spray
1 medium green bell pepper, thinly sliced
1/2 teaspoon minced jalapeño chili
1/4 teaspoon cayenne pepper
Enchilada Sauce (see p. 553)
1 1/2 cups cooked black beans *or* 1 can (15 ounces) black beans, rinsed, drained
1 cup fresh, *or* frozen, thawed whole-kernel corn
12-16 ounces cooked chicken breast, shredded
1 large tomato, thinly sliced
Jalapeño con Queso Sauce (recipe follows)
Medium, *or* hot, salsa

Per Serving
Calories: 292
% Calories from fat: 16
Fat (gm): 5.4
Saturated fat (gm): 2.6
Cholesterol (mg): 46.1
Sodium (mg): 634
Protein (gm): 30.1
Carbohydrate (gm): 32.5
Exchanges
Milk: 0.0
Vegetable: 1.0
Fruit: 0.0
Bread: 1.5
Meat: 3.0
Fat: 0.0

1. Spray both sides of tortillas lightly with cooking spray; cook in small skillet over medium-high heat to brown lightly, 30 to 60 seconds per side. Cool slightly; cut into 1/2-inch strips.

2. Spray small skillet with cooking spray; heat over medium heat until hot. Saute bell pepper and jalapeño chili until tender, 2 to 3 minutes; sprinkle with cayenne pepper. Stir in Enchilada Sauce; heat until hot.

3. Arrange 1/3 of the tortilla strips in bottom of 2-quart casserole; top with 1/2 cup black beans, 1/3 cup corn, 1/3 of the chicken, 1/3 of the tomato slices, and 2/3 cup Jalapeño con Queso Sauce. Repeat layers 2 times.

4. Bake casserole, uncovered, at 350 degrees until hot through, 25 to 30 minutes. Serve hot with salsa.

Jalapeño con Queso Sauce

makes about 2 cups

    Vegetable cooking spray
  1 teaspoon finely chopped jalapeño chili
  1 teaspoon ground cumin
  $^1/_2$ teaspoon dried oregano leaves
  8 ounces reduced-fat pasteurized processed cheese product, cubed
$^1/_3$-$^1/_2$ cup fat-free milk
1$^1/_4$ cups (5 ounces) shredded fat-free Cheddar cheese

1. Spray medium saucepan with cooking spray; heat over medium heat until hot. Saute jalapeño chili until tender, about 2 minutes; stir in cumin and oregano.

2. Add processed cheese product; cook over low heat, stirring frequently, until melted. Stir in 1/3 cup milk and Cheddar cheese. Stir in additional milk if needed for desired consistency, cooking until hot, 1 to 2 minutes.

ENCHILADA STACK

A quick and easy casserole. Corn tortillas are layered with pork, beans, chilies, and cheese, then baked until hot—a Mexican fiesta of flavors, perfect for brunch!

4 servings

 12 ounces boneless pork tenderloin, cut into 1-inch slices
    Vegetable cooking spray
  1 medium onion, chopped
  1 can (15 ounces) pinto beans, rinsed, drained
  1 medium tomato, chopped
  1 can (4 ounces) chopped green chilies, drained
1$^1/_2$ teaspoons ground cumin
  $^1/_4$ teaspoon pepper
  5 corn tortillas
    Enchilada Sauce (recipe follows)

Per Serving
Calories: 379
% Calories from fat: 16
Fat (gm): 7.2
Saturated fat (gm): 2.2
Cholesterol (mg): 56.7
Sodium (mg): 793
Protein (gm): 33.1
Carbohydrate (gm): 49.4
Exchanges
Milk: 0.0
Vegetable: 2.0
Fruit: 0.0
Bread: 2.5
Meat: 2.5
Fat: 0.0

¹/₂ cup (2 ounces) shredded reduced-fat
Cheddar cheese

¹/₃ cup fat-free sour cream

1. Heat pork tenderloin in saucepan with 2 inches water to boiling; reduce heat and simmer, covered, until pork is tender, about 10 minutes. Drain; cool slightly and shred finely.

2. Spray medium skillet with cooking spray; heat over medium heat until hot. Saute onion until tender, 3 to 4 minutes. Add shredded pork, beans, tomato, chilies, cumin, and pepper; cook over medium heat until hot, 3 to 4 minutes.

3. Place 1 tortilla in bottom of 1-quart soufflé dish or casserole; spoon ¹/₄ of bean mixture over tortilla. Spoon ¹/₃ cup Enchilada Sauce over. Repeat layers three times, ending with tortilla and remaining ²/₃ cup Enchilada Sauce. Sprinkle with cheese.

4. Bake, covered, at 350 degrees until hot through, 25 to 30 minutes. Let stand 5 minutes; cut into 4 wedges. Serve with sour cream.

Enchilada Sauce

makes about 2 cups

1 ancho chili, stem, seeds, and veins
discarded

2 medium tomatoes, chopped

1 red bell pepper, chopped

1 small onion, chopped

2 cloves garlic, minced

¹/₂ teaspoon dried marjoram leaves

¹/₈ teaspoon ground allspice
Vegetable cooking spray

1 bay leaf
Salt, to taste

1. Cover ancho chili with boiling water in small bowl; let stand until softened, 10 to 15 minutes. Drain.

2. Process ancho chili, tomatoes, bell pepper, onion, garlic, marjoram, and allspice in food processor or blender until almost smooth.

3. Spray small skillet with cooking spray; heat over medium heat until hot. Cook sauce and bay leaf over medium heat until thickened to a medium sauce consistency; discard bay leaf and season with salt. Serve hot.

TAMALE PIE

Have the flavor and goodness of tamales the easy way with this delicious casserole.

4 servings

1 pound lean ground beef
1 medium onion, chopped
1 clove garlic, minced
2 teaspoons chili powder
1¼ teaspoons ground cumin, divided
1 can (15 ounces) reduced-sodium tomato sauce
1 can (4 ounces) diced green chilies, drained
1 cup yellow cornmeal
  Hot pepper sauce, to taste
2 cups water
1 package (10 ounces) frozen whole-kernel corn
1 cup (4 ounces) shredded fat-free Cheddar cheese

Per Serving
Calories: 493
% Calories from fat: 28
Fat (gm): 15.5
Saturated fat (gm): 5.7
Cholesterol (mg): 70.4
Sodium (mg): 423
Protein (gm): 37.3
Carbohydrate (gm): 52.6
Exchanges
Milk: 0.0
Vegetable: 3.0
Fruit: 0.0
Bread: 3.0
Meat: 3.0
Fat: 1.0

1. Saute ground beef, onion, and garlic in large skillet until beef is browned, crumbling meat as it cooks; drain excess fat. Stir in chili powder, 1 teaspoon cumin, tomato sauce, and chilies; simmer over low heat, stirring occasionally.

2. Combine cornmeal, remaining ¼ teaspoon cumin, hot pepper sauce, and water in medium saucepan. Stir until well blended. Heat to boiling, stirring constantly; reduce heat and simmer until thickened, about 3 minutes.

3 Stir corn and cheese into meat mixture and simmer 1 minute. Pour meat mixture into 2-quart baking dish; spoon cornmeal mixture over. Bake, uncovered, at 375 degrees until browned, about 40 minutes.

AUTUMN POT PIE

Choose ingredients from your garden or produce market for this savory pie.

6 servings

Olive oil cooking spray
8 ounces pork tenderloin, cubed
1¹/₂ cups frozen stir-fry pepper blend
2 teaspoons minced garlic
3 tablespoons flour
³/₄ teaspoon dried sage leaves
2 pinches ground nutmeg
2 cups reduced-sodium fat-free beef broth
2 medium sweet potatoes, peeled, cubed (¹/₂ inch)
2 medium russet potatoes, peeled, cubed (¹/₂ inch)
1 cup cubed (¹/₂ inch), peeled turnip *or* parsnip
1 cup halved Brussels sprouts
Salt and pepper, to taste
Pastry for 9-inch pie, purchased

Per Serving
Calories: 318
% Calories from fat: 30
Fat (gm): 10.9
Saturated fat (gm): **4.5**
Cholesterol (mg): **28.6**
Sodium (mg): **287**
Protein (gm): **13.6**
Carbohydrate (gm): **43.1**
Exchanges
Milk: 0.0
Vegetable: 1.0
Fruit: 0.0
Bread: 2.5
Meat: 1.5
Fat: 1.0

1. Spray large saucepan with cooking spray; heat over medium heat until hot. Saute pork until browned, about 5 minutes; add pepper blend and garlic and cook until tender, about 5 minutes. Stir in flour, sage, and nutmeg and cook 1 to 2 minutes longer. Add broth and remaining vegetables; heat to boiling. Reduce heat and simmer, covered, until vegetables are tender, about 10 minutes. Season to taste with salt and pepper. Pour mixture into 1¹/₂-quart casserole or soufflé dish.

2. Place pastry on top of casserole; fold edge of pastry under and flute or press with tines of fork. Bake pie at 425 degrees until pastry is browned, about 20 minutes. Cool on wire rack 5 minutes before serving.

VEGGIE SHEPHERD'S PIE

Topped with traditional mashed potatoes, this comfort food is sure to please.

4 servings (about 1¹/₄ cups each)

Vegetable cooking spray
1¹/₂ cups frozen onion seasoning blend
¹/₂ cup sliced celery
1 teaspoon minced garlic
³/₄ teaspoon dried savory leaves
3 tablespoons flour
2 cups reduced-sodium vegetable broth
1 cup thinly sliced cabbage
1 cup sliced carrots
2 medium Idaho potatoes, unpeeled, cubed
³/₄ cup sliced mushrooms
Salt and pepper, to taste
³/₄ package (22-ounce size) frozen mashed potatoes

Per Serving
Calories: 235
% Calories from fat: 11
Fat (gm): 2.9
Saturated fat (gm): 0.9
Cholesterol (mg): 2.3
Sodium (mg): 354
Protein (gm): 6.1
Carbohydrate (gm): 47.7
Exchanges
Milk: 0.0
Vegetable: 3.0
Fruit: 0.0
Bread: 2.0
Meat: 0.0
Fat: 0.5

1. Spray large saucepan with cooking spray; heat over medium heat until hot. Saute onion seasoning blend, celery, garlic, and savory 5 minutes. Sprinkle with flour and cook 1 minute. Stir in broth and remaining vegetables and heat to boiling; reduce heat and simmer, covered, until vegetables are tender, about 10 minutes. Season to taste with salt and pepper. Pour mixture into 1¹/₂-quart soufflé dish or casserole.

2. Make mashed potatoes according to package directions. Spoon or pipe mashed potatoes around edge of casserole; bake at 375 degrees until potatoes are lightly browned, about 20 minutes.

TORTA RUSTICA

An Italian pizza in a crust-lined deep-dish pie.

6 to 8 servings

Olive oil cooking spray
1¹/₂ cups chopped onions
1¹/₂ teaspoons minced roasted garlic
6-8 ounces turkey Italian sausage, casing removed
1 can (16 ounces) reduced-sodium whole tomatoes, undrained, coarsely chopped
2 medium zucchini, sliced
1¹/₂ cups sliced mushrooms
Salt and pepper, to taste
1 package (16 ounces) hot roll mix
1 cup very hot water (120 degrees)
1 egg
1¹/₂ cups (6 ounces) shredded low-sodium mozzarella cheese
Fat-free milk

Per Serving
Calories: 457
% Calories from fat: 23
Fat (gm): 11.5
Saturated fat (gm): 4.2
Cholesterol (mg): 65.8
Sodium (mg): 760
Protein (gm): 23.5
Carbohydrate (gm): 63.7
Exchanges
Milk: 0.0
Vegetable: 1.0
Fruit: 0.0
Bread: 4.0
Meat: 2.0
Fat: 1.0

1. Spray large skillet with cooking spray; heat over medium heat until hot. Saute onions, garlic, and sausage until onions are tender, about 5 minutes; drain any fat. Stir in tomatoes, zucchini, and mushrooms; heat to boiling. Reduce heat and simmer, covered, 5 minutes. Simmer, uncovered, until excess liquid is gone, about 10 minutes. Season to taste with salt and pepper.

2. Make hot roll mix according to package directions, using hot water and egg, and omitting margarine. Roll ²/₃ of the dough on floured surface to fit 2-quart casserole or soufflé dish. Ease dough into casserole, allowing dough to extend 1 inch over edge. Spoon half the vegetable mixture into casserole; sprinkle with half the cheese. Top with remaining vegetable mixture and cheese.

3. Roll remaining dough into circle to fit top of casserole; place over vegetable mixture. Bring outside edges of dough together and crimp. Cut 1 or 2 slits in top of dough with sharp knife. Brush top of dough with milk.

4. Bake at 400 degrees until crust is browned, about 30 minutes. Let stand 5 to 10 minutes before serving.

WILD RICE, CHEESE, AND VEGETABLE CASSEROLE

Delicious, with a generous amount of melty cheese. The vegetables can vary according to season and availability.

4 servings (about 1¹/₄ cups each)

1 package (6¹/₄ ounces) wild and white rice mix, cooked without spice packet

1¹/₂ cups cut asparagus spears, blanched

1¹/₂ cups halved small Brussels sprouts, blanched

3 ounces fat-free cream cheese, cubed

³/₄ cup (3 ounces) shredded fat-free mozzarella cheese

3-4 ounces goat cheese, crumbled
Salt and pepper, to taste

Per Serving
Calories: 307
% Calories from fat: 21
Fat (gm): 7.2
Saturated fat (gm): 4.3
Cholesterol (mg): 9.7
Sodium (mg): 200
Protein (gm): 21.7
Carbohydrate (gm): 39
Exchanges
Milk: 0.0
Vegetable: 2.0
Fruit: 0.0
Bread: 2.0
Meat: 1.5
Fat: 0.5

1. Mix rice, vegetables, and cheeses; season to taste with salt and pepper. Spoon into 1¹/₂-quart casserole.

2. Bake, covered, at 350 degrees until casserole is hot and cheese is melted, about 30 minutes.

BEEF AND NOODLE BAKE

This old-fashioned pot-luck dish makes a great cold weather meal, quick to fix and hearty.

6 servings

1¹/₂ pounds lean ground beef
1 large onion, finely chopped
1 large green bell pepper, coarsely chopped
1 package (10 ounces) frozen corn
1 can (14¹/₂ ounces) reduced-sodium diced tomatoes
¹/₂ teaspoon black pepper
12 ounces thin egg noodles, cooked al dente
¹/₄ cup seasoned dry bread crumbs

Per Serving
Calories: 495
% Calories from fat: 30
Fat (gm): 16.5
Saturated fat (gm): 6
Cholesterol (mg): 119.4
Sodium (mg): 118
Protein (gm): 31.3
Carbohydrate (gm): 55.6
Exchanges
Milk: 0.0
Vegetable: 2.0
Fruit: 0.0
Bread: 3.0
Meat: 3.0
Fat: 1.5

1. Brown beef and onion in large skillet, crumbling as meat browns; drain fat. Stir in bell pepper, corn, tomatoes, and black pepper.

2. Combine noodles and beef mixture in 2¹/₂-quart casserole; sprinkle bread crumbs over top. Bake, uncovered, at 350 degrees 45 minutes.

BEEF STROGANOFF CASSEROLE

Always add the sour cream to this casserole near the end of baking time to avoid curdling. No-yolk noodles can be substituted for the egg noodles in the recipe.

6 servings

12   ounces wide egg noodles

1¹/₂ pounds beef round, *or* sirloin, steak, cut into 1-inch strips

¹/₂ cup all-purpose flour

1   pound mushrooms, coarsely chopped

2   tablespoons finely chopped onion

¹/₂ teaspoon ground nutmeg

¹/₂ teaspoon dried parsley flakes

1   tablespoon paprika

1   can (13³/₄ ounces) reduced-sodium fat-free beef broth

1   container (8 ounces) fat-free sour cream

Salt and pepper, to taste

Per Serving
Calories: 409
% Calories from fat: 14
Fat (gm): 6.4
Saturated fat (gm): 1.9
Cholesterol (mg): 103.6
Sodium (mg): 132
Protein (gm): 33.7
Carbohydrate (gm): 52.4
Exchanges
Milk: 0.0
Vegetable: 1.0
Fruit: 0.0
Bread: 3.0
Meat: 3.0
Fat: 0.0

1. Place uncooked noodles in 2¹/₂-quart casserole. Coat beef with flour; arrange on top of noodles. Arrange mushrooms over meat; sprinkle with onion, nutmeg, parsley, and paprika. Pour beef broth over. Bake, covered, at 325 degrees 1 hour; stir in sour cream and bake, uncovered, 15 minutes longer. Season to taste with salt and pepper.

SPICY BEEF AND ASPARAGUS WITH RICE NOODLES

Much preparation time is saved by using frozen stir-fry vegetables with the fresh asparagus. Rice noodles are found in the ethnic foods section of your market.

6 servings

1	pound lean top beef round steak, cut into thin strips
8	ounces rice noodles, soaked in cold water 10 minutes
12	ounces fresh asparagus, cut into 1-inch pieces
1	package (16 ounces) frozen stir-fry vegetables, thawed, drained
2	tablespoons flour
2	tablespoons water
1/4	teaspoon black pepper
	Hot pepper sauce, to taste
1	beef bouillon cube, dissolved in 3/4 cup hot water
1	tablespoon reduced-sodium soy sauce
1	tablespoon catsup
1	teaspoon minced garlic

Per Serving
Calories: 291
% Calories from fat: 11
Fat (gm): 3.5
Saturated fat (gm): 1.2
Cholesterol (mg): 37.3
Sodium (mg): 274
Protein (gm): 25.8
Carbohydrate (gm): 38
Exchanges
Milk: 0.0
Vegetable: 2.0
Fruit: 0.0
Bread: 2.0
Meat: 2.0
Fat: 0.0

1. Place beef, rice noodles, asparagus, and stir-fry vegetables in 2 1/2-quart casserole. Whisk flour and water in small bowl until smooth; whisk in with remaining ingredients. Pour over casserole. Bake, covered, at 350 degrees 45 minutes.

SALMON, PEA POD, AND NEW POTATO CASSEROLE

The lemon in this casserole gives a light, delicate flavor accent.

4 servings

- 4 salmon fillets (about 4 ounces each)
- 2 tablespoons margarine, softened
- 1 tablespoon dried tarragon leaves
- 1 small lemon, thinly sliced
- 1 package (8 ounces) frozen pea pods, thawed
- 6 small new potatoes, peeled, quartered
- 1/2 tablespoon black pepper
- 1/3 cup apple cider

Per Serving
Calories: 404
% Calories from fat: 22
Fat (gm): 10.1
Saturated fat (gm): 1.9
Cholesterol (mg): 57.1
Sodium (mg): 156
Protein (gm): 28.1
Carbohydrate (gm): 53
Exchanges
Milk: 0.0
Vegetable: 2.0
Fruit: 0.0
Bread: 3.0
Meat: 2.0
Fat: 1.0

1. Place salmon in lightly greased 13 x 9-inch baking dish; spread each fillet with margarine. Sprinkle with tarragon and cover with lemon slices.

2. Place pea pods and potatoes around fish; sprinkle with pepper and pour cider over. Bake, covered, at 350 degrees until fish flakes easily with fork and potatoes are tender, 20 to 30 minutes.

TWELVE

Vegetable Side Dishes

BRAISED WHOLE ARTICHOKES

After the artichokes are tender, continue to cook them slowly until the bottoms are browned and crusty—the resulting flavor is marvelous!

4 servings

    4 medium artichokes
       Salt, to taste
2-4 teaspoons extra-virgin olive oil

Per Serving
Calories: 80
% Calories from fat: 24
Fat (gm): 2.4
Saturated fat (gm): 0.3
Cholesterol (mg): 0
Sodium (mg): 114
Protein (gm): 4.2
Carbohydrate (gm): 13.4
Exchanges
Milk: 0.0
Vegetable: 2.0
Fruit: 0.0
Bread: 0.0
Meat: 0.0
Fat: 0.5

1. Cut 1 inch from tops of artichokes and trim off stems. Place artichokes in medium saucepan and sprinkle lightly with salt; add 1 inch water. Heat to boiling; reduce heat and simmer, covered, until artichokes are tender, 30 to 40 minutes (bottom leaves will pull out easily).

2. Remove artichokes from pan; discard any remaining water. Holding artichokes with a towel or hot pad, brush bottom of each with olive oil; return to saucepan. Cook, uncovered, over medium to medium-low heat until bottoms of artichokes are deeply browned, 10 to 15 minutes.

ARTICHOKES WITH HOLLANDAISE SAUCE

The Hollandaise Sauce is also excellent served over steamed asparagus spears or broccoli.

4 to 6 servings

4-6 whole artichokes, stems trimmed
    Mock Hollandaise Sauce (see p. 209)

Per Serving
Calories: 114
% Calories from fat: **2**
Fat (gm): 0.3
Saturated fat (gm): 0.1
Cholesterol (mg): 0.2
Sodium (mg): 396
Protein (gm): 11.9
Carbohydrate (gm): 17.5
Exchanges
Milk: 0.5
Vegetable: 2.0
Fruit: 0.0
Bread: 0.0
Meat: 0.5
Fat: 0.0

1. Slice 1 inch off tops of artichokes and discard. Trim tips of remaining leaves with scissors. Place artichokes in medium saucepan with 2 inches of water; heat to boiling. Reduce heat and simmer, covered, until artichoke leaves pull off easily and bottom is tender when pierced with a fork, about 30 minutes.

2. Place artichokes on serving plates with Mock Hollandaise Sauce on the side for dipping.

ASPARAGUS WITH PEANUT SAUCE

Oriental flavors are the perfect complement to spring's freshest asparagus.

6 servings

2 tablespoons reduced-fat peanut butter
1/4 cup sugar
2-3 tablespoons reduced-sodium tamari soy sauce
3-4 teaspoons rice wine (sake) *or* dry sherry
1 teaspoon grated gingerroot
1/2 pounds asparagus spears, cooked until crisp-tender, chilled

Per Serving
Calories: 95
% Calories from fat: 21
Fat (gm): 2.3
Saturated fat (gm): 0.5
Cholesterol (mg): 0
Sodium (mg): 246
Protein (gm): 4.8
Carbohydrate (gm): 15
Exchanges
Milk: 0.0
Vegetable: 3.0
Fruit: 0.0
Bread: 0.0
Meat: 0.0
Fat: 0.5

1. Mix peanut butter, sugar, soy sauce, rice wine, and gingerroot until smooth.

2. Arrange asparagus on serving platter; spoon peanut sauce over.

ASPARAGUS AND WHITE BEANS, ITALIAN-STYLE

Imagine yourself in a medieval town in Tuscany while you enjoy this spring asparagus, bean, and pasta side-dish. A lovely accompaniment to grilled or roasted meat, this dish will also serve 4 as a meatless main course.

8 servings

1 pound asparagus, cut into 2-inch pieces
2 teaspoons minced garlic
2-3 teaspoons olive oil
2 cups chopped Italian plum tomatoes
1 can (15 ounces) cannellini *or* Great Northern, beans, rinsed, drained
1 teaspoon dried rosemary leaves *or* Italian seasoning
1 cup canned reduced-sodium vegetable broth

Per Serving
Calories: 169
% Calories from fat: 16
Fat (gm): 3.1
Saturated fat (gm): 0.7
Cholesterol (mg): 2
Sodium (mg): 229
Protein (gm): 7.9
Carbohydrate (gm): 29.4
Exchanges
Milk: 0.0
Vegetable: 1.0
Fruit: 0.0
Bread: 1.0
Meat: 0.0
Fat: 0.5

Salt and pepper, to taste

8 ounces linguine *or* thin spaghetti, cooked, warm

1/4-1/2 cup (1-2 ounces) shredded Parmesan cheese

1. Saute asparagus and garlic in oil in large skillet until crisp-tender, 3 to 4 minutes. Stir in remaining ingredients, except salt, pepper, linguine, and cheese; heat to boiling; reduce heat and simmer rapidly until mixture has thickened, 3 to 5 minutes. Season to taste with salt and pepper.

2. Toss vegetable mixture with pasta; sprinkle with cheese.

GREEN BEAN CASSEROLE

Reduced-fat cream of mushroom soup and fat-free sour cream make this old favorite possible in a new form. We've used fresh green beans, but canned or frozen may be used if you prefer.

6 servings

1 can (10³/₄ ounces) reduced-fat cream of mushroom soup

1/2 cup fat-free sour cream

1/4 cup fat-free milk

1¹/₄ pounds green beans, cut into 1¹/₂-inch pieces, cooked until crisp-tender

1/2 cup canned French-fried onions

Per Serving
Calories: 81
% Calories from fat: 31
Fat (gm): 2.9
Saturated fat (gm): 0.8
Cholesterol (mg): 1.3
Sodium (mg): 172
Protein (gm): 3
Carbohydrate (gm): 11.6
Exchanges
Milk: 0.0
Vegetable: 2.0
Fruit: 0.0
Bread: 0.0
Meat: 0.0
Fat: 0.5

1. Mix soup, sour cream, and milk in 2-quart casserole; stir in beans.

2. Bake, uncovered, at 350 degrees until mixture is bubbly, about 45 minutes. Sprinkle onions on top during last 5 minutes of baking time.

GREEK-STYLE GREEN BEANS

Fresh green beans are long simmered with tomatoes, herbs, and garlic in traditional Greek style.

4 to 6 servings

1/2	cup chopped onion
4	cloves garlic, minced
1	tablespoon olive oil
3/4	teaspoon dried oregano leaves
1/2	teaspoon dried basil leaves
1	can (28 ounces) reduced-sodium tomatoes, undrained, coarsely chopped
1	pound green beans
	Salt and pepper, to taste

Per Serving
Calories: 123
% Calories from fat: 28
Fat (gm): 4.3
Saturated fat (gm): 0.6
Cholesterol (mg): 0
Sodium (mg): 30
Protein (gm): 4.5
Carbohydrate (gm): 20.5
Exchanges
Milk: 0.0
Vegetable: 4.0
Fruit: 0.0
Bread: 0.0
Meat: 0.0
Fat: 0.5

1. Saute onion and garlic in oil in large skillet until tender, 3 to 4 minutes. Stir in herbs and cook 1 to 2 minutes longer.

2. Add tomatoes and liquid and green beans and heat to boiling; reduce heat and simmer, covered, until beans are very tender, 30 to 40 minutes. Season to taste with salt and pepper.

ORIENTAL GREEN BEANS

Serve these beans with grilled marinated chicken or fish.

4 servings

	Oriental-flavored vegetable cooking spray
1/4	cup chopped onion
1/4	cup chopped red bell pepper
2	teaspoons finely chopped gingerroot
2	cloves garlic, minced
8	ounces green beans, cut into halves
1/2	cup sliced water chestnuts
1	cup cooked dried, *or* canned, adzuki *or* black beans
1	tablespoon rice wine vinegar
1-2	teaspoons reduced-sodium tamari soy sauce
	Salt and pepper, to taste

Per Serving
Calories: 109
% Calories from fat: 2
Fat (gm): 0.2
Saturated fat (gm): 0
Cholesterol (mg): 0
Sodium (mg): 64
Protein (gm): 5.8
Carbohydrate (gm): 22.5
Exchanges
Milk: 0.0
Vegetable: 1.5
Fruit: 0.0
Bread: 1.0
Meat: 0.0
Fat: 0.0

1. Spray wok or large skillet with cooking spray; heat over medium heat until hot. Add onion, bell pepper, gingerroot, and garlic; spray with cooking spray and stir-fry until tender, 3 to 4 minutes.

2. Add green beans and water chestnuts to wok; stir-fry until beans are crisp-tender, 5 to 8 minutes. Stir in adzuki beans, vinegar, and soy sauce; cook 1 to 2 minutes longer. Season to taste with salt and pepper.

NEW ENGLAND BAKED BEANS

Long-baked and savory, these beans are the best! Bacon replaces the higher-fat salt pork traditionally used in the recipe. If you prefer soaking beans overnight, omit Step 1 and proceed with Step 2.

8 to 10 servings

8 ounces dried navy, *or* Great Northern, beans, washed, sorted

4 slices bacon, fried crisp, well drained, cut into 1-inch pieces

3/4 cup chopped onion

1 clove garlic

3 tablespoons tomato paste

3 tablespoons dark molasses

3 tablespoons packed light brown sugar

1/2 teaspoon dry mustard

1/4 teaspoon dried thyme leaves

1/2 teaspoon salt

Per Serving
Calories: 161
% Calories from fat: 11
Fat (gm): 2.1
Saturated fat (gm): 0.7
Cholesterol (mg): 2.7
Sodium (mg): 246
Protein (gm): 7.8
Carbohydrate (gm): 29.1
Exchanges
Milk: 0.0
Vegetable: 0.0
Fruit: 0.0
Bread: 2.0
Meat: 0.0
Fat: 0.5

1. Cover beans with 2 inches of water in large saucepan; heat to boiling and boil, uncovered, 2 minutes. Remove from heat and let stand, covered, 1 hour.

2. Add more water to beans to cover, if necessary. Heat to boiling; reduce heat and simmer, covered, until beans are tender, about 1 1/4 hours. Drain beans; reserve liquid.

3. Mix beans, bacon, onion, garlic, tomato paste, molasses, brown sugar, dry mustard, thyme, and salt in 1 1/2-quart casserole; add enough reserved cooking liquid to cover beans. Bake, covered, at 325 degrees, stirring occasionally, 3 hours. Bake, uncovered, until beans are desired consistency, about 1 hour more.

HARVARD BEETS

Sweet yet tart, the sauce can also be served over cooked carrots or pearl onions. Vary the amount of vinegar for the tartness you like.

4 servings

3	tablespoons sugar
1¹/2	tablespoons cornstarch
³/4	cup water
3-4	tablespoons cider vinegar
2	teaspoons margarine
	Salt and white pepper, to taste
1	pound beets, cooked, sliced or julienned, warm

Per Serving
Calories: 94
% Calories from fat: 18
Fat (gm): 1.9
Saturated fat (gm): 0.4
Cholesterol (mg): 0
Sodium (mg): 70
Protein (gm): 1.1
Carbohydrate (gm): 19.3
Exchanges
Milk: 0.0
Vegetable: 2.0
Fruit: 0.0
Bread: 0.5
Meat: 0.0
Fat: 0.0

1. Mix sugar and cornstarch in small saucepan; whisk in water and vinegar. Heat to boiling, whisking constantly; boil, whisking constantly, until thickened, about 1 minute. Add margarine, whisking until melted. Season to taste with salt and white pepper.

2. Pour sauce over beets in serving bowl and toss gently.

BEETS DIJON

The easiest way to cook beets is with the skins on; after cooking, the skins slip off easily!

4 servings

	Butter-flavored vegetable cooking spray
¹/3	cup finely chopped onion
2	cloves garlic, minced
¹/3	cup fat-free sour cream
2	tablespoons Dijon-style mustard
2-3	teaspoons lemon juice
	Salt and white pepper, to taste
1¹/2	pounds beets, cooked, peeled, cubed or sliced, warm
	Minced parsley, as garnish

Per Serving
Calories: 71
% Calories from fat: 7
Fat (gm): 0.6
Saturated fat (gm): 0.1
Cholesterol (mg): 0
Sodium (mg): 185
Protein (gm): 3.5
Carbohydrate (gm): 13.8
Exchanges
Milk: 0.0
Vegetable: 3.0
Fruit: 0.0
Bread: 0.0
Meat: 0.0
Fat: 0.0

1. Spray small saucepan with cooking spray; heat over medium heat until hot. Saute onion and garlic until tender, 3 to 4 minutes. Stir in sour cream, mustard, and lemon juice; heat over low heat until hot. Season to taste with salt and white pepper.

2. Spoon sour cream mixture over beets; stir gently. Sprinkle with parsley.

HERB-CRUMBED BROCCOLI

Herb-seasoned breadcrumbs and pecans offer new flavor and texture contrasts in this favorite broccoli dish.

6 servings

Butter-flavored vegetable cooking spray
2-4 tablespoons chopped pecans
1/4 cup dry unseasoned breadcrumbs
1/2 teaspoon dried marjoram leaves
1/4 teaspoon dried chervil leaves
2 tablespoons finely chopped parsley
1 1/2 pounds broccoli, cut into florets and stalks sliced, cooked
Salt and pepper, to taste

Per Serving
Calories: 61
% Calories from fat: 28
Fat (gm): 2.1
Saturated fat (gm): 0.2
Cholesterol (mg): 0
Sodium (mg): 64
Protein (gm): 3.7
Carbohydrate (gm): 8.7
Exchanges
Milk: 0.0
Vegetable: 1.5
Fruit: 0.0
Bread: 0.0
Meat: 0.0
Fat: 0.5

1. Spray small skillet with cooking spray; heat over medium heat until hot. Add pecans and spray with cooking spray; cook over medium heat until toasted, 2 to 3 minutes, stirring frequently. Add breadcrumbs, marjoram, and chervil to skillet; cook until crumbs are toasted, 3 to 4 minutes, stirring frequently. Remove from heat and stir in parsley.

2. Season broccoli with salt and pepper to taste; arrange in serving bowl. Spoon crumb mixture over broccoli.

BROCCOLI RABE SAUTEED WITH GARLIC

A simple but flavorful vegetable recipe that can also be made with asparagus spears.

4 to 6 servings

Garlic-flavored vegetable cooking spray
1 pound broccoli rabe, cooked until crisp-tender
4 cloves garlic, minced
Salt and pepper, to taste

Per Serving
Calories: 32
% Calories from fat: 8
Fat (gm): 0.4
Saturated fat (gm): 0.1
Cholesterol (mg): 0
Sodium (mg): 25
Protein (gm): 3.1
Carbohydrate (gm): 5.9
Exchanges
Milk: 0.0
Vegetable: 1.0
Fruit: 0.0
Bread: 0.0
Meat: 0.0
Fat: 0.0

1. Spray large skillet with cooking spray; heat over medium heat until hot. Add broccoli rabe and garlic; spray lightly with cooking spray. Saute over medium to medium-low heat until broccoli is beginning to brown, 4 to 5 minutes. Season to taste with salt and pepper.

TINY PEAS AND PEARL ONIONS

Mint and dill offer refreshing flavor and are often used together in Mediterranean dishes.

6 servings

1 package (8 ounces) frozen tiny peas
1/2 package (16-ounce size) frozen small whole onions
1/4 cup water
2-3 teaspoons margarine
1/4-1/2 teaspoon dried mint leaves
1/4-1/2 teaspoon dried dill weed
Salt and pepper, to taste

Per Serving
Calories: 63
% Calories from fat: 20
Fat (gm): 1.4
Saturated fat (gm): 0.3
Cholesterol (mg): 0
Sodium (mg): 57
Protein (gm): 2.5
Carbohydrate (gm): 10.4
Exchanges
Milk: 0.0
Vegetable: 0.0
Fruit: 0.0
Bread: 1.0
Meat: 0.0
Fat: 0.0

1. Heat peas, onions, and water to boiling in medium saucepan; reduce heat and simmer until vegetables are tender, 8 to 10 minutes. Drain. Add margarine and herbs to vegetables, stirring until margarine is melted. Season to taste with salt and pepper.

BRAISED CABBAGE

You'll enjoy the combination of aromatic anise and caraway seeds in this cabbage dish.

4 to 6 servings

Vegetable cooking spray
- ³/₄ cup chopped onion
- ¹/₂ cup chopped green bell pepper
- 3 cloves garlic, minced
- ¹/₂ teaspoon caraway seeds, crushed
- ¹/₂ teaspoon anise seeds, crushed
- 1 medium head cabbage, thinly sliced
- 1 cup reduced-sodium vegetable broth
- 2 slices bacon, fried crisp, drained, crumbled

Salt and pepper, to taste

Per Serving
Calories: 123
% Calories from fat: 15
Fat (gm): 2.3
Saturated fat (gm): 0.6
Cholesterol (mg): 2.7
Sodium (mg): 116
Protein (gm): 6.4
Carbohydrate (gm): 18.4
Exchanges
Milk: 0.0
Vegetable: 3.0
Fruit: 0.0
Bread: 0.0
Meat: 0.0
Fat: 1.0

1. Spray large saucepan with cooking spray; heat over medium heat until hot. Saute onion, bell pepper, and garlic 3 to 4 minutes; add caraway and anise seeds and cook 1 minute longer.

2. Add cabbage and vegetable broth to saucepan; heat to boiling. Reduce heat and simmer, covered, until cabbage is wilted, about 5 minutes. Simmer, uncovered, until cabbage is tender, 10 to 15 minutes. Stir in bacon; season to taste with salt and pepper.

GINGERED CARROT PUREE

Cooked until thick, this intensely flavored puree owes its creamy texture to the additions of Idaho potato and fat-free half-and-half.

6 servings (about ¹/₂ cup each)

2 pounds carrots, sliced
1 medium Idaho potato (8 ounces), peeled, cubed
1-2 tablespoons margarine
¹/₄-¹/₂ cup fat-free half-and-half *or* fat-free milk, warm
¹/₄-¹/₂ teaspoon ground ginger
Salt and white pepper, to taste
Ground nutmeg, as garnish
1 tablespoon chopped crystallized ginger

Per Serving
Calories: 122
% Calories from fat: 16
Fat (gm): 2.2
Saturated fat (gm): 0.4
Cholesterol (mg): 0
Sodium (mg): 132
Protein (gm): 2.4
Carbohydrate (gm): 24.1
Exchanges
Milk: 0.0
Vegetable: 2.5
Fruit: 0.0
Bread: 0.5
Meat: 0.0
Fat: 0.5

1. Cook carrots and potato in 2 inches simmering water until very tender, about 15 minutes; drain.

2. Process carrots and potato in food processor until smooth; transfer mixture to large skillet. Cook mixture over medium to medium-low heat, stirring frequently, until mixture is the consistency of thick mashed potatoes (do not brown), about 15 minutes.

3. Beat margarine and enough half-and-half into carrot mixture to make creamy consistency. Stir in ground ginger; season to taste with salt and white pepper. Spoon into serving bowl; sprinkle with nutmeg and crystallized ginger.

ORANGE-GLAZED BABY CARROTS

The sweet-spiced orange glaze is also delicious over sweet potatoes or beets.

6 servings

1 package (16 ounces) baby carrots
³/4 cup orange juice
¹/2 cup packed light brown sugar
2 tablespoons cornstarch
¹/2 teaspoon ground cinnamon
¹/4 teaspoon ground allspice
¹/4 teaspoon ground mace
1 tablespoon margarine
Salt and white pepper, to taste
Finely chopped parsley, as garnish

Per Serving
Calories: 127
% Calories from fat: 13
Fat (gm): 2
Saturated fat (gm): 0.4
Cholesterol (mg): 0
Sodium (mg): 97
Protein (gm): 1.2
Carbohydrate (gm): 28.2
Exchanges
Milk: 0.0
Vegetable: 1.5
Fruit: 1.5
Bread: 0.0
Meat: 0.0
Fat: 0.5

1. Cook carrots in 1 inch simmering water in covered medium saucepan until crisp-tender, 10 to 12 minutes; drain.

2. Mix orange juice, brown sugar, cornstarch, and spices in small saucepan; heat to boiling. Boil, stirring constantly, until thickened, about 1 minute. Stir in margarine until melted; season to taste with salt and white pepper.

3. Arrange carrots in serving bowl; pour orange sauce over and sprinkle with parsley.

CARROT PUDDING

This sweetly spiced carrot pudding will become a family favorite!

8 servings

2 pounds carrots, cooked, mashed
$1/2$ cup sugar
$1^1/2$ tablespoons margarine, melted
$1/2$ cup all-purpose flour
$1^1/2$ teaspoons baking powder
$1/2$ teaspoon ground cinnamon
$1/2$ teaspoon salt
$1/2$ cup raisins
$1/2$ cup (2 ounces) shredded fat-free
Cheddar cheese
4 egg whites, beaten to stiff peaks
$1/4$ cup sliced almonds, optional

Per Serving
Calories: 191
% Calories from fat: 11
Fat (gm): 2.5
Saturated fat (gm): 0.5
Cholesterol (mg): 1.3
Sodium (mg): 339
Protein (gm): 6.3
Carbohydrate (gm): 37.9
Exchanges
Milk: 0.0
Vegetable: 1.5
Fruit: 0.5
Bread: 1.5
Meat: 0.0
Fat: 0.5

1. Mix carrots, sugar, and margarine in medium bowl; mix in combined flour, baking powder, cinnamon, and salt. Mix in raisins and cheese; fold in beaten egg whites. Spoon mixture into 8-inch square baking pan; sprinkle with almonds.

2. Bake at 475 degrees 10 minutes; reduce temperature to 350 degrees and bake until browned and set, 50 to 60 minutes. Cut into squares.

CAULIFLOWER WITH CREAMY CHEESE SAUCE

Try making the cheese sauce with other reduced-fat cheeses, such as Havarti, Gruyère, American, or blue, for new flavor variations.

6 servings

1 whole cauliflower (2 pounds)
Creamy Cheese Sauce (recipe follows)
Paprika, as garnish
Finely chopped parsley leaves, as garnish

Per Serving
Calories: 102
% Calories from fat: 31
Fat (gm): 3.6
Saturated fat (gm): 1.5
Cholesterol (mg): 5.7
Sodium (mg): 194
Protein (gm): 6.5
Carbohydrate (gm): 11.7
Exchanges
Milk: 0.0
Vegetable: 2.0
Fruit: 0.0
Bread: 0.0
Meat: 0.5
Fat: 0.5

1. Place cauliflower in saucepan with 2 inches of water; heat to boiling. Reduce heat and simmer, covered, until cauliflower is tender, 20 to 25 minutes.

2. Place cauliflower on serving plate; spoon Creamy Cheese Sauce over and sprinkle with paprika and parsley.

Creamy Cheese Sauce

makes about 1¹/₄ cups

2 tablespoons minced onion
1 tablespoon margarine
2 tablespoons flour
1 cup fat-free milk
¹/₂ cup (2 ounces) cubed reduced-fat pasteurized processed cheese product *or* shredded reduced-fat Cheddar cheese
¹/₄ teaspoon dry mustard
2-3 drops hot pepper sauce
Salt and white pepper, to taste

1. Saute onion in margarine in small saucepan 2 to 3 minutes. Stir in flour; cook over medium-low heat, stirring constantly, 1 minute. Whisk in milk and heat to boiling; boil, whisking constantly, until thickened, about 1 minute.

2. Reduce heat to low. Add cheese, dry mustard, and pepper sauce, whisking until cheese is melted. Season to taste with salt and pepper.

CAULIFLOWER-FENNEL PUREE

Cooking a pureed vegetable mixture until thick intensifies the flavor of the vegetable.

6 servings (about ½ cup each)

2	pounds cauliflower, cut into pieces
1	medium Idaho potato (8 ounces), peeled, cubed
1-1½	teaspoons fennel, *or* caraway, seeds, crushed
1-2	tablespoons margarine
¼-½	cup fat-free half-and-half *or* fat-free milk, warm
	Salt and white pepper, to taste
	Finely chopped parsley, as garnish

Per Serving
Calories: 90
% Calories from fat: 21
Fat (gm): 2.2
Saturated fat (gm): 0.4
Cholesterol (mg): 0
Sodium (mg): 43
Protein (gm): 3.7
Carbohydrate (gm): 14.8
Exchanges
Milk: 0.0
Vegetable: 1.5
Fruit: 0.0
Bread: 0.5
Meat: 0.0
Fat: 0.5

1. Cook cauliflower and potato in 2 inches simmering water, covered, until very tender, 10 to 12 minutes. Drain.

2. Process vegetables in food processor until smooth; transfer mixture to large skillet and stir in fennel seeds. Cook mixture over medium to medium-low heat, stirring frequently, until mixture is the consistency of very thick mashed potatoes (do not brown), about 15 minutes.

3. Beat margarine and enough half-and-half into mixture to make creamy consistency. Season to taste with salt and white pepper. Spoon into serving bowl; sprinkle with parsley.

CELERY ROOT PUREE

Sometimes the flavor of celery root can be slightly bitter, which a few pinches of sugar will correct.

6 servings (about ¹/₂ cup each)

2	pounds peeled celery root, cubed
1	medium Idaho potato, peeled, cubed
¹/₄	cup cubed sweet onion
1-2	tablespoons margarine
¹/₄-¹/₂	cup fat-free half-and-half *or* fat-free milk, warm
	Ground nutmeg, to taste
	Salt and white pepper, to taste
	Finely chopped parsley, as garnish

Per Serving
Calories: 115
% Calories from fat: 17
Fat (gm): 2.4
Saturated fat (gm): 0.4
Cholesterol (mg): 0
Sodium (mg): 185
Protein (gm): 3.3
Carbohydrate (gm): 22.4
Exchanges
Milk: 0.0
Vegetable: 0.0
Fruit: 0.0
Bread: 1.5
Meat: 0.0
Fat: 0.5

1. Cook celery root, potato, and onion in 2 inches simmering water, covered, until very tender, about 15 minutes; drain.

2. Process vegetables in food processor until smooth; transfer mixture to large skillet. Cook mixture over medium to medium-low heat, stirring frequently, until mixture is the consistency of thick mashed potatoes (do not brown), about 15 minutes.

3. Beat margarine and enough half-and-half into vegetable mixture to make creamy consistency. Stir in nutmeg, salt, and white pepper to taste. Spoon into serving bowl; sprinkle with parsley.

CORN PUDDING

Cut fresh corn from the cob for best flavor, though frozen corn can be used for convenience.

6 servings

Vegetable cooking spray

2 tablespoons plain dry bread crumbs

2 cups fresh, *or* frozen, thawed, whole-kernel corn

1/2 cup fat-free milk

3 tablespoons flour

1 1/2 tablespoons margarine, softened

1 egg

2 egg whites

1 teaspoon sugar

1/2 teaspoon dried thyme leaves

1/2 teaspoon salt

1/8 teaspoon pepper

Per Serving
Calories: 122
% Calories from fat: 28
Fat (gm): 3.9
Saturated fat (gm): 0.9
Cholesterol (mg): 35.8
Sodium (mg): 272
Protein (gm): 5.3
Carbohydrate (gm): 17.9
Exchanges
Milk: 0.0
Vegetable: 0.0
Fruit: 0.0
Bread: 1.0
Meat: 0.5
Fat: 0.5

1. Spray 1-quart casserole or soufflé dish with cooking spray; coat dish with bread crumbs.

2. Process corn, milk, and flour in food processor or blender until a coarse puree. Beat margarine, egg, and egg whites in medium bowl until smooth; mix in sugar, thyme, salt, and pepper. Stir in corn mixture, and pour into prepared casserole.

3. Bake, uncovered, at 350 degrees until pudding is set and beginning to brown, about 35 minutes. Serve warm.

SUCCOTASH

Fat-free half-and-half contributes richness without the fat calories in this old-fashioned favorite. Fresh crisp-tender cooked or frozen green beans can be substituted for the baby lima beans.

4 servings

1 small onion, chopped
1 tablespoon margarine
2 cups frozen baby lima beans
2 cups fresh, *or* frozen, whole-kernel corn
1/2 cup reduced-sodium vegetable broth
1/2 cup fat-free half-and-half *or* fat-free milk
Salt and pepper, to taste

Per Serving
Calories: 146
% Calories from fat: 13
Fat (gm): 2.1
Saturated fat (gm): 0.4
Cholesterol (mg): 0
Sodium (mg): 69
Protein (gm): 6.6
Carbohydrate (gm): 26.7
Exchanges
Milk: 0.0
Vegetable: 0.0
Fruit: 0.0
Bread: 1.5
Meat: 0.0
Fat: 0.5

1. Saute onion in margarine in medium saucepan until tender, 5 to 8 minutes. Stir in lima beans, corn, broth, and half-and-half; heat to boiling. Reduce heat and simmer, covered, until vegetables are tender, about 5 minutes. Season to taste with salt and pepper.

FRIED CORN

Lightly flavored with mesquite, and wonderfully delicious! Use fresh corn, if you can.

6 servings

Mesquite-flavored vegetable cooking spray
3 cups fresh corn cut from the cob (3-4 ears) *or* frozen, thawed whole-kernel corn
1 green bell pepper, sliced
1 red bell pepper, sliced
3 cloves garlic, minced
1/4 cup water
Salt and pepper, to taste

Per Serving
Calories: 85
% Calories from fat: 2
Fat (gm): 0.2
Saturated fat (gm): 0
Cholesterol (mg): 0
Sodium (mg): 5
Protein (gm): 3.3
Carbohydrate (gm): 21
Exchanges
Milk: 0.0
Vegetable: 1.0
Fruit: 0.0
Bread: 1.0
Meat: 0.0
Fat: 0.0

1. Spray large skillet with cooking spray; heat over medium heat until hot. Add corn, bell pepper, and garlic to skillet; spray generously with cooking spray. Cook, covered, over medium-low heat until vegetables are very tender and browned, about 25 minutes, stirring occasionally.

2. Stir water into skillet; cook, covered, over low heat until water is absorbed, about 15 minutes. Season to taste with salt and pepper.

TEX-MEX SWEET CORN

Flavors of the Southwest make corn-on-the-cob better than ever!

6 servings

2-3 tablespoons margarine
1/2 teaspoon chili powder
1/2 teaspoon ground cumin
1/4 teaspoon dried oregano leaves
1/4 teaspoon garlic powder
1/8 teaspoon cayenne pepper
6 ears fresh corn, cooked, warm
Salt, to taste
Finely chopped cilantro, as garnish

Per Serving
Calories: 153
% Calories from fat: 25
Fat (gm): 4.8
Saturated fat (gm): 0.9
Cholesterol (mg): 0
Sodium (mg): 52
Protein (gm): 4.1
Carbohydrate (gm): 28.5
Exchanges
Milk: 0.0
Vegetable: 0.0
Fruit: 0.0
Bread: 0.0
Meat: 0.0
Fat: 1.0

1. Melt margarine in small saucepan; stir in chili powder, cumin, oregano, garlic powder, and cayenne pepper.

2. Brush margarine mixture on corn; sprinkle lightly with salt and cilantro.

SEASONED EGGPLANT SAUTE

Simple, good, and easy to make!

4 servings

Olive oil cooking spray
1 large eggplant (about 1½ pounds), unpeeled, cut into scant ¾-inch cubes
1 cup chopped onion
½ cup chopped green bell pepper
1 large tomato, chopped
6 cloves garlic, minced
2 tablespoons finely chopped parsley
1 teaspoon dried oregano leaves
½ teaspoon dried thyme leaves
¼ teaspoon crushed red pepper
½ cup reduced-sodium vegetable, *or* chicken, broth
Salt and pepper, to taste

Per Serving
Calories: 83
% Calories from fat: 6
Fat (gm): 0.6
Saturated fat (gm): 0.1
Cholesterol (mg): 0
Sodium (mg): 18
Protein (gm): 2.8
Carbohydrate (gm): 19.3
Exchanges
Milk: 0.0
Vegetable: 3.0
Fruit: 0.0
Bread: 0.0
Meat: 0.0
Fat: 0.0

1. Spray large skillet with cooking spray; heat over medium heat until hot. Saute vegetables until crisp-tender, 8 to 10 minutes; add herbs and red pepper and cook 1 to 2 minutes longer.

2. Add broth to skillet and heat to boiling; reduce heat and simmer, covered, until vegetables are tender and broth absorbed, 15 to 20 minutes. Season to taste with salt and pepper.

EGGPLANT AND VEGETABLE SAUTE

Minced roasted garlic is available in jars in your produce section; substitute fresh minced garlic if desired.

6 servings

1 large eggplant (about 1¹/₄ pounds), unpeeled, cut into ¹/₂-inch cubes
3 cups frozen stir-fry pepper blend
4 teaspoons minced roasted garlic
³/₄ teaspoon dried rosemary leaves
¹/₂ teaspoon dried thyme leaves
2 teaspoons olive oil
1 can (15 ounces) cannellini beans *or* Great Northern beans, rinsed, drained
Salt and pepper, to taste

Per Serving
Calories: 109
% Calories from fat: 16
Fat (gm): 2
Saturated fat (gm): 0.3
Cholesterol (mg): 0
Sodium (mg): 114
Protein (gm): 4.1
Carbohydrate (gm): 19.1
Exchanges
Milk: 0.0
Vegetable: 2.0
Fruit: 0.0
Bread: 1.0
Meat: 0.0
Fat: 0.5

1. Cook eggplant, pepper blend, garlic, and herbs in oil in large saucepan over medium heat, covered, until vegetables are tender, 8 to 10 minutes, stirring occasionally.

2. Stir in beans; cook until hot through, 1 to 2 minutes. Season to taste with salt and pepper.

EGGPLANT AND TOMATO CASSEROLE

Assemble the casserole up to a day in advance, then bake before serving—perfect pot-luck fare!

8 servings

1 large eggplant (2 pounds), peeled, cut into 1-inch cubes
¹/₂ cup seasoned dry bread crumbs
¹/₃ cup chopped onion
3 cloves garlic, minced
1¹/₂ teaspoons dried oregano leaves, divided
¹/₂ teaspoon dried basil leaves
¹/₄ teaspoon dried thyme leaves
Salt and pepper, to taste
2 eggs

Per Serving
Calories: 98
% Calories from fat: 16
Fat (gm): 1.9
Saturated fat (gm): 0.5
Cholesterol (mg): 53.3
Sodium (mg): 245
Protein (gm): 5.1
Carbohydrate (gm): 16.9
Exchanges
Milk: 0.0
Vegetable: 2.0
Fruit: 0.0
Bread: 0.5
Meat: 0.0
Fat: 0.5

3 medium tomatoes, sliced
$^1/_4$ cup grated fat-free Parmesan cheese

1. Cook eggplant in 2 inches simmering water in covered medium saucepan until tender, 5 to 8 minutes. Drain well. Mash eggplant with fork; mix in bread crumbs, onion, garlic, 1 teaspoon oregano, basil, and thyme. Season to taste with salt and pepper. Mix in eggs.

2. Spoon eggplant mixture into 11 x 7-inch baking dish. Arrange tomatoes in rows over eggplant; sprinkle with cheese and remaining $^1/_2$ teaspoon oregano.

3. Bake, uncovered, at 350 degrees until hot through, about 20 minutes.

FENNEL PUREE

We've included a number of puree recipes, as we love the creamy textures and intense flavors gained from this cooking method.

6 servings (about $^1/_2$ cup each)

2 pounds fennel bulbs, cubed
1 large Idaho potato (12 ounces), peeled, cubed
$^1/_2$ cup cubed sweet onion
1-2 tablespoons margarine
$^1/_4$-$^1/_2$ cup fat-free half-and-half *or* fat-free milk, warm
Salt and white pepper, to taste
Paprika, as garnish

Per Serving
Calories: 117
% Calories from fat: 16
Fat (gm): 2.3
Saturated fat (gm): 0.4
Cholesterol (mg): 0
Sodium (mg): 113
Protein (gm): 3.2
Carbohydrate (gm): 22.9
Exchanges
Milk: 0.0
Vegetable: 0.0
Fruit: 0.0
Bread: 1.5
Meat: 0.0
Fat: 0.5

1. Cook fennel, potato, and onion in 2 inches simmering water, covered, until very tender, about 15 minutes; drain.

2. Process vegetables in food processor until smooth; transfer mixture to large skillet. Cook mixture over medium to medium-low heat, stirring frequently, until mixture is the consistency of thick mashed potatoes (do not brown), about 15 minutes.

3. Beat margarine and enough half-and-half into vegetable mixture to make creamy consistency. Season to taste with salt and white pepper. Spoon into serving bowl; sprinkle with paprika.

LEMON SPIKED GARLIC GREENS

Kale, collard, turnip, or beet greens are excellent choices for this quick-and-easy healthy vegetable.

4 servings

Garlic-flavored vegetable cooking spray
$^1/_3$ cup finely chopped onion
4 cloves garlic, minced
$1^1/_2$ pounds greens, washed, stems removed, coarsely chopped
$^1/_3$ cup water
1-2 tablespoons lemon juice
Salt and pepper, to taste

Per Serving
Calories: 58
% Calories from fat: 23
Fat (gm): 1.7
Saturated fat (gm): 0.4
Cholesterol (mg): 53.3
Sodium (mg): 43
Protein (gm): 5.9
Carbohydrate (gm): 7
Exchanges
Milk: 0.0
Vegetable: 2.0
Fruit: 0.0
Bread: 0.0
Meat: 0.0
Fat: 0.0

1. Spray large saucepan with cooking spray; heat over medium heat until hot. Saute onion and garlic until tender, 3 to 4 minutes.

2. Add greens and water to saucepan; heat to boiling. Reduce heat and simmer, covered, until greens are wilted and tender, about 5 to 8 minutes, adding more water if necessary. Season to taste with lemon juice, salt, and pepper.

BRAISED KALE

Packed with vitamins and minerals, kale and other dark leafy greens offer a nutritional bonus. Use other greens, such as beet, turnip, or mustard, with this recipe, too.

4 servings

1 medium leek (white part only) *or* 6 green onions and tops, sliced
2-3 teaspoons olive oil
1 pound kale, rinsed, torn into pieces
$^1/_2$ cup water
$^1/_2$-1 teaspoon vegetable bouillon crystals
$^1/_2$ cup fat-free sour cream
1 teaspoon Dijon-style mustard

Per Serving
Calories: 131
% Calories from fat: 26
Fat (gm): 3.8
Saturated fat (gm): 0.7
Cholesterol (mg): 1.4
Sodium (mg): 221
Protein (gm): 5.7
Carbohydrate (gm): 18.6
Exchanges
Milk: 0.0
Vegetable: 4.0
Fruit: 0.0
Bread: 0.0
Meat: 0.0
Fat: 0.5

1-2 slices bacon, fried crisp, drained, crumbled
    Salt and pepper, to taste

1. Saute leek in oil in large saucepan until tender, 3 to 4 minutes. Add kale, water, and bouillon crystals; heat to boiling. Reduce heat and simmer, covered, until kale is wilted and tender, about 5 minutes. Drain and discard any excess liquid.

2. Stir sour cream, mustard, and bacon into kale mixture; cook over low heat 2 to 3 minutes. Season to taste with salt and pepper.

SAUTEED LEEKS AND PEPPERS

A colorful side dish that will brighten any meal!

6 servings

Olive oil cooking spray
3 medium leeks (white parts only), cut into ¹/₂-inch slices
1 small yellow bell pepper, sliced
1 small red bell pepper, sliced
1 small green bell pepper, sliced
¹/₂ teaspoon bouquet garni
    Salt and pepper, to taste

Per Serving
Calories: 63
% Calories from fat: **5**
Fat (gm): 0.4
Saturated fat (gm): **0**
Cholesterol (mg): **0**
Sodium (mg): 13
Protein (gm): 2
Carbohydrate (gm): 14.6
Exchanges
Milk: 0.0
Vegetable: 2.5
Fruit: 0.0
Bread: 0.0
Meat: 0.0
Fat: 0.0

1. Spray large skillet with cooking spray; heat over medium heat until hot. Add vegetables to skillet; spray with cooking spray. Cook, covered, over medium heat until vegetables are wilted, 5 to 8 minutes.

2. Stir in bouquet garni and cook, uncovered, over medium to medium-low heat until vegetables are tender. Season to taste with salt and pepper.

MUSHROOMS WITH SOUR CREAM

Cooking the mushrooms very slowly until deeply browned intensifies their flavor. Especially delicious served with pierogi, ravioli, or grilled steaks!

4 servings

Butter-flavored vegetable cooking spray
12 ounces shiitake, *or* cremini, mushrooms, sliced, tough stems discarded
¼ cup finely chopped onion
1 teaspoon minced garlic
¼ cup dry white wine *or* reduced-sodium vegetable broth
¼ teaspoon dried thyme leaves
½ cup fat-free sour cream
Salt and cayenne pepper, to taste

Per Serving
Calories: 80
% Calories from fat: 2
Fat (gm): 0.2
Saturated fat (gm): 0.1
Cholesterol (mg): 0
Sodium (mg): 24
Protein (gm): 3.5
Carbohydrate (gm): 16.5
Exchanges
Milk: 0.0
Vegetable: 2.0
Fruit: 0.0
Bread: 0.5
Meat: 0.0
Fat: 0.0

1. Spray large skillet with cooking spray; heat over medium heat until hot. Add mushrooms, onion, and garlic to skillet; spray with cooking spray and saute 3 to 4 minutes.

2. Add wine and thyme to skillet; heat to boiling. Reduce heat and simmer, covered, until mushrooms are very tender, 8 to 10 minutes. Cook, uncovered, on low heat until mushrooms are dry and well browned, 20 to 25 minutes. Stir in sour cream; season to taste with salt and cayenne pepper.

GULF PORTS OKRA

A Cajun recipe I remember fondly from the Gulf Ports Diner. Select small okra for best flavor and tenderness.

6 servings

1½ pounds fresh, *or* frozen, thawed okra
Garlic-flavored vegetable cooking spray
Garlic powder, to taste
Salt and pepper, to taste

Per Serving
Calories: 37
% Calories from fat: 24
Fat (gm): 0.2
Saturated fat (gm): 0.1
Cholesterol (mg): 0
Sodium (mg): 6
Protein (gm): 2.1
Carbohydrate (gm): 8.2
Exchanges
Milk: 0.0
Vegetable: 1.5
Fruit: 0.0
Bread: 0.0
Meat: 0.0
Fat: 0.0

1. Trim okra stems without cutting into tops of okra. Cook okra in boiling water 1 to 2 minutes; drain well.

2. Spray large skillet with cooking spray; heat over medium heat until hot. Add okra and spray with cooking spray; cook over medium heat until well browned, almost blackened, stirring occasionally. Sprinkle okra generously with garlic powder; season to taste with salt and pepper.

QUARTET OF ONIONS

Cooked slowly until caramelized, the onion mixture is scented with a combination of mint and sage.

6 servings

    Vegetable cooking spray

2 pounds sweet onions, sliced

1 small leek (white part only), thinly sliced

4 ounces shallots, finely chopped

1/2 cup sliced green onions and tops

1/2 cup reduced-sodium vegetable broth

1 1/2 teaspoons dried mint leaves

1/4 teaspoon dried sage leaves

    Salt and white pepper, to taste

Per Serving
Calories: 90
% Calories from fat: 4
Fat (gm): 0.4
Saturated fat (gm): 0.1
Cholesterol (mg): 0
Sodium (mg): 16
Protein (gm): 2.7
Carbohydrate (gm): 20.1
Exchanges
Milk: 0.0
Vegetable: 4.0
Fruit: 0.0
Bread: 0.0
Meat: 0.0
Fat: 0.0

1. Spray large skillet with cooking spray; heat over medium heat until hot. Saute onions, leek, shallots, and green onions 3 to 4 minutes, stirring frequently. Stir in broth and heat to boiling; reduce heat and simmer, covered, 5 minutes.

2. Stir in herbs and cook, uncovered, over medium-low heat until onion mixture is golden, about 15 minutes. Season to taste with salt and white pepper.

SAUTEED SUMMER SQUASH WITH SNOW PEAS

The vegetables are best when crisp-tender, so don't overcook! Zucchini or chayote squash may also be used in the recipe.

4 servings

Butter-flavored vegetable cooking spray
2 green onions and tops, sliced
2 cloves garlic, minced
2 medium yellow squash, sliced
2 ounces snow peas, strings trimmed
2 tablespoons finely chopped lovage *or* tarragon
Salt and white pepper, to taste

Per Serving
Calories: 27
% Calories from fat: 10
Fat (gm): 0.3
Saturated fat (gm): 0.1
Cholesterol (mg): 0
Sodium (mg): 2
Protein (gm): 1.4
Carbohydrate (gm): 5.7
Exchanges
Milk: 0.0
Vegetable: 1.0
Fruit: 0.0
Bread: 0.0
Meat: 0.0
Fat: 0.0

1. Spray a large skillet with cooking spray; heat over medium heat until hot. Saute green onions and garlic 2 to 3 minutes.

2. Add squash, snow peas, and lovage to skillet; spray with cooking spray and cook over medium heat until vegetables are crisp-tender, about 5 minutes. Season to taste with salt and pepper.

BRAISED PARSNIPS AND WINTER VEGETABLES

Idaho or sweet potatoes, winter squash, or Brussels sprouts would be flavorful additions to this colorful vegetable side-dish.

6 servings

Olive oil cooking spray
1/4 cup minced onion
2 teaspoons minced garlic
2 medium parsnips, peeled, cubed
2 medium carrots, sliced
1 cup julienned celery root *or* celery
1 cup shredded red, *or* green, cabbage
1/2 cup dry red wine *or* reduced-sodium vegetable broth
2 tablespoons light brown sugar

Per Serving
Calories: 92
% Calories from fat: 3
Fat (gm): 0.3
Saturated fat (gm): 0.1
Cholesterol (mg): 0
Sodium (mg): 47
Protein (gm): 1.5
Carbohydrate (gm): 19.3
Exchanges
Milk: 0.0
Vegetable: 2.0
Fruit: 0.0
Bread: 0.5
Meat: 0.0
Fat: 0.0

1 teaspoon balsamic, *or* red wine, vinegar
1 teaspoon dried sage leaves
$^1/_2$ teaspoon dried thyme leaves
Salt and pepper, to taste

1. Spray large skillet with cooking spray; heat over medium heat until hot. Saute onion and garlic 2 to 3 minutes; add parsnips, carrots, celery root, and cabbage and continue to saute until beginning to brown, 4 to 5 minutes.

2. Add remaining ingredients, except salt and pepper, to skillet; heat to boiling; reduce heat and simmer, covered, until vegetables are tender, 8 to 10 minutes. Season to taste with salt and pepper.

PEPERONATA

Peperonata is Italian-inspired. Sweet bell peppers and onions are slowly cooked until tender and creamy.

8 servings

Olive oil cooking spray
2 cups sliced onions
1 cup sliced green bell pepper
1 cup sliced red bell pepper
6 cloves garlic, minced
$^1/_4$ cup water
Salt and pepper, to taste

Per Serving
Calories: 36
% Calories from fat: 5
Fat (gm): 0.2
Saturated fat (gm): 0
Cholesterol (mg): 0
Sodium (mg): 2
Protein (gm): 1.3
Carbohydrate (gm): 8.2
Exchanges
Milk: 0.0
Vegetable: 2.0
Fruit: 0.0
Bread: 0.0
Meat: 0.0
Fat: 0.0

1. Spray medium skillet with cooking spray; heat over medium heat until hot. Add onions, bell peppers, and garlic to skillet; cook over medium heat 5 minutes, stirring occasionally.

2. Add water to skillet; cook, covered, over medium-low to low heat until vegetables are very tender and creamy, 20 to 25 minutes, stirring occasionally. Season to taste with salt and pepper.

REAL MASHED POTATOES

Just like grandma used to make! For a country-style variation, leave potatoes unpeeled.

8 servings

2 pounds Idaho potatoes, peeled, quartered, cooked until tender

1/2 cup fat-free sour cream

1/4 cup fat-free milk, hot

2 tablespoons margarine

Salt and pepper, to taste

Per Serving
Calories: 124
% Calories from fat: 21
Fat (gm): 2.9
Saturated fat (gm): 0.6
Cholesterol (mg): 0.2
Sodium (mg): 53
Protein (gm): 3.1
Carbohydrate (gm): 22.2
Exchanges
Milk: 0.0
Vegetable: 0.0
Fruit: 0.0
Bread: 1.5
Meat: 0.0
Fat: 0.5

1. Mash potatoes, or beat until smooth, in medium bowl, adding sour cream, milk, and margarine. Season to taste with salt and pepper.

Variations: **Garlic-Mashed Potatoes**—Cook 10 peeled cloves of garlic with the potatoes. Follow recipe above, mashing garlic with potatoes.

Horseradish-Mashed Potatoes—Make Real or Garlic-Mashed Potatoes, beating in 2 teaspoons horseradish.

Potato Pancakes—Make any of the mashed potato recipes above; refrigerate until chilled. Mix in 2 egg whites (or 1/4 cup no-cholesterol real egg product), 4 chopped green onions and tops, and 1/4 cup grated fat-free Parmesan cheese (optional). Form mixture into 8 patties, using about 1/2 cup mixture for each. Coat patties in flour, dip in beaten egg white, and coat with plain dry bread crumbs. Cook over medium-high heat in lightly greased large skillet until browned, 3 to 5 minutes on each side.

GREENS AND SMASHED POTATOES

The potatoes are not peeled, giving this dish a rustic character.

4 servings

Butter-flavored vegetable cooking spray
1/4 cup finely chopped onion
3 cloves garlic, minced
1 1/2 cups thinly sliced greens (kale, mustard, or turnip greens)
1/4 cup water
3 medium Idaho potatoes, cubed, cooked
1/4 cup fat-free sour cream
2-4 tablespoons fat-free milk
1-2 tablespoons margarine, softened
Salt and pepper, to taste
Paprika, as garnish

Per Serving
Calories: 141
% Calories from fat: 19
Fat (gm): 3.1
Saturated fat (gm): 0.6
Cholesterol (mg): 0.1
Sodium (mg): 60
Protein (gm): 3.8
Carbohydrate (gm): 25.4
Exchanges
Milk: 0.0
Vegetable: 2.0
Fruit: 0.0
Bread: 1.0
Meat: 0.0
Fat: 0.5

1. Spray medium skillet with cooking spray; heat over medium heat until hot. Saute onion and garlic until tender, 3 to 4 minutes.

2. Add greens and water to skillet; heat to boiling. Cook, covered, until greens are tender, about 5 minutes. Cook, uncovered, until water has evaporated and greens are almost dry.

3. Mash potatoes in bowl; mix in sour cream, milk, and margarine. Stir into greens mixture and cook over low heat until hot through. Season to taste with salt and pepper. Spoon potatoes into serving bowl; sprinkle lightly with paprika.

ROOT VEGGIES AND MASHED POTATOES

A selection of winter root vegetables, roasted to perfection and served with garlic-spiked mashed potatoes.

8 servings

Vegetable cooking spray

3 medium beets, peeled, sliced

3 medium turnips, peeled, sliced

1 cup baby carrots

1 leek (white part only), cut into 1-inch pieces

2¹/₂ cups halved Brussels sprouts

1 tablespoon caraway seeds

Salt and pepper, to taste

1¹/₂ pounds Idaho potatoes, unpeeled, cubed

4 cloves garlic, peeled

¹/₄ cup fat-free milk, hot

2 tablespoons margarine, cut in pieces

Per Serving
Calories: 194
% Calories from fat: 15
Fat (gm): 3.5
Saturated fat (gm): 0.7
Cholesterol (mg): 0.1
Sodium (mg): 164
Protein (gm): 6.2
Carbohydrate (gm): 37.8
Exchanges
Milk: 0.0
Vegetable: 1.0
Fruit: 0.0
Bread: 2.0
Meat: 0.0
Fat: 0.5

1. Line large jelly roll pan with aluminum foil; spray with cooking spray. Arrange beets, turnips, carrots, leek, and Brussels sprouts on pan in single layer; spray generously with cooking spray. Sprinkle vegetables with caraway seeds; sprinkle lightly with salt and pepper. Bake at 450 degrees until vegetables are tender and lightly browned, about 25 minutes.

2. Cook potatoes and garlic in 2 inches simmering water in covered saucepan until tender, 10 to 15 minutes; drain. Mash potatoes and garlic with masher or electric mixer, adding milk and margarine. Season to taste with salt and pepper.

3. Spoon potatoes onto plates; spoon vegetables over potatoes.

TWICE-BAKED POTATOES WITH CHEESE

The potatoes can be prepared and refrigerated 24 hours in advance; then bake 5 to 10 minutes longer than indicated in recipe.

4 servings

2 large Idaho potatoes (8 ounces each)
1/4 cup fat-free sour cream
1/4 cup fat-free milk
3/4 cup (3 ounces) shredded reduced-fat sharp, *or* mild, Cheddar cheese, divided
Salt and pepper, to taste
Paprika, as garnish

Per Serving
Calories: 177
% Calories from fat: 16
Fat (gm): 3.2
Saturated fat (gm): 1.6
Cholesterol (mg): 11.6
Sodium (mg): 314
Protein (gm): 8.4
Carbohydrate (gm): 29.2
Exchanges
Milk: 0.0
Vegetable: 0.0
Fruit: 0.0
Bread: 2.0
Meat: 0.5
Fat: 0.0

1. Pierce potatoes with a fork and bake at 400 degrees until tender, about 1 hour. Cut into halves lengthwise; let cool enough to handle.

2. Scoop out inside of potatoes, being careful to leave shells intact. Mash warm potatoes, or beat until smooth, in medium bowl, adding sour cream, milk, and 1/2 cup cheese. Season to taste with salt and pepper.

3. Spoon potato mixture into potato shells; sprinkle with remaining 1/4 cup cheese and paprika. Bake at 400 degrees until hot through, 15 to 20 minutes.

VEGGIE-STUFFED BAKERS

Cheesy and topped with a vegetable medley, these potatoes are oven-baked for a crispy skin. The potatoes can be made through Step 3 and refrigerated a day in advance; then increase baking time to 30 to 40 minutes.

6 servings

3 large Idaho potatoes (8-10 ounces each)
  Vegetable cooking spray
1 cup chopped onion
1/3 cup fresh, *or* frozen, whole-kernel corn
1 medium red bell pepper, chopped
4 cloves garlic, minced
1/3 cup fat-free sour cream *or* plain fat-free yogurt
3/4 cup (3 ounces) shredded fat-free Cheddar cheese, divided
  Salt and pepper, to taste
1 cup broccoli florets, cooked until crisp-tender

Per Serving
Calories: 160
% Calories from fat: 2
Fat (gm): 0.3
Saturated fat (gm): 0
Cholesterol (mg): 0
Sodium (mg): 119
Protein (gm): 9
Carbohydrate (gm): 32.4
Exchanges
Milk: 0.0
Vegetable: 1.0
Fruit: 0.0
Bread: 1.5
Meat: 0.5
Fat: 0.0

1. Grease potatoes lightly and bake at 400 degrees until tender, 45 to 60 minutes; let stand until cool enough to handle. Cut potatoes lengthwise into halves; scoop out potato, leaving shells intact.

2. Spray medium skillet with cooking spray; heat over medium heat until hot. Saute onion, corn, bell pepper, and garlic until tender, about 5 minutes.

3. Mash potatoes, adding sour cream and half the Cheddar cheese. Mix in sauteed vegetables; season to taste with salt and pepper. Spoon mixture into potato shells; arrange broccoli on top and sprinkle with remaining cheese.

4. Arrange potatoes in baking pan; bake, uncovered, at 350 degrees until hot through, 20 to 30 minutes.

POTATOES WITH POBLANO CHILIES

In this recipe, roasted poblano chilies are combined with potatoes for a hearty side dish. Serve with a fried egg and salsa for brunch.

4 servings (about 2/3 cup each)

4 medium poblano chilies
   Vegetable cooking spray
1 medium onion, sliced
1 pound Idaho potatoes, unpeeled, cooked, cut into 1/2-inch cubes
   Salt and pepper, to taste

Per Serving
Calories: 147
% Calories from fat: 2
Fat (gm): 0.3
Saturated fat (gm): 0.1
Cholesterol (mg): 0
Sodium (mg): 11
Protein (gm): 3.7
Carbohydrate (gm): 34
Exchanges
Milk: 0.0
Vegetable: 1.0
Fruit: 0.0
Bread: 1.5
Meat: 0.0
Fat: 0.0

1. Cut chilies into halves; discard stems, seeds, and veins. Place chilies, skin sides up, on broiler pan; broil 6 inches from heat source until skin is blackened and blistered. Wrap chilies in plastic bag or paper toweling 5 minutes; peel off skin and discard. Cut chilies into strips.

2. Spray large skillet with cooking spray; heat over medium heat until hot. Saute onion 2 to 3 minutes; add chilies and potatoes. Cook over medium heat until onion is tender and potatoes browned, 5 to 8 minutes. Season to taste with salt and pepper.

POTATOES GRATIN

These potatoes are so rich and creamy you'll never believe they were made without heavy cream!

8 servings

2 tablespoons margarine

3 tablespoons flour

1³/4 cups fat-free milk

2 ounces light pasteurized processed cheese product, cubed

1/2 cup (2 ounces) shredded reduced-fat Cheddar cheese

Salt and pepper, to taste

2 pounds Idaho potatoes, peeled, cut into scant 1/4-inch slices

1/4 cup very thinly sliced onion

Ground nutmeg, to taste

Per Serving
Calories: 202
% Calories from fat: 23
Fat (gm): 5.1
Saturated fat (gm): 1.7
Cholesterol (mg): 8.5
Sodium (mg): 259
Protein (gm): 7.6
Carbohydrate (gm): 31.7
Exchanges
Milk: 0.0
Vegetable: 0.0
Fruit: 0.0
Bread: 2.0
Meat: 0.5
Fat: 0.5

1. Melt margarine in medium saucepan; stir in flour and cook over medium heat, stirring constantly, 2 minutes. Whisk in milk and heat to boiling; boil, stirring constantly, until thickened. Remove from heat; add cheeses, stirring until melted. Season to taste with salt and pepper.

2. Layer 1/3 of the potatoes and onion in bottom of 2-quart casserole; sprinkle lightly with salt, pepper, and nutmeg. Spoon 2/3 cup sauce over. Repeat layers 2 times, using remaining ingredients.

3. Bake, covered, at 350 degrees for 45 minutes; uncover and bake until potatoes are fork-tender and browned, 20 to 30 minutes more.

Variations: **Scalloped Potatoes**—Make sauce as in Step 1 above, increasing margarine to 3 tablespoons, flour to 1/4 cup, and milk to 2¹/4 cups; omit cheeses. Assemble and bake as directed.

Scalloped Potatoes and Ham—Trim visible fat from 1 pound lean smoked ham; cut into cubes. Make Scalloped Potatoes as above, layering ham between potatoes.

POTATOES AND WILD MUSHROOMS AU GRATIN

A time-savvy casserole that utilizes frozen and dried vegetables to speed preparation.

6 servings

Vegetable cooking spray

1/2 red, *or* green, bell pepper, chopped

1/2 cup chopped onion

2 cups water

11/2 cups frozen, *or* fresh, broccoli florets

1/2 cup frozen tiny peas

11/2 ounces dried shiitake mushrooms, broken into small pieces (about 6 mushrooms)

1 package (41/2 ounces) dried julienned potatoes

3/4 cup fat-free milk

1-11/2 cups (4-6 ounces) shredded reduced-fat Swiss, *or* Cheddar, cheese

Per Serving
Calories: 199
% Calories from fat: 20
Fat (gm): 4.5
Saturated fat (gm): 2.1
Cholesterol (mg): 14.1
Sodium (mg): 572
Protein (gm): 12.5
Carbohydrate (gm): 28.7
Exchanges
Milk: 0.0
Vegetable: 3.0
Fruit: 0.0
Bread: 1.0
Meat: 0.0
Fat: 1.0

1. Spray medium saucepan with cooking spray; heat over medium heat until hot. Saute bell pepper and onion until tender, about 5 minutes. Add water, broccoli, peas, and dried mushrooms; heat to boiling.

2. Pour potato and sauce mix into 2-quart casserole; pour boiling vegetable mixture over and mix well. Stir in milk and cheese. Bake, uncovered, at 400 degrees until golden, 20 to 30 minutes.

CRISPY FRIES

Golden brown, delicious, and crisp, these potatoes look and taste like they have been deep-fried; the secret is salting the raw potatoes! Potatoes can be held in a 200-degree oven for up to 1 hour.

4 to 6 servings

1 pound Idaho potatoes, unpeeled
2 teaspoons salt
Vegetable cooking spray
Salt and pepper, to taste

Per Serving
Calories: 166
% Calories from fat: 1
Fat (gm): 0.2
Saturated fat (gm): 0
Cholesterol (mg): 0
Sodium (mg): 12
Protein (gm): 3.5
Carbohydrate (gm): 38.6
Exchanges
Milk: 0.0
Vegetable: 0.0
Fruit: 0.0
Bread: 2.5
Meat: 0.0
Fat: 0.0

1. Cut potatoes into sticks 3 to 4 inches long and a scant $1/2$ inch wide. Sprinkle lightly with 2 teaspoons salt and let stand 10 minutes. Rinse potatoes in cold water and dry well on paper toweling.

2. Spray non-stick jelly roll pan with cooking spray. Arrange potatoes in single layer on pan; spray generously with cooking spray, tossing to coat all sides. Sprinkle potatoes lightly with salt and pepper.

3. Bake at 350 degrees until potatoes are golden brown and crisp, 40 to 45 minutes, turning halfway through cooking time.

Variations: **Parmesan Fries**—Follow recipe, sprinkling potatoes lightly with grated fat-free Parmesan cheese before baking.

Steak Fries—Cut potatoes into wedges 4 inches long and 1 inch wide. Follow recipe as above, baking until golden brown and crisp, 1 to $1^1/4$ hours.

ORANGE-LIME SWEET POTATOES

Sweet potatoes are gently sauced with citrus juices; use fresh squeezed juices for best flavor.

6 servings (about ¹/₂ cup each)

Butter-flavored vegetable cooking spray
1 cup chopped onion
1 teaspoon minced garlic
1 pound sweet potatoes, peeled, cut into 1-inch pieces
1 cup orange juice
¹/₄ cup lime juice
Salt and pepper, to taste

Per Serving
Calories: 95
% Calories from fat: 3
Fat (gm): 0.3
Saturated fat (gm): 0.1
Cholesterol (mg): 0
Sodium (mg): 9
Protein (gm): 1.7
Carbohydrate (gm): 22.3
Exchanges
Milk: 0.0
Vegetable: 0.0
Fruit: 0.5
Bread: 1.0
Meat: 0.0
Fat: 0.0

1. Spray medium skillet with cooking spray; heat over medium heat until hot. Saute onion and garlic 3 to 4 minutes.

2. Add sweet potatoes and juices to skillet; heat to boiling. Reduce heat and simmer, covered, until potatoes are tender, about 10 minutes. Cook, uncovered, until sauce is thickened, 8 to 10 minutes. Season to taste with salt and pepper.

SWEET POTATO PONE

More of a country-style pudding than a soufflé, this comfort food will become a favorite. Serve with a drizzle of warm maple syrup, if you like.

4 servings

1 small onion, finely chopped
1 tablespoon margarine
3 tablespoons flour
1 cup fat-free milk
1/2 cup no-cholesterol real egg product *or* 2 eggs
1 large sweet potato (about 8 ounces), unpeeled, cut into 1-inch cubes, cooked
2 tablespoons packed light brown sugar
1/4 teaspoon ground cinnamon
1/8 teaspoon ground nutmeg
1/8 teaspoon ground cloves
1/4 teaspoon salt
2-3 dashes white pepper
4 egg whites, beaten to stiff peaks

Per Serving
Calories: 179
% Calories from fat: 16
Fat (gm): 3.1
Saturated fat (gm): 0.7
Cholesterol (mg): 1.0
Sodium (mg): 303
Protein (gm): 5.5
Carbohydrate (gm): 27.7
Exchanges
Milk: 0.0
Vegetable: 0.5
Fruit: 0.0
Bread: 1.0
Meat: 0.5
Fat: 0.0

1. Saute onion in margarine in medium saucepan until tender, 3 to 5 minutes. Stir in flour; cook 2 to 3 minutes. Stir in milk; heat to boiling, stirring constantly, until thickened.

2. Beat egg product in small bowl until thick and lemon colored, 2 to 3 minutes. Slowly whisk about half the milk mixture into egg; then whisk egg mixture into saucepan. Cook over low heat, whisking constantly, 1 minute; remove from heat.

3. Coarsely mash sweet potato with fork. Mix sweet potato, brown sugar, spices, salt, and pepper into milk and egg mixture. Mix in half the egg whites; fold mixture into remaining egg whites.

4. Spoon mixture into lightly greased 1-quart soufflé dish or casserole. Bake at 375 degrees until puffed and golden (sharp knife inserted halfway between center and edges will come out almost clean), 30 to 35 minutes.

SWEET POTATOES WITH PINEAPPLE BROTH

8 servings

4 medium sweet potatoes, unpeeled
1 teaspoon low-fat margarine
1/4 cup unsweetened pineapple juice
2 tablespoons low-sodium chicken broth
1 tablespoon chopped unsweetened pineapple
Pinch of cinnamon
Pinch of allspice
Vegetable cooking spray

Per Serving
Calories: 67
% Calories from fat: 3
Fat (gm): 0.3
Saturated fat (gm): 0
Cholesterol (mg): 0
Sodium (mg): 14
Protein (gm): 1.1
Carbohydrate (gm): 15.2
Exchanges
Milk: 0.0
Vegetable: 0.0
Fruit: 0.0
Bread: 1.0
Meat: 0.0
Fat: 0.0

1. Preheat oven to 375 degrees. Boil potatoes in water in large saucepan until tender, about 30 minutes; remove skins. Mash pulp in large bowl; add margarine, fruit juice, and broth and whip until fluffy. Add chopped pineapple and spices; transfer to 1-quart baking dish coated with cooking spray. Bake for 30 minutes or until lightly browned.

CREAMED SPINACH

Easy to prepare, this sauced spinach dish is rich in flavor—a perfect accompaniment to chicken or fish.

4 servings

2 packages (10 ounces each) fresh spinach, stems trimmed
1/4 cup finely chopped onion
2 teaspoons margarine
2 tablespoons flour
1 cup fat-free milk *or* fat-free half-and-half
1/4 cup fat-free sour cream
Ground nutmeg, to taste
Salt and pepper, to taste

Per Serving
Calories: 92
% Calories from fat: 20
Fat (gm): 2.2
Saturated fat (gm): 0.5
Cholesterol (mg): 1
Sodium (mg): 145
Protein (gm): 6.6
Carbohydrate (gm): 13.3
Exchanges
Milk: 0.0
Vegetable: 2.5
Fruit: 0.0
Bread: 0.0
Meat: 0.0
Fat: 0.5

1. Rinse spinach and place in large saucepan with water clinging to leaves. Cook, covered, over medium-high heat until spinach is wilted, 3 to 4 minutes. Drain excess liquid.

2. Saute onion in margarine in small saucepan until tender, 3 to 5 minutes. Stir in flour; cook over medium-low heat 1 minute, stirring constantly. Whisk in milk; heat to boiling. Boil, whisking constantly, until thickened, about 1 minute. Remove from heat and stir in sour cream.

3. Pour sauce over spinach and mix lightly; season to taste with nutmeg, salt, and pepper.

Variation: **Spinach au Gratin**—Make recipe as above, mixing spinach with all but 1/4 cup of the sauce and spoon into a small casserole. Spoon 1/4 cup of sauce over the top, and sprinkle with 2 to 3 tablespoons of grated Parmesan cheese or reduced-fat mild Cheddar cheese. Bake at 425 degrees until cheese is melted, 2 to 3 minutes.

ACORN SQUASH AND APPLE BAKE

4 servings

  2 acorn squash, cut into 1/4–inch rings, seeded
  2 apples, cored and sliced
  1 teaspoon sugar-free pancake syrup
  1/2 teaspoon ground cinnamon
  1 teaspoon water

Per Serving
Calories: 99
% Calories from fat: 3
Fat (gm): 0.4
Saturated fat (gm): 0.1
Cholesterol (mg): 0
Sodium (mg): 6
Protein (gm): 1.3
Carbohydrate (gm): 25.8
Exchanges
Milk: 0.0
Vegetable: 0.0
Fruit: 0.5
Bread: 1.0
Meat: 0.0
Fat: 0.0

1. Preheat oven to 375 degrees. Layer rings of squash and apple in casserole dish, top with pancake syrup, cinnamon, and water. Cover and bake 30 minutes or until squash is tender.

CHAYOTE WITH PEPITAS

The pumpkin seeds, or "pepitas," will begin to pop and jump in the skillet, signaling that they are toasted! Chayote squash have the crisp texture of an apple when raw and are delicious sauteed or steamed until crisp-tender.

4 servings

Vegetable cooking spray
4 teaspoons pumpkin seeds
$^1/_2$ cup finely chopped onion
2 cloves garlic, minced
2 chayote squash, peeled, pitted, cut into $^1/_2$-inch cubes
Salt and pepper, to taste

Per Serving
Calories: 35
% Calories from fat: 16
Fat (gm): 0.7
Saturated fat (gm): 0.1
Cholesterol (mg): 0
Sodium (mg): 2
Protein (gm): 1.1
Carbohydrate (gm): 7
Exchanges
Milk: 0.0
Vegetable: 1.5
Fruit: 0.0
Bread: 0.0
Meat: 0.0
Fat: 0.0

1. Spray small skillet with vegetable cooking spray; heat over medium heat until hot. Cook pumpkin seeds over medium heat until they are toasted and begin to pop, 3 to 5 minutes. Reserve.

2. Spray large skillet with vegetable cooking spray; heat over medium heat until hot. Saute onion and garlic until tender, 3 to 5 minutes; add squash and cook over medium heat until squash is crisp-tender, about 20 minutes, stirring occasionally. Season to taste with salt and pepper. Spoon squash into serving bowl; sprinkle with reserved pumpkin seeds.

PARMESAN-HERB SPAGHETTI SQUASH

The delicate flavor of the squash is complemented by the combination of herbs and Parmesan cheese.

4 servings

1   spaghetti squash (2¹/₂-3 pounds), cut lengthwise into halves, seeded
2   tablespoons sliced green onions and tops
1   teaspoon minced garlic
1-2 tablespoons margarine
¹/₄ cup reduced-sodium vegetable broth
1   teaspoon Italian seasoning
¹/₃ cup grated fat-free Parmesan cheese
   Salt and pepper, to taste

Per Serving
Calories: 99
% Calories from fat: 29
Fat (gm): 3.6
Saturated fat (gm): 0.7
Cholesterol (mg): 0
Sodium (mg): 102
Protein (gm): 5.1
Carbohydrate (gm): 14.3
Exchanges
Milk: 0.0
Vegetable: 2.0
Fruit: 0.0
Bread: 0.0
Meat: 0.5
Fat: 0.5

1. Place squash, cut sides down, in baking pan; add ¹/₂ inch hot water. Bake, covered, at 400 degrees until squash is fork-tender, 30 to 40 minutes. Remove squash from pan and turn cut sides up. Fluff strands of squash with tines of fork.

2. Saute green onions and garlic in margarine in small saucepan until tender, 3 to 4 minutes. Stir in broth and Italian seasoning; heat to boiling. Spoon half the mixture into each squash half and toss; sprinkle with Parmesan cheese and toss. Season to taste with salt and pepper.

FRIED TOMATOES

Either green or red tomatoes can be used in this recipe—do try both!

4 servings

Butter-flavored vegetable cooking spray

4 medium green, *or* red, tomatoes, sliced ¹/₄ inch thick

¹/₄ cup all-purpose flour

Salt and pepper, to taste

Per Serving
Calories: 58
% Calories from fat: 5
Fat (gm): 0.3
Saturated fat (gm): 0
Cholesterol (mg): 0
Sodium (mg): 16
Protein (gm): 2.3
Carbohydrate (gm): 12.2
Exchanges
Milk: 0.0
Vegetable: 1.0
Fruit: 0.0
Bread: 0.5
Meat: 0.0
Fat: 0.0

1. Spray large skillet with cooking spray; heat over medium heat until hot. Coat tomato slices lightly with flour; cook over medium heat until browned, 2 to 3 minutes on each side. Sprinkle lightly with salt and pepper.

Variations: **Sugar-Glazed Fried Tomatoes**—Cook tomatoes as above, but do not coat with flour. After tomatoes are browned, sprinkle lightly with sugar and cook until caramelized, about 1 minute on each side. Do not season with salt and pepper.

Cornmeal Fried Tomatoes—Cook tomatoes as above, substituting yellow cornmeal for the flour.

TOMATO PUDDING

Use a good quality, firm French, Italian, or sourdough bread for the croutons, as a soft bread will become too soggy in baking.

4 servings

1¹/₂ cups cubed firm bread, such as French or Italian
Vegetable cooking spray
¹/₂ cup thinly sliced celery
¹/₂ cup chopped onion
¹/₂ cup chopped green bell pepper
1 can (16 ounces) reduced-sodium whole tomatoes, undrained, coarsely chopped
¹/₂ teaspoon celery seeds
¹/₂ teaspoon dried marjoram leaves
1 tablespoon light brown sugar
Salt and pepper, to taste

Per Serving
Calories: 85
% Calories from fat: 9
Fat (gm): 0.9
Saturated fat (gm): 0.1
Cholesterol (mg): 0
Sodium (mg): 88
Protein (gm): 2.6
Carbohydrate (gm): 17.9
Exchanges
Milk: 0.0
Vegetable: 2.0
Fruit: 0.0
Bread: 0.5
Meat: 0.0
Fat: 0.0

1. Spray bread cubes generously with cooking spray; arrange in single layer in baking pan. Bake at 375 degrees until browned, stirring occasionally, 8 to 10 minutes.

2. Spray medium skillet with cooking spray; heat over medium heat until hot. Saute celery, onion, and bell pepper until tender, about 8 minutes. Stir in tomatoes, celery seeds, marjoram, and brown sugar and heat to boiling. Reduce heat and simmer, covered, 2 to 3 minutes; season to taste with salt and pepper. Pour mixture into 1-quart soufflé dish or casserole.

3. Stir bread cubes into tomato mixture, leaving some on the top. Bake at 425 degrees until hot through, about 20 minutes. Serve hot.

Tips: Dry "stuffing" cubes can be substituted for the toasted bread cubes. Two cups coarsely chopped fresh tomatoes can be substituted for the canned tomatoes; simmer as above until tomatoes wilt and release juices, 5 to 8 minutes.

ZUCCHINI FROM PUEBLA

If the Mexican white cheese, "queso blanco," is not available, farmer's cheese can be readily substituted. Purchased roasted peppers can be used.

6 servings

Vegetable cooking spray

1 cup chopped onion

2 pounds zucchini, cut diagonally into ¹/₄-inch slices

4 roasted red peppers, cut into strips (about 1 cup)

¹/₂ cup reduced-sodium fat-free chicken broth

¹/₂-1 teaspoon ground cumin

¹/₂ cup fat-free milk

Salt and pepper, to taste

2 tablespoons crumbled Mexican white cheese *or* farmer's cheese

Per Serving
Calories: 100
% Calories from fat: 11
Fat (gm): 0.4
Saturated fat (gm): 0
Cholesterol (mg): 2.6
Sodium (mg): 36
Protein (gm): 5.1
Carbohydrate (gm): 20.3
Exchanges
Milk: 0.0
Vegetable: 4.0
Fruit: 0.0
Bread: 0.0
Meat: 0.0
Fat: 0.0

1. Spray large skillet with cooking spray; heat over medium heat until hot. Saute onion until tender, 5 to 8 minutes; stir in zucchini, roasted peppers, broth, and cumin. Heat to boiling. Reduce heat and simmer, covered, just until the zucchini is crisp-tender, 5 to 8 minutes.

2. Add milk; cook until hot, 1 to 2 minutes. Season to taste with salt and pepper. Spoon zucchini into serving bowl; sprinkle with cheese.

ZUCCHINI FANS PROVENÇAL

Zucchini are thinly sliced, then spread out to form "fans."

4 servings

2 medium sweet onions, thinly sliced, divided

6 cloves garlic, minced, divided

4 small zucchini, cut lengthwise into halves

3 medium tomatoes, thinly sliced

1/2 cup dry white wine *or* reduced-sodium vegetable broth

Olive oil cooking spray

Salt and pepper, to taste

3/4 teaspoon dried basil leaves

1/2 teaspoon dried oregano leaves

1/2 teaspoon dried marjoram leaves

1/4 teaspoon dried thyme leaves

Per Serving
Calories: 89
% Calories from fat: 6
Fat (gm): 0.6
Saturated fat (gm): 0.1
Cholesterol (mg): 0
Sodium (mg): 16
Protein (gm): 3.4
Carbohydrate (gm): 15.3
Exchanges
Milk: 0.0
Vegetable: 3.0
Fruit: 0.0
Bread: 0.0
Meat: 0.0
Fat: 0.0

1. Separate onions into rings; arrange half the onions and garlic in bottom of 11 x 7-inch baking pan.

2. Cut zucchini halves lengthwise into scant 1/4-inch slices, cutting to, but not through, small ends. Alternate zucchini and tomato slices in rows over the onions, spreading zucchini slices into "fans." Arrange remaining onions and garlic on top.

3. Heat wine to simmering in small saucepan; pour over vegetables. Spray top of vegetables with cooking spray; sprinkle lightly with salt and pepper and combined herbs.

4. Bake, covered, at 350 degrees until zucchini is crisp-tender, about 25 minutes.

THIRTEEN

Salads

AND

Dressings

TROPICAL FRUIT SALAD

This can also be served as a light dessert.

24 servings

1 can (20 ounces) unsweetened crushed pineapple in juice, drained, juice reserved

18 ounces frozen unsweetened pineapple-orange-banana juice concentrate, thawed

2 medium bananas, diced

1 can (15 ounces) mandarin oranges, drained, rinsed, and halved

24 paper baking cups
   Lettuce leaves, optional

Per Serving
Calories: 77
% Calories from fat: 1
Fat (gm): 0.1
Saturated fat (gm): 0
Cholesterol (mg): 0
Sodium (mg): 5
Protein (gm): 1.4
Carbohydrate (gm): 18.7
Exchanges
Milk: 0.0
Vegetable: 0.0
Fruit: 1.0
Bread: 0.0
Meat: 0.0
Fat: 0.0

1. Add water to reserved pineapple juice to make 1^1/$_2$ cups liquid. Pour liquid into large mixing bowl; add pineapple, juice concentrate, bananas, and mandarin oranges; mix well.

2. Line muffin tins with paper baking cups; spoon in fruit mixture, filling cups ^{3}/$_4$ full. Cover tightly with plastic wrap and freeze two hours or until firm.

3. Before serving, remove desired number of cups from freezer and let stand 20 minutes; remove from baking cups and serve on lettuce leaf, if desired.

FROZEN FRUIT SALAD

So simple, but so very tasty—serve as a dessert too!

8 servings

1 package (8 ounces) fat-free cream cheese

1 cup fat-free sour cream

^{1}/$_3$ cup sugar

1 tablespoon grated lemon rind
   Pinch salt

5 cups assorted fresh, frozen, *or* canned fruit (drained crushed pineapple, sliced strawberries, blueberries, raspberries,

Per Serving
Calories: 126
% Calories from fat: 2
Fat (gm): 0.3
Saturated fat (gm): 0
Cholesterol (mg): 0
Sodium (mg): 191
Protein (gm): 6.6
Carbohydrate (gm): 25.2
Exchanges
Milk: 0.0
Vegetable: 0.0
Fruit: 1.0
Bread: 0.0
Meat: 0.5
Fat: 0.0

cherries, chopped peaches, etc.)
Lettuce leaves, as garnish

1. Beat cream cheese, sour cream, sugar, lemon rind, and salt in large bowl until smooth. Mix in fruit. Spread in 11 x 7-inch baking dish and freeze until firm, 8 hours or overnight.

2. Let stand at room temperature until softened enough to cut, 10 to 15 minutes. Cut into squares and serve on lettuce-lined plates.

SPINACH AND MELON SALAD

An unusual salad, with melon adding color and flavor contrasts.

12 servings

8 cups torn spinach
1 cup watermelon balls
1 cup honeydew balls
1 cup cantaloupe balls
1/3 cup thinly sliced cucumber
1/3 cup thinly sliced red onion
Honey Dressing (recipe follows)

Per Serving
Calories: 40
% Calories from fat: 27
Fat (gm): 1.4
Saturated fat (gm): 0.2
Cholesterol (mg): 0
Sodium (mg): 33
Protein (gm): 1.5
Carbohydrate (gm): 6.9
Exchanges
Milk: 0.0
Vegetable: 0.5
Fruit: 0.0
Bread: 0.0
Meat: 0.0
Fat: 0.0

1. Combine spinach, melon balls, cucumber, and onion in salad bowl; drizzle with Honey Dressing and toss.

Honey Dressing

makes 1/4 cup

1-2 tablespoons honey
1 tablespoon red wine vinegar
1 tablespoon olive oil
1-2 tablespoons orange juice
1-2 teaspoons lime juice
1/2 teaspoon dried tarragon leaves
2-3 dashes salt
2-3 dashes pepper

1. Mix all ingredients; refrigerate until ready to use. Mix again before using.

WALDORF SALAD

Using both red and green apples adds color and flavor interest. If your family enjoys this salad with miniature marshmallows, please add them!

4 servings

2 cups cored, cubed red and green apples
1 cup sliced celery
1/4 cup raisins
1/4 cup coarsely chopped toasted walnuts
   or pecans
1/4 cup fat-free mayonnaise
1/4 cup fat-free sour cream
2-3 teaspoons lemon juice
1-2 tablespoons honey
   Lettuce leaves, as garnish

Per Serving
Calories: 149
% Calories from fat: 26
Fat (gm): 4.7
Saturated fat (gm): 0.3
Cholesterol (mg): 0
Sodium (mg): 227
Protein (gm): 3.5
Carbohydrate (gm): 26.5
Exchanges
Milk: 0.0
Vegetable: 0.5
Fruit: 1.5
Bread: 0.0
Meat: 0.0
Fat: 1.0

1. Combine apples, celery, raisins, and walnuts in medium bowl. Mix remaining ingredients, except lettuce leaves, and stir into apple mixture. Serve on lettuce-lined plates.

WHEAT BERRY WALDORF

Wheat berries have a wonderful "toothsome" texture. They can be purchased at health food stores and many supermarkets. Two-thirds cup bulgur can be substituted. Soak bulgur in 1¹/₃ cups water until tender; do not cook.

8 servings

1¹/₄ cups wheat berries
1¹/₂ cups peeled, cored, cubed pineapple
2 medium oranges, peeled, cut into
   segments
1 large apple, cored, cubed
1 cup thinly sliced fennel bulb
3 tablespoons coarsely chopped walnuts
2 tablespoons finely chopped parsley
   leaves
1/3 cup fat-free mayonnaise

Per Serving
Calories: 159.2
% Calories from fat: 12
Fat (gm): 2.3
Saturated fat (gm): 0.2
Cholesterol (mg): 0
Sodium (mg): 155
Protein (gm): 3.9
Carbohydrate (gm): 32.9
Exchanges
Milk: 0.0
Vegetable: 0.0
Fruit: 1.0
Bread: 1.5
Meat: 0.0
Fat: 0.0

2¹/₂ teaspoons Dijon-style mustard
1¹/₂ tablespoons lemon juice
   2 teaspoons sugar
 ³/₄ teaspoon crushed fennel seeds
     Lettuce leaves, as garnish

1. Heat wheat berries to boiling in water to cover in medium saucepan; reduce heat and simmer, covered, until wheat berries are tender, 45 to 55 minutes. Drain and cool.

2. Combine wheat berries, fruit, fennel, walnuts, and parsley in bowl. In separate bowl, combine remaining ingredients, except lettuce; spoon over salad and toss. Serve on lettuce-lined plates.

CARROT-RAISIN SALAD

Comfort food at its best! A small can of drained pineapple tidbits can be added to the salad, if you like.

6 servings

2¹/₂ cups shredded carrots (about 3 large)
 ³/₄ cup chopped celery
 ¹/₃ cup raisins
 ¹/₃ cup coarsely chopped walnuts
 ³/₄ cup fat-free mayonnaise
 ¹/₂ teaspoon Dijon-style mustard
 1-2 teaspoons sugar
 ¹/₈ teaspoon salt
   6 lettuce leaves

Per Serving
Calories: 115
% Calories from fat: 30
Fat (gm): 4.1
Saturated fat (gm): 0.3
Cholesterol (mg): 0
Sodium (mg): 460
Protein (gm): 2.6
Carbohydrate (gm): 19.2
Exchanges
Milk: 0.0
Vegetable: 2.0
Fruit: 0.5
Bread: 0.0
Meat: 0.0
Fat: 1.0

1. Combine carrots, celery, raisins, and walnuts in medium bowl. Add remaining ingredients, except lettuce, stirring until blended. Serve on lettuce-lined salad plates.

PERFECTION SALAD

For quick and easy preparation, packaged coleslaw ingredients can be used.

12 servings

1 can (8 ounces) unsweetened crushed pineapple in juice, undrained

1 package (0.6 ounces) sugar-free lemon, lime, *or* orange-flavor gelatin

1/4 teaspoon salt

1 1/2 cups thinly sliced, *or* shredded, cabbage

1/2 cup chopped celery

1/2 cup shredded carrot

1/4 cup chopped red, *or* green, bell pepper

1/4-1/2 cup sliced pimiento-stuffed olives
      Lettuce leaves

3/4 cup fat-free mayonnaise

Per Serving
Calories: 36
% Calories from fat: 11
Fat (gm): 0.4
Saturated fat (gm): 0.1
Cholesterol (mg): 0
Sodium (mg): 265
Protein (gm): 1.1
Carbohydrate (gm): 6.9
Exchanges
Milk: 0.0
Vegetable: 1.0
Fruit: 0.0
Bread: 0.0
Meat: 0.0
Fat: 0.0

1. Drain pineapple, reserving juice. Prepare gelatin in large bowl according to package directions, adding salt and using reserved pineapple juice as part of the liquid.

2. Mix pineapple, cabbage, celery, carrot, bell pepper, and olives into gelatin mixture. Pour into ungreased 13 x 9-inch baking dish. Refrigerate until firm, 4 to 5 hours.

3. Cut salad into squares; arrange on lettuce-lined plates. Top each serving with a tablespoon of mayonnaise.

SPROUTS AND VEGETABLE SALAD

Use any sprouted beans or grains you like in this salad, mixing flavors and textures.

4 side-dish servings (about 1 cup each)

1 medium tomato, chopped
1 cup broccoli florets
1/2 cup each: sprouted wheat berries, chickpeas, and lentils (sprouting directions follow)
2 green onions and tops, sliced
Salt and pepper, to taste
1/2 cup fat-free blue cheese, *or* other flavor salad dressing
Lettuce leaves, for garnish
1/4 cup (1 ounce) crumbled blue cheese

Per Serving
Calories: 129
% Calories from fat: 16
Fat (gm): 2.5
Saturated fat (gm): 1.4
Cholesterol (mg): 5.2
Sodium (mg): 452
Protein (gm): 5.7
Carbohydrate (gm): 23.5
Exchanges
Milk: 0.0
Vegetable: 1.5
Fruit: 0.0
Bread: 1.0
Meat: 0.0
Fat: 0.5

1. Combine tomato, broccoli, wheat berry sprouts, chickpea sprouts, lentil sprouts, and green onions in salad bowl; sprinkle lightly with salt and pepper. Pour dressing over salad and toss.

2. Spoon salad on lettuce-lined plates; sprinkle with blue cheese.

Sprouted Lentils

makes about 2 cups

1/2 cup dried lentils
Water

1. Place lentils in quart jar; add water to cover lentils by 2 to 3 inches and soak overnight. Drain.

2. Return drained lentils to jar and cover with cheesecloth. Let stand at room temperature until lentils have sprouted, about 2 days. Rinse lentils and drain well 3 to 4 times a day until they have sprouted; return to jar and cover with cheesecloth.

3. Refrigerate sprouted lentils until ready to use. Check sprouts daily; if they appear dry, rinse and drain, then return to refrigerator.

Notes: All grains and beans can be sprouted according to the directions above, although they may require shorter or longer times to sprout. The various grains and beans will also yield different amounts.

Wheat berries—1/2 cup dry wheat berries yields about 1 1/2 cups sprouted wheat berries.

Chickpeas—1/2 cup dry chickpeas yields about 1 1/2 cups sprouted chickpeas.

TEN-LAYER SALAD

Or make this salad as many layers as you want! Add a layer of cubed chicken breast or lean smoked ham for an entrée salad, using 3 ounces of cooked meat per person.

8 servings

2 cups thinly sliced romaine lettuce
1 cup thinly sliced red cabbage
1 medium red, *or* green, bell pepper, sliced
1 cup broccoli, *or* cauliflower, florets
1 cup sliced mushrooms
1 cup sliced carrots
1 cup halved cherry tomatoes
1/2 cup sliced cucumber
1/2 cup sliced red onion
    Herbed Sour Cream Dressing (recipe follows)
    Finely chopped parsley leaves, as garnish

Per Serving
Calories: 68
% Calories from fat: 4
Fat (gm): 0.4
Saturated fat (gm): 0.1
Cholesterol (mg): 0
Sodium (mg): 380
Protein (gm): 3.3
Carbohydrate (gm): 14.8
Exchanges
Milk: 0.0
Vegetable: 1.5
Fruit: 0.0
Bread: 0.0
Meat: 0.0
Fat: 0.0

1. Arrange lettuce in bottom of 1 1/2-quart glass bowl; arrange remaining vegetables in layers over lettuce. Spread Herbed Sour Cream Dressing over top of salad and sprinkle with parsley. Refrigerate, loosely covered, 8 hours or overnight. Toss before serving.

Herbed Sour Cream Dressing

makes about 1¹/2 cups

- ³/4 cup fat-free mayonnaise
- ³/4 cup fat-free sour cream
- 2-3 cloves garlic, minced
- ¹/2 teaspoon dried basil leaves
- ¹/2 teaspoon dried tarragon leaves
- ¹/4 teaspoon salt
- ¹/8 teaspoon pepper

1. Mix all ingredients in small bowl.

BROCCOLI SALAD WITH SOUR CREAM-MAYONNAISE DRESSING

Serve this hearty salad on a bed of salad greens, spinach, thinly sliced red cabbage, or in scooped-out tomato halves. The blue cheese can be omitted from the dressing, if desired.

12 servings

- 4¹/2 cups sliced broccoli florets and stalks
- 1¹/2 cups sliced zucchini
- 1¹/2 cups chopped green bell peppers
- 1¹/2 cups sliced mushrooms
- 12 cherry tomatoes, cut into halves
- 3 green onions and tops, sliced
- 2 tablespoons dark raisins
  Sour Cream-Mayonnaise Dressing (recipe follows)
- 12 lettuce leaves

Per Serving
Calories: 50
% Calories from fat: 13
Fat (gm): 0.9
Saturated fat (gm): 0.4
Cholesterol (mg): 1.4
Sodium (mg): 129
Protein (gm): 2.9
Carbohydrate (gm): 9.4
Exchanges
Milk: 0.0
Vegetable: 2.0
Fruit: 0.0
Bread: 0.0
Meat: 0.0
Fat: 0.0

1. Combine all ingredients in salad bowl; toss with Sour Cream-Mayonnaise Dressing. Serve in lettuce-lined salad bowls.

Sour Cream-Mayonnaise Dressing

makes about 1 1/4 cups

   1/3 cup fat-free sour cream
   1/3 cup fat-free mayonnaise
   3 cloves garlic, minced
   3 tablespoons fat-free milk
   3 tablespoons crumbled blue cheese

1. Mix all ingredients.

TABBOULEH AND VEGETABLE SALAD MEDLEY

Two salads—a tabbouleh salad dressed with Lemon-Cinnamon Vinaigrette, and a mixed vegetable salad with chunky Cucumber-Sour Cream Dressing—are lightly combined for a contrast of flavors. If desired, the salads can be arranged side by side on serving plates.

8 servings

   1 package (5 1/4 ounces) tabbouleh wheat salad mix
   1 cup cold water
   1/2 cup finely chopped celery
   1/3 cup sliced green onions and tops
   8 pitted prunes, chopped
   2 tablespoons finely chopped parsley
   1 tablespoon finely chopped fresh, *or* 1 teaspoon dried, basil leaves
   1 clove garlic, minced
   Lemon-Cinnamon Vinaigrette (recipe follows)
   Salt and pepper, to taste
   2 cups cauliflower florets
   3/4 cup coarsely chopped red bell pepper
   2 medium carrots, diagonally sliced
   8 cherry tomatoes, halved
   Cucumber-Sour Cream Dressing (recipe follows)
   Salad greens
   1/4 cup (1 ounce) crumbled feta cheese

Per Serving
Calories: 191
% Calories from fat: 28
Fat (gm): 6.3
Saturated fat (gm): 1.3
Cholesterol (mg): 3.3
Sodium (mg): 300
Protein (gm): 5.7
Carbohydrate (gm): 30.8
Exchanges
Milk: 0.0
Vegetable: 1.5
Fruit: 0.5
Bread: 0.5
Meat: 0.0
Fat: 1.0

1. Mix tabbouleh and cold water in small bowl (discard spice packet); let stand 30 minutes. Stir celery, green onions, prunes, parsley, basil, and garlic into tabbouleh; add Lemon-Cinnamon Vinaigrette and toss. Season to taste with salt and pepper.

2. Combine cauliflower, bell pepper, carrots, and tomatoes; spoon Cucumber-Sour Cream Dressing over and toss. Season to taste with salt and pepper.

3. Add vegetable salad to tabbouleh salad and toss lightly. Spoon salad onto greens-lined serving plates; sprinkle with feta cheese.

Lemon-Cinnamon Vinaigrette

makes about 1/2 cup

- 1/3 cup lemon juice
- 3 tablespoons olive oil *or* vegetable oil
- 1/4 teaspoon ground cinnamon

1. Mix all ingredients; refrigerate until ready to serve. Mix again before using.

Cucumber-Sour Cream Dressing

makes about 1 cup

- 1/2 cup fat-free sour cream
- 1/4 cup plain fat-free yogurt
- 1 teaspoon white wine vinegar
- 1 teaspoon dried dill weed
- 1/2 medium cucumber, peeled, seeded, chopped

1. Combine all ingredients; refrigerate until ready to serve.

WILTED SPINACH SALAD

A delicious favorite that includes the bacon but not the fat!

4 servings

1 package (10 ounces) salad spinach, rinsed, dried
4 green onions and tops, sliced
4 slices bacon, fried crisp, well drained, crumbled
1 cup fat-free bottled French dressing *or* sweet-sour salad dressing
1 hard-cooked egg, chopped
  Salt and pepper, to taste

Per Serving
Calories: 95
% Calories from fat: 26
Fat (gm): 2.6
Saturated fat (gm): 0.8
Cholesterol (mg): 38.2
Sodium (mg): 418
Protein (gm): 3.4
Carbohydrate (gm): 12.6
Exchanges
Milk: 0.0
Vegetable: 1.0
Fruit: 0.0
Bread: 0.5
Meat: 0.0
Fat: 0.5

1. Combine spinach, onions, and bacon in salad bowl. Heat French dressing to boiling in small saucepan; immediately pour over salad and toss. Sprinkle egg over salad. Season to taste with salt and pepper.

CAESAR SALAD

Although anchovies are traditional in this salad we've made them option-al because of their high sodium content. If you use anchovies, drain them well, as they are packed in oil.

4 servings

4 thick slices French, *or* Italian, bread
1 clove garlic, cut in half
6 cups torn romaine lettuce
2 tablespoons lemon juice
2 tablespoons no-cholesterol real egg product
1 tablespoon olive oil
1/2 teaspoon Worcestershire sauce
2-3 anchovies, well drained, chopped, optional
2 tablespoons grated fat-free Parmesan cheese
1/8 teaspoon dry mustard
  Dash hot pepper sauce
  Freshly ground pepper, to taste

Per Serving
Calories: 127
% Calories from fat: 30
Fat (gm): 4.4
Saturated fat (gm): 0.6
Cholesterol (mg): 0
Sodium (mg): 200
Protein (gm): 5.3
Carbohydrate (gm): 17.1
Exchanges
Milk: 0.0
Vegetable: 1.0
Fruit: 0.0
Bread: 1.0
Meat: 0.0
Fat: 0.5

1. Rub both sides of bread slices with cut side of garlic; mince remaining garlic and reserve. Cut bread into $1/2$ to $3/4$-inch cubes. Bake on jelly roll pan at 425 degrees until croutons are toasted, about 5 minutes.

2. Place lettuce in salad bowl. Beat together lemon juice, reserved garlic, and remaining ingredients, except croutons and pepper. Pour dressing over lettuce and toss; season to taste with pepper. Add croutons and toss again.

JICAMA SALAD

Jicama adds a marvelous crispness to salads, complementing both fruits and vegetables.

6 servings

$1/2$ large jicama, peeled (about 12 ounces)
$1^1/2$ medium zucchini, sliced
1 small orange, peeled, cut into segments
2-3 thin slices red onion
Cilantro Lime Dressing (recipe follows)
Salt and pepper, to taste
Lettuce leaves

Per Serving
Calories: 77
% Calories from fat: 27
Fat (gm): 2.4
Saturated fat (gm): 0.3
Cholesterol (mg): 0
Sodium (mg): 1
Protein (gm): 1.3
Carbohydrate (gm): 13.5
Exchanges
Milk: 0.0
Vegetable: 1.0
Fruit: 0.5
Bread: 0.0
Meat: 0.0
Fat: 0.5

1. Cut jicama into sticks about $1^1/2$ x $1/2$ inches. Combine jicama, zucchini, orange, and onion in bowl. Pour Cilantro Lime Dressing over and toss; season to taste with salt and pepper. Serve on lettuce-lined plates.

Cilantro Lime Dressing

makes about $1/4$ cup

2 tablespoons lime juice
1 tablespoon orange juice
1-2 tablespoons olive, *or* vegetable, oil
2 tablespoons finely chopped cilantro
2 teaspoons sugar

1. Mix all ingredients; refrigerate until serving time. Mix again before using.

CACTUS SALAD

The tender cactus paddles, "nopales," are readily available in large supermarkets today—be sure all the thorns have been removed! If not, they can be pulled out easily with tweezers.

6 servings

2 quarts water
1¹/2 pounds cactus paddles, cut into ¹/2-inch pieces
1 tablespoon salt
¹/4 teaspoon baking soda
1¹/2 cups cherry tomato halves
¹/2 cup thinly sliced red onion
Lime Dressing (recipe follows)
Lettuce leaves

Per Serving
Calories: 78
% Calories from fat: 28
Fat (gm): 2.5
Saturated fat (gm): 0.3
Cholesterol (mg): 0
Sodium (mg): 131
Protein (gm): 2.4
Carbohydrate (gm): 12.5
Exchanges
Milk: 0.0
Vegetable: 2.0
Fruit: 0.0
Bread: 0.0
Meat: 0.0
Fat: 0.5

1. Heat water to boiling in large saucepan; add cactus, salt, and baking soda. Reduce heat and simmer, uncovered, until cactus is crisp-tender, about 20 minutes. Rinse well in cold water and drain thoroughly.

2. Combine cactus, tomatoes, and onion in salad bowl; pour Lime Dressing over and toss. Serve on lettuce-lined plates.

Lime Dressing

makes about ¹/4 cup

2 tablespoons lime juice
1-2 tablespoons olive, *or* vegetable, oil
1 tablespoon water
1 teaspoon cider vinegar
2 teaspoons sugar
¹/2 teaspoon dried oregano leaves

1. Combine all ingredients; refrigerate until serving time. Mix again before using.

CREAMY POTATO SALAD

Thanks to fat-free mayonnaise, it's possible to include hard-cooked egg and crisp bacon pieces in this low-fat salad. For the creamiest salad, toss the potatoes with the dressing while they're still slightly warm.

10 servings

1¹/₂ pounds russet potatoes, peeled, cut into
     ³/₄-inch cubes
   1 cup sliced celery
¹/₂ cup thinly sliced green onions and tops
¹/₄ cup chopped green bell pepper
¹/₄ cup chopped red bell pepper
¹/₂ cup chopped sweet pickle *or* pickle
     relish
   2 hard-cooked eggs, chopped
   4 slices bacon, fried, well drained, crumbled
   1 cup fat-free mayonnaise
¹/₂ cup fat-free sour cream
   2 tablespoons cider vinegar
   1 tablespoon prepared mustard
¹/₂ teaspoon celery seeds
     Salt and pepper, to taste

Per Serving
Calories: 132
% Calories from fat: 16
Fat (gm): 2.5
Saturated fat (gm): 0.8
Cholesterol (mg): 44.7
Sodium (mg): 495
Protein (gm): 4.3
Carbohydrate (gm): 24.5
Exchanges
Milk: 0.1
Vegetable: 0.2
Fruit: 0.0
Bread: 1.3
Meat: 0.3
Fat: 0.3

1. Cook potatoes, covered, in 2 inches simmering water until fork-tender, about 10 minutes. Drain and cool until just warm.

2. Combine potatoes, celery, green onions, green and red bell pepper, sweet pickle, eggs, and bacon in large bowl. In small bowl, mix remaining ingredients, except salt and pepper; spoon over vegetable mixture and toss. Season to taste with salt and pepper.

GERMAN POTATO SALAD

Tart and tangy in flavor, this salad is best served warm from the skillet.

6 servings

3 slices bacon
1 cup chopped onion
1 tablespoon flour
1/2 cup reduced-sodium beef broth
1/4 cup cider vinegar
1 tablespoon sugar
1/2 teaspoon celery seeds
1 1/2 pounds russet potatoes, peeled, sliced, and cooked, warm
   Salt and pepper, to taste
2 tablespoons finely chopped parsley

Per Serving
Calories: 133
% Calories from fat: 11
Fat (gm): 1.8
Saturated fat (gm): 0.6
Cholesterol (mg): 2.7
Sodium (mg): 64
Protein (gm): 3.6
Carbohydrate (gm): 29.5
Exchanges
Milk: 0.0
Vegetable: 0.0
Fruit: 0.0
Bread: 2.0
Meat: 0.0
Fat: 0.0

1. Cook bacon in medium skillet until crisp; drain and crumble. Discard all but 1 tablespoon bacon fat; add onion to skillet and saute until tender and browned, about 5 minutes. Stir in flour; cook 1 minute.

2. Add broth, vinegar, sugar, and celery seeds to onion mixture and heat to boiling; boil, stirring constantly, until thickened, 1 to 2 minutes. Pour mixture over warm potatoes in bowl and toss. Season to taste with salt and pepper; sprinkle with parsley.

CARIBBEAN POTATO SALAD

Sweet and white potatoes combine with a creamy cumin-lime mayonnaise dressing; olives provide a pungent accent.

8 servings

1 1/2 pounds sweet potatoes, peeled, cut into 1 to 1 1/2-inch pieces
1 1/2 pounds russet potatoes, peeled, cut into 1 to 1 1/2-inch pieces
3/4 cup fat-free mayonnaise
1/2 cup fat-free milk
2 teaspoons lime juice
1 teaspoon ground cumin

Per Serving
Calories: 167
% Calories from fat: 5
Fat (gm): 1
Saturated fat (gm): 0.2
Cholesterol (mg): 0.3
Sodium (mg): 416
Protein (gm): 3.1
Carbohydrate (gm): 37.2
Exchanges
Milk: 0.0
Vegetable: 0.0
Fruit: 0.0
Bread: 2.5
Meat: 0.0
Fat: 0.0

1/8 teaspoon cayenne pepper
Salt, to taste
2 green onions and tops, sliced
1/4 cup small pimiento-stuffed olives

1. Cook potatoes in simmering water in separate large saucepans until just tender, but not soft; drain and cool. Combine potatoes in large bowl.

2. Mix mayonnaise, milk, lime juice, cumin, and cayenne pepper; mix gently into potatoes. Season to taste with salt. Gently stir in green onions and olives. Refrigerate 2 to 3 hours to chill and for flavors to blend.

MACARONI SALAD

Fourth of July signals fried chicken, apple pie, and, of course, homemade macaroni salad! Add 1 cup halved or quartered summer-ripe cherry tomatoes for festive color.

6 servings

2 cups cooked elbow macaroni
1 cup frozen baby peas, thawed
1/2 cup chopped onion
1/2 cup chopped celery
1/3 cup shredded carrot
1/4 cup chopped red bell pepper
1/4 cup sliced ripe, *or* pimiento-stuffed, olives
3/4 cup fat-free mayonnaise
2 teaspoons yellow mustard
1 teaspoon sugar
Salt and pepper, to taste

Per Serving
Calories: 129
% Calories from fat: 9
Fat (gm): 1.3
Saturated fat (gm): 0.2
Cholesterol (mg): 0
Sodium (mg): 583
Protein (gm): 4
Carbohydrate (gm): 25.6
Exchanges
Milk: 0.0
Vegetable: 0.0
Fruit: 0.0
Bread: 1.5
Meat: 0.0
Fat: 0.0

1. Combine macaroni, peas, onion, celery, carrot, bell pepper, and olives in medium bowl. Add mayonnaise, mustard, and sugar and stir until blended. Season to taste with salt and pepper.

MACARONI-BLUE CHEESE SALAD

A not-so-traditional macaroni salad with blue cheese pizazz!

8 servings

1 cup (4 ounces) elbow macaroni, cooked, room temperature
³/4 cup chopped red bell pepper
¹/2 cup chopped cucumber
¹/2 cup shredded carrots
¹/4 cup thinly sliced green onions and tops
Blue Cheese Dressing (recipe follows)

Per Serving
Calories: 82
% Calories from fat: 9
Fat (gm): 0.9
Saturated fat (gm): 0.4
Cholesterol (mg): 1.3
Sodium (mg): 159
Protein (gm): 2.6
Carbohydrate (gm): 16.3
Exchanges
Milk: 0.0
Vegetable: 2.0
Fruit: 0.0
Bread: 0.5
Meat: 0.0
Fat: 0.0

1. Combine macaroni, bell pepper, cucumber, carrots, and green onions in bowl; stir in Blue Cheese Dressing.

Blue Cheese Dressing

makes about ¹/2 cup

¹/2 cup fat-free mayonnaise
2 tablespoons crumbled blue cheese
1 tablespoon red wine vinegar
1 teaspoon celery seeds
¹/2 teaspoon salt, optional
¹/8 teaspoon cayenne pepper
¹/8 teaspoon black pepper

1. Mix all ingredients.

PASTA COLESLAW

The addition of pasta updates a traditional cabbage slaw.

4 servings

1¹/2 cups (4 ounces) fusilli (spirals) *or*
        farfalle (bow ties), cooked, room
        temperature
    1 cup thinly sliced green cabbage
    1 medium tomato, chopped
    1 medium green bell pepper, chopped
 ¹/4 cup sliced celery
        Creamy Dressing (recipe follows)

Per Serving
Calories: 139
% Calories from fat: 8
Fat (gm): 1.2
Saturated fat (gm): 0.3
Cholesterol (mg): 0.9
Sodium (mg): 156
Protein (gm): 5.4
Carbohydrate (gm): 27.3
Exchanges
Milk: 0.0
Vegetable: 1.0
Fruit: 0.0
Bread: 1.5
Meat: 0.0
Fat: 0.0

1. Combine pasta, cabbage, tomato, bell pepper, and celery in bowl; stir in Creamy Dressing.

Creamy Dressing

makes about ¹/2 cup

 ¹/4 cup fat-free mayonnaise
 ¹/4 cup plain low-fat yogurt
    1 tablespoon lemon juice
    2 cloves garlic, minced
 ¹/2 teaspoon dried tarragon leaves
 ¹/4 teaspoon salt, optional
 ¹/4 teaspoon pepper

1. Mix all ingredients.

MANGO AND BLACK BEAN SALAD

Any tropical fruit, such as banana, kiwi, papaya, or star fruit, can be used in this refreshing salad.

8 servings

4	large ripe mangoes, peeled, pitted, cubed
1	cup cubed pineapple
1/2	medium cucumber, seeded, sliced
1/4	cup finely chopped red bell pepper
4	small green onions and tops, thinly sliced
1	can (15 ounces) black beans, rinsed, drained
	Herbed Lime Dressing (recipe follows)
	Romaine lettuce leaves
	Mint sprigs, as garnish

Per Serving
Calories: 164
% Calories from fat: 20
Fat (gm): 4.3
Saturated fat (gm): 0.6
Cholesterol (mg): 0
Sodium (mg): 169
Protein (gm): 5.2
Carbohydrate (gm): 32.7
Exchanges
Milk: 0.0
Vegetable: 0.0
Fruit: 1.0
Bread: 1.0
Meat: 0.0
Fat: 1.0

1. Combine mangoes, pineapple, cucumber, bell pepper, green onions, and black beans in bowl; drizzle with Herbed Lime Dressing and toss gently.

2. Spoon salad mixture onto lettuce-lined plates. Garnish with mint.

Herbed Lime Dressing

makes about 1/3 cup

2	tablespoons olive oil
1	tablespoon honey
3-4	teaspoons lime juice
1	teaspoon grated lime rind
1	tablespoon tarragon wine vinegar
2	tablespoons water
1/2	teaspoon dried mint leaves
	Pinch salt

1. Mix all ingredients; refrigerate until ready to use. Mix again before using.

BEAN, TOMATO, AND BREAD SALAD

Use summer ripe tomatoes for best flavor. A favorite purchased salad dressing can be substituted for the homemade.

8 servings

3 cups cubed sourdough bread (¹/₂-inch cubes)
Olive oil cooking spray
2 large tomatoes, cubed
¹/₂ small red onion, thinly sliced
2 cans (15 ounces each) navy, *or* Great Northern, beans, rinsed, drained
1 cup chopped roasted red peppers
Parmesan Vinaigrette (recipe follows) *or*
¹/₂ cup prepared reduced-fat vinaigrette
Salt and pepper, to taste

Per Serving
Calories: 199
% Calories from fat: 19
Fat (gm): 4.2
Saturated fat (gm): 0.7
Cholesterol (mg): 0
Sodium (mg): 454
Protein (gm): 9.8
Carbohydrate (gm): 30.4
Exchanges
Milk: 0.0
Vegetable: 0.0
Fruit: 0.0
Bread: 2.0
Meat: 0.0
Fat: 1.0

1. Spray bread cubes generously with cooking spray; arrange in single layer on jelly roll pan. Bake at 350 degrees until golden, about 10 minutes, stirring occasionally. Cool.

2. Combine tomatoes, onion, beans, and roasted red peppers in bowl; pour Parmesan Vinaigrette over and toss. Season to taste with salt and pepper. Add croutons to salad and toss; serve immediately.

Parmesan Vinaigrette

makes about ¹/₂ *cup*

2-4 tablespoons olive oil
4 tablespoons red wine vinegar
2 tablespoons grated fat-free Parmesan cheese
¹/₄ cup finely chopped fresh, *or* 1 teaspoon dried, basil leaves
1 teaspoon minced garlic

1. Mix all ingredients; refrigerate until serving time. Mix again before using.

LENTIL SALAD WITH FETA CHEESE

There are lots of flavor and texture contrasts in this colorful salad. Cook the lentils just until tender so they retain their shape.

10 servings

1¹/2 cups dried brown lentils
3 cups reduced-sodium vegetable broth
2 medium tomatoes, coarsely chopped
¹/2 cup thinly sliced celery
¹/2 cup sliced yellow bell pepper
¹/2 cup chopped, seeded cucumber
¹/2 cup chopped onion
¹/2-³/4 cup (2-3 ounces) crumbled reduced-fat feta cheese
Balsamic Dressing (recipe follows)
Salt and pepper, to taste
Lettuce leaves

Per Serving
Calories: 169
% Calories from fat: 21
Fat (gm): 4.0
Saturated fat (gm): 1.0
Cholesterol (mg): 2.0
Sodium (mg): 110
Protein (gm): 9.8
Carbohydrate (gm): 24.8
Exchanges
Milk: 0.0
Vegetable: 0.5
Fruit: 0.0
Bread: 1.5
Meat: 0.5
Fat: 0.0

1. Wash and sort lentils, discarding any stones. Heat lentils and broth to boiling in large saucepan; reduce heat and simmer, covered, until lentils are just tender, about 20 minutes. Drain any excess liquid; cool to room temperature.

2. Combine lentils, vegetables, and cheese in salad bowl; drizzle Balsamic Dressing over and toss. Season to taste with salt and pepper. Serve on lettuce-lined plates.

Balsamic Dressing

makes about ¹/3 cup

3 tablespoons balsamic, *or* red wine, vinegar
1-2 tablespoons olive oil
2 tablespoons lemon juice
2 cloves garlic, minced
¹/2 teaspoon dried thyme leaves

1. Mix all ingredients; refrigerate until serving time. Mix again before using.

VEGETABLE SALAD WITH TWO BEANS

Enjoy the fresh flavors of cilantro and orange and the accent of jalapeño chili in this bean and vegetable salad.

8 servings

1 package (10 ounces) frozen baby lima beans, cooked

1 can (15 ounces) garbanzo beans, rinsed, drained

1 large Idaho potato (10-12 ounces), peeled, cubed, cooked

1 medium cucumber, peeled, seeded, chopped

1 medium zucchini, sliced

1 small green bell pepper, chopped

¼ cup chopped cilantro leaves
   Citrus Vinaigrette (recipe follows)
   Salt and pepper, to taste
   Salad greens

Per Serving
Calories: 170
% Calories from fat: 24
Fat (gm): 4.7
Saturated fat (gm): 0.7
Cholesterol (mg): 0
Sodium (mg): 232
Protein (gm): 6.3
Carbohydrate (gm): 27.4
Exchanges
Milk: 0.0
Vegetable: 1.0
Fruit: 0.0
Bread: 1.5
Meat: 0.0
Fat: 1.0

1. Combine vegetables and cilantro in salad bowl. Pour Citrus Vinaigrette over vegetables and toss; season to taste with salt and pepper.

2. Spoon vegetable mixture over salad greens on salad plates.

Citrus Vinaigrette

makes about ⅔ cup

¼ cup fresh orange juice

¼ cup fresh lime juice

2 tablespoons olive oil *or* vegetable oil

1 teaspoon ground cumin

1 teaspoon minced jalapeño chili

½ teaspoon paprika

¼ teaspoon cayenne pepper

1. Mix all ingredients; refrigerate until ready to use. Mix again before using.

SPROUTED LENTIL SALAD

All kinds of dried beans and grains can be sprouted. Sprouts are delicious for salads, as garnishes on main dishes and side dishes, or just to eat as snacks. Any favorite sprouted bean or grain can be used in this salad.

4 side-dish servings (about 1 cup each)

2   cups Sprouted Lentils (see p. 617)
1   cup torn radicchio leaves
1   cup chopped tomato
1/2 cup chopped cucumber
1/2 cup chopped yellow bell pepper
1/2-2/3 cup fat-free, *or* reduced-fat, salad
    dressing
    Salt and pepper, to taste

Per Serving
Calories: 86
% Calories from fat: 18
Fat (gm): 1.9
Saturated fat (gm): 0.2
Cholesterol (mg): 0
Sodium (mg): 41
Protein (gm): 6.3
Carbohydrate (gm): 14.3
Exchanges
Milk: 0.0
Vegetable: 3.0
Fruit: 0.0
Bread: 0.0
Meat: 0.0
Fat: 0.5

1.   Combine lentils and vegetables in salad bowl; spoon salad dressing over and toss. Season to taste with salt and pepper.

BEAN AND PASTA SALAD WITH WHITE BEAN DRESSING

Pureed beans, fat-free sour cream, and seasonings combine to make a rich, delicious salad dressing—use on green salads too!

10 servings

4   ounces tri-color radiatore *or* rotini,
    cooked, cooled
1   can (14 1/4 ounces) baby lima beans,
    rinsed, drained
1/2 can (15-ounce size) Great Northern
    beans, rinsed, drained
1/2 package (9-ounce size) frozen artichoke
    hearts, cooked, cooled, cut into halves
2   cups cut green beans, cooked, cooled
1/2 cup sliced red bell pepper
1/4 cup sliced black olives

Per Serving
Calories: 188
% Calories from fat: 19
Fat (gm): 4.0
Saturated fat (gm): 0.8
Cholesterol (mg): 3.1
Sodium (mg): 313
Protein (gm): 9.7
Carbohydrate (gm): 30.1
Exchanges
Milk: 0.0
Vegetable: 1.0
Fruit: 0.0
Bread: 1.5
Meat: 0.5
Fat: 0.5

$^{1}/_{2}$ cup (2 ounces) julienned reduced-fat
    brick cheese
White Bean Dressing (recipe follows)
Lettuce leaves
Finely chopped parsley, as garnish

1. Combine pasta, vegetables, and cheese in salad bowl; pour
White Bean Dressing over and toss. Serve on lettuce-lined plates;
sprinkle with parsley.

White Bean Dressing

makes about 1$^{1}/_{2}$ cups

$^{1}/_{2}$ can (15-ounce size) Great Northern
    beans, rinsed, drained
$^{1}/_{2}$ cup fat-free sour cream
 1 tablespoon olive oil
2-3 tablespoons red wine vinegar
 2 cloves garlic
 1 teaspoon dried oregano leaves
1-2 green onions and tops, sliced
 2 tablespoons finely chopped parsley
   Salt and pepper, to taste

1. Process beans, sour cream, olive oil, vinegar, garlic, and oregano in food processor or blender until smooth. Stir in green onions
and parsley; season to taste with salt and pepper. Refrigerate several
hours for flavors to blend.

PASTA, WHITE BEAN, AND RED CABBAGE SALAD

A hearty salad with a caraway accent. The salad can be made 1 day in advance; stir in the cabbage just before serving for fresh color.

6 servings

2^1/$_4$ cups (6 ounces) rotini (corkscrews), cooked, room temperature

1 cup coarsely chopped, *or* sliced, red cabbage

1 cup canned, drained Great Northern beans

^{1}/$_2$ small onion, chopped

^{1}/$_2$ small red bell pepper, chopped
Caraway Dressing (recipe follows)

Per Serving
Calories: 185
% Calories from fat: 5
Fat (gm): 1.1
Saturated fat (gm): 0.2
Cholesterol (mg): 0
Sodium (mg): 268
Protein (gm): 8.7
Carbohydrate (gm): 35.9
Exchanges
Milk: 0.0
Vegetable: 1.5
Fruit: 0.0
Bread: 2.0
Meat: 0.0
Fat: 0.0

1. Combine pasta, cabbage, beans, onion, and bell pepper in bowl; stir in Caraway Dressing.

Caraway Dressing

makes about 1 cup

^{1}/$_2$ cup fat-free mayonnaise

^{1}/$_2$ cup fat-free sour cream

2 teaspoons lemon juice

2 cloves garlic, minced

1 teaspoon caraway seeds, crushed

^{1}/$_4$ teaspoon salt, optional

^{1}/$_4$ teaspoon pepper

1. Mix all ingredients.

LIGHT SUMMER PASTA

The fragrant aroma and flavor of fresh herbs and garlic accent summer ripe tomatoes in this salad.

8 servings

8 ounces spaghetti, cooked, room temperature

1 pound Italian plum tomatoes, chopped

3/4 cup (3 ounces) cubed reduced-fat mozzarella cheese (1/4-inch cubes)

3 tablespoons finely chopped fresh, *or* 2 teaspoons dried, basil leaves

2 tablespoons finely chopped parsley

Garlic Vinaigrette (recipe follows)

Per Serving
Calories: 150
% Calories from fat: 30
Fat (gm): 5.7
Saturated fat (gm): 0.5
Cholesterol (mg): 3.8
Sodium (mg): 176
Protein (gm): 7.4
Carbohydrate (gm): 19.7
Exchanges
Milk: 0.0
Vegetable: 1.0
Fruit: 0.0
Bread: 1.0
Meat: 0.0
Fat: 1.0

1. Combine spaghetti, tomatoes, cheese, and herbs in salad bowl; pour Garlic Vinaigrette over and toss.

Garlic Vinaigrette

makes about 1/3 cup

3 tablespoons red wine vinegar

2 tablespoons olive oil

2 teaspoons minced garlic

1/4 teaspoon salt

1/8 teaspoon pepper

1. Mix all ingredients; refrigerate until serving time. Mix again before using.

SESAME PASTA WITH SUMMER VEGETABLES

These garden vegetables signal the end of summer harvest. Vary the vegetable selection according to seasonal availability.

6 servings

1 small eggplant

1 cup sliced carrots, steamed until crisp-tender

1 cup sliced summer yellow squash, steamed until crisp-tender

1 cup broccoli florets, steamed until crisp-tender

1 medium red bell pepper, sliced

¹/4 cup sliced green onions and tops
   Sesame Dressing (recipe follows)

8 ounces thin spaghetti, cooked, room temperature

2 teaspoons toasted sesame seeds

Per Serving
Calories: 192
% Calories from fat: 30
Fat (gm): 6.6
Saturated fat (gm): 0.7
Cholesterol (mg): 0
Sodium (mg): 428
Protein (gm): 7.2
Carbohydrate (gm): 28.3
Exchanges
Milk: 0.0
Vegetable: 1.5
Fruit: 0.0
Bread: 1.5
Meat: 0.0
Fat: 1.0

1. Pierce eggplant 6 to 8 times with fork; place in baking pan. Bake, uncovered, at 400 degrees until tender, about 20 minutes. Cool until warm enough to handle easily. Cut eggplant in half; scoop out pulp with a large spoon and cut into ³/4-inch pieces.

2. Combine eggplant and remaining vegetables in bowl; pour Sesame Dressing over and toss. Add pasta and toss; sprinkle with sesame seeds.

Sesame Dressing

makes about ¹/3 cup

2 tablespoons reduced-sodium soy sauce

2 tablespoons sesame oil

1 teaspoon hot chili oil, optional

1 tablespoon balsamic, *or* red wine, vinegar

1¹/2 tablespoons sugar

1 clove garlic, minced

1 tablespoon finely chopped cilantro *or* parsley

1. Mix all ingredients; refrigerate until serving time. Mix again before using.

MIXED VEGETABLES AND ORZO VINAIGRETTE

The spice, turmeric, used in the salad dressing gives this salad its unusual yellow color. Curry powder can be used instead, imparting the same color but adding a delicate curry flavor.

8 servings

2 medium zucchini, thinly sliced

8 ounces asparagus, cut into 1¹/₂-inch pieces, steamed until crisp-tender, cooled

1 cup frozen, thawed peas

¹/₂ cup sliced carrots, steamed

³/₄ cup (6 ounces) orzo, cooked
Mustard-Turmeric Vinaigrette
(recipe follows)

2 cups torn lettuce leaves

4 cherry tomatoes, cut into halves

Per Serving
Calories: 142
% Calories from fat: 27
Fat (gm): 4.2
Saturated fat (gm): 0.6
Cholesterol (mg): 0
Sodium (mg): 112
Protein (gm): 5.5
Carbohydrate (gm): 20.9
Exchanges
Milk: 0.0
Vegetable: 1.0
Fruit: 0.0
Bread: 1.0
Meat: 0.0
Fat: 1.0

1. Combine zucchini, asparagus, peas, carrots, and orzo in bowl; pour Mustard-Turmeric Vinaigrette over and toss. Spoon onto lettuce on salad plates; garnish with tomatoes.

Mustard-Turmeric Vinaigrette

makes about ¹/₂ cup

¹/₄ cup red wine vinegar

¹/₄ teaspoon ground turmeric

2-3 tablespoons lemon juice

2 tablespoons olive, *or* vegetable, oil

2 teaspoons Dijon-style mustard

2 cloves garlic, minced

¹/₄ teaspoon salt

¹/₄ teaspoon pepper

1. Heat vinegar and turmeric in small saucepan over medium heat until turmeric is dissolved, stirring constantly, 2 to 3 minutes; cool.

2. Mix vinegar mixture and remaining ingredients; refrigerate until serving time. Mix again before using.

GARDEN VEGETABLE AND PASTA SALAD

Steaming is a healthful, fat-free method of cooking vegetables. Steam broccoli and cauliflower florets just until crisp-tender for this delicious salad.

6 servings

1 medium eggplant, cut into $^1/_2$-inch slices
   Vegetable cooking spray
2 cups cauliflower florets, steamed, cooled
2 cups broccoli florets, steamed, cooled
10 cherry tomatoes
$^1/_2$ medium green bell pepper, sliced
8 ounces fettuccine *or* linguine, cooked, room temperature
   Basil Vinaigrette (recipe follows)
2 ounces feta cheese, crumbled

Per Serving
Calories: 202
% Calories from fat: 25
Fat (gm): 6
Saturated fat (gm): 1.8
Cholesterol (mg): 8.3
Sodium (mg): 282
Protein (gm): 8.5
Carbohydrate (gm): 31.5
Exchanges
Milk: 0.0
Vegetable: 1.0
Fruit: 0.0
Bread: 1.5
Meat: 0.0
Fat: 1.0

1. Spray both sides of eggplant with cooking spray; arrange on cookie sheet. Bake at 400 degrees until eggplant is tender, about 15 minutes. Cool. Cut into $^1/_2$-inch pieces.

2. Combine eggplant, remaining vegetables, and fettuccine in large bowl; pour Basil Vinaigrette over and toss. Sprinkle with cheese.

Basil Vinaigrette

makes about $^1/_3$ cup

$^1/_4$ cup balsamic vinegar
1 tablespoon olive oil
2 tablespoons finely chopped fresh, *or* 2 teaspoons dried, basil leaves
2 tablespoons finely chopped parsley
$^1/_4$ teaspoon salt
$^1/_4$ teaspoon pepper

1. Mix all ingredients; refrigerate until serving time. Mix again before using.

FUSILLI WITH FRESH TOMATOES AND CORN

A perfect salad, especially when homegrown tomatoes, corn, and basil are available!

8 servings

2 cups chopped plum tomatoes
1 cup fresh whole-kernel corn, cooked
1/2 cup sliced green onions and tops
2²/3 cups (6 ounces) fusilli (spirals) *or* corkscrews, cooked, room temperature
Fresh Basil Dressing (recipe follows)

Per Serving
Calories: 135
% Calories from fat: 26
Fat (gm): 4
Saturated fat (gm): 0.6
Cholesterol (mg): 0
Sodium (mg): 141
Protein (gm): 4.1
Carbohydrate (gm): 21.8
Exchanges
Milk: 0.0
Vegetable: 1.0
Fruit: 0.0
Bread: 1.0
Meat: 0.0
Fat: 1.0

1. Combine tomatoes, corn, onions, and pasta in salad bowl; pour Fresh Basil Dressing over and toss.

Fresh Basil Dressing

makes about ¹/₄ cup

1/3 cup red wine vinegar
2 tablespoons olive oil *or* vegetable oil
3 tablespoons finely chopped fresh, *or* 1 teaspoon dried, basil leaves
2 cloves garlic, minced
1/2 teaspoon salt
1/4 teaspoon pepper

1. Mix all ingredients; refrigerate until serving time. Mix again before using.

FETTUCCINE SALAD WITH ROASTED GARLIC, ONIONS, AND PEPPERS

A salad that is deceptively simple to make, incredibly delicious to eat.

8 servings

2 bulbs garlic
   Olive oil cooking spray
3 medium onions, cut into wedges
2 large red bell peppers, cut into 1/2-inch slices
2 tablespoons olive oil *or* vegetable oil
2 tablespoons lemon juice
2 tablespoons finely chopped parsley
1/2 teaspoon salt
1/4 teaspoon pepper
8 ounces fettuccine, cooked, warm

Per Serving
Calories: 151
% Calories from fat: 26
Fat (gm): 4.5
Saturated fat (gm): 0.5
Cholesterol (mg): 0
Sodium (mg): 184
Protein (gm): 5
Carbohydrate (gm): 24.4
Exchanges
Milk: 0.0
Vegetable: 1.5
Fruit: 0.0
Bread: 1.0
Meat: 0.0
Fat: 1.0

1. Cut a scant 1/2 inch off tops of garlic bulbs, exposing ends of cloves. Wrap garlic heads loosely in aluminum foil. Spray jelly roll pan with cooking spray. Arrange garlic, onions, and bell peppers on pan. Bake vegetables, uncovered, at 400 degrees until garlic is very soft and vegetables are tender, 30 to 40 minutes.

2. Cool garlic slightly; squeeze pulp into small bowl. Stir in oil, lemon juice, parsley, salt, and pepper. Spoon garlic mixture over pasta and toss; add onions and peppers and toss. Serve warm.

BRUSSELS SPROUTS AND GNOCCHI SALAD

Enjoy the first fall harvest of Brussels sprouts in this colorful salad. Pasta shells can be substituted for the gnocchi, if preferred.

8 servings

2	cups (8 ounces) gnocchi, cooked, room temperature
8	ounces Brussels sprouts, cut into halves, steamed, cooled
1	cup seeded, chopped tomato
1	medium purple, *or* green, bell pepper, sliced
1/4	cup thinly sliced red onion
	Sun-Dried Tomato and Goat Cheese Dressing (recipe follows)
2	tablespoons grated Romano cheese

Per Serving
Calories: 172
% Calories from fat: 27
Fat (gm): 5.4
Saturated fat (gm): 0.9
Cholesterol (mg): 3.5
Sodium (mg): 179
Protein (gm): 6.3
Carbohydrate (gm): 26.3
Exchanges
Milk: 0.0
Vegetable: 1.0
Fruit: 0.0
Bread: 1.5
Meat: 0.0
Fat: 1.0

1. Combine gnocchi and vegetables in salad bowl. Pour Sun-Dried Tomato and Goat Cheese Dressing over salad and toss; sprinkle with grated cheese.

Sun-Dried Tomato and Goat Cheese Dressing

makes about 1/2 cup

3	sun-dried tomatoes (not in oil)
2	tablespoons olive oil
2	tablespoons white wine vinegar
2	tablespoons lemon juice
1	tablespoon goat cheese *or* reduced-fat cream cheese, room temperature
2	cloves garlic, minced
1/2	teaspoon dried marjoram leaves
1/8	teaspoon dried thyme leaves
1/4	teaspoon salt
1/8	teaspoon pepper

1. Place sun-dried tomatoes in small bowl; pour hot water over to cover. Let tomatoes stand until softened, about 15 minutes; drain and finely chop.

2. Mix tomatoes, oil, and remaining ingredients; refrigerate until serving time. Mix again before using.

ORZO WITH SUN-DRIED TOMATOES AND MUSHROOMS

A simple salad, intensely flavored with sun-dried tomatoes, fresh rosemary, and sherry. If desired, the sherry can be omitted.

4 servings

2 sun-dried tomatoes (not in oil)
Olive oil cooking spray
1¹/₂ cups sliced mushrooms
¹/₄ cup thinly sliced green onions and tops
2 cloves garlic, minced
¹/₂ cup reduced-sodium chicken broth
2 tablespoons dry sherry, optional
¹/₂ cup (4 ounces) orzo, cooked, room temperature
2 tablespoons finely chopped fresh, *or* 1 teaspoon dried, rosemary leaves
2 tablespoons finely chopped parsley
¹/₄ teaspoon salt
¹/₄ teaspoon pepper

Per Serving
Calories: 122
% Calories from fat: 8
Fat (gm): 1.2
Saturated fat (gm): 0.2
Cholesterol (mg): 0
Sodium (mg): 239
Protein (gm): 5.4
Carbohydrate (gm): 23.5
Exchanges
Milk: 0.0
Vegetable: 0.5
Fruit: 0.0
Bread: 1.5
Meat: 0.0
Fat: 0.0

1. Place sun-dried tomatoes in small bowl; pour hot water over to cover. Let tomatoes stand until softened, about 15 minutes; drain and slice.

2. Spray large skillet with cooking spray; heat over medium heat until hot. Saute mushrooms, green onions, and garlic until mushrooms are tender, 5 to 7 minutes.

3. Add chicken broth and sherry to skillet; heat to boiling. Reduce heat and simmer, uncovered, until liquid is reduced by half, about 5 minutes. Cool to room temperature.

4. Combine orzo and mushroom mixture in bowl; add tomatoes and remaining ingredients and toss.

ORIENTAL NOODLE SALAD

If you enjoy the flavor of sesame oil, substitute 2 teaspoons sesame oil and 1 tablespoon plus 1 teaspoon vegetable oil for the olive oil.

8 servings

2/3 package (12-ounce size) rice noodles
2 cups snow peas, steamed
2 cups sliced red bell pepper
2 medium oranges, peeled, cut into segments
1 cup sliced mushrooms
1/2 cup fresh, *or* canned, bean sprouts, rinsed and drained
1/3 cup orange juice
2 tablespoons olive oil
2 cloves garlic, minced
1/2 teaspoon five-spice powder
1/4 teaspoon salt
1/4 teaspoon pepper

Per Serving
Calories: 198
% Calories from fat: 16
Fat (gm): 3.7
Saturated fat (gm): 0.5
Cholesterol (mg): 0
Sodium (mg): 72
Protein (gm): 5.9
Carbohydrate (gm): 36.9
Exchanges
Milk: 0.0
Vegetable: 0.5
Fruit: 0.5
Bread: 2.0
Meat: 0.0
Fat: 0.5

1. Place noodles in large bowl; pour boiling water over to cover. Let stand until noodles separate and are tender, about 10 minutes; drain. Cool.

2. Combine noodles, snow peas, bell pepper, oranges, mushrooms, and bean sprouts in large bowl. Combine orange juice and remaining ingredients; pour over noodle mixture and toss.

TOSSED GREENS WITH RICE NOODLES AND VEGETABLES

Tender rice noodles and vegetables are bedded on gourmet greens.

4 servings

$^1/_2$ package (4-ounce size) rice noodles
4 cups mesclun *or* other mixed greens
$^1/_4$ cup finely chopped mint
$^1/_4$ cup finely chopped cilantro
Warm Lime Dressing (recipe follows)
1 cup peeled, seeded, chopped cucumber
1 cup chopped tomato
1 cup snow peas, trimmed, cooked until crisp-tender, cooled

Per Serving
Calories: 146
% Calories from fat: 10
Fat (gm): 1.7
Saturated fat (gm): 0.2
Cholesterol (mg): 0
Sodium (mg): 228
Protein (gm): 4.9
Carbohydrate (gm): 29.8
Exchanges
Milk: 0.0
Vegetable: 3.0
Fruit: 2.0
Bread: 2.0
Meat: 0.0
Fat: 1.5

1. Place noodles in large bowl; pour boiling water over to cover. Let stand until noodles are separate and tender, about 10 minutes; drain. Cool.

2. Toss mesclun and herbs with half the Warm Lime Dressing; arrange on large salad plates and top with rice noodles. Toss cucumber, tomato, and snow peas with remaining Warm Lime Dressing and spoon over greens.

Warm Lime Dressing

makes about $^3/_4$ cup

$^1/_2$ cup water
$^1/_2$ cup lime juice
1 teaspoon cornstarch
2 tablespoons sugar
2 teaspoons minced garlic
2-3 teaspoons reduced-sodium tamari soy sauce
1 teaspoon dark sesame oil
1 teaspoon black bean sauce
$^1/_2$ teaspoon hot chili paste

1. Combine water, lime juice, and cornstarch in small saucepan; stir in remaining ingredients. Heat to boiling; boil, whisking constantly, until thickened, about 1 minute.

WARM PAPPARDELLE SALAD WITH CAJUN SHRIMP

Pappardelle is a very wide pasta, measuring about 1 inch in width. Any of the wide, flat pastas, such as mafalde or trenette, are also appropriate for this highly spiced dish.

4 main-dish servings

Olive oil cooking spray
1/2 medium red bell pepper, sliced
1/4 cup sliced onion
2 teaspoons dried oregano leaves
2 teaspoons dried basil leaves
2 teaspoons dried thyme leaves
1/2 teaspoon garlic powder
1/2 teaspoon paprika
1/4 teaspoon cayenne pepper
1/4 teaspoon black pepper
1/4 teaspoon salt
12 ounces peeled, deveined shrimp
1 cup reduced-sodium chicken broth
1/4 cup dry white wine *or* reduced-sodium chicken broth
1 tablespoon tomato paste
8 ounces pappardelle, cooked, warm

Per Serving
Calories: 292
% Calories from fat: 7
Fat (gm): 2.2
Saturated fat (gm): 0.5
Cholesterol (mg): 130.6
Sodium (mg): 329
Protein (gm): 22.7
Carbohydrate (gm): 41.4
Exchanges
Milk: 0.0
Vegetable: 0.5
Fruit: 0.0
Bread: 3.0
Meat: 1.0
Fat: 0.0

1. Spray large skillet with cooking spray; heat over medium heat until hot. Saute bell pepper and onion until tender. Stir in herbs, garlic powder, paprika, cayenne, black pepper, and salt.

2. Add shrimp to skillet; cook over medium heat until shrimp just begin to turn pink. Stir in broth, wine, and tomato paste; heat to boiling. Reduce heat and simmer 5 minutes. Serve over pasta.

"LITTLE EARS" WITH SHRIMP AND VEGETABLES

For variety, cooked cubed chicken breast, lean beef, or lean pork can be substituted for the shrimp in this entrée salad.

4 main-dish servings

12 ounces peeled, deveined shrimp, cooked
 3 cups broccoli florets, steamed
 1 medium yellow, *or* green, bell pepper, sliced
12 cherry tomatoes, cut into halves
 2 cups (8 ounces) orrechiette (little ears) *or* small pasta shells, cooked
    Mustard Seed Vinaigrette
    (recipe follows)

Per Serving
Calories: 367
% Calories from fat: 23
Fat (gm): 9.6
Saturated fat (gm): 1.4
Cholesterol (mg): 130.6
Sodium (mg): 451
Protein (gm): 24.7
Carbohydrate (gm): 47.3
Exchanges
Milk: 0.0
Vegetable: 2.0
Fruit: 0.0
Bread: 2.5
Meat: 2.0
Fat: 0.5

1. Combine shrimp, vegetables, and pasta in serving bowl; pour Mustard Seed Vinaigrette over and toss.

Mustard Seed Vinaigrette

makes about 1/3 cup

 2 tablespoons olive oil
 2 tablespoons white wine vinegar
 2 tablespoons lemon juice
 2 medium shallots, finely chopped
 2 cloves garlic, finely chopped
 2 tablespoons finely chopped cilantro *or* parsley
1/2 teaspoon salt
1/4 teaspoon pepper

1. Mix all ingredients; refrigerate until serving time. Mix again before using.

CHILI-DRESSED TUNA SALAD WITH RADIATORE

A fun pasta, radiatore look like the tiny radiators for which they are named! Other shaped pastas can be used, if preferred.

4 main-dish servings

Chili Dressing (recipe follows)
3 cups (8 ounces) radiatore (radiators), cooked, room temperature
1 can (9¼ ounces) white tuna in water, drained, flaked
2 medium tomatoes, cut into wedges
½ medium avocado, peeled, pitted, cut into ¾-inch pieces
2 tablespoons finely chopped cilantro *or* parsley
2 cups torn salad greens

Per Serving
Calories: 388
% Calories from fat: 30
Fat (gm): 12.9
Saturated fat (gm): 1.9
Cholesterol (mg): 18.7
Sodium (mg): 238
Protein (gm): 25.5
Carbohydrate (gm): 43.2
Exchanges
Milk: 0.0
Vegetable: 2.0
Fruit: 0.0
Bread: 2.5
Meat: 2.0
Fat: 1.0

1. Pour dressing over pasta in medium bowl and toss. Add tuna, tomatoes, avocado, and cilantro; toss. Spoon salad over greens on serving plate.

Chili Dressing

makes about ¼ cup

3 tablespoons lemon juice
2 tablespoons olive oil
½ teaspoon chili powder
¼ teaspoon crushed red pepper

1. Mix all ingredients; refrigerate until serving time. Mix again before using.

FOURTEEN

Breads, Coffee Cakes, Muffins

AND

More

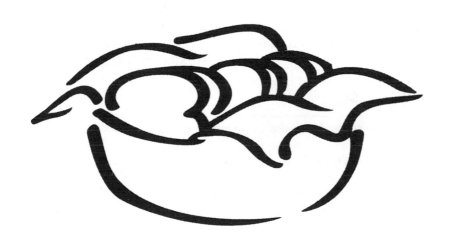

EASY HERB LAVOSH

Quick, easy, delicious, and versatile!

6 servings

  1 whole wheat, *or* plain, lavosh
     Vegetable cooking spray
$^{1}/_{2}$-$^{3}/_{4}$ teaspoon caraway seeds *or* dried herb
     leaves (see Tip below)

Per Serving
Calories: 132
% Calories from fat: 3
Fat (gm): 0.6
Saturated fat (gm): 0.1
Cholesterol (mg): 0
Sodium (mg): 1
Protein (gm): 5
Carbohydrate (gm): 29.2
Exchanges
Milk: 0.0
Vegetable: 0.0
Fruit: 0.0
Bread: 2.0
Meat: 0.0
Fat: 0.0

1. Spray top of lavosh generously with cooking spray and sprinkle with caraway seeds. Bake on a cookie sheet or piece of aluminum foil at 350 degrees until browned, 4 to 6 minutes (watch carefully as lavosh can burn easily).

Tip: Use any dried herb leaves you want, or a mix of herbs, such as Italian seasoning, bouquet garni, or creole seasoning. Grated fat-free Parmesan cheese can be sprinkled over the lavosh too.

PITA CHIPS

Perfect to serve with any dip, or to eat as a snack.

6 to 8 servings (6 to 8 chips each)

  3 whole wheat, *or* plain, pita breads
     Butter-flavored, *or* olive oil, cooking
     spray
3-4 teaspoons Italian seasoning *or* other
     dried herb leaves

Per Serving
Calories: 86
% Calories from fat: 8
Fat (gm): 0.9
Saturated fat (gm): 0.1
Cholesterol (mg): 0
Sodium (mg): 171
Protein (gm): 3.2
Carbohydrate (gm): 17.7
Exchanges
Milk: 0.0
Vegetable: 0.0
Fruit: 0.0
Bread: 1.0
Meat: 0.0
Fat: 0.0

1. Open pita breads and separate each into 2 halves. Stack pita halves and cut into 8 wedges. Arrange pita wedges, soft sides up, in single layer on jelly roll pan. Spray generously with cooking spray and sprinkle with Italian seasoning.

2. Bake at 425 degrees until pita wedges are browned and crisp, 5 to 10 minutes.

Variation: **Seasoned Pita Chips**—Make recipe as above, substituting 1 to 2 teaspoons chili powder, ground cumin, or garlic powder, or 1 to 2 tablespoons grated fat-free Parmesan cheese for the Italian seasoning.

BRUSCHETTA

These simple-to-make Italian garlic toasts are perfect for serving with many kinds of savory appetizer spreads.

12 servings (2 each)

1 loaf French bread (8 ounces, about 15 inches long)
 Olive oil cooking spray
2 cloves garlic, cut into halves

Per Serving
Calories: 53
% Calories from fat: **10**
Fat (gm): 0.6
Saturated fat (gm): 0.1
Cholesterol (mg): 0
Sodium (mg): 115
Protein (gm): 1.7
Carbohydrate (gm): 10
Exchanges
Milk: 0.0
Vegetable: 0.0
Fruit: 0.6
Bread: 1.0
Meat: 0.0
Fat: 0.0

1. Cut bread into 24 slices; spray both sides of bread lightly with cooking spray. Broil on cookie sheet 4 inches from heat source until browned, 2 to 3 minutes on each side.

2. Rub top sides of bread slices with cut sides of garlic.

Tip: Bread slices can be sprinkled with herbs, such as basil, oregano, or Italian seasoning, before broiling. Bread can also be sprinkled lightly with grated fat-free Parmesan cheese before broiling; watch carefully so cheese does not burn.

CROUSTADES

These crisp toast cups can be filled with just about any hot or cold filling. Try Eggplant Marmalade or Chutney Cheese Spread (see pp. 8, 9). Croustades can be baked up to a week in advance and stored in an airtight container.

8 servings (2 each)

16 slices soft bread
     Butter-flavored vegetable cooking spray

Per Serving
Calories: 67
% Calories from fat: 12
Fat (gm): 0.9
Saturated fat (gm): 0.2
Cholesterol (mg): 0
Sodium (mg): 135
Protein (gm): 2.1
Carbohydrate (gm): 12.4
Exchanges
Milk: 0.0
Vegetable: 0.0
Fruit: 0.0
Bread: 1.0
Meat: 0.0
Fat: 0.0

1. Cut 2^1/$_2$-inch rounds out of bread slices with cookie cutter (remaining bread can be used for croutons or bread crumbs).

2. Spray 16 mini-muffin tins with cooking spray; press 1 round of bread firmly into each. Spray bread generously with cooking spray.

3. Bake at 350 degrees until browned and crisp, 10 to 12 minutes.

CROUTONS

Croutons can brighten a soup, add crunch to a salad, and provide flavor accent for many dishes. Store croutons up to 2 weeks, or freeze; bake at 300 degrees 5 to 7 minutes if they need freshening.

12 servings (¼ cup each)

3 cups cubed firm or day-old French, *or* Italian, bread (¹/₂-³/₄-inch cubes)
Butter-flavored, *or* olive oil, cooking spray

Per Serving
Calories: 20
% Calories from fat: 13
Fat (gm): 0.3
Saturated fat (gm): 0.1
Cholesterol (mg): 0
Sodium (mg): 39
Protein (gm): 0.6
Carbohydrate (gm): 3.7
Exchanges
Milk: 0.0
Vegetable: 0.0
Fruit: 0.0
Bread: 0.0
Meat: 0.0
Fat: 0.0

1. Spray bread cubes generously with cooking spray; arrange in single layer on jelly roll pan. Bake at 375 degrees until browned, 8 to 10 minutes, stirring occasionally. Cool; store in airtight container.

Variations: **Italian-Style Croutons**—Spray bread cubes with olive oil cooking spray; sprinkle generously with combined 1 teaspoon garlic powder and 1 teaspoon Italian seasoning. Bake as above.

Sourdough Croutons—Spray sourdough bread cubes with cooking spray and sprinkle with 2 teaspoons bouquet garni. Bake as above.

Parmesan Croutons—Spray bread cubes with cooking spray and sprinkle with 1 to 2 tablespoons grated fat-free Parmesan cheese. Bake as above.

Rye Caraway Croutons—Spray rye bread cubes with cooking spray, and sprinkle with 2 teaspoons crushed caraway seeds. Bake as above.

Sesame Croutons—Spray bread cubes with cooking spray and sprinkle with 2 to 3 teaspoons sesame seeds. Bake as above.

Herb Croutons—Spray multi-grain or whole wheat bread cubes with cooking spray and sprinkle with 2 teaspoons dried herb or herb combinations, such as basil, tarragon, oregano, savory, rosemary, etc. Bake as above.

SOFT PRETZELS

To achieve their typical dense, chewy texture, the pretzels are cooked in boiling water before baking.

12 servings (1 each)

1 package active dry yeast

$^1/_2$ cup warm water (110-115 degrees)

1 tablespoon sugar

1 cup fat-free milk, heated to simmering, cooled

3$^1/_2$-4 cups all-purpose flour

1 teaspoon salt

2 quarts water

1 tablespoon baking soda

1 egg, beaten

1 tablespoon cold water

Toppings: Poppy seeds, sesame seeds, coarse salt, herbs, dried onion flakes, etc. (Not included in nutritional data)

Per Serving
Calories: 152
% Calories from fat: 5
Fat (gm): 0.8
Saturated fat (gm): 0.2
Cholesterol (mg): 18.1
Sodium (mg): 509
Protein (gm): 5.2
Carbohydrate (gm): 30.2
Exchanges
Milk: 0.0
Vegetable: 0.0
Fruit: 0.0
Bread: 2.0
Meat: 0.0
Fat: 0.0

1. Mix yeast, warm water, and sugar in large bowl; let stand 5 minutes. Add milk, 2 cups flour, and salt, beating until mixture is smooth. Mix in enough remaining 2 cups flour to make smooth dough.

2. Knead dough on floured surface until smooth and elastic, about 5 minutes. Place dough in greased bowl; let rise, covered, in warm place until double in size, 45 to 60 minutes. Punch dough down.

3. Roll dough on floured surface to rectangle 16 x 12 inches. Cut dough lengthwise into 12 strips, 1 inch wide. Roll one strip dough with palms of hands until rounded and 18 to 20 inches long. Form loop, holding ends of strip and twisting strips 2 times. Bring ends of strips down and fasten at opposite sides of loop to form pretzel shape. Repeat with remaining dough. Transfer pretzels to floured surface and let stand, lightly covered, 30 minutes (they may not double in size).

4. Heat 2 quarts water to boiling in large saucepan; stir in baking soda. Transfer pretzels, a few at a time, into boiling water; boil until dough feels firm, about 1 minute. Remove pretzels from boiling water with slotted spoon, allowing them to drain well. Place on well-greased aluminum foil-covered cookie sheets.

5. Mix egg and cold water; brush on tops of pretzels and sprinkle with desired toppings. Bake at 400 degrees until pretzels are golden, 18 to 20 minutes. Remove from pans; cool on wire racks.

GARLIC BREAD

Select a good quality French or Italian loaf for this aromatic bread, or use a sourdough bread for an interesting flavor variation.

4 servings

4 thick slices French, *or* Italian, bread
   Olive oil cooking spray
2 cloves garlic, cut into halves

Per Serving
Calories: 71
% Calories from fat: 10
Fat (gm): 0.8
Saturated fat (gm): 0.2
Cholesterol (mg): 0
Sodium (mg): 152
Protein (gm): 2.3
Carbohydrate (gm): 13.5
Exchanges
Milk: 0.0
Vegetable: 0.0
Fruit: 0.0
Bread: 1.0
Meat: 0.0
Fat: 0.0

1. Spray both sides of bread generously with cooking spray. Broil on cookie sheet 4 inches from heat source until browned, about 1 minute on each side.

2. Rub both sides of hot toast with cut sides of garlic.

Variation: **Parmesan Garlic Bread**—Combine 2 teaspoons grated Parmesan cheese and 1 teaspoon minced garlic. Spray bread with cooking spray as above and spread top of each slice with cheese mixture. Broil as above, or wrap loosely in aluminum foil and bake at 350 degrees until warm, about 5 minutes.

PITA BREADS

Also called Syrian bread and pocket breads, pitas can be eaten plain or split and filled. The breads freeze well, so make lots!

12 servings (1 each)

1 package active dry yeast
1¹/₃ cups warm water (110-115 degrees)
¹/₄ teaspoon sugar
1¹/₂ tablespoons olive oil
3-4 cups all-purpose flour
1 teaspoon salt

Per Serving
Calories: 131
% Calories from fat: 14
Fat (gm): 2
Saturated fat (gm): 0.3
Cholesterol (mg): 0
Sodium (mg): 178
Protein (gm): 3.5
Carbohydrate (gm): 24.2
Exchanges
Milk: 0.0
Vegetable: 0.0
Fruit: 0.0
Bread: 2.0
Meat: 0.0
Fat: 0.0

1. Combine yeast, water, and sugar in large bowl; let stand 5 minutes. Add oil, 3 cups flour, and salt, mixing until smooth. Mix in enough remaining 1 cup flour to make smooth dough.

2. Knead dough on floured surface until smooth and elastic, about 5 minutes. Place dough in greased bowl; let stand, covered, in warm place until double in size, about 1 hour. Punch dough down.

3. Shape dough into 12 balls; let stand, loosely covered, 30 minutes (dough will not double in size). Roll balls of dough on floured surface into rounds 5 to 6 inches in diameter. Place rounds, 2 to 3 inches apart, on cookie sheets; let stand 30 minutes.

4. Bake breads, 1 pan at a time, at 500 degrees until breads are puffed and brown, 3 to 5 minutes. Cool on wire racks.

WHOLE WHEAT LAVOSH

A flat cracker bread that is perfect to serve with dips and spreads, or as an accompaniment to soups and salads.

6 servings (1 each)

$^1/_2$ cup warm fat-free milk (110-115 degrees)

1 package active dry yeast

2$^1/_3$ cups whole wheat flour

1 cup all-purpose flour

$^1/_2$ teaspoon salt

1 egg white

1 tablespoon water

Per Serving
Calories: 186
% Calories from fat: **4**
Fat (gm): 0.8
Saturated fat (gm): 0.2
Cholesterol (mg): 0.3
Sodium (mg): 150
Protein (gm): 7.7
Carbohydrate (gm): 38.5
Exchanges
Milk: 0.0
Vegetable: 0.0
Fruit: 0.0
Bread: 2.5
Meat: 0.0
Fat: 0.0

1. Mix milk and yeast in large bowl; let stand 5 minutes. Mix in whole wheat flour, $^1/_2$ cup all-purpose flour, and salt; mix in enough remaining $^1/_2$ cup all-purpose flour to make a smooth dough. Let stand, covered, 15 to 20 minutes.

2. Divide dough into 6 equal pieces. Roll each piece on lightly floured surface into a 3 to 4-inch round; place on greased cookie sheet. Beat egg white and water; brush over tops of dough.

3. Bake lavosh at 425 degrees until crisp and browned, 5 to 8 minutes, turning lavosh halfway through baking time. (Lavosh will become crisper upon cooling, so do not overbake.) Cool on wire rack.

SPINACH-MUSHROOM FLATBREAD

This attractive bread is made in a freeform shape and topped with spinach and Parmesan cheese. The bread can be made in advance and reheated at 300 degrees, loosely wrapped in aluminum foil, 15 to 20 minutes.

1 loaf (12 servings)

3-3¹/₂	cups all-purpose flour
1¹/₂	cups whole wheat flour
2	tablespoons sugar
1¹/₂	teaspoons dried rosemary leaves, crushed
¹/₂	teaspoon dried thyme leaves
¹/₂	teaspoon salt
1	package fast-rising yeast
2	cups very hot water (125-130 degrees) Olive oil cooking spray
¹/₄	cup sliced onion
3	cloves garlic, minced
2	cups torn spinach leaves
1	cup sliced cremini, *or* white, mushrooms
¹/₄	cup (2 ounces) shredded reduced-fat mozzarella cheese
2-3	tablespoons grated fat-free Parmesan cheese

Per Serving
Calories: 190
% Calories from fat: 5
Fat (gm): 1
Saturated fat (gm): 0.4
Cholesterol (mg): 1.3
Sodium (mg): 123
Protein (gm): 7
Carbohydrate (gm): 38.8
Exchanges
Milk: 0.0
Vegetable: 0.0
Fruit: 0.0
Bread: 2.5
Meat: 0.0
Fat: 0.0

1. Combine 2¹/₂ cups all-purpose flour, whole wheat flour, sugar, herbs, salt, and yeast in large mixing bowl; add hot water, mixing until smooth. Mix in enough remaining 1 cup all-purpose flour to make soft dough.

2. Knead dough on floured surface until smooth and elastic, about 5 minutes. Place dough in greased bowl; let rise, loosely covered, in warm place until double in size, 30 to 45 minutes. Punch dough down.

3. Pat dough on floured surface into a round. Pull the edges of the dough into a free form shape, about 10 x 14 inches. Transfer dough to greased cookie sheet and let stand 20 minutes (dough will rise, but will not double in size).

4. Spray medium skillet with cooking spray; heat over medium heat until hot. Saute onion and garlic until tender, 3 to 4 minutes. Add spinach and mushrooms; cook, covered, over medium to medium-low heat until spinach is wilted, about 5 minutes. Cook, uncovered, until mushrooms are tender, about 5 minutes. Remove from heat and reserve.

5. Bake bread at 350 degrees until golden, about 20 minutes. Arrange spinach mixture over top of bread; sprinkle with cheeses. Continue baking until spinach mixture is hot and cheese melted, 5 to 10 minutes. Remove from cookie sheet and cool on wire rack.

FOCACCIA

This delicious Italian bread is very versatile and can be used in many ways—try Leek and Onion Focaccia or Fruit Focaccia (p. 663, 662). Focaccia can be frozen, so bake extra to have on hand.

2 focaccia (10 servings each)

5¹/₂ cups bread flour, divided
1 package fast-rising yeast
1 teaspoon sugar
1 teaspoon salt
1³/₄ cups very hot water (125-130 degrees)
   Olive oil cooking spray
¹/₄ cup grated Parmesan cheese

Per Serving
Calories: 139
% Calories from fat: 5
Fat (gm): 0.8
Saturated fat (gm): 0.2
Cholesterol (mg): 1
Sodium (mg): 131
Protein (gm): 5.2
Carbohydrate (gm): 28.2
Exchanges
Milk: 0.0
Vegetable: 0.0
Fruit: 0.0
Bread: 2.0
Meat: 0.0
Fat: 0.0

1. Combine 4 cups flour, yeast, sugar, and salt in large mixing bowl. Add water, mixing until smooth. Mix in enough remaining 1¹/₂ cups flour to make soft dough.

2. Knead dough on floured surface until dough is smooth and elastic, about 5 minutes. Place dough in greased bowl; turn greased side up and let rise, covered, in warm place until double in size, about 1 hour. Punch dough down.

3. Divide dough into halves. Roll 1 piece dough on floured surface to fit jelly roll pan, 15 x 10 inches. Grease pan lightly; ease dough into pan. Repeat with remaining dough. Let dough rise until double in size, 45 to 60 minutes.

4. Make ¹/₄-inch-deep indentations with fingers to "dimple" the dough; spray lightly with cooking spray and sprinkle with Parmesan cheese.

5. Bake focaccia at 425 degrees until browned, about 30 minutes. Cool in pans on wire racks. Serve warm, or at room temperature.

FRUIT FOCACCIA

Dried blueberries would be an excellent addition to this focaccia. Serve for breakfast, or even dessert.

1 focaccia (12 servings)

¹/₂ cup dried cranberries *or* cherries
¹/₂ cup dried fruit bits
1 cup boiling water
1 Focaccia (¹/₂ recipe) (see p. 661)
2 tablespoons granulated sugar
1 tablespoon melted margarine
¹/₃ cup packed light brown sugar
Butter-flavored vegetable cooking spray

Per Serving
Calories: 168.7
% Calories from fat: 8
Fat (gm): 1.6
Saturated fat (gm): 0.4
Cholesterol (mg): 0.8
Sodium (mg): 125
Protein (gm): 4.4
Carbohydrate (gm): 35.1
Exchanges
Milk: 0.0
Vegetable: 0.0
Fruit: 0.5
Bread: 2.0
Meat: 0.0
Fat: 0.0

1. Combine dried fruits in bowl; pour boiling water over and let stand until softened, 10 to 15 minutes. Drain.

2. Make Focaccia, adding granulated sugar to the flour mixture. After first rising, spread dough in greased baking pan, 11 x 7 inches. Let rise until double in size, about 30 minutes.

3. Make ¹/₄-inch indentations with fingers to "dimple" dough. Brush margarine over dough; sprinkle with fruit and brown sugar. Spray with cooking spray.

4. Bake focaccia at 425 degrees until browned, 20 to 25 minutes.

LEEK AND ONION FOCACCIA

This bread would make a perfect addition to a soup and salad supper.

1 focaccia (8 servings)

1 Focaccia (¹/₂ recipe) (see p. 661)
¹/₂ cup thinly sliced leek (white part only)
¹/₂ cup thinly sliced yellow onion
¹/₂ cup thinly sliced red onion
¹/₂ teaspoon dried sage leaves
1-2 teaspoons olive oil
    Salt and pepper, to taste
1-2 tablespoons grated fat-free Parmesan
    cheese

Per Serving
Calories: 193
% Calories from fat: 7
Fat (gm): 1.6
Saturated fat (gm): 0.4
Cholesterol (mg): 1.2
Sodium (mg): 171
Protein (gm): 7.1
Carbohydrate (gm): 38.4
Exchanges
Milk: 0.0
Vegetable: 1.0
Fruit: 0.0
Bread: 2.5
Meat: 0.0
Fat: 0.0

1. Make Focaccia; after first rising, spread dough in greased jelly roll pan, 15 x 10 inches. Let stand until dough is doubled in size, about 30 minutes.

2. Make ¹/₄-inch indentations with fingers to "dimple" the dough. Combine leek, onions, and sage; toss with oil and spread over dough. Sprinkle lightly with salt and pepper; sprinkle with Parmesan cheese.

3. Bake focaccia at 425 degrees until golden, 20 to 25 minutes.

POTATO BREAD

Breads made with mashed potatoes are very moist and retain their fresh-ness well. This dough can be conveniently made in advance and refriger-ated up to 5 days.

2 loaves (16 servings each)

1	package active dry yeast
1¹/₂	cups warm water (110-115 degrees)
2	tablespoons sugar
3	tablespoons margarine, softened
2	eggs
1	cup mashed potatoes, lukewarm
6-6¹/₂	cups all-purpose flour
1	cup whole wheat flour
1	teaspoon salt
	Fat-free milk

Per Serving
Calories: 121
% Calories from fat: 13
Fat (gm): 1.7
Saturated fat (gm): 0.4
Cholesterol (mg): 13.4
Sodium (mg): 103
Protein (gm): 3.6
Carbohydrate (gm): 22.7
Exchanges
Milk: 0.0
Vegetable: 0.0
Fruit: 0.0
Bread: 1.5
Meat: 0.0
Fat: 0.5

1. Mix yeast and warm water in large bowl; let stand 5 minutes. Mix in sugar, margarine, eggs, and mashed potatoes; mix in 5¹/₂ cups all-purpose flour, whole wheat flour, and salt; mix in enough remaining 1 cup all-purpose flour to make smooth dough.

2. Knead dough on floured surface until smooth and elastic, about 5 minutes. Place dough in greased bowl; let rise, covered, in warm place until double in size, 1 to 1¹/₂ hours. Punch down dough.

3. Divide dough into 2 equal pieces; shape into loaves and place in greased 9 x 5-inch loaf pans. Let stand, loosely covered, until double in size, about 45 minutes.

4. Brush tops of loaves with milk. Bake at 375 degrees until loaves are golden and sound hollow when tapped, about 45 minutes. Remove from pans and cool on wire racks.

PEASANT BREAD

Six grains and ground nuts are combined in this hearty, dense-textured, country-style bread.

2 small loaves (8 servings each)

2 packages active dry yeast
1/2 cup warm water (110-115 degrees)
1 1/4 cups whole wheat flour
1/2 cup millet
1/2 cup cracked wheat
1/2 cup yellow cornmeal
1/2 cup bulgur wheat
1/2 cup quick-cooking oats
1/2 cup ground pecans
1 teaspoon salt
1 1/4 cups lukewarm water
1/4 cup honey
2 tablespoons vegetable oil
1-2 cups unbleached all-purpose flour

Per Serving
Calories: 197
% Calories from fat: 22
Fat (gm): 5
Saturated fat (gm): 0.6
Cholesterol (mg): 0
Sodium (mg): 137
Protein (gm): 5.4
Carbohydrate (gm): 34.2
Exchanges
Milk: 0.0
Vegetable: 0.0
Fruit: 0.0
Bread: 2.0
Meat: 0.0
Fat: 1.0

1. Mix yeast and 1/2 cup warm water in small bowl; let stand 5 minutes. Mix whole wheat flour, millet, cracked wheat, cornmeal, bulgur, oats, pecans, and salt in large bowl; stir in yeast mixture, 1 1/4 cups water, honey, and oil. Mix in enough all-purpose flour to make dough easy to handle.

2. Knead dough on floured surface until smooth and elastic, about 5 minutes (dough will be heavy and difficult to handle). Place bread in greased bowl; let rise, covered, in warm place until double in size, about 1 1/2 hours. Punch down dough.

3. Divide dough in half; shape into 2 round loaves on greased baking sheet. Let stand, loosely covered, until double in size, about 1 1/2 hours.

4. Bake bread at 350 degrees until loaves are deep golden brown and sound hollow when tapped, about 40 minutes. Transfer to wire racks to cool.

HEARTY VEGETABLE-RYE BREAD

Cauliflower adds a subtle flavor to this aromatic rye loaf.

1 loaf (10 servings)

1	package active dry yeast
1/3	cup warm water (110-115 degrees)
1	teaspoon sugar
1	cup pureed cooked cauliflower
1	tablespoon margarine, melted
1	tablespoon light molasses
1	tablespoon spicy brown mustard
2 1/2-3	cups all-purpose flour
1	cup rye flour
1/2	teaspoon salt
1 1/2	teaspoons caraway seeds, crushed, divided
1 1/2	teaspoons fennel seeds, crushed, divided
1	teaspoon dried dill weed
1	egg white, beaten

Per Serving
Calories: 177
% Calories from fat: 9
Fat (gm): 1.9
Saturated fat (gm): 0.3
Cholesterol (mg): 0
Sodium (mg): 149
Protein (gm): 5.3
Carbohydrate (gm): 34.8
Exchanges
Milk: 0.0
Vegetable: 0.0
Fruit: 0.0
Bread: 2.0
Meat: 0.0
Fat: 0.5

1. Mix yeast, water, and sugar in large bowl; let stand 5 minutes. Mix in cauliflower, margarine, molasses, and mustard. Mix in 2 cups all-purpose flour, rye flour, salt, 1 teaspoon caraway seeds, 1 teaspoon fennel seeds, and dill weed. Mix in enough remaining 1 cup all-purpose flour to make smooth dough.

2. Knead dough on floured surface until smooth and elastic, about 5 minutes. Place dough in greased bowl; let stand, covered, in warm place until double in size, about 1 hour. Punch dough down.

3. Shape dough into long or round loaf on greased cookie sheet. Let rise, loosely covered, until double in size, 45 to 60 minutes. Slash top of loaf with sharp knife; brush with egg white and sprinkle with remaining 1/2 teaspoon caraway seeds and 1/2 teaspoon fennel seeds. Bake at 350 degrees until bread is golden and sounds hollow when tapped, 40 to 50 minutes. Cool on wire rack.

ROASTED RED PEPPER BREAD

Bake in freeform long or round loaves, or in pans. For convenience, use a jarred fire-roasted red pepper.

2 loaves (8 servings each)

2¹/₄-2³/₄   cups all-purpose flour
      ³/₄   cup whole wheat flour
      ¹/₄   cup grated fat-free Parmesan cheese
       1   teaspoon Italian seasoning
      ¹/₂   teaspoon salt
       1   package fast-rising active dry yeast
    1¹/₄   cups very hot water (125-130 degrees)
       1   tablespoon olive oil
       4   ounces reduced-fat mozzarella cheese, cut into ¹/₂-inch cubes
      ¹/₂   cup coarsely chopped roasted red pepper
       1   egg white, beaten
       2   teaspoons water
          Italian seasoning

Per Serving
Calories: 119
% Calories from fat: 16
Fat (gm): 2.2
Saturated fat (gm): 0.9
Cholesterol (mg): 3.8
Sodium (mg): 133
Protein (gm): 5.6
Carbohydrate (gm): 19
Exchanges
Milk: 0.0
Vegetable: 0.0
Fruit: 0.0
Bread: 1.5
Meat: 0.0
Fat: 0.5

1. Combine 2¹/₄ cups all-purpose flour, whole wheat flour, Parmesan cheese, Italian seasoning, salt, and yeast in large bowl; add water and oil, mixing until smooth. Mix in mozzarella cheese and red pepper; mix in enough remaining ¹/₂ cup all-purpose flour to make smooth dough.

2. Knead dough on floured surface until smooth and elastic, about 5 minutes. Place dough in greased bowl; let rise, covered, in warm place until double in size, about 30 minutes. Punch dough down.

3. Divide dough into 2 equal pieces. Shape each into loaf and place in greased 9 x 5-inch loaf pan, or shape into round or long loaf on greased cookie sheets. Let stand, covered, until double in size, about 30 minutes.

4. Slash top of loaves with sharp knife. Mix egg white and water; brush over dough and sprinkle with Italian seasoning. Bake at 375 degrees until loaves are golden and sound hollow when tapped, 35 to 40 minutes. Remove from pans and cool on wire racks.

LIMA BEAN WHEAT BREAD

Any kind of pureed bean can be used in this moist, dense bread.

3 loaves (10 servings each)

2 packages active dry yeast
1/2 cup warm water (110-115 degrees)
1 cup cooked dried lima beans *or*
   canned lima beans, rinsed, drained
1 cup water
2 cups fat-free milk
4-6 tablespoons margarine, melted
1/3 cup sugar
4¹/2-5¹/2 cups all-purpose flour
1¹/2 cups whole wheat flour
1¹/2 teaspoons salt
   Fat-free milk

Per Serving
Calories: 125
% Calories from fat: 13
Fat (gm): 1.9
Saturated fat (gm): 0.4
Cholesterol (mg): 0.3
Sodium (mg): 133
Protein (gm): 4
Carbohydrate (gm): 23.2
Exchanges
Milk: 0.0
Vegetable: 0.0
Fruit: 0.0
Bread: 1.5
Meat: 0.0
Fat: 0.5

1. Mix yeast and warm water in small bowl; let stand 5 minutes. Process beans and 1 cup water in food processor or blender until smooth. Mix bean puree, 2 cups milk, margarine, and sugar in large bowl; mix in yeast mixture, 4¹/2 cups all-purpose flour, whole wheat flour, and salt. Mix in enough remaining 1 cup all-purpose flour to make soft dough.

2. Knead dough on floured surface until smooth and elastic, about 5 minutes. Place dough in greased bowl and let rise, covered, in warm place until double in size, about 1 hour. Punch dough down.

3. Divide dough into 3 equal pieces. Shape each piece into oval loaf on greased cookie sheet. Let rise, loosely covered, until double in size, about 45 minutes.

4. Brush loaves with milk. Bake until loaves are golden and sound hollow when tapped, about 1 hour. Transfer to wire racks and cool.

SWEET POTATO BRAIDS

Canned pumpkin can be substituted for the sweet potatoes, if desired. For variation, add $^1/_2$ cup raisins and/or $^1/_2$ cup coarsely chopped nuts to the bread dough.

2 loaves (12 servings each)

2	packages active dry yeast
$^1/_4$	cup warm fat-free milk (110-115 degrees)
1	cup mashed cooked sweet potatoes
$1^3/_4$	cups fat-free milk
$^1/_4$	cup vegetable oil
1	egg
4	cups all-purpose flour
2	cups whole wheat flour
1	teaspoon salt

Per Serving
Calories: 156
% Calories from fat: 17
Fat (gm): 2.9
Saturated fat (gm): 0.5
Cholesterol (mg): 9.2
Sodium (mg): 105
Protein (gm): 4.9
Carbohydrate (gm): 27.7
Exchanges
Milk: 0.0
Vegetable: 0.0
Fruit: 0.0
Bread: 2.0
Meat: 0.0
Fat: 0.5

1. Mix yeast and warm milk in large bowl; let stand 5 minutes. Stir in sweet potatoes, milk, oil, and egg; add 3 cups all-purpose flour, whole wheat flour, and salt, mixing until smooth. Mix in enough remaining 1 cup all-purpose flour to make smooth dough.

2. Knead dough on floured surface until smooth and elastic, about 5 minutes. Place dough in bowl; let rise, covered, in warm place until double in size, about 1 hour. Punch down dough.

3. Divide dough into 2 equal halves; divide each half into thirds. Roll pieces of dough into strips, 12 inches long. Braid 3 strips; fold ends under and place on greased cookie sheet. Repeat with remaining dough strips. Let rise, loosely covered, until double in size, 30 to 45 minutes.

4. Bake until breads are golden and sound hollow when tapped, 45 to 55 minutes. Transfer to wire racks and cool.

SQUASH DINNER ROLLS

Use pumpkin, Hubbard, or acorn squash for these rolls; mashed sweet potatoes can be substituted for the squash. If a loaf is preferred, shape and bake the dough in a greased 8¹/₂ x 4¹/₂-inch loaf pan.

24 servings (1 each)

1¹/₂-2¹/₂ cups all-purpose flour
    1 cup whole wheat flour
    2 packages fast-rising yeast
  1-2 teaspoons salt
   ¹/₂ cup fat-free milk
   ¹/₄ cup honey
  1-2 tablespoons margarine
   ³/₄ cup mashed cooked winter squash
    1 egg

Per Serving
Calories: 70
% Calories from fat: 11
Fat (gm): 0.9
Saturated fat (gm): 0.2
Cholesterol (mg): 9
Sodium (mg): 100
Protein (gm): 2.2
Carbohydrate (gm): 13.5
Exchanges
Milk: 0.0
Vegetable: 0.0
Fruit: 0.0
Bread: 1.0
Meat: 0.0
Fat: 0.0

1. Combine 1¹/₂ cups all-purpose flour, whole wheat flour, yeast, and salt in large mixing bowl. Heat milk, honey, and margarine in small saucepan until very hot (125-130 degrees). Add milk mixture to flour mixture, mixing until smooth. Mix in squash and egg. Mix in enough remaining 1 cup all-purpose flour to make smooth dough.

2. Knead dough on floured surface until smooth and elastic, about 5 minutes. Place dough in greased bowl; let stand, covered, in warm place until double in size, 30 to 45 minutes. Punch down dough.

3. Divide dough into 24 pieces; shape into balls and place in greased muffin tins. Let rise until almost double in size, about 30 minutes. Bake at 375 degrees until browned, 20 to 25 minutes.

CRANBERRY-NUT WHEAT LOAF

Dried cranberries and walnuts make this bread a perfect fall and winter offering.

1 loaf (16 servings)

1 package active dry yeast
³/4 cup warm water (110-115 degrees)
3 tablespoons honey
2-3 tablespoons vegetable shortening
2 egg whites
1¹/2-2 cups all-purpose flour
1 cup whole wheat flour
1 teaspoon salt
1 cup dried cranberries
²/3 cup coarsely chopped walnuts
Fat-free milk

Per Serving
Calories: 153
% Calories from fat: 27
Fat (gm): 4.7
Saturated fat (gm): 0.6
Cholesterol (mg): 0
Sodium (mg): 141
Protein (gm): 4.1
Carbohydrate (gm): 24.6
Exchanges
Milk: 0.0
Vegetable: 0.0
Fruit: 0.5
Bread: 1.0
Meat: 0.0
Fat: 1.0

1. Mix yeast, warm water, and honey in large bowl; let stand 5 minutes. Add shortening, egg whites, 1 cup all-purpose flour, the whole wheat flour, and salt, mixing until smooth. Mix in cranberries, walnuts, and enough remaining 1 cup all-purpose flour to make smooth dough.

2. Knead dough on floured surface until smooth and elastic, about 5 minutes. Place dough in greased bowl; let rise, covered, in warm place until double in size, 1 to 1¹/2 hours. Punch down dough.

3. Shape dough into loaf and place in greased 9 x 5-inch loaf pan. Let stand, loosely covered, until double in size, about 45 minutes.

4. Brush top of loaf with milk. Bake at 375 degrees until loaf is golden and sounds hollow when tapped, 35 to 40 minutes. Remove from pan and cool on wire rack.

GRANOLA BREAD

A wonderful breakfast bread—serve with plenty of Spiced Rhubarb Jam (see p. 694). For convenience this bread is mixed with an electric mixer and has only 1 rise.

2 loaves (16 servings each)

2	packages active dry yeast
3/4	cup warm water (110-115 degrees)
2	tablespoons light brown sugar
1¼	cups buttermilk
3	cups all-purpose flour
3/4-1½	cups whole wheat flour
2	teaspoons baking powder
1	teaspoon salt
2-3	tablespoons margarine, softened
1½	cups low-fat granola
	Buttermilk

Per Serving
Calories: 87
% Calories from fat: 13
Fat (gm): 1.3
Saturated fat (gm): 0.2
Cholesterol (mg): 0.4
Sodium (mg): 111
Protein (gm): 2.6
Carbohydrate (gm): 16.7
Exchanges
Milk: 0.0
Vegetable: 0.0
Fruit: 0.0
Bread: 1.0
Meat: 0.0
Fat: 0.5

1. Mix yeast, warm water, and brown sugar in large mixer bowl; let stand 5 minutes. Add buttermilk, all-purpose flour, 3/4 cup whole wheat flour, baking powder, salt, and margarine, mixing on low speed until smooth. Mix in granola and enough remaining 3/4 cup whole wheat flour to make smooth dough (dough will be slightly sticky).

2. Knead dough on floured surface until smooth and elastic, about 5 minutes. Divide dough into 2 equal pieces. Roll each piece into a rectangle 18 x 10 inches. Roll up, beginning at short ends; press each end to seal. Place loaves, seam sides down, in greased 9 x 5-inch loaf pans. Let rise, covered, in warm place until double in size, about 1 hour.

3. Brush tops of loaves with buttermilk. Bake at 375 degrees until loaves are golden and sound hollow when tapped, 40 to 45 minutes. Remove from pans and cool on wire racks.

ENGLISH MUFFIN BREAD

This quick and easy single-rise bread has a coarse texture similar to English muffins. Delicious warm from the oven or toasted.

1 loaf (16 servings)

Vegetable cooking spray
1-2 teaspoons yellow cornmeal
2-2¹/₂ cups all-purpose flour
¹/₂ cup quick-cooking oats
1 package active dry yeast
1 teaspoon salt
1¹/₄ cups fat-free milk
1 tablespoon honey
¹/₄ teaspoon baking soda

Per Serving
Calories: 79
% Calories from fat: 4
Fat (gm): 0.4
Saturated fat (gm): 0.1
Cholesterol (mg): 0.3
Sodium (mg): 163
Protein (gm): 2.9
Carbohydrate (gm): 15.9
Exchanges
Milk: 0.0
Vegetable: 0.0
Fruit: 0.0
Bread: 1.0
Meat: 0.0
Fat: 0.0

1. Spray 8 x 4 x 2-inch loaf pan with cooking spray; coat with cornmeal.

2. Combine 1¹/₂ cups flour, oats, yeast, and salt in large bowl. Heat milk and honey until warm (110-115 degrees) in small saucepan; stir in baking soda. Add milk mixture to flour mixture, mixing until smooth. Stir in enough remaining ¹/₂ cup flour to make a thick batter. Pour into prepared pan. Let rise, covered, in warm place until doubled in size, 45 to 60 minutes.

3. Bake at 400 degrees until bread is golden and sounds hollow when tapped, 25 to 30 minutes. Remove from pan immediately and cool on wire rack.

Variation: **Raisin Bread**—Spray loaf pan, but do not coat with cornmeal. Stir 1 teaspoon cinnamon and ¹/₂ cup raisins into batter.

MULTI-GRAIN BATTER BREAD

Batter breads are quick and easy to make, requiring no kneading and only one rise.

2 loaves (16 servings each)

3¹/₄ cups all-purpose flour

1 cup whole wheat flour

¹/₄ cup soy flour *or* quick-cooking oats

³/₄ cup quick-cooking oats

¹/₄ cup sugar

¹/₂ teaspoon salt

2 packages fast-rising yeast

1 cup cooked brown rice

2¹/₄ cups very hot fat-free milk (125-130 degrees)

2 tablespoons vegetable oil

Per Serving
Calories: 97
% Calories from fat: 13
Fat (gm): 1.4
Saturated fat (gm): 0.2
Cholesterol (mg): 0.3
Sodium (mg): 43
Protein (gm): 3.5
Carbohydrate (gm): 17.9
Exchanges
Milk: 0.0
Vegetable: 0.0
Fruit: 0.0
Bread: 1.0
Meat: 0.0
Fat: 0.5

1. Combine flours, oats, sugar, salt, and yeast in large bowl; stir in rice. Add milk and oil, mixing until smooth. Spoon batter into 2 greased 8¹/₂ x 4¹/₂-inch bread pans; let stand, loosely covered, until double in size, about 30 minutes.

2. Bake bread at 375 degrees until loaves are browned and sound hollow when tapped, 35 to 40 minutes. Remove from pans and cool on wire racks.

BUBBLE LOAF

Also called Bath Buns and Monkey Bread, this pull-apart loaf is easy to make, fun to eat, and perfect for pot-luck offerings and parties. The recipe can be halved and baked in a 6-cup fluted cake pan.

1 loaf (16 servings)

2 packages active dry yeast
1 cup warm fat-free milk (110-115 degrees)
6 tablespoons margarine, softened
1/4 cup sugar
3 eggs
4 cups all-purpose flour
1/2 teaspoon salt

Per Serving
Calories: 186
% Calories from fat: 27
Fat (gm): 5.5
Saturated fat (gm): 1.2
Cholesterol (mg): 40.2
Sodium (mg): 137
Protein (gm): 5.3
Carbohydrate (gm): 28.3
Exchanges
Milk: 0.0
Vegetable: 0.0
Fruit: 0.0
Bread: 2.0
Meat: 0.0
Fat: 1.0

1. Stir yeast into milk; let stand 2 to 3 minutes. In a large bowl, beat margarine and sugar until fluffy; beat in eggs, 1 at a time. Mix in combined flour and salt alternately with milk mixture, beginning and ending with dry ingredients and beating well after each addition. Let stand, covered, in warm place until dough is double in size, about 1 hour. Punch dough down.

2. Drop dough by large spoonfuls into greased 10-inch tube pan. Let rise, covered, until dough is double in size, about 30 minutes. Bake at 350 degrees until browned, 25 to 30 minutes. Cool in pan on wire rack 10 minutes; remove from pan. Serve warm.

BANANA BREAD

Brown sugar gives this banana bread a caramel flavor, and the apple-sauce adds moistness. It's the best!

1 loaf (16 servings)

   4 tablespoons margarine, softened

  1/4 cup unsweetened applesauce

   2 eggs

   2 tablespoons fat-free milk *or* water

  3/4 cup packed light brown sugar

   1 cup mashed bananas (2-3 medium bananas)

1 3/4 cups all-purpose flour

   2 teaspoons baking powder

  1/2 teaspoon baking soda

  1/4 teaspoon salt

  1/4 cup coarsely chopped walnuts *or* pecans

Per Serving
Calories: 151
% Calories from fat: 28
Fat (gm): 4.8
Saturated fat (gm): 0.9
Cholesterol (mg): 26.7
Sodium (mg): 160
Protein (gm): 2.9
Carbohydrate (gm): 24.9
Exchanges
Milk: 0.0
Vegetable: 0.0
Fruit: 0.5
Bread: 1.0
Meat: 0.0
Fat: 1.0

1. Beat margarine, applesauce, eggs, milk, and brown sugar in large mixing bowl until smooth. Add bananas and blend at low speed; beat at high speed 1 to 2 minutes.

2. Combine flour, baking powder, baking soda, and salt; mix into batter. Mix in walnuts. Pour batter into greased loaf pan, 8 x 4 x 2 inches.

3. Bake at 350 degrees until bread is golden and toothpick inserted in center comes out clean, 55 to 60 minutes. Cool in pan on wire rack 10 minutes; remove from pan and cool to room temperature.

GREEN CHILI CORN BREAD

Corn bread, Southwest-style! If using mild canned chilies, consider adding a teaspoon or so of minced jalapeño chili for a piquant accent. Serve this flavorful corn bread warm.

9 servings

Vegetable cooking spray
1/4 cup chopped red bell pepper
2 cloves garlic, minced
1/2 teaspoon cumin seeds, crushed
1 1/4 cups yellow cornmeal
3/4 cup all-purpose flour
2 teaspoons baking powder
1/2 teaspoon baking powder
1 teaspoon sugar
1/2 teaspoon salt
1 1/4 cups buttermilk
1/2 cup canned cream-style corn
1 can (4 ounces) chopped hot, *or* mild, green chilies, well drained
1 egg
2 egg whites
3 1/2 tablespoons margarine, melted

Per Serving
Calories: 184
% Calories from fat: 29
Fat (gm): 6.1
Saturated fat (gm): 1.3
Cholesterol (mg): 24.9
Sodium (mg): 563
Protein (gm): 5.6
Carbohydrate (gm): 27.6
Exchanges
Milk: 0.0
Vegetable: 0.0
Fruit: 0.0
Bread: 2.0
Meat: 0.0
Fat: 1.0

1. Spray small skillet with cooking spray; heat over medium heat until hot. Saute bell pepper, garlic, and cumin seeds until pepper is tender, 2 to 3 minutes.

2. Combine cornmeal, flour, baking powder, baking soda, sugar, and salt in large bowl. Add buttermilk, bell pepper mixture, and remaining ingredients; mix until smooth. Spread batter in a greased 8-inch-square baking pan.

3. Bake at 425 degrees until corn bread is golden, about 30 minutes. Cool in pan on wire rack.

FRUITED BRAN BREAD

Use any combination of dried fruit you want in this quick and healthy no-rise batter bread.

1 loaf (16 servings)

1¼ cups all-purpose flour
½ cup whole wheat flour
2 teaspoons baking powder
½ teaspoon baking soda
½ teaspoon salt
1½ cups whole bran cereal
1⅓ cups buttermilk
¾ cup packed light brown sugar
3 tablespoons margarine, softened
1 egg
1 cup coarsely chopped mixed dried fruit
¼-½ cup chopped walnuts

Per Serving
Calories: 169
% Calories from fat: 20
Fat (gm): 4.2
Saturated fat (gm): 0.8
Cholesterol (mg): 14.1
Sodium (mg): 261
Protein (gm): 4.1
Carbohydrate (gm): 33.1
Exchanges
Milk: 0.0
Vegetable: 0.0
Fruit: 0.0
Bread: 2.0
Meat: 0.0
Fat: 0.5

1. Combine all-purpose flour, whole wheat flour, baking powder, baking soda, salt, and bran cereal in medium bowl. Add buttermilk, brown sugar, margarine, and egg to bowl; stir just until dry ingredients are moistened. Gently fold in dried fruit and walnuts.

2. Spread batter in greased and floured 9 x 5-inch loaf pan. Bake at 350 degrees until wooden pick inserted in center comes out clean, about 1 hour. Remove from pan; cool completely on wire rack before slicing.

MINT AND CITRUS TEA BREAD

Fine textured and lightly scented with mint, orange, and lemon, this bread is a delicious addition to any meal.

1 loaf (12 servings)

1/2	cup fat-free milk
2	tablespoons finely chopped fresh, *or* 2 teaspoons dried, mint leaves
2	tablespoons grated orange rind
1	tablespoon grated lemon rind
5	tablespoons margarine, softened
3/4	cup sugar
2	eggs
1 1/2	cups all-purpose flour
1/2	cup whole wheat flour
1 1/2	teaspoons baking powder
1/2	teaspoon salt
1/4	cup orange juice
1/2	cup powdered sugar
	Fat-free milk
	Ground nutmeg, as garnish

Per Serving
Calories: 153
% Calories from fat: 25
Fat (gm): 4.4
Saturated fat (gm): 0.9
Cholesterol (mg): 26.8
Sodium (mg): 151
Protein (gm): 2.9
Carbohydrate (gm): 26
Exchanges
Milk: 0.0
Vegetable: 0.0
Fruit: 0.0
Bread: 1.5
Meat: 0.0
Fat: 1.0

1. Heat milk, mint, orange rind, and lemon rind in small saucepan to simmering; strain and cool.

2. Beat margarine and sugar until smooth in medium bowl; beat in eggs. Mix in combined all-purpose and whole wheat flour, baking powder, and salt alternately with cooled milk mixture and orange juice, beginning and ending with dry ingredients.

3. Pour batter into greased 8 1/2 x 4 1/2-inch loaf pan. Bake at 325 degrees until bread is golden and toothpick inserted in center comes out clean, about 45 minutes. Remove from pan and cool on wire rack.

4. Mix powdered sugar with enough milk to make medium glaze consistency; drizzle glaze over bread and sprinkle lightly with nutmeg.

QUICK SELF-RISING BISCUITS

*Two cups all-purpose flour can be substituted for the self-rising flour;
add 3 teaspoons baking powder and 1/2 teaspoon salt.*

18 biscuits (1 per serving)

2 cups self-rising flour
1 tablespoon vegetable shortening
3/4-1 cup fat-free milk
1 tablespoon margarine, melted

Per Serving
Calories: 65
% Calories from fat: 21
Fat (gm): 1.4
Saturated fat (gm): 0.3
Cholesterol (mg): 0.2
Sodium (mg): 189
Protein (gm): 1.7
Carbohydrate (gm): 10.8
Exchanges
Milk: 0.0
Vegetable: 0.0
Fruit: 0.0
Bread: 1.0
Meat: 0.0
Fat: 0.0

1. Measure flour into medium bowl; cut in shortening until mixture resembles coarse crumbs. Stir enough milk into flour mixture to make a soft dough. Roll dough on floured surface to 1/2 inch thickness; cut into biscuits with 2-inch cutter.

2. Place biscuits in greased 13 x 9-inch baking pan; brush with melted margarine. Bake at 425 degrees until golden, about 15 minutes.

Variations: **Chive Biscuits**—Mix 3 tablespoons snipped fresh or dried chives into biscuit dough.

Parmesan Biscuits—Brush biscuits with melted margarine as above; sprinkle with 2 tablespoons grated fat-free Parmesan cheese.

SWEET POTATO BISCUITS

Sweet potatoes offer moistness and a delicate sweetness to these biscuits. For a nonsweet biscuit, mashed potatoes can be substituted for the sweet potatoes.

18 biscuits (1 per serving)

<table>
<tr><td>3/4</td><td>cup mashed, cooked sweet potatoes</td></tr>
<tr><td>3-4</td><td>tablespoons margarine, melted</td></tr>
<tr><td>2/3</td><td>cup fat-free milk</td></tr>
<tr><td>1 3/4-2</td><td>cups all-purpose flour</td></tr>
<tr><td>4</td><td>teaspoons baking powder</td></tr>
<tr><td>1</td><td>tablespoon brown sugar</td></tr>
<tr><td>1/2</td><td>teaspoon salt</td></tr>
<tr><td></td><td>Fat-free milk</td></tr>
<tr><td></td><td>Ground nutmeg, as garnish</td></tr>
</table>

Per Serving
Calories: 82
% Calories from fat: 23
Fat (gm): 2.1
Saturated fat (gm): 0.4
Cholesterol (mg): 0.1
Sodium (mg): 161
Protein (gm): 1.8
Carbohydrate (gm): 14
Exchanges
Milk: 0.0
Vegetable: 0.0
Fruit: 0.0
Bread: 1.0
Meat: 0.0
Fat: 0.5

1. Mix sweet potatoes and margarine in medium bowl; stir in 2/3 cup milk. Mix in 1 3/4 cups flour, baking powder, brown sugar, and salt. Mix in remaining 1/4 cup flour if dough is too sticky to handle easily.

2. Knead dough on floured surface 5 to 6 times. Roll on floured surface to 1/2 inch thickness; cut with 2-inch biscuit cutter and place close together on greased baking sheet. Brush biscuits lightly with milk and sprinkle lightly with nutmeg.

3. Bake biscuits at 425 degrees until golden, 12 to 15 minutes.

VINEGAR BISCUITS

Every grandmother, no doubt, has her version of this old-fashioned biscuit recipe.

12 biscuits (1 per serving)

<table>
<tr><td>

³/₄ cup fat-free milk

¹/₄ cup cider vinegar

2 cups all-purpose flour

1¹/₂ teaspoons baking soda

1 teaspoon cream of tartar

¹/₂ teaspoon salt

3 tablespoons vegetable shortening, melted

</td><td>

Per Serving
Calories: 109
% Calories from fat: 27
Fat (gm): 3.2
Saturated fat (gm): 0.8
Cholesterol (mg): 0.3
Sodium (mg): 255
Protein (gm): 2.7
Carbohydrate (gm): 17.1
Exchanges
Milk: 0.0
Vegetable: 0.0
Fruit: 0.0
Bread: 1.0
Meat: 0.0
Fat: 0.5

</td></tr>
</table>

1. Mix milk and vinegar in glass measure. Combine flour, baking soda, cream of tartar, and salt in medium bowl; add milk mixture and shortening, mixing until blended.

2. Knead dough on generously floured surface 1 to 2 minutes. Pat dough into ¹/₂ inch thickness; cut into biscuits with 3-inch round cutter. Bake on greased cookie sheet at 425 degrees until golden, 10 to 12 minutes.

WILD RICE MUFFINS

Wild rice adds crunchy texture and a nutritional boost to these hearty muffins.

12 muffins (1 per serving)

<table>
<tr><td>

¹/₂ cup uncooked wild rice

2 cups water

1 teaspoon salt, divided

1 cup fat-free milk

4 tablespoons margarine, melted

1 egg, beaten

2 egg whites

1 cup all-purpose flour

¹/₂ cup whole wheat flour

</td><td>

Per Serving
Calories: 136
% Calories from fat: 30
Fat (gm): 4.5
Saturated fat (gm): 0.9
Cholesterol (mg): 18.1
Sodium (mg): 494
Protein (gm): 4.6
Carbohydrate (gm): 19.4
Exchanges
Milk: 0.0
Vegetable: 0.0
Fruit: 0.0
Bread: 1.5
Meat: 0.0
Fat: 0.5

</td></tr>
</table>

> 3 tablespoons baking powder
> 1 tablespoon sugar

1. Heat rice, water, and ¹/₂ teaspoon salt to boiling in small saucepan; reduce heat and simmer, covered, until rice is tender, 45 to 50 minutes. Drain, if necessary, and cool.

2. Mix milk, margarine, egg, egg whites, and rice. Add combined all-purpose and whole wheat flour, baking powder, sugar, and remaining ¹/₂ teaspoon salt, mixing just until dry ingredients are moistened.

3. Spoon batter into 12 greased muffin cups. Bake at 400 degrees until muffins are browned, 20 to 25 minutes. Remove from pans and cool on wire racks.

CARDAMOM-PEAR MUFFINS

Any dried fruit you like can be substituted for the pears.

12 muffins (1 per serving)

> 1 cup fat-free milk
> 4 tablespoons margarine, melted
> 1 egg
> 2 cups all-purpose flour
> ¹/₃ cup plus 2 tablespoons sugar, divided
> 3 teaspoons baking powder
> ¹/₂ teaspoon salt
> 1 cup chopped dried pears
> 1 teaspoon grated orange, *or* lemon, rind
> ¹/₂ teaspoon ground cardamom *or* nutmeg

Per Serving
Calories: 193
% Calories from fat: **21**
Fat (gm): 4.5
Saturated fat (gm): **1**
Cholesterol (mg): 18.1
Sodium (mg): 232
Protein (gm): 3.7
Carbohydrate (gm): 35.4
Exchanges
Milk: 0.0
Vegetable: 0.0
Fruit: 0.0
Bread: 2.0
Meat: 0.0
Fat: 1.0

1. Mix milk, margarine, and egg in medium bowl. Add combined flour, ¹/₃ cup sugar, baking powder, and salt, mixing just until dry ingredients are moistened; gently mix in pears and orange rind.

2. Spoon batter into 12 greased muffin cups; sprinkle with remaining 2 tablespoons sugar and cardamom. Bake at 400 degrees until muffins are browned and toothpicks inserted in centers of muffins come out clean, 20 to 25 minutes. Remove from pans and cool on wire racks.

"LITTLE PANTS" BISCUITS

These Mexican-inspired sugar and cinnamon-topped breads are sort of a cross between a biscuit and a cookie. They are usually made into "pants" shapes but can be cut into rounds or squares if you prefer.

18 servings (1 per serving)

   4 tablespoons vegetable shortening
1/2 cup sugar, divided
   2 cups all-purpose flour
   2 teaspoons baking powder
1/2 salt
1/2 cup plus 2 tablespoons skim milk, divided
1/2 teaspoon ground cinnamon

Per Serving
Calories: 101
% Calories from fat: 27
Fat (gm): 3
Saturated fat (gm): 0.8
Cholesterol (mg): 0.1
Sodium (mg): 100
Protein (gm): 1.7
Carbohydrate (gm): 16.7
Exchanges
Milk: 0.0
Vegetable: 0.0
Fruit: 0.0
Bread: 1.0
Meat: 0.0
Fat: 0.5

1. Beat shortening and 6 tablespoons sugar in medium bowl until smooth. Beat in combined flour, baking powder, and salt alternately with 1/2 milk to form soft dough.

2. Roll dough on floured surface into a rectangle, a scant 1/2 inch thick. Cut dough into 18 trapezoid shapes, 2 1/2 inches long on the bottom, 1 1/2 inches on the top, and 3 inches on the sides. Cut out a small wedge of dough from the bottom, center of each piece to form "pants legs."

3. Lightly brush biscuits with remaining 2 tablespoons of milk. Mix the remaining 2 tablespoons of sugar with the cinnamon; sprinkle over biscuits.

4. Bake at 350 degrees on lightly greased cookie sheet until browned, 15 to 20 minutes. Serve warm.

VERY BERRY MUFFINS

These muffins can be made any time of year since they use frozen blueberries instead of fresh.

18 muffins (1 per serving)

2^1/$_2$ cups all-purpose flour
^{1}/$_2$ teaspoon baking soda
2 teaspoons baking powder
^{1}/$_4$ teaspoon salt
^{1}/$_2$ cup light brown sugar
1^1/$_2$ cups low-fat buttermilk
^{1}/$_4$ cup vegetable oil
1 egg, beaten
^{1}/$_2$ teaspoon lemon extract
1 teaspoon vanilla extract
^{1}/$_2$ teaspoon butter flakes
1 package (12 ounces) frozen, unsweetened blueberries
   Vegetable cooking spray

Per Serving
Calories: 137
% Calories from fat: 24
Fat (gm): 3.7
Saturated fat (gm): 0.6
Cholesterol (mg): 12.5
Sodium (mg): 151
Protein (gm): 2.9
Carbohydrate (gm): 22.7
Exchanges
Milk: 0.0
Vegetable: 0.0
Fruit: 0.0
Bread: 1.5
Meat: 0.0
Fat: 0.5

1. Preheat oven to 350 degrees. Combine flour, baking soda, baking powder, salt, and brown sugar in large bowl.

2. In a separate bowl, combine remaining ingredients, except blueberries and cooking spray; pour this mixture into a well made in the dry ingredients and mix until dry ingredients are just moistened; fold in blueberries. Spoon batter into 18 muffin cups coated with cooking spray, filling cups ^{3}/$_4$ full. Bake for 23 minutes or until muffins spring back when touched.

BOLILLOS

Bolillos are the crusty, "bobbin-shaped" yeast rolls that are popular throughout Mexico. The dough is similar to French bread dough.

12 servings (1 per serving)

1 package active dry yeast
1/2 teaspoon sugar
1 cup hot water (110-115 degrees)
2 tablespoons vegetable shortening,
   room temperature
3 1/2-4 cups all-purpose flour
1/2 teaspoon salt
2 tablespoons fat-free milk

Per Serving
Calories: 155
% Calories from fat: 15
Fat (gm): 2.5
Saturated fat (gm): 0.6
Cholesterol (mg): 0
Sodium (mg): 91
Protein (gm): 4.1
Carbohydrate (gm): 28.4
Exchanges
Milk: 0.0
Vegetable: 0.0
Fruit: 0.0
Bread: 2.0
Meat: 0.0
Fat: 0.5

1. Mix yeast, sugar, and hot-water in medium mixing bowl; add shortening, stirring until melted. Let stand 5 minutes. Mix in 3 1/2 cups of flour and the salt; mix in enough remaining flour to make soft dough.

2. Knead dough on floured surface until smooth and elastic, about 5 minutes. Place dough in greased bowl; let stand, covered, in warm place until dough is double in size, 1 to 1 1/2 hours. Punch dough down.

3. Divide dough into 12 equal pieces. Roll or pat 1 piece into an oval shape, a scant 1/2–inch thick. Fold 1/3 of the dough (long edge) toward the center and flatten with palm of hand; fold dough in half in same direction and flatten with palm of hand. Place, seam side up, on lightly greased cookie sheet. Repeat with remaining dough. Let rolls stand, loosely covered, until double in size, about 1 hour.

4. Brush tops of bolillos lightly with milk. Bake at 375 degrees until lightly browned, about 25 minutes.

APPLE HONEY KUCHEN

Use your favorite baking apple, tart or sweet, for this special brunch bread.

2 kuchen (16 servings each)

1	package active dry yeast
3/4	cup warm fat-free milk (110-115 degrees)
6	tablespoons granulated sugar, divided
4	tablespoons margarine, divided
1	egg
2-3	cups all-purpose flour
3/4	teaspoon salt
1	pound tart, *or* sweet, baking apples, peeled, sliced
1/2	cup raisins
1/4	cup light brown sugar
2	tablespoons grated orange rind
1/4	teaspoon ground cinnamon
1/8	teaspoon ground nutmeg
2-4	tablespoons honey
	Fat-free milk

Per Serving
Calories: 81
% Calories from fat: 19
Fat (gm): 1.8
Saturated fat (gm): 0.4
Cholesterol (mg): 6.8
Sodium (mg): 73
Protein (gm): 1.4
Carbohydrate (gm): 15.5
Exchanges
Milk: 0.0
Vegetable: 0.0
Fruit: 0.0
Bread: 1.0
Meat: 0.0
Fat: 0.5

1. Mix yeast, 3/4 cup milk, and 2 tablespoons granulated sugar in large bowl; let stand 5 minutes. Add 2 tablespoons margarine, egg, 2 cups flour, and salt, mixing until smooth. Mix in enough remaining 1 cup flour to make smooth dough.

2. Knead dough on floured surface until smooth and elastic, about 5 minutes. Place dough in greased bowl; let rise, covered, in warm place until double in size, 1 to 1 1/2 hours. Punch down dough.

3. Heat remaining 2 tablespoons margarine in large skillet until melted; add apples and cook over medium heat until apples are tender, 5 to 8 minutes. Stir in raisins; remove from heat. Mix brown sugar, orange rind, cinnamon, and nutmeg; sprinkle over apple mixture and toss.

4. Divide dough into 2 equal pieces. Roll each piece of dough on floured surface into 12-inch round. Arrange apple mixture on half of each round; drizzle each with 1 to 2 tablespoons honey. Brush edges of dough with milk; fold dough over filling and press edges with tines of fork to seal.

5. Transfer kuchen to greased cookie sheets; sprinkle with remaining 4 tablespoons granulated sugar. Let rise, loosely covered, until impression of finger remains in dough when touched, about 1 hour. Reseal edges of kuchen, if necessary. Bake kuchen at 375 degrees until golden, about 20 minutes. Slide onto wire racks to cool; serve warm.

CRANBERRY COFFEE CAKE

Quick and easy to make, this sweet-tart coffee cake can be ready to bake in less than 10 minutes.

1 coffee cake (8 servings)

1 1/2 cups fresh, *or* frozen, thawed, cranberries
1 cup sugar, divided
1 teaspoon grated orange rind
1 1/2 cups all-purpose flour
2 teaspoons baking powder
1/2 teaspoon salt
1 egg
1/4 cup orange juice
1/4 cup fat-free milk
3 tablespoons margarine, softened
1/4-1/2 cup chopped pecans

Per Serving
Calories: 135
% Calories from fat: 25
Fat (gm): 3.8
Saturated fat (gm): 0.6
Cholesterol (mg): 13.3
Sodium (mg): 139
Protein (gm): 2
Carbohydrate (gm): 23.9
Exchanges
Milk: 0.0
Vegetable: 0.0
Fruit: 0.0
Bread: 1.5
Meat: 0.0
Fat: 1.0

1. Arrange cranberries in greased 8-inch square baking pan; sprinkle with 1/2 cup sugar and the orange rind. Mix remaining ingredients until just moistened in medium bowl; drop by spoonfuls onto cranberries, spreading batter evenly to sides of pan.

2. Bake coffee cake at 400 degrees until wooden pick inserted in center comes out clean, 25 to 30 minutes. Immediately invert coffee cake onto serving plate. Serve warm.

PUMPKIN CINNAMON-SPICE MUFFINS

18 muffins (1 per serving)

1 1/2 cups all-purpose flour
1/2 cup whole wheat flour
1 1/2 teaspoons baking powder
1/2 teaspoon baking soda
1 1/2 teaspoons ground cinnamon
1/8 teaspoon ground cloves
1/2 teaspoon ground nutmeg
1/2 teaspoon allspice
3/4 cup brown sugar
1 cup canned pumpkin
1/4 cup liquid egg substitute
1/3 cup fat-free milk
1/4 cup corn oil
3 ounces frozen unsweetened orange
 juice concentrate, thawed
 Vegetable cooking spray

Per Serving
Calories: 99
% Calories from fat: 2
Fat (gm): 0.2
Saturated fat (gm): 0.1
Cholesterol (mg): 0
Sodium (mg): 87
Protein (gm): 2.2
Carbohydrate (gm): 22.6
Exchanges
Milk: 0.0
Vegetable: 0.0
Fruit: 0.0
Bread: 1.5
Meat: 0.0
Fat: 0.0

1. Preheat oven to 400 degrees. Sift together flours, baking powder, baking soda, cinnamon, cloves, nutmeg, and allspice into a large bowl; add brown sugar.

2. In a separate bowl, combine remaining ingredients, except cooking spray. Add wet ingredients to dry ingredients, stirring until just moistened. Spoon into 18 muffin cups coated with cooking spray; bake 14 minutes.

BLUEBERRY PANCAKES WITH BLUEBERRY SYRUP

For special occasions or just for fun, drizzle pancake batter into heart or other shapes in the skillet!

4 servings

3/4 cup fat-free milk

1 egg

1 tablespoon margarine, melted

3/4 cup all-purpose flour

1/4 cup whole wheat flour

1-2 tablespoons sugar

2 teaspoons baking powder

1/2 teaspoon salt

1/8 teaspoon ground nutmeg

3/4 cup fresh, *or* frozen, thawed, unsweetened blueberries

Blueberry Syrup (recipe follows) *or* sugar-free pancake syrup, warm

Per Serving
Calories: 221
% Calories from fat: 19
Fat (gm): 4.7
Saturated fat (gm): 1.1
Cholesterol (mg): 53.8
Sodium (mg): 654
Protein (gm): 6.9
Carbohydrate (gm): 39.6
Exchanges
Milk: 0.0
Vegetable: 0.0
Fruit: 0.5
Bread: 2.0
Meat: 0.0
Fat: 1.0

1. Mix milk, egg, and margarine in medium bowl; add remaining ingredients, except blueberries and Blueberry Syrup, and beat until almost smooth. Gently mix in blueberries.

2. Pour batter into lightly greased large skillet, using about 1/4 cup batter for each pancake. Cook over medium heat until bubbles form in pancakes and they are browned on the bottoms, 3 to 5 minutes. Turn pancakes; cook until browned on other side, 3 to 5 minutes.

3. Serve pancakes with Blueberry Syrup.

Blueberry Syrup

makes about 1 cup

> 1/2 cup sugar-free pancake syrup
> 1/2 cup fresh, *or* frozen, blueberries
> 1 teaspoon grated orange rind
> 1 teaspoon grated lemon rind

1. Heat all ingredients in small saucepan over medium-high heat until hot through, 3 to 5 minutes.

BUTTERMILK BUCKWHEAT PANCAKES

Whole wheat flour can be substituted for the buckwheat flour if you want.

4 servings

> 1 cup buttermilk
> 1 egg
> 1-2 tablespoons vegetable oil
> 1/2 cup all-purpose flour
> 1/2 cup buckwheat flour
> 1 tablespoon sugar
> 1 teaspoon baking powder
> 1/2 teaspoon baking soda
> 1/2 teaspoon salt
> 1 teaspoon grated orange rind
> 1/2-1 cup sugar-free pancake syrup, *or* Blueberry Syrup (see above), warm

Per Serving
Calories: 204
% Calories from fat: 25
Fat (gm): 5.8
Saturated fat (gm): 1.3
Cholesterol (mg): 55.1
Sodium (mg): 695
Protein (gm): 7.1
Carbohydrate (gm): 32.6
Exchanges
Milk: 0.0
Vegetable: 0.0
Fruit: 0.0
Bread: 2.0
Meat: 0.0
Fat: 1.0

1. Mix buttermilk, egg, and oil in medium bowl; add remaining ingredients, except syrup, and beat until almost smooth.

2. Pour batter into lightly greased large skillet, using about 1/4 cup batter for each pancake. Cook over medium heat until bubbles form in pancakes and they are browned on the bottoms, 3 to 5 minutes. Turn pancakes; cook until browned on other side, 3 to 5 minutes.

3. Serve pancakes with warm syrup.

CREPES

These thin French pancakes can be made ahead. Just cool, stack between layers of waxed paper or plastic wrap, and refrigerate or freeze. Double or triple the recipe if desired.

4 servings

1/2 cup all-purpose flour
1/2 cup fat-free milk
  1 egg
  2 egg whites
  1 tablespoon margarine, melted
  2 tablespoons sugar
1/4 teaspoon salt
    Vegetable cooking spray

Per Serving
Calories: 144
% Calories from fat: 27
Fat (gm): 4.3
Saturated fat (gm): 1
Cholesterol (mg): 53.6
Sodium (mg): 238
Protein (gm): 6
Carbohydrate (gm): 20
Exchanges
Milk: 0.0
Vegetable: 0.0
Fruit: 0.0
Bread: 1.5
Meat: 0.0
Fat: 1.0

1. Combine all ingredients, except cooking spray, in small bowl; beat until smooth (batter will be thin).

2. Spray 8-inch crepe pan or small skillet with cooking spray; heat over medium heat until hot. Pour scant 1/4 cup batter into pan, tilting to coat bottom evenly with batter.

3. Cook over medium heat until browned on the bottom, 2 to 3 minutes. Turn crepe and cook until browned on the other side, 2 to 3 minutes. Repeat with remaining batter.

SWEET-STUFFED FRENCH TOAST

A rich breakfast entrée with a sweet surprise inside! Serve with warm maple syrup or a drizzle of honey.

4 servings

  3 eggs *or* 3/4 cup no-cholesterol real egg product
1/3 cup fat-free milk
  1 teaspoon ground cinnamon
1/4 teaspoon ground nutmeg
  4 thick (1 inch) slices sourdough, *or* Italian, bread
  4 tablespoons fat-free cream cheese

Per Serving
Calories: 207
% Calories from fat: 32
Fat (gm): 7.7
Saturated fat (gm): 2.1
Cholesterol (mg): 160.6
Sodium (mg): 410
Protein (gm): 9.8
Carbohydrate (gm): 26.2
Exchanges
Milk: 0.0
Vegetable: 0.0
Fruit: 0.0
Bread: 2.0
Meat: 0.0
Fat: 1.5

4 teaspoons strawberry, *or* other flavor,
sugar-free spreadable fruit

1-2 tablespoons margarine

1 cup sugar-free pancake syrup, warm

1. Combine eggs, milk, and spices in shallow bowl.

2. Cut a pocket in the side of each bread slice, cutting to center of bread. Fill with cream cheese and spreadable fruit. Dip bread in egg mixture, turning to generously coat both sides.

3. Cook bread in margarine in large skillet on low to medium-low heat until browned, about 5 minutes on each side. Serve with warm syrup.

FRUITY APPLE-PEAR BUTTER

Use ripe pears that are still firm for this gently spiced spread.

36 servings (2 tablespoons each)

1 pound firm, ripe pears, peeled, cored, chopped

1 pound Rome apples, peeled, cored, chopped

1 can (12 ounces) frozen apple juice concentrate

1 tablespoon lemon juice

1 teaspoon orange peel, finely shredded

1/4 teaspoon ground ginger

1/4 teaspoon ground cinnamon

Per Serving
Calories: 31
% Calories from fat: **3**
Fat (gm): 0.1
Saturated fat (gm): 0
Cholesterol (mg): 0
Sodium (mg): 2
Protein (gm): 0.1
Carbohydrate (gm): 7.8
Exchanges
Milk: 0.0
Vegetable: 0.0
Fruit: 0.5
Bread: 0.0
Meat: 0.0
Fat: 0.0

1. Preheat oven to 300 degrees. Combine pears, apples, and apple juice concentrate in a large saucepan and heat to boiling. Reduce heat and simmer, covered, about 20 minutes or until pears and apples are tender. Process pear-apple mix in food processor until smooth, in batches if necessary.

2. Pour into a 9-inch baking pan; add remaining ingredients. Bake for 2 to 2 1/2 hours, stirring every half hour, until thick enough to mound on a spoon.

3. Serve warm or cold on biscuits or toast. Can also be used in recipes as a substitute for sugar.

SPICED RHUBARB JAM

Cook this jam to desired consistency, as it is not made with pectin.

2 pints

1½ pounds rhubarb, cut into 1- to 2-inch pieces (about 6 cups)

2 cups Splenda

1 cup water

2 inch piece of gingerroot, cut lengthwise in half

1 cinnamon stick

¼ teaspoon ground cardamom

Per Serving
Calories: 5
% Calories from fat: 4
Fat (gm): 0
Saturated fat (gm): 0
Cholesterol (mg): 0
Sodium (mg): 1
Protein (gm): 0.1
Carbohydrate (gm): 1.2
Exchanges
Milk: 0.0
Vegetable: 0.0
Fruit: 0.0
Bread: 0.0
Meat: 0.0
Fat: 0.0

1. Combine rhubarb, Splenda, and water in large saucepan; heat to boiling. Reduce heat and simmer, covered, until rhubarb is tender, about 10 minutes. Strain rhubarb, reserving juice.

2. Return juice to saucepan; add gingerroot, cinnamon, and cardamom and heat to boiling. Simmer rapidly, stirring occasionally, until very thick, 10 to 15 minutes. Discard cinnamon stick and gingerroot.

3. Stir rhubarb into juice mixture; simmer longer, if necessary to achieve desired thickness, stirring constantly to prevent sticking and burning.

4. Pour jam into sterilized pint jars and seal; cool. Store in refrigerator up to 2 weeks.

ORANGE-ROSEMARY JELLY

A subtle herb-flavored jelly that's especially wonderful with biscuits.

2 pints

1 cup boiling water

2 tablespoons rosemary leaves, crushed

1 can (6 ounces) frozen orange juice concentrate

1 package (1³/₄ ounces) powdered fruit pectin

¹/₄ cup lemon juice

1 tablespoon white distilled vinegar

Pinch salt

1 drop red food color, optional

3¹/₃ cups Splenda

Per Serving
Calories: 12
% Calories from fat: 1
Fat (gm): 0
Saturated fat (gm): 0
Cholesterol (mg): 0
Sodium (mg): 1
Protein (gm): 0.1
Carbohydrate (gm): 3
Exchanges
Milk: 0.0
Vegetable: 0.0
Fruit: 0.0
Bread: 0.0
Meat: 0.0
Fat: 0.0

1. Pour boiling water over rosemary in small bowl; let stand until cool. Strain; discard rosemary. Combine rosemary water and orange juice concentrate in 2-cup measure; add water to measure 2 cups.

2. Combine orange juice mixture and remaining ingredients, except sugar, in large saucepan; heat to boiling. Stir in Splenda and return to boiling, stirring constantly. Boil hard 1 minute, stirring constantly.

3. Pour jelly into sterilized pint jars and seal; cool. Store in refrigerator 2 to 3 weeks.

CINNAMON-RAISIN CREAM CHEESE

10 servings (1 tablespoon each)

4 ounces light cream cheese, softened
2 tablespoons chopped raisins
1 tablespoon brown sugar
1/4 teaspoon cinnamon
2 teaspoons fat-free milk

Per Serving
Calories: 37
% Calories from fat: 45
Fat (gm): 1.8
Saturated fat (gm): 1.2
Cholesterol (mg): 5.3
Sodium (mg): 54
Protein (gm): 1.2
Carbohydrate (gm): 3.8
Exchanges
Milk: 0.0
Vegetable: 0.0
Fruit: 0.0
Bread: 0.0
Meat: 0.0
Fat: 0.5

1. Combine all ingredients, except milk, in small bowl. Add enough milk to make the mixture spreadable. Cover and refrigerate to store.

ROSE GERANIUM JELLY

Simply delicious, and perfect for gift giving. Serve with plain crackers, biscuits, or bread.

2 pints

1 cup boiling water
1/2 cup packed torn rose geranium leaves
1 can (6 ounces) unsweetened frozen apple juice concentrate
1 package (1³/4 ounces) powdered fruit pectin
2-3 tablespoons lemon juice
1 tablespoon white distilled vinegar
Pinch salt
3¹/2 cups Splenda

Per Serving
Calories: 15
% Calories from fat: 0
Fat (gm): 0
Saturated fat (gm): 0
Cholesterol (mg): 0
Sodium (mg): 2
Protein (gm): 0
Carbohydrate (gm): 3.6
Exchanges
Milk: 0.0
Vegetable: 0.0
Fruit: 0.0
Bread: 0.0
Meat: 0.0
Fat: 0.0

1. Pour boiling water over rose geranium leaves in small bowl; let stand until cool. Strain; discard rose geranium leaves. Combine rose geranium water and apple juice in 2-cup measure; add water to measure 2 cups.

2. Combine apple juice mixture and remaining ingredients, except sugar, in large saucepan; heat to boiling. Stir in Splenda and return to boiling, stirring constantly. Boil hard 1 minute, stirring constantly.

3. Pour jelly into sterilized pint jars and seal; cool. Store in refrigerator 2 to 3 weeks.

Variation: **Apple-Mint Jelly**—Make recipe as above, substituting 1/2 cup loosely packed mint leaves, or 3 tablespoons dried mint leaves, for the rose geranium leaves.

CRAN-RAISIN CHUTNEY

40 servings (1 tablespoon each)

1   can (10 ounces) whole cranberries
    Peel of 1 lemon
1/4 cup raisins
1   teaspoon grated ginger
1   teaspoon dry mustard
1   tart green apple, peeled, cored, diced
1   onion, chopped
1/2 red, green, *or* yellow bell pepper, chopped
1/2 cup apple cider vinegar
1/4 cup brown sugar
1/2 teaspoon salt
1   clove garlic, minced

Per Serving
Calories: 24
% Calories from fat: 2
Fat (gm): 0
Saturated fat (gm): 0
Cholesterol (mg): 0
Sodium (mg): 34
Protein (gm): 0.1
Carbohydrate (gm): 6
Exchanges
Milk: 0.0
Vegetable: 0.0
Fruit: 0.5
Bread: 0.0
Meat: 0.0
Fat: 0.0

1. Combine all ingredients in a saucepan; simmer, stirring frequently, until mixture thickens, about 1 hour. Cool and store in refrigerator until ready to serve.

CINNAMON-APPLE-PRUNE JELLY

The perfect breakfast treat for muffins and bagels.

64 servings (1 tablespoon each)

4 large Granny Smith apples, peeled, cored, sliced
1 package (12 ounces) pitted prunes
1 cup unsweetened apple juice
1¹/₂ teaspoons cinnamon
¹/₂ teaspoon allspice
¹/₂ teaspoon lemon juice

Per Serving
Calories: 20
% Calories from fat: 3
Fat (gm): 0.1
Saturated fat (gm): 0
Cholesterol (mg): 0
Sodium (mg): 0
Protein (gm): 0.2
Carbohydrate (gm): 5.2
Exchanges
Milk: 0.0
Vegetable: 0.0
Fruit: 0.0
Bread: 0.0
Meat: 0.0
Fat: 0.0

1. Combine all ingredients, except lemon juice, in large saucepan and heat to boiling. Reduce heat and simmer, covered, 10 minutes. Simmer, uncovered, 15 minutes longer or until most of liquid is absorbed and fruit is tender. Remove from heat and add lemon juice. Beat with electric mixer on high speed until smooth.

2. Serve warm or transfer to storage container, cover, and store in refrigerator. Will keep for about 3 weeks.

FIFTEEN

Sandwiches, Snacks

AND

Beverages

GORP, BY GOLLY!

The right kind of snack mix for curing the munchies, or for sharing with a gathering of friends.

16 servings (about ¹/2 cup each)

3 cups low-fat granola
2 cups pretzel goldfish
¹/2 cup sesame sticks, broken into halves
3 cups coarsely chopped mixed dried fruit
Butter-flavored vegetable cooking spray
1 teaspoon ground cinnamon
¹/2 teaspoon ground nutmeg
¹/4 teaspoon ground allspice

Per Serving
Calories: 172
% Calories from fat: 13
Fat (gm): 2.6
Saturated fat (gm): 0.2
Cholesterol (mg): 0
Sodium (mg): 82
Protein (gm): 2.7
Carbohydrate (gm): 37.8
Exchanges
Milk: 0.0
Vegetable: 0.0
Fruit: 2.0
Bread: 0.5
Meat: 0.0
Fat: 0.5

1. Mix granola, pretzel goldfish, sesame sticks, and dried fruit on large jelly roll pan. Spray mixture generously with cooking spray; sprinkle with combined spices and toss to coat.
2. Bake at 350 degrees 15 to 20 minutes, stirring after 10 minutes. Cool; store in covered container at room temperature.

HOT STUFF!

And if this snack mix is not hot enough for you, add a few sprinkles of red pepper sauce! Use 2 cups purchased plain pita chips, or make your own.

16 servings (¹/2 cup each)

2 cups oyster crackers
Pita Chips (see p. 652)
¹/2 cup dry-roasted smoked almonds
1 cup coarsely chopped mixed dried fruit
1 cup dried pineapple chunks
Butter-flavored vegetable cooking spray
1 teaspoon dried oregano leaves
1 teaspoon garlic powder
1 teaspoon chili powder
1-1¹/4 teaspoons cayenne pepper
1-1¹/4 teaspoons black pepper

Per Serving
Calories: 120
% Calories from fat: 22
Fat (gm): 3.2
Saturated fat (gm): 0.2
Cholesterol (mg): 0
Sodium (mg): 160
Protein (gm): 3.2
Carbohydrate (gm): 21.7
Exchanges
Milk: 0.0
Vegetable: 0.0
Fruit: 0.5
Bread: 1.0
Meat: 0.0
Fat: 0.5

1. Mix crackers, Pita Chips, almonds, and fruit on large jelly roll pan. Spray mixture generously with cooking spray; sprinkle with combined herbs and peppers and toss to coat.

2. Bake at 350 degrees 15 to 20 minutes, stirring after 10 minutes. Cool; store in covered container at room temperature.

CHILI BANZOS

These highly spiced crisp snackers are great tasting and good for you too!

8 servings (¼ cup each)

2 cans (15 ounces each) garbanzo beans
Olive oil cooking spray
1 tablespoon reduced-sodium Worcestershire sauce
1-2 teaspoons chili powder
1-2 teaspoons garlic powder
1-2 teaspoons onion powder
1 teaspoon paprika
2-3 dashes hot pepper sauce
Salt, to taste

Per Serving
Calories: 109
% Calories from fat: 16
Fat (gm): 2.0
Saturated fat (gm): 0.3
Cholesterol (mg): 0
Sodium (mg): 440
Protein (gm): 5.1
Carbohydrate (gm): 18.5
Exchanges
Milk: 0.0
Vegetable: 0.0
Fruit: 0.0
Bread: 1.5
Meat: 0.0
Fat: 0.0

1. Rinse beans, drain, and dry well on paper toweling. Arrange beans in large skillet; spray generously with cooking spray. Cook over medium heat, stirring frequently, until beans begin to brown, about 10 minutes. Remove from heat.

2. Combine Worcestershire sauce, spices, and hot pepper sauce; pour over beans and stir to coat evenly. Sprinkle lightly with salt.

3. Transfer beans to jelly roll pan; bake at 325 degrees until beans are very crisp on the outside, 20 to 25 minutes, stirring twice. Cool; store in airtight container.

VEGGIE CRISPS

So delicious and colorful, with intense vegetable flavors! Cut veggies as thinly as you can to ensure even cooking for crispness. And be sure they are completely dried; if slightly moist inside, spoilage can develop.

8 servings (about ½ cup each)

2 pounds assorted vegetables (sweet potatoes, russet potatoes, large radishes, butternut squash, large carrots, turnips, parsnips, rutabaga, beets)
Salt, to taste
Vegetable cooking spray

Per Serving
Calories: 87
% Calories from fat: 1
Fat (gm): 0.2
Saturated fat (gm): 0.1
Cholesterol (mg): 0
Sodium (mg): 22
Protein (gm): 1.8
Carbohydrate (gm): 20
Exchanges
Milk: 0.0
Vegetable: 0.5
Fruit: 0.0
Bread: 1.0
Meat: 0.0
Fat: 0.0

1. Peel vegetables and slice very thinly, about ¹/₁₆ inch thick. Sprinkle vegetable slices lightly and evenly with salt. Let stand 20 to 30 minutes, allowing vegetables to release moisture. Rinse well in cold water and dry completely on paper toweling.

2. To dry vegetables in the microwave, arrange slices in single layer on large microwave-safe plate sprayed with cooking spray. Spray vegetables lightly with cooking spray. Microwave on high power until vegetables are dried, 5 to 7 minutes, checking and rearranging after 4 or 5 minutes and removing vegetables as they dry. The vegetables will become crisper as they cool.

3. To dry vegetables in the oven, arrange slices in single layer on jelly roll pan sprayed with cooking spray. Spray vegetables lightly with cooking spray. Bake at 275 degrees for 40 to 50 minutes, checking occasionally and removing vegetables as they dry. The vegetables will become crisper as they cool.

4. Store cooled chips in airtight container at room temperature.

Note: Different kinds of vegetables cook in different times, so it is important to check for doneness frequently. In microwave cooking it is better to cook 1 kind of vegetable at a time.

FRUIT NUGGETS

Bite-size and perfect for high-energy snacking or for a sweet ending to a meal.

36 nuggets (1 per serving)

2 cups finely ground low-fat graham crackers

1/2 cup finely ground gingersnaps *or* low-fat graham crackers

1/2 teaspoon ground cinnamon

1/2 teaspoon ground nutmeg

1/4 teaspoon ground ginger

1/2 cup dried apples

1/2 cup dried apricots

1/2 cup pitted dates

1/2 cup golden raisins

1/2 cup orange juice

2-3 tablespoons honey

3 tablespoons sugar

Per Serving
Calories: 57
% Calories from fat: 8
Fat (gm): 0.5
Saturated fat (gm): 0.1
Cholesterol (mg): 0
Sodium (mg): 29
Protein (gm): 0.8
Carbohydrate (gm): 12.8
Exchanges
Milk: 0.0
Vegetable: 0.0
Fruit: 0.5
Bread: 0.5
Meat: 0.0
Fat: 0.0

1. Combine graham cracker and gingersnap crumbs and spices in medium bowl. Finely chop fruit in food processor, using pulse technique, or by hand; add to crumb mixture.

2. Add orange juice and honey to fruit mixture, stirring until mixture holds together. Roll into 36 balls, about 1 inch in diameter.

3. Measure 1 tablespoon sugar into large plastic bag; add 1 dozen nuggets and shake to coat with sugar. Repeat with remaining sugar and nuggets. Store in covered container at room temperature.

TOASTED ONION DIP

Remember the popular onion dip made with packaged soup mix? This dip will bring back memories! Toasting the dried onion flakes is the flavor secret.

12 servings (generous 2 tablespoons each)

3-4	tablespoons dried onion flakes
1	package (8 ounces) fat-free cream cheese
1/3	cup plain reduced-fat yogurt
1/3	cup fat-free mayonnaise
2	small green onions and tops, chopped
2	cloves garlic, minced
1/4	teaspoon crushed beef bouillon cube
2-3	tablespoons fat-free milk
1/2-1	teaspoon lemon juice
2-3	drops hot pepper sauce
	Salt and white pepper, to taste
	Assorted vegetable relishes and bread sticks, as dippers (not included in nutritional data)

Per Serving
Calories: 32
% Calories from fat: 4
Fat (gm): 0.1
Saturated fat (gm): 0.1
Cholesterol (mg): 0.4
Sodium (mg): 223
Protein (gm): 3.3
Carbohydrate (gm): 3.9
Exchanges
Milk: 0.0
Vegetable: 0.0
Fruit: 0.0
Bread: 0.0
Meat: 0.5
Fat: 0.0

1. Cook onion flakes in small skillet over medium to medium-low heat until toasted, 3 to 4 minutes, stirring frequently. Cool.

2. Mix cream cheese, yogurt, mayonnaise, green onions, garlic, and bouillon in medium bowl until smooth, adding enough milk to make desired dipping consistency. Season to taste with lemon juice, pepper sauce, salt, and white pepper.

3. Spoon dip into serving bowl; serve with vegetable relishes and bread sticks.

BLACK BEAN HUMMUS

Tahini, a ground sesame paste, and soy sauce season this unusual bean dip.

6 servings (about ¹/₄ cup each)

> 1 can (15 ounces) black beans, rinsed, drained
> ¹/₄ cup vegetable broth *or* water
> 2-4 tablespoons tahini (sesame seed paste)
> 3 cloves garlic
> 2-2¹/₂ tablespoons lemon juice
> 1¹/₂ tablespoons soy sauce
> Salt and cayenne pepper, to taste
> Pita Chips (see p. 652) *or* pita breads, cut into wedges for dippers

Per Serving
Calories: 100
% Calories from fat: 30
Fat (gm): 4
Saturated fat (gm): 0
Cholesterol (mg): 0
Sodium (mg): 480
Protein (gm): 7.6
Carbohydrate (gm): 13.9
Exchanges
Milk: 0.0
Vegetable: 0.0
Fruit: 0.0
Bread: 1.0
Meat: 0.0
Fat: 0.5

1. Process beans, broth, tahini, garlic, lemon juice, and soy sauce in food processor until smooth; season to taste with salt and cayenne pepper. Refrigerate 1 to 2 hours for flavors to blend.

2. Spoon hummus into serving bowl; serve with Pita Chips.

SLOPPY JOES

Toasted buns are a must for this sweet-sour beef filling.

4 servings

1 pound ground beef eye of round steak *or* 95% lean ground beef

$^1/_2$ cup chopped onion

$^1/_2$ cup finely chopped celery

$^1/_2$ cup finely chopped red, *or* green, bell pepper

2 cloves garlic, minced

1 cup reduced-sodium catsup

$^1/_2$ cup water

2 tablespoons prepared mustard

1 tablespoon cider vinegar

2 teaspoons packed light brown sugar

Salt and pepper, to taste

4 hamburger buns, toasted

Per Serving
Calories: 385
% Calories from fat: 17
Fat (gm): 7.4
Saturated fat (gm): 2.2
Cholesterol (mg): 64
Sodium (mg): 423
Protein (gm): 32.5
Carbohydrate (gm): 48.2
Exchanges
Milk: 0.0
Vegetable: 2.0
Fruit: 0.0
Bread: 2.0
Meat: 3.5
Fat: 0.0

1. Cook ground beef, onion, celery, bell pepper, and garlic in medium skillet over medium heat until beef is browned and vegetables tender, about 10 minutes.

2. Stir in catsup, water, mustard, vinegar, and brown sugar; heat to boiling. Reduce heat and simmer, uncovered, until mixture is thickened, about 5 minutes. Season to taste with salt and pepper. Spoon into toasted buns.

Variation: **Baked Sloppy Potatoes**—Instead of buns, use 4 large baked potatoes. Loosen the potato flesh with a fork; spoon meat filling over.

CHEESEBURGERS SUPREME

Top these moist burgers with your choice of catsup, mustard, raw or sauteed onions, sauteed mushrooms, or chopped olives, and serve with plenty of dill pickles and Crispy Fries (see p. 600).

4 servings

1	pound ground beef eye of round steak *or* 95% lean ground beef
2-4	tablespoons finely chopped onion
3	tablespoons water
1/2	teaspoon salt
1/4	teaspoon pepper
	Vegetable cooking spray
4	slices (1 ounce each) fat-free, *or* reduced-fat, Cheddar, *or* Swiss, cheese
4	hamburger buns, toasted

Per Serving
Calories: 326
% Calories from fat: 19
Fat (gm): 6.7
Saturated fat (gm): 2.2
Cholesterol (mg): 64
Sodium (mg): 768
Protein (gm): 39.5
Carbohydrate (gm): 24.1
Exchanges
Milk: 0.0
Vegetable: 0.0
Fruit: 0.0
Bread: 1.5
Meat: 4.0
Fat: 0.0

1. Mix ground beef, onion, water, salt, and pepper in medium bowl just until blended. Shape mixture into four 1-inch-thick patties.

2. Spray skillet with cooking spray; heat over medium heat until hot. Cook burgers to desired degree of doneness, 3 to 4 minutes per side for medium. Top each burger with slice of cheese; cover skillet and cook until cheese is beginning to melt, 1 to 2 minutes. Serve burgers in buns.

COUNTRY EGG AND GREEN ONION SANDWICH

A simple, unsophisticated sandwich that is super quick to make and re-markably satisfying. Use the best coarse-grained bread you can find, and the freshest eggs.

2 servings

Butter-flavored vegetable cooking spray
4 slices coarse-grained, *or* homemade, whole wheat bread
2 large eggs
Salt and pepper, to taste
1 tablespoon chili sauce
2 green onions and tops, sliced

Per Serving
Calories: 215
% Calories from fat: 29
Fat (gm): 7.1
Saturated fat (gm): 2
Cholesterol (mg): 212
Sodium (mg): 442
Protein (gm): 11.1
Carbohydrate (gm): 26.8
Exchanges
Milk: 0.0
Vegetable: 0.0
Fruit: 0.0
Bread: 2.0
Meat: 1.0
Fat: 0.5

1. Spray small skillet with cooking spray; heat over medium heat until hot. Cook bread slices until toasted on both sides; re-move from skillet. Add eggs to skillet and cook, covered, over low heat until white is set and yolk still somewhat runny. Sprin-kle lightly with salt and pepper.

2. Spread 2 slices of bread with chili sauce; top with eggs, green onions, and remaining bread slices.

TUNA PAN BAGNA

This Mediterranean specialty consists of tuna tossed with a savory dress-ing and spooned onto French bread halves. The bread absorbs the season-ing, giving the sandwich its name, literally, bathed bread.

4 servings

2 cans (6 ounces each) no-salt, oil-packed solid white tuna
1/2 cup chopped roasted red peppers
1 1/2 tablespoons capers
2 tablespoons balsamic, *or* red wine, vinegar
2 tablespoons chopped fresh chives *or* green onions

Per Serving
Calories: 443
% Calories from fat: 20
Fat (gm): 9.7
Saturated fat (gm): 1.9
Cholesterol (mg): 15.3
Sodium (mg): 802
Protein (gm): 33
Carbohydrate (gm): 52.5
Exchanges
Milk: 0.0
Vegetable: 2.0
Fruit: 0.0
Bread: 3.0
Meat: 3.0
Fat: 0.0

1 loaf (12 ounces) French bread, halved
   horizontally
4 leaves romaine lettuce
1 tomato, sliced
2 slices red onion
2-4 pepperoncini

1. Drain tuna, reserving 3 tablespoons oil. Combine tuna, peppers, capers, reserved oil, vinegar, and chives in medium bowl, stirring well to mix thoroughly. Spread tuna mixture over bottom half of bread. Cover with lettuce, tomato, onion, pepperoncini, and top half of bread.

2. Wrap sandwich tightly in plastic wrap, pressing to compact sandwich. Refrigerate at least 10 minutes, or up to 8 hours, to allow flavors to blend.

EGGPLANT PARMESAN SANDWICHES

Thick-sliced eggplant, breaded and sauteed, topped with roasted red peppers, and served in buns with a flavorful tomato sauce. Purchased sauce can be substituted.

4 servings

4 thick slices eggplant (scant $^3/_4$ inch
   thick)
$^1/_4$ cup no-cholesterol real egg product
$^1/_3$ cup seasoned dry bread crumbs
2 tablespoons grated fat-free Parmesan
   cheese
   Vegetable cooking spray
4 ounces sliced fat-free mozzarella cheese
2 roasted red peppers, cut into halves
4 French rolls *or* Hoagie buns, toasted
   Easy Tomato Sauce (recipe follows)

Per Serving
Calories: 262
% Calories from fat: 8
Fat (gm): 2.2
Saturated fat (gm): 0.5
Cholesterol (mg): 0
Sodium (mg): 765
Protein (gm): 19.4
Carbohydrate (gm): 42.1
Exchanges
Milk: 0.0
Vegetable: 3.0
Fruit: 0.0
Bread: 2.0
Meat: 1.0
Fat: 0.0

1. Dip eggplant slices in egg product and coat generously with combined bread crumbs and Parmesan cheese.

2. Spray large skillet with cooking spray; heat over medium heat until hot. Cook eggplant slices over medium heat until browned on the bottoms, about 5 minutes. Spray eggplant slices generously with cooking spray and turn. Cook over medium heat until eggplant slices are tender and browned on other side, about 5 minutes. Top each eggplant slice with 1 ounce mozzarella cheese; cook, covered, until cheese is melted, 2 to 3 minutes.

3. Place red peppers on bottoms of rolls; top with eggplant, Easy Tomato Sauce, and roll tops.

Easy Tomato Sauce

makes about 1 cup

> Olive oil cooking spray
> 1 small onion, chopped
> 1/4 cup chopped green bell pepper
> 2 cloves garlic, minced
> 1 can (8 ounces) reduced-sodium tomato sauce
> 1/2 teaspoon dried basil leaves
> 1/4 teaspoon dried oregano leaves
> Salt and pepper, to taste

1. Spray medium saucepan with cooking spray; heat over medium heat until hot. Saute onion, bell pepper, and garlic until tender, about 5 minutes.

2. Stir in tomato sauce and herbs; heat to boiling. Reduce heat and simmer, uncovered, until sauce thickens, about 5 minutes. Season to taste with salt and pepper.

HERBED VEGGIE BURGERS

These fabulous meatless burgers can star in any meal.

4 servings

Vegetable cooking spray
³/4 cup finely chopped broccoflower florets
³/4 cup finely chopped mushrooms
¹/4 cup finely chopped onion
2 cloves garlic
1¹/2 teaspoons dried basil leaves, divided
¹/2 teaspoon dried marjoram leaves
¹/4 teaspoon dried thyme leaves
²/3 cup cooked wild, *or* brown, rice
¹/3 cup quick-cooking oats
¹/3 cup coarsely chopped toasted walnuts
¹/2 cup 1% low-fat cottage cheese
¹/2 cup (2 ounces) fat-free Cheddar cheese
Salt and pepper, to taste
2 egg whites
¹/2 cup fat-free mayonnaise
4 multi-grain, *or* whole wheat, buns, toasted
Lettuce leaves, as garnish

Per Serving
Calories: 322
% Calories from fat: 26
Fat (gm): 9.5
Saturated fat (gm): 1.3
Cholesterol (mg): 1.3
Sodium (mg): 828
Protein (gm): 19.7
Carbohydrate (gm): 42
Exchanges
Milk: 0.0
Vegetable: 2.0
Fruit: 0.0
Bread: 2.0
Meat: 1.5
Fat: 1.7

1. Spray medium skillet with cooking spray; heat over medium heat until hot. Saute broccoflower, mushrooms, onion, and garlic until tender, 8 to 10 minutes. Add ¹/2 teaspoon basil, marjoram, and thyme and cook 1 to 2 minutes longer. Remove from heat and cool slightly.

2. Stir rice, oats, walnuts, and cheeses into vegetable mixture; season to taste with salt and pepper. Stir in egg whites. Form mixture into 4 burgers.

3. Spray large skillet with cooking spray; heat over medium heat until hot. Add burgers and cook over medium to medium-low heat until browned on the bottoms, 3 to 4 minutes. Spray tops of burgers with cooking spray and turn; cook until browned, 3 to 4 minutes.

4. Mix mayonnaise and remaining 1 teaspoon basil; spread on bottoms of buns and top with lettuce, burgers, and bun tops.

FALAFEL BURGERS WITH TAHINI DRESSING

The falafel mixture can also be shaped into "meatballs," if preferred. Coat lightly with dry unseasoned bread crumbs and place in baking pan. Spray generously with cooking spray; bake at 375 degrees until browned, about 15 minutes.

4 servings

1½ cups cooked garbanzo beans *or* 1 can (15 ounces) rinsed, drained garbanzo beans, coarsely pureed

¼ cup loosely packed parsley leaves, finely chopped

2 tablespoons chopped green onions and tops

2 cloves garlic, minced

1-2 tablespoons lemon juice

¼ cup all-purpose flour

1¼ teaspoons ground cumin

Salt and pepper, to taste

Olive oil cooking spray

2 pita breads, cut into halves

Tahini Dressing (recipe follows)

¼ cup chopped tomato

¼ cup chopped cucumber

¼ cup thinly sliced green onions and tops

Per Serving
Calories: 291
% Calories from fat: 23
Fat (gm): 7.6
Saturated fat (gm): 0.3
Cholesterol (mg): 0.3
Sodium (mg): 194
Protein (gm): 13.2
Carbohydrate (gm): 45.0
Exchanges
Milk: 0.0
Vegetable: 2.0
Fruit: 0.0
Bread: 2.5
Meat: 0.5
Fat: 1.0

1. Mix garbanzo beans, parsley, chopped green onions, garlic, lemon juice, flour, and cumin in bowl; season to taste with salt and pepper. Shape mixture into 4 burgers.

2. Spray large skillet with cooking spray; heat over medium heat until hot. Cook burgers until browned on the bottoms, 3 to 4 minutes. Spray tops of burgers with cooking spray; turn and cook until browned on other side, 3 to 4 minutes.

3. Arrange burgers in pita breads; drizzle scant 2 tablespoons Tahini Dressing over each burger. Spoon combined tomato, cucumber, and sliced green onions into pitas.

Tahini Dressing

makes about 1/2 cup

    1/3 cup plain fat-free yogurt
    2-3 tablespoons tahini (sesame seed paste)
      1 small clove garlic, minced
  1/2-1 teaspoon lemon juice

1. Combine all ingredients; refrigerate until ready to use.

BARBECUE VEGETABLE PITA ROUNDS

4 servings

      1 tablespoon vegetable oil
      1 large onion, thinly sliced into rings
      1 green bell pepper, julienned
      3 cups sliced fresh mushrooms
      1 zucchini, sliced into 3-inch strips
    1/2 cup barbecue sauce
      4 pita breads, halved, warmed
      1 cup shredded reduced-fat Monterey
         Jack cheese

Per Serving
Calories: 343
% Calories from fat: 28
Fat (gm): 11
Saturated fat (gm): 4.4
Cholesterol (mg): 20.3
Sodium (mg): 822
Protein (gm): 18.1
Carbohydrate (gm): 47.2
Exchanges
Milk: 0.0
Vegetable: 3.0
Fruit: 0.0
Bread: 2.0
Meat: 1.0
Fat: 1.5

1. Heat vegetable oil in large skillet over medium heat until hot. Saute onion and pepper in skillet for 3 minutes, until onion is tender; add mushrooms and zucchini and saute for an additional 3 minutes. Stir in barbecue sauce and cook until heated through, about 5 minutes. Distribute vegetable mixture evenly in pita pockets. Sprinkle cheese on top.

CRAB MELT

Canned tuna, boiled shrimp, or surimi (imitation crabmeat) can be used in place of the crab.

2 servings

- 4 ounces cooked crabmeat, flaked
- 2 tablespoons chopped red bell pepper
- 1 medium green onion and top, thinly sliced
- 2 tablespoons fat-free mayonnaise
- 2 tablespoons fat-free sour cream
- 1/4-1/2 teaspoon dried dill weed
- 1-2 teaspoons lemon juice
  Salt and pepper, to taste
- 2 slices white, *or* whole wheat, bread
- 2 slices (3/4 ounce each) fat-free American cheese

Per Serving
Calories: 182
% Calories from fat: 10
Fat (gm): 2
Saturated fat (gm): 0.3
Cholesterol (mg): 56.7
Sodium (mg): 786
Protein (gm): 19.9
Carbohydrate (gm): 20.4
Exchanges
Milk: 0.0
Vegetable: 0.0
Fruit: 0.0
Bread: 1.0
Meat: 2.0
Fat: 0.0

1. Mix crabmeat, red bell pepper, green onion, mayonnaise, sour cream, and dill weed in small bowl; season to taste with lemon juice, salt, and pepper. Spread on bread slices and top with cheese.

2. Bake at 400 degrees, or broil, until sandwiches are warm and cheese melted.

MONTE CRISTO

The sourdough bread and egg-batter coating make this grilled sandwich special. Substitute any desired meat and cheese for variety.

4 servings

- 4 slices (3 ounces) lean smoked ham
- 4 slices (3 ounces) turkey, *or* chicken, breast
- 4 slices (4 ounces) fat-free Cheddar cheese
- 8 slices sourdough, *or* Italian, bread
- 1/2 cup no-cholesterol real egg product *or* 4 egg whites, beaten
  Vegetable cooking spray

Per Serving
Calories: 248
% Calories from fat: 9
Fat (gm): 2.4
Saturated fat (gm): 0.5
Cholesterol (mg): 27.7
Sodium (mg): 756
Protein (gm): 26.8
Carbohydrate (gm): 28.9
Exchanges
Milk: 0.0
Vegetable: 0.0
Fruit: 0.0
Bread: 2.0
Meat: 2.0
Fat: 0.0

1. Arrange meats and cheese on 4 slices of bread; top with remaining bread. Pour egg product into pie pan; dip sandwiches in egg, coating both sides of sandwiches.

2. Spray large skillet with cooking spray; heat over medium heat until hot. Cook sandwiches over medium to medium-low heat until browned, about 5 minutes on each side.

SMOKED TURKEY AND GOAT CHEESE HOAGIES

A sandwich full of surprise flavors!

4 servings

Olive oil cooking spray
4 cups sliced onions
2 cups sliced green bell peppers
2 teaspoons minced garlic
1/3 cup water
1/4 cup raisins
1-1 1/2 tablespoons balsamic vinegar
Salt and pepper, to taste
1/4-1/2 package (8-ounce size) fat-free cream cheese, softened
1/2 cup goat cheese
4 French rolls *or* hoagie buns
16 spinach leaves
4 ounces thinly sliced smoked turkey breast

Per Serving
Calories: 330
% Calories from fat: 18
Fat (gm): 6.7
Saturated fat (gm): 3.5
Cholesterol (mg): 12.3
Sodium (mg): 792
Protein (gm): 18.3
Carbohydrate (gm): 52.1
Exchanges
Milk: 0.0
Vegetable: 3.0
Fruit: 0.0
Bread: 2.0
Meat: 2.0
Fat: 0.0

1. Spray large skillet with cooking spray; heat over medium heat until hot. Cook onions, bell peppers, and garlic over medium to medium-low heat, covered, until softened and beginning to brown, 15 to 20 minutes. Add water, raisins, and vinegar; heat to boiling. Reduce heat and simmer, covered, until water has evaporated, 5 to 8 minutes. Season to taste with salt and pepper.

2. Mix cheeses; spread on tops and bottoms of rolls. Arrange spinach leaves and turkey on bottoms of rolls; fill with onion mixture and replace tops of rolls.

TURKEY AND CRANBERRY CHEESE MELT

The latest in grilled cheese, with cranberry and walnut accents.

4 servings

$^1/_4$ package (8-ounce size) fat-free cream cheese, softened

$^1/_4$ cup (1 ounce) shredded smoked Gouda, *or* Swiss, cheese

$^1/_4$ cup chopped walnuts

8 slices whole wheat bread

8 ounces thinly sliced turkey breast

$^1/_2$ medium onion, thinly sliced

$^1/_4$ cup whole-berry cranberry sauce

$^1/_2$ cup (2 ounces) fat-free shredded Cheddar cheese

   Butter-flavored vegetable cooking spray

Per Serving
Calories: 336
% Calories from fat: 28
Fat (gm): 10.6
Saturated fat (gm): 2.7
Cholesterol (mg): 32.9
Sodium (mg): 734
Protein (gm): 27.8
Carbohydrate (gm): 34.2
Exchanges
Milk: 0.0
Vegetable: 0.0
Fruit: 0.5
Bread: 2.0
Meat: 3.0
Fat: 0.0

1. Mix cream cheese, Gouda cheese, and walnuts; spread on 4 slices bread. Arrange turkey and onion slices over cheese; top with cranberry sauce, Cheddar cheese, and the remaining bread slices.

2. Spray large skillet with cooking spray; heat over medium heat until hot. Cook sandwiches over medium heat until browned on the bottoms, about 5 minutes. Spray tops of sandwiches with spray and turn; cook until browned on other side, about 5 minutes.

CUCUMBER CHEESE MELT

A marvelous combination of flavors that will keep you coming back for more!

4 servings

1/4 package (8-ounce size) fat-free cream cheese, softened

2 tablespoons crumbled blue cheese

8 slices multi-grain bread

1/4 cup sugar-free apricot spreadable fruit

16 cucumber slices

2 ounces shaved reduced-sodium ham

4 slices (3 ounces) fat-free Swiss cheese
Butter-flavored vegetable cooking spray

Per Serving
Calories: 237
% Calories from fat: 9
Fat (gm): 2.7
Saturated fat (gm): 0.9
Cholesterol (mg): 10.4
Sodium (mg): 692
Protein (gm): 18.4
Carbohydrate (gm): 39.5
Exchanges
Milk: 0.0
Vegetable: 0.0
Fruit: 0.5
Bread: 2.0
Meat: 1.0
Fat: 0.0

1. Mix cream cheese and blue cheese; spread on 4 slices bread. Spread 1 tablespoon spreadable fruit over cheese on each slice; top each with 4 cucumber slices, ham, Swiss cheese, and remaining bread slices.

2. Spray large skillet with cooking spray; heat over medium heat until hot. Cook sandwiches over medium heat until browned on the bottoms, about 5 minutes. Spray tops of sandwiches with cooking spray and turn; cook until browned on other side, about 5 minutes.

TURKEY AND SUN-DRIED TOMATO PESTO GRILL

Cilantro Pesto (see p. 287) can also be used. Thin onion slices can be added to the sandwich or substituted for the tomato slices.

4 servings

8 slices sourdough bread
1/2 cup prepared sun-dried tomato pesto
8 slices (6 ounces) fat-free mozzarella cheese
4 ounces thinly sliced turkey breast
8 thin slices ripe tomato
Butter-flavored vegetable cooking spray

Per Serving
Calories: 366
% Calories from fat: 30
Fat (gm): 12.2
Saturated fat (gm): 1.8
Cholesterol (mg): 23.5
Sodium (mg): 777
Protein (gm): 28.1
Carbohydrate (gm): 35.8
Exchanges
Milk: 0.0
Vegetable: 1.0
Fruit: 0.0
Bread: 2.0
Meat: 3.0
Fat: 1.0

1. Spread each bread slice with 1 tablespoon pesto. Top 4 slices of bread with a cheese slice, a turkey slice, and 2 tomato slices. Top with remaining cheese slices and bread.

2. Spray large skillet with cooking spray; heat over medium heat until hot. Cook sandwiches over medium to medium-low heat until browned on the bottoms, about 5 minutes. Spray tops of sandwiches generously with cooking spray and turn. Cook until browned on other side, 3 to 5 minutes.

BLUE CHEESE AND PEAR MELT

Blue cheese and pears are perfect flavor companions any way they are served.

4 servings

8 slices honey wheat, *or* light rye, bread
4 slices (3 ounces) fat-free Swiss cheese
1/4 cup mango chutney
1 medium pear, cored, cut into 1/4-inch slices
1/2 cup (2 ounces) crumbled blue cheese
Butter-flavored vegetable cooking spray

Per Serving
Calories: 284
% Calories from fat: 20
Fat (gm): 6.6
Saturated fat (gm): 3.2
Cholesterol (mg): 10.5
Sodium (mg): 780
Protein (gm): 13.6
Carbohydrate (gm): 44.6
Exchanges
Milk: 0.0
Vegetable: 0.0
Fruit: 1.0
Bread: 2.0
Meat: 1.0
Fat: 0.5

1. Top 4 slices bread with Swiss cheese and spread each with 1 tablespoon chutney; arrange pear slices on chutney and sprinkle with blue cheese. Top sandwiches with remaining bread slices.

2. Spray large skillet with cooking spray; heat over medium heat until hot. Cook sandwiches until browned on the bottoms, about 5 minutes. Spray tops of sandwiches with cooking spray and turn; cook until browned on other side, about 5 minutes.

GAZPACHO PIZZA

The refreshing flavors of gazpacho, served on a crust!

8 servings

1¼ packages (8-ounce size) fat-free cream cheese, softened

2 tablespoons fat-free mayonnaise

½ teaspoon dry mustard

2 teaspoons finely chopped parsley

2 teaspoons finely chopped chives

1 large whole wheat lavosh *or* cracker bread (5¼ ounces)

½ cup chopped avocado

1 cup chopped seeded tomato

1 cup chopped seeded cucumber

½ cup chopped onion

½ cup chopped yellow pepper

½ cup chopped green pepper

¼ cup fat-free Italian salad dressing

1 teaspoon minced garlic

1 teaspoon minced jalapeño chili

Salt and pepper, to taste

Per Serving
Calories: 153
% Calories from fat: 29
Fat (gm): 5.1
Saturated fat (gm): 0.4
Cholesterol (mg): 0
Sodium (mg): 415
Protein (gm): 7.4
Carbohydrate (gm): 19.9
Exchanges
Milk: 0.0
Vegetable: 1.5
Fruit: 0.0
Bread: 1.0
Meat: 0.0
Fat: 1.0

1. Mix cream cheese, mayonnaise, dry mustard, parsley, and chives. Spread mixture on lavosh.

2. Combine vegetables in large bowl. Combine salad dressing, garlic, and jalapeño chili; pour over vegetables and toss. Add salt and pepper to taste. Spoon mixture onto lavosh and serve immediately.

TOMATO FILLO PIZZA

Use summer's ripest tomatoes for this delectable pizza.

8 servings

Olive oil cooking spray
8 sheets frozen, thawed fillo pastry
2 cups (8 ounces) shredded fat-free mozzarella cheese
1/2 cup thinly sliced onion
1 pound tomatoes, thinly sliced
Salt and pepper, to taste
1/4 cup (1 ounce) grated Parmesan cheese
3/4 teaspoon dried dill weed
1/2 teaspoon dried basil leaves

Per Serving
Calories: 79
% Calories from fat: 14
Fat (gm): 1.2
Saturated fat (gm): 0.6
Cholesterol (mg): 2.5
Sodium (mg): 270
Protein (gm): 12
Carbohydrate (gm): 5.4
Exchanges
Milk: 0.0
Vegetable: 0.0
Fruit: 0.0
Bread: 0.5
Meat: 1.0
Fat: 0.0

1. Spray jelly roll pan with cooking spray; place sheet of fillo on pan and spray generously with spray. Repeat with remaining sheets fillo.

2. Sprinkle mozzarella cheese and onion over fillo; arrange tomato slices on top. Sprinkle lightly with salt and pepper. Sprinkle with Parmesan cheese and herbs.

3. Bake pizza at 375 degrees until fillo is browned and cheese melted, about 15 minutes.

GARDEN PATCH PIZZA

Pick the best from the season's bounty for this good-for-you pizza!

8 servings

1¼ packages (8-ounce size) fat-free cream cheese, softened
2 tablespoons fat-free sour cream
1 teaspoon Italian seasoning
1 large whole wheat lavosh *or* cracker bread (5¼ ounces)
1 cup small broccoli florets
1 cup chopped, seeded cucumber
2-3 marinated artichoke hearts, drained, sliced

Per Serving
Calories: 149
% Calories from fat: 28
Fat (gm): 4.6
Saturated fat (gm): 0.8
Cholesterol (mg): 5.1
Sodium (mg): 419
Protein (gm): 9.3
Carbohydrate (gm): 17.2
Exchanges
Milk: 0.0
Vegetable: 2.0
Fruit: 0.0
Bread: 0.5
Meat: 0.0
Fat: 0.5

1/4 cup sliced carrot

1/4 cup thinly sliced green onion

2-4 tablespoons sliced ripe olives

2 ounces reduced-fat Havarti cheese, shredded

1/4 cup red French, *or* other flavor, fat-free salad dressing

1. Mix cream cheese, sour cream, and Italian seasoning; spread mixture on lavosh. Arrange vegetables attractively on cream cheese; sprinkle with Havarti cheese.

2. Serve immediately, or refrigerate no longer than 1 hour; drizzle with salad dressing just before serving.

SPINACH SALAD PIZZA

This salad on a crust is made with the large, crisp lavosh crackers. Serve with any salad dressing flavor—red French or honey Dijon are also good choices.

8 servings

1 1/2 packages (8-ounce size) fat-free cream cheese, softened

5-6 tablespoons sweet-sour salad dressing, divided

1 large whole wheat lavosh *or* cracker bread (5 1/4 ounces)

2 cups packed spinach leaves, torn into bite-size pieces

1 cup sliced mushrooms

1/2 cup thinly sliced red onion

2 hard-cooked eggs, sliced

2 slices bacon, cooked crisp, crumbled

Per Serving
Calories: 178
% Calories from fat: 30
Fat (gm): 6.1
Saturated fat (gm): 1.6
Cholesterol (mg): 57.7
Sodium (mg): 450
Protein (gm): 10.6
Carbohydrate (gm): 21.4
Exchanges
Milk: 0.0
Vegetable: 1.0
Fruit: 0.0
Bread: 1.0
Meat: 1.0
Fat: 0.5

1. Mix cream cheese and 2 tablespoons sweet-sour dressing. Spread mixture on lavosh; top with spinach, mushrooms, onion, hard-cooked eggs, and bacon.

2. Serve immediately, or refrigerate no longer than 1 hour; drizzle with remaining sweet-sour dressing just before serving.

CALZONES

These Italian-style turnovers, filled with cheese and vegetables, can also be served for a lunch or supper. A package mix makes a quick and easy dough.

16 servings

Olive oil cooking spray
1 cup chopped zucchini
1 cup sliced mushrooms
1/2 cup chopped onion
1/4 cup chopped green bell pepper
1 can (14 1/2 ounces) diced tomatoes with roasted garlic, undrained
2 teaspoons Italian seasoning
1 cup fat-free ricotta cheese
2 cups (8 ounces) shredded reduced-fat mozzarella cheese
Salt and pepper, to taste
1 package (16 ounces) hot roll mix
1 1/4 cups hot water
1 tablespoon olive oil
Fat-free milk

Per Serving
Calories: 185
% Calories from fat: 28
Fat (gm): 5.8
Saturated fat (gm): 1.6
Cholesterol (mg): 7.6
Sodium (mg): 379
Protein (gm): 9.4
Carbohydrate (gm): 23.6
Exchanges
Milk: 0.0
Vegetable: 1.5
Fruit: 0.0
Bread: 1.0
Meat: 1.0
Fat: 0.5

1. Spray large skillet with cooking spray; heat over medium heat until hot. Saute zucchini, mushrooms, onion, and bell pepper 5 minutes.

2. Add tomatoes and liquid and Italian seasoning to skillet; simmer until vegetables are tender and excess liquid is gone, about 10 minutes. Cool slightly; stir in cheeses and season to taste with salt and pepper.

3. Make hot roll mix according to package directions, using hot water and oil. Divide dough into 8 parts; roll each into 7-inch circle. Place about 1/2 cup vegetable mixture on each; fold in half and seal edges with tines of fork. Brush tops of pastries with milk.

4. Bake at 350 degrees until browned, about 15 minutes. Cut each calzone in half and arrange on serving platter. Serve warm.

SWEET FENNEL CALZONES

Fresh fennel, onion, sour cream, and melty cheese are combined in these golden calzones.

8 servings

Vegetable cooking spray

6 cups thinly sliced fennel bulb

1¹/₂ cups chopped onions

²/₃ cup chopped red bell pepper

2 cloves garlic, minced

1 cup (4 ounces) shredded fat-free mozzarella cheese

¹/₂ cup fat-free sour cream

2 tablespoons finely chopped fennel leaves

Salt and pepper, to taste

1 package (16 ounces) hot roll mix

1¹/₄ cups hot water

1 tablespoon olive oil

Fat-free milk

Per Serving
Calories: 307
% Calories from fat: 15
Fat (gm): 5.3
Saturated fat (gm): 0.28
Cholesterol (mg): 3.4
Sodium (mg): 378
Protein (gm): 13.8
Carbohydrate (gm): 52
Exchanges
Milk: 0.0
Vegetable: 1.5
Fruit: 0.0
Bread: 3.0
Meat: 0.5
Fat: 0.5

1. Spray large skillet with cooking spray; heat over medium heat until hot. Add fennel, onions, bell pepper, and garlic; cook, covered, over medium to medium-low heat until tender, 15 to 20 minutes, stirring occasionally. Cool until warm; stir in cheese, sour cream, and fennel leaves; season to taste with salt and pepper.

2. Make hot roll mix according to directions for pizza, using 1¹/₄ cups hot water and 1 tablespoon olive oil. Divide dough into 8 equal pieces. Roll 1 piece dough on floured surface into 6 to 7-inch circle; spoon about ²/₃ cup fennel mixture on dough. Brush edge of dough with milk and fold in half. Flute edges of dough or press together with tines of fork. Place on greased cookie sheet. Repeat with remaining dough and filling.

3. Brush tops of calzones with milk. Bake calzones at 375 degrees until browned, 15 to 20 minutes. Let cool on wire rack 5 minutes before serving.

NACHOS

This high-fat restaurant favorite can be made in a healthy "skinny" version at home! Canned refried beans can be substituted for the pinto beans, and purchased salsa can be substituted for the homemade. Cooked, crumbled Chorizo (see p. 166) can be added to make these nachos grande!

6 servings

48 baked tortilla chips

1 can (15½ ounces) pinto beans, rinsed, drained, coarsely mashed

Red Tomato Salsa (recipe follows), divided

½-1 teaspoon chili powder

¾ teaspoon dried oregano leaves

2-3 cloves garlic, minced

Salt, to taste

½ cup (2 ounces) shredded reduced-fat Cheddar, *or* Monterey Jack, cheese

1 medium tomato, chopped

½ small avocado, chopped

2 green onions and tops, sliced

6 pitted ripe olives, sliced, optional

¼ cup fat-free sour cream

Per Serving
Calories: 200
% Calories from fat: 22
Fat (gm): 5.4
Saturated fat (gm): 1.2
Cholesterol (mg): 5.1
Sodium (mg): 455
Protein (gm): 10.5
Carbohydrate (gm): 32.5
Exchanges
Milk: 0.0
Vegetable: 1.0
Fruit: 0.0
Bread: 2.0
Meat: 0.0
Fat: 1.0

1. Spread tortilla chips in single layer in jelly roll pan. Mix beans, ¼ cup salsa, chili powder, oregano, and garlic; season to taste with salt. Spoon beans over tortilla chips; sprinkle with cheese. Bake at 350 degrees until beans are hot and cheese melted, 5 to 10 minutes.

2. Sprinkle with tomato, avocado, onions, and olives; garnish with dollops of sour cream. Serve with remaining salsa.

Red Tomato Salsa

makes about 2 cups

2 large tomatoes, cut into wedges

1 small onion, finely chopped

1 small poblano chili *or* green bell pepper, veins and seeds discarded, chopped

1/4 jalapeño chili, seeds and veins discarded,
  chopped
1 clove garlic, minced
1/4 cup loosely packed cilantro, finely
  chopped
  Salt, to taste

1. Process tomatoes, onion, chilies, and garlic in food processor
or blender until finely chopped. Mix in cilantro; season to taste
with salt.

QUESADILLAS

*The simplest quesadillas are made only with cheese. Our version adds the
Mexican poblano chili, onion, and cilantro; Chorizo (see p. 166) would be
a flavorful addition.*

6 servings

  Vegetable cooking spray
1 poblano chili *or* green bell pepper,
  sliced
1 medium onion, finely chopped
1 teaspoon ground cumin
2 tablespoons finely chopped cilantro
1 cup (4 ounces) shredded reduced-fat
  Cheddar cheese
6 flour tortillas
  Green Tomato Salsa (recipe follows)
6 tablespoons fat-free sour cream

Per Serving
Calories: 165
% Calories from fat: 26
Fat (gm): 4.8
Saturated fat (gm): 1.7
Cholesterol (mg): 10.1
Sodium (mg): 393
Protein (gm): 8.3
Carbohydrate (gm): 22.9
Exchanges
Milk: 0.0
Vegetable: 1.5
Fruit: 0.0
Bread: 1.0
Meat: 0.5
Fat: 0.5

1. Spray large skillet with cooking spray; heat over medium
heat until hot. Saute poblano chili, onion, and cumin until vegetables are tender, 3 to 5 minutes; stir in cilantro.

2. Sprinkle cheese on half of each tortilla; spoon vegetable mixture over. Fold tortillas in half.

3. Spray large skillet with cooking spray; heat over medium
heat until hot. Cook quesadillas over medium to medium-high
heat until browned on the bottoms, 2 to 3 minutes. Spray tops
of quesadillas with cooking spray; turn and cook until browned
on other side. Cut into wedges and serve warm with salsa and
sour cream.

Green Tomato Salsa

makes about 2 cups

1¹/₂ pounds tomatillos
¹/₂ medium onion, finely chopped
2 cloves garlic, minced
¹/₄ small jalapeño chili, seeds and veins discarded, very finely chopped
2 tablespoons finely chopped cilantro
¹/₂ teaspoon ground cumin
¹/₄ teaspoon dried oregano leaves
¹/₈-¹/₄ teaspoon sugar
Salt, to taste

1. Remove and discard husks from tomatillos; simmer tomatillos in water to cover in large saucepan until tender, 5 to 8 minutes. Cool; drain, reserving liquid.

2. Process tomatillos, onion, garlic, jalapeño chili, cilantro, cumin, and oregano in food processor or blender, using pulse technique, until almost smooth, adding enough reserved liquid to make medium dipping consistency. Season to taste with sugar and salt.

TORTILLA WEDGES

Fun to make and eat—our Mexican version of a pizza perhaps! Lean ground beef can replace the Chorizo, if you prefer.

12 servings

Vegetable cooking spray
Chorizo (see p. 166)
¹/₂ cup chopped green bell pepper
¹/₂ cup chopped onion
4 large flour tortillas (10-inch)
1 cup (4 ounces) shredded reduced-fat Monterey Jack cheese
1 cup (4 ounces) shredded fat-free Cheddar cheese
1 cup Red Tomato Salsa (see p. 724) *or* prepared salsa
³/₄ cup fat-free sour cream

Per Serving
Calories: 135
% Calories from fat: 24
Fat (gm): 3.7
Saturated fat (gm): 1.5
Cholesterol (mg): 24.8
Sodium (mg): 313
Protein (gm): 14.4
Carbohydrate (gm): 11.4
Exchanges
Milk: 0.0
Vegetable: 0.5
Fruit: 0.0
Bread: 0.5
Meat: 1.5
Fat: 0.0

1. Spray medium skillet with cooking spray; heat over medium heat until hot. Add Chorizo and cook over medium heat until brown, crumbling with fork; add green pepper and onion and cook until tender, 2 to 3 minutes.

2. Place tortillas on baking sheets; sprinkle evenly with Monterey Jack cheese. Sprinkle with Chorizo mixture and top with Cheddar cheese. Bake at 450 degrees until edges of tortillas are browned and cheese is melted, 6 to 8 minutes. Top with Red Tomato Salsa and sour cream. Cut each tortilla into 6 wedges.

GOAT CHEESE QUESADILLAS WITH TROPICAL SALSA

Goat cheese and tropical fruits combine for a new flavor in quesadillas.

8 servings

4	ounces fat-free cream cheese, softened
2	ounces goat cheese
1/2	small jalapeño chili, minced
1/2	teaspoon dried marjoram leaves
1/4	teaspoon dried thyme leaves
1/8	teaspoon white pepper
8	whole wheat, *or* white flour, tortillas
	Butter-flavored vegetable cooking spray
	Tropical Salsa (see p. 280)

Per Serving
Calories: 186
% Calories from fat: 25
Fat (gm): 5.2
Saturated fat (gm): 2.2
Cholesterol (mg): 7.5
Sodium (mg): 285
Protein (gm): 8
Carbohydrate (gm): 26.3
Exchanges
Milk: 0.0
Vegetable: 1.0
Fruit: 0.5
Bread: 1.0
Meat: 0.5
Fat: 0.5

1. Combine cream cheese, goat cheese, jalapeño chili, herbs, and white pepper; spread about 3 tablespoons mixture on each of 4 tortillas. Top with remaining tortillas.

2. Spray medium skillet with cooking spray; heat over medium heat until hot. Cook 1 quesadilla on medium to medium-low heat until browned on the bottom, 2 to 3 minutes. Spray top of quesadilla with cooking spray; turn and cook until browned on other side. Repeat with remaining quesadillas.

3. Cut quesadillas into wedges; serve warm with Tropical Salsa.

BLACK BEAN QUESADILLAS

Substitute pinto beans for the black beans if you like, and vary the amount of jalapeño chili to taste.

12 servings

  1   cup cooked dried black beans *or* canned, rinsed and drained black beans

  1   cup mild, *or* hot, salsa, divided

 ¹/4   cup thinly sliced green onions and tops

  3   tablespoons finely chopped cilantro

2-3   teaspoons minced jalapeño chili

 12   whole wheat, *or* white flour, tortillas

 ³/4   cup (3 ounces) reduced-fat Monterey Jack cheese

 ³/4   cup (3 ounces) fat-free Cheddar cheese Butter-flavored vegetable cooking spray

Per Serving
Calories: 169
% Calories from fat: 21
Fat (gm): 3.9
Saturated fat (gm): 1.2
Cholesterol (mg): 5.1
Sodium (mg): 427
Protein (gm): 9
Carbohydrate (gm): 24.2
Exchanges
Milk: 0.0
Vegetable: 0.0
Fruit: 0.0
Bread: 1.5
Meat: 0.5
Fat: 0.5

1. Mash beans slightly; mix in ¹/4 cup salsa, green onions, cilantro, and chili. Divide mixture on 6 tortillas, spreading almost to edges. Sprinkle with cheeses and top with remaining tortillas.

2. Spray medium skillet with cooking spray; heat over medium heat until hot. Cook 1 quesadilla on medium to medium-low heat until browned on the bottom, 2 to 3 minutes. Spray top of quesadilla with cooking spray; turn and cook until browned on other side. Repeat with remaining quesadillas.

3. Cut quesadillas into wedges; serve warm with remaining ³/4 cup salsa.

THREE-CHILI TAMALES

Packaged ancho chilies are sometimes called New Mexico chilies; ancho chilies are fresh poblano chilies that have been dried. Corn husks and masa harina (corn flour) can be purchased in large supermarkets or Mexican groceries.

6 servings (2 each)

12 corn husks
    Hot water
 2 ancho chilies, stems, seeds, and veins
    discarded
1/3 cup boiling water
 1 large poblano chili, seeds and veins
    discarded, chopped
 1 can (4 ounces) chopped green chilies,
    drained
3/4 teaspoon dried oregano leaves
1/2 teaspoon dried thyme leaves
    Salt and pepper, to taste
    Tamale Dough (recipe follows)

Per Serving
Calories: 117
% Calories from fat: 27
Fat (gm): 3.6
Saturated fat (gm): 0.5
Cholesterol (mg): 0
Sodium (mg): 267
Protein (gm): 3.0
Carbohydrate (gm): 18.9
Exchanges
Milk: 0.0
Vegetable: 0.5
Fruit: 0.0
Bread: 1.0
Meat: 0.0
Fat: 0.5

1. Soak corn husks in hot water until softened, about 1 hour; drain well on paper toweling.

2. Crumble ancho chilies into bowl; pour boiling water over and let stand until softened, 15 to 20 minutes. Cook ancho chilies and liquid, poblano chili, green chilies, and herbs over medium heat in medium skillet until chilies are tender, 5 to 8 minutes, stirring frequently. Season to taste with salt and pepper. Mix in Tamale Dough.

3. Spoon about 1/4 cup tamale mixture onto center of each corn husk; fold sides of husks over filling. Tie ends of tamales, making "bundles."

4. Place tamales on steamer rack in saucepan with 2 inches water; steam, covered, 2 hours, adding more water to saucepan if necessary.

Tamale Dough

makes about 1 cup

> 1 cup masa harina
> 3/4 teaspoon baking powder
> 1 1/2 tablespoons margarine, softened
> 1/4-1/2 teaspoon salt
> 1 cup reduced-sodium fat-free chicken broth

1. Combine masa harina, baking powder, margarine, and salt; gradually stir in broth (mixture will be soft).

CHICKEN AND POBLANO TAMALES

Red and Green Tomato Salsas (pp. 724, 726) would be excellent accompaniments to these delicious tamales.

6 servings (2 each)

> 12 corn husks
> Hot water
> 12 ounces boneless, skinless chicken breast
> Vegetable cooking spray
> 1 medium poblano chili, seeds and veins discarded, chopped
> 1 medium onion, chopped
> 1 large tomato, chopped
> 1/2 teaspoon minced jalapeño chili
> 2 cloves garlic, minced
> 2 tablespoons finely chopped cilantro
> 3/4-1 teaspoon ground cumin
> Salt and pepper, to taste
> Tamale Dough (see above)

Per Serving
Calories: 190
% Calories from fat: 24
Fat (gm): 5.2
Saturated fat (gm): 1.0
Cholesterol (mg): 34.4
Sodium (mg): 214
Protein (gm): 16.3
Carbohydrate (gm): 20.0
Exchanges
Milk: 0.0
Vegetable: 1.0
Fruit: 0.0
Bread: 1.0
Meat: 1.5
Fat: 0.5

1. Soak corn husks in hot water until softened, about 1 hour; drain well on paper toweling.

2. Cover chicken with water in small saucepan; heat to boiling. Reduce heat and simmer, covered, until chicken is tender and no longer pink in the center, 8 to 10 minutes. Drain, reserving 1/2 cup cooking liquid. Cool chicken slightly; shred into small pieces.

3. Spray medium skillet with cooking spray; heat over medium heat until hot. Saute vegetables until tender, about 5 minutes; stir in chicken, cilantro, and cumin and season to taste with salt and pepper. Stir in Tamale Dough and 1/2 cup reserved cooking liquid.

4. Spoon about ¹/₄ cup tamale mixture onto center of each corn husk; fold sides of husks over filling. Tie ends of tamales with string, making "bundles."

5. Place tamales on steamer rack in saucepan with 2 inches water; steam, covered, 2 hours, adding more water to saucepan if necessary.

BEEF PINTO BEAN TAMALES

Tamales can be tied in "bundles," as the Three-Chili Tamales (see p. 729) are, or tied in "envelopes" as in this recipe.

6 servings (2 each)

12	corn husks
	Hot water
12	ounces boneless beef eye of round steak, cut into 1-inch pieces
	Vegetable cooking spray
1	medium onion, chopped
3	cloves garlic, minced
³/₄	teaspoon dried marjoram leaves
¹/₄	teaspoon ground allspice
¹/₈-¹/₂	teaspoon cayenne pepper
¹/₂	can (15-ounce size) pinto beans, rinsed, drained, coarsely mashed
	Salt, to taste
	Tamale Dough (see p. 730)

Per Serving
Calories: 204
% Calories from fat: 25
Fat (gm): 5.7
Saturated fat (gm): 1.3
Cholesterol (mg): 27.3
Sodium (mg): 328
Protein (gm): 15.8
Carbohydrate (gm): 23.6
Exchanges
Milk: 0.0
Vegetable: 0.5
Fruit: 0.0
Bread: 1.0
Meat: 1.0
Fat: 0.5

1. Soak corn husks in hot water until softened, about 1 hour; drain well on paper toweling.

2. Cover beef with water in small saucepan; heat to boiling. Reduce heat and simmer, covered, until beef is tender, 15 to 20 minutes. Drain, reserving ¹/₂ cup cooking liquid. Cool beef slightly; shred into small pieces.

3. Spray medium skillet with cooking spray; heat over medium heat until hot. Saute onion, garlic, marjoram, allspice, and pepper until onion is tender, about 5 minutes. Stir in beans and beef and cook 2 to 3 minutes; season to taste with salt. Mix in Tamale Dough and ¹/₂ cup reserved cooking liquid.

4. Spoon about ¹/₄ cup tamale mixture onto center of each corn husk. Fold sides of husks over filling; fold top and bottom of husks toward center and tie in the center with string.

5. Place tamales on steamer rack in saucepan with 2 inches water; steam, covered, 2 hours, adding more water to saucepan if necessary.

TACOS WITH CHORIZO AND POTATOES

In many parts of Mexico, tacos are made by pan-sauteing folded filled tortillas—a delectable alternative to the crisp taco shells we are accustomed to!

8 servings (1 each)

Vegetable cooking spray
Chorizo (see p. 166)
1 cup chopped onion
1 cup cubed cooked potato
1 cup (4 ounces) shredded fat-free Cheddar cheese
2 tablespoons finely chopped cilantro
Salt and pepper, to taste
8 corn, *or* flour, tortillas
¹/₂ cup Tomatillo Sauce (see p. 203)
¹/₄ cup fat-free sour cream

Per Serving
Calories: 179
% Calories from fat: 13
Fat (gm): 2.5
Saturated fat (gm): 0.7
Cholesterol (mg): 27
Sodium (mg): 303
Protein (gm): 16.5
Carbohydrate (gm): 23.3
Exchanges
Milk: 0.0
Vegetable: 1.0
Fruit: 0.0
Bread: 1.0
Meat: 1.5
Fat: 0.0

1. Spray large skillet with cooking spray; heat over medium heat until hot. Cook Chorizo over medium heat 2 to 3 minutes; add onion and potato and cook until onion is tender and Chorizo cooked, about 5 minutes. Remove from heat; stir in cheese and cilantro. Season to taste with salt and pepper.

2. Heat tortillas in skillet or microwave oven until soft enough to fold. Spoon about ¹/₂ cup Chorizo mixture on each tortilla and fold in half to make tacos. Spray large skillet with cooking spray; heat over medium heat until hot. Saute tacos until lightly browned, 1 to 2 minutes on each side. Serve with Tomatillo Sauce and sour cream.

TACOS PICADILLO

Chicken breast or lean beef can be substituted for the pork. Serve these tacos with Red or Green Tomato Salsa (see pp. 724, 726).

12 servings (1 each)

1½ pounds pork tenderloin, cut into 1-inch cubes

Vegetable cooking spray

½ cup chopped onion

4 cloves garlic, minced

1 small jalapeño chili, seeds and veins discarded, minced

2 medium tomatoes, chopped

¼ cup dark raisins

2 tablespoons slivered almonds, toasted

1-2 tablespoons cider vinegar

1½-2 teaspoons ground cinnamon

½ teaspoon ground cloves

½ teaspoon dried oregano leaves

¼ teaspoon ground allspice

Salt and pepper, to taste

12 flour, *or* corn, tortillas

Per Serving
Calories: 176
% Calories from fat: 23
Fat (gm): 4.5
Saturated fat (gm): 1.0
Cholesterol (mg): 327
Sodium (mg): 151
Protein (gm): 14.6
Carbohydrate (gm): 18.9
Exchanges
Milk: 0.0
Vegetable: 1.0
Fruit: 0.0
Bread: 1.0
Meat: 1.5
Fat: 0.0

1. Cover pork with water in medium saucepan; heat to boiling. Reduce heat and simmer, covered, until pork is tender, about 10 minutes. Drain; cool pork slightly and shred into small pieces.

2. Spray medium skillet with cooking spray; heat over medium heat until hot. Saute onion, garlic, and jalapeño chili until tender, about 5 minutes. Add pork, tomatoes, raisins, almonds, vinegar, cinnamon, cloves, oregano, and allspice; cook over medium heat, stirring occasionally, until pork is hot through and mixture is dry, about 5 minutes. Season to taste with salt and pepper.

3. Spoon about ⅓ cup mixture on each tortilla and fold in half to make tacos. Spray large skillet with cooking spray; heat over medium heat until hot. Saute tacos until lightly browned, 1 to 2 minutes on each side.

MARGARITAS

Mexico's favorite libation! For best flavor, use fresh lime juice.

2 servings

  1 lime wedge
     Coarse salt, optional
 1/2 cup tequila
 1/4 cup fresh lime juice
  2 tablespoons orange liqueur
     Ice cubes

Per Serving
Calories: 185
% Calories from fat: 0
Fat (gm): 0
Saturated fat (gm): 0
Cholesterol (mg): 0
Sodium (mg): 1
Protein (gm): 0.2
Carbohydrate (gm): 8.6
Exchanges
Milk: 0.0
Vegetable: 0.0
Fruit: 0.5
Bread: 0.0
Meat: 0.0
Fat: 3.5

1. Rub rims of 2 margarita or stemmed glasses with lime wedge; dip rims in salt.

2. Mix tequila, lime juice, and orange liqueur; pour over ice cubes in glasses.

Variation: **Strawberry Margaritas**—Process tequila, lime juice, orange liqueur, and 12 to 14 fresh, *or* frozen, strawberries in food processor or blender; pour over ice cubes in margarita or stemmed glasses.

SANGRIA

America has adopted this famous Spanish wine punch; it also can be made with the addition of sparkling water. Serve well chilled.

6 servings

   4 cups dry red wine, chilled
   2 cups orange juice, chilled
  1/4 cup lime juice
 3/4-1 cup Splenda *or* artificial sweetener
  1/2 lime, thinly sliced
  1/2 orange, thinly sliced
     Ice cubes

Per Serving
Calories: 88
% Calories from fat: 1
Fat (gm): 0.1
Saturated fat (gm): 0
Cholesterol (mg): 0
Sodium (mg): 6
Protein (gm): 0.6
Carbohydrate (gm): 9
Exchanges
Milk: 0.0
Vegetable: 0.0
Fruit: 0.5
Bread: 0.0
Meat: 0.0
Fat: 1.5

1. Mix wine, juices, and Splenda in large pitcher, stirring until Splenda is dissolved. Add fruit slices to pitcher; pour over ice cubes in tall glasses.

CRAN-ORANGE TEA

A refreshing punch that is especially nice for the holidays.

12 servings (about ³/₄ cup each)

6 cups boiling water
2 tea bags
4 whole cloves
3 sticks cinnamon
2 cups diet cranberry juice cocktail
2 cups orange juice
¹/₄ cup sugar
2 tablespoons lemon juice
Ice cubes

Per Serving
Calories: 43
% Calories from fat: 1
Fat (gm): 0.1
Saturated fat (gm): 0
Cholesterol (mg): 0
Sodium (mg): 14
Protein (gm): 0.3
Carbohydrate (gm): 10.6
Exchanges
Milk: 0.0
Vegetable: 0.0
Fruit: 1.0
Bread: 0.0
Meat: 0.0
Fat: 0.0

1. Pour water over tea bags, cloves, and cinnamon in large saucepan. Let stand, covered, 10 minutes; discard tea bags. Stir in remaining ingredients except ice cubes. Heat to boiling; reduce heat and simmer 10 minutes. Cool; refrigerate until chilled. Pour over ice cubes in tall glasses.

SPARKLING GREEN PUNCH

Remember this punch for St. Patrick's Day and winter holidays!

16 servings (about ¹/₂ cup each)

1 can (6 ounces) frozen lemonade concentrate, thawed
2 cans (6 ounces each) frozen limeade concentrate, thawed
2 cups cold water
Few drops green food coloring
2 bottles (28 ounces each) diet ginger ale, chilled
Ice cubes

Per Serving
Calories: 59
% Calories from fat: 1
Fat (gm): 0
Saturated fat (gm): 0
Cholesterol (mg): 0
Sodium (mg): 16
Protein (gm): 0.1
Carbohydrate (gm): 15.6
Exchanges
Milk: 0.0
Vegetable: 0.0
Fruit: 1.0
Bread: 0.0
Meat: 0.0
Fat: 0.0

1. Mix concentrates, water, and food coloring in large pitcher and refrigerate until serving time. At serving time, pour into punch bowl and stir in ginger ale. Serve over ice cubes.

EGGNOG WITH RUM

A holiday favorite—thick, rich, and creamy!

12 servings

    $1/2$ cup Splenda *or* artificial sweetener
    2 tablespoons cornstarch
    1 quart fat-free milk, divided
    2 eggs, beaten
1-$1^1/_2$ cups light rum
    1 cup light whipped topping
    Ground cinnamon *or* nutmeg

Per Serving
Calories: 106
% Calories from fat: 14
Fat (gm): 1.6
Saturated fat (gm): 1
Cholesterol (mg): 36.8
Sodium (mg): 57
Protein (gm): 3.8
Carbohydrate (gm): 7.6
Exchanges
Milk: 0.5
Vegetable: 0.0
Fruit: 0.0
Bread: 0.0
Meat: 0.0
Fat: 1.5

1. Mix Splenda, cornstarch, and 3 cups milk in medium saucepan; heat to boiling, stirring frequently. Boil, stirring constantly, until thickened, about 1 minute.

2. Stir about half the milk mixture into the eggs; stir egg mixture back into saucepan. Cook over low heat, stirring constantly, 1 minute. Cool; refrigerate until chilled, 3 to 4 hours.

3. Stir remaining 1 cup milk and rum into egg nog; stir in whipped topping. Serve eggnog in small glasses or mugs; sprinkle with cinnamon.

SWEET CINNAMON COFFEE

This spiced coffee is also wonderful chilled and served over ice.

8 servings

> 4 cups water
> 1/3-1/2 cup packed brown sugar
> 1 small cinnamon stick
> 4 whole cloves
> 1/4 cup dark roast regular grind coffee

Per Serving
Calories: 37
% Calories from fat: 0
Fat (gm): 0
Saturated fat (gm): 0
Cholesterol (mg): 0
Sodium (mg): 6
Protein (gm): 0.1
Carbohydrate (gm): 9.4
Exchanges
Milk: 0.0
Vegetable: 0.0
Fruit: 0.0
Bread: 0.5
Meat: 0.0
Fat: 0.0

1. Heat water, brown sugar, and spices to boiling in medium saucepan; stir in coffee. Reduce heat and simmer, covered, 2 to 3 minutes. Remove from heat and let stand 2 to 3 minutes for grounds to settle.

2. Strain coffee; serve in small mugs.

CINNAMON-SPICE TEA

32 servings (about 1 cup each)

> 2 packages (0.3 ounces each) sugar-free strawberry gelatin
> 1/2 gallon boiling water
> 6 cinnamon sticks
> 12 cloves
> 1 pint water
> 1 quart weak tea
> 1 cup pure lemon juice
> 1 quart water
> 8 packets Splenda
> 1 can (46 ounces) unsweetened pineapple juice

Per Serving
Calories: 28
% Calories from fat: 1
Fat (gm): 0
Saturated fat (gm): 0
Cholesterol (mg): 0
Sodium (mg): 15
Protein (gm): 0.5
Carbohydrate (gm): 6.7
Exchanges
Milk: 0.0
Vegetable: 0.0
Fruit: 0.5
Bread: 0.0
Meat: 0.0
Fat: 0.0

1. Dissolve gelatin in boiling water in a large saucepan.

2. Simmer cinnamon sticks and cloves in 1 pint water for 30 minutes.

3. Combine all ingredients. Add more water or juice if desired. Serve warm but do not boil.

WARM WINE PUNCH

This is a wonderful beverage for all the winter holidays. It's also good chilled in the summer.

12 servings (about ½ cup each)

- 4 cups sweet red wine
- 3 cups orange juice
- ½ cup Splenda
- ¼ cup lemon juice
- 4 whole cloves
- 1 whole cinnamon stick

Per Serving
Calories: 90
% Calories from fat: 1
Fat (gm): 0.1
Saturated fat (gm): 0
Cholesterol (mg): 0
Sodium (mg): 5
Protein (gm): 0.6
Carbohydrate (gm): 9.3
Exchanges
Milk: 0.0
Vegetable: 0.0
Fruit: 0.5
Bread: 0.0
Meat: 0.0
Fat: 1.5

1. Heat all ingredients just to simmering in large saucepan, stirring occasionally; do not boil. Serve warm.

AUTUMN APPLE-SPICED COFFEE

8 servings (1 cup each)

- 1 quart unsweetened apple juice
- 1 quart hot, strong coffee
- 6 oranges, sliced wafer thin
- 2 3-inch cinnamon sticks
  Pinch ground allspice
  Pinch grated nutmeg
  Pinch ground cloves
  Brown sugar substitute to equal ⅓ cup brown sugar

Per Serving
Calories: 66
% Calories from fat: 2
Fat (gm): 0.1
Saturated fat (gm): 0
Cholesterol (mg): 0
Sodium (mg): 6
Protein (gm): 0.3
Carbohydrate (gm): 16.2
Exchanges
Milk: 0.0
Vegetable: 0.0
Fruit: 1.0
Bread: 0.0
Meat: 0.0
Fat: 0.0

1. Mix all ingredients, except brown sugar substitute in large saucepan. Heat to boiling; reduce heat and simmer, covered, 10 minutes. Remove from heat and add brown sugar substitute. Serve warm.

BREAKFAST SHAKE

Great for breakfast on the run, or for an afternoon pick-me-up. Freeze bananas when you have extra, or use any frozen fruit.

4 servings (about ³/₄ cup each)

    1 large banana, cut into chunks and frozen
    1 cup orange juice
    1 cup fat-free milk
  ¹/₄ cup wheat germ
    1 teaspoon vanilla
    4 ice cubes

Per Serving
Calories: 104
% Calories from fat: 7
Fat (gm): 1.8
Saturated fat (gm): 0.2
Cholesterol (mg): 1.1
Sodium (mg): 32
Protein (gm): 4.8
Carbohydrate (gm): 19.4
Exchanges
Milk: 1.0
Vegetable: 0.0
Fruit: 1.0
Bread: 0.0
Meat: 0.0
Fat: 0.0

1. Process all ingredients in blender until smooth; serve immediately.

STRAWBERRY-BANANA SMOOTHIE

3 servings (²/₃ cup each)

    1 banana
    1 cup plain fat-free yogurt
 1¹/₂ cups unsweetened orange juice, chilled
 1¹/₄ cups hulled strawberries
  ¹/₂ teaspoon vanilla extract
    1 packet Splenda *or* artificial sweetener

Per Serving
Calories: 155
% Calories from fat: 4
Fat (gm): 0.8
Saturated fat (gm): 0.2
Cholesterol (mg): 1.4
Sodium (mg): 60
Protein (gm): 6
Carbohydrate (gm): 32.4
Exchanges
Milk: 0.5
Vegetable: 0.0
Fruit: 2.0
Bread: 0.0
Meat: 0.0
Fat: 0.0

1. Process all ingredients in blender until smooth. Pour into three 5-ounce glasses.

TROPICAL ORANGE JUICE

16 servings (¹/₂ cup each)

1   quart unsweetened pineapple juice
1   quart fresh unsweetened orange juice
3   3-inch cinnamon sticks
20   whole cloves
3   tablespoons grated orange peel
8   packets Splenda

Per Serving
Calories: 65
% Calories from fat: 2
Fat (gm): 0.2
Saturated fat (gm): 0
Cholesterol (mg): 0
Sodium (mg): 2
Protein (gm): 0.7
Carbohydrate (gm): 15.6
Exchanges
Milk: 0.0
Vegetable: 0.0
Fruit: 1.0
Bread: 0.0
Meat: 0.0
Fat: 0.0

1. Combine all ingredients, except the Splenda, in a large saucepan; heat to boiling. Reduce heat and simmer 5 minutes. Strain mixture through colander into a large pitcher and add sweetener.

TOFRUITY

A delicious way to get your serving of nutritious tofu! Make it up to 24 hours in advance for convenience, then shake or stir before serving.

4 servings (³/₄ cup each)

¹/₂   package (14-ounce size) light silken
        tofu, drained
1   cup cubed, pitted, peeled mango
³/₄   cup frozen strawberries *or* raspberries
1-1¹/₂   cups orange juice

Per Serving
Calories: 92
% Calories from fat: 8
Fat (gm): 0.9
Saturated fat (gm): 0.1
Cholesterol (mg): 0
Sodium (mg): 44
Protein (gm): 3.8
Carbohydrate (gm): 18.4
Exchanges
Milk: 0.0
Vegetable: 0.0
Fruit: 1.0
Bread: 0.0
Meat: 0.5
Fat: 0.0

1. Process all ingredients in blender or food processor until smooth, adding enough orange juice to make desired consistency. Serve in tall glasses.

SIXTEEN

Cakes, Pies, Cookies
AND
Other Desserts

DARK FLOURLESS CHOCOLATE CAKE

A chocolate indulgence, incredibly fudgey and sumptuous.

6 to 8 servings

4   tablespoons margarine, softened
1/4 cup raspberry spreadable fruit
1   egg
7 1/4 teaspoons Equal® for Recipes *or* 24
     packets Equal® sweetener
1/2 cup fat-free milk
3   tablespoons Dutch process cocoa
1   cup all-purpose flour
1   teaspoon baking powder
1/2 teaspoon baking soda
1/4 teaspoon salt
     Chocolate Glaze (recipe follows)

Per Serving
Calories: 291
% Calories from fat: 47
Fat (gm): 16.2
Saturated fat (gm): 6.7
Cholesterol (mg): 36.7
Sodium (mg): 417
Protein (gm): 13.3
Carbohydrate (gm): 27.2
Exchanges
Milk: 0.0
Vegetable: 0.0
Fruit: 0.0
Bread: 2.0
Meat: 0.0
Fat: 3.0

1. Beat margarine, spreadable fruit, egg, and Equal® for Recipes in medium bowl until smooth. Mix milk and cocoa in glass measuring cup until smooth.

2. Mix combined flour, baking powder, baking soda, and salt into margarine mixture alternately with milk mixture, beginning and ending with dry ingredients.

3. Lightly grease bottom and side of 8-inch round cake pan; line bottom with parchment paper; pour batter into pan. Bake in preheated 350 degree oven until toothpick inserted in center of cake comes out clean, about 20 minutes. Cool in pan; refrigerate, covered, 8 hours or overnight.

4. Place cake on serving plate. Within 1 hour of serving, spread with Chocolate Glaze.

Chocolate Glaze

makes about $^1/_2$ *cup*

> $^1/_3$ cup 2% reduced-fat milk
>
> 3 ounces unsweetened baking chocolate, cut into small pieces
>
> $5^1/_2$ teaspoons Equal® for Recipes *or* 18 packets Equal® sweetener

1. Heat milk in small saucepan until very hot (do not boil). Remove pan from heat; immediately add chocolate, stirring until melted. Stir in Equal® for Recipes; return saucepan to low heat, stirring constantly, until smooth.

2. Cool to room temperature; refrigerate glaze until thickened enough to spread, about 15 minutes.

Variation: **Chocolate Lace Cake**—Make cake as above, omitting Chocolate Glaze. Place cake on serving plate. Melt 2 ounces unsweetened baking chocolate over low heat in small saucepan, stirring frequently; drizzle over top of cake in "lace" pattern. Refrigerate until chocolate has hardened, about 10 minutes. Garnish cake with dollops or rosettes of light whipped topping, raspberries, and mint sprigs.

GLAZED APPLESAUCE-RAISIN CAKE

Cream cheese glaze is a perfect topping for this moist cake—or serve plain with scoops of sugar-free, fat-free frozen yogurt.

12 to 16 servings

> 1 cup unsweetened applesauce
>
> $^2/_3$ cup vegetable oil
>
> 2 eggs
>
> 1 teaspoon maple extract *or* vanilla
>
> $^3/_4$ cup raisins
>
> $^1/_2$ cup coarsely chopped walnuts, optional
>
> 2 cups all-purpose flour
>
> $7^1/_4$ teaspoons Equal® for Recipes *or* 24 packets Equal® sweetener
>
> 1 teaspoon baking soda
>
> $^1/_4$ teaspoon salt

Per Serving
Calories: 263
% Calories from fat: 50
Fat (gm): 14.7
Saturated fat (gm): 2.9
Cholesterol (mg): 39.7
Sodium (mg): 211
Protein (gm): 6.6
Carbohydrate (gm): 26.5
Exchanges
Milk: 0.0
Vegetable: 0.0
Fruit: 0.0
Bread: 2.0
Meat: 0.0
Fat: 2.5

1½ teaspoons ground cinnamon
¼ teaspoon ground nutmeg
⅛ teaspoon ground cloves
  Vanilla Cream Cheese Glaze
  (recipe follows)

1. Mix applesauce, oil, eggs, maple extract, raisins, and walnuts in large bowl. Add combined flour, Equal® for Recipes, baking soda, salt, and spices, mixing until blended.

2. Spoon batter into greased 13 x 9-inch baking pan. Bake at 350 degrees until cake is browned and toothpick inserted in center comes out clean, 18 to 20 minutes (do not overbake!). Cool on wire rack. Drizzle with Vanilla Cream Cheese Glaze.

Vanilla Cream Cheese Glaze

makes about ½ cup

½ package (8-ounce size) reduced-fat cream
  cheese, softened
½ teaspoon vanilla
1 teaspoon Equal® for Recipes *or* 3 packets
  Equal® sweetener
  Fat-free milk

1. Beat cream cheese, vanilla, Equal® for Recipes, and enough milk to make desired consistency.

BLUEBERRY CRUMB CAKE

Best served warm with light whipped topping or sugar-free frozen yogurt!

9 to 12 servings

4 tablespoons margarine
1 egg
5½ teaspoons Equal® for Recipes *or* 18
  packets Equal® sweetener
1 cup all-purpose flour
1½ teaspoons baking powder
½ teaspoon baking soda
¼ teaspoon salt

Per Serving
Calories: 196
% Calories from fat: 50
Fat (gm): 11
Saturated fat (gm): 2.3
Cholesterol (mg): 24
Sodium (mg): 358
Protein (gm): 6.5
Carbohydrate (gm): 18
Exchanges
Milk: 0.0
Vegetable: 0.0
Fruit: 0.0
Bread: 1.0
Meat: 0.0
Fat: 2.5

    1 teaspoon ground cinnamon
    1/2 cup reduced-fat buttermilk
    1/2 teaspoon vanilla
        Blueberry Crumb Topping (recipe
        follows)

1. Beat margarine, egg, and Equal® for Recipes until smooth in medium bowl. Mix in combined flour, baking powder, baking soda, salt, and cinnamon alternately with combined buttermilk and vanilla, beginning and ending with dry ingredients.

2. Pour batter into greased and floured 8-inch square cake pan; sprinkle Blueberry Crumb Topping evenly over batter. Bake at 350 degrees until toothpick inserted in cake comes out clean, 35 to 40 minutes. Serve warm.

Blueberry Crumb Topping

    1/3 cup all-purpose flour
    3 1/2 teaspoons Equal® for Recipes *or* 12
        packets Equal® sweetener
    1 teaspoon ground cinnamon
    1/2 teaspoon maple extract
    4 tablespoons cold margarine, cut into
        pieces
    1 cup fresh, *or* frozen, blueberries

1. Combine flour, Equal® for Recipes, and cinnamon in small bowl; sprinkle with maple extract. Cut in margarine until mixture resembles coarse crumbs. Add blueberries and toss.

PEACH-ALMOND UPSIDE-DOWN CAKE

Best served slightly warm, topped with sugar-free, fat-free ice cream, of course!

8 servings

1 can (8^1/$_4$ ounces) peaches in juice, well drained

^{1}/$_2$ cup unsweetened applesauce

5^1/$_2$ teaspoons Equal® for Recipes *or* 18 packets Equal® sweetener

1 egg

^{1}/$_2$ teaspoon vanilla

1 cup cake flour

1 teaspoon baking powder

^{1}/$_4$ teaspoon baking soda

^{1}/$_2$ teaspoon ground cinnamon

^{1}/$_8$-^{1}/$_4$ teaspoon ground nutmeg

^{1}/$_4$ teaspoon salt

^{1}/$_2$ cup reduced-fat buttermilk

Fruit Topping (recipe follows)

^{1}/$_4$ cup sliced almonds, toasted

Per Serving
Calories: 136
% Calories from fat: 18
Fat (gm): 2.6
Saturated fat (gm): 0.4
Cholesterol (mg): 27
Sodium (mg): 207
Protein (gm): 6.1
Carbohydrate (gm): 19.8
Exchanges
Milk: 0.0
Vegetable: 0.0
Fruit: 0.5
Bread: 1.0
Meat: 0.0
Fat: 0.5

1. Cut peach slices into thirds; arrange in bottom of lightly greased 8-inch round cake pan.

2. Mix applesauce, Equal® for Recipes, egg, and vanilla until smooth in medium bowl. Mix in combined flour, baking powder, baking soda, cinnamon, nutmeg, and salt alternately with buttermilk, beginning and ending with dry ingredients. Pour batter over peach slices in pan.

3. Bake at 350 degrees until cake is browned and toothpick inserted in center comes out clean, about 20 minutes. Invert cake immediately onto serving plate. Cool 10 to 15 minutes; spread Fruit Topping over cake and sprinkle with almonds.

COFFEE-FROSTED COCOA CAKE

A perfect cake to carry for shared dinners and picnics.

16 servings

1¹/₂ cups sugar
¹/₂ cup margarine, softened
2 eggs
1 teaspoon vanilla
2 cups all-purpose flour
³/₄ cup unsweetened cocoa
2 teaspoons baking soda
1 teaspoon salt
1 cup skim milk
Coffee Frosting (recipe follows)

Per Serving
Calories: 240
% Calories from fat: 27
Fat (gm): 7.6
Saturated fat (gm): 1.6
Cholesterol (mg): 26.9
Sodium (mg): 385
Protein (gm): 3.9
Carbohydrate (gm): 41.9
Exchanges
Milk: 0.0
Vegetable: 0.0
Fruit: 0.0
Bread: 2.5
Meat: 0.0
Fat: 1.5

1. Combine sugar and margarine in large bowl; beat until light and fluffy. Add eggs one at a time, beating well after each addition. Stir in vanilla.

2. Combine flour, cocoa, baking soda, and salt in medium bowl. Mix dry ingredients into egg mixture alternately with milk, blending well. Spread batter in greased and floured 13 x 9-inch cake pan.

3. Bake cake at 350 degrees 25 to 35 minutes or until toothpick inserted in center comes out clean and cake begins to pull away from sides of pan. Cool completely on wire rack. Frost with Coffee Frosting.

Coffee Frosting

makes about ¹/₂ cup

1 tablespoon instant coffee granules
1 tablespoon hot water
1 tablespoon margarine, softened
1 cup powdered sugar
2-3 tablespoons skim milk

1. Dissolve coffee in hot water in medium bowl. Beat in margarine, powdered sugar, and enough milk for spreading consistency.

CHOCOLATE MOUSSE TORTE

This cake is more complex to make, but the soufflé-like flourless cake layers, filled and frosted with rich chocolate mousse, will make any occasion special.

12 servings

  5 egg yolks
2/3 cup sugar, divided
  1 teaspoon almond extract
  5 egg whites
1/4 teaspoon cream of tartar
1/4 cup Dutch process cocoa
      Chocolate Mousse (recipe follows)
1/4 cup sliced almonds, toasted

Per Serving
Calories: 247
% Calories from fat: 29
Fat (gm): 8.3
Saturated fat (gm): 3.2
Cholesterol (mg): 125.3
Sodium (mg): 54
Protein (gm): 7.1
Carbohydrate (gm): 39.2
Exchanges
Milk: 0.0
Vegetable: 0.0
Fruit: 0.0
Bread: 2.5
Meat: 0.0
Fat: 1.5

1. Grease bottoms of three 8- or 9-inch round cake pans and line with parchment paper; grease and flour lightly.

2. Beat egg yolks and 1/3 cup sugar in large bowl until thick and lemon colored, about 5 minutes; mix in almond extract.

3. With clean beaters and bowl, beat egg whites and cream of tartar to soft peaks; beat to stiff peaks, adding remaining 1/3 cup sugar gradually. Mix 1/4 of the egg whites into the egg yolk mixture; fold egg yolk mixture into egg whites. Fold in cocoa.

4. Spread batter in cake pans; bake at 350 degrees until toothpick inserted in center comes out clean, 15 to 18 minutes. Cool cakes in pans on wire racks; remove from pans.

5. Place 1 cake layer, parchment side up, in bottom of 9-inch springform pan; discard parchment. Spread cake with 1/3 of the Chocolate Mousse; repeat with remaining cake layers and Chocolate Mousse. Sprinkle top of cake with almonds. Refrigerate 8 hours or overnight.

6. Loosen cake from side of pan with sharp knife; remove side of pan and place cake on serving plate.

Chocolate Mousse

makes about 4 cups

1 envelope ($^1/_4$ ounce) unflavored gelatin
$^1/_4$ cup cold water
1 cup sugar, divided
$^1/_2$ cup Dutch process cocoa
$1^1/_4$ cups 1% low-fat milk
2 egg yolks
4 ounces semisweet chocolate, finely chopped
2 egg whites
$^1/_8$ teaspoon cream of tartar

1. Sprinkle gelatin over cold water in small saucepan; let stand 3 to 4 minutes. Heat over low heat until gelatin is dissolved, stirring constantly.

2. Mix $^1/_2$ cup sugar and cocoa in small saucepan; whisk in milk. Heat to boiling over medium-high heat; reduce heat and simmer briskly, whisking constantly, until thickened, 3 to 4 minutes. Whisk about $^1/_2$ the milk mixture into egg yolks; whisk yolk mixture into milk mixture in saucepan. Cook over low heat 1 to 2 minutes, whisking constantly. Remove from heat; add gelatin mixture and chocolate, whisking until chocolate is melted. Refrigerate until cool, but not set, about 20 minutes.

3. Beat egg whites, remaining $^1/_2$ cup sugar, and cream of tartar until foamy in medium bowl; place bowl over pan of simmering water and beat at medium speed until egg whites reach 160 degrees on candy thermometer. Remove from heat and beat at high speed until very thick and cool, about 5 minutes. Mix $^1/_4$ of the egg whites into chocolate mixture; fold chocolate mixture into remaining egg whites.

CHEESECAKE CUPCAKES

No need to frost, as these chocolate cupcakes are baked with a topping of cream cheese.

20 servings (1 cupcake each)

³/₄	cup all-purpose flour
³/₄	cup sugar
¹/₃	cup unsweetened cocoa
³/₄	teaspoon baking soda
¹/₂	teaspoon salt
³/₄	cup reduced-fat buttermilk
¹/₄	cup shortening
1	egg
1	teaspoon vanilla
	Cheesecake Topping (recipe follows)
¹/₂	cup reduced-fat semisweet chocolate morsels

Per Serving
Calories: 136
% Calories from fat: 29
Fat (gm): 4.6
Saturated fat (gm): 2.3
Cholesterol (mg): 22.5
Sodium (mg): 186
Protein (gm): 3.4
Carbohydrate (gm): 21.7
Exchanges
Milk: 0.0
Vegetable: 0.0
Fruit: 0.0
Bread: 1.5
Meat: 0.0
Fat: 0.5

1. Combine all ingredients, except Cheesecake Topping and chocolate morsels, in large bowl. Beat at low speed until blended; beat at high speed 3 minutes, scraping side of bowl occasionally.

2. Pour batter into paper-lined muffin cups, filling each about ¹/₂ full. Spread about 1 tablespoon Cheesecake Topping over batter in each, covering completely. Sprinkle each with about 1 teaspoon chocolate morsels.

3. Bake at 350 degrees until golden, about 30 minutes. Cool in pans on wire rack.

Cheesecake Topping

1	package (8 ounces) fat-free cream cheese, room temperature
¹/₂	cup sugar
1	egg

1. Mix all ingredients until smooth.

GINGERED PEAR CAKE

We serve this cake simply topped with sweetened sour cream and ginger; a drizzle of Citrus Glaze (see p. 755) is also delicious.

12 servings

1 cup packed light brown sugar
1/4 cup margarine, softened
3 egg whites
1 1/2 cups all-purpose flour
1 1/2 teaspoons baking soda
1/4 teaspoon salt
1 teaspoon ground ginger
1/4 teaspoon ground cloves
2 tablespoons chopped crystallized ginger
2 small pears, unpeeled, cored, shredded
Gingered Sour Cream Topping (recipe follows)

Per Serving
Calories: 228
% Calories from fat: 22
Fat (gm): 5.7
Saturated fat (gm): 2.1
Cholesterol (mg): 6.7
Sodium (mg): 287
Protein (gm): 4
Carbohydrate (gm): 40.7
Exchanges
Milk: 0.0
Vegetable: 0.0
Fruit: 0.0
Bread: 2.5
Meat: 0.0
Fat: 1.0

1. Beat brown sugar, margarine, and egg whites in large bowl until thoroughly mixed. Mix in combined flour, baking soda, salt, ground ginger, cloves, and crystallized ginger. Gently mix in pears.

2. Pour batter into greased and floured 6-cup fluted tube pan. Bake at 350 degrees until toothpick inserted in center comes out clean, 50 to 60 minutes. Cool cake in pan on wire rack 10 minutes; remove from pan and cool completely.

3. Serve cake slices with Gingered Sour Cream Topping.

Gingered Sour Cream Topping

makes 1 to 1 1/2 cups

1-1 1/2 cups reduced-fat sour cream
2-3 tablespoons sugar
2-4 tablespoons coarsely chopped crystallized ginger

1. Mix all ingredients.

PEACH MERINGUE CAKE

Meringues, light as clouds, are layered with cake and peach cream filling.

12 servings

8 tablespoons margarine, softened
1/2 cup sugar
4 egg yolks
1 teaspoon vanilla
1 cup all-purpose flour
2 teaspoons baking powder
1/4 teaspoon salt
1/3 cup fat-free milk
  Peach Cream Filling (recipe follows)
  Meringue Layers (recipe follows)

Per Serving
Calories: 263
% Calories from fat: 36
Fat (gm): 10.4
Saturated fat (gm): 3
Cholesterol (mg): 71.1
Sodium (mg): 243
Protein (gm): 3.5
Carbohydrate (gm): 38.8
Exchanges
Milk: 0.0
Vegetable: 0.0
Fruit: 0.0
Bread: 2.5
Meat: 0.0
Fat: 2.0

1. Beat margarine and sugar in large bowl until fluffy; beat in egg yolks and vanilla. Mix in combined flour, baking powder, and salt alternately with milk, beginning and ending with dry ingredients.

2. Spread batter in 2 greased and floured 9-inch round cake pans; bake at 350 degrees until toothpick inserted in center comes out clean, 35 to 40 minutes. Cool cakes in pans on wire rack 10 minutes; remove from pans and cool completely.

3. Place 1 cake layer on serving plate; spread with 1/2 cup Peach Cream Filling, top with 1 Meringue Layer, and spread with another 1/2 cup Peach Cream Filling. Top with remaining cake layer, Peach Cream Filling, and Meringue Layer.

Peach Cream Filling

makes about 1 1/2 cups

1 1/2 cups light whipped topping
2 tablespoons peach preserves
1 tablespoon powdered sugar

1. Mix all ingredients.

Meringue Layers

makes 2

> 4 egg whites
> 1/8 teaspoon cream of tartar
> 1 cup sugar

1. Beat egg whites and cream of tartar to soft peaks in large bowl; beat to stiff peaks, adding sugar gradually.

2. Spread mixture onto greased and floured bottoms of 2 inverted 9-inch round cake pans, spreading to edges of pans. Bake at 350 degrees until meringues are golden and crisp, about 40 minutes. Carefully remove meringues from pan bottoms with metal spatula; cool on wire rack.

RICH LEMON POUND CAKE

Savor the richness of this cake—balanced perfectly by the Lemon Syrup accompaniment.

12 servings

> 3/4 cup sugar
> 1/3 cup margarine, softened
> 1 cup reduced-fat sour cream
> 3 egg whites
> 2 teaspoons lemon juice
> 1 tablespoon grated lemon rind
> 2 1/2 cups cake flour
> 1 teaspoon baking soda
> 1/4 teaspoon salt
> Lemon Syrup (recipe follows)
> Powdered sugar, as garnish

Per Serving
Calories: 234
% Calories from fat: 27
Fat (gm): 6.9
Saturated fat (gm): 2.4
Cholesterol (mg): 6.7
Sodium (mg): 240
Protein (gm): 4.2
Carbohydrate (gm): 39
Exchanges
Milk: 0.0
Vegetable: 0.0
Fruit: 0.0
Bread: 2.5
Meat: 0.0
Fat: 1.0

1. Beat sugar and margarine in large bowl until light and fluffy. Beat in sour cream, egg whites, lemon juice, and lemon rind until smooth. Mix in combined flour, baking soda, and salt, beating until smooth, about 1 minute. Spoon batter into greased and floured 6-cup fluted tube pan.

2. Bake cake 40 to 50 minutes or until toothpick inserted in center comes out clean. Cool in pan on wire rack 20 minutes; invert onto wire rack.

3. With a skewer or tines of fork, pierce cake top at 1-inch intervals. Spoon warm Lemon Syrup over cake; sprinkle with powdered sugar.

Lemon Syrup

makes about 2/3 cup

> 2/3 cup powdered sugar
> 1/4 cup lemon juice
> 3 tablespoons water

1. Combine sugar, lemon juice, and water in small saucepan. Heat to boiling, stirring constantly until sugar is dissolved. Cool slightly.

MOIST RAISIN CAKE

Thank you, Mrs. Rosencrans, for sharing your dairy-free recipe! The cake is also excellent without the spices.

12 servings

> 1 cup raisins
> 2 cups water
> 1/2 cup margarine, room temperature
> 13/4 cup all-purpose flour
> 1 cup granulated sugar
> 1 teaspoon baking soda
> 1 teaspoon salt
> 1/2 teaspoon ground cinnamon
> 1/2 teaspoon ground nutmeg
>   Powdered sugar, as garnish

Per Serving
Calories: 235
% Calories from fat: 29
Fat (gm): 7.8
Saturated fat (gm): 1.6
Cholesterol (mg): 0
Sodium (mg): 389
Protein (gm): 2.4
Carbohydrate (gm): 40.3
Exchanges
Milk: 0.0
Vegetable: 0.0
Fruit: 0.0
Bread: 2.5
Meat: 0.0
Fat: 1.5

1. Heat raisins and water to boiling in medium saucepan; reduce heat and simmer, uncovered, 10 minutes. Add margarine, stirring until melted. Cool.

2. Add combined remaining ingredients, except powdered sugar, mixing well. Pour batter into greased 13 x 9-inch baking pan. Bake at 350 degrees until cake springs back when touched, about 35 minutes. Cool on wire rack; sprinkle with powdered sugar.

CITRUS POPPY SEED ANGEL FOOD CAKE

My all-time favorite angel food cake—tall, tender, and bursting with sweet citrus flavor!

16 servings

13 egg whites, room temperature
1 teaspoon cream of tartar
2 teaspoons lemon juice
1½ cups sugar, divided
1 cup cake flour
½ teaspoon salt
2 tablespoons finely grated orange rind
1 tablespoon finely grated lemon rind
2 tablespoons poppy seeds
Citrus Glaze (recipe follows)

Per Serving
Calories: 149
% Calories from fat: 3
Fat (gm): 0.5
Saturated fat (gm): 0.1
Cholesterol (mg): 0
Sodium (mg): 118
Protein (gm): 3.6
Carbohydrate (gm): 32.8
Exchanges
Milk: 0.0
Vegetable: 0.0
Fruit: 0.0
Bread: 2.0
Meat: 0.0
Fat: 0.0

1. Beat egg whites and cream of tartar to soft peaks in large bowl. Beat in lemon juice; beat just to stiff peaks, adding ½ cup sugar gradually (do not overbeat). Sprinkle ½ cup sugar over egg whites and fold in. Combine remaining ½ cup sugar, flour, and salt; sift half the flour mixture over egg whites and fold in. Repeat with remaining flour mixture. Fold in citrus rinds and poppy seeds.

2. Pour batter into ungreased 12-cup tube pan. Bake until cake is golden and cracks look dry, about 40 minutes. Invert pan on funnel and cool completely. Loosen side of cake from pan with metal spatula and invert onto serving plate. Drizzle with Citrus Glaze.

Citrus Glaze

makes about ½ cup

1 cup powdered sugar
3-4 tablespoons orange juice

1. In small bowl, combine powdered sugar and enough orange juice to make glaze consistency.

CLASSIC SPONGE CAKE

This luscious, very low-fat cake can be adapted to make many desserts—use your imagination and combine different fillings and frostings to create your own masterpiece! Simply sprinkle with powdered sugar and serve with a medley of berries, or frost with Chocolate Glaze (see p. 743).

12 servings

3   egg yolks
1   cup sugar, divided
2   teaspoons vanilla
1/4   cup water
1   cup cake flour
1   teaspoon baking powder
1/4   teaspoon salt
5   egg whites
1/4   teaspoon cream of tartar

Per Serving
Calories: 122
% Calories from fat: 10
Fat (gm): 1.4
Saturated fat (gm): 0.4
Cholesterol (mg): 53.2
Sodium (mg): 114
Protein (gm): 2.9
Carbohydrate (gm): 24.3
Exchanges
Milk: 0.0
Vegetable: 0.0
Fruit: 0.0
Bread: 1.5
Meat: 0.0
Fat: 0.0

1.   Beat egg yolks in large mixing bowl, gradually adding 3/4 cup sugar; beat at high speed until yolks are thick and lemon colored, about 5 minutes. Mix in vanilla and water; add combined flour, baking powder, and salt, beating on low speed just until blended.

2.   With clean beaters and in separate large bowl, beat egg whites and cream of tartar to soft peaks. Beat to stiff peaks, gradually adding remaining 1/4 cup sugar. Stir 1/4 of the egg whites into batter; fold batter into remaining whites.

3.   Pour batter into ungreased 12-cup tube pan. Bake at 350 degrees 35 minutes or until cake springs back when touched lightly. Invert pan onto funnel and cool to room temperature. Loosen side of cake with small metal spatula and remove from pan.

Tip: Cake can be baked in an ungreased 10-inch springform pan. Invert on wire rack or balance on 4 cans or custard cups to cool.

LEMON CUSTARD SPONGE CAKE

A beautiful cake that will make any special occasion one to remember.

12 servings

3 egg yolks
3/4 cup sugar, divided
1 teaspoon vanilla
3 egg whites
1/8 teaspoon cream of tartar
1/3 cup all-purpose flour
1/3 cup cornstarch
1/8 teaspoon salt
    Lemon Custard (recipe follows)
2 1/2 cups light whipped topping, divided
1/2 cup raspberries
    Lemon rind twists, as garnish
    Mint sprigs, as garnish

Per Serving
Calories: 196
% Calories from fat: 25
Fat (gm): 5.4
Saturated fat (gm): 2.6
Cholesterol (mg): 71.5
Sodium (mg): 126
Protein (gm): 3.2
Carbohydrate (gm): 33
Exchanges
Milk: 0.0
Vegetable: 0.0
Fruit: 0.0
Bread: 2.0
Meat: 0.0
Fat: 1.0

1. Grease 9-inch round cake pan; line with parchment paper and grease and flour.

2. Beat egg yolks and 1/2 cup sugar in small bowl until thick and lemon colored, 3 to 5 minutes; mix in vanilla.

3. With clean, medium bowl and beaters, beat egg whites and cream of tartar to soft peaks; beat to stiff peaks, adding remaining 1/4 cup sugar gradually. Fold egg yolk mixture into egg whites. Gently fold in combined flour, cornstarch, and salt.

4. Spread batter in prepared pan. Bake at 350 degrees until toothpick inserted in center of cake comes out clean, about 30 minutes. Cool cake in pan 10 minutes; remove from pan and cool completely. Remove parchment.

5. Cut cake horizontally in half. Place bottom of cake on serving plate. Spread 1 cup Lemon Custard on cake and top with second layer. Spread remaining 1 cup Lemon Custard on top of cake. Spread 2 cups whipped topping on side of cake. Place remaining 1/2 cup whipped topping in pastry bag with star tip and pipe rosettes around top edge of cake. Garnish rosettes with raspberries, lemon rind twists, and mint sprigs. Refrigerate until serving time.

Lemon Custard

makes about 2 cups

1/3 cup sugar
1/4 cup cornstarch
1/4 teaspoon salt
1 1/3 cups fat-free milk
1 egg yolk
2 tablespoons margarine
2 teaspoons grated lemon rind
1/3 cup lemon juice

1. Combine sugar, cornstarch, and salt in medium saucepan; whisk in milk. Heat to boiling over medium-high heat, whisking constantly; boil, whisking constantly, until thickened, about 1 minute.

2. Whisk about 1/2 cup milk mixture into egg yolk; whisk yolk mixture back into milk mixture. Cook over low heat, whisking constantly, 1 to 2 minutes. Remove from heat; stir in margarine, lemon rind, and lemon juice. Cool; refrigerate until chilled.

Variation: **Sponge Cake with Rosemary Syrup and Blueberries—** Make cake as above; do not make Lemon Custard. Cool uncut cake on wire rack 20 minutes; remove from pan and place on serving plate. To make **Rosemary Syrup,** heat 3/4 cup sugar, 3/4 cup water, 2 tablespoons crushed dried rosemary leaves, and 1 tablespoon lemon juice to boiling in small saucepan. Reduce heat and simmer, uncovered, 10 minutes. Pierce top of cake with tines of fork; drizzle 1/2 cup warm syrup over warm cake. Mix remaining syrup with 1 1/2 quarts blueberries; serve over cake slices.

ORANGE POPPY SEED CAKE

This citrus-fresh cake is a perfect addition to any brunch menu.

12 servings

1/2 cup sugar
6 tablespoons margarine, softened
2 egg whites
1 egg
3/4 cup reduced-fat sour cream
2 tablespoons frozen orange juice concentrate, thawed
2 cups cake flour
2 tablespoons poppy seeds
1 teaspoon baking powder
1/2 teaspoon baking soda
1/4 teaspoon salt

Per Serving
Calories: 227
% Calories from fat: 31
Fat (gm): 7.8
Saturated fat (gm): 1.3
Cholesterol (mg): 22.5
Sodium (mg): 215
Protein (gm): 3.5
Carbohydrate (gm): 35.5
Exchanges
Milk: 0.0
Vegetable: 0.0
Fruit: 0.0
Bread: 2.5
Meat: 0.0
Fat: 1.0

1. In large bowl, beat sugar and margarine until smooth and fluffy. Beat in egg whites, egg, sour cream, and orange juice concentrate until smooth.

2. Mix in combined cake flour, poppy seeds, baking powder, baking soda, and salt; beat on medium-high speed until smooth, 1 to 2 minutes. Pour batter into greased and floured 6-cup fluted cake pan.

3. Bake cake at 350 degrees 40 to 55 minutes or until toothpick inserted in center comes out clean. Cool in pan on wire rack 25 to 30 minutes; invert onto wire rack and cool.

HOT FUDGE PUDDING CAKE

For the ultimate treat serve warm, topped with scoops of low-fat ice cream or frozen yogurt.

6 servings

  1 cup all-purpose flour
 1/2 cup packed light brown sugar
  6 tablespoons Dutch process cocoa, divided
1 1/2 teaspoons baking powder
 1/4 teaspoon salt
 1/2 cup fat-free milk
  2 tablespoons vegetable oil
  1 teaspoon vanilla
 1/3 cup granulated sugar
1 1/2 cups boiling water

Per Serving
Calories: 259
% Calories from fat: 18
Fat (gm): 5.2
Saturated fat (gm): 0.9
Cholesterol (mg): 0.4
Sodium (mg): 240
Protein (gm): 4.1
Carbohydrate (gm): 49.1
Exchanges
Milk: 0.0
Vegetable: 0.0
Fruit: 0.0
Bread: 3.0
Meat: 0.0
Fat: 1.0

1. Combine flour, brown sugar, 3 tablespoons cocoa, baking powder, and salt in medium bowl. Add combined milk, oil, and vanilla to flour mixture, mixing well. Spoon batter into greased 8- or 9-inch square baking pan.

2. Mix remaining 3 tablespoons cocoa and granulated sugar; sprinkle over cake batter. Pour boiling water over batter; do not stir.

3. Bake at 350 degrees until cake springs back when touched, about 30 minutes. Cool on wire rack 5 to 10 minutes; serve warm.

Variation: **Mocha Latte Pudding Cake**—Make cake as above, substituting granulated sugar for the brown sugar and adding 1 tablespoon instant espresso coffee powder and 1/2 teaspoon ground cinnamon to flour mixture. Serve warm pudding cake with a scoop of fat-free vanilla or chocolate ice cream and light whipped topping.

LEMON PUDDING CAKE

A luscious combination of moist cake and creamy pudding—for best flavor, use fresh lemon juice.

8 servings

1¹/₄ cups sugar, divided
¹/₂ cup all-purpose flour
¹/₈ teaspoon salt
1 cup reduced-fat 2% milk
¹/₃ cup lemon juice
2 tablespoons margarine, melted
1 egg
1 tablespoon grated lemon rind
3 egg whites
¹/₈ teaspoon cream of tartar

Per Serving
Calories: 208
% Calories from fat: 17
Fat (gm): 4.1
Saturated fat (gm): 1.1
Cholesterol (mg): 28.8
Sodium (mg): 114
Protein (gm): 4
Carbohydrate (gm): 39.9
Exchanges
Milk: 0.0
Vegetable: 0.0
Fruit: 0.0
Bread: 2.5
Meat: 0.0
Fat: 0.5

1. Combine 1 cup sugar, flour, and salt in large bowl. Combine milk, lemon juice, margarine, egg, and lemon rind; mix into dry ingredients.

2. Beat egg whites and cream of tartar to soft peaks in large bowl; beat to stiff peaks, adding remaining ¹/₄ cup sugar gradually. Fold egg whites into cake batter (batter will be slightly lumpy and thin).

3. Pour batter into greased 1¹/₂-quart casserole or soufflé dish. Place casserole in roasting pan on oven rack; add 1 to 2 inches boiling water to pan. Bake at 350 degrees until cake is golden and springs back when touched, about 40 minutes. Cool on wire rack 15 minutes; serve warm.

BASIC PIE CRUST (ALL-PURPOSE FLOUR)

This pastry contains a minimum of margarine yet is not difficult to handle or roll. Use cold margarine and ice water, as the recipe directs.

8 servings (one 8- or 9-inch pie crust)

1¼   cups all-purpose flour
2   tablespoons sugar
¼   teaspoon salt
4-5   tablespoons cold margarine *or* vegetable shortening
3-5   tablespoons ice water

Per Serving
Calories: 134
% Calories from fat: 39*
Fat (gm): 5.8
Saturated fat (gm): 1.1
Cholesterol (mg): 0
Sodium (mg): 140
Protein (gm): 2.1
Carbohydrate (gm): 18
Exchanges
Milk: 0.0
Vegetable: 0.0
Fruit: 0.0
Bread: 1.0
Meat: 0.0
Fat: 1.0

1. Combine flour, sugar, and salt in medium bowl. With pastry blender or 2 knives, cut in margarine until mixture resembles coarse crumbs. Sprinkle with water, 1 tablespoon at a time, mixing lightly with a fork after each addition until pastry just holds together.

2. Roll dough on lightly floured surface into circle 2 inches larger in diameter than pie pan. Wrap pastry around rolling pin and unroll into 8- or 9-inch pie or tart pan, easing it into bottom and side of pan. Trim edges, fold under, and flute. Bake as pie recipe directs.

Tip: To bake pie crust before filling it, line bottom of pastry with aluminum foil and fill with a single layer of pie weights or dried beans. Bake at 425 degrees until browned, about 15 minutes, removing weights and foil 5 minutes before end of baking time. If not using weights or dried beans, piercing the bottom of the pastry with the tines of a fork will help crust remain flat.

*The percentage of calories from fat will decrease in servings of actual pie.

BASIC PIE CRUST (CAKE FLOUR)

This pastry also contains a minimum of margarine but uses cake flour, which is lower in calories than all-purpose flour.

8 servings (one 8- or 9-inch pie crust)

1¼ cups cake flour
1 tablespoon sugar
¼ teaspoon salt
4-5 tablespoons cold margarine
3-5 tablespoons ice water

Per Serving
Calories: 119
% Calories from fat: 44*
Fat (gm): 5.8
Saturated fat (gm): 1.1
Cholesterol (mg): 0
Sodium (mg): 140
Protein (gm): 1.5
Carbohydrate (gm): 14.9
Exchanges
Milk: 0.0
Vegetable: 0.0
Fruit: 0.0
Bread: 1.0
Meat: 0.0
Fat: 1.0

1. Combine cake flour, sugar, and salt in medium bowl. With pastry blender or 2 knives, cut in margarine until mixture resembles coarse crumbs. Sprinkle in water, 1 tablespoon at a time, mixing lightly with a fork after each addition until pastry just holds together.

2. Roll dough on lightly floured surface into a circle 2 inches larger in diameter than pie pan. Wrap pastry around rolling pin and unroll into 8- or 9-inch pie or tart pan, easing it into bottom and side of pan. Trim edges, fold under, and flute. Bake as pie recipe directs.

Tip: To bake pie crust before filling it, line bottom of pastry with aluminum foil and fill with a single layer of pie weights or dried beans. Bake at 425 degrees until browned, about 15 minutes, removing weights and foil 5 minutes before end of baking time. If not using weights or dried beans, piercing the bottom of the pastry with the tines of a fork will help crust remain flat.

*The percentage of calories from fat will decrease in servings of actual pie.

DOUBLE PIE CRUST

Perfect for fresh fruit pie!

8 servings (one 8- or 9-inch double pie crust)

1³/₄ cups all-purpose flour
3 tablespoons sugar
¹/₂ teaspoon salt
5-6 tablespoons cold margarine, cut into pieces
5-7 tablespoons ice water

Per Serving
Calories: 181
% Calories from fat: 36*
Fat (gm): 7.3
Saturated fat (gm): 1.4
Cholesterol (mg): 0
Sodium (mg): 229
Protein (gm): 2.9
Carbohydrate (gm): 25.6
Exchanges
Milk: 0.0
Vegetable: 0.0
Fruit: 0.0
Bread: 1.5
Meat: 0.0
Fat: 1.5

1.   Combine flour, sugar, and salt in medium bowl; cut in margarine with pastry blender or two knives until mixture resembles coarse crumbs. Add water, a tablespoon at a time, mixing with fork, until dough forms.

2.   Roll and bake as recipe directs.

*The percentage of calories from fat will decrease in servings of actual pie.

CORNMEAL DOUBLE PIE CRUST

This unusual Italian-Style crust is particularly good with fruit pies.

8 servings (one 8- or 9-inch double pie crust)

2 cups all-purpose flour
¹/₃ cup yellow cornmeal
1 teaspoon baking powder
¹/₂ teaspoon salt
5 tablespoons cold margarine, cut into pieces
¹/₄ package (8-ounce size) cold fat-free cream cheese, cut into pieces
3 egg whites *or* ¹/₃ cup no-cholesterol real egg product

Per Serving
Calories: 209
% Calories from fat: 33*
Fat (gm): 7.6
Saturated fat (gm): 1.5
Cholesterol (mg): 0.6
Sodium (mg): 351
Protein (gm): 6.1
Carbohydrate (gm): 28.4
Exchanges
Milk: 0.0
Vegetable: 0.0
Fruit: 0.0
Bread: 2.0
Meat: 0.0
Fat: 1.5

1. Combine flour, cornmeal, baking powder, and salt in bowl; cut in margarine and cream cheese until mixture resembles coarse crumbs. Add egg whites, mixing until dough is moist and crumbly.

2. Roll and bake as pie recipe directs.

*The percentage of calories from fat will decrease in servings of actual pie.

SHORTBREAD CRUST

A tender, sweet crust that is almost like a cookie.

12 servings (one 10- or 12-inch tart crust)

1¹/₃ cups all-purpose flour
¹/₂ cup powdered sugar
Pinch salt
5 tablespoons cold margarine, cut into pieces
1 egg, lightly beaten
1 teaspoon vanilla

Per Serving
Calories: 120
% Calories from fat: 40*
Fat (gm): 5.3
Saturated fat (gm): 1.1
Cholesterol (mg): 17.7
Sodium (mg): 61
Protein (gm): 2
Carbohydrate (gm): 15.7
Exchanges
Milk: 0.0
Vegetable: 0.0
Fruit: 0.0
Bread: 1.0
Meat: 0.0
Fat: 1.0

1. Combine flour, sugar, and salt in medium bowl. Cut in margarine until mixture resembles coarse crumbs. Mix in combined egg and vanilla with fork, stirring just until mixture forms a dough.

2. Form dough into a ball; flatten slightly and wrap in plastic wrap. Chill 1 hour or longer before using.

3. Roll and bake as recipe directs.

*The percentage of calories from fat will decrease in servings of actual pie.

GRAHAM CRACKER CRUMB CRUST

Mix crumb crust right in the pan—quick and easy!

8 servings (one 8- or 9-inch pie crust)

1¼ cups graham cracker crumbs
2 tablespoons sugar
3 tablespoons margarine, melted
1-2 tablespoons honey

Per Serving
Calories: 144
% Calories from fat: 47*
Fat (gm): 7.8
Saturated fat (gm): 1.6
Cholesterol (mg): 0
Sodium (mg): 125
Protein (gm): 1.3
Carbohydrate (gm): 18
Exchanges
Milk: 0.0
Vegetable: 0.0
Fruit: 0.0
Bread: 1.0
Meat: 0.0
Fat: 1.5

1. Combine graham crumbs, sugar, and margarine in 8- or 9-inch pie pan; add enough honey for mixture to stick together. Pat mixture evenly on bottom and side of pan.

2. Bake at 350 degrees 8 to 10 minutes or until edge of crust is lightly browned. Cool on wire rack.

*The percentage of calories from fat will decrease in servings of actual pie.

CHOCOLATE COOKIE CRUMB CRUST

You can choose chocolate wafer crumbs, or chocolate sandwich cookie crumbs.

8 servings (one 8- or 9-inch pie crust)

1¼ cups chocolate cookie crumbs
2 tablespoons sugar
3 tablespoons margarine, melted
1-2 tablespoons honey

Per Serving
Calories: 158
% Calories from fat: 44*
Fat (gm): 8
Saturated fat (gm): 1.5
Cholesterol (mg): 0
Sodium (mg): 225
Protein (gm): 1.3
Carbohydrate (gm): 21.6
Exchanges
Milk: 0.0
Vegetable: 0.0
Fruit: 0.0
Bread: 1.5
Meat: 0.0
Fat: 1.0

1. Mix cookie crumbs, sugar, and margarine in bottom of 8- or 9-inch pie pan; add enough honey for mixture to stick together. Press evenly on bottom and side of pie pan.

2. Bake at 350 degrees 6 to 8 minutes. Cool on wire rack.

Variation: **Chocolate Pecan Crumb Crust**—Make crust as above, decreasing margarine to 1 tablespoon, increasing honey to 3 tablespoons, and adding 1/4 cup ground pecans.

*The percentage of calories from fat will decrease in servings of actual pie.

CINNAMON-APPLE PIE

One of the juiciest apple pies you'll ever taste! Use a tart baking apple—Granny Smith is our favorite.

8 servings

Double Pie Crust (see p. 764)

8 1/4 teaspoons Equal® for Recipes *or* 27 packets Equal® sweetener, divided

1/2 teaspoon ground cinnamon

2-3 pinches ground nutmeg

6 cups sliced, peeled baking apples (about 6 medium)

3/4 cup unsweetened apple juice

1 tablespoon cornstarch

1 teaspoon grated lemon rind

Per Serving
Calories: 246
% Calories from fat: 28
Fat (gm): 7.8
Saturated fat (gm): 1.5
Cholesterol (mg): 0
Sodium (mg): 232
Protein (gm): 6.2
Carbohydrate (gm): 39.1
Exchanges
Milk: 0.0
Vegetable: 0.0
Fruit: 1.0
Bread: 1.5
Meat: 0.0
Fat: 1.5

1. Make Double Pie Crust, substituting 1 teaspoon Equal® for Recipes for the sugar. Roll 2/3 of the pastry on lightly floured surface into circle 1 1/2 inches larger than inverted 9-inch pie pan. Ease pastry into pan.

2. Combine 5 1/2 teaspoons Equal® for Recipes, cinnamon, and nutmeg; sprinkle over apples in large bowl and toss.

3. Mix apple juice, remaining 1 3/4 teaspoons Equal® for Recipes, cornstarch, and lemon rind in small saucepan; heat to boiling, whisking constantly until thickened, about 1 minute. Pour mixture over apples and toss; arrange in pastry.

4. Roll remaining pastry on lightly floured surface to $^1/_8$ inch thickness and place over apples. Trim edges of pastry to within $^1/_2$ inch of pan; fold top pastry over bottom pastry and flute. Cut decorative slits in top of pastry.

5. Bake pie in preheated 425 degree oven until pastry is golden and apples are tender, 40 to 50 minutes; cover edge of pie with aluminum foil if browning too quickly. Cool on wire rack.

HEAVENLY PEACH PIE

Enjoy this pie in winter too, using frozen, thawed peaches, or drained canned peaches in juice.

8 servings

Double Pie Crust (see p. 764)
$8^1/_4$ teaspoons Equal® for Recipes *or* 27 packets Equal® sweetener, divided
6 cups sliced, pitted, peeled peaches
2 tablespoons flour
$^1/_2$ teaspoon ground cinnamon
2-3 pinches ground nutmeg

Per Serving
Calories: 238
% Calories from fat: 28
Fat (gm): 7.4
Saturated fat (gm): 1.5
Cholesterol (mg): 0
Sodium (mg): 230
Protein (gm): 7.2
Carbohydrate (gm): 36.6
Exchanges
Milk: 0.0
Vegetable: 0.0
Fruit: 1.0
Bread: 1.5
Meat: 0.0
Fat: 1.5

1. Make Double Pie Crust, substituting 1 teaspoon Equal® for Recipes for the sugar. Roll $^2/_3$ of the pastry on lightly floured surface to form circle $1^1/_2$ inches larger than inverted 9-inch pie pan. Ease pastry into pan.

2. Toss peaches with combined flour, remaining $7^1/_4$ teaspoons Equal® for Recipes, cinnamon, and nutmeg. Arrange fruit in pastry.

3. Roll remaining pastry on lightly floured surface to $^1/_8$ inch thickness; cut into $^1/_2$-inch strips. Lay pastry strips across top of pie and weave into lattice design. Trim ends of strips; fold edge of lower crust over ends of strips and seal and flute edge.

4. Bake pie at 425 degrees until bubbly, 30 to 40 minutes, covering edge of crust with aluminum foil if necessary to prevent excessive browning. Cool on wire rack.

TARTE TATIN

Caramelized sugar contributes special flavor to this French-style upside-down apple tart.

8 servings

5 cups Granny Smith apples (about 2^1/$_2$ pounds), peeled, cored, and cut into scant ^{1}/$_2$-inch slices

^{3}/$_4$ cup sugar, divided

^{1}/$_4$ teaspoon ground nutmeg

1 tablespoon lemon juice

2 tablespoons margarine

Tatin Crust (recipe follows)

Per Serving
Calories: 245
% Calories from fat: 27
Fat (gm): 7.6
Saturated fat (gm): 1.5
Cholesterol (mg): 0
Sodium (mg): 84
Protein (gm): 1.4
Carbohydrate (gm): 44.8
Exchanges
Milk: 0.0
Vegetable: 0.0
Fruit: 2.0
Bread: 1.0
Meat: 0.0
Fat: 1.0

1. Toss apples with ^{1}/$_2$ cup sugar and nutmeg; sprinkle with lemon juice. Set aside.

2. Place remaining ^{1}/$_4$ cup sugar in 10-inch skillet with oven-proof handle. Cook over medium heat until sugar melts and is golden brown, about 5 minutes, stirring occasionally (watch carefully as the sugar can burn easily). Add apple mixture and margarine; cook 5 minutes or until apples are just tender, stirring occasionally. Remove from heat.

3. Arrange apples in skillet so they are slightly mounded in the center.

4. On lightly floured surface, roll Tatin Crust into 11-inch circle and place on top of apples; tuck in edges. Cut vents in pastry to allow steam to escape.

5. Bake in skillet at 425 degrees 20 to 25 minutes or until lightly browned. Invert onto serving platter. Serve warm or at room temperature.

Tatin Crust

1 cup cake flour
2 tablespoons sugar
3 tablespoons cold margarine
2-3 tablespoons ice water

1. Combine cake flour and sugar in medium bowl. Cut in margarine until mixture resembles coarse crumbs. Sprinkle in water, 1 tablespoon at a time, mixing lightly with a fork until dough just holds together. Cover and refrigerate 15 minutes.

Variations: **Caramelized Pear and Almond Tarte Tatin**—Substitute pears for the apples, tossing with combined 1/2 cup sugar, 1/3 cup sliced almonds, 1 tablespoon flour, 1 teaspoon grated lemon rind, 1/2 teaspoon ground cinnamon, and 1/4 teaspoon ground nutmeg. Complete recipe as above, beginning with Step 2.

Apple-Cheddar Tarte Tatin—Make recipe as above, adding 1/3 cup raisins to apples in Step 1. Prepare Tatin Crust, substituting vegetable shortening for the margarine, and adding 1/3 cup shredded reduced-fat or fat-free Cheddar cheese before sprinkling with water; add additional water if necessary.

APPLE-CRANBERRY STREUSEL PIE

This pie will be a delicious addition to your holiday dessert table.

8 servings

Basic Pie Crust (All-Purpose Flour) (see p. 762)
10 teaspoons Equal® for Recipes *or* 33 packets Equal® sweetener, divided
1 tablespoon cornstarch
1 cup apple cider *or* unsweetened apple juice
1 1/2 cups cranberries, coarsely chopped
3/4 teaspoon ground cinnamon
1/4 teaspoon ground nutmeg
1/4 teaspoon salt
5 cups sliced, cored, peeled tart baking apples (about 5 medium)
Cinnamon Streusel (recipe follows)

Per Serving
Calories: 334
% Calories from fat: 36
Fat (gm): 13.7
Saturated fat (gm): 2.7
Cholesterol (mg): 0
Sodium (mg): 372
Protein (gm): 9.4
Carbohydrate (gm): 45.2
Exchanges
Milk: 0.0
Vegetable: 0.0
Fruit: 1.0
Bread: 2.0
Meat: 0.0
Fat: 2.5

1. Make Basic Pie Crust, substituting 1 teaspoon Equal® for Recipes for the sugar. Roll pastry on floured surface into circle 1¹/₂ inches larger than inverted 9-inch pie pan. Ease pastry into pan; trim and flute.

2. Combine cornstarch and remaining 9 teaspoons Equal® for Recipes in small saucepan; stir in apple cider and cranberries. Heat to boiling; reduce heat and simmer, stirring constantly, until thickened, about 1 minute. Stir in spices and salt. Toss cranberry mixture with apples; arrange in pastry and sprinkle evenly with Cinnamon Streusel.

3. Bake pie at 400 degrees until pastry is golden and apples are tender, 50 to 60 minutes, covering pie loosely with aluminum foil during last 20 to 30 minutes of baking time if needed to prevent excessive browning. Cool on wire rack; serve warm.

Cinnamon Streusel

makes about ¹/₂ cup

- ¹/₄ cup quick-cooking oats
- 3 tablespoons all-purpose flour
- 3¹/₂ teaspoons Equal® for Recipes *or* 12 packets Equal® sweetener
- 1 teaspoon ground cinnamon
- ¹/₂ teaspoon ground nutmeg
- 4 tablespoons cold margarine, cut into pieces

1. Combine oats, flour, Equal® for Recipes, cinnamon, and nutmeg in small bowl; cut in margarine until mixture resembles coarse crumbs.

BLUEBERRY PATCH PIE

Pastry strips weave a lattice topping for this garden fresh pie.

8 servings

Double Pie Crust (see p. 764)
11³/₄ teaspoons Equal® for Recipes *or* 39 packets Equal® sweetener, divided
4 tablespoons plus 2 teaspoons cornstarch, divided
¹/₃ cup apple juice
2 tablespoons lemon juice
6 cups fresh blueberries *or* 2 packages (16 ounces each) frozen unsweetened blueberries, thawed

Per Serving
Calories: 266
% Calories from fat: 26
Fat (gm): 7.7
Saturated fat (gm): 1.5
Cholesterol (mg): 0
Sodium (mg): 238
Protein (gm): 8.3
Carbohydrate (gm): 42
Exchanges
Milk: 0.0
Vegetable: 0.0
Fruit: 1.0
Bread: 2.0
Meat: 0.0
Fat: 1.5

1. Make Double Pie Crust, substituting 1 teaspoon Equal® for Recipes for the sugar. Roll ²/₃ of the pastry on lightly floured surface into circle 1¹/₂ inches larger than inverted 9-inch pie pan. Ease pastry into pan.

2. Mix remaining 10³/₄ teaspoons Equal® for Recipes, 2 teaspoons cornstarch, apple juice, and lemon juice in small saucepan; heat to boiling, whisking until thickened, about 1 minute.

3. Sprinkle remaining 4 tablespoons cornstarch over blueberries and toss; stir apple juice mixture into blueberries. Spoon blueberry mixture into pastry.

4. Roll remaining pastry on lightly floured surface to ¹/₈ inch thickness; cut into ¹/₂-inch strips. Lay pastry strips across top of pie and weave into lattice design. Trim ends of strips; fold edge of lower pastry over ends of strips and seal and flute edge.

5. Bake at 425 degrees until pastry is golden and pie is bubbly, 30 to 40 minutes; cover edge of pastry with aluminum foil if necessary to prevent excessive browning. Cool on wire rack.

MIXED BERRY TART

Select as many kinds of berries as you can for beautiful color and texture contrast.

8 servings

Shortbread Crust (see p. 765)
Mock Mascarpone (recipe follows)
3-4 cups mixed berries (raspberries, black-berries, strawberries, blueberries, gooseberries, currants, etc.)
¼ cup sugar-free currant, *or* apple, jelly, melted
Powdered sugar, as garnish

Per Serving
Calories: 264
% Calories from fat: 31
Fat (gm): 9
Saturated fat (gm): 2.3
Cholesterol (mg): 30.9
Sodium (mg): 255
Protein (gm): 8
Carbohydrate (gm): 37.9
Exchanges
Milk: 0.0
Vegetable: 0.0
Fruit: 0.5
Bread: 2.0
Meat: 0.0
Fat: 2.0

1. Roll Shortbread Crust between 2 sheets of waxed paper into 12-inch circle. Ease into 10-inch tart pan and trim. Pierce bottom with fork. Bake at 425 degrees until crisp and golden brown, 10 to 15 minutes. Cool on wire rack.

2. Spread Mock Mascarpone evenly on cooled crust; top with berries and drizzle with jam. Dust serving plates with powdered sugar; top with tart slices.

Mock Mascarpone

makes about 1¼ cups

1 package (8 ounces) fat-free cream cheese, softened
3 tablespoons reduced-fat sour cream
2-3 tablespoons 2% reduced-fat milk

1. Beat cream cheese until fluffy; mix in sour cream and milk. Refrigerate several hours, or up to several days.

LEMON CLOUD PIE

Other flavors of this wonderful dessert are easy. Just substitute another low-fat fruit yogurt for the lemon—strawberry, raspberry, or cherry are possible choices.

8 servings

Meringue Pie Crust (recipe follows)
1¹/₂ cups light whipped topping
1¹/₂ cups custard-style lemon low-fat yogurt
2 tablespoons grated lemon rind
Lemon slices, as garnish

Per Serving
Calories: 170
% Calories from fat: 17
Fat (gm): 3.5
Saturated fat (gm): 0.3
Cholesterol (mg): 2
Sodium (mg): 62
Protein (gm): 3.6
Carbohydrate (gm): 35.5
Exchanges
Milk: 0.5
Vegetable: 0.0
Fruit: 2.0
Bread: 0.0
Meat: 0.0
Fat: 0.5

1. Make Meringue Pie Crust.

2. Combine whipped topping, yogurt, and lemon rind in small bowl. Spoon into center of meringue shell. Garnish with lemon slices.

Meringue Pie Crust

makes one 9-inch crust

4 egg whites
¹/₂ teaspoon cream of tartar
1 cup sugar

1. Beat egg whites and cream of tartar in medium bowl to soft peaks. Gradually beat in sugar, beating to stiff peaks. Spoon mixture into ungreased 9-inch glass pie pan, spreading on bottom and up side to form a large bowl shape.

2. Bake at 350 degrees 40 minutes or until crust is firm to touch and very lightly browned. Cool on wire rack.

KEY LIME PIE

A Southern dessert that is famous for its smooth creamy texture and unique cool lime taste.

8 servings

1 cup reduced-fat graham cracker crumbs

3-4 tablespoons melted margarine

4¹/₂ teaspoons Equal® for Recipes *or* 15 packets Equal® sweetener, divided

1 envelope unflavored gelatin

1³/₄ cups fat-free milk, divided

1 package (8 ounces) fat-free cream cheese, softened

¹/₂ cup key lime, *or* Persian lime, juice
Light whipped topping, as garnish
Mint sprigs, as garnish

Per Serving
Calories: 147
% Calories from fat: 32
Fat (gm): 5.4
Saturated fat (gm): 1.4
Cholesterol (mg): 3.2
Sodium (mg): 320
Protein (gm): 8.7
Carbohydrate (gm): 16.6
Exchanges
Milk: 0.0
Vegetable: 0.0
Fruit: 0.0
Bread: 1.0
Meat: 1.0
Fat: 0.5

1. Combine graham cracker crumbs, margarine, and 1 teaspoon Equal® for Recipes in 7-inch springform pan; pat evenly on bottom and ¹/₂ inch up side of pan.

2. Sprinkle gelatin over ¹/₂ cup of the milk in small saucepan; let stand 2 to 3 minutes; heat just to simmering, stirring constantly; cool.

3. Beat cream cheese until fluffy in medium bowl; beat in remaining 1¹/₄ cups milk and the gelatin mixture. Mix in lime juice and remaining 3¹/₂ teaspoons Equal® for Recipes. Pour into pan; refrigerate until set, 3 to 4 hours.

4. Remove side of pan; place pie on serving plate. Garnish with light whipped topping and mint.

NECTARINE AND BERRY TART

Fresh apricots or fresh or frozen, thawed peaches can be substituted for the nectarines in this summer-fresh, country-style tart.

6 servings

Basic Pie Crust (All-Purpose Flour) (see p. 762)

8¼ teaspoons Equal® for Recipes *or* 27 packets Equal® sweetener, divided

5 cups sliced nectarines (about 5 medium)

1 cup raspberries *or* sliced strawberries

1 cup fresh, *or* frozen, partially thawed blueberries

2 teaspoons lemon juice

3 tablespoons cornstarch

1 teaspoon grated lemon rind

¼ teaspoon ground allspice

Per Serving
Calories: 275
% Calories from fat: 27
Fat (gm): 8.5
Saturated fat (gm): 1.6
Cholesterol (mg): 0
Sodium (mg): 189
Protein (gm): 8.5
Carbohydrate (gm): 42.9
Exchanges
Milk: 0.0
Vegetable: 0.0
Fruit: 1.0
Bread: 2.0
Meat: 0.0
Fat: 1.5

1. Make Basic Pie Crust, substituting 1 teaspoon Equal® for Recipes for the sugar. Roll pastry on floured surface into 12-inch circle; transfer to ungreased cookie sheet.

2. Toss fruit with lemon juice in large bowl; sprinkle with combined cornstarch, remaining 7¼ teaspoons Equal® for Recipes, lemon rind, and allspice and toss. Arrange fruit on pastry, leaving 2-inch border around edge of pastry. Fold edge of pastry over edge of fruit, overlapping as necessary.

3. Bake at 425 degrees until pastry is golden and fruit tender, 35 to 40 minutes. Cool on wire rack.

DOUBLE COCONUT CREAM MERINGUE PIE

Reduced-fat coconut milk, available in most large groceries, lends a subtle coconut flavor to the pie filling.

8 servings

Basic Pie Crust (All-Purpose Flour) (see p. 762)

^{1}/$_3$ cup plus ^{1}/$_4$ cup sugar, divided

^{1}/$_3$ cup cornstarch

^{1}/$_8$ teaspoon salt

2 cups fat-free milk

^{1}/$_2$ can (14-ounce size) light coconut milk

2 egg yolks

1 teaspoon vanilla

1 tablespoon margarine

^{1}/$_4$-^{1}/$_2$ cup plus 2 tablespoons flaked coconut, divided

3 egg whites

^{1}/$_4$ teaspoon cream of tartar

Per Serving
Calories: 298
% Calories from fat: 33
Fat (gm): 11
Saturated fat (gm): 2.9
Cholesterol (mg): 54.4
Sodium (mg): 248
Protein (gm): 6.5
Carbohydrate (gm): 43.2
Exchanges
Milk: 0.0
Vegetable: 0.0
Fruit: 0.0
Bread: 3.0
Meat: 0.0
Fat: 2.0

1. Bake Basic Pie Crust according to recipe, using 9-inch pie pan. Cool on wire rack.

2. Combine ^{1}/$_3$ cup sugar, cornstarch, and salt in medium saucepan; whisk in milk and coconut milk. Heat to boiling over medium-high heat, whisking constantly until thickened, 1 to 2 minutes. Whisk about ^{1}/$_2$ the milk mixture into egg yolks; whisk yolk mixture back into saucepan. Cook over medium-low heat, whisking constantly, 1 minute. Remove from heat; stir in vanilla, margarine, and ^{1}/$_4$ cup coconut. Pour into crust.

3. Beat egg whites and cream of tartar to soft peaks in medium bowl; beat to stiff peaks, adding remaining ^{1}/$_4$ cup sugar gradually. Spread meringue over hot filling, sealing to edge of crust; sprinkle with 2 tablespoons coconut.

4. Bake at 400 degrees until meringue is browned, about 5 minutes. Cool on wire rack. Refrigerate until chilled, 3 to 4 hours.

Variation: **Coconut-Banana Island Pie**—Slice 1 small banana and arrange in cooled pie crust. Make pie as above, substituting 1 cup fat-free milk for the coconut milk and adding 1/2 teaspoon coconut extract. Substitute chopped macadamia nuts for the coconut in the filling and in the meringue.

BANANA-STRAWBERRY CREAM PIE

Strawberries add a new twist to this old favorite.

8 servings

Graham Cracker Crumb Crust
(see p. 766)

- 1/4 cup graham cracker crumbs
- 1 tablespoon margarine
- 1/3 cup sugar
- 1/4 cup cornstarch
- 2 tablespoons flour
- 1/3 teaspoon salt
- 2 1/2 cups fat-free milk
- 3 egg yolks
- 1 teaspoon vanilla
- 1/4 teaspoon ground cinnamon
- 1/3 teaspoon ground nutmeg
- 1 cup sliced strawberries
- 2 medium bananas

Per Serving
Calories: 250
% Calories from fat: 30
Fat (gm): 8.5
Saturated fat (gm): 1.7
Cholesterol (mg): 81.1
Sodium (mg): 226
Protein (gm): 5.4
Carbohydrate (gm): 38.9
Exchanges
Milk: 0.0
Vegetable: 0.0
Fruit: 0.5
Bread: 2.0
Meat: 0.0
Fat: 1.5

1. Make pie crust, adding 1/4 cup graham cracker crumbs and 1 tablespoon margarine to recipe and using 9-inch pie pan.

2. Mix sugar, cornstarch, flour, and salt in medium saucepan; stir in milk. Cook over medium heat until mixture boils and thickens; boil 1 minute, stirring constantly.

3. Stir about 1/2 cup of mixture into egg yolks; stir egg mixture back into saucepan. Cook over low heat, stirring constantly until thickened. Remove from heat; stir in vanilla, cinnamon, and nutmeg. Cool to room temperature, stirring frequently. Refrigerate until chilled, 1 to 2 hours.

4. Set aside 4 to 6 strawberry slices. Slice 1 to 1 1/2 bananas and arrange in crust with remaining strawberries. Spoon custard into crust; refrigerate until set, 4 to 6 hours. Slice remaining banana and garnish pie with banana and strawberry slices.

CHERRY LATTICE PIE

This pie will disappear so quickly that you'd better bake two!

8 servings

Double Pie Crust (see pg. 764)
18 teaspoons Equal® for Recipes *or* 60 packets Equal® sweetener, divided
3 packages (16 ounces each) frozen no-sugar-added pitted tart cherries, thawed
3 tablespoons cornstarch, divided
2 tablespoons flour, divided
1/8 teaspoon ground nutmeg
6-8 drops red food color, optional

Per Serving
Calories: 290
% Calories from fat: 24
Fat (gm): 8.1
Saturated fat (gm): 1.6
Cholesterol (mg): 0
Sodium (mg): 233
Protein (gm): 12.2
Carbohydrate (gm): 43.9
Exchanges
Milk: 0.0
Vegetable: 0.0
Fruit: 1.5
Bread: 2.0
Meat: 0.0
Fat: 1.5

1. Make Double Pie Crust, substituting 1 teaspoon Equal® for Recipes for the sugar. Roll 1/2 of the pastry on lightly floured surface into circle 1 1/2 inches larger than inverted 9-inch pie pan. Ease pastry into pan.

2. Drain cherries, reserving 3/4 cup cherry juice. Mix remaining 17 teaspoons Equal® for Recipes, 1 tablespoon cornstarch, 1 tablespoon flour, reserved cherry juice, nutmeg, and food color in small saucepan; heat to boiling, whisking constantly. Boil, whisking constantly, until thickened, about 1 minute.

3. Sprinkle remaining 2 tablespoons cornstarch and 1 tablespoon flour over cherries and toss; stir cherry juice mixture into cherries. Spoon cherry mixture into pastry.

4. Roll remaining pastry on lightly floured surface to 1/8 inch thickness; cut into 1/2-inch strips. Lay pastry strips across top of pie and weave into lattice design. Trim ends of strips; fold edge of lower pastry over ends of strips and seal and flute edge.

5. Bake pie at 425 degrees until pastry is golden and pie is bubbly, 35 to 45 minutes; cover edge of pastry with aluminum foil if necessary to prevent excessive browning. Cool on wire rack.

OLD-FASHIONED CUSTARD PIE

One of the best custard pies we've tasted! For a richer custard, use 2% reduced-fat milk.

8 servings

Basic Pie Crust (All-Purpose Flour) (see p. 762)

6^1/$_2$ teaspoons Equal® for Recipes *or* 21 packets Equal® sweetener, divided

4 eggs

^{1}/$_4$ teaspoon salt

2^1/$_2$ cups fat-free milk

1^1/$_2$ teaspoons vanilla

^{1}/$_4$ teaspoon ground cinnamon

^{1}/$_8$ teaspoon ground nutmeg

Per Serving
Calories: 199
% Calories from fat: 39
Fat (gm): 8.5
Saturated fat (gm): 2
Cholesterol (mg): 107.4
Sodium (mg): 284
Protein (gm): 10.3
Carbohydrate (gm): 19.3
Exchanges
Milk: 0.0
Vegetable: 0.0
Fruit: 0.0
Bread: 1.5
Meat: 1.0
Fat: 1.0

1. Make Basic Pie Crust, substituting 1 teaspoon Equal® for Recipes for the sugar. Roll pastry on floured surface into circle 1^1/$_2$ inches larger than inverted 9-inch pie pan. Ease pastry into pan; trim and flute.

2. Beat eggs and salt until thick and lemon colored in large bowl, about 5 minutes. Mix in milk, remaining 5^1/$_2$ teaspoons Equal® for Recipes, and remaining ingredients; pour into pastry.

3. Bake at 425 degrees 15 minutes; reduce temperature to 350 degrees and bake until sharp knife inserted halfway between center and edge comes out clean, about 12 minutes. Cool on wire rack. Serve at room temperature, or refrigerate and serve chilled.

Variation: **Coconut Custard Pie**—Make recipe as above, reducing milk to 2 cups, adding ^{1}/$_2$ cup flaked coconut, and substituting 1 to 2 teaspoons coconut extract for the vanilla.

PECAN CRUNCH TART

We've reduced the calories and fat in this rich-tasting pecan pie.

8 servings

Basic Pie Crust (All-Purpose Flour) (see p. 762)

2 eggs

1 cup maple syrup *or* pancake syrup

1 tablespoon vanilla

1/8 teaspoon salt

2/3 cup reduced-fat granola

1/3 cup barley-wheat cereal (Grape-Nuts)

2/3 cup coarsely chopped pecans

Per Serving
Calories: 356
% Calories from fat: 22
Fat (gm): 8.9
Saturated fat (gm): 3.2
Cholesterol (mg): 56.2
Sodium (mg): 279
Protein (gm): 9.6
Carbohydrate (gm): 63.1
Exchanges
Milk: 0.0
Vegetable: 0.0
Fruit: 0.0
Bread: 4.0
Meat: 0.0
Fat: 1.5

1. Make Basic Pie Crust, using 10-inch tart pan.

2. Beat eggs, syrup, vanilla, and salt until smooth. Stir in remaining ingredients; pour into pastry. Bake at 350 degrees until set, about 35 minutes.

PUMPKIN CHIFFON PIE

The perfect addition to any holiday menu.

8 servings

Basic Pie Crust (All-Purpose Flour) (see p. 762)

3 1/2 teaspoons Equal® for Recipes *or* 12 packets Equal® sweetener, divided

1 envelope unflavored gelatin

1 teaspoon cornstarch

1/2 cup fat-free milk

2 egg yolks

2 cups canned pumpkin

1 teaspoon pumpkin pie spice

1 teaspoon vanilla

1/8 teaspoon salt

1 cup light whipped topping
Light whipped topping, as garnish

Per Serving
Calories: 196
% Calories from fat: 39
Fat (gm): 8.3
Saturated fat (gm): 2.7
Cholesterol (mg): 53.5
Sodium (mg): 191
Protein (gm): 5.5
Carbohydrate (gm): 24.1
Exchanges
Milk: 0.0
Vegetable: 0.0
Fruit: 0.0
Bread: 2.0
Meat: 0.0
Fat: 1.5

1. Make Basic Pie Crust, substituting 1 teaspoon Equal® for Recipes for the sugar. Roll pastry on floured surface to circle 1¹/₂ inches larger than inverted 9-inch pie pan. Ease pastry into pan; trim and flute. Pierce bottom of pastry with tines of a fork. Bake at 425 degrees until browned, about 15 minutes. Cool on wire rack.

2. Whisk remaining 2¹/₂ teaspoons Equal® for Recipes, gelatin, cornstarch, and milk over medium heat in medium saucepan until mixture boils and thickens, 2 to 3 minutes. Stir about ¹/₂ of the milk mixture into the egg yolks; whisk egg mixture into saucepan. Whisk over low heat until thickened, 1 to 2 minutes. Remove from heat and stir in pumpkin, pumpkin pie spice, vanilla, and salt. Cool to room temperature; refrigerate until mixture mounds when dropped from a spoon, about 20 minutes.

3. Whisk mixture gently until smooth; fold in 1 cup whipped topping and spoon into pie crust, smoothing top. Refrigerate until set, 3 to 4 hours. Garnish slices with dollops of whipped topping.

STRAWBERRY CREAM PIE

Celebrate spring with this colorful fresh berry pie.

8 servings

1¹/₄ cups reduced-fat graham cracker crumbs

4-5 tablespoons margarine, melted

6¹/₄ teaspoons Equal® for Recipes *or* 19 packets Equal® sweetener, divided

1 package (8 ounces) fat-free cream cheese, softened

1 teaspoon vanilla

1 cup boiling water

1 package (0.3 ounces) sugar-free strawberry gelatin

2 cups sliced strawberries

Light whipped topping, as garnish

Per Serving
Calories: 165
% Calories from fat: 38
Fat (gm): 6.9
Saturated fat (gm): 1.6
Cholesterol (mg): 2.3
Sodium (mg): 330
Protein (gm): 8.9
Carbohydrate (gm): 17.1
Exchanges
Milk: 0.0
Vegetable: 0.0
Fruit: 0.0
Bread: 1.0
Meat: 1.0
Fat: 1.0

1. Mix graham cracker crumbs, margarine, and 1 teaspoon Equal® for Recipes in 8-inch pie pan; pat evenly on bottom and side of pan. Bake at 350 degrees until lightly browned, 6 to 8 minutes. Cool.

2. Beat cream cheese, vanilla, and 1³/₄ teaspoons Equal® for Recipes in small bowl until fluffy; spread evenly in bottom of crust.

3. Pour boiling water over gelatin and remaining 3¹/₂ teaspoons Equal® for Recipes in bowl, whisking until gelatin is dissolved. Refrigerate until mixture is the consistency of unbeaten egg whites, 20 to 30 minutes.

4. Arrange half the strawberries over the cream cheese; spoon half the gelatin mixture over strawberries. Arrange remaining strawberries over pie and spoon remaining gelatin mixture over. Refrigerate until pie is set and chilled, 2 to 3 hours. Serve with light whipped topping.

Variations: **Double Berry Pie**—Make recipe as above, substituting 1 cup blueberries for 1 cup strawberries. Arrange 1 cup blueberries over cream cheese in pie crust; spoon half the gelatin mixture over berries; top with 1 cup sliced strawberries and spoon remaining gelatin mixture over.

Strawberry Banana Pie—Make recipe as above, substituting sugar-free strawberry-banana gelatin for the strawberry gelatin and 1 small sliced banana for 1 cup strawberries. Arrange banana over cream cheese; spoon half the gelatin mixture over; top with 1 cup sliced strawberries and spoon remaining gelatin mixture over.

PINEAPPLE CRUMB TART

The rich crumb mixture is used both as a crust and topping in this delectable French-style tart. Substitute other canned fruit for the pineapple, if desired.

10 to 12 servings

1¹/₄ cups all-purpose flour

5¹/₂ teaspoons Equal® for Recipes *or* 18 packets Equal® sweetener

4 teaspoons cornstarch

¹/₄ teaspoon salt

10 tablespoons cold margarine, cut into pieces

1¹/₂ teaspoons vanilla

2 cans (8 ounces each) sliced pineapple in juice, well drained

¹/₄ cup apricot spreadable fruit, warm

Per Serving
Calories: 207
% Calories from fat: 50
Fat (gm): 11.5
Saturated fat (gm): 2.3
Cholesterol (mg): 0
Sodium (mg): 201
Protein (gm): 3.7
Carbohydrate (gm): 22.3
Exchanges
Milk: 0.0
Vegetable: 0.0
Fruit: 0.5
Bread: 1.0
Meat: 0.0
Fat: 2.0

1. Combine flour, Equal® for Recipes, cornstarch, and salt in medium bowl; cut in margarine until mixture resembles coarse crumbs. Sprinkle vanilla over mixture and stir with fork to combine.

2. Reserve 1/2 cup crumb mixture. Pat remaining mixture evenly on bottom only of ungreased 10-inch tart pan or quiche dish. Bake at 350 degrees until browned, about 15 minutes. Cool on wire rack.

3. Cut pineapple slices in half and arrange on crust; sprinkle with reserved 1/2 cup crumb mixture. Bake at 400 degrees until topping is browned, about 10 minutes. Cool on wire rack; drizzle with spreadable fruit.

ALMOND CHEESECAKE SQUARES

Rich in flavor and texture, yet made with fat-free cream cheese!

24 servings

3 packages (8 ounces each) fat-free cream cheese, softened

5 1/2 teaspoons Equal® for Recipes *or* 18 packets Equal® sweetener

2 eggs

2 egg whites

2 tablespoons cornstarch

1 cup fat-free sour cream

1/2 teaspoon vanilla

1/4 teaspoon almond extract
Chocolate Crumb Crust
(recipe follows)

1/4 cup sliced almonds

Per Serving
Calories: 112
% Calories from fat: 34
Fat (gm): 4.1
Saturated fat (gm): 1
Cholesterol (mg): 19.9
Sodium (mg): 244
Protein (gm): 7.5
Carbohydrate (gm): 10.2
Exchanges
Milk: 0.0
Vegetable: 0.0
Fruit: 0.0
Bread: 1.0
Meat: 0.0
Fat: 1.0

1. Beat cream cheese until smooth in large bowl; beat in remaining ingredients, except Chocolate Crumb Crust and almonds, until smooth. Pour filling into crust; sprinkle with almonds.

2. Bake cheesecake at 300 degrees until set, about 30 minutes. Cool on wire rack; refrigerate until chilled, 6 hours or overnight. Cut into squares to serve.

Chocolate Crumb Crust

  1¹/2 cups ground reduced-fat graham crackers
    ¹/4 cup Dutch process cocoa
  2¹/2 teaspoons Equal® for Recipes *or* 8 packets
      Equal® sweetener
     5 tablespoons margarine, melted
¹/2-³/4 teaspoon chocolate extract

1. Mix graham cracker crumbs, cocoa, and Equal® for Recipes in bottom of 13 x 9-inch baking pan; mix in margarine and chocolate extract. Pat mixture evenly on bottom of pan.

PUMPKIN CHEESECAKE

A creamy smooth cheesecake, scented with holiday flavors of pumpkin and spices.

12 to 14 servings

    ³/4 cup ground reduced-fat graham crackers
    ³/4 cup ground gingersnap cookies
  8¹/4 teaspoons Equal® for Recipes *or* 27 packets Equal® sweetener, divided
  4-5 tablespoons margarine, melted
    2 packages (8 ounces each) fat-free cream cheese, softened
    1 package (8 ounces) reduced-fat cream cheese
    1 cup canned pumpkin
    2 eggs
    2 egg whites
    2 teaspoons ground cinnamon
    1 teaspoon ground cloves
    1 teaspoon ground ginger
    2 tablespoons cornstarch
    1 cup light whipped topping
      Chopped toasted pecans, as garnish

Per Serving
Calories: 213
% Calories from fat: 42
Fat (gm): 9.8
Saturated fat (gm): 4.3
Cholesterol (mg): 47.2
Sodium (mg): 444
Protein (gm): 12.1
Carbohydrate (gm): 18.2
Exchanges
Milk: 0.0
Vegetable: 0.0
Fruit: 0.0
Bread: 1.0
Meat: 1.0
Fat: 2.0

1. Mix graham cracker and gingersnap crumbs, 1 teaspoon Equal® for Recipes, and melted margarine in bottom of 9-inch springform pan; reserve 2 tablespoons crumb mixture. Pat remaining mixture evenly on bottom and ¹/2 inch up side of pan. Bake at 350 degrees until lightly browned, about 8 minutes. Cool on wire rack.

2. Beat cream cheese until smooth in large bowl; beat in pumpkin, eggs, and egg whites. Mix in remaining 7¹/₄ teaspoons Equal® for Recipes, spices, and cornstarch. Pour mixture into springform pan.

3. Bake at 300 degrees just until set in the center, 45 to 60 minutes; sprinkle with reserved crumbs and return to oven. Turn oven off and let cheesecake cool in oven with door ajar for 3 hours. Refrigerate 8 hours or overnight.

4. Remove side of springform pan; place cheesecake on serving plate. Spread with light whipped topping and sprinkle with pecans.

RICH CHOCOLATE CHEESECAKE

A chocolate lover's delight!

16 servings

1¹/₄ cups graham cracker crumbs
4-5 tablespoons margarine, melted
6¹/₂ teaspoons Equal® for Recipes *or* 21 packets Equal® sweetener, divided
2 packages (8 ounces each) fat-free cream cheese, softened
1 package (8 ounces) reduced-fat cream cheese, softened
2 eggs
2 egg whites
2 tablespoons cornstarch
1 cup fat-free sour cream
¹/₃ cup Dutch process cocoa
1 teaspoon vanilla
1 cup light whipped topping
Unsweetened chocolate shavings, as garnish

Per Serving
Calories: 182
% Calories from fat: 43
Fat (gm): 8.5
Cholesterol (mg): 3.6
Sodium (mg): 320
Protein (gm): 10
Carbohydrate (gm): 14.9
Exchanges
Milk: 0.0
Vegetable: 0.0
Fruit: 0.0
Bread: 1.0
Meat: 1.0
Fat: 1.0

1. Mix graham cracker crumbs, margarine, and 1 teaspoon Equal® for Recipes in 9-inch springform pan; pat evenly on bottom and ¹/₂ inch up side of pan.

2. Beat cream cheese and remaining 5^1/$_2$ teaspoons Equal® for Recipes until fluffy in large bowl; beat in eggs, egg whites, and cornstarch. Beat in sour cream, cocoa, and vanilla, blending well; pour into crust.

3. Bake cheesecake at 300 degrees just until set in the center, 45 to 50 minutes. Turn oven off and let cheesecake cool in oven with door ajar for 3 hours. Refrigerate 8 hours or overnight.

4. Remove side of pan; place cheesecake on serving plate. Spread light whipped topping over top and garnish with chocolate shavings.

CHOCOLATE CHIP COOKIES

Chocolate chip are, no doubt, America's favorite cookie—you'll love these.

5 dozen cookies (1 per serving)

8	tablespoons margarine, softened
1	cup packed light brown sugar
^{1}/$_2$	cup granulated sugar
1	egg
1	teaspoon vanilla
2^1/$_2$	cups all-purpose flour
^{1}/$_2$	teaspoon baking soda
^{1}/$_2$	teaspoon salt
^{1}/$_3$	cup fat-free milk
^{1}/$_2$	package (12-ounce size) reduced-fat semisweet chocolate morsels

Per Serving
Calories: 66
% Calories from fat: 27
Fat (gm): 2
Saturated fat (gm): 0.7
Cholesterol (mg): 3.6
Sodium (mg): 70
Protein (gm): 0.8
Carbohydrate (gm): 11.2
Exchanges
Milk: 0.0
Vegetable: 0.0
Fruit: 0.0
Bread: 0.5
Meat: 0.0
Fat: 0.5

1. Beat margarine and sugars in medium bowl until fluffy; beat in egg and vanilla. Mix in combined flour, baking soda, and salt alternately with milk, beginning and ending with dry ingredients. Mix in chocolate morsels.

2. Drop cookies by tablespoonfuls onto greased cookie sheets. Bake until browned, about 10 minutes. Cool on wire racks.

RAISIN OATMEAL COOKIES

Moist and chewy, just the way they should be!

2¹/₂ dozen cookies (1 per serving)

   6 tablespoons margarine, softened
 ¹/₄ cup fat-free sour cream
   1 egg
   1 teaspoon vanilla
   1 cup packed light brown sugar
 1¹/₂ cups quick-cooking oats
   1 cup all-purpose flour
 ¹/₂ teaspoon baking soda
 ¹/₄ teaspoon baking powder
   1 teaspoon ground cinnamon
 ¹/₂ cup raisins for baking

Per Serving
Calories: 90
% Calories from fat: 27
Fat (gm): 2.7
Saturated fat (gm): 0.5
Cholesterol (mg): 7.1
Sodium (mg): 57
Protein (gm): 1.5
Carbohydrate (gm): 15.3
Exchanges
Milk: 0.0
Vegetable: 0.0
Fruit: 0.0
Bread: 1.0
Meat: 0.0
Fat: 0.5

1. Mix margarine, sour cream, egg, and vanilla in large bowl; beat in brown sugar. Mix in combined oats, flour, baking soda, baking powder, and cinnamon. Mix in raisins.

2. Drop dough onto greased cookie sheets, using 2 tablespoons for each cookie. Bake at 350 degrees until browned, 12 to 15 minutes. Cool on wire racks.

SHORTBREAD COOKIES

A crisp yet tender cookie, with a wonderful buttery flavor.

1 dozen cookies (1 per serving)

   1 cup all-purpose flour
 3¹/₂ teaspoons Equal® for Recipes *or* 12 packets Equal® sweetener
   1 tablespoon cornstarch
 ¹/₈ teaspoon salt
   8 tablespoons cold margarine, cut into pieces
 ¹/₂-1 teaspoon butter extract
 ¹/₂ teaspoon vanilla

Per Serving
Calories: 113
% Calories from fat: 61
Fat (gm): 7.6
Saturated fat (gm): 1.5
Cholesterol (mg): 0
Sodium (mg): 113
Protein (gm): 2.1
Carbohydrate (gm): 8.7
Exchanges
Milk: 0.0
Vegetable: 0.0
Fruit: 0.0
Bread: 0.5
Meat: 0.0
Fat: 1.5

1. Combine flour, Equal® for Recipes, cornstarch, and salt in medium bowl; cut in margarine until mixture resembles coarse crumbs. Sprinkle butter extract and vanilla over mixture and mix with hands briefly until dough begins to hold together.

2. Pat dough evenly in bottom of greased 8-inch round cake pan. Lightly cut dough into 12 wedges with sharp knife, cutting about halfway through dough. Pierce each wedge 3 to 4 times with tines of fork.

3. Bake at 325 degrees until lightly browned, 25 to 30 minutes. Cool on wire rack; cut into wedges while warm.

Variations: **Almond Shortbread**—Make recipe as above, substituting almond extract for the butter extract and omitting vanilla. Separate 6 whole blanched almonds into halves; press 1 half into each shortbread wedge before baking.

Chocolate Shortbread—Make recipe as above, adding $1/4$ cup Dutch process cocoa, increasing Equal® for Recipes to $5^1/2$ teaspoons or 18 packets, and substituting vanilla for butter extract.

SOFT MOLASSES COOKIES

Fill your home with the scent of spices when you bake these cookies.

3 dozen cookies (1 per serving)

$1/4$ cup vegetable shortening	
$1/2$ cup packed dark brown sugar	
1 egg yolk	
$1^1/4$ cups all-purpose flour	
2 teaspoons baking soda	
$1/2$ teaspoon ground cinnamon	
$1/2$ teaspoon ground ginger	
$1/4$ teaspoon ground nutmeg	
$1/4$ teaspoon salt	
$1/4$ cup light molasses	
2 tablespoons water	
$1/2$ cup currants *or* chopped raisins	

Per Serving
Calories: 53
% Calories from fat: 25
Fat (gm): 1.5
Saturated fat (gm): 0.4
Cholesterol (mg): 5.9
Sodium (mg): 89
Protein (gm): 0.6
Carbohydrate (gm): 9.3
Exchanges
Milk: 0.0
Vegetable: 0.0
Fruit: 0.0
Bread: 0.5
Meat: 0.0
Fat: 0.0

1. Beat shortening, brown sugar, and egg yolk in medium bowl until blended. Mix in combined flour, baking soda, spices, and salt alternately with combined molasses and water, beginning and ending with dry ingredients. Mix in currants.

2. Drop mixture by rounded teaspoons onto greased cookie sheets. Bake at 350 until lightly browned on the bottoms (cookies will be soft), 8 to 10 minutes. Cool on wire racks.

CARDAMOM CUT-OUTS

Intensely flavored with cardamom, these delicate cookies are also delicious made with cinnamon. Cut into tiny 1-inch rounds for tea cookies.

5 dozen cookies (1 per serving)

1/2 cup vegetable shortening
1 cup plus 2 tablespoons sugar, divided
3 tablespoons fat-free milk
1 egg yolk
3/4 teaspoon ground cardamom, divided
2 cups all-purpose flour
1/4 teaspoon salt

Per Serving
Calories: 46
% Calories from fat: 34
Fat (gm): 1.7
Saturated fat (gm): 0.4
Cholesterol (mg): 3.6
Sodium (mg): 10
Protein (gm): 0.5
Carbohydrate (gm): 7
Exchanges
Milk: 0.0
Vegetable: 0.0
Fruit: 0.0
Bread: 0.5
Meat: 0.0
Fat: 0.0

1. Beat shortening, 1 cup sugar, milk, egg yolk, and 1/2 teaspoon cardamom in medium bowl until well blended; mix in flour and salt.

2. Roll 1/2 the dough on floured surface to scant 1/4 inch thickness; cut into rounds or decorative shapes with 2-inch cutter. Repeat with remaining dough.

3. Bake on greased baking sheets at 375 degrees until browned, 8 to 10 minutes. Combine remaining 2 tablespoons sugar and 1/4 teaspoon cardamom; sprinkle over warm cookies. Cool on wire racks.

TART LEMON DAINTIES

Enjoy the subtle lemon flavor of these tiny crisp cookies—perfect with coffee or tea.

4 dozen cookies (1 per serving)

4	tablespoons margarine, softened
1	cup granulated sugar
1	egg
3	tablespoons fat-free milk
2	teaspoons lemon juice
1	teaspoon finely grated lemon rind
2	cups all-purpose flour
1	teaspoon baking powder
1/4	teaspoon salt

Per Serving
Calories: 46
% Calories from fat: 22
Fat (gm): 1.1
Saturated fat (gm): 0.2
Cholesterol (mg): 4.4
Sodium (mg): 35
Protein (gm): 0.7
Carbohydrate (gm): 8.2
Exchanges
Milk: 0.0
Vegetable: 0.0
Fruit: 0.0
Bread: 0.5
Meat: 0.0
Fat: 0.0

1. Beat margarine, sugar, egg, milk, lemon juice, and lemon rind in bowl until blended. Mix in combined flour, baking powder, and salt. Refrigerate until chilled, 2 to 3 hours.

2. Roll 1/2 the dough on floured surface to 1/4 inch thickness; cut into rounds or decorative shapes with 1 1/2-inch cutter. Repeat with remaining dough.

3. Bake on greased cookie sheet at 375 degrees until lightly browned, 7 to 8 minutes. Cool on wire racks.

CHOCOLATE CRINKLES

These cookies have crinkled, crisp tops but are soft inside.

4¹/₂ dozen cookies (1 per serving)

8 tablespoons margarine, softened
1¹/₄ cups packed light brown sugar
¹/₃ cup reduced-fat sour cream
1 egg
1-2 ounces semisweet baking chocolate, melted
1 teaspoon vanilla
1³/₄ cups all-purpose flour
³/₄ cup unsweetened cocoa
1 teaspoon baking soda
1 teaspoon ground cinnamon
¹/₄ cup granulated sugar

Per Serving
Calories: 61
% Calories from fat: 31
Fat (gm): 2.1
Saturated fat (gm): 0.6
Cholesterol (mg): 4.5
Sodium (mg): 49
Protein (gm): 0.8
Carbohydrate (gm): 9.8
Exchanges
Milk: 0.0
Vegetable: 0.0
Fruit: 0.0
Bread: 0.5
Meat: 0.0
Fat: 0.5

1. Beat margarine and brown sugar in large bowl until fluffy. Mix in sour cream, egg, chocolate, and vanilla. Mix in combined flour, cocoa, baking soda, and cinnamon. Refrigerate, covered, 2 to 3 hours.

2. Measure granulated sugar into pie pan or shallow bowl. Drop dough by tablespoons into sugar and roll into balls. (Dough will be soft.) Place cookies on greased cookie sheets; flatten with fork or bottom of glass. Bake at 350 degrees until firm to touch, 10 to 12 minutes. Cool on wire racks.

GRANOLA LACE COOKIES

When cookies are still warm, they can be rolled or folded over the handle of a wooden spoon, or "pinched" in the center to form bow shapes; see recipe for Almond Tuiles, p. 794 for shaping directions. Bake only 4 to 6 cookies at a time as they must be handled quickly and carefully before cooling.

4 dozen cookies (1 per serving)

> 4 tablespoons margarine, softened
> 1/4 cup granulated sugar
> 1/4 cup packed light brown sugar
> 2 egg whites
> 1 tablespoon orange juice
> 1/4-1/2 teaspoon orange extract
> 1/2 cup reduced-fat granola without raisins, finely crushed
> 1/2 cup all-purpose flour
> 1/4 teaspoon baking soda
> 2 teaspoons finely grated orange rind
> 1/4 teaspoon salt

Per Serving
Calories: 27
% Calories from fat: 33
Fat (gm): 1
Saturated fat (gm): 0.2
Cholesterol (mg): 0
Sodium (mg): 35
Protein (gm): 0.4
Carbohydrate (gm): 4.1
Exchanges
Milk: 0.0
Vegetable: 0.0
Fruit: 0.0
Bread: 0.5
Meat: 0.0
Fat: 0.0

1. Beat all ingredients in large bowl until smooth.

2. Drop rounded 1/2 teaspoons dough 3 inches apart on parchment-lined cookie sheets, making 4 to 6 cookies per pan. Bake at 400 degrees until lightly browned, about 3 minutes. Let stand until firm enough to remove from pans, about 1 minute. Cool on wire racks.

ALMOND TUILES

These lacy cookies are crisp and delicate. They can be folded, rolled, or formed into small basket shapes for ice cream or other fillings (see Variation below).

3 dozen cookies (1 per serving)

 1/2 cup quick-cooking oats
 1/4 cup finely chopped blanched almonds
  4 tablespoons margarine, melted
 1/2 cup light corn syrup
 1/3 cup sugar
  1 teaspoon almond extract
 1/2 cup all-purpose flour
 1/4 teaspoon salt

Per Serving
Calories: 49
% Calories from fat: 33
Fat (gm): 1.7
Saturated fat (gm): 0.3
Cholesterol (mg): 0
Sodium (mg): 36
Protein (gm): 0.5
Carbohydrate (gm): 7.5
Exchanges
Milk: 0.0
Vegetable: 0.0
Fruit: 0.0
Bread: 0.5
Meat: 0.0
Fat: 0.5

1. Place oats and almonds in separate pie pans. Bake at 350 degrees until toasted, 5 to 8 minutes for the almonds and about 10 minutes for the oats. Cool.

2. Mix margarine and corn syrup in medium bowl; mix in sugar and almond extract. Mix in combined oats, almonds, flour, and salt.

3. Drop batter by well-rounded teaspoons, 3 inches apart, onto parchment-lined cookie sheets (4 to 6 cookies per pan). Bake at 350 degrees until golden and bubbly, 7 to 10 minutes. Let cookies cool just until firm enough to remove from pan, about 1 minute. Working quickly, remove each cookie and roll or fold over the handle of a wooden spoon, or leave flat; cool on wire rack. If cookies have cooled too much to shape, return to warm oven for about 1 minute to soften.

Variation: **Cream-Filled Tuiles**—Remove warm tuiles from cookie sheet 1 at a time and roll loosely around handle of wooden spoon; transfer to wire rack and cool. Mix 3 cups light whipped topping and 1/3 cup powdered sugar. Using pastry bag with medium star tip, fill cookies with mixture. Drizzle cookies with 1 ounce melted semisweet baking chocolate.

FUDGEY BROWNIES

Easy to make whenever you get an urge for something chocolate!

1¹/₄ dozen brownies (1 per serving)

- 6 tablespoons margarine
- 4 ounces unsweetened chocolate
- ¹/₃ cup fat-free milk
- ¹/₃ cup apricot spreadable fruit
- 1 egg yolk
- 1 teaspoon vanilla
- ¹/₂ cup all-purpose flour
- 10³/₄ teaspoons Equal® for Recipes *or* 36 packets Equal® sweetener
- ¹/₂ teaspoon baking powder
- ¹/₈ teaspoon salt
- 3 egg whites
- ¹/₈ teaspoon cream of tartar
- ¹/₂ cup coarsely chopped walnuts *or* pecans, optional

Per Serving
Calories: 120
% Calories from fat: 61
Fat (gm): 8.7
Saturated fat (gm): 3.4
Cholesterol (mg): 14.3
Sodium (mg): 111
Protein (gm): 4.7
Carbohydrate (gm): 7.9
Exchanges
Milk: 0.0
Vegetable: 0.0
Fruit: 0.0
Bread: 0.5
Meat: 0.0
Fat: 1.5

1. Heat margarine, chocolate, milk, and spreadable fruit in small saucepan, stirring frequently, until chocolate is almost melted. Remove from heat; continue stirring until chocolate is melted. Stir in egg yolk and vanilla; mix in combined flour, Equal® for Recipes, baking powder, and salt.

2. Beat egg whites and cream of tartar to stiff peaks in medium bowl; fold chocolate mixture into egg whites. Fold in walnuts, if using. Pour batter into greased 8-inch square baking pan.

3. Bake at 350 degrees until brownies are firm to touch and toothpick comes out clean, 18 to 20 minutes (do not overbake). Cool on wire rack. Serve warm or at room temperature.

RASPBERRY-ALMOND BARS

A pretty bar cookie with a rich-tasting shortbread pastry.

2 dozen cookies (1 per serving)

2 cups all-purpose flour

3¹/2 teaspoons Equal® for Recipes *or* 12 packets Equal® sweetener

¹/8 teaspoon salt

8 tablespoons cold margarine, cut into pieces

1 large egg, beaten

1 tablespoon fat-free milk *or* water

²/3 cup seedless raspberry spreadable fruit

1 teaspoon cornstarch

¹/4-¹/3 cup finely chopped almonds, walnuts, *or* pecans, toasted

Per Serving
Calories: 96
% Calories from fat: 45
Fat (gm): 4.6
Saturated fat (gm): 0.9
Cholesterol (mg): 8.8
Sodium (mg): 69
Protein (gm): 2.1
Carbohydrate (gm): 10.5
Exchanges
Milk: 0.0
Vegetable: 0.0
Fruit: 0.0
Bread: 0.5
Meat: 0.0
Fat: 1.0

1. Combine flour, Equal® for Recipes, and salt in medium bowl; cut in margarine until mixture resembles coarse crumbs. Mix in egg and milk.

2. Press mixture evenly in bottom of greased 11 x 7-inch baking dish. Bake at 400 degrees until edges of crust are browned, about 15 minutes. Cool on wire rack.

3. Mix spreadable fruit and cornstarch in small saucepan; heat to boiling. Boil until thickened, stirring constantly, 1 minute; cool 5 minutes. Spread mixture evenly over cooled crust; sprinkle with almonds. Bake at 400 degrees until spreadable fruit is thick and bubbly, about 15 minutes. Cool on wire rack.

PUTTING ON THE RITZ BARS

Never have these rice cereal treats been quite so glamorous!

2¹/₂ dozen bars (1 per serving)

1 package (10 ounces) marshmallows
4 tablespoons margarine
3 cups rice cereal (Rice Krispies)
¹/₂ cup flaked coconut
1 cup dried cranberries *or* raisins
1 cup chopped dried mixed fruit
¹/₂-³/₄ cup coarsely chopped walnuts
2 ounces semisweet baking chocolate, melted

Per Serving
Calories: 108
% Calories from fat: 30
Fat (gm): 3.7
Saturated fat (gm): 1.1
Cholesterol (mg): 0
Sodium (mg): 59
Protein (gm): 1.2
Carbohydrate (gm): 18.7
Exchanges
Milk: 0.0
Vegetable: 0.0
Fruit: 0.0
Bread: 1.0
Meat: 0.0
Fat: 1.0

1. Heat marshmallows and margarine in large saucepan over low heat until melted, stirring frequently. Stir in remaining ingredients, except chocolate, mixing well.

2. Spoon mixture into greased 15 x 10-inch jelly roll pan, pressing into an even layer. Refrigerate 1 hour.

3. Drizzle top with chocolate; refrigerate until set, about 15 minutes. Cut into bars.

LIGHT LEMON SQUARES

One of America's favorite bar cookies, made with no sugar added!

1 dozen cookies (1 per serving)

2 eggs
5¹/₂ teaspoons Equal® for Recipes *or* 18 packets Equal® sweetener
¹/₄ cup plus 2 tablespoons lemon juice
4 tablespoons margarine, melted, cooled
1 tablespoon grated lemon rind
Rich Pastry (recipe follows)

Per Serving
Calories: 138
% Calories from fat: 67
Fat (gm): 10.4
Saturated fat (gm): 2.1
Cholesterol (mg): 35.3
Sodium (mg): 146
Protein (gm): 3.9
Carbohydrate (gm): 7.5
Exchanges
Milk: 0.0
Vegetable: 0.0
Fruit: 0.0
Bread: 0.5
Meat: 0.0
Fat: 2.0

1. Beat eggs and Equal® for Recipes; mix in lemon juice, margarine, and lemon rind. Pour mixture into baked Rich Pastry.

2. Bake at 350 degrees until filling is set, about 15 minutes. Cool on wire rack.

Rich Pastry

> ³/₄ cup all-purpose flour
> 2¹/₂ teaspoons Equal® for Recipes *or* 8 packets Equal® sweetener
> 2¹/₄ teaspoons cornstarch
> ¹/₈ teaspoon salt
> 6 tablespoons cold margarine, cut into pieces
> ³/₄ teaspoon vanilla
> 1 teaspoon lemon rind

1. Combine flour, Equal® for Recipes, cornstarch, and salt in medium bowl; cut in margarine until mixture resembles coarse crumbs. Sprinkle with vanilla and lemon rind; mix with hands to form dough.

2. Press dough evenly on bottom and ¹/₄ inch up side of 8-inch square baking pan. Bake at 350 degrees until lightly browned, about 10 minutes. Cool on wire rack.

ANISE-ALMOND BISCOTTI

Crisp biscotti are perfect for dunking into coffee, tea, or Vin Santo, the Italian way!

60 biscotti (1 per serving)

> 4 tablespoons margarine, softened
> ³/₄ cup sugar
> 2 eggs
> 2 egg whites
> 2¹/₂ cups all-purpose flour
> 2 teaspoons anise seeds, crushed
> 1¹/₂ teaspoons baking powder
> ¹/₂ teaspoon baking soda
> ¹/₄ teaspoon salt
> ¹/₃ cup whole blanched almonds

Per Serving
Calories: 41
% Calories from fat: 26
Fat (gm): 1.2
Saturated fat (gm): 0.2
Cholesterol (mg): 7.1
Sodium (mg): 40
Protein (gm): 1
Carbohydrate (gm): 6.7
Exchanges
Milk: 0.0
Vegetable: 0.0
Fruit: 0.0
Bread: 0.5
Meat: 0.0
Fat: 0.0

1. Beat margarine, sugar, eggs, and egg whites until smooth in medium bowl. Mix in combined flour, anise seeds, baking powder, baking soda, and salt. Mix in almonds.

2. Shape dough on greased cookie sheets into 4 slightly flattened rolls 1¹/₂ inches in diameter. Bake at 350 degrees until lightly browned, about 20 minutes. Let stand on wire rack until cool enough to handle; cut bars into ¹/₂-inch slices. Arrange the slices, cut sides down, on ungreased cookie sheets.

3. Bake biscotti at 350 degrees until toasted on the bottom, 7 to 10 minutes; turn and bake until biscotti are golden on other side and feel almost dry, 7 to 10 minutes. Cool on wire racks.

HAZELNUT MACAROONS

Use any favorite nuts in these moist and crunchy macaroons.

30 cookies (1 per serving)

   4 egg whites
¹/₈ teaspoon cream of tartar
¹/₄ teaspoon salt
   1 cup sugar
   1 cup canned sweetened coconut
¹/₄ cup hazelnuts *or* pecans, finely chopped

Per Serving
Calories: 44
% Calories from fat: 28
Fat (gm): 1.4
Saturated fat (gm): 0.8
Cholesterol (mg): 0
Sodium (mg): 25.6
Protein (gm): 0.7
Carbohydrate (gm): 7.6
Exchanges
Milk: 0.0
Vegetable: 0.0
Fruit: 0.0
Bread: 0.5
Meat: 0.0
Fat: 0.5

1. Beat egg whites, cream of tartar, and salt to soft peaks in medium bowl. Beat in sugar gradually, beating to stiff, shiny peaks. Fold in coconut; fold in hazelnuts.

2. Drop mixture by tablespoons onto parchment- or aluminum foil-lined cookie sheets. Bake at 300 degrees until cookies begin to brown and feel crisp when touched, 20 to 25 minutes. Cool in pans on wire racks.

STEWED RHUBARB AND BERRIES

A great team of flavors—serve with light whipped topping and a sprinkle of toasted chopped pecans.

6 servings (about ²/₃ cup each)

1	pound fresh, *or* frozen, rhubarb, cut into 1-inch pieces
¹/₄	cup water
2	cups sliced strawberries
2¹/₂	teaspoons Equal® for Recipes *or* 8 packets Equal® sweetener

Per Serving
Calories: 36
% Calories from fat: 7
Fat (gm): 0.3
Saturated fat (gm): 0.1
Cholesterol (mg): 0
Sodium (mg): 4
Protein (gm): 2.3
Carbohydrate (gm): 6.9
Exchanges
Milk: 0.0
Vegetable: 0.0
Fruit: 0.5
Bread: 0.0
Meat: 0.0
Fat: 0.0

1. Combine rhubarb and water in medium saucepan; cook, covered, over medium heat until soft, about 10 minutes. Stir in strawberries and Equal® for Recipes; cook until hot through, 1 to 2 minutes. Serve warm, or refrigerate and serve chilled.

SPICED CUSTARD

Pumpkin pie spice adds an extraordinary flavor to this smooth custard.

4 servings

2	cups fat-free milk
¹/₄	cup sugar
¹/₈	teaspoon salt
2	eggs, beaten
¹/₂	teaspoon vanilla
2-3	teaspoons pumpkin pie spice

Per Serving
Calories: 133
% Calories from fat: 19
Fat (gm): 2.8
Saturated fat (gm): 1
Cholesterol (mg): 108.2
Sodium (mg): 168
Protein (gm): 7.4
Carbohydrate (gm): 19.5
Exchanges
Milk: 0.5
Vegetable: 0.0
Fruit: 0.0
Bread: 1.0
Meat: 0.5
Fat: 0.0

1. Whisk all ingredients until well blended in medium bowl; pour mixture into 1¹/₂-quart casserole. Place casserole in large pan on middle oven rack; add 1 inch hot water to pan.

2. Bake at 325 degrees until knife inserted near center of custard comes out clean, about 1 hour; cool on wire rack.

CINNAMON BREAD PUDDING

For best texture, use day-old firm bread, such as French, Italian, or Vienna. Or, try sourdough bread, which lends a robust flavor.

8 servings

2 cups fat-free milk
4 tablespoons margarine, cut into pieces
1 egg
2 egg whites
3¹/₂ teaspoons Equal® for Recipes *or* 12 packets Equal® sweetener
1¹/₂ teaspoons ground cinnamon
¹/₈ teaspoon ground cloves
3 dashes ground nutmeg
¹/₄ teaspoon salt
6 cups cubed day-old French, *or* Italian, bread (³/₄-inch cubes)

Per Serving
Calories: 153
% Calories from fat: 43
Fat (gm): 7.2
Saturated fat (gm): 1.7
Cholesterol (mg): 27.6
Sodium (mg): 308
Protein (gm): 6.8
Carbohydrate (gm): 14.8
Exchanges
Milk: 0.0
Vegetable: 0.0
Fruit: 0.0
Bread: 1.0
Meat: 0.5
Fat: 1.0

1. Heat milk and margarine to simmering in medium saucepan; remove from heat and stir until margarine is melted. Cool 10 minutes.

2. Beat egg and egg whites in large bowl until foamy; mix in Equal® for Recipes, spices, and salt. Mix in milk mixture and bread.

3. Spoon mixture into ungreased 1¹/₂-quart casserole. Place casserole in roasting pan on middle oven rack; pour 1 inch hot water into pan. Bake, uncovered, at 350 degrees until pudding is set and sharp knife inserted halfway between center and edge comes out clean, 40 to 45 minutes.

CREAMY FRUIT FREEZE MELBA

A medley of flavorful fruit, frozen with cream cheese and sour cream, and served with brilliant-hued raspberry sauce.

12 servings

1	package (8 ounces) fat-free cream cheese
1	cup fat-free sour cream
2¹/₂	teaspoons Equal® for Recipes *or* 8 packets Equal® sweetener
2-3	teaspoons lemon juice
1	cup coarsely chopped fresh, *or* canned, peaches
1	cup fresh, *or* frozen, blueberries
1	cup fresh, *or* unsweetened frozen, raspberries *or* halved *or* quartered strawberries
1	cup canned, drained pineapple wedges in juice
1	can (11 ounces) Mandarin orange segments, drained
	Chopped pecans, as garnish
	Melba Sauce (recipe follows)

Per Serving
Calories: 102
% Calories from fat: 5
Fat (gm): 0.7
Saturated fat (gm): 0.2
Cholesterol (mg): 1.5
Sodium (mg): 122
Protein (gm): 6.5
Carbohydrate (gm): 18.2
Exchanges
Milk: 0.0
Vegetable: 0.0
Fruit: 1.0
Bread: 0.0
Meat: 1.0
Fat: 0.0

1. Beat cream cheese, sour cream, Equal® for Recipes, and lemon juice in medium bowl until smooth; gently mix in fruit. Spoon mixture into 10 x 6-inch baking dish and sprinkle with pecans. Freeze until firm, 6 to 8 hours.

2. Let stand at room temperature until slightly softened, 10 to 15 minutes; cut into squares. Serve with Melba Sauce.

Melba Sauce

makes about 2 cups

| 4 | cups fresh, *or* frozen, thawed unsweetened raspberries |
| 3¹/₂-5 | teaspoons Equal® for Recipes *or* 12 to 16 packets Equal® sweetener |

1. Process raspberries in food processor or blender until smooth; strain and discard seeds. Stir in Equal® for Recipes.

BAKED CUSTARD WITH ORANGE SAUCE

The custard has a shimmery light texture and lovely flavor, complemented with a lovely orange sauce.

6 servings (about ²/₃ cup each)

1 quart fat-free milk
5 eggs
5 teaspoons Equal® for Recipes *or* 16 packets Equal® sweetener
2 teaspoons vanilla
Orange Sauce (recipe follows)
Mint sprigs, as garnish

Per Serving
Calories: 174
% Calories from fat: 24
Fat (gm): 4.6
Saturated fat (gm): 1.5
Cholesterol (mg): 179.6
Sodium (mg): 138
Protein (gm): 14.3
Carbohydrate (gm): 17.7
Exchanges
Milk: 1.0
Vegetable: 0.0
Fruit: 0.0
Bread: 0.5
Meat: 1.0
Fat: 0.0

1. Heat milk just to simmering in medium saucepan. Beat eggs until foamy in medium bowl; gradually whisk milk into eggs. Stir in Equal® for Recipes and vanilla. Pour mixture through strainer into ungreased 1-quart casserole or soufflé dish.

2. Cover casserole with lid or aluminum foil and place in roasting pan on middle rack of oven. Pour 2 inches hot water into roasting pan. Bake at 325 degrees until custard is set and sharp knife inserted halfway between center and edge of custard comes out clean, 1 to 1¹/₄ hours.

3. Remove casserole from roasting pan; cool to room temperature on wire rack. Refrigerate until chilled, 6 hours or overnight. Spoon custard into dishes; spoon Orange Sauce over and garnish with mint.

Orange Sauce

makes about 1³/₄ cups

³/₄ cup orange juice
1 tablespoon cornstarch
1 teaspoon Equal® for Recipes *or* 3 packets Equal® sweetener
1 cup orange segments

1. Mix orange juice and cornstarch in small saucepan; whisk until mixture boils and thickens, 2 to 3 minutes. Stir in Equal® for Recipes and orange segments. Cool to room temperature; refrigerate until chilled.

Variation: **Baked Chocolate Custard**—Make recipe as above, increasing Equal® for Recipes to 6¹/4 teaspoons and adding ¹/3 cup Dutch process cocoa to the milk mixture. Omit Orange Sauce and mint sprigs.

APRICOT BAVARIAN

This delicately flavored dessert is party perfect.

4 servings (about ²/3 cup each)

  2¹/2 teaspoons Equal® for Recipes *or* 8 packets Equal® sweetener
    1 tablespoon cornstarch
    1 envelope unflavored gelatin
    1 cup apricot nectar
    2 egg yolks
    2 teaspoons finely grated lemon rind
    2 cups light whipped topping
      Light whipped topping, as garnish

Per Serving
Calories: 168
% Calories from fat: 38
Fat (gm): 6.6
Saturated fat (gm): 4.8
Cholesterol (mg): 106.5
Sodium (mg): 11
Protein (gm): 3.9
Carbohydrate (gm): 20.7
Exchanges
Milk: 0.0
Vegetable: 0.0
Fruit: 1.5
Bread: 0.0
Meat: 0.0
Fat: 1.0

1. Mix Equal® for Recipes, cornstarch, and gelatin in small saucepan; whisk in apricot nectar and heat to boiling, whisking until thickened. Whisk about ¹/2 of the apricot juice mixture into the egg yolks; whisk egg yolk mixture into saucepan. Whisk over low heat until thickened, 2 to 3 minutes. Whisk in lemon rind. Cool to room temperature.

2. Fold 2 cups whipped topping into apricot mixture and spoon into serving bowl or individual dishes. Refrigerate until set, 3 to 4 hours. Garnish with light whipped topping.

Variation: **Orange Bavarian**—Make recipe as above, substituting orange juice for the apricot nectar, 1 tablespoon finely grated orange rind for the lemon rind, and adding ¹/2 teaspoon orange extract. Garnish with light whipped topping and orange slices.

LIME MELON COMPOTES

A medley of melon, served with subtle-flavored Minted Lime Sauce.

6 servings (about 1 cup each)

2 cups each: cubed honeydew, cantaloupe, and watermelon
1 teaspoon Equal® for Recipes *or* 3
packets Equal® sweetener
Minted Lime Sauce (recipe follows)
Mint sprigs, as garnish

Per Serving
Calories: 86
% Calories from fat: 23
Fat (gm): 2.3
Saturated fat (gm): 0.5
Cholesterol (mg): 0
Sodium (mg): 34
Protein (gm): 2.6
Carbohydrate (gm): 15.5
Exchanges
Milk: 0.0
Vegetable: 0.0
Fruit: 1.0
Bread: 0.0
Meat: 0.0
Fat: 0.5

1. Combine melon in serving bowl; sprinkle with Equal® for Recipes and toss. Serve with Minted Lime Sauce and garnish with mint.

Minted Lime Sauce

makes 1¹/₄ cups

1 tablespoon cornstarch
1³/₄ teaspoons Equal® for Recipes *or* 6 packets
Equal® sweetener
1 cup water
3 tablespoons lime juice
1 teaspoon dried mint leaves
1 tablespoon margarine, softened

1. Whisk all ingredients, except margarine, in small saucepan over medium-high heat until mixture boils and thickens, 2 to 3 minutes. Stir in margarine.

OLD-FASHIONED APPLE CRISP

Juicy apples baked with a crisp sweet-spiced topping will warm hearts in any season.

6 servings

3¹/₂ teaspoons Equal® for Recipes *or* 12 packets Equal® sweetener
1 tablespoon cornstarch
³/₄ cup unsweetened apple juice
1 teaspoon finely grated lemon rind
4 cups sliced peeled apples
Crispy Spiced Topping (recipe follows)

Per Serving
Calories: 198
% Calories from fat: 41
Fat (gm): 9.3
Saturated fat (gm): 2.5
Cholesterol (mg): 0
Sodium (mg): 93
Protein (gm): 4.8
Carbohydrate (gm): 25.7
Exchanges
Milk: 0.0
Vegetable: 0.0
Fruit: 1.0
Bread: 1.5
Meat: 0.0
Fat: 2.0

1. Whisk Equal® for Recipes, cornstarch, apple juice, and lemon rind over medium heat in medium saucepan until mixture boils and thickens, 2 to 3 minutes; add apples and simmer, uncovered, until apples begin to lose their crispness, about 5 minutes. Transfer mixture to 8-inch square baking pan.

2. Sprinkle Crispy Spiced Topping over apples. Bake at 400 degrees until topping is browned and apples are tender, about 25 minutes. Serve warm.

Crispy Spiced Topping

makes about ³/₄ cup

¹/₄ cup all-purpose flour
2¹/₂ teaspoons Equal® for Recipes *or* 8 packets Equal® sweetener
1 teaspoon ground cinnamon
¹/₂ teaspoon ground nutmeg
3 dashes ground allspice
4 tablespoons cold margarine, cut into pieces
¹/₄ cup quick-cooking oats
¹/₄ cup flaked coconut

1. Combine flour, Equal® for Recipes, and spices in small bowl; cut in margarine until mixture resembles coarse crumbs. Stir in oats and coconut.

FROZEN YOGURT FRUIT CUPS

The texture of this frozen dessert is luxuriously creamy.

6 to 8 servings

1 can (9 ounces) pineapple tidbits in juice, drained

2 medium bananas, cut into scant $1/2$-inch pieces

$1/2$ cup quartered small strawberries

2 cups fat-free plain yogurt

2 tablespoons lemon juice

$5^1/2$ teaspoons Equal® for Recipes *or* 18 packets Equal® sweetener

$1/3$ cup walnut pieces

$1/4$ teaspoon salt

6-8 walnut halves, as garnish

Per Serving
Calories: 161
% Calories from fat: 23
Fat (gm): 4.3
Saturated fat (gm): 0.4
Cholesterol (mg): 1.4
Sodium (mg): 157
Protein (gm): 9.5
Carbohydrate (gm): 23.5
Exchanges
Milk: 0.5
Vegetable: 0.0
Fruit: 1.5
Bread: 0.0
Meat: 0.0
Fat: 0.5

1. Mix pineapple tidbits, bananas, and strawberries into yogurt; mix in lemon juice, Equal® for Recipes, walnut pieces, and salt.

2. Spoon mixture into small custard cups and garnish with walnut halves; freeze until firm, 4 to 6 hours. Let stand at room temperature 5 to 10 minutes before serving.

PEARS BELLE HÉLÈNE

Serve Almond Shortbread Cookies (see p. 789) with this lovely dessert. To make Pears Melba, substitute Melba Sauce (see p. 802) for the Bittersweet Chocolate Sauce.

6 servings

2 cups unsweetened apple juice

1³/₄ teaspoons Equal® for Recipes *or* 6 packets Equal® sweetener, divided

3 large pears, peeled, cored, cut into halves

3 cups sugar-free, fat-free ice cream
Bittersweet Chocolate Sauce (recipe follows)
Mint sprigs, as garnish

Per Serving
Calories: 235
% Calories from fat: 11
Fat (gm): 3
Saturated fat (gm): 0.8
Cholesterol (mg): 0.4
Sodium (mg): 85
Protein (gm): 9.7
Carbohydrate (gm): 45.3
Exchanges
Milk: 0.0
Vegetable: 0.0
Fruit: 1.0
Bread: 2.0
Meat: 0.0
Fat: 0.5

1. Heat apple juice and Equal® for Recipes to simmering in large skillet; add pear halves, cut sides down. Simmer, covered, until pears are tender, 10 to 15 minutes. Remove pears with slotted spoon.

2. Spoon ice cream into 6 serving dishes; top with pear halves. Spoon Bittersweet Chocolate Sauce over; garnish with mint sprigs.

Bittersweet Chocolate Sauce

makes about 1 cup

¹/₂ cup fat-free milk

¹/₂ cup Dutch process cocoa

3¹/₂ teaspoons Equal® for Recipes *or* 12 packets Equal® sweetener

1-2 tablespoons margarine

1¹/₂ teaspoons vanilla

1. Whisk milk, cocoa, and Equal® for Recipes until blended in small saucepan; add margarine and vanilla and whisk over medium heat just until simmering. Serve warm, or refrigerate and serve chilled.

INDEX

809